Reader's Digest
Complete Guide to Needlework

Reader's Digest

COMPLETE GUIDE TO NEEDLEWORK

The Reader's Digest Association, Inc.
Pleasantville, New York/Montreal

Contents

7 Embroidery
8 Embroidery tools and supplies
12 Designing for embroidery
16 General embroidery techniques
21 Embroidery stitches
54 Finishing embroidered pieces
56 Blackwork embroidery
66 Cross stitch embroidery
70 Huck embroidery
74 Openwork/pulled thread embroidery
78 Openwork/drawn threadwork
86 Openwork/Hardanger embroidery
90 Openwork/cutwork embroidery
92 Smocking
98 Machine embroidery

Embroidery projects
103 Monogramming/machine embroidery
104 Crewel picture
106 Place mat and napkin/pulled thread
107 Table runner/huck embroidery
108 Cutwork embroidery on caftan
109 Cross stitch for a child's dress
110 Corded pillow/blackwork

111 Needlepoint
112 Needlepoint basics
118 Needlepoint stitches
162 Designing and working needlepoint
173 Designing and working Bargello
183 General working techniques

Needlepoint projects
186 Initialed eyeglass case/Bargello
188 Oriental-design footstool cover
189 Man's belt
190 Address book cover

191 Appliqué
192 Appliqué basics
201 Reverse appliqué

207 Patchwork
208 Patchwork basics
218 Preparing and sewing a block-unit patchwork
232 Preparing and sewing a one-shape patchwork

235 Quilting
236 Quilting and quilts
238 Quilting designs
246 Basic quilting techniques
252 Other quilting techniques
257 Finishing edges
261 Care of quilts

Appliqué/Patchwork/Quilting projects
262 Man's patchwork vest
263 Boy's coveralls/machine appliqué
264 Baby quilt
266 Cut-through appliqué wall hanging
267 Patchwork floor pillow
268 Quilted evening bag

269 Knitting
270 Knitting supplies
274 Knitting basics
286 Following knitting instructions
300 Knitting stitches
324 Knitting a garment
342 Assembling and finishing

Knitting projects
285 Scarf
315 Aran-pattern pullover
326 Man's pullover
350 Children's sweaters and hats
352 Sport socks
353 Mittens and hat
354 Evening skirt, top, and shawl
356 Knitted trims for sheets and pillowcases

357 Crochet
358 Crochet basics
366 Following crochet instructions
372 Crochet stitches
393 Crocheting a garment
400 Assembling and finishing

Crochet projects
367 Tote bag
371 Three hats
385 Irish crochet pillow top
394 Woman's cardigan
402 Afghan

403 Lacework
404 Needle lace
413 Tatting
420 Filet netting
426 Bobbin lace
435 Lace weaves
440 Hairpin lace

Lacework projects
411 Needle lace butterfly
418 Shawl with tatted border
424 Chinese folk design pillow top
432 Bobbin lace-trimmed apron
439 Woven lace place mat
442 Hairpin lace shawl

443 Macramé
444 Introduction to macramé
447 Basic macramé knots
452 Additional techniques
456 Fringing

Macramé projects
459 Woman's macramé belt
460 Window screen

461 Rug-making
462 Hooking and knotting
470 Preparing for and working a hooked rug
476 Preparing for and working a knotted rug
480 Finishing techniques
485 Care of handmade rugs
486 Braiding

Projects using rug methods
494 Chair cushion
495 Wall hanging
496 Braided rug

497 Index

Staff

Editor
Virginia Colton

Art director
David Trooper

Associate art director
Albert D. Burger

Associate editors
Linda Hetzer
Susan C. Hoe
Therese L. Hoehlein
Gayla Visalli

Designers
Larissa Lawrynenko
Marta Norman
Marta M. Strait
Virginia Wells

Copy editor
Elizabeth T. Salter

Art-production associate
Carol Claar

Art assistant
Lisa Grant

Picture researcher
Margaret Mathews

Project secretary
Annette Koshut

Photography
Ernest Coppolino

Contributors

Consulting editors and designers
Louise Ambler
Peggy Bendel
Sherry De Leon
Rosemary Drysdale
Katherine Enzmann
Phoebe Fox
Zuelia Ann Hurt
Barbara H. Jacksier
Joyce D. Lee
Susanna E. Lewis
Claudia Librett
Victoria Mileti
Edna Adam Walker
Monna Weinman
Joanne Whitwell

Technical assistance
Linda Blyer
Charlotte Feng-Veshi
Arlene Mintzer
Erwin Rowland
Cathie Strunz
Valentina Watson

Contributing artists
Roberta W. Frauwirth
Susan Frye
John A. Lind Corp.
Marilyn MacGregor
Mary Ruth Roby
Jim Silks;
Randall Lieu
Ray Skibinski
Lynn E. Yost

Contributing photographers
J. D. Barnell
Joel Elkins
Ken Korsh
Russ McCann/
Conrad-Dell-McCann, Inc.
Michael A. Vaccaro

The editors are grateful for the cooperation of the organizations listed below

Research assistance
C. J. Bates & Son
Emile Bernat & Sons Co.
Boye Needle Company
Brunswick Worsted Mills, Inc.
Coats & Clark Inc.
The D.M.C. Corporation
Dritz Art Needlework /
Scovill Manufacturing Company
Frederick J. Fawcett, Incorporated
Harry M. Fraser Company
Kreinik Mfg. Co.
Paternayan Bros., Inc.
Reynolds Yarns Inc.
Talon/Donahue Sales, Div. of Textron
Joan Toggitt, Ltd.
Wm. E. Wright Co.

Special credits
Page 12:   Flower-and-bird design, The Bagshaws of St. Lucia Ltd.
Silk-screen bamboo-print wallpaper, Janovic/Plaza
Page 103: Alphabet, from *New Art Deco Alphabets* by Marcia Loeb
New York: Dover Publications, Inc.
Page 208: Rose design quilt, The Gazebo
Page 233: Baby Blocks quilt, The Gazebo
Page 234: Grandmother's Flower Garden quilt, Thos. K. Woodard

Embroidery

8 Embroidery tools and supplies
Yarns and threads; fabrics
10 Hoops and frames; needles; accessories
12 Designing for embroidery
Design sources; interpretation
13 Choosing colors
14 Enlarging and reducing designs
16 General embroidery techniques
Cutting and binding edges
Transferring designs
18 Using an embroidery hoop
19 Yarn preparation; threading
20 Working tips
21 Embroidery stitches
Selecting stitches; charting
22 Backstitches
25 Blanket stitches
28 Chain stitches
32 Couching
35 Cross stitches
39 Featherstitches
42 Filling stitches
46 Running stitches
48 Satin stitches
51 Weaving stitches
54 Finishing embroidered pieces
Cleaning and pressing
55 Blocking
56 Blackwork embroidery
57 Blackwork stitches
58 Typical blackwork patterns
63 Creating your own pattern
64 Working blackwork
66 Cross stitch embroidery
Forming the basic cross stitch
67 Cross stitch guides and grids
68 Cross stitch on gingham
69 Assisi embroidery
70 Huck embroidery
71 Four basic huck motifs
72 Basic stitch movements
Working huck embroidery

74 Openwork/pulled threadwork
Working pulled threadwork
75 Typical pulled thread patterns
78 Openwork/drawn threadwork
Hemstitching
80 Grouping variations
Knotting variations
81 Lacing variations
82 Handling drawn corners
84 Needleweaving
Basic needleweaving stitches
Needleweaving variations
86 Openwork/Hardanger
87 Kloster blocks
Working a motif
88 Covered bars
Filling stitches
90 Openwork/cutwork
91 Basic procedure
Making a cutwork piece
92 Smocking
Fabrics and grids
93 Adding smocking to a garment
94 English smocking
Smocking stitches
98 Machine embroidery
Straight stitching
99 Zigzag stitching
Decorative stitch patterns
100 Free-motion embroidery
101 Machine hemstitching
102 Machine cutwork
Machine smocking

Embroidery projects
103 Monogramming/machine embroidery
104 Crewel picture
106 Place mat and napkin/ pulled thread embroidery
107 Table runner/huck embroidery
108 Cutwork embroidery on caftan
109 Cross stitch for a child's dress
110 Corded pillow/blackwork

Detail of bedspread, crewel on black wool twill, by Lucretia Hall, mid-19th century, from the collection of Historic Deerfield, Inc., Deerfield, Massachusetts.

Embroidery tools and supplies

Yarns and threads
Embroidery fabrics
Hoops and frames
Needles
Design transfer materials
Accessories

Yarns and threads

Embroidery offers an enormous variety of finished effects, and that calls for a wide range of yarns and threads. Several of the types popular for embroidery are pictured below. Although they differ individually in texture, fiber content, number of plies, separable strands, etc., all of the types shown have one feature in common: whatever their character, it remains uniform throughout. Uneven or nubby novelty yarns (see Knitting and Crochet) are generally not recommended, except for occasional special effects.

Some yarns and threads come in more than one fiber, with new ones constantly being introduced, especially synthetic varieties. Some yarns and threads are easier to find than others; you may need to check several sources—needlework departments as well as special shops and catalogs—to find what you want.

In this section, as each form of embroidery is introduced, we specify the yarn or thread traditional for working it. This should not discourage experiment with different yarns and threads—that is what produces original pieces.

Embroidery floss, a loosely twisted 6-strand thread, works well in many types of embroidery. Strands can be separated for finer work. Cotton is most popular; made also in silk and rayon. Many colors (fewer for rayon).

Pearl cotton, a twisted 2-ply thread suitable for all embroidery types, has high sheen, good colors. Comes in sizes 3, 5, and 8 (3 is the heaviest).

Matte embroidery cotton, a tightly twisted 5-ply thread, gives embroidery a muted look. Usually reserved for heavier fabrics. Good color choice.

Crewel yarn, of fine 2-ply wool (also some acrylic), resembles one strand of Persian yarn. For fine embroidery and needlepoint. Many soft, subtle colors.

Persian yarn is loosely twisted 3-strand wool (sometimes acrylic); each strand is 2-ply. Used in needlepoint and embroidery. Good color choice.

Tapestry yarn is a tightly twisted 4-ply yarn appropriate for embroidery and needlepoint. Choice of wool (in many colors) or acrylic (considerably fewer).

Knitting yarn is a 4-ply yarn, like tapestry yarn but less twisted. Usable also for crochet. May be wool or acrylic.

Rug yarn, a thick 3-ply yarn, can also be used for texture variation in embroidered pieces; works best when it is couched down (fastened with small stitches). May be wool, acrylic, or cotton/rayon blend.

Machine embroidery thread is extra fine (size 50 or A). Silk is most popular for its sheen.

Metallic threads, available in many weights and textures, are used only for special effects.

Embroidery fabrics

Embroidery fabrics fall basically into three categories. The first, **common-weave fabrics**, includes most tightly woven fabrics with a relatively smooth surface. Although medium-weight linens and wools are the traditional preferences, fabrics of other weights and fibers (such as cotton and synthetics) are also acceptable as long as the working yarn or thread is not too heavy. Most standard free-form embroidery (including crewel) is worked on common-weave fabrics.

Even-weave fabrics, the next of the classifications, are all essentially plain weaves, but with a distinguishing difference: the number of threads per square inch is the same for both warp and weft. One type, the *single even-weave*, is made from single strands of intersecting threads; the thread count can vary from a coarse 14 to a fine 36 threads per inch. In *Hardanger*, another of the even-weave types, pairs of threads intersect; 22 pairs of threads per inch is the usual count. Still another type is *Aida cloth*, which consists of intersecting thread groups, generally 11 to the inch. As a rule, even-weave fabrics are used for thread-counting techniques, such as blackwork and openwork. They may be cotton, linen, wool, or blends of these with synthetics.

What the fabrics in the third group have in common is an evenly spaced **surface pattern** (see examples at right) that supplies guidelines for certain kinds of embroidery, such as cross stitch and smocking. As the swatches show, the surface pattern may be printed on or woven in. The method of producing the effect is not important; what matters is its usefulness as a grid. The fabric *type*, however, is important. Select woven fabrics for this purpose; knits are rarely satisfactory.

The list of embroidery fabrics is far from fixed—new ones are always appearing. Look for the damasks and other woven fabrics specially created to permit original embroidery motifs to be incorporated into their woven-in designs.

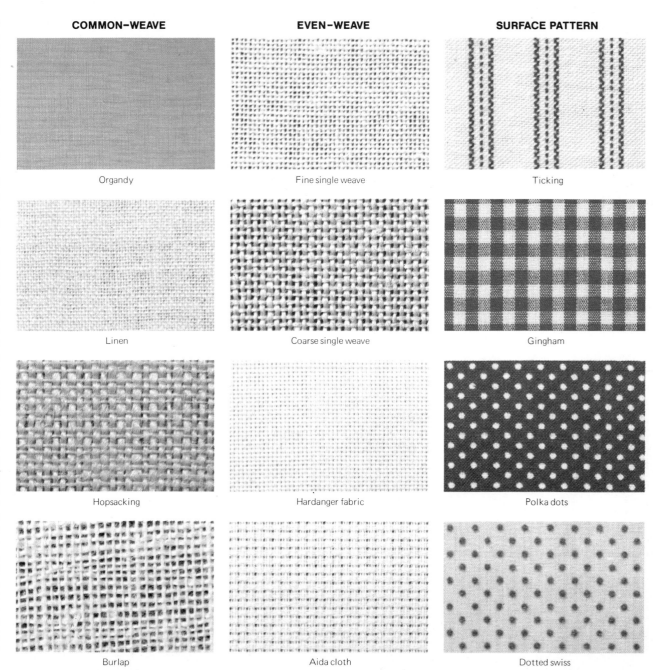

COMMON-WEAVE	EVEN-WEAVE	SURFACE PATTERN
Organdy	Fine single weave	Ticking
Linen	Coarse single weave	Gingham
Hopsacking	Hardanger fabric	Polka dots
Burlap	Aida cloth	Dotted swiss

Embroidery tools and supplies

Hoops and frames

A hoop or frame is necessary for most types of embroidery work to hold the fabric taut for stitching. **Embroidery hoops** keep a section of fabric stretched between two rings. The outer ring usually has an adjustable screw or a spring that allows the hoop to hold different weights of fabric. Hoops come in many sizes and may be hand-held or attached to a stand. **Frames** work by keeping the entire fabric taut. There are two basic types, the scroll or square frame and the stretcher frame. *Scroll frames* stretch the fabric between top and bottom rollers, which are then tightened. On the *stretcher frames*, which are basically four-sided units that you make with precut wooden slats, the fabric is stretched around the framework and tacked down on the back. For further details about frames and their uses, see the Needlepoint chapter.

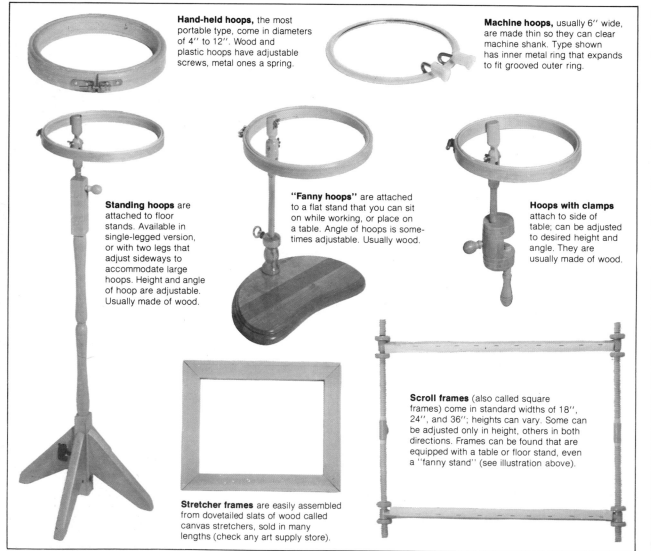

Hand-held hoops, the most portable type, come in diameters of 4″ to 12″. Wood and plastic hoops have adjustable screws, metal ones a spring.

Machine hoops, usually 6″ wide, are made thin so they can clear machine shank. Type shown has inner metal ring that expands to fit grooved outer ring.

Standing hoops are attached to floor stands. Available in single-legged version, or with two legs that adjust sideways to accommodate large hoops. Height and angle of hoop are adjustable. Usually made of wood.

"Fanny hoops" are attached to a flat stand that you can sit on while working, or place on a table. Angle of hoops is sometimes adjustable. Usually wood.

Hoops with clamps attach to side of table; can be adjusted to desired height and angle. They are usually made of wood.

Stretcher frames are easily assembled from dovetailed slats of wood called canvas stretchers, sold in many lengths (check any art supply store).

Scroll frames (also called square frames) come in standard widths of 18″, 24″, and 36″; heights can vary. Some can be adjusted only in height, others in both directions. Frames can be found that are equipped with a table or floor stand, even a "fanny stand" (see illustration above).

Needles

Hand needles for embroidery are of three basic types: **crewel**, **chenille**, and **tapestry**. Each has a specific purpose and comes in its own range of sizes (the larger the number, the shorter and finer the needle). Which needle type you should use depends largely on the embroidery technique being worked (see below). Another consideration is the yarn or thread; the needle should be large enough that the yarn does not fray excessively when it is pulled through the fabric.

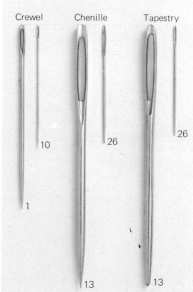

Crewels (sizes 1 to 10) are sharp-pointed, medium-length needles with large eyes for easy threading. They are the type used for most standard embroidery stitchery.
Chenilles (sizes 13 to 26) are also sharp-pointed needles, but they are thicker and longer, and have larger eyes. Chenilles are the appropriate choice for embroidery that is worked with heavier yarns.
Tapestry needles (sizes 13 to 26) are similar in size to chenilles, but are blunt rather than sharp. This makes them best for thread-counting embroidery techniques and for needlepoint as well.

Design transfer materials

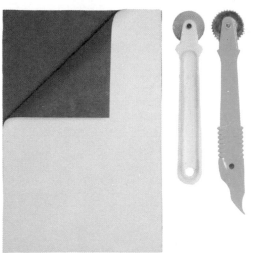

Hot-iron transfers are heat-sensitive patterns that come in a wide range of designs, usually several different designs printed on one sheet.

Dressmaker's carbon and tracing wheel aid in the transfer of designs to fabric. Paper comes in limited selection of colors. Wheel can be either smooth-edged or serrated.

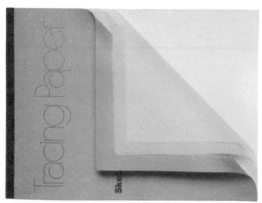

Pounce is fine powder used in transferring design by pricking method (see p. 17).

Tracing paper is useful for transferring original designs. Comes in a choice of tablet sizes and in several weights.

Dressmaker's marking pencils enable you to mark fabric directly; will not smudge and are usually pastel-colored.

Transfer pencil enables you to make a hot-iron transfer from any design of your choice.

Accessories

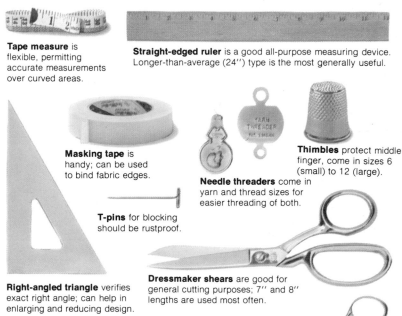

Tape measure is flexible, permitting accurate measurements over curved areas.

Straight-edged ruler is a good all-purpose measuring device. Longer-than-average (24'') type is the most generally useful.

Masking tape is handy; can be used to bind fabric edges.

Thimbles protect middle finger, come in sizes 6 (small) to 12 (large).

Needle threaders come in yarn and thread sizes for easier threading of both.

T-pins for blocking should be rustproof.

Right-angled triangle verifies exact right angle; can help in enlarging and reducing design.

Dressmaker shears are good for general cutting purposes; 7'' and 8'' lengths are used most often.

Embroidery scissors are small and sharp, good for fine work.

Blocking board can be made from soft pine or composition board; 24'' x 24'' is handy size. Board is usually covered with muslin, and is sometimes padded as well.

Magnifier helps you to see fine work. Model shown comes with cord (detached in photo) for hanging unit around neck.

11

Designing for embroidery

Design sources
and interpretation
Choosing colors
Enlarging a design
Reducing a design

Sources and interpretation

Many needleworkers who have become quite skilled still do not consider themselves designers. Yet all of us, if we try, can manage some degree of designing. One person might take a first creative step by simply changing the yarn colors dictated by a kit. Another may go a step further and make all of the color and stitch decisions. Still another may carry out an original design. It is hoped that this section will encourage more people to try introducing their own ideas into the embroidery they do.

Most embroidery designs are nothing but personal interpretations of designs from such sources as books, magazines, posters, china, fabric prints, wallpaper, and photographs. Examine such possible sources carefully, studying elements *within* a composition as well as the overall composition itself; you may find that you can single out a part of the larger design (see below) with excellent results.

Take note of designs that draw the eye naturally up and down or from side to side. This can determine whether the overall line direction of a finished piece will be vertical or horizontal.

When you find a design that you like, place tracing paper over it, and carefully draw its outlines. You may want to omit some of the finer details, perhaps stylize certain lines as well; you can even rearrange elements within the composition. Make several different tracings and select the best one. Remember you are not trying to copy the original design, but to interpret it in embroidery. As you become more experienced at design interpretation, you will begin to recognize what has possibilities for embroidery and—just as important—what does not.

A portion of a composition can be isolated for an embroidery design. From design below, bird and flower have been singled out and traced; note the interpretive changes made in the tracing.

The strong horizontal lines in the full design direct the eye naturally to move from side to side.

Vertical lines draw the eye up and down.

Choosing colors

Once your design is chosen, you are ready to select colors, a decision that will greatly affect the mood of your finished project. With color, as with most design problems, there are guidelines that can help you to make a successful choice. Most color schemes are one of three basic types. The first, called **monochromatic,** is a color scheme consisting of different values (light and dark hues) of the *same* color (e.g., a design done in a "family" of blues). The second type, the **analogous** color scheme, employs colors that are *similar,* and "neighbors" on the color wheel (e.g., blues and greens or violets). A **complementary** color scheme, the third combination, brings together two or more *contrasting* colors, the strongest contrasts being those that are opposites on the color wheel (e.g., red and green, purple and yellow).

These color guidelines, though simple in theory, can be more difficult to put into practice. You will find the task far easier if you make yourself a *color plan*—a colored-in version of your traced design. You may have to color more than one drawing before you hit upon a satisfactory combination. Once you have one you like, take it along when you go to buy yarns. Be prepared to make slight modifications in tones and shades when you see what yarn colors are actually available.

Monochromatic (one-color) schemes can achieve surprising variety if the values (tints and shades) are imaginatively chosen and used, as illustrated.

Analogous schemes combine closely related colors, a characteristic that almost assures a harmonious blend, no matter how varied your choices.

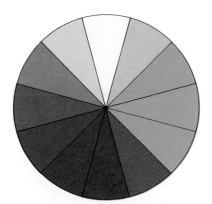

Color wheel

Complementary schemes, with their contrasting colors, can be difficult to bring off. Surest way: experiment with colors until you are satisfied.

13

Designing for embroidery

Enlarging a design

What do you do if the design you like is not the right size for your project? If there is a commercial photostat service nearby, you can give them your drawing or the original art and have the size changed to your specifications. The cost for this service is nominal. If there is no such service in your community, or you prefer to "do things yourself," you can make your own size change, using the grid methods illustrated—enlargement on this page, reduction on the page opposite. Basically, this method involves simply transposing design lines from one grid to another grid of a different size.

1. Trace design onto center of paper.

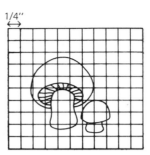

2. Draw a small (¼") grid over the traced design.

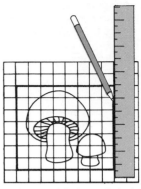

3. Mark perimeters of design to desired size.

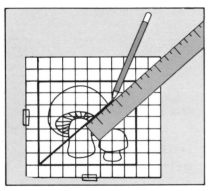

4. Tape grid to lower left corner of a large sheet of paper. Draw a corner-to-corner line diagonally across design area, extending line beyond grid.

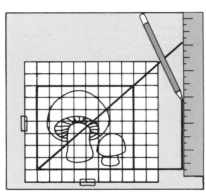

5. Extend the bottom line of the design area to desired width. Draw a line straight up to form a right angle, extending line to intersect diagonal.

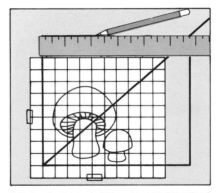

6. Using the finished width and height determined in Step 5, draw in remaining two sides of rectangle (left-hand line will join line of original grid).

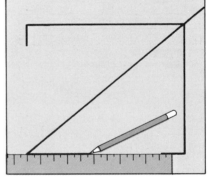

7. Remove the grid. Fill in the area that was covered by the grid, extending the diagonal, side, and bottom lines to complete the enlarged rectangle.

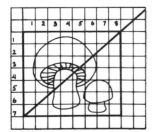

8. Along the design perimeter of the small grid, number each square across top and down side.

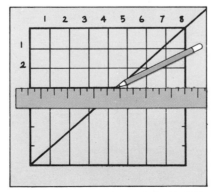

9. Count the squares within marked grid; divide large rectangle into same number of squares.

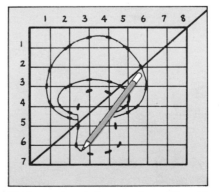

10. To reproduce design, copy lines within small squares onto corresponding squares of large grid.

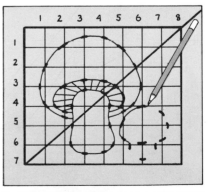

To make copying easier, place a mark where design lines intersect a square; connect marks.

Reducing a design

When a design is too large, you have the same choices as when it is too small. It can be reduced to your specifications by a commercial photostat service, as mentioned on the opposite page. Or you can reduce the design yourself, by means of the grid technique shown here. The basic principle—copying square by square—is the same for reducing as for enlarging, but the actual steps differ. Essentially, they are the reverse of what is done for enlargement. Follow directions carefully when using either method; for drawing accurate angles, a plastic right-angled triangle can be a great convenience.

1. Trace design onto center of paper.

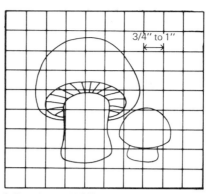
2. Draw large grid (¾'' to 1'') over traced design.

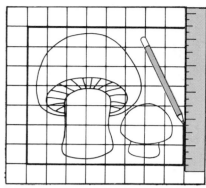
3. Mark perimeters of design to desired size.

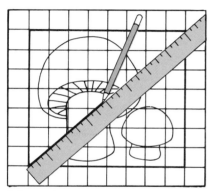
4. Draw a diagonal line from corner to corner of the design area marked off on the grid. Tape a smaller sheet of paper to the lower left corner.

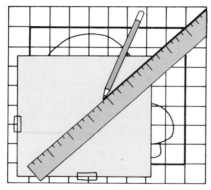
5. Extend the diagonal line at the upper right-hand corner of the grid straight down to the lower left-hand corner of the taped sheet of paper.

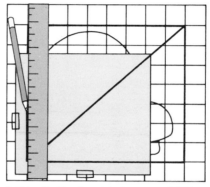
6. Extend bottom line of design area until it intersects diagonal. Connect intersected point with perimeter line at left side to form right angle.

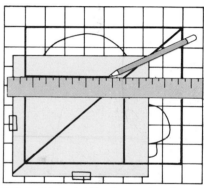
7. Mark off desired width at bottom of small sheet; draw line up at right angle to intersect diagonal. Mark height at left; draw connecting line at top.

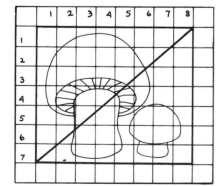
8. Along the design perimeter of the large grid, number each square across top and down side.

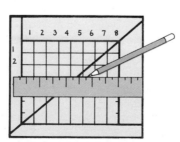
9. Count the number of squares within marked grid; divide small rectangle into same number.

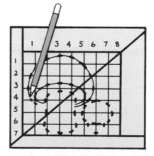
10. To reproduce design, copy lines within large squares onto equivalent squares of small grid.

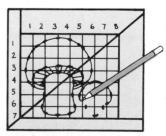
To make copying easier, place a mark where design lines intersect a square; connect marks.

General embroidery techniques

Cutting and binding fabric edges
Transferring designs
Using an embroidery hoop
Preparing yarns
Threading the needle
Working tips

Cutting and binding edges

To determine cutting size of fabric, measure the overall design and to this measurement add 2 inches all around. Add twice as much allowance if the embroidered piece is to be framed. Cut fabric to the desired size, following the fabric's grainline; a straight grain is especially important for counted-thread embroidery. To keep the fabric from raveling during any lengthy embroidering process, finish off the raw edges, using one of the methods shown below.

Use masking tape over raw edges of fabric.

Overcast raw edges by hand to prevent raveling.

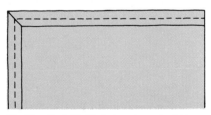

Machine straight-stitch along turned edges.

Machine zigzag raw edges for easy finish.

Transferring designs

Transfer of a design to a fabric can be accomplished by any of three different methods. The first, and probably the easiest, is to use a **hot-iron transfer,** which is simply a printed, heat-sensitive pattern. When the pattern is placed against the fabric and heat from an iron is applied, the design comes off onto the fabric. Commercial hot-iron transfers are produced in quite a variety of appealing designs; check the dress pattern catalogs as well as those expressly for needlework. Though most hot-iron transfers are good for only a single printing, there are some specially made to be used more than once. If you prefer to use a design of your own, you can make your own hot-iron transfer with a special transfer pencil (see the opposite page).

Another method of design transfer involves the use of **dressmaker's carbon** and a tracing wheel. Do not confuse this type of carbon with typing carbon paper, which can smear badly. The method is basically the same as that used to transfer pattern markings in standard sewing procedures. Dressmaker's carbon is suitable for marking only very smooth fabrics.

Pricking is one of the oldest and still an effective means of transferring a design. Little holes are pricked along the outline of the design pattern, which is then laid over the fabric and rubbed with a light-colored powder called *pounce.* When the pattern is lifted away, a fine dotted line remains on the fabric. The dotted lines are then drawn over with a dressmaker's pencil; on fabrics that cannot be penciled (such as velvet), this step can be done with a fine paintbrush and opaque watercolors. The pricked patterns can be used more than once and are especially well suited to slightly textured fabrics. This method is also suitable for transferring quilting designs.

No matter which method of transference you decide on, be sure that the design of the pattern is properly positioned on the fabric (see right).

POSITIONING DESIGN

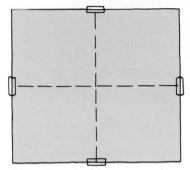

Fold and quarter fabric; crease along folds. If crease will not hold, baste center foldlines. Pin or tape fabric to flat surface.

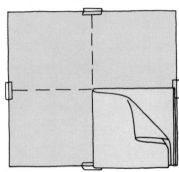

Fold and quarter pattern (design should be centered). Place pattern in one quadrant of fabric, center points aligned.

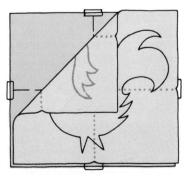

Carefully open out the pattern so its foldlines match the crease lines of fabric. Anchor pattern down, then transfer design.

HOT-IRON TRANSFERS

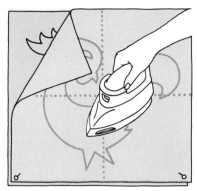

To use hot-iron transfer, first cut off any waste lettering and test on scrap of fabric. If test piece takes, position main transfer face down on fabric, and pin at corners. Turn iron to low setting and press down on transfer for a few seconds; lift, then move to next area. Do not glide iron over transfer. Lift up corner to make sure transfer is taking.

To make your own hot-iron transfer, copy design on heavy tracing paper. Turn paper to back and trace over lines with transfer pencil. With traced side down on fabric, press transfer as described at left. A wax crayon can be used as a transfer pencil, but usually produces a thick line, so it is recommended only for large designs on coarse fabrics.

DRESSMAKER'S CARBON

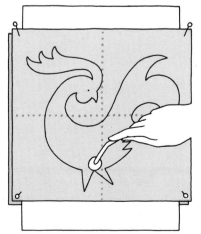

To use dressmaker's carbon, position pattern right side up on fabric, and pin at each corner. Carefully slip carbon paper, carbon side down, between fabric and pattern.

Draw over design lines of pattern, using a tracing wheel. You may find that a knitting needle, used like a pencil, will give you more control when you are drawing over lines.

PRICKING METHODS

To transfer a design by pricking method, lay pattern on a thick wad of fabric (an old sheet will do). Using a sharp pin or an awl, prick along design lines of pattern; keep holes close together. **For a quick pricking job,** use your sewing machine. Remove top and bobbin threads, and set stitch length to 8. Stitch along the design lines.

Position pricked design, right side up, on fabric, and pin along all edges. Using a small felt pad, gently rub pounce (special powder for the purpose) over pricked holes.

Remove pattern carefully to avoid smudging the pounce, then blow off any excess powder from fabric. Use a sharp dressmaker's pencil to connect dots that form design outline.

17

General embroidery techniques

Using an embroidery hoop

The purpose of an embroidery hoop is to hold the fabric taut during stitching so stitch tension can be kept even and consistent. Hoops may be made of wood, plastic, or metal and are available in different diameter sizes ranging from 4 inches to 12 inches. The wood and plastic hoops usually have a screw on the outer ring for adjusting their fit; the metal hoops only have springs.

To secure the fabric in a hoop, follow the instructions below, making certain that fabric threads are running straight in both directions. When you think the fabric is properly secured, tap it lightly; it should feel like a drum. Such delicate fabrics as satin, or such highly textured stitches as bullion knots, can be marred by the pressure of the rings. Tissue paper between rings will prevent this. Sometimes moisture causes wooden hoops to warp, making the outer ring very loose. To remedy, wrap fabric around inner ring as shown.

Although there is no set rule as to which part of a design to center first, always try to get a full motif within the hoop. For example, if your design is of a flower garden, try centering one full flower within the hoop. If the flower is too large, center only a portion of it, like three complete petals.

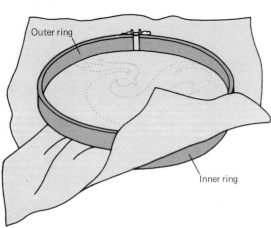

1. With the design side up, place fabric over inner ring of hoop. Adjust screw on outer ring so it fits snugly over inner ring and fabric.

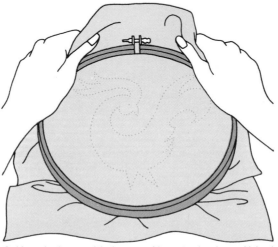

2. Move slowly around the hoop, pushing outer ring down with heels of hands while pulling fabric taut between thumb and fingers.

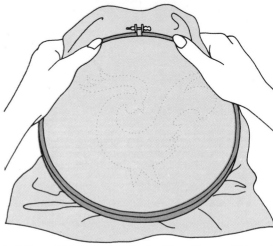

3. Pulling on fabric can make outer ring ride up. To correct this, push outer ring down over inner ring until it is secure.

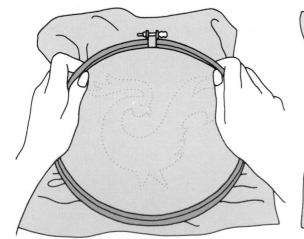

4. Always release fabric from hoop before storing away. Press down fabric at edges of hoop with thumbs, lifting outer ring at same time.

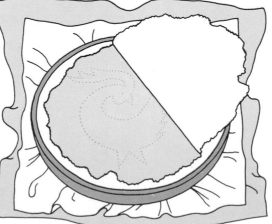

To protect fabric or stitches pressed between rings, place tissue paper over fabric, then secure as usual. Tear away paper as shown.

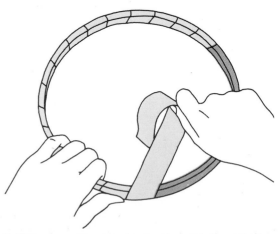

To tighten warped hoop, wrap cotton blanket binding or bias tape tightly around inner ring as shown; secure ends with masking tape.

Preparing yarns

Working yarns and threads should be no longer than 18 inches; an extremely long thread, pulled too often through the fabric, tends to fray toward the end.

Embroidery floss and Persian yarn are both loosely twisted yarns that can be separated into finer strands (see below for separating techniques). It is best to separate these yarns as you need them rather than all at once.

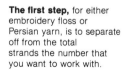

The first step, for either embroidery floss or Persian yarn, is to separate off from the total strands the number that you want to work with.

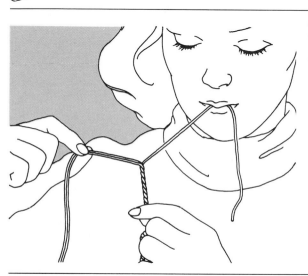

To separate embroidery floss, after dividing strands as shown above, hold one group of strands in your mouth, the other in one hand. Hold rest of floss length with your free hand. Then gently pull the divided strands apart, moving your free hand slowly down the floss length to control its twisting action.

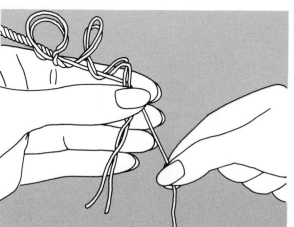

When strands of Persian yarn have been isolated as in top illustration, lay the yarn over your left hand; gently pull out a small quantity of the selected strand with your right hand. Stop, then straighten the remaining strands of yarn with left hand to keep them from tangling. Continue pulling and straightening in this way until the entire length is separated.

Threading the needle

There are several ways to simplify needle threading. One is to use a **needle threader,** a handy device specially designed for the purpose. If a threader is not available, try either the **paper strip** or the **looping** method below. Whichever method you choose, be sure that the selected yarn can ride easily through the eye of the needle, but not so easily that it will constantly slip out.

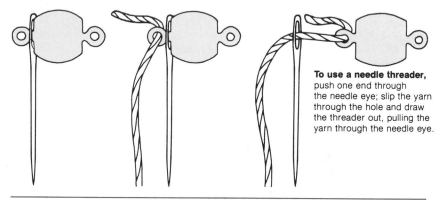

To use a needle threader, push one end through the needle eye; slip the yarn through the hole and draw the threader out, pulling the yarn through the needle eye.

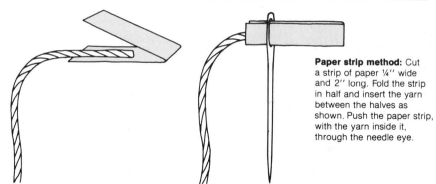

Paper strip method: Cut a strip of paper ¼" wide and 2" long. Fold the strip in half and insert the yarn between the halves as shown. Push the paper strip, with the yarn inside it, through the needle eye.

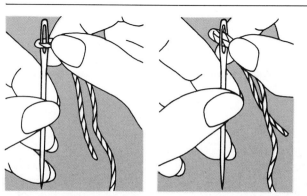

Loop method: Loop end of yarn over eye of needle and pull it tight. Slip the loop off the needle and force the fold of the yarn through the needle eye.

General embroidery techniques

Working embroidery

Above all else, it takes patience and care to create a successful piece of embroidery. Nothing else will produce the characteristic effects in the stitches that make up the design. You should aim for stitches that are executed at just the right tension and a finished result that is neat and even on the wrong as well as the right side. The pointers at the right will help you to reach these goals. Some techniques may seem awkward at first, but they will become easier as practice makes you more proficient.

When you are starting or ending a length of yarn, never use a knot; it might show through the finished piece or cause lumps on the right side. This is especially true if your embroidery is to be framed. The adjoining illustrations suggest ways of securing yarn at the beginning and end. Do not skimp on yarn in either process; the ends can begin to work loose after a few washings.

Whether you use an embroidery hoop or a frame, make the most use you can of both hands as you work. You will find the stabbing motion easier to master when your hoop or frame is on a stand—it frees both hands for the push and pull of the needle action.

Before you start to embroider, study your design carefully and notice which of its parts appear to lie on top of other parts. Work first the parts that are lowest (farthest down), then work the elements above these so that the two overlap. This will give your piece subtle realism, and also avoid the possibility of fabric showing between parts.

If you are working on one area of the design and would like to move to another in which the same color yarn is used, it is best to secure the yarn at the first point and start again rather than trail the yarn over a wide space.

Follow the transferred design lines precisely, remembering that they are merely guides and are not meant to be seen when the embroidery is completed.

STARTING AND ENDING

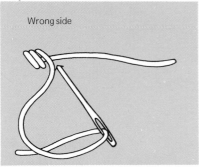

To secure yarn at the start of stitching, hold the end of the yarn on the wrong side of the fabric and work stitches over 2″ of yarn end.

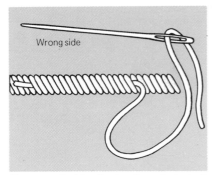

If some embroidery is already worked, simply slide needle under wrong side of laid stitches, securing 2″ of yarn end under the stitching.

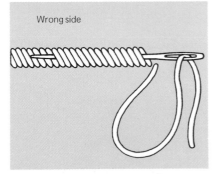

To secure yarn at the end of stitching, slide the needle under 2″ of laid stitches on the wrong side and then cut the yarn.

HANDLING NEEDLE

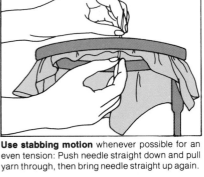

Use stabbing motion whenever possible for an even tension: Push needle straight down and pull yarn through, then bring needle straight up again.

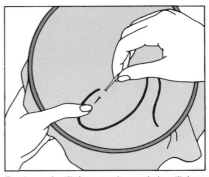

For looped stitches, such as chain stitches, bring needle up before yarn is pulled through, and use free hand to guide yarn around needle.

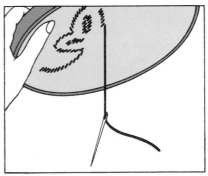

Twisting and eventual tangling often occur with constant needle action. To remedy this, drop needle and let it dangle freely until yarn unwinds.

FOLLOWING DESIGN LINES

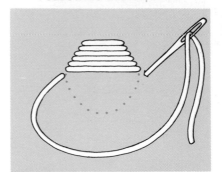

When following design markings on fabric, insert needle on the outside edge of transferred line so that all markings are completely covered.

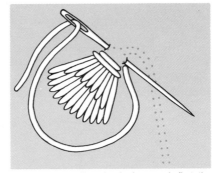

For greater realism in design, work first the parts that lie lowest, then work the parts that lie above them so that the two overlap slightly.

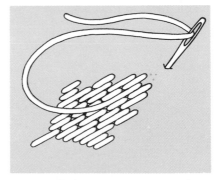

For finer definition of pointed shapes (such as a leaf tip as shown), exaggerate the point by extending the stitch past the transferred line.

Embroidery stitches

Selecting embroidery stitches
Charting your design
Backstitches
Blanket stitches
Chain stitches
Couching stitches
Cross stitches
Featherstitches
Filling stitches/detached
Filling stitches/laid
Running stitches
Satin stitches
Weaving stitches

Selecting embroidery stitches

Embroidery stitches are the basic components with which a design is carried out. Although the number may seem unlimited, actually each stitch is a part of a stitch family and, as such, has its origin in the basic family stitch. There are 11 such family groups; the pages that follow give step-by-step illustrations for each stitch in each group.

To help you understand the family relationship of one stitch to another, and to provide a means of practicing the stitches, we suggest that you work a sampler of all or some of the stitches you will see on the following pages. You can then keep the sampler as a stitch "dictionary" for future reference or, if you prefer, you can finish it to use as a decorative wall hanging.

Embroidery stitches are used in basically two ways: they either *outline* or *fill* in a particular shape in a design. The shape can be solidly filled so that none of the fabric shows through, or it can be filled with opened stitches for a lacy effect. Some stitches have natural configurations or textures that make them ideal for particular effects. An example is the Vandyke stitch (see p. 38), which gives a natural impression of a leaf when it is worked.

When you make your first attempt at stitch selection, try to limit your choice to a few stitches, and remember that there is no "right" combination of stitches for a design, only one that pleases you and carries out the design to your satisfaction. Notice how the design below has been interpreted in two different ways. Both are lovely pieces, yet each of them was worked with a totally different stitch combination.

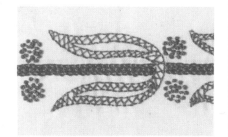

Different stitch interpretations of the identical design can produce two very different impressions.

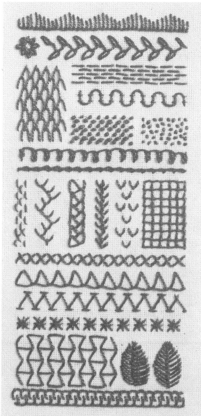

Sampler can serve as a "dictionary" of stitches.

Charting your design

Prepare a guide for your embroidery work by mapping out a chart that indicates the selected stitches as well as the yarn colors for each part of the design. Use your original traced drawing as the basis for the chart. First assign a *letter* to each stitch and list those stitch symbols at the side. Then print the identifying letters on the appropriate parts of the drawing. Indicate with simple pencil lines the direction in which each stitch will be worked. If colors are not present in your drawing, color-code the yarns in a similar way: assign a *number* to each colored yarn and put the numbers on the appropriate parts of the drawing. If there are any other variables, such as the number of yarn strands that are to be used with each stitch, indicate those in your list as well. An example of a charted design is shown below.

A – Long and short stitch
B – Wave stitch
C – Basic satin stitch
D – Threaded chain stitch

1 – Pale orange
2 – Lavender
3 – Black
4 – Tan

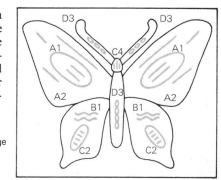

Embroidery stitches

Backstitches

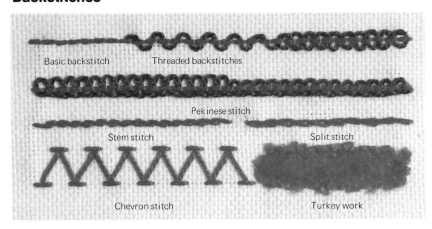

Basic backstitch Threaded backstitches

Pekinese stitch

Stem stitch Split stitch

Chevron stitch Turkey work

Though each of the stitches in the backstitch group has its own distinctive look, they are related in the stitching motion that produces a stitch row. In every case, the needle must be moved a step backward before a step is taken forward along the stitch row. This is true whether stitches are being worked from left to right or from right to left.

Some of the stitches shown are narrow, and so are ideal for outlining. In general, the *basic backstitch* is used to outline areas bounded by straight lines, and the *stem* and *split* stitches are preferred when the boundary line is curved. Worked in close rows, these thin stitches can be used to fill an area. Some of the other stitches, such as the *chevron* and *threaded backstitches,* are wider, and therefore perfect for decorative borders and bands. Most of the stitches shown are flat and not highly textured; the exception is *Turkey work,* which creates a soft pile when trimmed.

When working each stitch, be sure to carefully follow the sequence of steps. Because of the backward movement, the needle will often re-enter at a point already established by a previous step; it is important in these instances to insert the needle exactly in the hole that was previously made.

Basic backstitch is most often used as a straight outline stitch. Its simple line effect is often seen in blackwork embroidery. This stitch also forms the base line for other decorative stitches. Work basic stitch from right to left. Bring needle out at 1. Insert at 2 and exit at 3; distance between 3–1 and 1–2 should be equal. Repeat sequence for next stitch; needle entering at point 2 should go into hole made by thread emerging from point 1 of previous stitch. Keep length of backstitches consistent.

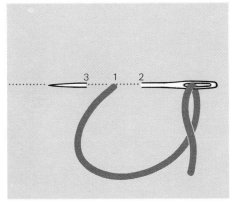
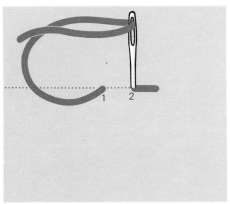
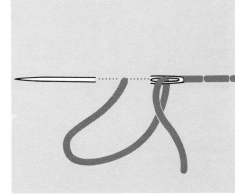

Single- or double-threaded backstitches add another dimension to the basic stitch. Worked in contrasting yarns, each new row can alter the overall effect. Lay down basic backstitch first. To work *single-threaded* line, use a blunt needle to lace the yarn under each stitch; do not catch fabric below. To work *double-threaded* line, lace second yarn in opposite direction, keeping loops even on both sides of backstitch line; do not catch or split yarns already laid.

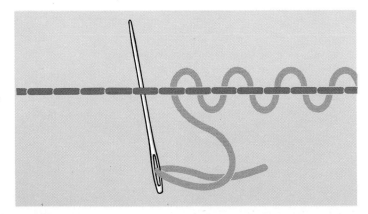
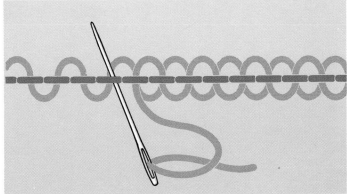

Pekinese stitch (also known as Chinese stitch), like the threaded backstitches, uses simple backstitch as a base. Its interlacing technique, however, produces an effect reminiscent of braiding. The stitch is often used for outlining and for decorative borders. Lay down the basic backstitch first. Then, using a blunt needle, lace yarn under laid stitches as shown; do not catch fabric below, and keep loops even. Lacing yarns can be pulled tighter to eliminate loops above the base line for an even finer braid-like effect.

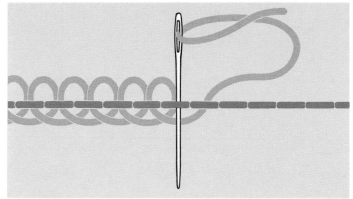 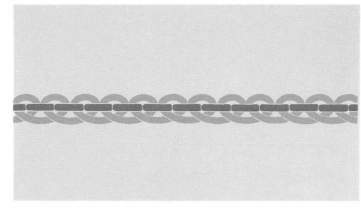

Stem stitch is primarily an outlining stitch, but is often used to work stems in floral designs as well. Working from left to right, bring needle out at 1. Insert at 2 and exit a half stitch length back at 3; distance 1–3 and 3–2 should be equal. Repeat sequence. Note that point 3 of previous stitch is now point 1, and the needle emerging at 3 is coming from hole made by thread entering at point 2 of the previous stitch. For a broader stem stitch, angle the needle slightly when entering at 2 and exiting at 3 as shown in the last drawing.

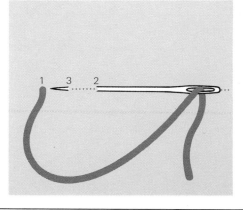 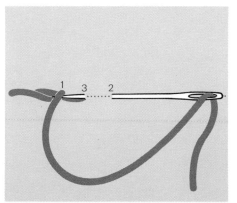 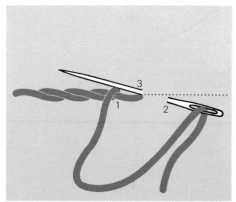

Split stitch is worked like the stem stitch, except when the needle emerges, it splits the working yarn; the final effect resembles a thin chain stitch. Although outlining is its most common use, split stitch can be used in solid rows as well. Working stitch from left to right, bring needle up at 1 and down at 2. Bring needle back up at 3, splitting center of laid yarn. Repeat sequence. Note that point 3 of previous stitch is now point 1. Keep stitch length even; when going around curves, however, shorten length slightly.

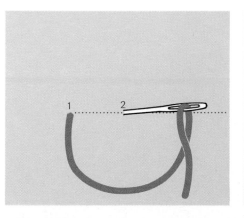 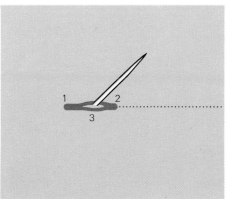 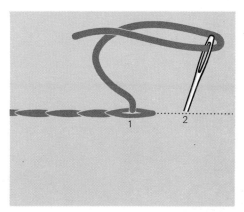

Embroidery stitches

Backstitches

Chevron stitch is often used as a decorative border. The stitch is worked from left to right between double lines. To work stitch, bring needle up at 1 along bottom line. Insert at 2; exit a half stitch length back at 3. Insert needle at point 4 and bring up at 5 along top line; distance between 4–5 is equal to a half stitch length. Bring needle down at 6 (whole stitch length from 5) and back out again at point 4.

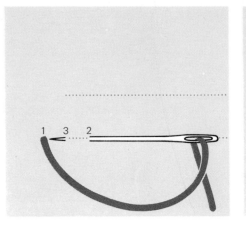

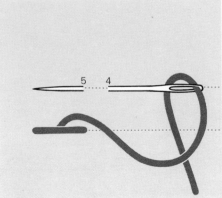

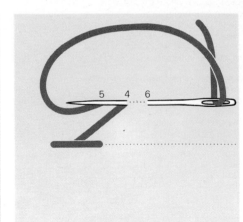

To position needle for repeat, insert needle at 7 on bottom line and exit a half stitch length back at 8; distance between 4–7 is same as 3–4. Continue this 1 to 8 sequence. Note that point 8 is point 1 at start of new sequence.

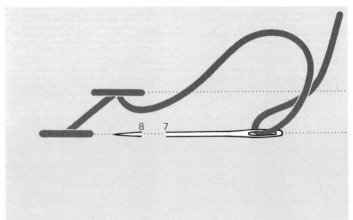

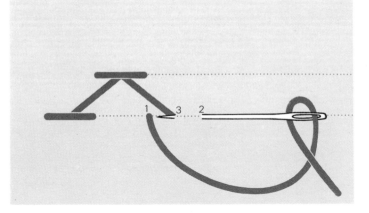

Turkey work is made up of backstitches alternately pulled tight and looped. A series of rows forms a pile, which may be trimmed for an even fuzzier effect. Stitch is worked from left to right. Bring the needle out at 1. Insert it at 2 and exit a half stitch length back at 3. Insert the needle at 4, a full stitch length away, and bring it back up at 2; carry yarn above stitch line and leave a short loop. Proceed with next backstitch, carrying yarn below the stitch line.

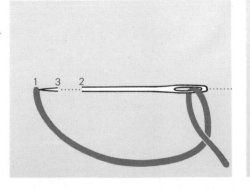

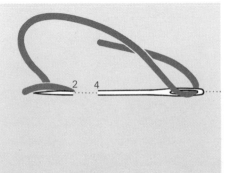

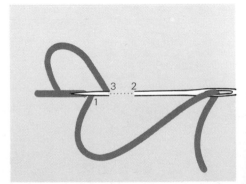

Continue sequence with another looped stitch, then a stitch pulled tight, until row is completed. Cover entire design area with the Turkey work, starting from the top and working toward the bottom. If existing loops get in the way, pin them down. For fuzzy pile, cut loops. Do not cut each row individually; instead, trim the entire area at once to a uniform length

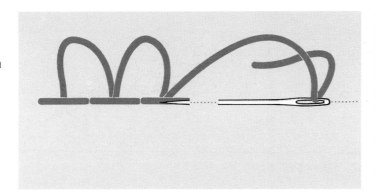 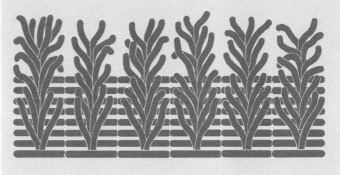

Blanket stitches

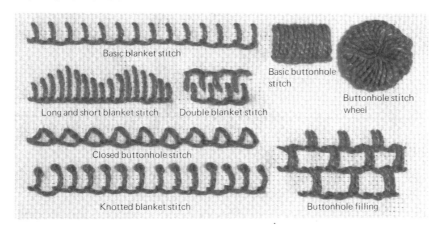

Basic blanket stitch

Long and short blanket stitch Double blanket stitch

Closed buttonhole stitch

Knotted blanket stitch

Basic buttonhole stitch

Buttonhole stitch wheel

Buttonhole filling

Blanket stitches, which consist basically of edging stitches, comprise the next stitch group. The name probably derived from the finishing worked around the edges of woolen blankets. Today, however, these stitches are often used as outlines and as functional decorative borders as well. One in particular, the *buttonhole filling,* can also be worked to cover an entire area, producing an almost crochet-like effect. Blanket stitches are basically flat stitches, neither raised nor textured, and can vary in size depending on the requirements of your design. Because of their adaptability to decorative purposes and the simplicity and speed of working them, they appear in many peasant embroideries, and are often seen in crazy patchwork and in appliqué. They are especially useful in hemstitching embroidery and are also a popular finishing choice for non-woven fabrics, such as felt, that do not require a hem.

You will note that all blanket stitches have a scroll-like base with "legs" extending from it. This base is formed by looping the yarn under the point of the needle before the stitch is pulled up tight. Work carefully to keep stitch height even (unless otherwise specified) and to keep the scroll base at an even tension all the way across.

Basic blanket stitch is a popular finishing stitch for edges. When worked small, it can be used for outlining as well. Stitch is worked from left to right. Bring needle out at 1 on bottom line. Insert at 2 on top line and slightly to the right, then exit at 3, directly below. Before pulling needle through, carry yarn under point of needle as shown. Proceed to next stitch. Note point 3 of previous stitch is now point 1. Work entire row in the same way, keeping height of stitches even throughout.

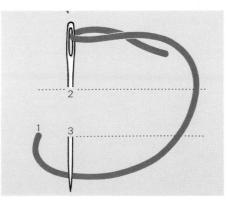 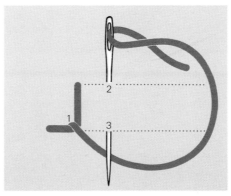 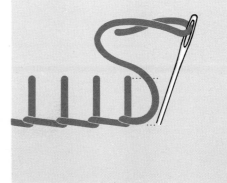

Embroidery stitches

Blanket stitches

Variations of blanket stitch:
The first variation is called the *long and short blanket stitch.* It is worked exactly like the basic stitch except that heights of stitches range from short to tall, creating a pyramid effect. The *double blanket stitch* is simply two rows of the basic stitch. Work is turned after one row is completed so the stitches of the second row can fall between the stitches of the first. Both rows should be the same height and should overlap slightly at the center.

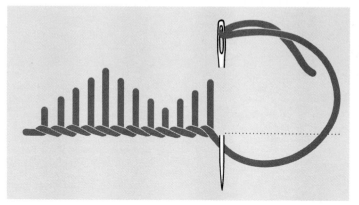
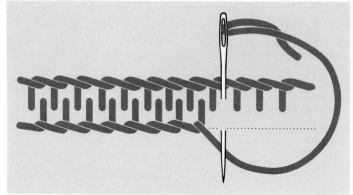

Basic buttonhole stitch is worked like basic blanket stitch, except that the stitches are placed very close together to form a firm edge. This tight little band of stitches is used extensively in cutwork embroidery. For added firmness along an edge, a row of split stitches (p.23) can be laid along the bottom line first. A *buttonhole stitch wheel* is a popular method for doing flowered motifs. The basic buttonhole stitch is worked in a circle with the needle entering the same hole in the center each time.

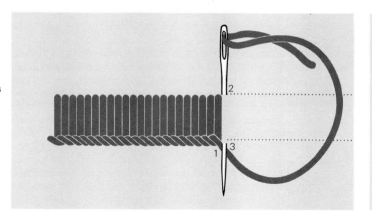
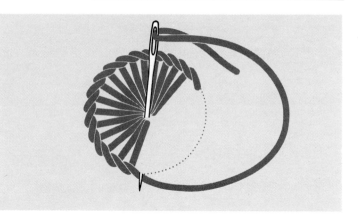

Closed buttonhole stitch is a decorative edging that is worked from left to right. The extending "legs" form small triangles along the row. Bring needle out at 1 on bottom line. Insert at 2 on top line, slightly to the right, then exit at 3 on bottom line. Before pulling needle through, carry yarn under needle point. To complete triangle, insert needle back into 2 again and come out at 4, carrying yarn below needle point as usual. Continue sequence as shown. Note that point 4 of the previous stitch is now point 1.

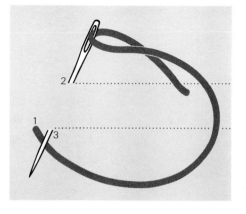
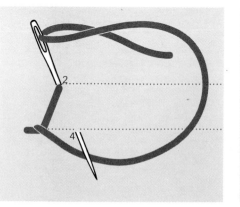
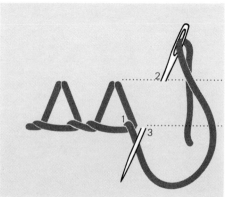

Buttonhole filling consists of several stitched rows that produce a lacy effect. Pairs of buttonhole stitches mesh between other pairs in the row above. (If desired, a group can be three or four stitches.) The buttonhole filling is first worked from left to right, then right to left on the next row. Work the first pair of stitches close together; start the second pair two spaces (width of two stitches) to the right. Continue this way to end of row. Insert needle at end of bottom line, then bring it out at next line directly below to start next row.

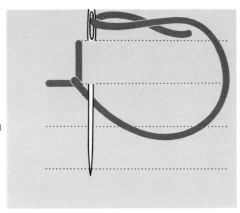 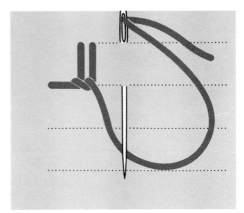 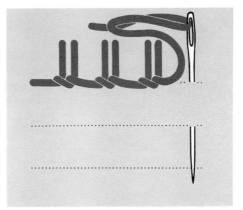

Work the next row from right to left. The basic 1 to 3 buttonhole stitch sequence is still used, but now the yarn is carried under the needle point from right to left as shown. Work the pairs of buttonhole stitches over the open spaces on the row above. At end of second row, insert needle in bottom line, then out at next line directly below. Continue working rows in this way until desired area is covered.

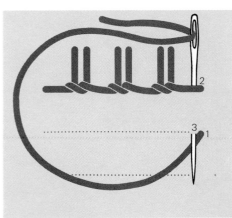 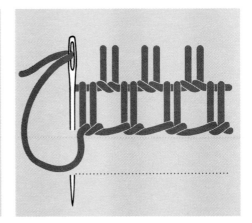 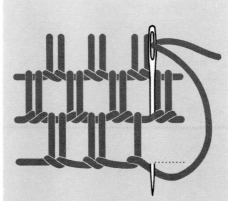

Knotted blanket stitch resembles basic blanket stitch, but with a knot formed at the top of each one. Working from left to right, bring needle out at 1. Wrap yarn around left thumb and place needle point under loop. Slip loop off thumb. With needle inside loop, insert needle at 2 and exit at 3; carry yarn under needle point, then pull yarn end to tighten loop around needle. Pull needle through to form knot at top of stitch. Continue along entire row. Worked back to back, knotted blanket stitch makes an attractive tree or leaf design.

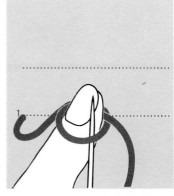 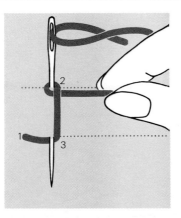 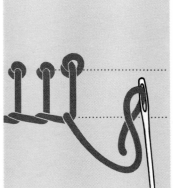 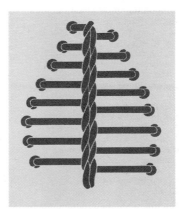

Embroidery stitches

Chain stitches

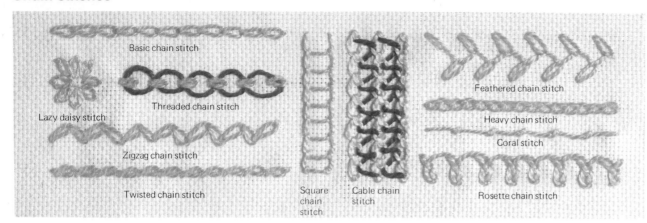

Basic chain stitch

Threaded chain stitch

Lazy daisy stitch

Zigzag chain stitch

Twisted chain stitch

Square chain stitch

Cable chain stitch

Feathered chain stitch

Heavy chain stitch

Coral stitch

Rosette chain stitch

As the name implies, most of the stitches in this group resemble the links in a chain. Each stitch has its own special configuration and particular use, but together they form one of the most indispensable of the stitch groups. Chain stitches, like the blanket stitch group, are looped: The working yarn is always carried under the needle point before the stitch is pulled tight.

For the most part, these stitches are worked vertically and are used basically for outlining and decorative borders. If worked in rows to fill an area, each row is usually stitched in the same direction to give a fabric-like texture.

Basic chain stitch is one of the most popular embroidery stitches for outlining or, if worked in close rows, for filling an area. Bring needle out at 1. Insert back into same hole at point 1 and bring out at 2, carrying yarn under needle point, then pull it through. Point 2 is now point 1 of next stitch. Work all stitches the same way, always inserting needle into the hole made by the emerging thread. To end row, take a small stitch over last chain loop to hold it down.

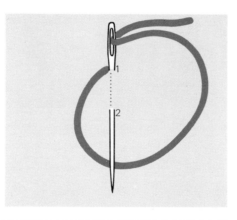

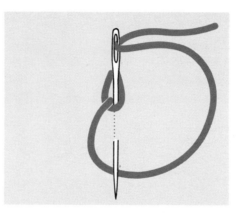

Lazy daisy stitch (or the detached chain) is a single unattached stitch worked in a circle to give an impression of petals. Bring needle out at 1. Insert back into same hole at point 1, and exit at 2; carry yarn under needle point, then pull through. Insert needle at 3 over chain loop, then bring needle out at point 1 for next chain stitch. Continue this way until all petals are completed. Stitches may be scattered at random over an area provided yarn does not have to be carried too far on wrong side.

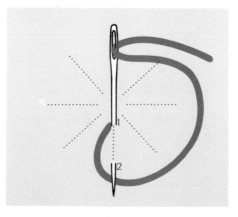

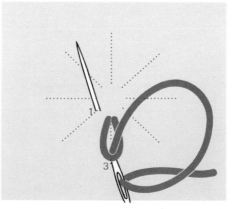

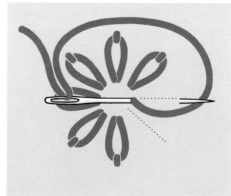

Threaded chain stitch resembles a chain with two link sizes. To achieve this double link effect, detached chain stitches are threaded with a contrasting yarn. This makes a pretty border or it can be used as an outline stitch. First work a row of detached chain stitches. Using a blunt needle and contrasting yarn, bring needle up under last chain. Lace yarn back and forth under each chain; do not catch fabric. Start again at bottom and lace in opposite direction, keeping loops even on both sides of the detached chain stitches.

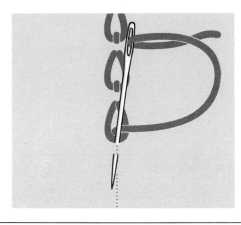 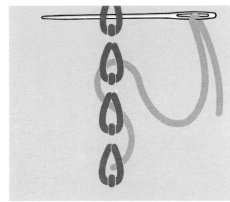 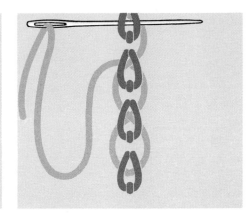

Zigzag chain stitch is worked with the chains positioned at alternating angles to give a decorative zigzag effect. Work first stitch exactly like a basic chain stitch, angling it as shown between double lines. The hole from which thread emerges becomes point 1 for next stitch. Insert needle at 2, piercing loop end to anchor it, and exit at 3; carry yarn under needle point, then pull through. Continue sequence, always piercing loop end and keeping angle of stitches consistent. To end, take small stitch over last chain loop.

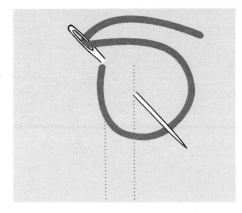 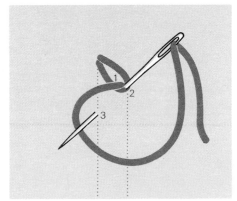 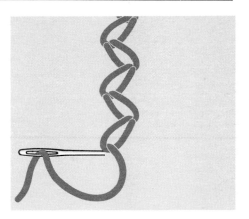

Twisted chain stitch makes an unusual textured outline. To work, bring needle out at 1. Insert needle at 2, which is slightly lower and to the left of 1, then exit at 3, which is in line with 1; carry yarn under point of needle, then pull through. Work next stitch the same way. Note that point 3 of previous stitch is point 1 of new stitch. Complete row of chains. To end, take a small stitch over the last chain loop to hold it down.

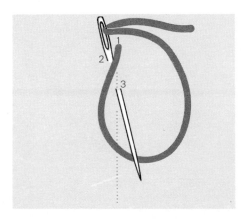 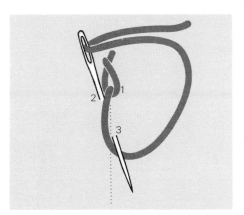 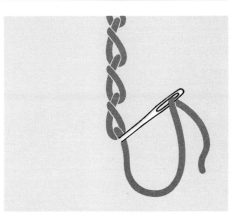

Embroidery stitches

Chain stitches

Square chain stitch (or ladder stitch) provides broad outline that may be laced with ribbon or yarn. Stitch is worked between double lines. Bring needle out at 1 on left line. Insert at 2, directly across, and exit at 3; carry yarn under needle point, then pull through. Do not pull yarn tight; leave a bit of slack so needle can be inserted inside wide loop for next stitch. Continue this way until row is completed. To anchor last chain, take a small stitch over left side of loop, then take a small stitch over right side.

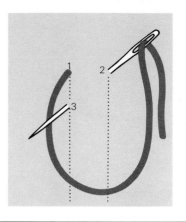 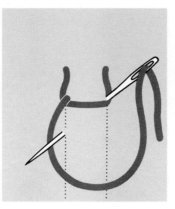 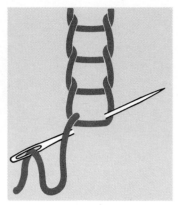 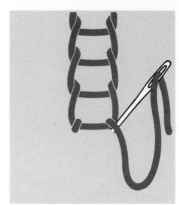

Cable chain stitch resembles a metal chain. It can be used for outlining or interlaced for a filling as in the last illustration. Bring needle out at 1. Loop yarn over needle as shown. Insert needle at 2, just below point 1, and exit at 3; carry yarn under needle point. As you pull needle through, both small and large links are formed. Continue this way until the row is completed. To interlace, work several rows of cable chain stitch, then use a blunt needle with contrasting yarn to weave in and out.

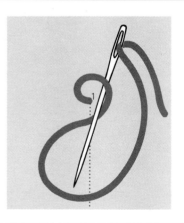 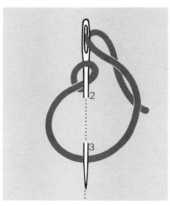 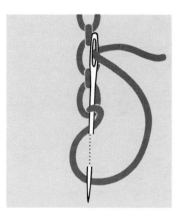 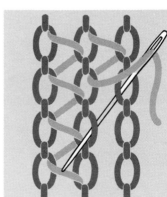

Feathered chain stitch is a delicate border stitch that resembles a vine. It is worked between double lines. Starting at one side of double line, work a slanted chain stitch in the basic 1 to 2 sequence shown. Insert needle in the same slanting direction at 3, then bring it back up at 4, approximately across from 2. Work subsequent chain stitches the same way, keeping alternating slants of chains consistent on each side.

 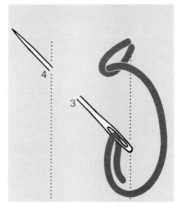 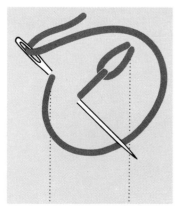 

Heavy chain stitch (also known as braid stitch) makes a pretty outline stitch. Because of its braid-like quality, it can also be used for stems, twigs, and narrow leaves. To start, work a basic chain stitch by bringing needle out at 1, then inserting needle back in same hole and coming up at 2. Insert needle down at 3 over chain loop, then come back up at 4, which is same distance from 2 as 1 is from 2. Slide needle under first chain stitch from right to left without picking up any fabric. Re-insert needle at 4, and exit at 5.

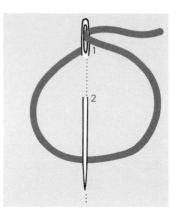
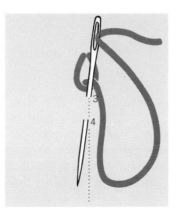
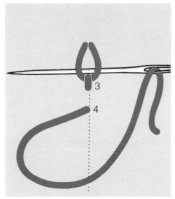

Slide needle from right to left under the second chain stitch and the small anchoring stitch, then re-insert needle at 5, and bring out at 6. Slide needle from right to left under the two preceding chain stitches as shown, then re-insert needle at 6. Continue in this way, always sliding needle under the last two chain stitches.

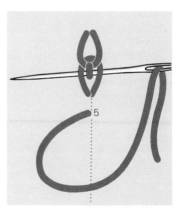
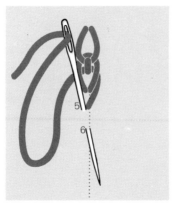
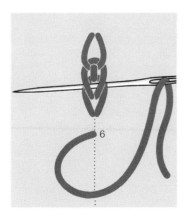
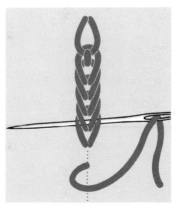

Coral stitch is a simple outline stitch, punctuated with small knots along the row. It is particularly effective used for stems and twigs. If worked in many rows, coral stitch can also fill an area with an unusual texture. Work stitch from right to left. Bring needle up at 1. Insert needle at 2, then take a small bite of fabric, slanting needle out at 3. Loop yarn over and around needle point, then pull needle through to secure stitch and form knot. Continue in this way for entire row, spacing knots evenly or at random as you wish.

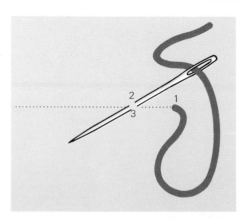
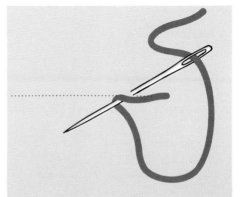
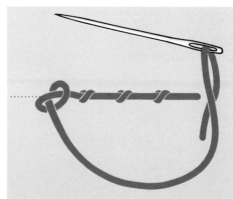

Embroidery stitches

Chain stitches

Rosette chain stitch, a pretty edging, is worked small and close together. Work stitch from right to left between double lines. Bring needle out at 1. To make rosette, insert at 2, slightly to the left, then out at 3 directly below; carry yarn under needle and pull through. Slide needle under yarn at 1; leave a little slack along top. Work next stitch a short distance away, entering at 2 and exiting at 3; slide needle under slack yarn at top. To end row, insert needle back into point 2 of last rosette.

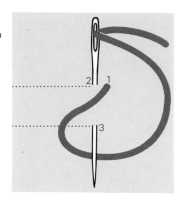
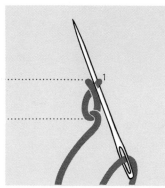
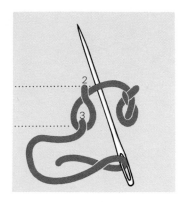
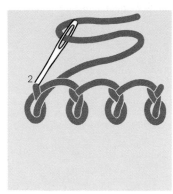

Couching

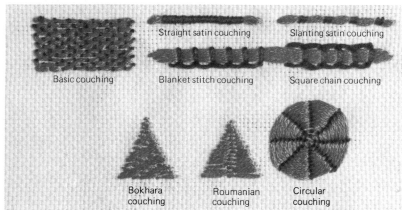

Straight satin couching

Slanting satin couching

Basic couching

Blanket stitch couching

Square chain couching

Bokhara couching

Roumanian couching

Circular couching

This group of stitches, known as couching stitches, are particularly useful in outlining an area or in giving more weight to a single line. Usually, there are two working yarns, the laid yarn (which can be one or more strands) and the couching yarn. The couching yarn is stitched over the laid yarn to attach it to the fabric. Often the laid yarn and the couching yarn are of contrasting colors. The actual effect of couching varies with the specific stitch and the number of laid yarns that are used.

The more strands you lay down, the heavier the outline. Experiment to determine how many strands should be laid.

You will need more strands to outline a heavily embroidered shape than to define a fragile pattern. Or you could use a single, heavyweight laid yarn.

In addition to outlining, whole areas can be filled in with couching. To create textural variety, lay the yarns so they run in different directions.

Two unique types of couching are *Bokhara* and *Roumanian*. Both employ only one length of yarn for both the laying and the couching instead of separate lengths of yarn for each.

To create more unusual effects, couch over finished needlepoint and appliqué. Or try couching with metallic yarns.

Basic couching is used to outline a design. To start, bring up desired number of laid yarns at right. Use left thumb to hold and guide laid yarns as you couch over them. Bring working yarn up at 1 just below laid yarns. Insert at 2 directly above laid yarns, and exit at 3 farther along the line. Point 3 is now point 1 for next stitch. Continue until laid yarns are completely anchored; keep distance between stitches consistent. Bring ends of laid yarns to back and secure.

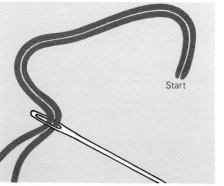

Start

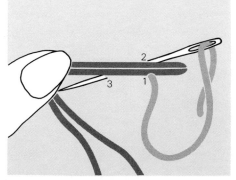
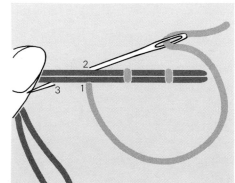

To fill an area, work first line as in basic couching. At end of line, turn trailing laid yarns to the right. Take a horizontal stitch at turning point. Turn work *upside down* and couch second row of yarns from right to left, placing stitches between stitches of preceding row. At end of second row, turn trailing laid yarns to the right and again take a horizontal stitch. Turn work *upright* and work third row, alternating vertical stitches with those in the row above. Continue this way until entire area is covered.

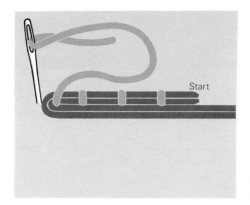

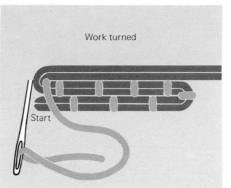

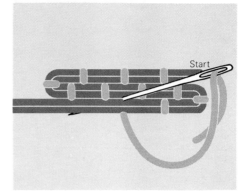

Variations can be achieved by working some basic embroidery stitches over the laid yarns. Four are shown at the right. The first is similar to basic couching except that *straight satin stitches* are worked close together to completely cover the laid yarns; this produces a raised, textured line. The next is couched with pairs of *slanting satin stitches.* The third and fourth types are couched with *blanket stitches* and *square chain stitches,* respectively, over several laid yarns.

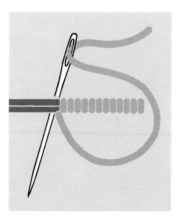

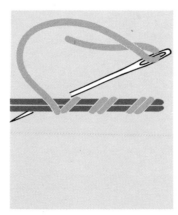

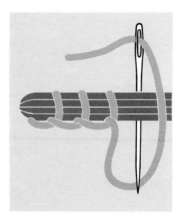

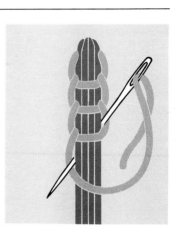

Bokhara couching is used to fill an area with a woven effect. Unlike the previous couching, both the laid and the couching yarns are the *same* length of yarn. The yarn is laid from left to right and couched from right to left. Bring yarn up at 1. Insert at 2, and exit at 3 above laid yarn. Insert needle at 4 over laid yarn and slightly ahead of 3. Come up at 5 (in line with 3). Continue slanted stitches to end of laid yarn. Bring needle out at 1 to begin next row. Place slanted stitches in each row between those in previous row.

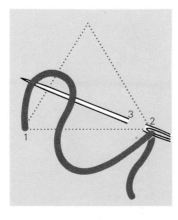

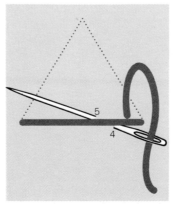

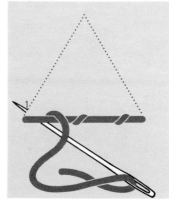

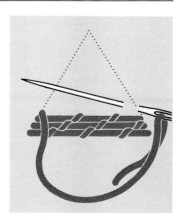

Embroidery stitches

Couching

Roumanian couching, like Bokhara, uses same yarn length for laid and couching yarns. The two stitches are worked similarly but the Roumanian stitches are longer. Bring yarn up at 1. Insert at 2, exit at 3 above laid yarn. Take a long slanting stitch over laid yarn to 4; exit at 1 for start of next row. Continue taking laid and couching stitches, keeping yarns slack so that the two stitch types appear indistinguishable. Place each new slanting stitch above one in previous row.

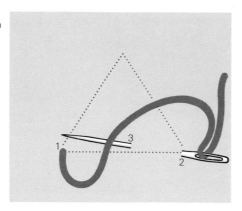
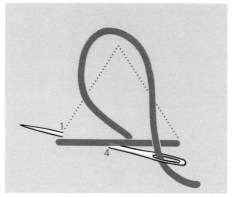
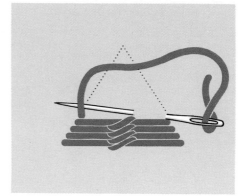

Circular couching produces a solid spoked-wheel effect. It is particularly effective in contrasting yarns. Bring couching yarn up at 1 in center of marked circle. Loop laid yarn over couching yarn as shown, and re-insert needle at 1 to secure laid yarn. Bring needle out at 2 along one of the spoke lines, then take a small stitch over the laid yarns by inserting needle at 3 directly above 2. Bring needle out at 4 along next spoke line. Take another stitch at 5 over laid yarns.

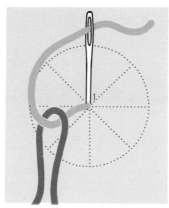
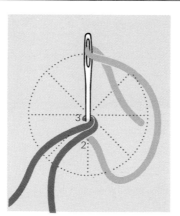
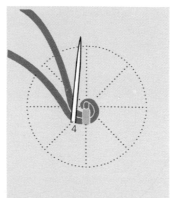
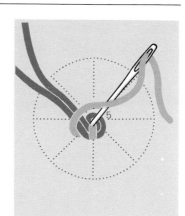

Continue taking small stitches over laid yarns at each marked spoke line while guiding the laid yarns around center in a clockwise direction. Be careful not to pull laid yarns too tightly or work will pucker. When circle is completed, fasten off couching yarn on wrong side. Thread one of the laid yarns; take to back of fabric and secure. Thread second laid yarn and wind around circle past end of first laid yarn (to make circle end gradually). Bring to back and secure as before.

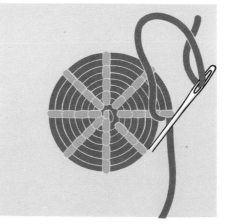

Cross stitches

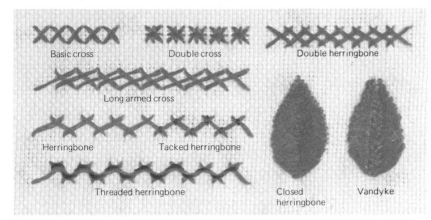

Basic cross   Double cross   Double herringbone

Long armed cross

Herringbone   Tacked herringbone

Threaded herringbone   Closed herringbone   Vandyke

Cross stitches make up the next group of embroidery stitches. As their name implies, all the stitches in this category are formed in one way or another by two crossing arms. The uses of cross stitches are numerous; they can be worked as outlines, as borders, or to fill in an entire area. Sometimes crossing stitches overlap, as in the *herringbone stitches*. Two such overlapping stitches, the *closed herringbone stitch* and the *Vandyke stitch*, are particularly well suited to the formation of leaves.

The basic cross stitch is, of course, the best known stitch and in itself encompasses an embroidery technique. Its even passes an embroidery technique. Its even stitch formation makes it ideal for working on even-weave and printed fabrics, such as gingham (see p. 68). Unlike cross stitch variations, the basic cross stitch (when worked in a row) can be stitched in two journeys. Half of the stitch is laid on one journey, then the crossing arm is laid on the return. This stitching technique helps to assure an even stitch tension. For stitch consistency, make sure that all of the top yarns lie in the same direction.

The basic cross stitch can be used to create an intaglio effect (see Assisi embroidery). This is a technique that involves covering the background, leaving the design free of stitching.

Basic cross stitch's simplicity and versatility make it a highly popular stitch. Cross stitches are usually *worked in rows* of even, slanted stitches, first from right to left laying down half the crosses, then back from left to right to complete them. Bring needle up at 1. Insert at 2 and exit at 3 directly below 2. At end of row, work back, entering at 4 and exiting at 5. To *work one cross stitch* at a time, bring needle up at 1. Insert at 2 and exit at 3 directly below 2. Insert needle at 4, above 1.

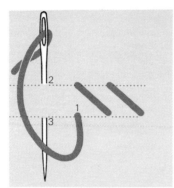
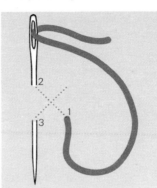
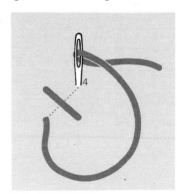

Double cross stitch resembles a star and can be scattered as a filling stitch or worked in a row to provide a decorative border. It is worked very similarly to the basic single cross stitch above. Bring needle out at 1. Insert at 2 and exit at 3 directly below 2. Enter at 4 and exit at 5 (halfway between points 1 and 3). Insert at 6 directly above 5 (halfway between points 2 and 4) and exit at 7 (halfway between 2 and 3). Insert at 8 directly across from 7 to complete stitch.

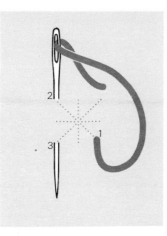
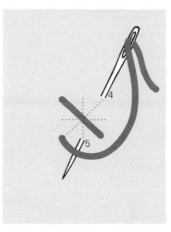
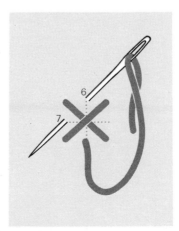

Embroidery stitches

Cross stitches

Long-armed cross stitch gives an almost plaited effect as each cross stitch overlaps the next. The first arm of the cross is longer and has a more extreme slant than the second. Work stitch from left to right. Bring needle up at 1. Take a long slanting stitch to top right, inserting needle at 2; exit half a step back at 3. Insert needle at 4 directly below point 2; then bring needle up at 1 directly below point 3, for start of next stitch. Repeat sequence. Note that each stitch touches the previous one at the top and overlaps it at the bottom.

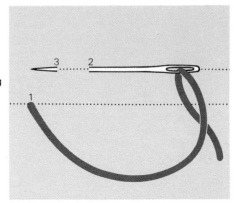
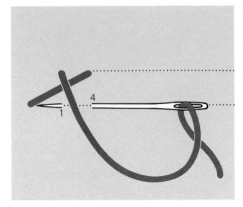
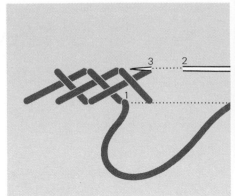

Herringbone stitch is a popular embroidery stitch often used for borders. This basic overlapping stitch (sometimes referred to as a catchstitch when used in sewing) forms a foundation that can be decorated with a second color. Keep the spacing and length of stitches even. Work from left to right. Bring needle up at 1. Take a slanting stitch to the top right, inserting needle at 2. Exit a short distance back at 3; insert needle at 4 to complete stitch. Bring needle up at 1 to start new stitch. Repeat sequence for each subsequent stitch.

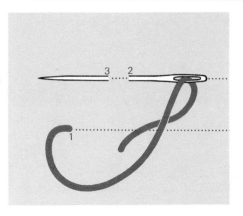
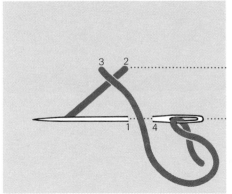
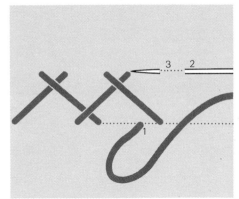

Tacked herringbone stitch adds another dimension to the basic herringbone stitch above; each cross of the stitch is tacked down with a small vertical stitch of a contrasting color yarn. Work a row of herringbone stitch first, using the 1 to 4 sequence above. To tack down crosses, work from right to left. Bring needle out at A just above top, right-hand cross. Insert at B and exit at C below next cross. Insert needle at D; exit at point A for the start of a new sequence. Continue in this way until all crosses are tacked down.

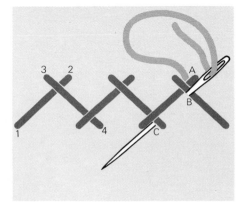
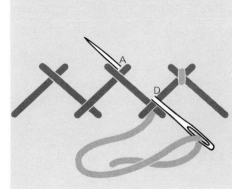
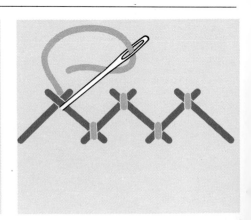

Threaded herringbone stitch is another variation of the basic herringbone stitch. Here, a contrasting color yarn is laced over and under the crosses. The needle does not pierce the fabric, so use a blunt needle for the lacing. Start lacing from the left side so that the needle passes under each arm of the cross and over the intersecting points as shown. Do not pull lacing too tightly or you will distort the basic herringbone stitch.

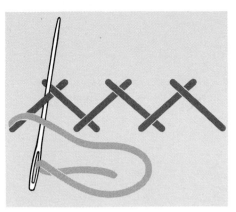
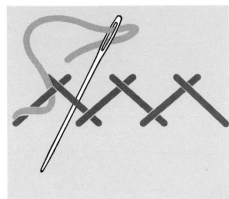
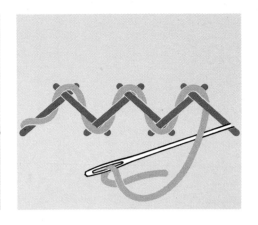

Double herringbone stitch is two rows of herringbone stitches that interlace. Rows worked in contrasting colors are especially attractive. For interlaced look, each row is worked slightly differently from the regular herringbone stitch. Work both rows from left to right. Bring needle up at 1. Take a slanting stitch to top right, inserting needle at 2. Exit a short distance back at 3. Slip needle *under first slanting arm.* Insert at 4 to complete stitch. Repeat sequence, always slipping needle under first slanting arm of each cross.

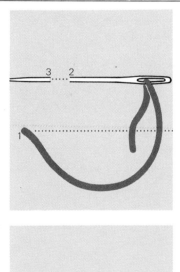
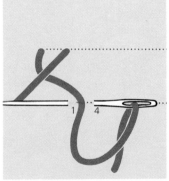
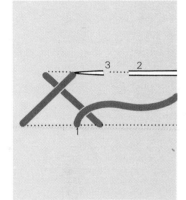

Change to contrasting yarn. To get into position for second herringbone sequence, come out at A directly above point 1, and insert at B directly below point 2, crossing over arm 1-2 in original color. Bring needle out at C directly below point 3, and pass needle under arm 3-4 (original color). Insert needle at D and exit at E. Pass needle under arm C-D; insert at F. To complete sequence, bring needle out at C for start of next repeat. Continue in this way, repeating sequence C to F, passing each time over and under appropriate slanting arms.

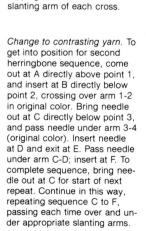
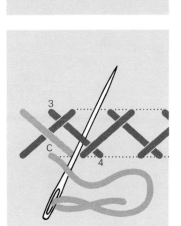
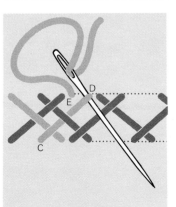
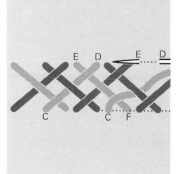

37

Embroidery stitches

Cross stitches

Closed herringbone is a type of cross stitch used primarily for leaf designs. The crosses are not immediately evident because the crossing points occur at the base of the arms. To establish tip of leaf, bring needle up at 1 and take a short stitch down center to 2. Bring needle up at 3 close to first stitch; insert at 4 just to right of middle line. Emerge at 5 directly across from 3. Insert needle at 6 just to left of center line. Repeat the 3 to 6 sequence by bringing needle up at the new point 3. Continue this sequence until leaf shape is completely filled.

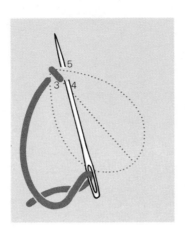
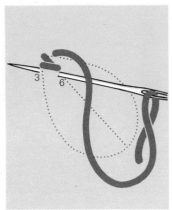

Vandyke stitch is another variation of cross stitch used for leaf designs. As the stitch is worked, a thin braided line is formed in the center to represent the central vein of the leaf. The first four steps in the following series start the design; the fifth and sixth steps are repeated in sequence thereafter. Bring needle out at 1 on left side below tip. Insert at 2 and exit at 3, taking a small bite at leaf tip. Insert needle at 4 directly across from 1. Bring needle out at 5 on left side. Pass needle *under the pair of crossed yarns* above.

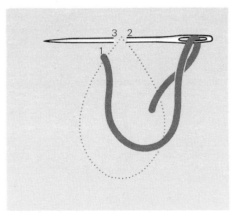
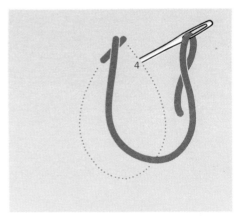
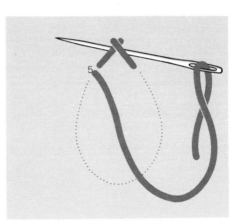

Insert needle at 6 on the right side and bring needle out at left side again for next stitch. Continue 5 to 6 sequence until leaf design is filled, always passing needle under last two crossed yarns. Worked between narrow parallel lines, stitch forms a fine raised braid for a decorative outline or border. When worked in adjacent rows, it produces a pebbly texture. Squares or rectangles of this stitch worked at right angles can convey the texture of bricks or paving stones.

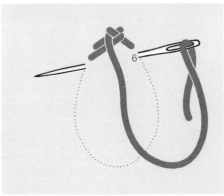

Featherstitches

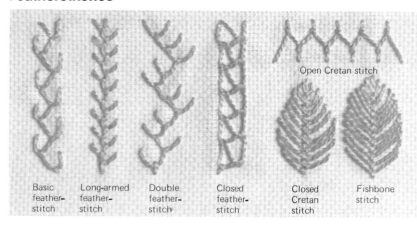

Basic feather-stitch

Long-armed feather-stitch

Double feather-stitch

Closed feather-stitch

Open Cretan stitch

Closed Cretan stitch

Fishbone stitch

The featherstitches make up the next category of embroidery stitches. Originally used to decorate nineteenth century English smocks, most of the featherstitches are used today for borders on edges and hems. Their feather-like look comes from their being open, looped stitches taken alternately to the right and the left from a central core.

A couple of the featherstitch variations, the *closed Cretan* and the *fishbone* stitches, are often used for filling leaf and fern designs. When worked, they both have a textured center that resembles the main vein of a leaf.

The basic featherstitch and its vari-ations are often seen in crazy patchwork (stitched over the adjoining edges of patches) and in appliqué. Their thin lines are also used to add a delicate edge to children's and babies' clothes.

Like the earlier blanket and chain stitches, featherstitches are looped; the working yarn must be carried under the point of the needle before it is pulled tight. Because of the back-and-forth movement of the needle, care must be taken to keep the stitches even on both sides of the center line. Before stitching, it is useful to lightly draw guidelines for the center line as well as the side lines of leaf edges.

Basic featherstitch is a looped stitch that is evenly worked with stitches alternating to the left and to the right. Work stitches from top to bottom. Bring needle up at 1 in center. Insert needle at 2 slightly lower and to the right. Then angle needle out at 3 along center line, carrying working yarn under point; pull through. Insert needle at 4 slightly below and to left of 3. Angle out at 5 along center line; carry yarn under point and pull through. Continue, alternating angle of looped stitches. To end row, take a small stitch over last loop.

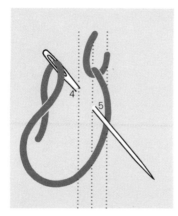  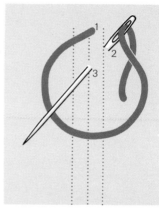 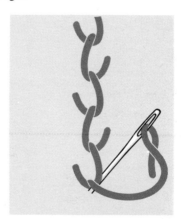

Long-armed featherstitch is worked like the basic stitch except that the longer half of each loop is on the outside rather than in the center. Bring needle up at 1 in center. Insert needle at 2 slightly higher and to the right, then angle needle out at 3 along center line. Carry working yarn under needle point and pull through. Insert needle at 4 slightly higher and to left of 3 (distance between 1-2 and 3-4 should be equal), then angle needle out at 5 along center. Carry yarn under needle and pull through. Repeat 1-5 to end.

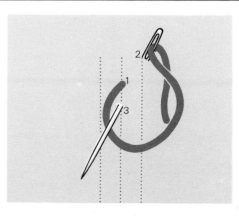 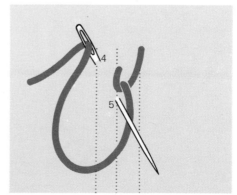 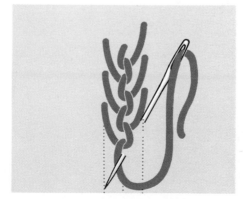

Embroidery stitches

Featherstitches

Double featherstitch makes an airy, zigzag border. Instead of a single looped stitch placed alternately left and right, two stitches are made consecutively to one side and then to the other. Keep the loops even. To start, bring needle up at 1 in center. Insert at 2 directly across. Angle needle left and out at 3; carry yarn under point of needle and pull. Insert at 4 directly across from 3. Angle right, coming out at 5; carry yarn under needle and pull. Insert needle at 6. Angle right, coming out at 7; carry yarn under needle and pull.

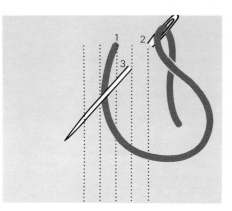 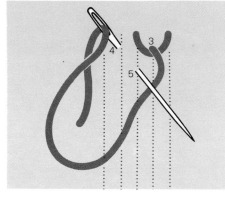 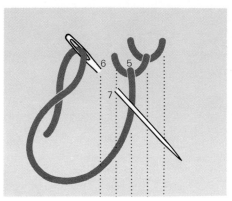

To complete sequence, insert needle at 8 directly across from 7 and below 3. Angle left and out at 9; carry yarn under needle point and pull. Two sets of looped stitches are now complete. Repeat sequence from start. Note that point 9 of last sequence is point 1 of the new sequence. Continue with 1 to 9 series until row is completed.

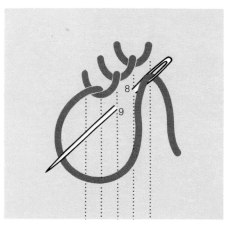 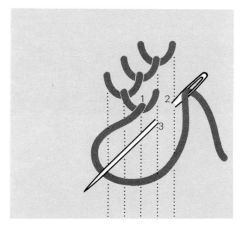 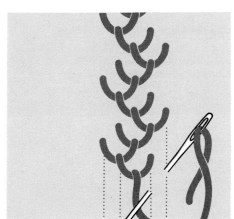

Closed featherstitch is a simple variation of the basic stitch in which each stitch *touches the previous one,* leaving no space between. To achieve this, the stitches are made *vertically* rather than at an angle. Bring needle up at 1. Insert at 2, half a step up and to the right of 1; emerge at 3 a full step below. Carry yarn under needle point and pull through. Insert needle at point 4 just below 1, so that the yarns touch. Emerge a full step below at 5. Repeat sequence, always inserting needle just below previous stitch to form an unbroken line.

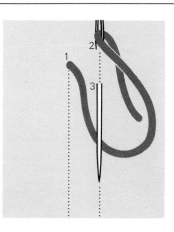 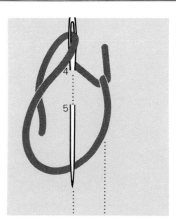 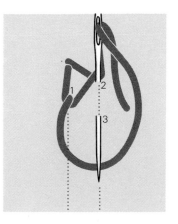 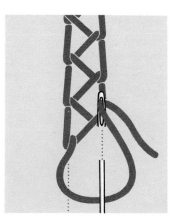

Open Cretan stitch is a type of featherstitch that produces a decorative border. Unlike most featherstitches, it is worked horizontally. Bring needle up at 1. Insert at 2 above and to right; exit at 3 directly below 2. Carry yarn under point and pull through. Insert needle at 4 on bottom and farther to the right; exit at 5 directly above 4. Carry yarn under point and pull through. Continue in this way, always placing each stitch to the right of the last one and keeping the distance between stitches even.

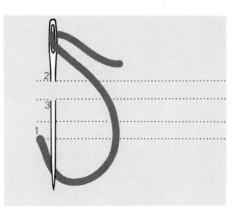
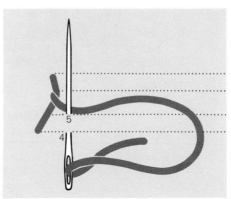
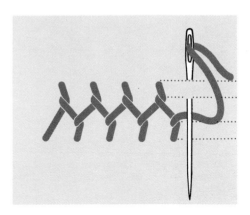

Closed Cretan stitch is usually used as a leaf-filling stitch as it forms a natural plait down the center. Bring needle up at leaf top, 1. Insert at 2 and exit at 3, slightly to the right of the center line. Carry yarn under needle point and pull through. Insert needle at 4 directly across from 2; exit at 5 directly across from 3 and slightly to the left of center. Carry yarn under needle and pull. Start next stitch on right side, then alternate, bringing needle out either to the left or to the right of the center line to create center braid.

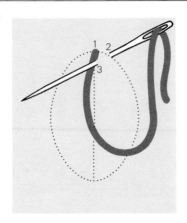
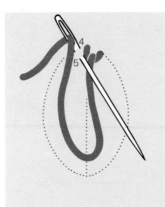
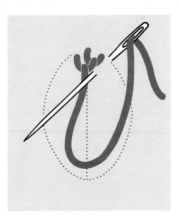

Fishbone stitch is another leaf-filling stitch. Its finished effect is similar to a fishbone with a "spine" down the center. Bring needle up at 1 and take a small stitch down center to 2. Bring needle up at 3; insert at 4 directly across from 3. Exit at hole originally made at 2; carry yarn under needle point and pull through. Proceed to next stitch. Note that point 2 of previous stitch (where yarn emerges) is point 1 of next stitch. Continue this way until leaf design is filled.

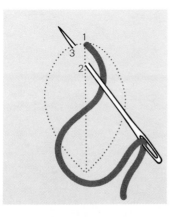

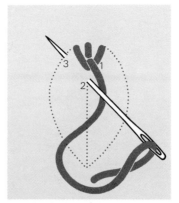

41

Embroidery stitches

Filling stitches/detached

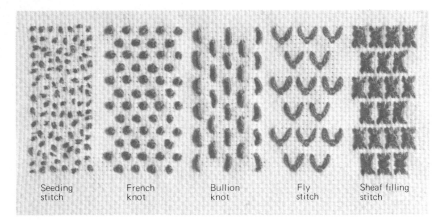

Seeding stitch   French knot   Bullion knot   Fly stitch   Sheaf filling stitch

Although all the stitches in this next set are quite different from one another, each having its own unique look, they have one thing in common: They are all detached, single stitches used primarily as a means of filling in a design area. All the stitches presented here contribute great textural variation to an embroidered piece. Certain especially raised stitches, among them the *French knot* and the *bullion knot,* can be flattened by an embroidery hoop. When using a hoop, take care to avoid crushing raised stitches (see p.18).

Because each of these stitches has such an individual look, they can serve many purposes besides filling. The French knot is a particular favorite of embroiderers because its rounded, raised look can create flower centers and eyes on an embroidered figure. It can also be used to give a woolly look to a lamb. Another versatile stitch is the *seeding stitch,* which can be scattered lightly or heavily to give a shaded effect. The *fly stitch* and *sheaf filling stitch* both require a little more planning in their placement. Worked in rows, they can be used as a border. They can also be worked singly. Scattered fly stitches resemble distant birds in flight; sheaf filling stitches look very much like bundles of wheat.

Seeding stitch is one of the simplest filling stitches. It can be used in clusters or scattered. If worked close together, groups of seeding stitches can even be a means of shading. Bring needle up at 1 and take a tiny stitch down at 2. For a heavier stitch, bring needle up at 3 and take another small stitch at 4 close to the first stitch. Scatter seeding stitches as desired, changing the direction of the stitches for a varied effect. If all stitches are worked in one direction, filling will be uniform.

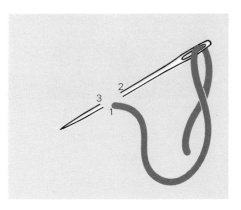
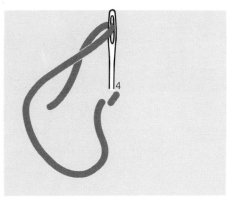
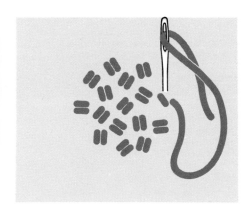

French knot is used like the seeding stitch, but it is considerably more textured and raised. Knots can be worked close together to completely fill an area, producing a nubby effect. Bring needle up at 1. Holding yarn taut with left hand, wrap yarn around needle twice as shown; gently pull the yarn so the twists are tightened against the needle. Carefully insert needle near point 1 and pull through; be sure yarn end is still held taut. Scatter knots as desired within design area. French knots can be made larger by increasing number of yarn twists around needle.

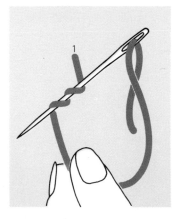
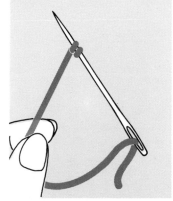
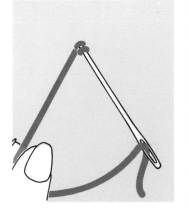

42

Bullion knot can be used as a filling or as an outline stitch. Bring needle up at 1. Insert at 2 and exit at 1 again, but do not pull yarn through. Twist yarn around needle point five to seven times depending on length of stitch (distance from 1 to 2). Then carefully pull needle through both fabric and twists; take care not to distort twists. Pull yarn toward point 2 so coil can lie flat. Pull working yarn tight and use point of needle to pack yarns in coil together evenly. Re-insert needle into point 2.

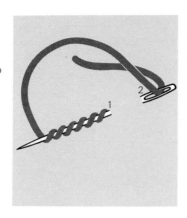  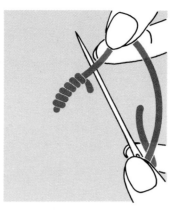 

Fly stitch is a single, looped stitch not unlike the basic featherstitch. When completed it resembles a Y. It can be scattered about as a filling or lined up for a border. Bring needle up at 1. Insert at 2 directly across, then angle needle out at 3. Points 1, 2, and 3 should be equidistant. Carry the yarn under the needle point and pull through. Complete stitch by inserting at 4 over loop. Work as many fly stitches as necessary to fill desired design area.

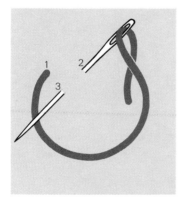 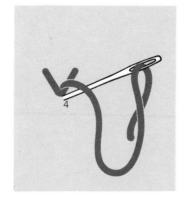  

Sheaf filling stitch resembles a tied bundle of wheat. Stitches can be arranged in alternate rows or set close together, one right below another. Bring needle out at 1. Work three satin stitches, following numbered sequence shown. Bring needle up at point 7, midway between 5 and 6. Pass needle around the stitch bundles twice without piercing fabric and pull yarn taut. Insert needle under bundle and through fabric; secure stitch at back. For a different effect, work the tying stitches in a contrasting yarn color.

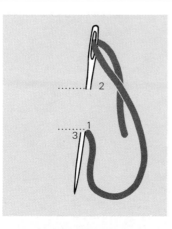 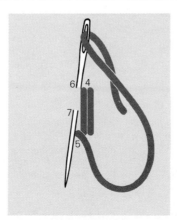 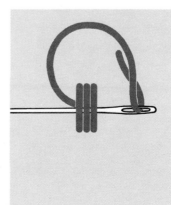 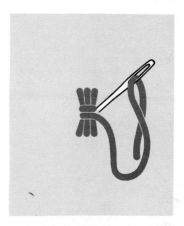

43

Embroidery stitches

Filling stitches/laid

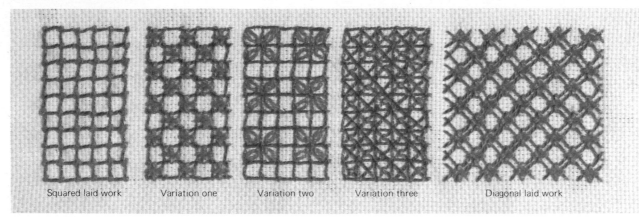

Squared laid work   Variation one   Variation two   Variation three   Diagonal laid work

A fairly large design area can be attractively filled with this next group of embroidered filling stitches. These stitches are longer than the preceding detached ones and are laid to create the effect of a grid or lattice. The basic lattice is laid down, then tacked down at its intersections to keep them in place. Embellishments can then be added: this is usually done with contrasting yarn. In laying down the long, grid-like stitches, take care to insure even and consistent spacing. The spacing between long stitches will depend on the size of the area you are filling as well as the overall effect that is desired.

Squared laid work is made up of long stitches that form a lattice over which other stitches are worked. This basic structure is anchored by small, slanting stitches at each yarn crossing. To form lattice, bring needle up at 1; take a long stitch to 2. Bring needle up at 3 below 2; insert at 4 below 1. Work stitches until area is covered, keeping spacing even. Lay vertical stitches over the horizontal ones the same way. Take small slanting stitch over each intersection. Start at upper left. Work across and back, coming up at A, inserting at B.

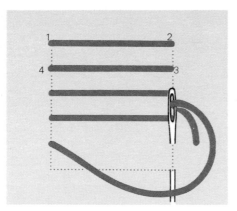

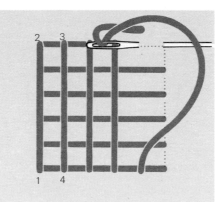

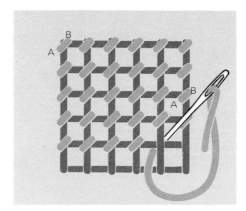

Variation I: Here upright cross stitches are worked over every other square of the lattice made from the basic laid work shown above. Work entire lattice with one color, cross stitches with a contrasting color. Starting at upper left corner, bring needle up at 1; insert at 2. Exit at 3 and complete stitch at 4. Work the second row using the same numbered sequence, moving from right to left. Continue in this way, working each row until the laid work is filled.

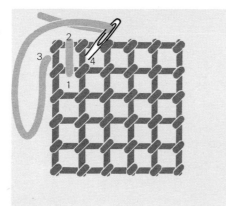

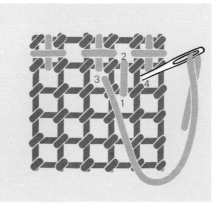

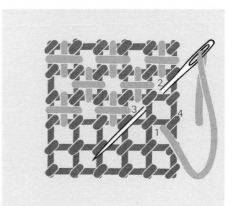

44

Variation II: Here a series of four detached chain stitches are worked within a set of four lattice squares. Depending on the total squares, the placement and number of sets will vary. Make each chain stitch so the anchoring stitch over the loop is at the center of the four lattice squares. Bring needle up at 1; insert back into 1 and emerge at 2. Carry yarn under point and pull through. With yarn over loop, insert at 3. Work the next and subsequent stitches counterclockwise until the set is complete. Work all other sets in the same way.

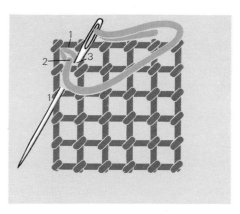
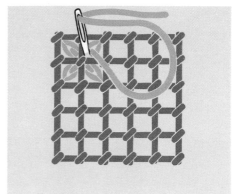
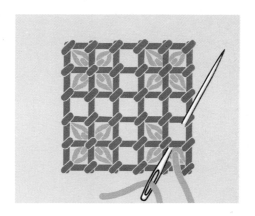

Variation III: This time, diagonal yarns are laid over basic yarns, then tacked down at each intersection. Starting at top left corner of laid work, bring needle up at 1; insert at 2. Bring needle up at 3, two squares to the right. Take a diagonal stitch to 4, two squares below 1. Work remainder; keep spacing even. Lay diagonal yarns in opposite direction. Start at top right and follow same sequence. At each crossing, take a small stitch, A to B. Start at upper left corner; work across, then back, until all intersections are covered.

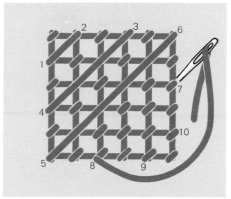
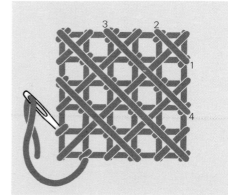
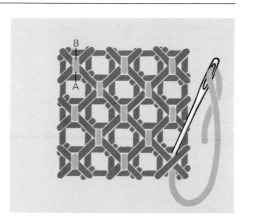

Diagonal laid work is made up of pairs of yarns laid diagonally to form a lattice base. Each intersection is tacked down with four small straight stitches. To form lattice, bring needle up at 1 in upper left corner; insert diagonally at 2. Bring up at 3 near 2; take another stitch to 4. Work pairs of stitches back and forth, keeping spacing even. Then, starting at upper right corner, lay pairs of yarns on the opposite diagonal. At each intersection, take four stitches, all out at A and in at center point B. Work these sets across and then back.

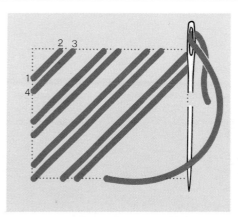
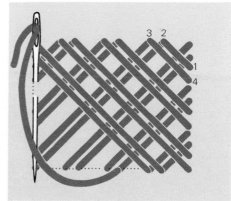
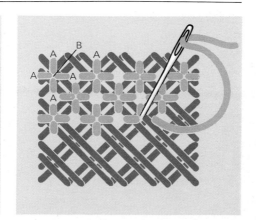

Embroidery stitches

Running stitches

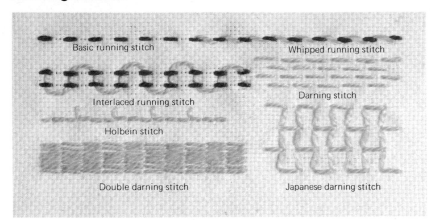

Basic running stitch
Whipped running stitch
Interlaced running stitch
Darning stitch
Holbein stitch
Double darning stitch
Japanese darning stitch

Running stitches would appear to be the simplest of all the stitch types to work, and in many ways they are. There is nothing at all complicated about the basic movements of the needle. Special diligence is required, however, to keep the stitch lengths uniform. This is why the running stitch and its variants are frequently worked on fabrics that have an even weave, with every stitch length covering a predetermined number of fabric threads. Unlike the majority of embroidery stitches, almost all the running stitches can be worked by picking up several stitches on the needle before pulling the needle and thread through.

This makes the stitching go much faster.

The *basic running stitch* is primarily used for outlining, and it is the basic stitch in quilting. Worked in rows with contrasting yarns laced through it, it can also be used as a border or band. The *Holbein* or *double running stitch* is often used for outlining. Carefully worked, a piece embroidered with only Holbein stitch can be reversible; right and wrong sides will be identical.

The *darning stitches* are usually used to fill a space. By changing the lengths of the stitches and the arrangements of the rows, many different patterns are possible (see Blackwork, p. 56).

Basic running stitch, the easiest outline stitch, can be same length on right and wrong sides or longer on right side. Work basic stitch right to left. Bring needle up at 1; down at 2. Pick up several stitches on needle before pulling it through. *For whipped variation,* weave contrast yarn through stitch base (second illustration); do not pick up fabric below. *For interlaced variation,* work two rows of running stitches and thread contrast yarn up and down through rows (last illustration).

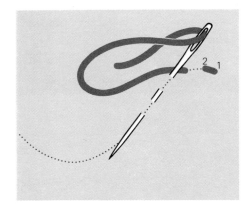
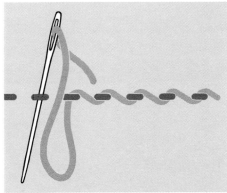
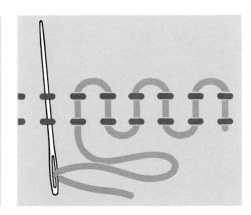

Darning stitch is basically several rows of running stitches any desired length. Surface floats usually form a design like the type found in blackwork embroidery. We show a "brick" design. Each row of running stitches consists of a long float on top with only a few fabric threads picked up by the needle. The long floats of each row are evenly stitched so they lie just below short spaces of row directly above. Work rows as needed to fill area.

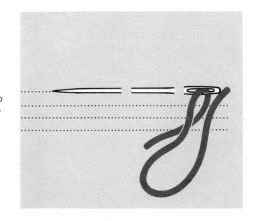
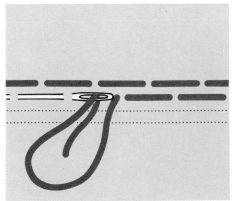
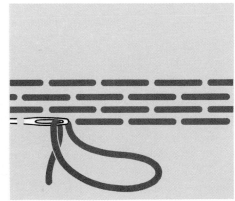

Holbein or double running stitch is an outline stitch used often in blackwork embroidery. This stitch is worked with two journeys of running stitches. On first journey, work evenly spaced running stitches. Turn work and stitch second journey so top floats are stitched over spaces left by first journey; enter and exit at same holes.
If design has offshoot stitch, work it on first journey. Bring needle up at 3, base of stray stitch. Insert at 4; exit at 3 again. Continue to next stray. Turn, and work second journey.

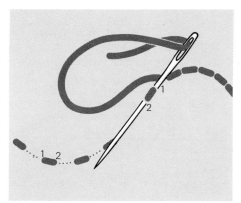

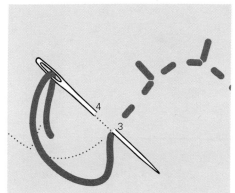

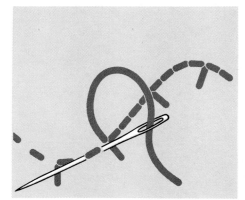

Double darning combines the techniques of both darning and Holbein stitches. This entails working several rows of evenly spaced Holbein stitches. To start, work the first journey of the first row with evenly spaced running stitches. Turn work, then stitch second journey over first so top floats are over spaces left by first journey. Work each subsequent row in the same manner, lining up stitches of each row directly below the stitches in the row above. Leave enough space between rows so the threads do not overlap each other.

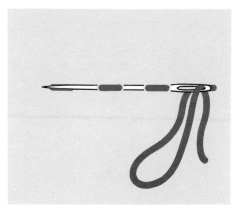

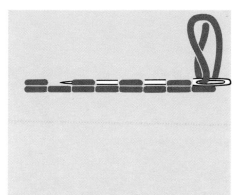

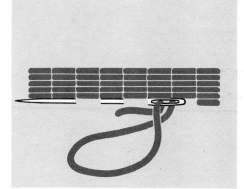

Japanese darning can be a filling stitch or a border. Work several rows of darning stitch in "brick" pattern but with more space between rows than in darning shown opposite. Work each row so the top float of each stitch is slightly longer than the intervening spaces. To connect rows, come up at 1 on top row. Insert at 2; exit at 3, with needle picking up fabric between 2 and 3. Continue, alternating pickup stitches from row to row. Connect the subsequent rows in the same way until all have been joined.

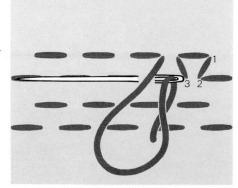

Embroidery stitches

Satin stitches

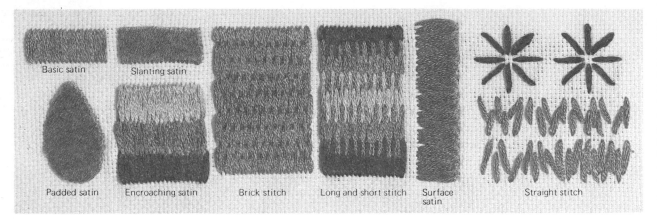

Basic satin | Slanting satin

Padded satin | Encroaching satin | Brick stitch | Long and short stitch | Surface satin | Straight stitch

This group of satin stitches is the most popular set of embroidery stitches for solidly filling in a design with a smooth surface. Although the main stitch movements are fairly simple, it still takes practice to get the floats to lie flat and close together, and the edges of the stitches to align evenly. When working satin stitches, be sure none of the fabric below shows through. An important aspect of satin stitching is the direction in which the stitches fall within a design. Decide this ahead of time; the stitch direction will influence the way the light reflects on the filled area and thus will determine its ultimate look.

Basic satin stitch is a solid filling stitch that covers the design area with long, straight stitches placed close together. Care must be taken to keep the stitches smooth and at an even tension. This simple version of satin stitching is the basic stitch in Hardanger embroidery. The stitch is usually worked from left to right. Bring needle up at 1. Insert at 2 directly above; exit at 3 close to point 1. Continue until area is filled. The stabbing method of stitching (see p. 20) will help to keep the stitches even.

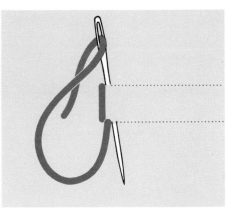

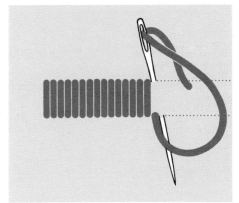

To slant satin stitches, start work in the center of the shape to establish the angle of slant. Work across to fill one side, then start again at the center and work across the other way to fill other side. When shape is large, slanting stitches tend to flatten out (becoming too horizontal) by the time you reach the end. To prevent this, work satin stitches so that needle is always inserted at upper edge (point 2) *very close* to preceding stitch; exit at 3 *slightly farther* from exit point of preceding stitch.

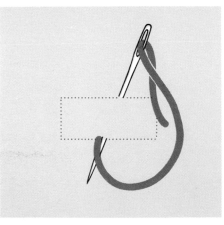

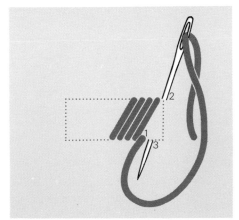

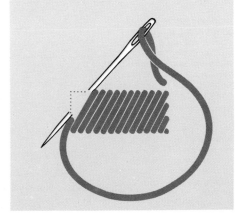

48

Padded satin stitch gives the same effect as the basic satin stitch, except that the stitched area is slightly raised for texture variation or design emphasis. The padded area consists of an outline of split stitches and two "layers" of satin stitching. Work one row of split stitches (see p. 23) around the shape. Carefully work basic satin stitch horizontally across, covering the split stitches. Then work upper satin stitch layer in desired direction. Take special care to keep the outline edges even; work slowly.

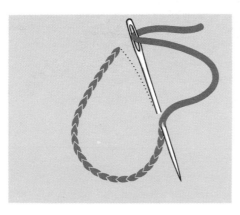 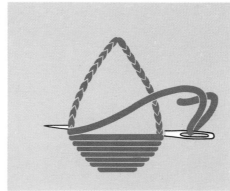 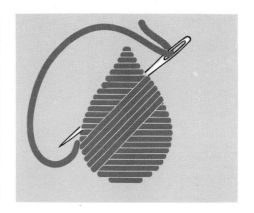

Encroaching satin stitch offers systematic color shading within a shape. Several rows of basic satin stitches are worked to give an almost woven effect. The colors of the rows can go from dark to light. Work a basic satin stitch along first row. Start second row so its first stitch falls between first two stitches in row above. Continue stitching second row so stitches fall between the stitches above them. Work next rows the same way. If you use shaded yarn, and want precise shading, start each row with the same tint portion of yarn.

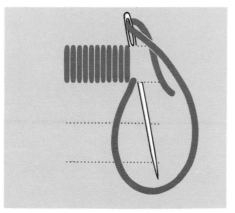 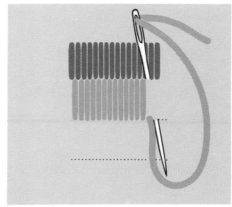 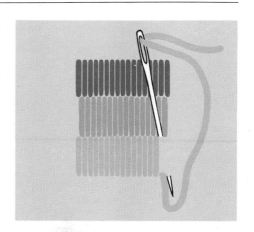

Brick stitch is a type of satin stitch with a texture like that of a woven basket. Stitching is done alternately left to right, then right to left. To work first row, alternate long and short satin stitches across; each short stitch should be approximately half the length of the long stitches. Work all other rows in long satin stitch. On last row, fill in the half-spaces with short satin stitches. Make sure that the top of each stitch touches the base of the stitches directly above it.

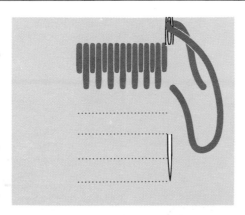 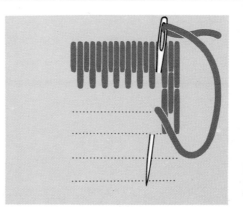 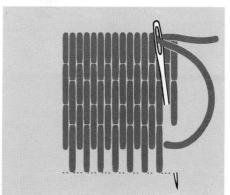

Embroidery stitches

Satin stitches

Long and short stitch is a popular stitch for shading areas in a design. The stitch is worked very similarly to the brick stitch, but there is more stitch blending. Each stitch from the second row onward pierces the stitch right above it in the preceding row. Work first row as for brick stitch (preceding page). Change color and work long satin stitches along second row, staggering them so top of each stitch splits base of stitch directly above. Work each subsequent row in this way. Fill in the last row with short satin stitches.

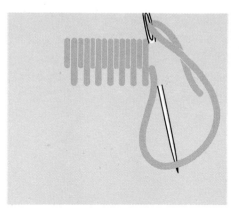 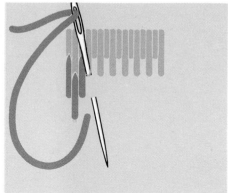 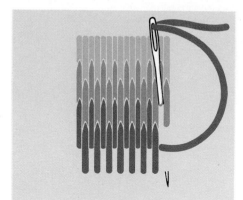

The direction in which long and short stitches fall is very important for proper shading effect. Before starting, decide direction stitches will take within each separate shape. Pencil in some direction lines. Here are three designs that have been partially worked with the long and short stitches running in different directions. Note the radiating colored effect achieved in the first and last illustrations by fanning the first row of stitch color.

 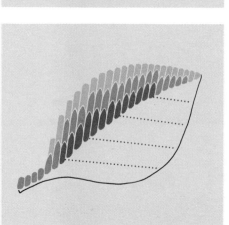 

Surface satin stitch is an economical way to obtain the look of the basic satin stitch; it eliminates the long floats on the wrong side. It takes careful stitching, however, to get the stitches to lie close to each other. Use the stabbing motion (see p.20) to work this stitch. Bring needle up at 1. Insert at 2 directly across; bring needle up at 3 as close as possible to 2 (no more than a fabric thread away). Insert needle at 4 directly across from 3. Continue until area is covered. Always work this stitch with a hoop.

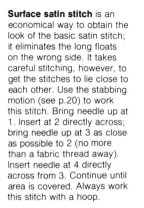 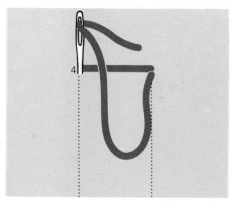 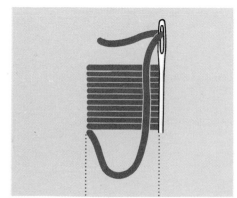

Straight stitch is a single satin stitch that can be of any length and worked in any direction. It can be used to cover straight design lines or scattered for an open filling. Be sure yarn is not carried too far on wrong side between stitches. Worked in a circle (last illustration), the cluster of straight stitches resembles a stylized flower, the center of which can be filled in with French knots (see p.42). Bring needle up at 1; insert it at 2. Work as many as needed for desired design.

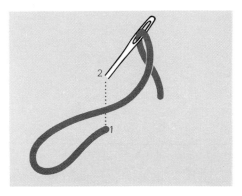

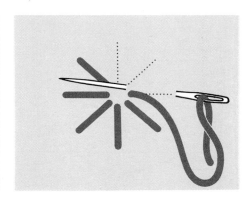

Weaving stitches

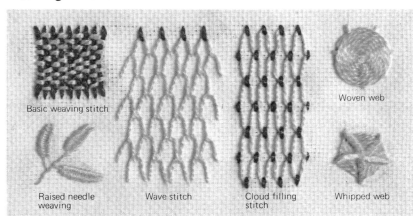

Basic weaving stitch

Raised needle weaving

Wave stitch

Cloud filling stitch

Woven web

Whipped web

The next embroidery stitch group, the weaving stitches, consists entirely of stitches based upon a network of yarns that are first laid down and then woven over. The yarn used for weaving may be the same or a contrasting color. The effect, and therefore the choice, varies considerably from one stitch to another. The *basic weaving stitch,* for example, can fill an area solidly with its subtle texture; *raised needle weaving,* on the other hand, produces a particular motif, such as a single leaf or petal. *Spider web stitches* are special in that the finished stitch assumes a definite circular shape. Both the *wave stitch* and the *cloud filling stitch* will serve as lacy fillings for different areas in a design. The filling can appear closed or quite open, however, depending on the placement of the base yarns. The yarn weight, too, affects stitch appearance, the same stitch looking very different in two different weights of yarn. Experiment until you find the particular effect you want in a given area.

Although a regular sharp needle is used for laying down the base yarns, it is recommended that you exchange it for a tapestry needle when you come to the weaving portion of these stitches. This will help to avoid piercing the fabric or splitting the laid yarns.

Basic weaving stitch is a solid filling stitch with a basket-like texture. Lay down the lengthwise yarns first, working right to left. Bring needle up at 1; insert at 2 directly above and exit at 3 to left. Insert at 4 and repeat for as many yarns as needed. Change to tapestry needle. Starting at upper right corner, come up at A and weave across, going over and under alternate lengthwise yarns. Insert needle at B; exit at C for next crosswise run. Continue until all lengthwise yarns are interwoven.

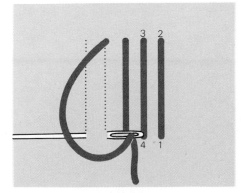
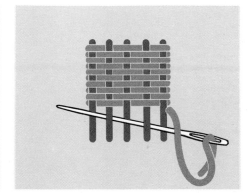

Embroidery stitches

Weaving stitches

Raised needleweaving is a weaving stitch that lies on top of fabric with only laid yarns attached. Bring needle out at 1. Insert at 2 directly below; emerge at 1. Insert needle at 2 again and bring needle up at 1. Change to a tapestry needle; begin weaving over and under the two laid yarns alternately without picking up any fabric below. Continue to work back and forth over the laid yarns until they are completely covered. Take care to keep the tension even so the shape of the stitches is not distorted.

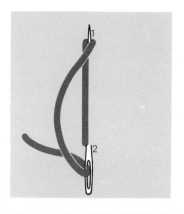 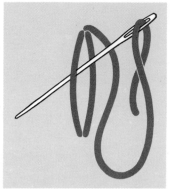 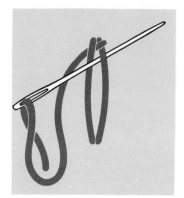 

Wave stitch is a lacy filling stitch that gives a honeycomb effect. Depending on the spacing of the stitches, this lace-like effect can look open or closed. To start, work a row of small, vertical satin stitches that are evenly spaced. Come up at 1; insert at 2. At end of row, bring needle up at 3, below and to right of last satin stitch. Pass needle back under satin stitch without picking up any fabric below; insert at 4. Bring needle up right next to point 4 and repeat the sequence until all satin stitches are threaded.

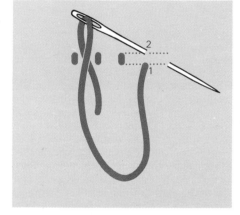 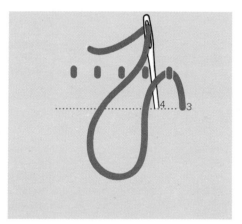 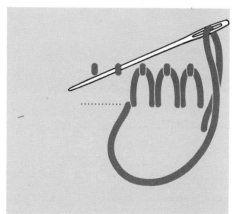

To work next row, bring needle up at 5 slightly to the left of the last stitch above. Pass needle under stitch above without picking up fabric. Insert at 6. Bring needle up right next to point 6 and repeat the sequence across, this time slipping needle under the pairs of stitch bases directly above. On following row, bring needle up at 7 directly under end stitch of first weaving row, and end at point 8, directly under end stitch of first weaving row. Work subsequent rows the same way, passing needle under the stitch bases in row directly above.

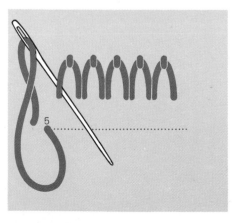 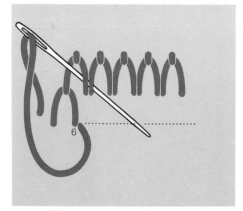 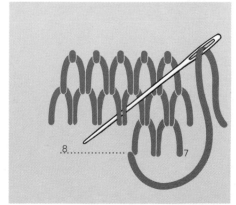

Cloud filling stitch is much like the wave stitch in texture. To start, work several rows of small, vertical, evenly spaced satin stitches checkerboard style. Change to tapestry needle and contrasting yarn. Bring needle up at A; lace yarn back and forth through satin stitches of first two rows. End lacing at B, securing yarn at back. Lace second and third rows (C to D) and all subsequent pairs of rows until all satin stitches are threaded. Different impressions can be achieved by the use of contrasting yarns and by varying spacing of satin stitches.

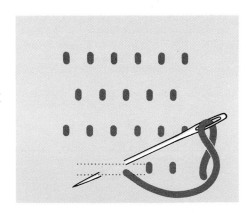
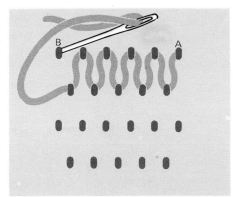
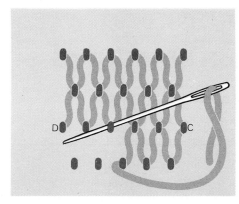

Spider webs are embroidered circular motifs that can be used as design accents or to represent stylized flowers. Spokes of the web are laid, then *woven over and under* for a smooth webbing or *whipped* to produce a pronounced rib. Before starting, divide circle into nine equal parts; mentally number each. Bring needle up at spoke 1. Insert at 4 and bring out at center; carry yarn under needle and pull through. Insert at 7 and bring out at 9. Insert at 3 and bring out at center; carry yarn under needle and pull through. Insert at 6 and bring out at 8.

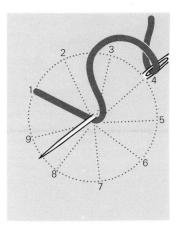
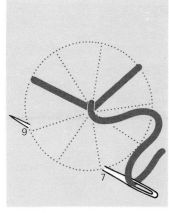
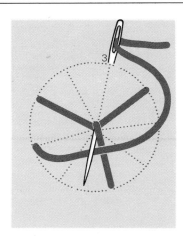

Insert needle at spoke 2 and bring out at center; carry yarn under needle, pull through. To complete last spoke, insert needle at 5 and exit at center. To *weave* over spokes, start from center and pass needle over and under spokes, moving around and outward counterclockwise until spokes are covered. To *whip* over spokes (last illustration), carry needle under and back over a spoke, then under that spoke and next spoke ahead. Work around, always moving needle back over one spoke and forward under two until all spokes are covered.

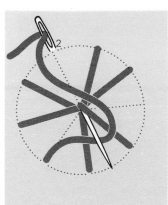
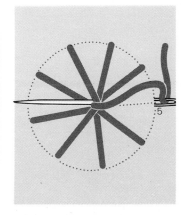
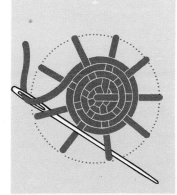
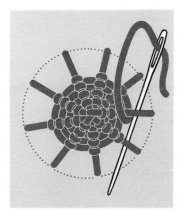

Finishing embroidered pieces

Cleaning, pressing, and blocking embroidery

Cleaning

Because of all the handling involved in the embroidering process, your finished piece may get very soiled and need cleaning before it is pressed or blocked. Embroidered pieces made with washable fabrics and yarns can simply be washed out in your bathroom basin as illustrated below. Swish the embroidery around in the cool, soapy water—never scrub embroidery harshly—rinse thoroughly, and roll in a towel to blot up the excess water. If the piece is not washable, you can use a good spot remover—which you have first tested on a scrap of fabric—or take the piece to a reliable dry cleaner.

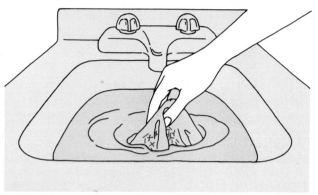 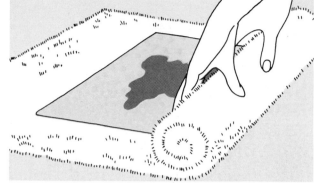

Gently wash the embroidered piece in cool water and mild soap. Rinse thoroughly (do not wring or twist); **roll in towel** to absorb excess moisture.

Pressing

When an embroidered piece is completed, it must be either **pressed** or **blocked** to help remove any wrinkles and to straighten fabric distortions that may have been caused by embroidering. If a piece is not seriously distorted, pressing is usually sufficient. Pressing, rather than blocking, is also recommended for embroidered clothing. Before pressing, pad the ironing board with a layer or two of towels. If your board is too narrow to accommodate the work satisfactorily, lay towels over your blocking board. Place the embroidered piece face down and cover it with a press cloth. If the article has been washed (see above) and is still damp, you can use a dry press cloth; if the piece is dry, use a damp press cloth. Press very lightly over the embroidered area, letting iron just touch the cloth. Press surrounding fabric in usual way.

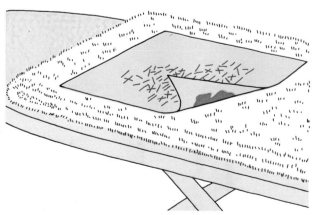 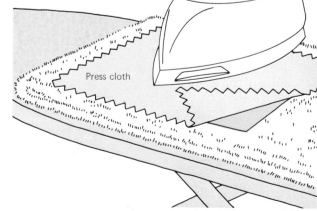

Press cloth

To press an embroidered piece, lay it face down on a padded ironing board, and cover with a press cloth. **Press lightly** so iron barely touches the cloth.

Blocking

Blocking is a corrective process in which embroidery pieces are stretched over a board to remove fabric wrinkles and distortions. To make a blocking board, see below. If you would like to pad the board, cut an old mattress cover into board-size pieces, and place a couple of them between the board and the muslin.

To block embroidery, you first soak the piece in cold water. If the stitches are flat, lay the piece face down on the board; if many stitches are raised and highly textured, lay it face up to prevent crushing. Stretch the fabric and hold it in place with heavy-duty T-pins or tacks. Pieces that cannot be soaked should be stretched dry. Moisten areas around embroidery with a damp sponge, and use tip of iron to lightly press moistened areas; let fabric dry before removing.

If the embroidered area is small enough to fit within a hoop or the whole piece is on a stretcher frame, sprinkle with water; let dry in hoop or frame.

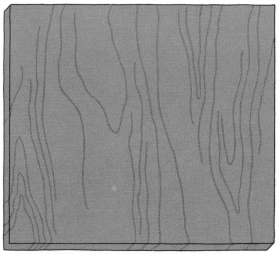

1. To make blocking board, purchase a piece of ½″ thick pine or soft composition board that is approximately 24″ × 24″.

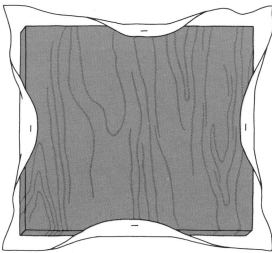

2. Cut a piece of muslin 2″ wider all around. Center board over fabric, and stretch fabric over edge, stapling at center of each side.

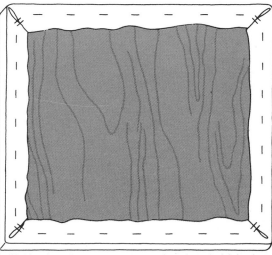

3. Working from the centers out, stretch and staple fabric along each edge. Neatly fold excess fabric at corners and staple in place.

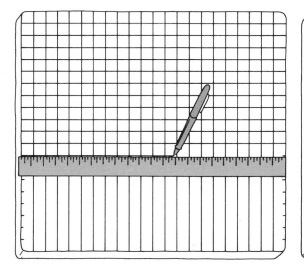

4. Turn board to right side and mark off a 1″ grid, using an indelible marking pen that absolutely will not run when wet.

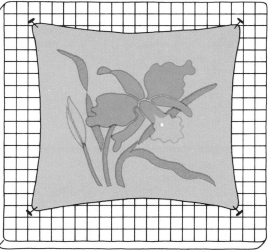

5. Soak embroidered piece in cold water and lay on top of board, face up or down as explained above. Tack at each corner.

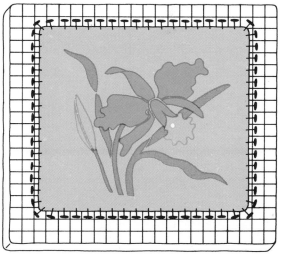

6. Pull sides out to desired measurements, using grid as a guide, and tack in place. Let dry completely before removing.

Even-weave fabrics 9   Buttonhole stitch 26   French knot 42
Couching 32   Laid work 44
Herringbone stitch 36   Long and short stitch 50

Blackwork embroidery

Introduction to blackwork
Basic stitches
Examples of blackwork patterns
Creating your own blackwork pattern
Working block designs
Working free-form shapes

Introduction

Blackwork is a special category of counted thread embroidery in which so-called *diaper* or repetitive patterns are used to fill design areas. It is called blackwork because, traditionally, black silk thread was worked on white linen.

Blackwork is said to have originated in Spain, becoming very popular in England during the sixteenth century when Catherine of Aragon married King Henry VIII. At that time, blackwork appeared on clothing and bed covers.

The play of one diaper pattern upon another creates dark, medium, and light areas within a design; a mixture of all three shades adds interest to a piece. Today, blackwork patterns are used in working two different types of designs: **block designs,** in which the patterns themselves form a simple geometric shape; and **free-form designs,** in which the patterns are used to fill predetermined shapes in a design.

Blackwork is done on even-weave fabric (see p. 9), typically even-weave linen or Hardanger fabric. For exact pattern repetition, stitches are counted over a precise number of threads. The more threads there are per inch of fabric, the smaller (and darker) the embroidered blackwork area will be.

Embroidery floss is usually used in blackwork; depending on the weave of the fabric, the number of strands can vary. Finer pearl cottons can also be used on the coarser woven fabrics. Although black floss on white linen is the traditional color choice, other colors can be used to give blackwork a more modern look. Brown floss on beige linen or deep blue on eggshell are popular (see examples at right). Gold or silver metallic threads create a fancier look.

Because blackwork is worked over an exact number of threads, the needle must go between threads rather than pierce them. For this purpose, fine tapestry needles are best. Select a size that corresponds to the floss you choose.

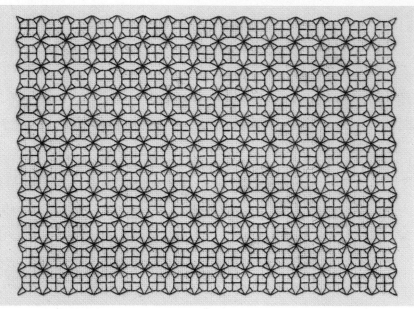

Block designs consist of a simple geometric shape that is formed by the blackwork pattern itself.

Free-form designs are shapes filled with blackwork, plus other stitches for contrast.

Basic stitches

Blackwork patterns are built upon a few basic embroidery stitches worked over a definite number of threads. The stitches that are used most often are shown below. Included are the **backstitch, Holbein stitch, darning stitch, double cross stitch,** and the **Algerian eye stitch.**

In addition to the stitches that create the patterns, other stitches are often used as embellishments to add textural interest and variety to the overall design. The free-form design on the opposite page features such supplementary stitching. One excellent contrast to the intricate blackwork lines is a completely filled area; the **satin stitch** will provide a smooth, solid filling where such an effect is wanted. To add definition to a free-form shape, outline it with a linear embroidery stitch. **Stem stitch, chain stitch,** and **couching stitches** are all good for this purpose.

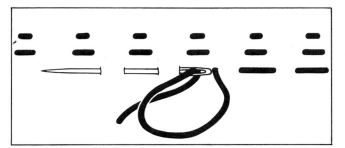

Darning stitch is often used alone in blackwork patterns. A running stitch worked in parallel rows, its floats may be any length. Stitch rows create the patterns.

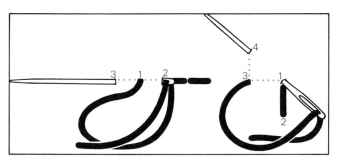

Basic backstitch is worked right to left. Bring needle out at 1, go in at 2 and exit at 3. To stitch corners, come up at 1, take a backstitch at 2 and come up at 3. Insert at 1; come up at 4; re-insert at 3 to complete stitch.

Double cross stitch is star-like. To work, bring needle up at 1, go in at 2 and exit at 3 below 2. Enter at 4, exit at 5 between 2 and 3. Insert at 6 across from 5; exit at 7 between 2 and 4. Insert at 8 below to complete stitch.

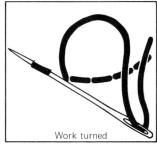

Work turned

Holbein stitch is worked in two runs. The first consists of a simple running stitch. The return run is made along the same stitching line with running stitch filling in spaces left from the first.

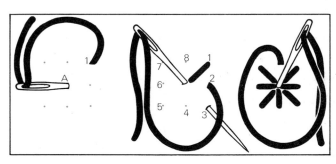

Algerian eye stitch produces an eyelet effect. To work, bring the needle up at 1 and insert at center, A. Bring out at 2 and insert at A. Continue to work in clockwise direction until all points are stitched.

Additional stitches

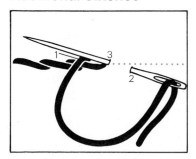

Stem stitch is worked left to right. Bring needle out at 1. Insert at 2 and bring out at 3. The distance between 1-3 and 3-2 is the same. Repeat sequence for next stitch. Keep length of stitches even.

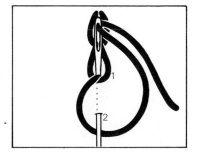

Chain stitch is worked as follows: Bring needle up at 1. Holding yarn down to left of 1, re-insert needle at 1, bring out at 2, looping yarn around needle point. Pull needle through and repeat the sequence.

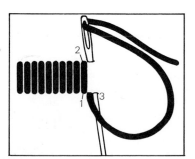

Satin stitch is used to fill small areas. Bring needle up at 1, down at 2. Emerge at 3 right next to 1. Repeat same sequence until area is filled. Keep yarn smooth and even.

Blackwork embroidery

Examples of blackwork patterns

Blackwork patterns consist of repetitive geometric motifs made from basic embroidery stitches. The original blackwork patterns probably were derived from Arabic embroidery designs. Later, when blackwork reached the height of its popularity in sixteenth-century England, the original geometric patterns were influenced by English design. At that time, fruits and figures were used as repeated motifs, with twining stems giving a cohesive look to the design. Elizabethan portraits of both men and women show this kind of blackwork pattern covering sleeves, cuffs, and collars. Some of the patterns are reminiscent of engravings or wrought iron work.

Even in the sixteenth century, blackwork was not always done in black floss on white or cream linen. Sometimes gold and black floss were used together in one piece. Even red floss, on occasion, was substituted for black.

We have selected twelve patterns to illustrate the range of possibilities. The number of patterns, however, is infinite. They are simple to design on your own (see p. 63) or to adapt from an existing design. Look to fabric prints or mosaic tile designs for inspiration. Or choose any blackwork pattern that appeals to you and simply change its scale or the thickness of the embroidery floss.

Each pattern will tend to have a dark, medium, or light value according to the relative openness or compactness of its lines. Note the differences on the sampler. A sampler like this one will serve as a pattern dictionary for future use and will provide you with practice in working the patterns. Any pattern can be adapted to either free-form or block use. The best pattern combinations are those that create textural contrast.

To show the order of steps necessary to work the patterns, each sequence begins in black and continues in color. On the grids, spaces between dots represent individual fabric threads.

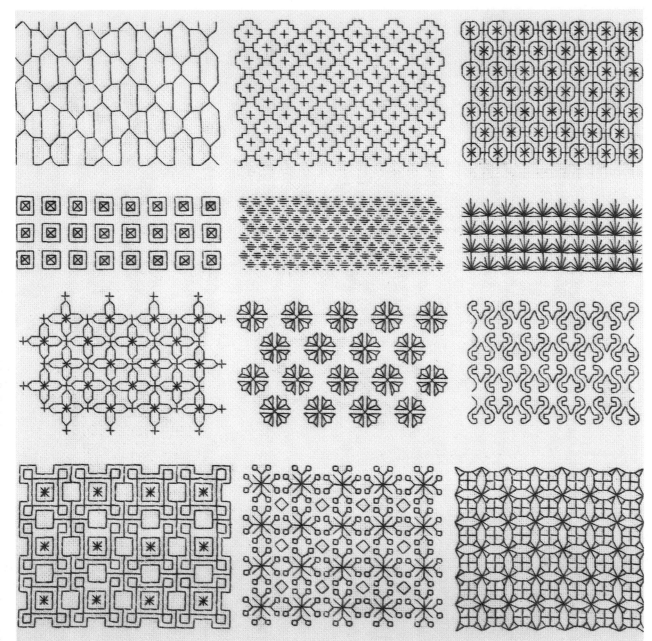

Representative sampler of twelve blackwork patterns illustrates the three values of light, medium, and dark.

This light, honeycomb pattern is worked completely in *backstitch* or *Holbein*. Work the pattern from left to right, stitching vertical rows in stitch lengths as indicated on grid (second illustration). Work first line from top down. Work second line (shown in color) from bottom up. Continue in this way until desired area is completely filled.

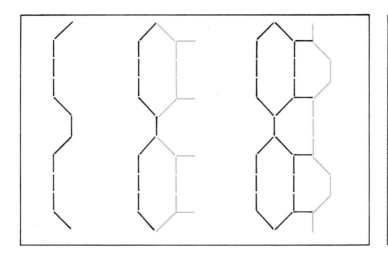

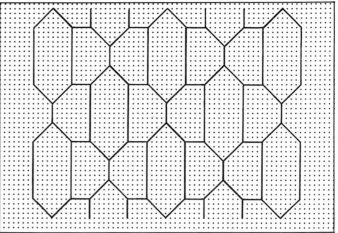

Step design is darker than the honeycomb because its lines are closer, its motif smaller. Work the basic shapes in *backstitch* in the sequence shown. Then fill centers with a single, vertical *cross stitch*. This pattern can be used as a border or filling.

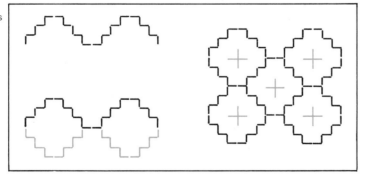

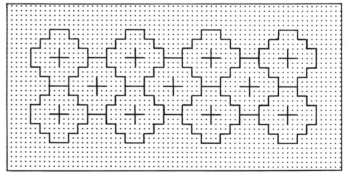

Octagonal trellis is a compact pattern worked in *backstitch* and *cross stitch*. The vertical lines, horizontal lines, and octagons are all worked in backstitch. The octagons are filled with cross stitch. The horizontal stitches add a third arm to the crosses and connect the octagons.

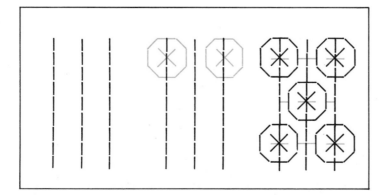

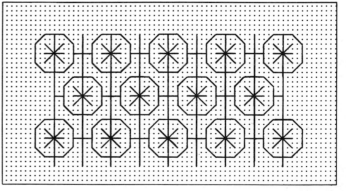

Blackwork embroidery

Examples of blackwork patterns

Delicate diamonds of medium value are worked entirely in *darning stitch*. The top floats, worked in rows, create the patterns. To begin, work the top row of either pattern from right to left, spacing stitches as shown on grid. Work subsequent rows, following stitch pattern, until desired area is filled.

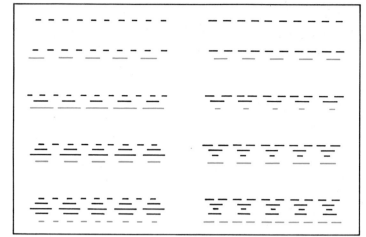

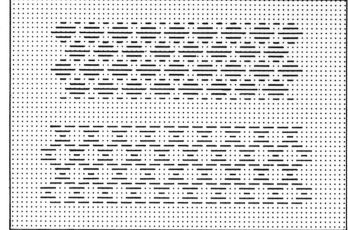

Dark fern pattern is made of closely stitched motifs. Each motif is worked like the *Algerian eye stitch*, coming up at the end of each line and entering at same center hole. Work across one row and return on next row until area is filled. Note stitch lengths as indicated on grid.

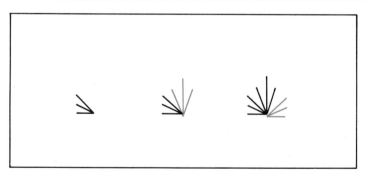

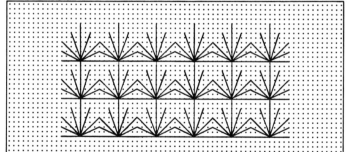

A simple geometric like this filled double square can be given a light or dark value depending on its filling. To work this pattern, stitch the squares in *backstitch* and fill with *cross stitch*. For a darker pattern, use a *double cross stitch* or work blocks closer together.

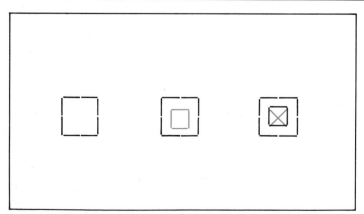

This Greek scroll, though it looks complex, is easy to work. *Backstitch* or *Holbein* can be used. Work the first row as shown. For the next row, invert motif to create a mirror-image effect. This pattern can be used as a filling or as a border.

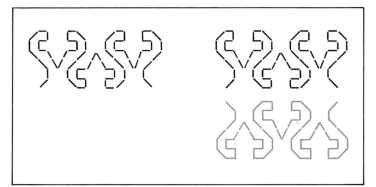

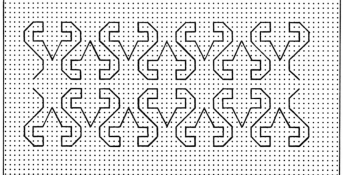

Crossed star motif is composed of a network of intersecting stars. Begin each star with a central *double cross stitch.* Add the points in *backstitch* and join the stars with a single vertical *cross stitch* at each point.

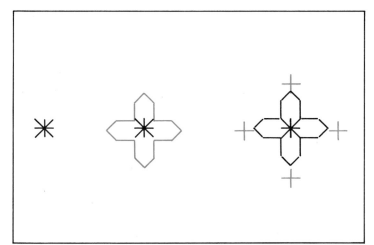

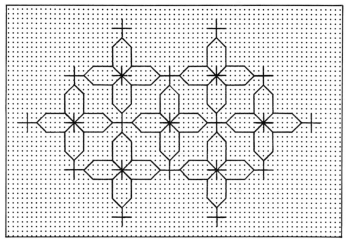

Flower arrangement creates a medium value with large motifs. To work this pattern, stitch center *cross stitch* of each group. Then work the outline of one bloom, in *backstitch,* adding the detail lines last. Work the other three blooms in the same way.

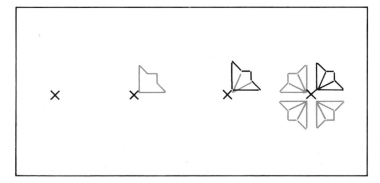

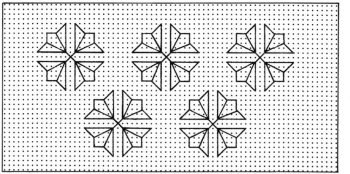

Blackwork embroidery

Examples of blackwork patterns

Scattered snowflakes produce an open pattern of medium value. Work snowflake center in *Algerian eye stitch*. Then work the adjoining lines and shapes in *backstitch*. When all rows of pattern are complete, add the diamond shapes in backstitch.

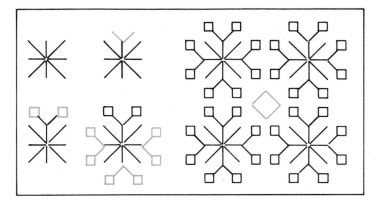

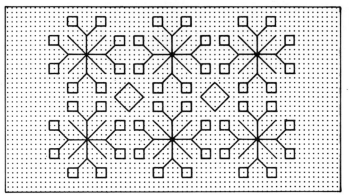

Stacked "H" shapes are worked from outside in. The main motifs are worked in *backstitch* (see p. 57 for the way to work corners). Fill in the centers of the "H" shapes with *Algerian eye stitch*.

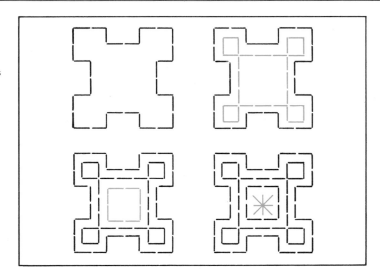

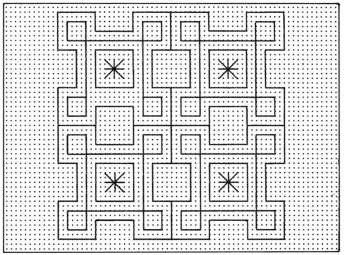

Stained glass impression is created by this dark, delicate pattern. Though its lines look intricate, pattern is easy to work. Begin by stitching a *backstitch* cross. Add an octagonal ring and four corner triangles (all backstitch).

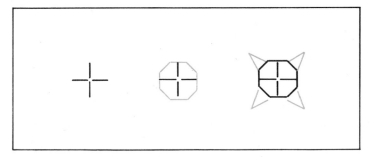

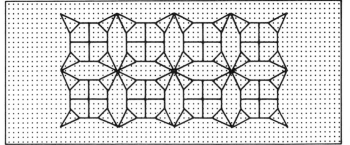

Creating your own blackwork pattern

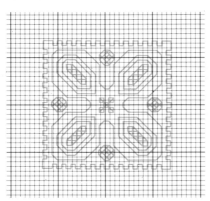

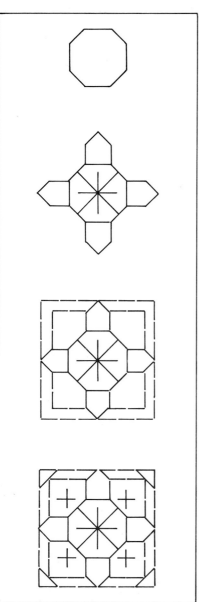

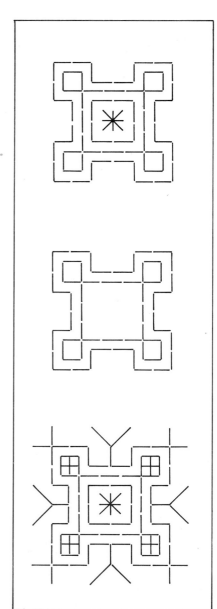

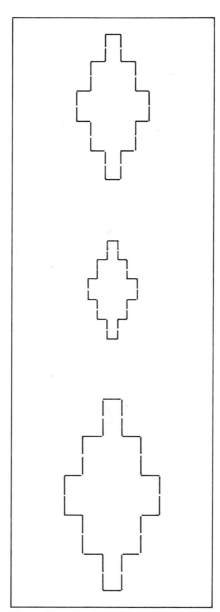

A geometric motif from a fabric print or a ceramic tile can be adapted for blackwork. Following the basic lines of the motif, draw it on graph paper; stylize for blackwork technique. Pattern shown is worked in backstitch and cross stitch.

Develop your own pattern from any simple geometric shape, adding lines and other shapes to fill in or extend the original shape. Pattern above combines Algerian eye stitch, backstitch, and cross stitch.

Modify an existing blackwork pattern to your taste. Simplify the motif by removing some of its lines. Or add lines for a larger or more complex pattern. Algerian eye stitch, backstitch, and cross stitch are used above.

Change the scale of an existing pattern to give it a new look. Enlarge the motif by lengthening the stitches. To make the motif smaller than the original, shorten the stitches. Motif shown is worked in backstitch, over 1, 2, or 3 threads.

Blackwork embroidery

Working blackwork in block designs

When working a blackwork piece to form a block or all-over design (see block design on p. 56), the blackwork pattern must be symmetrically placed. To accomplish this, you must carefully measure and divide the area to be stitched.

First determine the approximate size the finished blackwork design is to be. Then cut even-weave fabric on grain to the dimensions of the projected design **plus** four inches on all sides. Bind or finish the raw edges of the cut fabric to prevent raveling and fraying as you embroider (see p. 16). Count the threads within the area to be worked and mark the perimeters clearly.

Since blackwork patterns are worked from the center out, the center point of the design must be located and marked. Place the initial motif in relation to the center point so that as many *whole motifs* as possible fit into the worked area. This positioning is particularly important if the motifs are large.

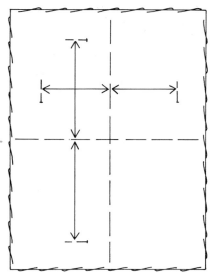

1. Fold fabric in half lengthwise; baste along center line with thread. Fold fabric in half crosswise and baste along that center line. Intersecting basting lines mark center of fabric.

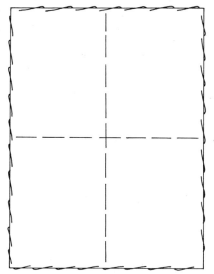

2. Measure desired width on one side of vertical center line; mark with pins. Count same number of threads from center on opposite side and mark. Measure and mark length from crosswise center.

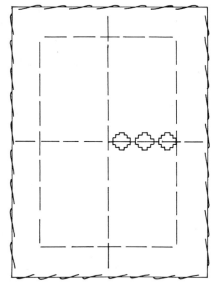

3. Baste along pinned lines for perimeter of design. Using selected pattern, start from center point and work one row of pattern outward from vertical center line. Work other half the same way.

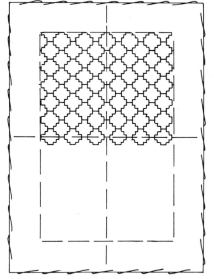

4. To fill remaining area, repeat rows of pattern above and below first row. Using it as a guide, subsequent rows can be worked from edge to edge, rather than from center out.

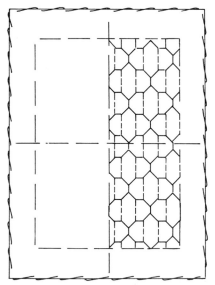

5. If the selected pattern is worked vertically, stitch first row out from crosswise center line. To fill remaining area, stitch subsequent rows, using first completed row as a guide.

POSITIONING LARGE MOTIF

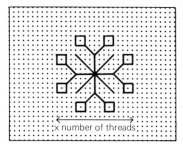

x number of threads

If a motif is large, whether it will be worked horizontally or vertically, as many motifs as possible should be worked on a line. To accomplish this, count fabric threads in a row, then fabric threads in one motif. Divide number of fabric threads by the number in one motif.

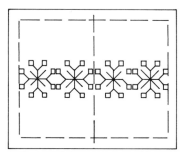

If the result is an even number, start motif *at* center line, working a complete motif on either side of center.

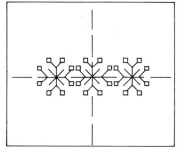

If result is an odd number, work half a motif *on either side* of center line so that one full motif is centered.

Working blackwork within free-form shapes

When design is to be free-form, patterns must be selected and placed with care. Choose patterns that have different values of light and dark, distinct enough so that the shapes in the piece do not become blurred. When combined thoughtfully, the lights and darks can add depth and realism to a free-form piece.

In choosing a pattern to fill any shape, consider the size of the shape in relation to the scale of the pattern. Make sure that there is enough space within the area to repeat the motif several times. Otherwise, the pattern will not be shown to its best advantage.

In addition to the basic stitches used to work patterns, consider working other embroidery stitches in a free-form piece. Use stitches such as the *chain stitch, stem stitch,* or *couching stitches* to emphasize and outline shapes that need definition. Or incorporate very dark areas of contrast into the design by filling small shapes with *satin stitch.*

1. Trace or draw design on heavy tracing paper. Color in different values of gray to represent light, medium, and dark patterns. Arrange them for balance and contrast; perhaps add shading for a realistic effect. Select the patterns that best represent the grays in the drawing.

2. Cut out even-weave fabric on grain four inches wider on all edges than desired finished size of design. Bind or finish the raw edges of the fabric to prevent raveling or fraying while the design is being worked (see p. 16). Transfer the design to the fabric (pp. 16-17).

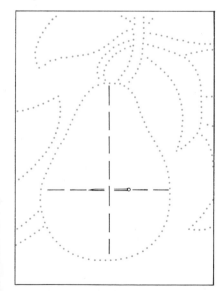

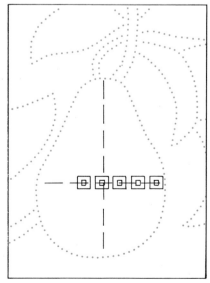

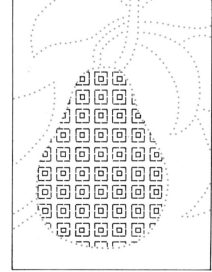

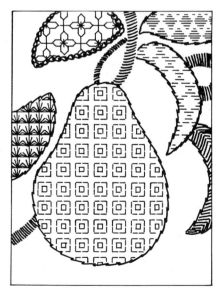

3. Determine approximate center of each shape to be filled; mark with a pin. Block designs must be centered exactly (by thread counting); center of a free-form shape can be determined by eye.

4. Start pattern at center, working the row out to marked edges. At edges where a whole motif may not fit, use part of a motif, perhaps shortening stitches, to keep pattern within outline.

5. Repeat the pattern rows, using the first completed row as a guide. As before, at edges where a whole motif does not fit, work a partial motif, shortening stitches as necessary.

6. When all shapes in design have been filled, outline them, using such stitches as the *stem stitch, chain stitch,* or *couching stitches.* Fill in solid areas with *satin stitch.*

65

Cross stitch embroidery

Introduction to cross stitch
Basic cross stitch
Cross stitch guides
Cross stitch on gingham
Assisi embroidery

Introduction

Cross stitch is a traditional type of embroidery adaptable to either simple or intricate designs. Cross stitch designs are often worked exclusively in basic cross stitch, as at right, though variations of the stitch can also be used.

Cross stitch can be worked on almost any fabric suitable for embroidery. The even-weave types are especially good because their even threads help guide the stitches. Gingham is popular for cross stitch for a similar reason—its squares form a natural grid (see p. 9).

Embroidery floss is the usual choice for working cross stitch, but other embroidery yarns can be used. Just be sure the floss you select is compatible with the weight of your embroidery fabric.

Choose a needle according to your fabric: a tapestry needle for an even-weave, to slip between threads; for other fabrics, a sharp-pointed needle (crewel or chenille) to pierce the fabric. To keep stitch tension even, it is best to use an embroidery hoop or frame.

Versatile basic cross stitch fills shapes, forms geometrics, outlines motifs.

Forming the basic cross stitch

Basic cross stitch can be formed in two ways. It can be worked **in rows** of even, slanted stitches, with one arm of the crosses laid down in one run, the other in a second, return run. Cross stitches can also be worked **one at a time.** Work cross stitches in a row when they are adjacent in a design. When they are scattered, it is best to work them singly; this way no long yarns will be trailed on the wrong side. With either stitching method, make sure that the top yarns all lie in the same direction. This is important to the even, neat look that is characteristic of cross stitch.

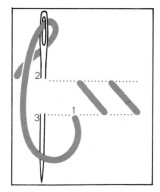
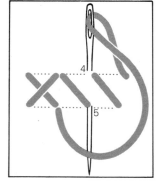
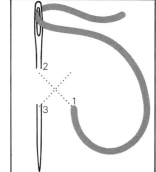
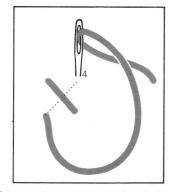

To work cross stitches in a row: Starting at right, come up at 1, insert at 2, exit at 3. At end of row, work back, inserting at 4, exiting at 5.

To work one cross stitch at a time: Bring needle up at 1, insert at 2, and exit at 3 below. To complete, insert needle at 4 above 1.

Even-weave fabrics 9
Hot-iron transfers 16-17
Needlepoint canvas 114

Cross stitch guides

There are two kinds of sources for cross stitch designs, **hot-iron transfers** and **charted designs.** Hot-iron transfers can be applied to any solid, tightly woven fabric. See pages 16-17 for details about them. Use charted designs on any fabric that offers a natural grid (even-weaves, or plain weaves with an even surface pattern, such as gingham).

With an iron-on transfer, your design will be the same size as the transfer. If you use a charted design, finished size will depend on the number of fabric threads or surface lines you work over.

Charted designs (both the colored key and symbol key types) are printed on a grid. Each block in the grid represents a single cross stitch. The scale of each stitch, however, is up to you.

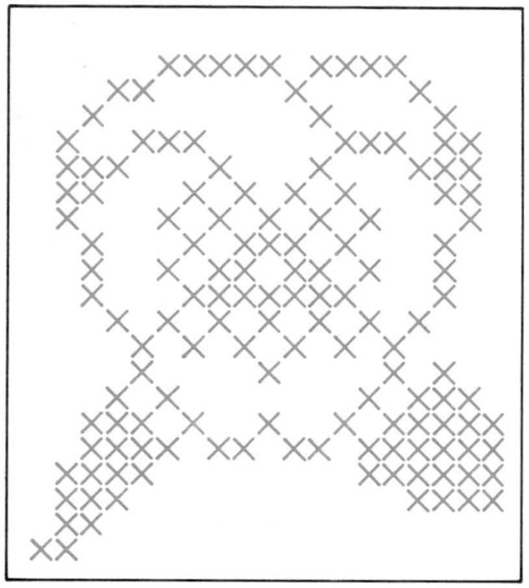

With iron-on transfers for cross stitch, simple crosses indicate stitch placement.

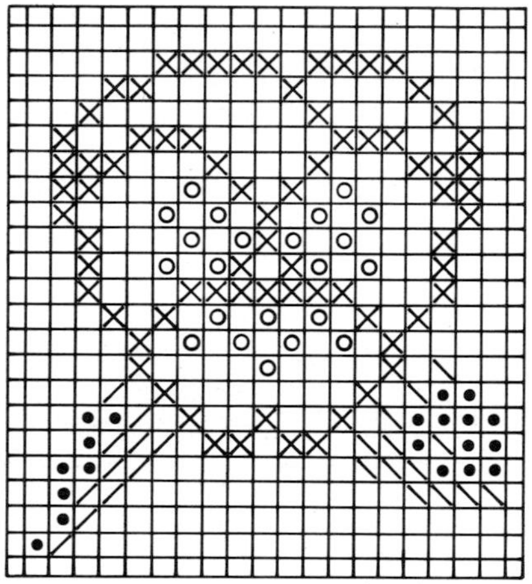

In charted designs with symbol keys, symbols represent stitch placement and color.

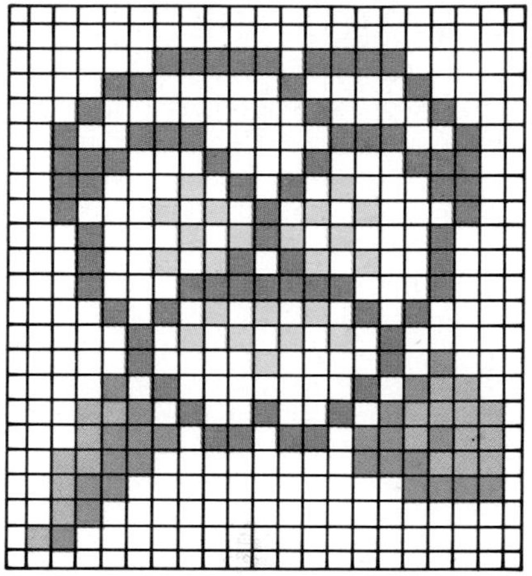

Charted designs with color keys show stitch placement and color with colored blocks.

Natural grids

Fabrics with natural grids (even-weaves, and plain weaves with even surface patterns) are ideal for cross stitch. With charted designs, fabrics of this type are indispensable. When the weave pattern is large, as in Aida fabric, each cross stitch can cover one thread intersection. When it is smaller, as in Hardanger fabric, each cross stitch can cover several fabric strands or thread intersections. Be sure each stitch crosses the same number of fabric threads.

When a fabric does not have a natural grid, **needlepoint canvas** can supply one. Choose a suitable size of either plain mono or penelope canvas (no interlocking meshes) and baste it to the embroidery fabric. Work the cross stitch design according to the chart. When the design is completed, remove the basting stitches and trim the excess canvas as close to the design as you can without cutting into the cross stitches. Carefully draw out the canvas threads with tweezers as follows: Start from one corner and pull all parallel threads in one direction. Then, working from another corner, pull out the remaining threads.

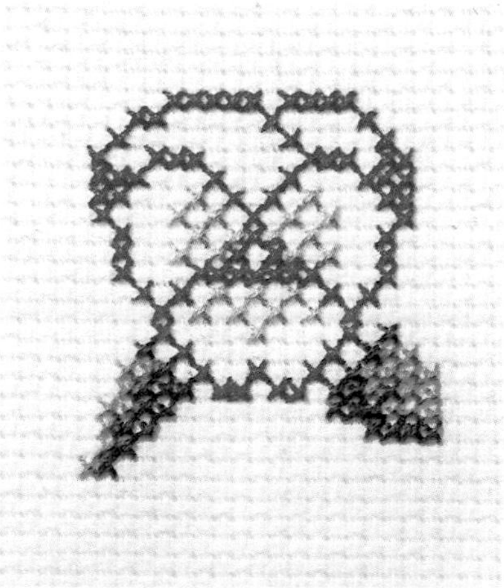

Cross stitch on a large even-weave shows each stitch worked over one thread group.

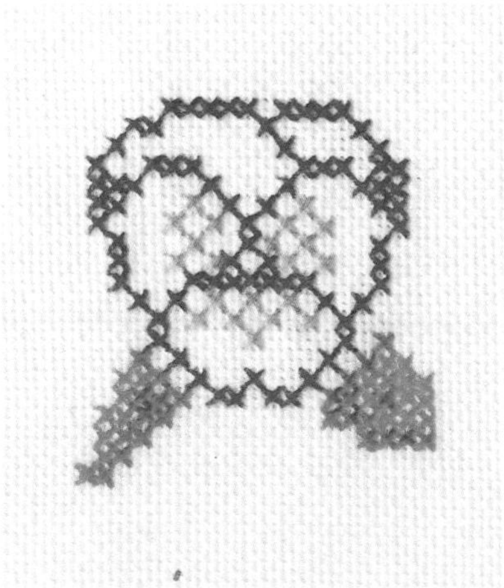

Cross stitch on a small even-weave shows each stitch worked over several threads.

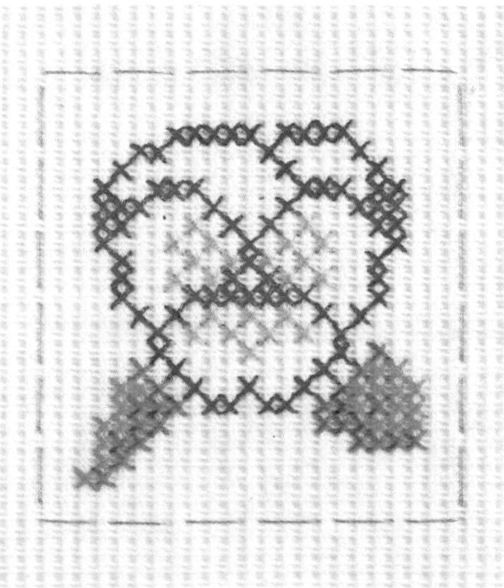

Needlepoint canvas, basted to embroidery fabric, can substitute for a fabric grid.

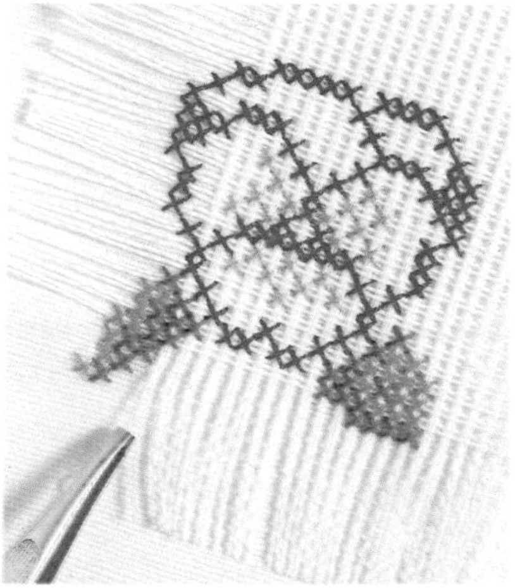

When the design is finished, the canvas threads are pulled out with tweezers.

Cross stitch embroidery

Cross stitch on gingham

Gingham is a highly popular fabric for cross stitch because of its natural grid. One cross is worked within each square, which keeps stitches uniform.

Any charted design that requires a fabric with a natural grid can be worked on gingham, but some designs are particularly effective on this fabric. The three tones of gingham (dark, light, and white) can be used to advantage (see below). A motif worked on only the dark squares will create a different effect, for example, than the same motif worked on the medium or the light gingham squares.

Gingham comes in many colors, and in check sizes from three to ten per inch. Since the check size determines the size of each cross, the larger the squares, the larger the overall design.

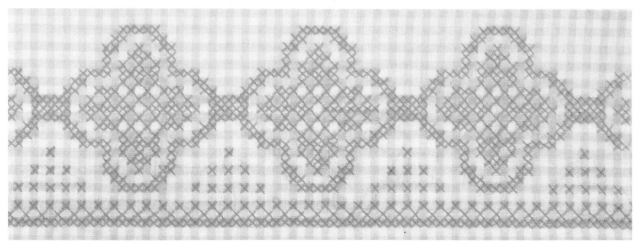

Cross stitch on gingham design features a repeated geometric motif, a favorite use of the technique and ideal for decorative borders.

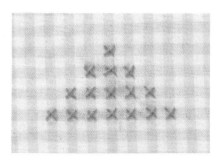

Crosses worked on the dark squares enhance the contrast between whites and darks.

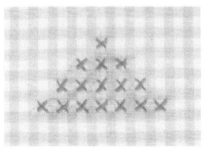

Crosses worked on the white squares give a more monochromatic look to the gingham.

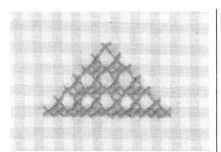

Crosses on both dark and light squares make shape more solid, whites more emphatic.

Variations of the basic cross stitch can be incorporated into the main motifs of a design or used to embellish a border pattern. The variations above are the *herringbone stitch* (p. 36) and the *double cross stitch* (p.35).

Working sample motif

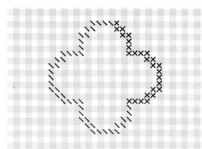

Individual flowers are stitched separately. Work outline as a row (in two journeys).

Next fill in center petals, working one petal at a time, again as a row.

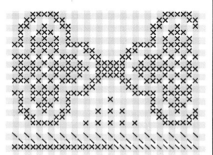

Work connecting blocks and border stitches as rows. Stitch triangle crosses one at a time.

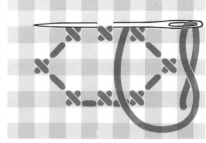

Work medallion with basic cross stitches, adding running stitches to connect them.

Assisi embroidery

Assisi embroidery is a variation of basic cross stitch in which design areas are left open and the background filled with basic cross stitch. Designs are usually outlined with Holbein stitch (see p. 47). Details and highlights within the open forms are also worked with either the Holbein or cross stitch.

The technique is named for the town in northern Italy where it originated. (Assisi is also the birthplace of Saint Francis, founder of the Franciscan order.) The first Assisi embroideries were worked at the beginning of this century. The designs, however, were adapted from centuries-old embroidered pieces preserved by local churches. The motifs in these early pieces were of primitively drawn animal shapes. As Assisi embroidery became more popular and greater variety of design was needed, elaborate patterns were adapted from the wood carvings in the churches of Assisi. The adaptations include, along with animal figures, geometric and floral motifs.

Traditionally, only one yarn color was used. Today, colors can be mixed. A particularly effective way of combining color is to use one for filling and another for outlining and detail.

Most regular cross stitch charts can be adapted for Assisi work. Simply select designs with strong shapes and reverse the open and filled areas.

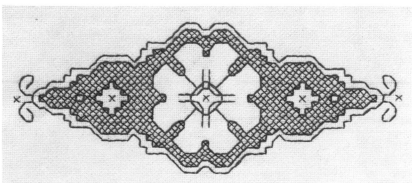

The first Assisi designs were roughly drawn animal shapes. Later, the designs were refined into more delicate shapes, abstracted florals, geometrics, and intertwining figures.

To work an Assisi piece, first stitch the outline of the shape in *Holbein stitch*, worked as two journeys of running stitches. On the first journey, stitch evenly spaced running stitches. Work the second journey so top floats are stitched over the spaces left by the first journey. Enter and exit at the same holes. When the outline is complete, fill in the background areas with cross stitch, worked as rows (see p. 66).

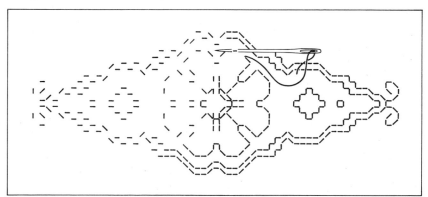

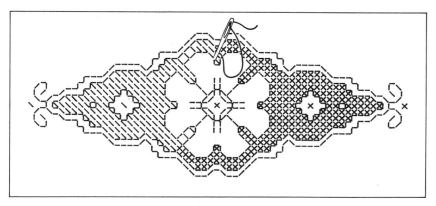

Huck embroidery

Introduction to huck embroidery
Kinds of huck motifs
Basic stitch movements
Working huck embroidery

Introduction

Huck embroidery, also called darning, is a type of needlework in which the surface of huckaback fabric is decorated. Huckaback is a toweling fabric most readily available in a 17-inch width and a limited number of colors, and distinguished by raised threads that occur at regular intervals on both sides. On one side, there are **single floats** that run **across;** this is considered the right side of the fabric. The reverse side has **double floats** running **up and down** and is the side usually embroidered.

Most huck designs are worked on the double floats, across the width of the fabric; some are worked on the single floats, across the fabric length (used crosswise to accommodate a project requiring unlimited width). Which of the floats are used depends on what article you are making. For example, a design for a hand towel would be worked on the double floats, across the width (see adjoining sample). Hand towels are a frequent huck project because the 17-inch width suits a towel's proportions. To work a design for a cafe curtain, you would turn the fabric to the other side and use the length crosswise (see sample at top of opposite page). When huck fabric is used this way, the single floats run up and down, and the width of the fabric becomes the height of the curtain.

Yarns used for huck work are usually pearl cotton and 6-strand embroidery floss, sometimes others such as Persian yarn and cotton tapestry yarn. Because the needle picks up the floats rather than piercing the fabric, a tapestry needle, in a size that suits your yarn, is recommended. An embroidery hoop is not needed.

Designs for huckaback embroidery are usually geometrics, used as a *single motif,* a *border, all-over or repetitive patterns,* or *stylized figures.* Examples appear at the far right, with drawings that show the order of working each type. For how-to drawings of the basic stitch movements, see page 72.

Used vertically, huckaback fabric is ideally proportioned for hand towels. Huck embroidery is worked on the double, vertical floats that appear at regular intervals on the fabric. Magnification shows number and direction of floats and the technique of securing yarn ends by weaving them back into stitching (see p. 73).

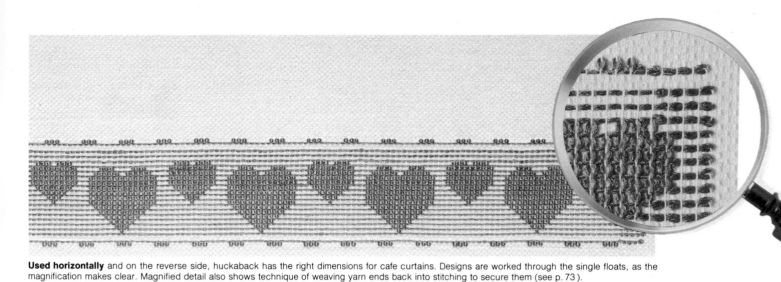

Used horizontally and on the reverse side, huckaback has the right dimensions for cafe curtains. Designs are worked through the single floats, as the magnification makes clear. Magnified detail also shows technique of weaving yarn ends back into stitching to secure them (see p. 73).

Four basic huck motifs

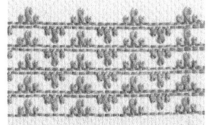

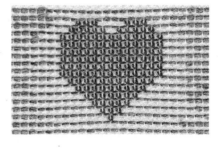

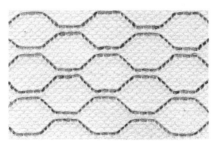

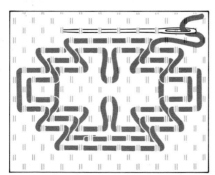

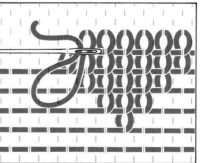

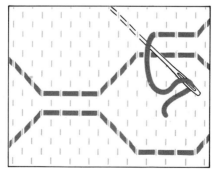

Single motif is worked from center out. Design above consists of straight stitches, offsets, and open loops.

Border is worked from bottom upward in rows from right to left. Stitches used are straight stitches and figure eights.

Stylized figure is worked from right to left in rows. The heart shape above is worked in rows of closed loops and straight stitches.

All-over pattern is worked in rows from right to left until desired area is filled. Pattern above is worked entirely in straight stitch.

For detailed stitch instructions, see next page.

Huck embroidery

Basic stitch movements

Straight stitches are the type used most often in huck darning. To work, move needle from right to left, picking up floats in a straight line. Needle can also move diagonally.

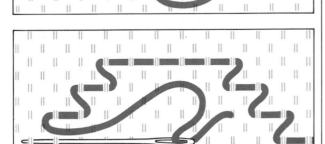

Offsets are huck stitches that create a stairway effect. To work, always move needle from right to left, and forward.

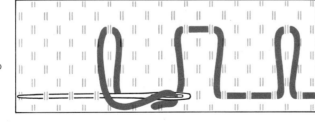

Open loops are huck stitches that are looped at the top and open at the base. Move needle from right to left, and forward at each pick-up point, to keep the loops open.

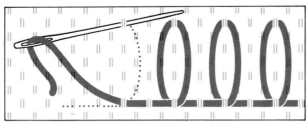

Closed loops are like open loops, but the stitch base is closed. To work, move needle from right to left at the base and from left to right at the top. *Re-enter same float at base, moving right to left.*

Figure eights are a combination of open and closed loops. Move from right to left at base, and at top of loop. Figure eight is formed by *re-entering the first base float* to complete the stitch.

Working huck embroidery

Most huck designs are worked in rows of stitches that start at the bottom and are built upward. The first row of a design, however, is worked from the center out to make sure the design is balanced on both sides. After this line is laid, rows can be worked from right to left.

Many huck patterns consist of large motifs that are repeated. In order to fit as many full motifs as possible within the width of the fabric (particularly on a narrow width), the initial motif must be carefully placed.

To determine placement of the first motif in relation to the center of the fabric, count the number of floats that are spanned by one motif, then the number across the fabric. Divide the number of floats per motif into the number available in the fabric. Drop all fractions from the result. If the answer is an even number, place the edge of a motif at the center line and work a complete motif on either side. If the answer is an odd number of floats, center the first motif—that is, work half a motif on either side.

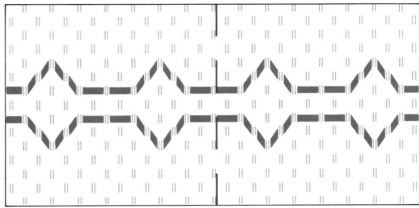

For an even number of huck embroidery motifs, start with two motifs, one on either side of the center line of the fabric.

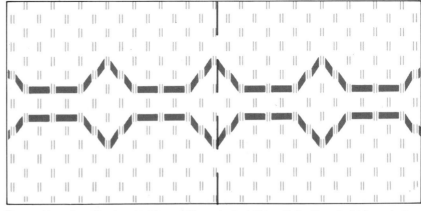

For an odd number of huck embroidery motifs, center the initial motif directly on the fabric center line, placing half on either side.

To start, fold fabric width in half; mark fold. Cut yarn about 30″ long (average length for one row across a towel). Do not knot yarn end. Leaving half of yarn length free at center, work first row from center to left.

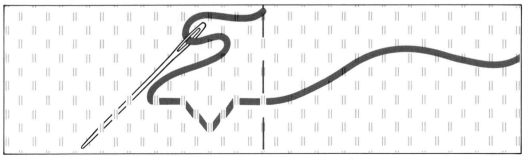

Turn work upside down. Thread needle with free yarn and work the other half of the row from the right to the left.

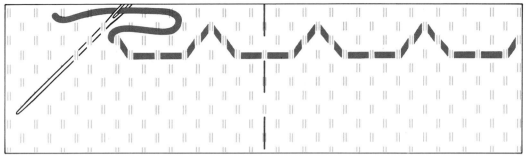

Turn work right side up again and work next row, going from right to left, using a continuous length of yarn.

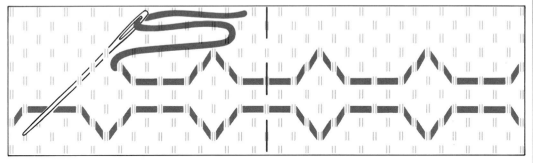

Work all other rows from right to left, using continuous lengths of yarn. Stitch carefully, using the laid rows as a guide.

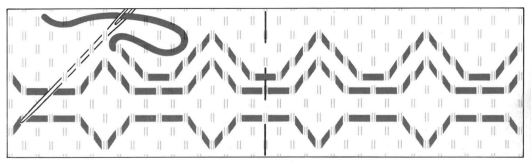

Finishing ends

If a design is complete within an open area, weave yarn ends back into final stitches.

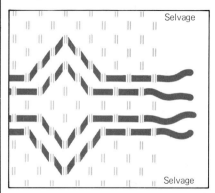

Selvage

Selvage

If a design runs all the way to a seam, leave ends free; they will be caught in seam.

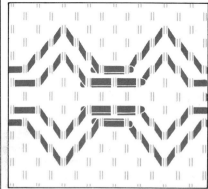

To join yarn ends within pattern, run yarn to very end. Start new yarn 1″ back.

Openwork/ Pulled thread embroidery

Introduction to pulled threadwork
Working a pulled threadwork piece
Stitch patterns

Introduction

Pulled thread embroidery (or drawn fabric work) is a type of openwork often employed to decorate linens. In pulled threadwork, each stitch pulls the fabric threads together, creating open, lace-like patterns. The many stitch patterns are used as borders, as geometrics, or to fill free-form shapes. Pulled threadwork pieces often include simple embroidery stitches as well, to outline motifs or to add textural interest.

Being a form of counted-thread embroidery, pulled threadwork is usually stitched on even-weave fabrics. Select a yarn similar in weight to a single fabric thread. Use the largest tapestry needle that will slip easily between fabric threads. This will exaggerate the openings. Use an embroidery hoop or frame.

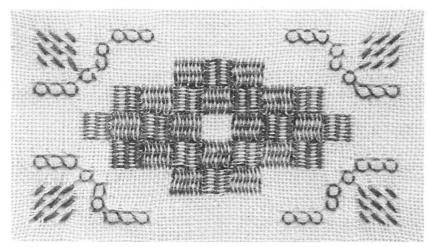

Pulled threadwork piece combining three stitch patterns from the selection illustrated.

Working a pulled threadwork piece

For any pulled threadwork piece, first locate the fabric center and mark with basting. Then position motifs, counting threads from center point out. If outer edges of motif will be covered with an embroidery stitch, you can *draw* the outline on right side of fabric. If outline will not be covered, use basting stitches. Work motifs one at a time, from center one out; work stitch patterns in rows (see next three pages). Always secure row ends as shown below. Do all patterns, then add embellishments.

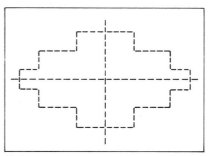

Mark center of fabric, then draw or baste motifs on fabric, counting threads from center.

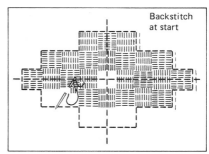

Work motif groups one at a time, from center of piece out; work stitch patterns in rows.

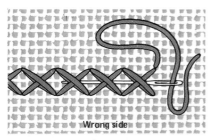

Always secure row ends by passing needle under worked stitches on wrong side. Then pull out the backstitches worked at the beginning and secure those thread ends the same way.

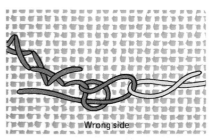

To tie in new yarn: Make loop for simple knot; hold twisted part with thumbnail close to last stitch; pull to small circle; insert yarn end to form second loop. Thread new yarn; pull through

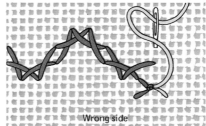

second loop. With nail holding first knot, tug on second loop to pull first partly closed. Pull old and new yarns opposite ways until second loop disappears and clicks through first. Trim ends.

Stitch patterns

Pulled thread embroidery offers quite a choice of stitch patterns. Here and on the next two pages, we show step-by-step instructions for six of the most popular. Each stitch pattern is worked in rows.

Depending on the pattern, rows may run from side to side, horizontally, or vertically. The needle movements are simple, though changing rows can be confusing. Follow each sequence carefully, noting the needle movements and direction in which the fabric is held. (Often it is turned for easier handling.) The last illustration in each sequence shows the look of the pulled threads. Begin with a few backstitches outside the area to be worked. End by weaving yarn into back of work. Finally, pull out the beginning backstitches and weave those, too, into the back of the work.

Four-sided stitch is worked in horizontal rows, always moving from right to left. To start, come up at 1, go in at 2, exit at 3 to the left of 1. Go in at 1 and come up at 4 above 3. Go in at 2, exit at 3. Pull each stitch tight. *Repeat sequence* until row is complete. For next row, turn fabric upside down and work second row as you did first. At end of row, turn fabric again for start of third row.

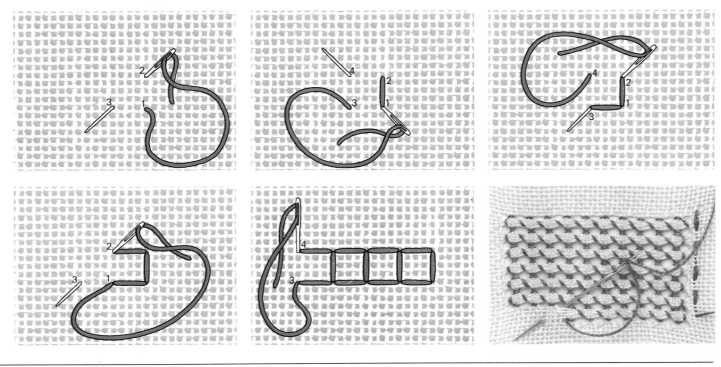

Coil filling stitch is made of groups of satin stitches worked in horizontal rows. To start, come up at 1 and work three satin stitches. Move to next group, four fabric threads to left, repeat Steps 1 to 6. At end of row, come up at 1 below for start of next row. Work second row left to right, third right to left.

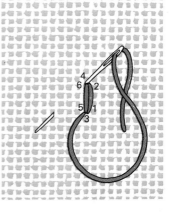
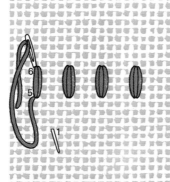
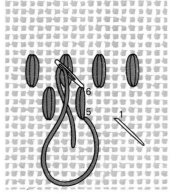
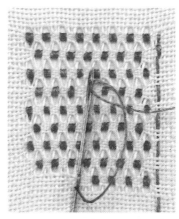

75

Openwork/Pulled thread embroidery

Stitch patterns

Chessboard filling stitch is worked in blocks. Each block is worked in three rows (8 stitches each) alternately right to left, then left to right. At end of third row, turn as shown and come up at 1 to start new block. *Work all subsequent blocks* like the first, turning as shown for each new block.

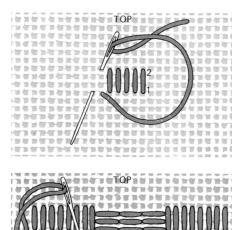 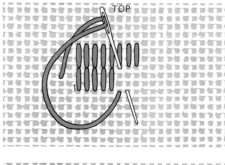 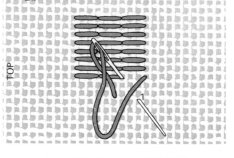

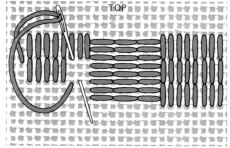 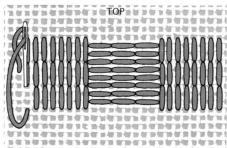 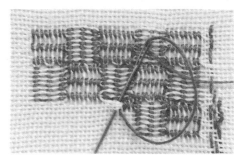

Framed cross is worked in two parts. First work the vertical pairs of stitches in rows alternately from right to left, then left to right, until desired number of rows are completed. *Then turn fabric* as shown and work pairs of stitches perpendicular to the first set, working rows alternately right to left, then left to right.

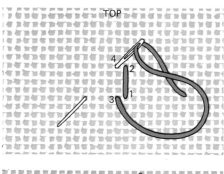 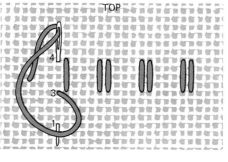 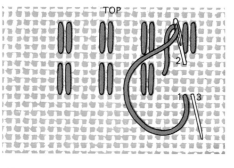

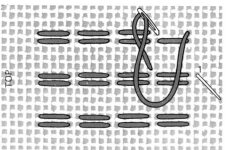 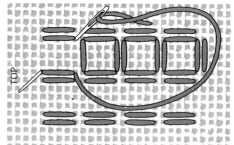 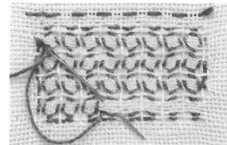

Ringed backstitch is worked in two journeys. On the first, a series of half-rings are formed. On the second journey, the rings are completed. To start, come up at 1, go in at 2, exit at 3. Continue working backstitches through Step 9. (A 1 to 9 sequence forms two half-rings or eight stitches.) *Repeat sequence* until desired number of half-rings are formed. At end of row, turn fabric and work other half of rings as shown. Always move from right to left; turn fabric to accomplish this.

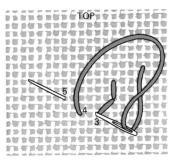
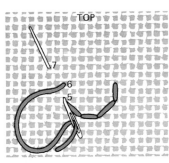
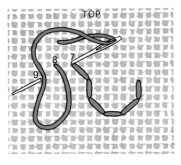

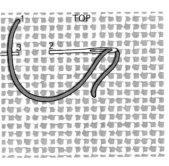
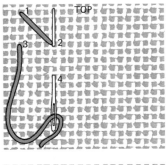
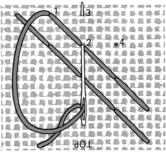

Reverse faggot stitch is worked in pairs of diagonal rows. Worked as shown, stitch fills a square area. Square is worked one half at a time. To start, come up at 1, go in at 2, exit at 3 directly across from 2. Go in at 4, exit at 2. Repeat the sequence until two rows are formed, having four and three stitches respectively. (Subsequent rows shorten similarly to form a corner of the square.) Turn fabric to begin next rows. *Using same 1 to 4 sequence*, work second pair of rows. Turn fabric upright for third pair. Work the other half of the square the same way.

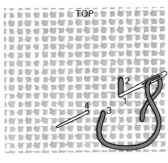
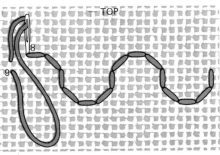
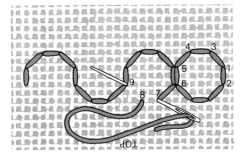
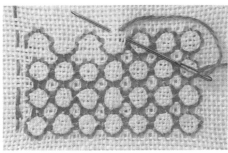

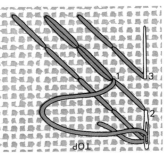
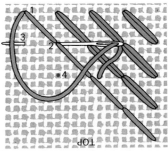
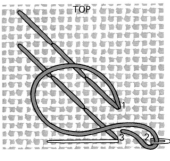
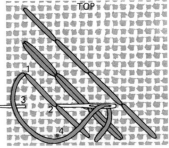

Openwork/ Drawn threadwork

Drawn threadwork techniques
Introduction to hemstitching
Preparing fabric for hemstitching
Working basic hemstitch
Hemstitching variations
Handling drawn corners
Introduction to needleweaving
Basic needleweaving stitches
Needleweaving variations

Drawn threadwork techniques

Drawn threadwork is a type of openwork embroidery in which some of the weft and warp threads are drawn out or removed from the fabric. The remaining threads in the drawn area are then grouped together by means of different stitches, creating an open, patterned effect. There are two basic types of drawn threadwork, **hemstitching** and **needleweaving,** both used primarily for border decorations on table linens and handkerchiefs. Fabric threads are drawn out the same way in both hemstitching and needleweaving. They differ in the way drawn threads are decorated.

Introduction to hemstitching

Hemstitching is the most common type of drawn threadwork. It is called hemstitching because as it groups threads within a drawn border, it hems the edge below the border. Hemstitching can also be used solely to group threads in a drawn border, without a hemmed edge.

Almost any woven fabric can be used, though an even-weave is easiest to handle. Select a yarn of a thickness comparable to one strand of your fabric. Use embroidery floss or fine pearl cotton and work with a tapestry needle.

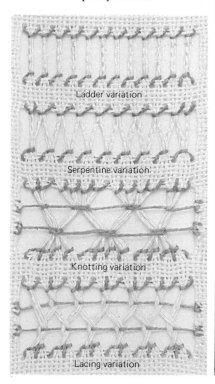

Ladder variation

Serpentine variation

Knotting variation

Lacing variation

Preparing fabric for hemstitching

To prepare an edge for hemstitching, you must first decide how deep and wide the border will be. Exact width and depth depend on the stitch variation you select (see pp. 80-81). Each one calls for the grouping of a certain number of vertical threads; a border's actual width will be a multiple of the threads in one group. Stitch variations differ, too, in depth, as the illustrations show.

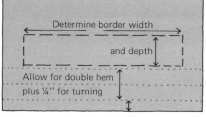

Decide how far border will be from finished edge. If hem is needed, allow twice hem depth plus ¼″ for turning. Baste-mark as explained below.

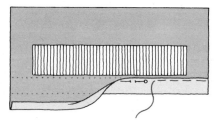

After drawing threads, press raw edge under; press hem up so top edge is one fabric thread from bottom of border. Pin and baste hem.

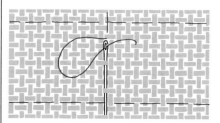

Drawing threads: 1. Baste along top and bottom of border between two horizontal threads. Baste-mark approximate width, then the center.

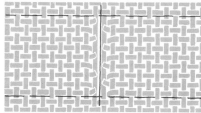

2. Using a pair of sharp embroidery scissors, carefully cut the horizontal fabric threads at the center of the marked border.

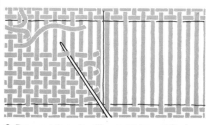

3. Draw out threads with a tapestry needle, leaving free the exact number of vertical threads for the stitch variation you plan to work.

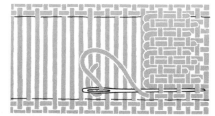

4. At border edges, weave fabric threads back into the wrong side of the fabric for 1″. Trim excess after weaving.

Working basic hemstitch

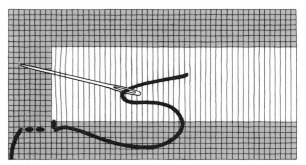

Without a hem, basic hemstitch is usually worked from wrong side of fabric. To start, leave 6″ yarn and work backstitches up to left edge of border. Take a small vertical stitch to right of edge. Then pass needle from right to left under fixed number (3-5) of vertical threads. Pull together into bundle.

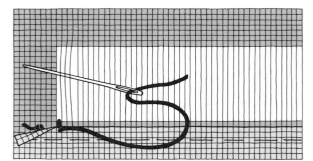

With a hem, too, basic hemstitch is usually worked from wrong side. To start, bring needle up at left edge of border, securing yarn in hem fold with a simple knot. Take small vertical stitch just to right of edge, being sure to catch hem. Then pass needle under fixed number of vertical threads (3-5) and pull together into bundle.

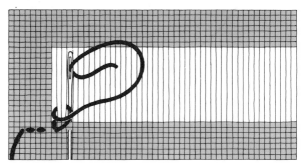

Take a small vertical stitch to the right of the bundle. Continue working in this way over the entire width of the border, keeping the small vertical stitches even throughout.

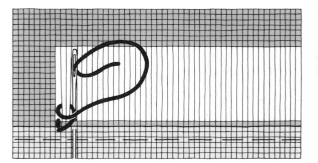

Take a small vertical stitch through right side, emerging at hem fold, to right of thread bundle. Continue working in this way across entire width of border.

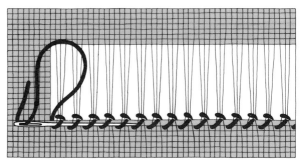

At end of border, still on the wrong (working) side, pass needle through completed stitches to secure. Pull out the backstitches at left edge of border and secure these as well by passing the yarn through the completed stitches there.

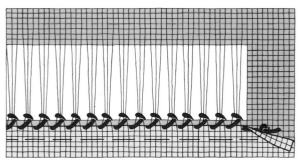

When the stitching is complete, secure it by passing needle through hem fold and knotting yarn. Trim excess yarn.

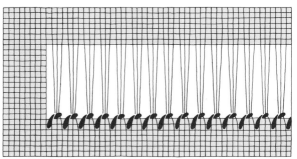

The finished effect on the right side (when work is done on the wrong side) is shown at left. If you prefer the look of the small loops formed on the working side, as shown immediately above, work hemstitching from right side of fabric. Secure thread ends on the wrong side; they should, of course, be invisible.

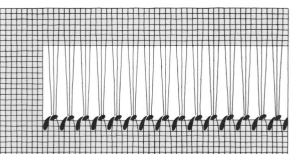

Look of right side (when worked from the wrong) is shown at left. If you prefer the looped effect shown above, work hemstitching from the right side of the fabric, being sure to catch hem, which will not be visible as you work. Knot thread ends, of course, on the wrong side.

Openwork/Drawn threadwork

Grouping variations

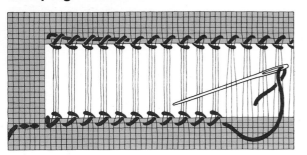

Ladder variation: To work, complete a row of basic hemstitch. Turn work upside down and work basic stitch on opposite edge. Stitch from left to right, catching the same threads in each bundle as were caught above to form a ladder-like pattern. Secure yarn at both ends as for basic hemstitch.

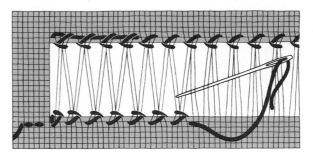

Serpentine variation: To work, complete a row of basic hemstitch, making sure each bundle has an *even* number of threads. Turn and work basic stitch on other edge, grouping halves of adjacent bundles together. First and last bundles will contain half as many threads as other bundles.

Knotting variations

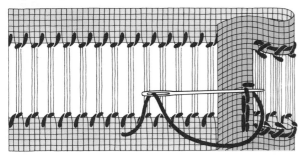

Simple knotted effect: To work, begin with a ladder variation on a border at least ½" deep. (Number of bundles must be a multiple of number grouped in second step.) Secure yarn by working backstitches along right edge of border. Then take whipstitches as shown, emerging at center, from wrong side, for next step.

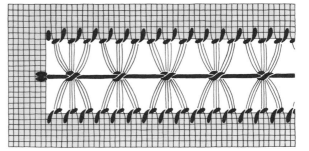

Continue working over remaining groups of bundles. When border is complete, whipstitch yarn at left edge to fasten, then weave end of yarn invisibly into back of fabric. Pull out the backstitches at opposite end and secure them the same way.

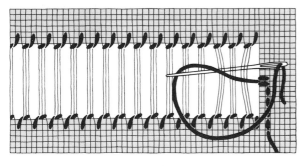

Working from right side of fabric, group the desired number of bundles (here three) as follows: Loop yarn as shown; pass needle behind yarn and under bundles; bring needle out with yarn under point.

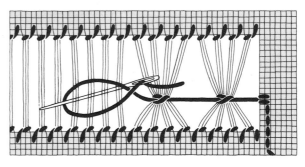

Double knotted effect: To work, draw out border at least ¾" deep. Work a ladder variation. (The number of ladder bundles must be a multiple of 4.) Then work a simple knot, grouping four bundles at bottom third of the drawn border.

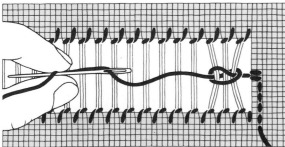

Pull needle through to form knot around bundles at the center of the border depth.

Work the same knot at the upper third of the border, taking adjacent halves of the bottom bundles in each knot. The first and last groups will contain half as many bundles as the others.

Lacing variations

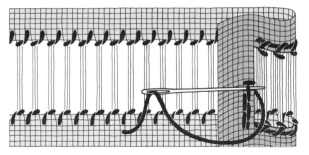

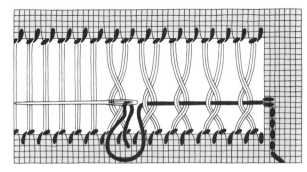

Simple laced effect:
To work, complete ladder variation on a border at least ½'' deep. (Work an even number of bundles.) Then, on right side of fabric, secure end of yarn by backstitching along the right edge. Take whipstitches as shown, emerging at center, from wrong side, for next step.

Multiple bundles can be laced in the same way that two are laced. (For the variation shown here, number of bundles must be a multiple of 4.)

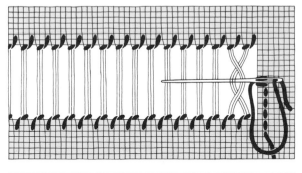

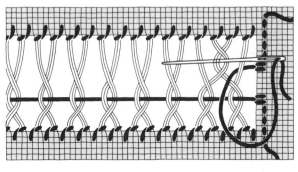

Working from right side of fabric, place needle over first two bundles. Then angle it down and toward the right, going under the second bundle and over the first with the tip of the needle.

Double laced effect:
Draw out a border at least ¾'' deep and work a ladder variation. (The number of bundles must be a multiple of 2.) Then work a simple lacing stitch at bottom third of the border, grouping two bundles together.

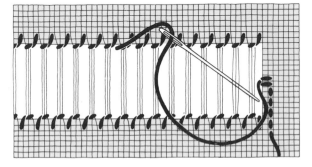

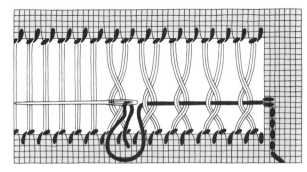

Press tip of needle against the first bundle and scoop it to the left, under the second bundle. Pulling the first bundle under the second causes the two to cross as shown.

Work the same simple lacing stitch at the top third of the border, but go under the first bundle before beginning actual lacing. The first bundle is skipped in order to stagger lacing points of the top and bottom rows.

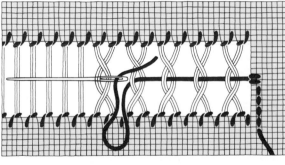

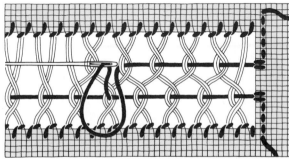

Pull needle through, keeping yarn taut to hold bundles in position. Continue working over pairs of bundles until entire border is laced. At left edge, fasten yarn with whipstitches, then weave end invisibly into back of fabric. Remove backstitches at opposite end; secure the same way.

Continue lacing in this way until border is completed. Be sure to keep yarn taut to hold intricate pattern in place. Fasten end of yarn on left edge of border with whipstitches. Weave end invisibly into back of fabric. Remove backstitches at opposite end and secure them in the same way.

Openwork/Drawn threadwork

Handling drawn corners

Often a drawn thread border of hemstitching (or of needleweaving) will run along all four edges of an article such as a napkin, a tablecloth, or a handkerchief. This will result in completely open corner areas where both warp and weft fabric threads have been drawn out. Drawn corners, depending on their size, can either be left open or decoratively filled with additional stitches. A small corner can be left open. A larger one should be filled to give it stability.

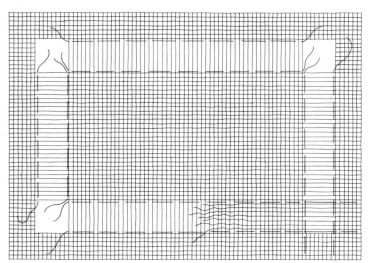

To prepare for corners, cut fabric to desired size, including hem allowance (see p. 78). Baste through horizontal and vertical centers. Measure and baste-mark border's outer edges, then its inner edges; keep bastings between fabric threads. Draw threads (p. 78), being sure that all sides contain the correct number for the stitch variation chosen. Hem as described at far right on opposite page.

Hemstitching to and around corners

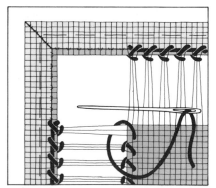

Hemstitch outer edges first, ending with small vertical stitch at corners. To secure, pass yarn through completed stitches; secure other end the same way, removing backstitches. Hemstitching

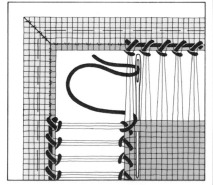

at the **inner edges** turns corners. Notice that yarn simply wraps the last bundle on the left edge, then the first one on the top edge, before the small vertical stitch is taken.

Decorating drawn corners

When the hemstitched border is shallow (less than ¾ inch), the open corners will be small and can be left open. The outer edges of the corner, however, should be reinforced with the **basic buttonhole stitch** or **tailor's buttonhole stitch.**

When the border is deep (¾ inch or more), the corners will be larger. These should be reinforced with a buttonhole stitch, then decorated as well. Decorative stitches help to stabilize large corners. Two such stitches are shown on these pages, the **loopstitch** and the **dove's eye filling.** The loopstitch forms a simple, flower-like motif and can be used with basic hemstitch or any hemstitch variation that has a straight bundle at each corner edge. The dove's eye filling forms an "X" with a circular center and can be used with any form of hemstitching.

BUTTONHOLE STITCHES

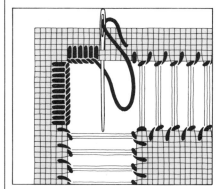

Basic buttonhole stitch: Work on outer edges of all corners, whether to be open or filled. Stitch from right side, two to three fabric threads deep, catching hem if one is involved.

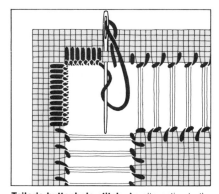

Tailor's buttonhole stitch: An alternative to the basic buttonhole stitch, and worked like it except that the yarn is wrapped around the needle as shown before it is pulled through.

DOVE'S EYE FILLING

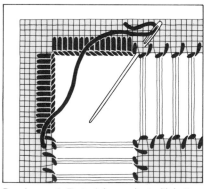

Dove's eye: 1. First reinforce edges with buttonhole stitch. Then bring needle up at lower left corner. Insert needle in fabric at upper right corner, coming out at corner opening.

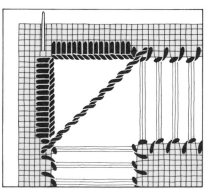

2. Overcast the laid yarn, working from upper right to lower left corner. Take needle to back of fabric and slip it through the buttonhole stitches, coming up at top left corner of square.

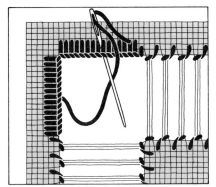

Buttonhole stitch reinforcing corner edges

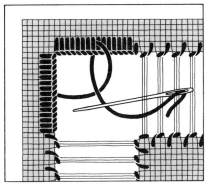

Loopstitch worked in large open corner

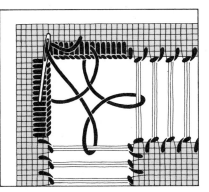

Dove's eye worked in large open corner

Hemming corners

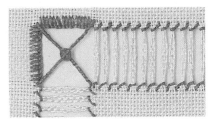

LOOPSTITCH

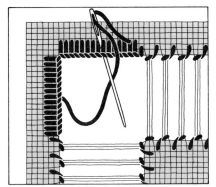

Loopstitch: 1. Work buttonhole stitch on outer edges. Then draw yarn through underside of stitches, coming up at left center. Take a stitch at top center (yarn passes under needle).

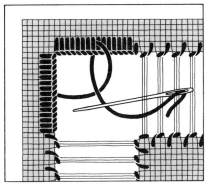

2. Loop needle over and under bundle at right edge; keep yarn under needle. Do not pull yarn too tightly; leave some slack to create open-looking loops and to avoid distorting bundle.

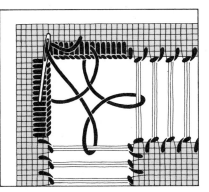

3. Loop needle over and under bundle at bottom edge. Pass needle under yarn at left edge and take a stitch at left center. Run needle through buttonhole stitches on wrong side to secure.

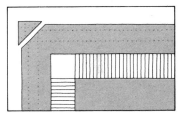

To hem corners, press under ¼″ on raw edges. Press hem up so fold is just below edge of border. Unfold pressed hem.

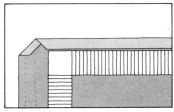

Trim off each corner diagonally as shown above, cutting along the diagonal of the corner square formed by the creases.

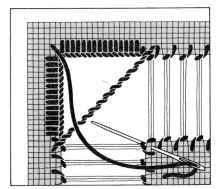

3. Bring needle over laid yarn and insert into fabric at lower right corner. Come out again at the opening, pulling the yarn tight enough to form an even ''X'' with the other laid yarn.

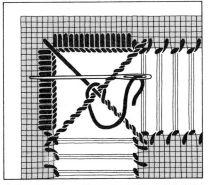

4. Overcast second laid yarn to the point where the two yarns cross. Weave under and over the laid yarns at center point, going counterclockwise, until dove's eye is desired size.

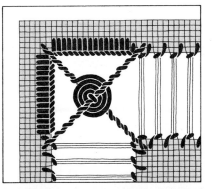

5. Overcast unwrapped remainder of diagonal yarn to upper left corner. Secure stitching yarn at back of fabric by running needle through buttonhole stitches along top edge of open square.

Turn down trimmed corner first. Then re-fold hem edges along the pressed lines to form neat, mitered corners.

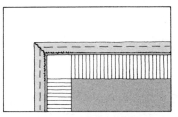

Pin and baste hem. Slipstitch mitered edges, also hem edge along outer corner. Hemstitch hem in place (p. 79).

83

Openwork/Drawn threadwork

Needleweaving

Needleweaving, like hemstitching, decorates threads in a drawn thread border. In needleweaving, however, thread bundles are covered one at a time, with the yarn ends secured under the covering.

The basic stitches are the *overcast stitch* and the *darning stitch*. Overcasting wraps the drawn threads, forming vertical bars. Darning weaves over and under them, giving a braid-like finish.

If needleweaving is "attached" (covers the bundles), the border is not usually hemstitched. (The hem, if there is one, must then be slipstitched.) Hemstitching is advised for "detached" types (see the darning variation on the opposite page).

Basic needleweaving stitches

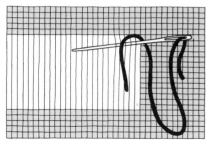 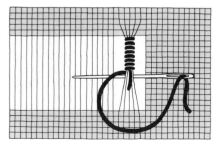 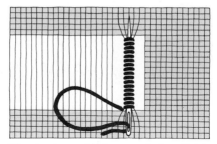

Basic overcast stitch: Place end of yarn over threads to be overcast (three to five; in this case five). Wrap yarn over threads and yarn end.

Pull yarns taut as you work. Pack them close together with the needle from time to time. Take care not to let wrapping yarns overlap.

When bar is completed, run needle through it to secure yarn. If fit is tight, change to a thinner, sharp-pointed needle. Trim excess yarn.

Needleweaving variations

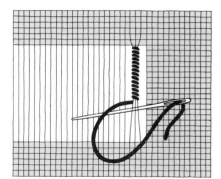 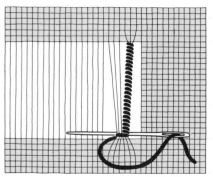 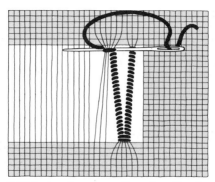

Overcast variation: Prepare drawn border, with total threads a multiple of 3. **1.** Work one basic overcast bar over three threads.

2. Just above bottom edge of border, overcast twice over six threads as shown, pulling first and second bundles together.

3. Work upward over second three-thread bundle. At top edge, overcast twice over six threads, pulling second and third bundles together.

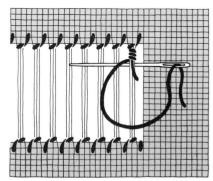 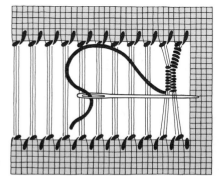 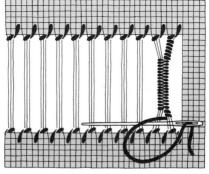

Overcast/darning variation: Bundles multiple of 4; three threads each (ladder hemstitch is helpful). **1.** Overcast one-fourth of first bundle.

2. Change to darning stitch and darn over and under first and second groups of threads until three-fourths of the border depth is covered.

3. Change back to overcasting stitch and wrap the remainder of the first group of threads to the bottom edge of the border.

The sample at left shows, from top to bottom:
- Basic overcast stitch
- Basic darning stitch
- Overcast variation
- Darning variation
- Overcast/darning variation

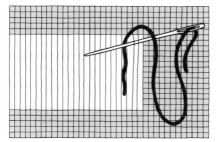

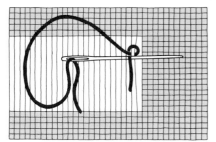

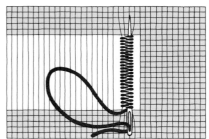

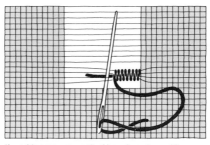

Basic darning stitch: Lay yarn end along first four threads. Pass needle under first two (have yarn end back of needle); pull it through. Then

pass needle back under second two threads, darning four threads (and yarn end) together. Continue weaving needle over and back, keeping

yarn taut, until bar is covered. To secure yarn, run needle through woven bar; if fit is tight, change to sharp, thinner needle. Trim excess yarn.

If working across vertical bars is awkward for you, **turn the work** so that the bar lies **horizontally**, and work darning stitch as shown.

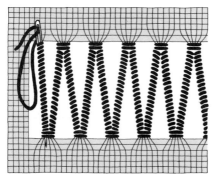

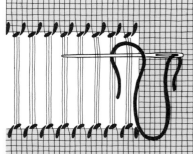

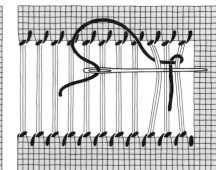

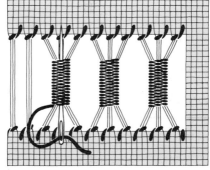

4. Continue this way to end of border, creating a zigzag effect. Run needle through last bar to secure yarn; change to thinner needle if fit is tight.

Darning variation: Work ladder hemstitch (see p. 80), with ladder bundles a multiple of 3. **1.** To begin darning, position needle and yarn as shown.

2. Darn three bundles together along center half, moving needle right to left, left to right until center half is darned. Pull yarn taut as you weave.

3. As each bar is completed, run the needle up through it to secure yarn; trim excess. If fit is tight, change to a thinner needle.

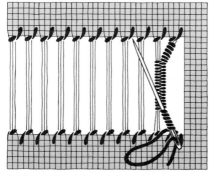

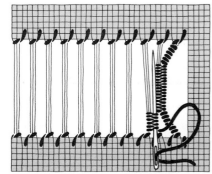

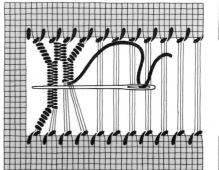

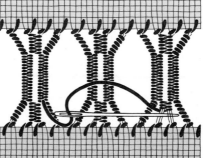

4. Slip needle up through these last overcasting stitches to get into position for next step. If fit is tight, change to thinner needle.

5. Darn second and third groups together to bottom edge. Run yarn through just-darned area; use thinner needle if necessary. Trim yarn close.

6. Turn work upside down and, using new length of yarn, repeat entire sequence to fill in other half of pattern. Turn right side up for next one.

7. Continue working individual units by halves, the first half right side up, the work turned for second half, until border is filled.

Openwork/Hardanger embroidery

Introduction to Hardanger
Kloster blocks
Working a motif
Covered bars
Filling stitches
Decorating a motif

Introduction

Hardanger embroidery is a type of openwork named for the district of Hardanger in Norway. It was first worked, however, in Persia centuries ago.

Hardanger is characterized by precisely worked blocks of satin stitch called **kloster blocks.** These are arranged to form the overall shapes of motifs and are often worked within these shapes as well. When blocks have been stitched, warp and weft threads are cut and drawn out in appropriate places (where there are opposing kloster blocks to secure ends).

Remaining fabric threads within the motifs are covered to form either **overcast** or **woven bars.** The open squares between bars can be decorated with various filling stitches. Often embroidery is added to enhance the overall design.

Because Hardanger is a type of counted thread embroidery, it is advisable to plot a piece on graph paper—first the shapes and locations of motifs, then bars, fillings, and embellishments. To prepare the piece for working, baste the outline of each motif on the fabric.

The work is generally done on Hardanger fabric, an even-weave with, as a rule, 22 pairs of threads per inch. Almost any even-weave fabric will do. Because kloster blocks are worked over a uniform number of fabric threads, the finer the fabric (the more threads per inch), the smaller a motif will be.

Ideally, two sizes of yarn are used. Yarn for kloster blocks should be slightly thicker than the threads of the fabric; the usual choice is a medium-weight pearl cotton. To cover bars and work filling stitches, yarn should be thinner—either a fine (#8) pearl cotton or a suitable number of embroidery floss strands. Originally, Hardanger was worked with white yarn on white fabric; today both yarn and fabric are often colored.

Select a fine tapestry needle with an eye that is large enough to accommodate your yarn. Always do this work with an embroidery hoop or frame.

Hardanger piece of overcast bars, woven bars, loopstitches, and dove's eyes (pp. 88-89).

Kloster blocks

The basic kloster block consists of five satin stitches worked over four fabric threads. In a motif, the blocks may be worked across in rows or diagonally in steps. In deciding on block placement, remember that there must be opposing blocks where warp and weft threads will be cut. While the basic kloster block is always worked in the same way, the movement from block to block varies with the arrangement. When blocks are in steps (see drawings below), stitching direction alternates from row to row.

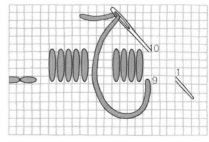

To work basic kloster block, secure yarn end with backstitches; come up at 1 and work five satin stitches, each over four fabric threads.

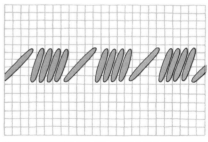

To work blocks in a row, stitch first block as usual. At end, come up four fabric threads to the right of point 9 to start the next block.

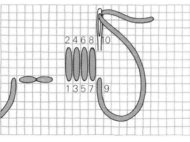

When kloster blocks are worked in a row, there should be single slanting yarns from block to block on the **wrong side** of the fabric.

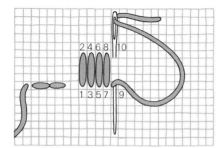

To work blocks diagonally in steps, stitch first block as usual. At the end, come up again at point 9 where the last satin stitch originated.

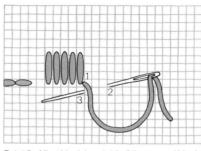

Point 9 of first block is point 1 of the second block. Start the second block by working a *horizontal* satin stitch over four fabric threads.

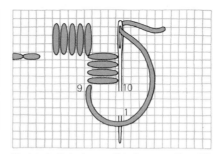

Work last stitch of second block as usual (up at 9, in at 10). Come up four fabric threads below 10 to start *vertical* stitches of third block.

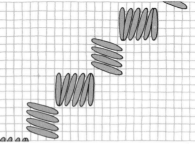

When kloster blocks are worked diagonally, there should be no trailing yarns between blocks on the **wrong side** of the fabric.

Working a motif

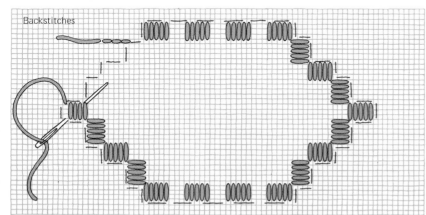

Backstitches

To work a motif: Baste shape onto fabric. Secure yarn end with backstitches. Working clockwise, go from block to block as instructed above. For every block where threads will be cut, another must be worked directly opposite, in the same direction, over the same fabric threads. At end of motif, run yarn under backs of five or more blocks to secure. Pull out backstitches and secure that yarn the same way.

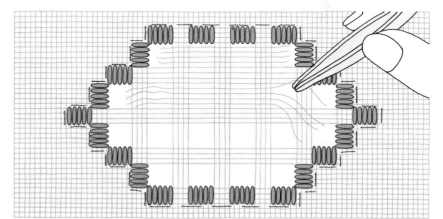

To remove threads: With sharp embroidery scissors, cut four threads at the base of a kloster block; cut same four threads at base of opposing block. (All cut threads must be secured at both ends by blocks.) Cut only threads that run the same way as satin stitches—never those the satin stitches cross. Remove threads with tweezers. Draw all appropriate threads running one way, then those running the other.

Openwork/Hardanger embroidery

Covered bars

When kloster blocks have been worked and threads drawn, motifs are usually decorated. The loose threads are **overcast** or **woven** into covered bars; *picots* (small loops) can be added to woven bars during weaving. Open areas are generally embellished with filling stitches (at right). Secure beginning yarn with backstitches. To start a new yarn, secure yarn end under next bar as you cover it.

Overcast bars   **Woven bars**   **Woven bars with picots**

Filling stitches

The three filling stitches shown in the sampler at the right and explained below are the **oblique loopstitch,** the **straight loopstitch,** and the **dove's eye filling.** These are basic filling techniques that, like other aspects of Hardanger embroidery, can be and are varied in many ways.

Fillings differ, too, in their usage. They can be worked to fill all the open areas in a motif, the intended result of the illustrations at the far right. Or squares can be filled intermittently or selectively. An area can be filled with one kind of stitch, or several.

The directional and other advice given earlier applies equally to the working of filling stitches. The recommendation that bars and fillings be worked diagonally is simply for convenience; it is generally easier to pass from bar to bar in this direction. If an area is to be worked in bars alone, many needleworkers recommend working all bars in one direction, then all bars in the other.

When all work on a motif is finished, run the yarn through the backs of five or more kloster blocks to secure it; remove the beginning backstitches and secure them the same way. Start a new yarn by working over its beginning end as you cover the next bar. For details of this maneuver, and some other useful similarities between Hardanger embroidery and needleweaving, refer to pages 84-85.

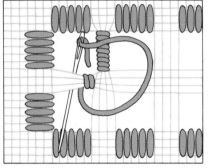

To overcast a bar, wrap yarn compactly around thread cluster; **to weave a bar,** bring needle up in center of cluster and weave yarn over and under pairs of threads. As clusters are covered, move in diagonal steps from bar to bar, passing yarn behind threads or through backs of kloster blocks.

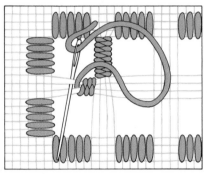

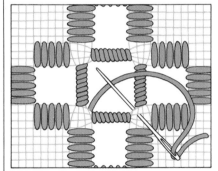

Oblique loopstitch: Come up at lower left, go in at lower right, come up at opening. With yarn under needle, pull it through, leaving a loop.

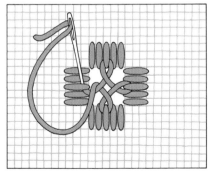

Insert needle into fabric at upper right corner, come up at opening. Making sure yarn is under needle, pull it through, again leaving a loop.

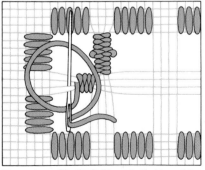

Woven bar with picot: Weave half of bar. Bring needle up through center; loop yarn under it as shown. Pull yarn through to form small loop.

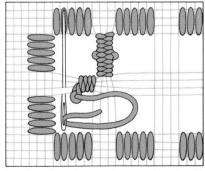

Insert needle under same two threads and pull it through. Work another picot through two threads on opposite side. Weave rest of bar.

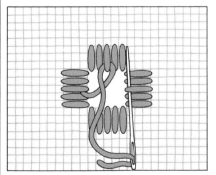

Straight loopstitch in area enclosed by kloster blocks: Come up at left below center stitch; loop yarn right to left through top center stitch.

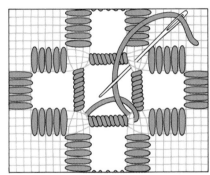

Continue working around square, looping yarn through center stitch at each side. Always carry yarn under needle. Stitch last loop as shown.

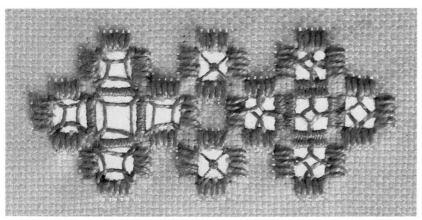

Filling stitches shown are, left to right: **oblique loopstitch; dove's eye; straight loopstitch.**

Decorating a motif

Because Hardanger designs vary so widely, it is difficult to give precise rules to suit all of them. It will help, however, especially on the first try, to understand some general principles that can be applied to most typical motifs. With those, and some practical experience, it should not be long before you can work Hardanger embroidery with the traditional precision and delicacy.

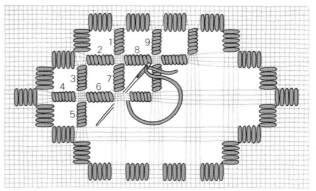

To work bars, most experts recommend the procedure shown, which progresses in diagonal steps from the upper left over four bars (1-4), then up in similar steps over five bars (5-9), and so on until all thread clusters are covered. Bars can be worked in two journeys: first all bars across, then, with work turned, all bars in the other direction.

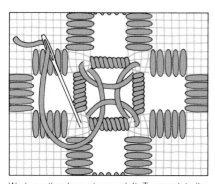

Work another loop at upper left. To complete the stitch, pass needle under first laid yarn and insert it into fabric at lower left corner.

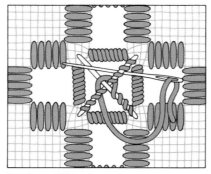

Dove's eye filling: Crossed laid yarns are woven over and under at center to form circular filling. For instructions, see Hemstitching, pages 82-83.

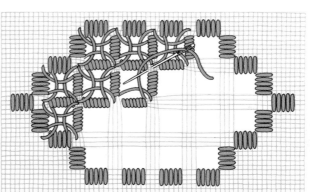

Oblique loops worked with bars go in the same general direction, the yarn being passed behind adjacent fabric threads to reach the next opening. It is important to pass the threads in such a way that they are hidden. To start a new yarn when needed, secure it in the most convenient bar.

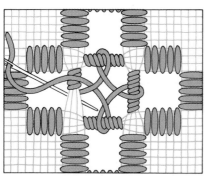

To work **straight loops with overcast bars,** work 3½ bars. Before working last half, make loops as at left. Finish overcasting of last bar.

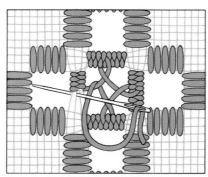

To work **straight loops with woven bars,** work 3½ bars. Then work loops, going through centers of bars (over two threads). Weave last half of bar.

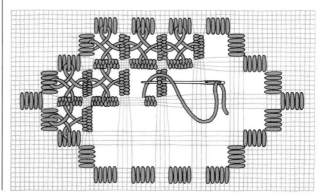

Straight loops with bars vary according to the sides of the opening that they are to fill—that is, whether individual loops go to a woven or overcast bar, or to a kloster block. The drawings at the left will refresh your memory as to placement.

Openwork/ Cutwork embroidery

Introduction to cutwork
Basic procedure
Making a cutwork piece

Introduction

Cutwork is a form of openwork embroidery that came into vogue in the sixteenth century and is still popular today, primarily for table linens and for decorative details on blouses and dresses. Despite its delicate look, cutwork is quite sturdy because each part of the design is outlined in a fine buttonhole stitch. After outlining, certain portions are cut away, giving the embroidery its characteristic airiness. Large cut-out areas are reinforced with embroidered bars, worked to bridge the areas and stabilize their sides. Other surface embroidery (such as French knot, stem stitch, and satin stitch) is often added to enhance a cutwork design.

Closely woven fabrics (those not likely to fray or ravel) should be used for cutwork. Stitch with pearl cotton or embroidery floss and a sharp-pointed needle (see Needles, p. 10) in a size that accommodates your yarn. Use an embroidery hoop or frame for cutwork.

Generally, the motifs in cutwork are florals, but other kinds can be used. In choosing a design, consider what areas will be cut away. If you are designing your own cutwork piece, think in terms of negative and positive (cut and uncut) areas, and try to balance the two.

There are three basic ways of arranging these positive and negative spaces. One is the stencil design, in which a motif is established by cutting away its main sections. (The small flowers in the sample are stencil designs.) Or a motif can be left intact and the background cut away, silhouetting the motif. (The stems and leaves in the sample are handled this way.) Buttonhole-stitch outlining gives the shapes further definition. The third approach leaves some of the motif whole, with only small, interior sections cut away. This technique must be employed to achieve the shaped edge that is so attractive a feature of cutwork—it is the only one that permits a motif to be positioned at the very edge. (See the large corner flower in the sample.)

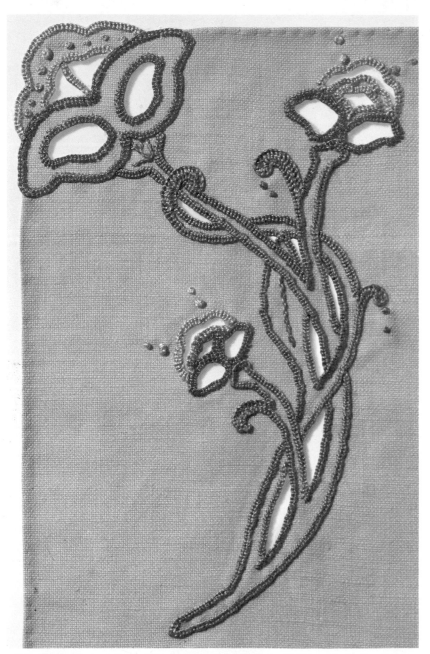

Cutwork piece features floral motifs. All outlining (in buttonhole stitch) is worked before cutting.

Basic procedure

The basic procedure for cutwork is quite simple, but the steps must be taken neatly and carefully to get professional results. The two main stitches in cutwork are the **buttonhole stitch** and the **running stitch**. The motifs are first "drawn" with running stitches, then buttonhole stitch is worked over these lines. Be sure you know which side of a motif line will be cut away; the buttonhole stitch must be worked so that the ridge lies along the cut edge. If the fabric will be cut away on both sides of a line, outlining can be done with a **double buttonhole stitch** (two facing rows of the basic stitch, slightly overlapped at the center).

To be sure that you will recognize the areas that are to be cut away, mark them before beginning to work the buttonhole stitch. On commercial transfers, open sections are often indicated by an "X" that transfers onto the fabric. If you are creating your own design, you may wish to use a similar method.

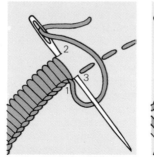

Buttonhole stitch is worked from left to right. Come up at 1, insert at 2, exit at 3 directly below 2. Carry yarn under needle point, pull through. Take care to keep stitches close together.
Double buttonhole stitch is two rows of the basic stitch. Work stitches in first row so that those of second row can go between them. Turn work to stitch second row.

Making a cutwork piece

First establish the design with *running stitches* (using either embroidery floss or pearl cotton).
Then cover the stitched shape of the motif with a fine, close *buttonhole stitch*. Make certain that the ridge of the stitch falls on the side of the line that is to be cut away. Tailor's buttonhole stitch may be also used for this purpose.
Cut away design areas indicated. Work from the *wrong side;* this makes it easier to cut close to the base of the stitches. Be careful not to cut into the buttonhole stitches.

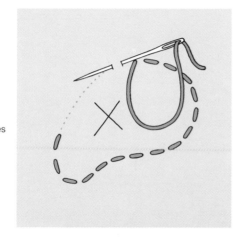

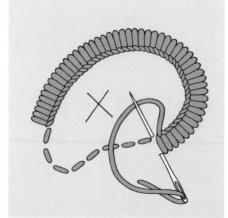

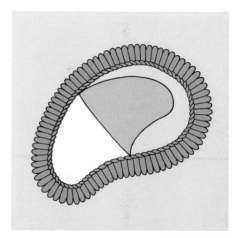

To work bars across an area, mark the design with running stitches until you come to a position for a bar. Carry yarn across the area, take a small stitch, bring the yarn back and take another stitch.
Work buttonhole stitch over the laid yarn without catching fabric beneath. Continue the running stitch around the rest of the motif, then outline it with fine buttonhole stitch. Cut away the fabric as above, taking care not to cut stitches.

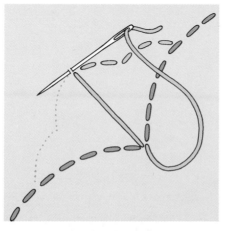

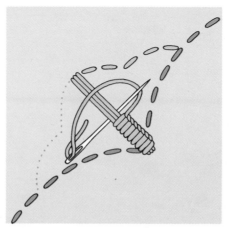

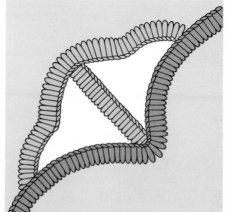

Smocking

Introduction to smocking
Fabrics and grids
Adding smocking to a garment
English smocking
Smocking stitches
Stitch variations
Embellishing stitches
Working stitch combinations

Introduction

Smocking is a type of embroidery that decorates as well as gathers the fabric on which it is worked. It is guided by a grid that is marked on the fabric in evenly spaced dots. Hot-iron transfers of smocking dots can be purchased, or you can make your own dotted grid.

There are two basic smocking methods, **regular** and **English.** In regular smocking, dots are marked on the *right* side of the fabric. The smocking stitches are worked from dot to dot, with the fabric gathered in each stitch. In English smocking, dots are marked on the *wrong* side of the fabric. Rows of uneven running stitches are worked from dot to dot, forming small, even pleats. (This is called *pregathering*.) Smocking stitches are then worked from the *right* side of the fabric, with a small stitch taken at each pleat formed by the pregathering. The look of the stitches is the same, regardless of the smocking method. The English method is particularly useful when different smocking stitches are being combined in a single piece (see p. 97).

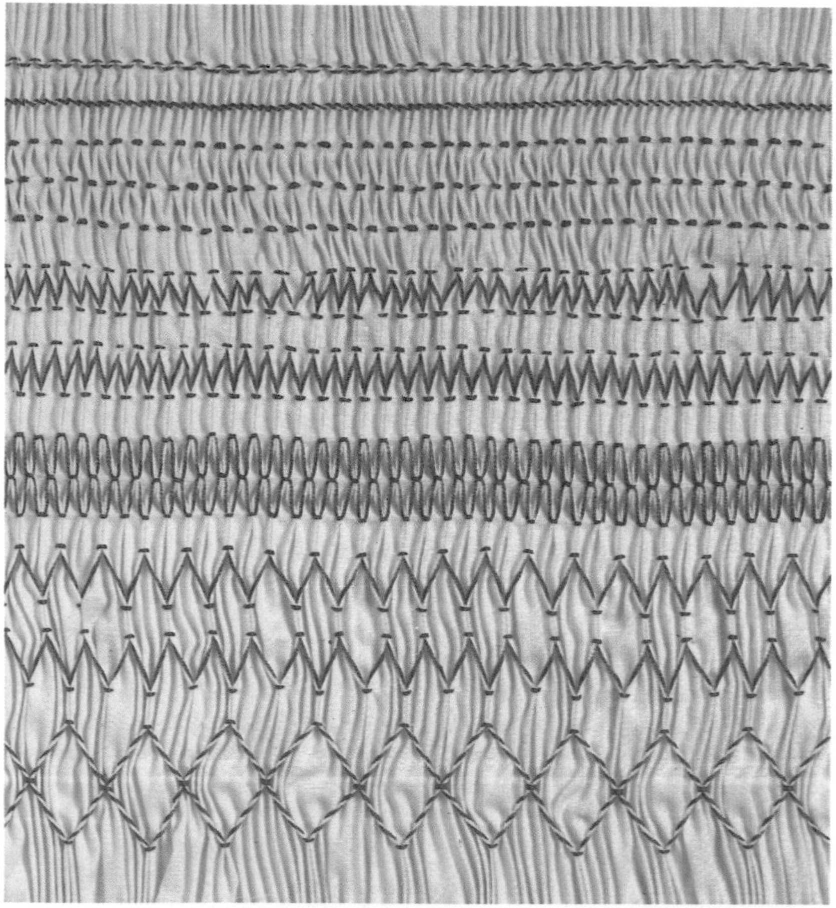

Fabrics and grids

Smocking, as a rule, is worked on soft, lightweight fabrics (cotton, lawn, fine wool) with pearl cotton or embroidery floss and a crewel or chenille needle.

Since smocking gathers the fabric, you should work on a piece 2½ to 3 times the desired finished width. This proportion of flat to gathered width is approximate. How much is actually drawn up depends on fabric weight, stitch tension, and the spacing between dots.

A smocking grid can be produced by means of a hot-iron transfer. You can

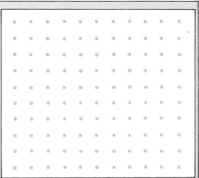

To use a transfer, cut it to fit the flat area to be smocked. Align the edges of the transfer with the fabric, leaving a seam allowance above the top row of dots. Press carefully.

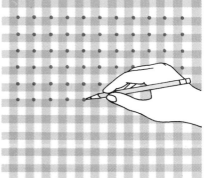

Even-weave fabrics or even prints such as polka dots or gingham need not be marked with a graph or transfer. The natural grid can guide your dot spacing. Mark dots on fabric in pencil.

Smocking sampler of cable, stem, honeycomb, surface honeycomb, Vandyke, wave, trellis stitches.

also plan your own on graph paper, or use an even-weave or an evenly printed fabric as a guide. Space between dots is usually from ¼ to ⅜ inch; between rows of dots, from ⅜ to ½ inch. The closer the dots, the more elasticity the finished smocking will have.

While most stitches can be worked on any smocking grid without their look being markedly altered, some stitches require grids of a specific proportion. For such special stitches, you may need to make your own grid.

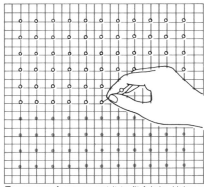

To use graph paper, cut it to fit fabric. Using a sharp awl or a needle or pin, pierce dots in paper to desired spacing. Position graph paper over area to be smocked and mark dots in pencil.

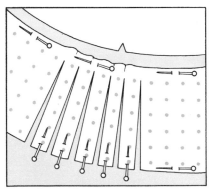

To mark curved area, use either a transfer or graph paper. On the grid, slash between dots to the top row. Align top edge of grid with curve, pin in place, and mark as usual.

Adding smocking to a garment

Smocking can be a most attractive decoration for a garment. It is easiest to apply in areas that have simple, rectangular pattern pieces—a yoke, band collar, cuffs—or along a hemline.

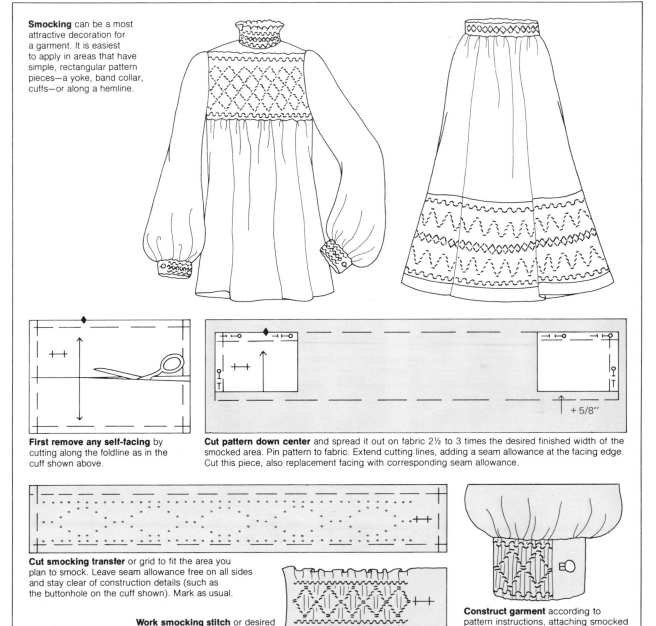

First remove any self-facing by cutting along the foldline as in the cuff shown above.

Cut pattern down center and spread it out on fabric 2½ to 3 times the desired finished width of the smocked area. Pin pattern to fabric. Extend cutting lines, adding a seam allowance at the facing edge. Cut this piece, also replacement facing with corresponding seam allowance.

+ 5/8″

Cut smocking transfer or grid to fit the area you plan to smock. Leave seam allowance free on all sides and stay clear of construction details (such as the buttonhole on the cuff shown). Mark as usual.

Work smocking stitch or desired stitch combinations (pp. 94-97).

Construct garment according to pattern instructions, attaching smocked piece and replacement facing.

Smocking

English smocking

English smocking is recommended for use by beginners because pregathering makes the actual smocking stitches easier to work. The rows of running stitches form even, secure pleats, gathering the fabric uniformly. This helps to regulate the tension of the smocking stitches. Pregathering does not, however, determine the width of the completed smocking. When the running stitches are removed, the area will relax, how much depending on how tightly the smocking is worked.

To prepare for pregathering, mark the dots on the wrong side of the fabric. Be sure that the grid you mark is appropriate for the stitch you plan to work (see smocking stitches). Do the pregathering by hand (following the instructions below) and work the smocking stitches from the right side of the fabric.

To pregather fabric, secure thread at right end of top row of dots. Work uneven running stitches from right to left, taking stitches so that the visible part of each stitch (the float) falls over a dot. Floats should be small and of uniform size. At end of row, leave a loose thread a few inches long. Work all other rows like the first.

Pull all thread ends together at left edge, forming parallel pleats. Pull the threads only tight enough to form even, stable rows. Leave a small space between pleats.

Tie pairs of threads together until all threads are secured at left edge of fabric.

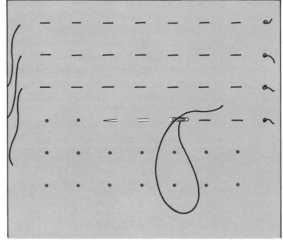
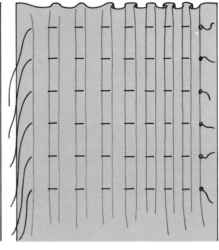
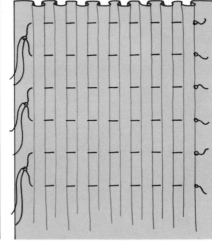

Smocking stitches

The stitch instructions that follow are illustrated in steps for regular smocking. The five stitches on these pages can be worked over any smocking grid. The last two stitches (stitch variations, p. 96) require grids of specific proportions; the grid proportions for these are indicated in the first step of their respective instructions. Be sure to follow these proportions carefully.

All of the stitches can also be worked in English smocking. The grid is the same (though the markings are placed on the wrong side of the fabric), and so are the stitch movements. Instead of taking a small stitch at a dot, however, take a stitch at the top of each pleat along a row of running stitches. Pick up only a couple of fabric threads at a uniform point on the top of each pleat. The last illustration in each sequence shows the stitches worked over the pregathered pleats of this method and is intended to help you visualize this way of working.

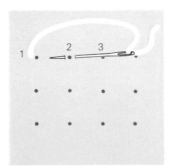

Cable stitch: Work this stitch from left to right. Come up at 1. Then take a small stitch at 2, keeping the yarn above the needle.

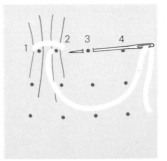

Pull the yarn taut so that points 1 and 2 are drawn together. Take another small stitch at 3, keeping the yarn below the needle.

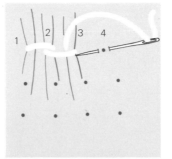

Take a stitch at 4, keeping the yarn above the needle. Continue this sequence, alternating placement of yarn above and below the needle.

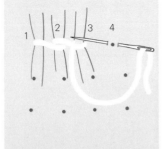

Stem stitch (also known as outline stitch): Worked as for cable stitch except that the yarn is always held below the needle.

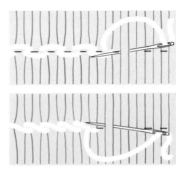

English method of working cable or stem stitch: Work across the rows of pregathering, taking a small stitch through the top of each pleat.

94

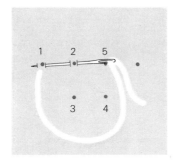

Honeycomb stitch: Work from left to right, with the needle pointing left. Come out at 1, take a small stitch at 2, another at 1. Pull yarn taut.

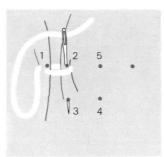

Re-insert the needle at 2, come up at 3 on the row below directly below 2. (This stitch is worked back and forth along two rows of smocking dots.)

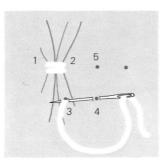

Take a small stitch at 4 and another at 3, keeping the needle pointing to the left. Pull the yarn taut so that 3 and 4 are drawn together.

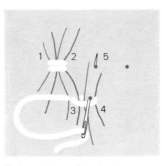

Re-insert the needle at 4 and come up at 5 directly above 4 in the top row. Point 5 is now point 1 for the start of the next sequence.

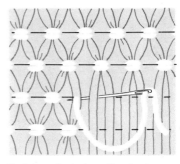

English method of working the honeycomb stitch: Work stitch back and forth along two rows of pregathering stitches, catching the pleat top as shown.

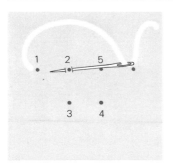

Surface honeycomb stitch: Work left to right, with needle pointing left. Come up at 1 and take a stitch at 2, keeping yarn above needle.

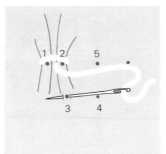

Pull yarn taut, drawing points 1 and 2 together. Then take a stitch at 3 directly below 2 on the second row of smocking dots.

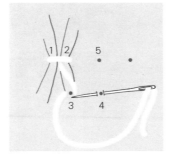

Take a small stitch at 4, to the right of 3 on second row. Keep yarn below needle. Pull yarn taut, drawing points 3 and 4 together.

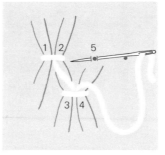

Return to top row and take a stitch at point 5 directly above 4. Point 5 is now point 1 for the beginning of the next sequence.

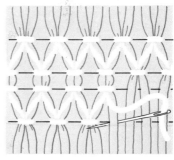

English method of working surface honeycomb stitch: Work back and forth along two rows of pregathering. Note the pattern created by two rows of this stitch.

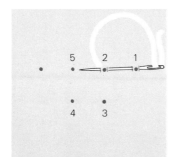

Vandyke stitch: Work from right to left, with needle pointing left. Come up at 2. Take a stitch at 1, another at 2. Keep yarn above needle.

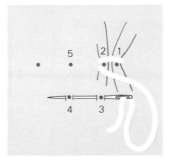

Pull the yarn taut so that 1 and 2 are drawn together. Then take a stitch at 3 directly below 2 and a stitch at 4 to the left of 3.

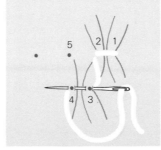

Take another stitch at point 3 and at point 4, keeping the yarn below the needle. Pull the yarn taut so that 3 and 4 are drawn together.

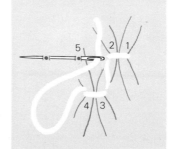

Return to the first row of dots and take a stitch at 5 (point 1 for the next sequence). Repeat Steps 1 to 5 until the row is complete.

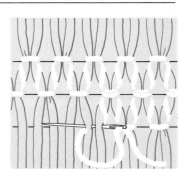

For English smocking, work Vandyke stitch along two rows of pregathering. Note how two rows are worked with the center stitches overlapping.

Smocking

Chain stitch 28 Cross stitch 35
Lazy daisy stitch 28 Satin stitch 48

Stitch variations

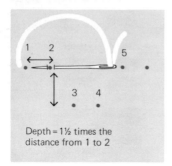 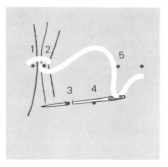 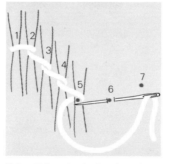 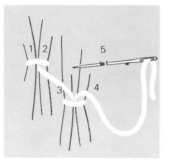 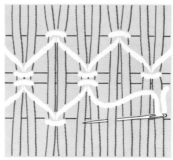

Depth = 1½ times the distance from 1 to 2

Wave stitch: Mark dots *only* where stitches will be taken. An all-over grid cannot be used. To work, come up at 1, take a stitch at 2.

Pull yarn taut. Take another stitch at 3 below and to the right of 2 in the second row of dots. Wave stitch is worked along two rows of dots.

Keeping yarn below needle, take another stitch at 4, directly to the right of 3. Pull yarn taut to draw 3 and 4 together.

Return to top row, taking a stitch at point 5. Point 5 is now point 1 for the beginning of the next sequence. Continue pattern to end of row.

For English smocking, you can use an all-over grid. Dots are skipped as required by the wave stitch, but they are on the wrong side, and so will not show.

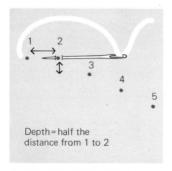 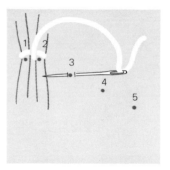 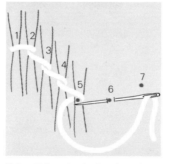 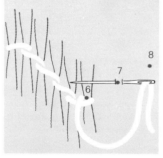 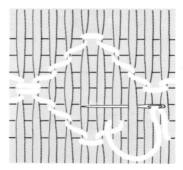

Depth = half the distance from 1 to 2

Trellis stitch: Mark dots as shown. An all-over grid cannot be used. To work, come up at 1, take a stitch at 2. Keep yarn above needle.

Pull yarn taut. Take another stitch at 3, keeping yarn above needle. The distance from 1 to 2 is the same as the distance from 2 to 3.

Take stitches at point 4 and at point 5, still keeping yarn above needle. Then take a stitch at 6, this time keeping yarn below needle.

Take a stitch up at 7 and continue working diagonally upward to the top row of dots. Repeat the sequence as needed to complete row.

For English smocking of this stitch, you can use an all-over grid. Though some dots will be unstitched, they are marked on the wrong side, and so will not show.

Embellishing stitches

Embroidery stitches are often added to smocking for texture and variety. The four stitches shown here (from left to right, lazy daisy, cross stitch, satin stitch, and chain stitch) are often worked between rows of smocking stitches or in the open areas formed by such stitches as trellis. Work all embellishments over two or more pleats. For detailed instructions, see basic embroidery, pages 22-53.

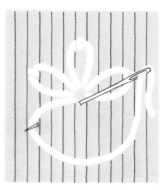 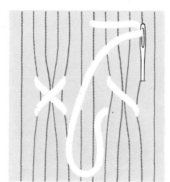 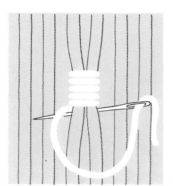 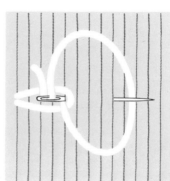

Working stitch combinations

Stitch combinations make the most interesting smocked pieces. If the stitches being combined can all be worked on the same grid, no special treatment is needed. Use the regular or the English method, as you wish. If, however, the stitches to be combined require different grids, as is true of the combination at the right, smocking must be done by the English method, applied in a specific way. The combination at the right is worked as follows: a row of cable stitch, two rows of overlapping wave stitch, and another row of cable, forming the borders; six rows of trellis in the center; satin stitch embellishments.

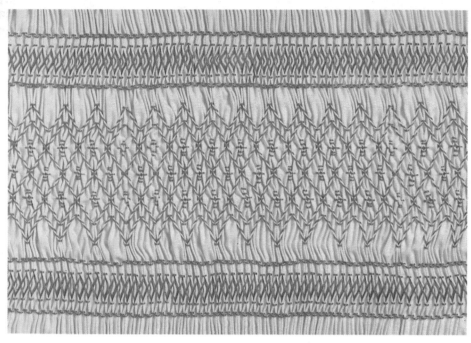

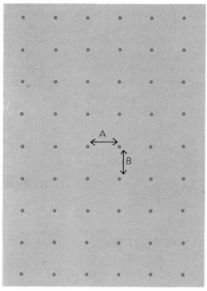

1. Choose a grid for this combination on which the distance between dots and between rows of dots is equal (above, A and B). Mark fabric and pregather for English smocking.

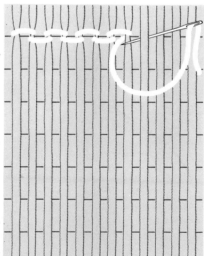

2. To work the stitches in the photographed sample, start at the top row of dots and work a row of cable stitch (refer to p. 94 for detailed instructions) along a row of pregathering.

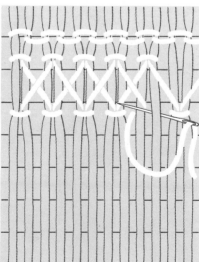

3. Place the wave stitches that follow so that they span *1½ times* the distance between rows of pregathering. This adjusts the proportions of the grid to those of the stitch.

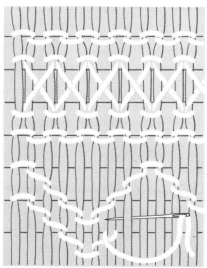

4. For the trellis stitch that forms the center pattern, place diagonal stitches to span *half* the distance between pregathering rows. This adjusts grid and stitch proportions.

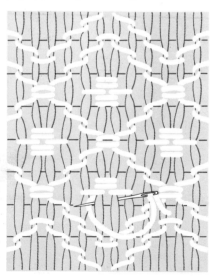

5. Complete six rows of trellis as shown. Repeat border pattern below. Then add embellishments in indicated positions. Satin stitches are used here; for other possibilities, see the facing page.

Machine embroidery

Introduction to machine
embroidery
Straight stitching
Zigzag stitching
Decorative stitch patterns
Free-motion embroidery
Machine hemstitching
Machine cutwork
Machine smocking

Introduction

Though machine embroidery effects are rooted in, and usually named for, traditional hand techniques, each has its own look and style. Except for a few that require a highly sophisticated machine, most of them can be achieved with any efficient zigzag model.

Even the *straight stitch*, the basic stitch on any machine, can produce several embroidery effects (including some free-motion embroidery, see p. 100). Most machine embroidery, however, calls for a *plain zigzag stitch*. Most present-day machines include both a zigzag and a straight stitch. In addition, there is an increasing number of *patterned zigzag stitches* that can only be worked by a machine equipped with the necessary adjustments or attachments.

Machine embroidery can be worked on almost any type of fabric. If the fabric you choose is lightweight, use a sheer backing, such as organza or a lightweight fusible interfacing, to prevent puckering. Use machine embroidery thread or regular sewing thread for basic stitching, metallics, pearl cotton, or silk twist for special effects. Make sure you know how to use your machine properly; consult the instruction booklet.

Border motifs can be worked on any straight stitch machine. Use a heavy thread such as silk twist, set stitch length at 6-8 per inch. Mark design on fabric, adjust tension (work a test piece first), and stitch along design lines, pivoting at corners. (To turn corners, see drawings at lower right.)

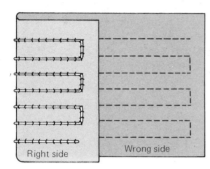

Mock couching can be achieved with straight stitching. Hand-wind a heavy thread (such as pearl cotton) on bobbin and loosen bobbin tension to accommodate thread. (Not all machines have this adjustment.) Then tighten upper tension. Stitch from wrong side to give couched effect on right side.

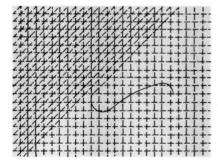

Textured fillings can be worked to resemble hand-embroidered laid work. Use the cross-hatching method shown. Stitch lines horizontally; stitch vertical lines over them. Add diagonal lines on top, following grid formed by the first stitching lines.

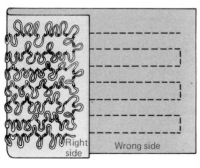

A looped stitch can be worked simply by adjusting (drastically reducing or completely disengaging) bobbin tension. Wind a heavy thread on bobbin. Then slowly stitch from wrong side of fabric. Small loops will form on right side. (Work a test piece; some machines also need top tension loosened.)

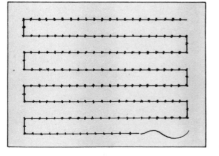

A beaded effect can be created by adjusting top tension so it is slightly tighter than usual. Stitch along design lines. Note how the tightened tension pulls the bobbin thread up, forming tiny beads.

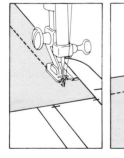

To turn corners, stop machine at corner with needle in fabric. Lift presser foot and turn fabric. Lower foot and continue stitching along design.

Zigzag stitching

Satin stitch, a plain zigzag with a very short stitch length, is popular for working along borders and bands. Stitch width can be varied to produce either *wide bands* of stitching or delicate *narrow lines* of satin stitch.
To turn corners, stitch to corner, stopping with needle in fabric at outer edge (for precise point, see drawings, far right). Lift presser foot, turn fabric. Lower foot, resume stitching.

Border design worked in a wide satin stitch.

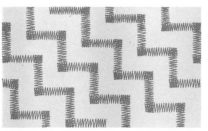

All-over design of narrow satin stitch lines.

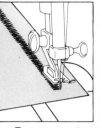

Turn a corner by stopping and pivoting.

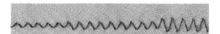

Zigzag filling can be produced with cross-hatching (near right). Work stitches horizontally, cross over these vertically, then diagonally.
A "wishbone" effect (center illustration) can be achieved by tightening top tension. Experiment until a satisfactory adjustment is found.
For couching, zigzag over heavy yarn or cord. Adjust stitch width to yarn thickness; lay yarn as you stitch. Thread can match or contrast.

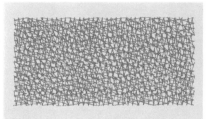

Zigzag filling done with cross-hatching.

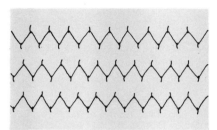

For "wishbone" effect tighten top tension.

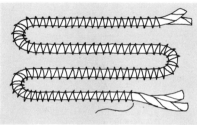

Zigzag couching over heavy yarn or cord.

Decorative stitch patterns

Sophisticated machines can work all the straight-stitch and zigzag embroidery, and produce fancy patterns as well. Each machine offers its own selection; some of the most common are shown below. Though these stitches are attractive on their own, they can be enhanced in various ways. We show several; these may suggest others. See your instruction booklet for basic stitching information and use of special embroidery feet.

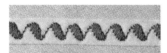

Embroidery over ribbon or braid increases texture and color impact. Select a stitch of appropriate width, center the ribbon or braid under the presser foot, and begin stitching. Guide the ribbon carefully so that the embroidery is worked evenly along its length.

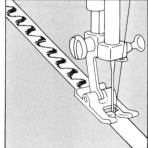

Working with a twin needle produces parallel rows of decorative stitching in one step. Carefully test for stitch width; it must be narrow enough that both needles will clear sides of hole in zigzag throat plate. Use either the same color thread for both rows, or contrasting colors.

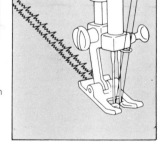

Stitching over a cord is another way to create texture. For the cord, select a contrasting shade of pearl cotton or yarn. Keep the cord centered under the presser foot, and guide it carefully as you stitch. There are machine feet with guide holes designed to hold cord in the proper position.

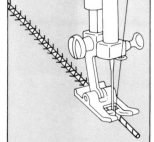

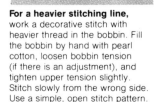

For a heavier stitching line, work a decorative stitch with heavier thread in the bobbin. Fill the bobbin by hand with pearl cotton, loosen bobbin tension (if there is an adjustment), and tighten upper tension slightly. Stitch slowly from the wrong side. Use a simple, open stitch pattern.

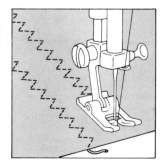

Machine embroidery

Free-motion embroidery

Free-motion embroidery offers unlimited stitching possibilities because fabric motion is not restricted by the presser foot (not used) or the feed dog (either lowered or covered, depending on the machine). An embroidery hoop holds the fabric taut and is moved in the desired stitch direction. Control of the hoop movement requires practice. Before beginning any kind of free-motion piece, experiment with thread tension, threads, and fabrics to create different effects. Free-motion embroidery can be worked on all machine types. For machine preparation, see the recommendations below, and your instruction booklet.

To prepare machine for free-motion work, remove presser foot and its shank. Drop feed dog or cover it with a plate. Set stitch length to 0. Loosen top tension slightly. Be sure needle is a proper size for thread.

Place fabric in embroidery hoop. (Be sure hoop is thin enough to clear presser bar.) Do not use a hoop larger than 8″ in diameter. Place fabric and backing right-side up over larger ring and press inner ring down into outer ring so fabric rests directly on machine bed.

To stitch, lower presser bar to engage upper tension. Holding upper thread taut, turn handwheel toward you to bring up bobbin loop.

Pull bobbin thread up and out so thread ends can be held taut. Hold both top and bobbin threads to the left of the needle as shown.

Take a few stitches to secure threads. Cut off ends as close as possible to stitching.

To maneuver hoop, hold it between fingers at edges. Keep elbows down and relaxed. Gently move and guide hoop in the desired direction. Keep machine running at an even, moderate speed. If machine has a speed range, set it at slow until you acquire some expertise. Keep the hoop moving evenly at all times to avoid a pile-up of stitches on the wrong side and possible thread breakage.

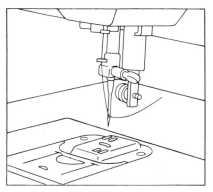
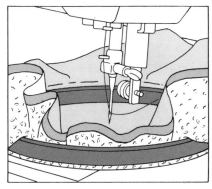
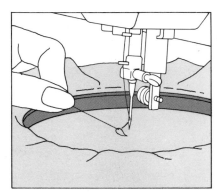
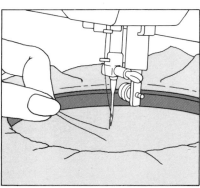
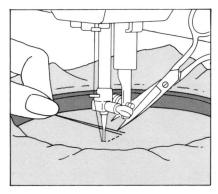
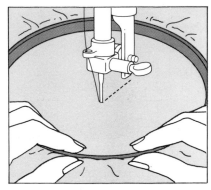

LINE DRAWING

Line drawing is one type of free-motion embroidery. It uses the machine needle to create linear designs. For line drawing, first mark a basic design outline on the fabric. Then improvise the details as you stitch. By altering the machine tension and by using different threads in upper and lower tensions, subtle textures can be created. Heavy threads (pearl cotton or metallics) set in the bobbin also result in interesting surface effects. (Wind heavy bobbin threads by hand, taking care not to stretch them.)

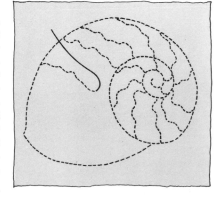

Simple stitch lines can create contour in a design, giving it a three-dimensional look. A shell is an excellent subject for line interpretation. First stitch along marked outline of design. Then stitch interior design lines, improvising as you go.

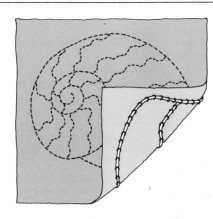

A couched effect can be produced by stitching a design from the wrong side of the fabric, with pearl cotton wound onto the bobbin by hand (do not stretch yarn as you wind it). Tighten the upper tension slightly. Move hoop slowly as you work.

SATIN STITCHING

Satin stitch, a plain zigzag set at a very short stitch length, lends itself beautifully to free-motion embroidery. Instead of precise lines merely being followed, stitch lines can be freely shaped and curved, and their widths varied to create interesting contours. This adaptability makes satin stitch ideal for outlining or filling shapes, working monograms, or shading in different colors.

The direction in which the stitches are worked varies the look of the line or filling; hoop movement determines the direction in which the stitches run. Keep the machine in constant motion.

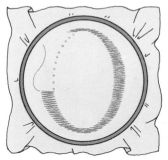

To outline with satin stitch, merely move along design lines. As lines change direction, contour will automatically be formed.

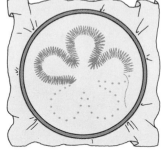

For designs with several parts, rotate hoop continually to work an even line of consistent width along all parts of the design.

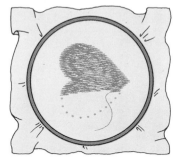

To fill a shape, move hoop slowly from one side to the other and backward. If you should miss a spot, go back and cover it. Keep the hoop moving.

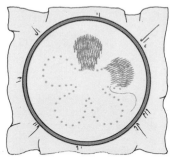

If a design has several parts, fill each part individually, rotating the hoop to move from one part of the design to another.

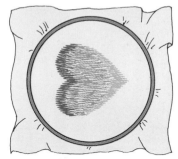

To shade, work several compact rows of satin stitch. Make edges jagged so that the next color will blend imperceptibly into the previous one.

Machine hemstitching

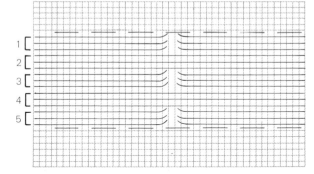

Machine hemstitching requires only a plain zigzag stitch. As in hand hemstitching, threads must be drawn out in a border.
1. Hand-baste upper edge of border. Count off 10 or 15 threads and baste lower edge. Divide threads into 5 groups (2 or 3 threads per group). Cut 1st, 3rd, and 5th groups of threads at center of border, leaving 2nd and 4th intact.

2. Draw out cut threads (groups 1, 3, and 5) to the edges of the border. To stabilize border edges, weave each drawn thread back into wrong side of fabric for 1″. Trim the excess thread length.

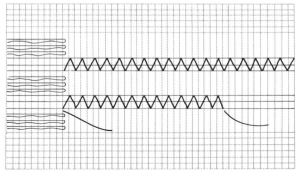

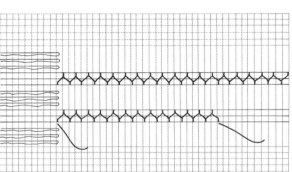

3. Stitch intact threads (groups 2 and 4) within drawn area. Use a regular machine needle, matching or contrasting thread. Hoop is not needed. Set machine to narrow zigzag; stitch over group 2, then group 4. This stitching decorates the border and fastens the threads in each group together.

4. For added texture, tighten the top tension so the zigzag is off-balance (see p. 99). Work this stitch over groups 2 and 4 as for a plain zigzag stitch shown above.

Machine embroidery

Transferring a design 16-17
Stencil designs 90

Hand smocking 92-97
Zigzag on curves 197

Embroidery scissors 11

Machine cutwork

Machine cutwork can be done on any sewing machine that is equipped for zigzag stitching. It is best to keep designs fairly large; very small and intricate ones can be difficult to work. Stencil designs (also used for hand-embroidered cutwork) work best for machine cutwork.

A satin stitch is used to outline the motifs; their centers are then trimmed away close to the stitching. Because of the heavy satin stitching that is worked around the shapes, the fabric needs a backing to give it additional body. A lightweight fusible interfacing is a good backing choice. Stitch with a fine mercerized thread to match or contrast.

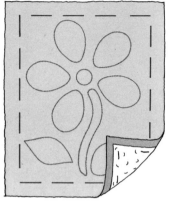

Transfer the design to the right side of the fabric. Cut a piece of interfacing large enough to cover the entire design. With wrong sides together, baste the interfacing to the fabric.

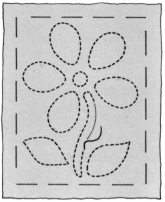

Set the sewing machine to a fine straight stitch (about 18 stitches to the inch). Then, working from the right side of the fabric, stitch carefully along the marked design lines of the motif.

Remove basting and trim away excess interfacing, leaving about ⅛″ around stitching lines of design. Press interfacing that remains; it will provide the necessary body around each shape.

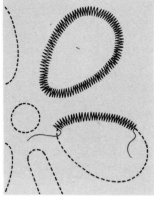

Set the machine for a narrow satin stitch. Work over the straight stitching around each shape. (See Appliqué section for zigzag stitching around curves and corners.)

Carefully trim design areas, using a pair of sharp embroidery scissors. Trim as close as possible to satin stitching without cutting the threads. Press entire piece on wrong side.

Machine smocking

A form of mock smocking can be done on any machine. Though machine smocking is similar in appearance to hand smocking, it does not offer the same elasticity, and so is best worked on garments or in areas where elasticity is not needed. Simple smocking can be produced with a straight stitch, a zigzag, or one or more decorative stitches. Fabric to be smocked must first be gathered on several rows of straight machine stitches (select a long stitch length on your machine; about 6 stitches to the inch is appropriate). The mock smocking stitches are then worked along the rows of gathering, which act as a guide for the stitching.

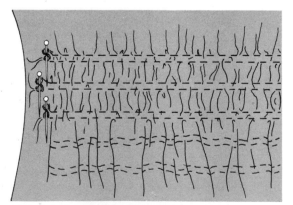

Work rows of gathering stitches in multiples of two, ¼″ apart. Work as many pairs of rows as needed to gather area to be smocked. Space the pairs ¾″ apart. Gather fabric to desired width.

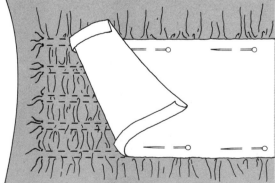

Cut an underlay 1″ wider than shirred area; fold the long edges under ½″ and pin or baste underlay to wrong side of fabric. Test decorative stitches (or plain zigzag) for maximum width of ¼″.

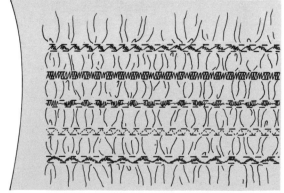

Work decorative, plain zigzag, or straight stitches between pairs of gathering stitches. For suitable span of straight stitching, work two rows of stitching between the pairs of gathering stitches.

102

Monogramming/Machine embroidery

A monogram adds an individual touch to a terry cloth robe and is quick to do on a sewing machine with zigzag capabilities. To make the letters easy to read, choose a thread color that contrasts emphatically with the color of the robe.

Materials needed

Paper and pencil for enlarging initials

Tissue paper

¼ yard interfacing

Machine embroidery thread *or* regular sewing thread

Embroidery scissors

Enlarging the initials

To enlarge the desired initials, make a grid with 1-inch squares and copy the letters square for square (see p. 14). Arrange the initials with the second one lower than the first, as shown at left, or place them side by side; trace them onto the tissue paper. Put the robe on and pin the traced monogram to the robe wherever it looks most pleasing to you.

Stitching

Pin the interfacing to the inside of the robe directly behind the monogram. Pin-baste the three layers together around the edges. Outline the letters with a straight stitch, then carefully tear the tissue paper away. With a pair of sharp embroidery scissors, trim the interfacing close to the stitching on the inside of the robe. Stitch over the straight stitches with satin stitch (see p. 99). This outlines the letters with a strong, straight edge. Bring the thread ends to the inside of the robe, knot them, and trim off the ends.

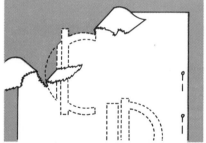

Straight stitch around the traced letters, stitching directly on top of the paper. Carefully tear away paper; trim interfacing close to stitches.

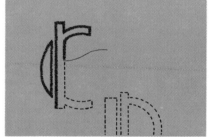

Carefully satin stitch around the letters, covering the straight stitching. This creates a strong outline with contrasting fabric showing through.

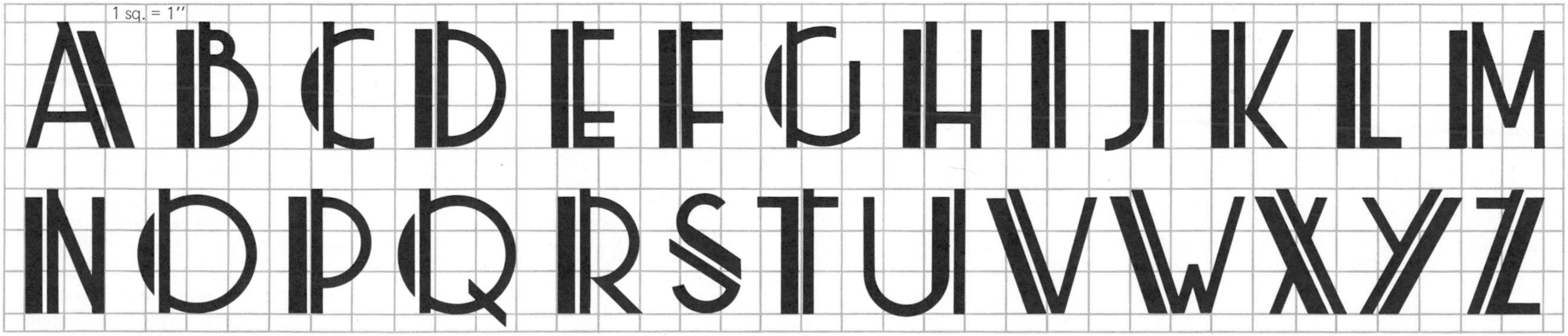

Initials personalize a robe, above; they could also be stitched on a skirt pocket or blazer lapel.

1 sq. = 1"

A B C D E F G H I J K L M
N O P Q R S T U V W X Y Z

To enlarge the desired initials, make a grid with 1" squares and copy the letters square for square (see p. 14). You can use one, two, or three initials, depending on the area you want to cover.

The fine wool yarn and soft colors give crewel embroidery its distinction; no special stitches are used. Design was adapted from print fabric on page 12.

Crewel picture

Framing crewel embroidery or any type of needlework is an attractive way of displaying and protecting your work.

Materials needed

½ yard linen twill
Yarn (see key below)
Crewel needle
Paper and pencil to transfer design
Embroidery hoop
Masking tape
Mat: 16″ × 24″ with 10″ × 18″ opening
Cardboard: 16″ × 24″
Polystyrene board, same size as above
Glass (optional), same size as above
Frame, same size as above
Straight pins
2 screw eyes
Wire for hanging

The embroidery

Needlework that is to be framed usually needs to be stretched onto a backing for support and to ensure that the work does not wrinkle or pucker. When planning for such a project, always allow 2 to 3 inches of fabric beyond the stitching area on all sides for stretching purposes. If you plan to add a mat, as was done here, allow enough extra so the fabric can be stretched onto a board that is the size of the embroidery and the mat combined.

The enlarged design (see p. 14 for instructions) will be 10 × 16 inches; to fit the 10 × 18-inch mat opening, add a 1-inch margin on both ends. Cut an 18 × 26-inch piece of linen (large enough to stretch onto a 16 × 24-inch board) and bind the edges (p. 16). Transfer the design to fabric (pp. 16-17). Work embroidery, following the chart below; use a hoop to keep the fabric taut. Wash and block finished embroidery (pp. 54-55).

Mounting the embroidery

Certain forms of wood, such as plywood or wood stretchers, contain acid that will discolor fabric and yarn in time. For mounting any needlework, use polystyrene or rag board, which are acid-free. Place the crewel face down on a clean,

1 sq. = 1″

To enlarge design, see page 14. Add 1″ to each side of enlarged (10″ × 16″) size to fit mat opening.

Colors and yarn amounts

▨	Brown	one 30-yard skein
▨	Dark leaf green	one 30-yard skein
▨	Light leaf green	two 30-yard skeins
▨	Mauve	one 30-yard skein
▨	Dull rose	one 30-yard skein
▨	Pink	one 30-yard skein
▨	Fuchsia	one 30-yard skein
▨	Light mauve	one 30-yard skein
▨	Light pink	one 30-yard skein
▨	Dark red	one 30-yard skein
▨	Signal green	one 30-yard skein
▨	Black	one 30-yard skein

List of stitches

A   stem stitch (p. 23)
B   slanted satin stitch (p. 48)
C   long and short satin stitch (p. 50)
D   coral stitch (p. 31), worked over satin stitch on odd-color petal of each flower
E   squared laid work (p. 44)
F   padded satin stitch (p. 49)
G   Turkey work (pp. 24-25)

flat surface. Center the board on top. When you are stretching the fabric, work two opposing sides at once so the fabric has something to pull against. Start in the center and work toward the corners: At the center of one side, pull the excess fabric around the board and put a pin into the edge of the board. Pull fabric at center of opposite side and pin it. Repeat with the other two sides. Turn the piece over to see if the embroidery is properly centered. If it is not, pull out the pins and start again. When centers are satisfactorily pinned, work toward corners, working as before on opposite sides. Turn the piece over occasionally to make sure that the grain of the fabric and any straight lines in the design are straight. Fold fabric at corners into pleats (see Step 3, below).

Assembling the frame
Whether you use glass to cover a framed needlework is a personal decision. Glass will keep the piece clean and free from handling marks, but it tends to obscure the texture, which is why we chose not to use it. If you decide to use glass, clean both sides. Place the frame face down and put the glass in it first; if you are not using glass, place the mat and the embroidery, in that order, in the frame first. Place the cardboard on top; seal the edges with masking tape. Insert screw eyes at back of frame, one-third of the way down the sides, and attach a hanging wire (Step 6, below).

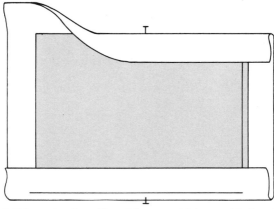

1. At the center of one side, pull the excess fabric around the board and put a pin into the edge of the board. Pull the fabric at center of opposite side and pin it. Repeat with two remaining sides.

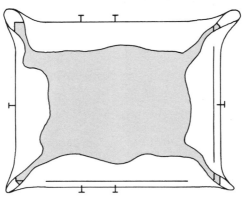

2. When all four centers are anchored, start pinning the area adjacent to the center pins, always working from the center out to the corners, and pulling opposite sides against each other.

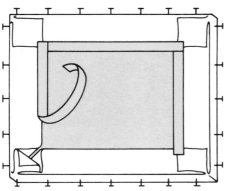

3. When all four sides are pinned taut, fold the excess fabric at the corners into pleats as shown. Secure the fabric to the board with masking tape, taping from pleat to pleat along the edges.

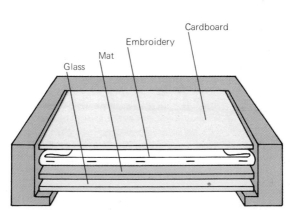

Glass Mat Embroidery Cardboard

4. To assemble, place frame face down on a flat surface. Insert glass first if you are using glass. Then place mat and mounted embroidery face down; put cardboard backing on top.

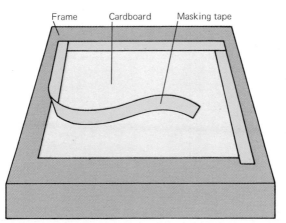

Frame Cardboard Masking tape

5. Carefully turn the assembled unit over to check that everything is correct from the front. Turn the unit to the back. On the back, secure the edges of the cardboard to the frame with masking tape.

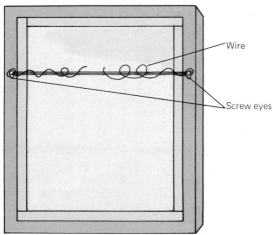

Wire Screw eyes

6. To attach a hanging wire, insert a screw eye on either side of frame 1/3 of the way down from top. Run a length of wire between screw eyes several times; wrap end of the wire around itself.

Place mat and napkin/Pulled thread

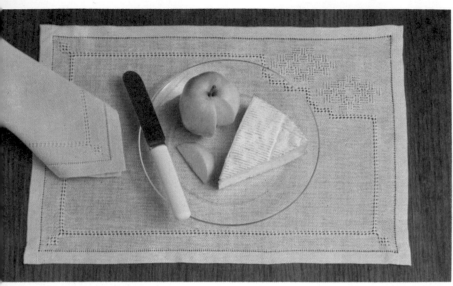

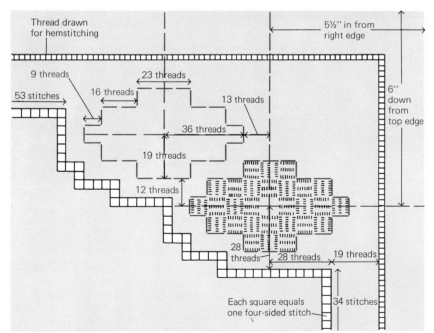

The design for the place mat and matching napkin was adapted from the pulled thread design on page 74.

Thread drawn for hemstitching

9 threads

53 stitches

16 threads

23 threads

13 threads

36 threads

19 threads

12 threads

5½" in from right edge

6" down from top edge

28 threads

28 threads

19 threads

34 stitches

Each square equals one four-sided stitch

To begin pulled threadwork, baste lines 5½" in from right side and 6" down from top. All embroidery is worked by counting threads from *intersection of fabric threads* where these two lines meet.

A pulled threadwork place mat and napkin are finished with a hemstitch edge.

Materials needed

¾ yard even-weave linen,
   20-22 threads per inch, for
   one place mat and one napkin
1 ball No. 8 pearl cotton
Embroidery hoop
Tapestry needle
Sharp needle and sewing thread

Pulled thread embroidery

Cut out a 24 × 18-inch rectangle for the place mat and a 24-inch square for the napkin; bind the edges (see p. 16). Mark with a pin the lengthwise grain of the napkin. Cut sizes allow extra fabric beyond hem allowance for an 18¾ × 13-inch mat and 15½-inch-square napkin.

To place the motif in the upper right corner of the place mat, baste one line 6 inches down from the top edge and another line 5½ inches in from the right edge. *The intersection of fabric threads where these basting lines cross is the center of the lower motif.* Baste motif outline, following thread counts given below, left. Locate center of upper motif; baste its outline. Work both motifs in chessboard filling stitch (p. 76).

To begin four-sided stitch (see p. 75)

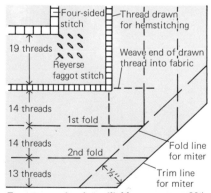

To prepare for hemstitching, remove 20th thread beyond four-sided stitch. Re-weave ends into fabric for 1". Make two folds beyond drawn-out threads for hem. Miters form at corners.

that outlines place mat, count 28 threads down and 28 threads to the right of center of lower motif (see below, left). Stitch is 4 threads high by 4 threads wide; each square in the drawing represents one stitch. Work the stepped line under the motifs from right to left, using the drawing to count the number of stitches. Along the top of the mat, work 53 stitches including corners; turn the mat so the left side is on top and work 52 stitches. With bottom edge on top, work 83 stitches. Work 34 stitches along right side to meet stepped line. Work a reverse faggot stitch (see p. 77) in the other three corners.

To embroider the napkin, baste a line 4¾ inches in from two adjoining sides. Begin the four-sided stitch where these two lines intersect. Work around all four sides, placing 64 stitches along the two sides that parallel the lengthwise grain, 65 stitches on the other sides; this compensates for the fact that even-weave fabric has more lengthwise than crosswise threads per inch. Work a reverse faggot stitch in one corner.

Hemstitching

To hemstitch both place mat and napkin, draw out the twentieth thread outside the four-sided stitch on all four sides until they intersect (see p. 78). Weave thread ends into wrong side of fabric for about one inch. With your fingers, press a crease 14 threads beyond the drawn-out thread on all four sides, folding toward the wrong side (see below, right). Make a diagonal crease at each corner at the point of the first crease. Trim corners ½ inch beyond this diagonal crease. Make a second crease 14 threads from the first. Trim away excess fabric 13 threads beyond second crease. Fold second crease, then fold first crease; pin and baste. Fold should line up with bottom of drawn-thread space. With sewing thread and sharp needle, slipstitch miters (see p. 83). Work hemstitching over groups of two threads (see p. 79), catching hem fold. Remove bastings.

Table runner/Huck embroidery

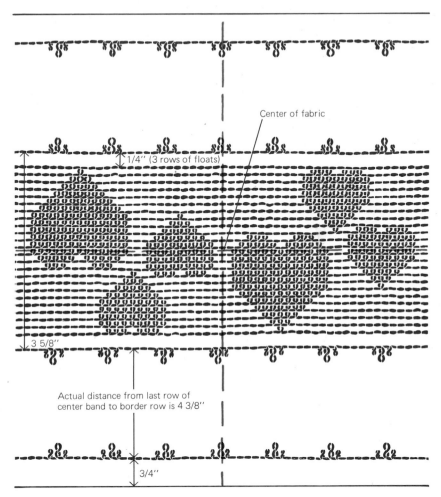

The design for the huck table runner was adapted from the huck design on page 71.

From sprightly designs to fabric width, huckwork is ideal for table runners.

Materials needed
1 yard huckaback fabric
8 skeins embroidery floss
Tapestry needle
Sharp needle and thread for hem

The fabric
Huckaback fabric comes in both 15- and 17-inch widths; either is suitable. Huck embroidery can be worked to any length. The longer pieces involve many thread changes, which can pose one problem: Thread ends are secured and new threads joined on the fabric front, and the joinings show. In this 33-inch runner, a good size for coffee table or buffet, rows are worked fully with a single thread length (half at a time, which is easily manageable), avoiding the problem of joinings.

The embroidery
Bind both cut edges with masking tape; you need not bind selvages. Embroidery is started at center and worked out to sides row by row; rows build from the center up to top and down to bottom.

Working on side of fabric that has single floats, locate center by folding the fabric in half both ways (diagram, right). Heart motif combines straight and closed loop stitches (see pp. 71-72). Cut a 45-inch length of floss (thread should be about one-and-one-half times as long as row). Start first row at fabric center, leaving half of the thread free; work first to left (see p. 73). Then turn the fabric around and, with free end of thread in needle, work other half of row. Work all rows the same way so you are always stitching with half a thread length. If you decide to make a longer runner, cut threads to different lengths so joinings do not appear in the same place on each row. To work borders, see drawing at the right and figure-eight stitch, page 72.

Hemming
Press selvages under ½ inch on 15-inch fabric; on wider fabric, press under any excess beyond design area. Hem the turned edges. Trim cut ends to ¾ inch beyond embroidery. Turn ends under ¼ inch, then ½ inch, and hem these as well.

Center of fabric

1/4" (3 rows of floats)

3 5/8"

Actual distance from last row of center band to border row is 4 3/8"

3/4"

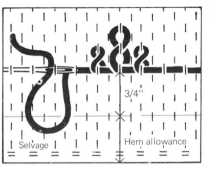

Selvage   Hem allowance   3/4"

Diagram above shows the design components and their relationship on the fabric. The design consists of right-side-up and upside-down hearts in a center band. Each motif is a grouping of one large and two small hearts that spans 3½". Allowing for three floats between motifs, nine repeats fit within the 33" length of the runner.

Detail at left shows border row of figure-eight stitches (p. 72); same stitch edges center panel as well. Allow for side hems; work border on each side, ¾" from point where hem fold will be.

Cutwork embroidery on caftan

Cutwork embroidery adds an elegant touch to a caftan; cut-out areas contrast with solid buttonhole-stitch outlines.

Materials needed

Paper and pencil for enlarging design
Dressmaker's carbon paper
Tracing wheel
No. 8 pearl cotton:
  1 ball blue
  1 ball rust
  1 ball green
Crewel needle
Embroidery hoop
Embroidery scissors

Preparation

To enlarge the design to the appropriate size, make a grid with ½-inch squares; copy the design square for square (see p. 14). Place the enlarged design under the front pattern piece of the pattern you are using to be sure the design fits within the seamlines. If it doesn't, adjust the design slightly. Then trace it directly onto the pattern piece.

The embroidery is worked on the fabric before pattern is cut out. To trace design onto fabric, pin pattern piece to fabric. Insert dressmaker's carbon between the two and trace around pattern piece and design with tracing wheel (see p. 17). To trace the other half of caftan front, turn pattern over, line up center front edge, and trace around pattern and design again (see below left).

Embroidery

Work cutwork embroidery, following the directions on pages 90 and 91. Press the completed embroidery before you cut the open areas. Press with a damp cloth, placing embroidery face down on a thick towel. Cut the open areas carefully from the back; press the embroidery again. Cut out the pattern pieces and construct caftan, following pattern directions.

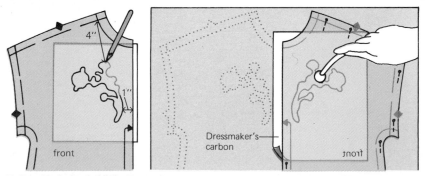

Caftan embroidery is the cutwork design on page 90; both the design and its mirror image are used.

To transfer design to fabric: Trace enlarged design onto pattern piece (left). Pin pattern to fabric. With dressmaker's carbon between pattern and fabric, trace around pattern and design with tracing wheel. Turn pattern over, align front edge, and trace mirror image of pattern and design (right).

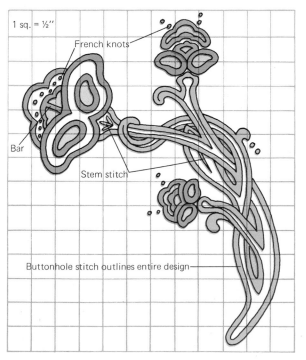

1 sq. = ½"

French knots

Bar

Stem stitch

Buttonhole stitch outlines entire design

To enlarge the graph, make grid with ½" squares and copy the design square for square (see p. 14).

To work the embroidery, see the cutwork section on pages 90-91. The design is outlined in buttonhole stitch, and embellished with French knots and stem stitch. To work the bar of buttonhole stitch that supports the large cutout area, see page 91. The gray areas indicate areas to be cut away when the embroidery is completed.

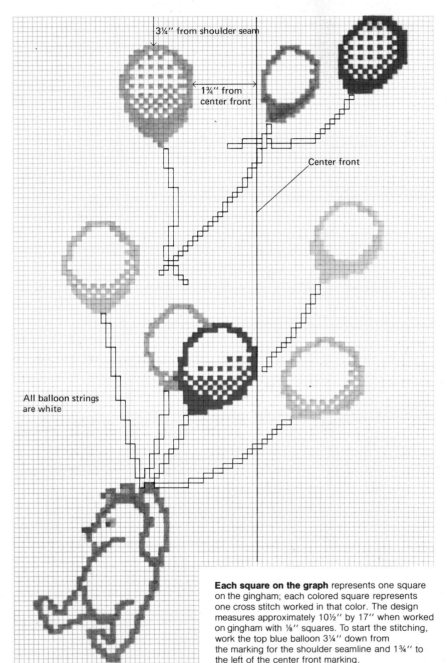

To cross stitch on gingham, a technique especially suited to children's clothing, see pages 66-68.

Cross stitch for a child's dress

3¼" from shoulder seam

1¾" from center front

Center front

All balloon strings are white

Each square on the graph represents one square on the gingham; each colored square represents one cross stitch worked in that color. The design measures approximately 10½" by 17" when worked on gingham with ⅛" squares. To start the stitching, work the top blue balloon 3¼" down from the marking for the shoulder seamline and 1¾" to the left of the center front marking.

Cross stitch on gingham makes a playful combination for a child's outfit.

Materials needed

Gingham with ⅛" checks; amount indicated on pattern envelope

1 skein embroidery floss in each color: red, blue, yellow, green, orange for balloons; white for string; light brown, dark brown, black for bear

Embroidery hoop

Crewel needle

Tailor's chalk

Design placement

The cross stitch design at the right measures about 10½ × 17 inches when worked on gingham with ⅛-inch squares. It was stitched on a child's size 4 dress; however, it will work on any pattern with a straight front, such as a sundress, pina-

fore, or apron. To work the design on coveralls that have a center front seam, work each half of the design on the corresponding front piece, keeping stitches within the seamlines, and making sure design parts meet at center front marking.

To be sure the design fits your pattern, measure the length and twice the width of the front pattern piece (which represents half the dress front), staying inside seamlines and hemline.

The embroidery

Trace around front pattern piece with tailor's chalk; do not cut it out. Mark seamlines and hemline. Using an embroidery hoop and following the chart, work design in cross stitch (see p. 35). Then cut out pattern pieces and construct the dress, following pattern directions.

Corded pillow/Blackwork

A simple way to show off embroidery— or needlepoint, appliqué, or patchwork, if you prefer. The backing and cording instructions apply equally to other tops.

Materials needed

½ yard even-weave linen
6 skeins embroidery floss
Tapestry needle
1 yard fabric for backing and cording
2 yards ¼-inch cable cord
12-inch zipper
14-inch-square pillow form

Preparing design for embroidery

To enlarge the design to the appropriate size, make a grid of 1-inch squares and copy the design square for square (see p. 14). Cut out an 18-inch square of linen, bind the edges (p. 16), and mark the horizontal and vertical centers with lines of basting. Transfer the design to the fabric (pp. 16-17).

Embroidery

Work the design, following the chart and key below for stitch placement and identification, and for the locations of detailed stitching instructions. Wash and block the finished embroidery (pp. 54-55). Trim fabric to a 15-inch square.

Cording

Cut two 8 × 15-inch rectangles for pillow backing; set aside. To make cording, cut 2-inch-wide bias strips (see p. 199) from remaining backing fabric. Seam them together into a 58-inch length. Fold the bias strip in half lengthwise with the wrong sides facing. Insert cable cord in the fold; stitch close to cord, by hand, or by machine using zipper foot. Trim cording seam allowance to ½ inch. Baste cording to right side of top at seamline (Step 1 below). Where cording ends meet, join them as shown in Step 2.

Backing

Pin the two backing rectangles together with right sides facing. To prepare the seam for inserting zipper, follow Step 3 below. Clip the basting threads at both ends to simplify later removal of bastings. Press the seam open. Insert zipper according to package directions. Remove basting stitches; open the zipper several inches. Join backing and embroidered top as specified in Step 4. Clip corners as illustrated to reduce bulk. Open zipper and turn the pillow cover inside out, squaring corners. Insert pillow form.

The design for this corded pillow was adapted from the blackwork design shown on page 56.

To enlarge design, follow instructions on page 14. Two basic embroidery stitches are used: the stem stitch (A), described on page 23; the satin stitch (B), on page 48. Directions for the seven blackwork stitches are given in that section: C & D, page 59; E, F, G, page 60; H, page 61; I, page 62.

To construct pillow. 1. Trim raw edges of cording to ½''; pin cording to pillow top at the stitching line and with raw edges aligned. At corners, clip into cording seam allowances so cording will turn corner neatly. Baste along stitching line of cording. To join cording where ends meet, see Step 2.

2. Trim cords so they butt. Trim fabric to ½'' overlap; fold the edge under ¼'' and wrap around starting end. Sew across both ends.

3. To prepare zipper seam, place backing pieces face to face. On one 15'' side, stitch 1½'', baste 12'', stitch to the end.

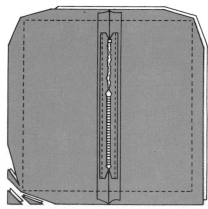

4. Attach zipper according to package directions. With zipper partway open, place backing and top fabrics together, with right sides facing and raw edges aligned; baste. Stitch around all four sides ½'' from raw edge. Remove bastings; clip corners to reduce bulk. Open zipper; turn pillow inside out.

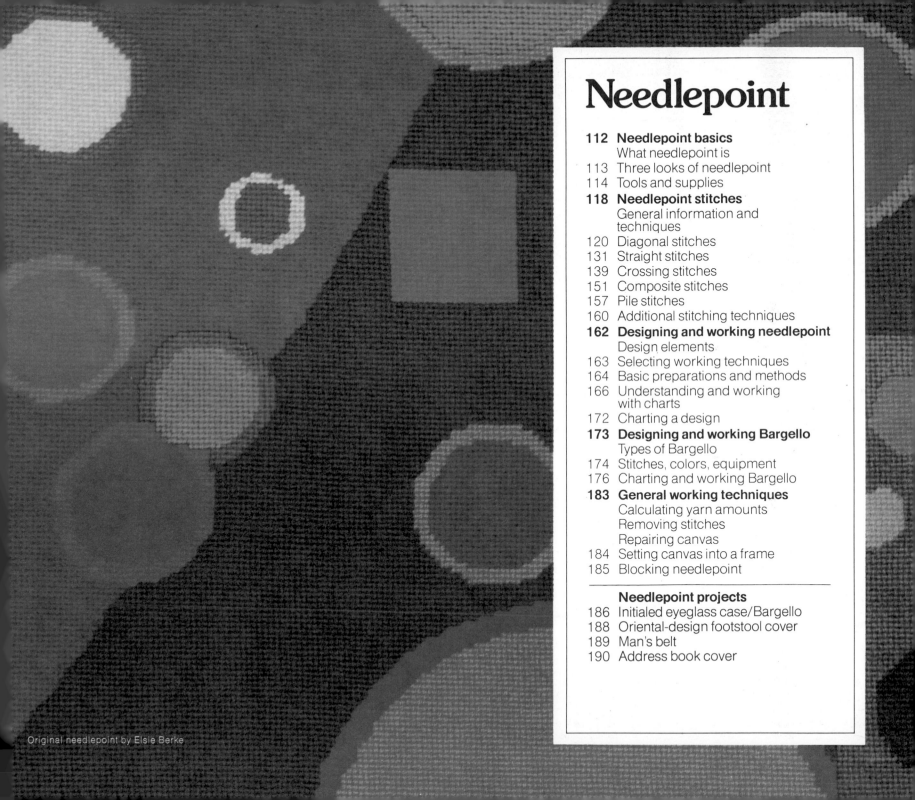

Needlepoint

112 Needlepoint basics
What needlepoint is
113 Three looks of needlepoint
114 Tools and supplies
118 Needlepoint stitches
General information and
techniques
120 Diagonal stitches
131 Straight stitches
139 Crossing stitches
151 Composite stitches
157 Pile stitches
160 Additional stitching techniques
162 Designing and working needlepoint
Design elements
163 Selecting working techniques
164 Basic preparations and methods
166 Understanding and working
with charts
172 Charting a design
173 Designing and working Bargello
Types of Bargello
174 Stitches, colors, equipment
176 Charting and working Bargello
183 General working techniques
Calculating yarn amounts
Removing stitches
Repairing canvas
184 Setting canvas into a frame
185 Blocking needlepoint

Needlepoint projects
186 Initialed eyeglass case/Bargello
188 Oriental-design footstool cover
189 Man's belt
190 Address book cover

Original needlepoint by Elsie Berke

Needlepoint basics

What needlepoint is
Three looks of needlepoint
Canvases
Yarns
Needles
Frames and holders
Design transfer needs
Miscellaneous equipment

What needlepoint is

Needlepoint is the technique of forming stitches on a special open-weave fabric known as canvas. Canvas is constructed of *lengthwise* and *crosswise* threads that are woven together to produce precisely spaced *holes* between threads. The points at which these threads intersect are known as *meshes*. All needlepoint stitches are worked in conformity with the grid-like structure of the canvas.

Basically, the yarn of any needlepoint stitch can go in only two directions, either diagonally across or parallel to the canvas threads and meshes (see the stitch direction sample below). The direction the yarn takes is dictated by the kind of stitch that is being worked. Several needlepoint stitches fall in only one direction; others require yarns to be laid in several directions or even require the yarns to be crossed over each other.

The size of a stitch depends upon two things. One of these is the character of the stitch. Certain of the stitches span only one canvas thread or mesh; other stitches span two or more. Stitch size also depends on the gauge of canvas that the stitch is being worked on. (The gauge of a canvas is the number of meshes to each inch of that canvas.) The more meshes per inch a canvas has, the smaller the stitches worked on it can be. Canvas is available in many gauges (see p. 114); this wide overall range breaks down into two subgroups, **petitpoint** and **grospoint.** A petitpoint canvas is one with 16 or more meshes to the inch; a grospoint canvas has fewer than 16 meshes per inch. Because a petitpoint canvas has more meshes per inch than a grospoint canvas, any stitch worked on a canvas in the petitpoint range will be smaller than it would be on a grospoint canvas. Petitpoint and grospoint stitching are shown actual size in the two samples below, right. The same stitch, the tent stitch, is used in both, and the linear amount of canvas, one square inch, is also the same. The first sample is done on a 24-gauge canvas, which is well within the petitpoint range of canvases; the second sample is on a 12-gauge canvas, which falls in the grospoint range.

Stitch size affects the amount of working time and the durability of the finished item. In general, the smaller the stitches, the more time will be spent in working them and the more durable the finished item will be. More time is required for small stitches, of course, because it takes more of them to cover each inch of canvas. Small stitches are more durable than large ones because they are less likely to be snagged or broken when the finished needlepoint is in use. How much stitch durability an item needs depends on its end use. A pillow, for example, will be subject to more abrasion than a wall hanging.

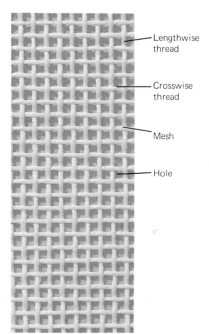

Lengthwise thread

Crosswise thread

Mesh

Hole

The parts of a needlepoint canvas

Directions stitches can take on canvas

Petitpoint stitches

Grospoint stitches

The three looks of needlepoint

The interpretation of the overall drawn design on which a finished needlepoint is based depends upon the stitches. They can affect a design in two ways. First, the stitches can alter the drawn lines of the design. Differences between drawn and stitched lines occur because the stitches must be worked to conform to the grid-like structure of the canvas. Drawn lines, of course, are free of such restrictions. How much deviation there is between the two lines depends on the character of the stitch and its size. The other way the stitch can affect a design arises from the texture or pattern the stitching produces. Interpretation in texture changes design elements drastically, greatly altering the design's visual impact. Needlepoint offers a wide choice of texture possibilities. For illustrations and explanations of a comprehensive assortment of needlepoint stitches and the textures and patterns they produce, see pages 118-161.

When you are deciding which stitches to use, bear in mind that three distinct visual impressions can be produced by means of needlepoint stitches (see the three stitched samples below). The first sample illustrates the effect of **tent stitches** on a design. The tent stitch is a small diagonal stitch that spans only a single canvas mesh. Though there are three ways of working tent stitches, each method produces the same stitch and even texture on the right side of the canvas. Because tent stitches are small, they can interpret a drawn line fairly precisely; the smaller the stitches, the truer the stitched line will be to the drawn line. A design to be executed in tent stitches, therefore, can be fairly detailed and include varying degrees of subtle shading.

All other needlepoint stitches are categorized as **novelty stitches.** This group embraces many stitches, each varying in size, texture, and pattern. A design intended for novelty stitches tends to be less detailed than one meant for tent stitches, usually relying on the structural elements of a design rather than on its details. There are two reasons for this. First, virtually all novelty stitches are large, and so less suited to following drawn lines. Second, the textures produced by novelty stitches interpret and enhance the physical reality of design elements exceptionally well. The second sample below follows the same basic design used for the tent stitch sample next to it. Notice how much more prominent major elements have become than design details, and how well the knotted stitch (see p. 145) suggests the texture of wood for the barn, the diamond eyelet (p. 153) the window of the barn, the leaf stitch (see p. 154) the tree. Stitch selection, however, is just one factor to consider when composing a design that will be rendered in needlepoint stitches. For a more thorough explanation of designing, see pages 162-163.

Included in the novelty stitch classification are the **Bargello stitches** that produce the third needlepoint look. Bargello stitches are straight needlepoint stitches placed parallel to the threads of the canvas. Many patterns can be produced with Bargello stitches, but one of the most familiar and classic is the pattern formed by a particular Bargello stitch, the Florentine stitch (see third sample below). The Florentine stitch is based on the customary straight stitches, but they are placed in a zigzag line across the canvas, a configuration that permits many variations. With many Bargello needlepoints, the overall finished design is determined by the structure of the stitch rather than the selection of a stitch to fill in a predetermined shape. For more details on Bargello and Florentine, see page 173.

Design done in tent stitches

Same design worked in novelty stitches

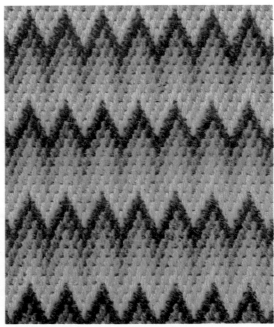

Arrangement of Bargello (Florentine) stitches

Needlepoint basics / Tools and supplies

Canvases

Canvas is fundamental to the success of any needlepoint project, and so should be selected with the utmost care. Be sure the threads are free of knots and cuts. Most canvases are made of cotton. Some newer ones are made of synthetics, such as nylon; some fine-gauge canvases come in silk. The gauge chosen should be suitable both for the proposed item and for the design being worked (see pp. 162-163).

To determine the gauge of a canvas, hold a ruler along a crosswise thread and count the meshes in one inch. In the photo above, this is being done on a 10-gauge mono canvas.

There are several different types of canvas. Those used most often are plain mono, interlock mono, and penelope. Both **plain and interlock mono** canvases have a single-mesh structure; the construction of the mesh, however, is different in each. A single mesh of the plain mono canvas is formed by the intersection of a single lengthwise and a single crosswise thread. With interlock mono canvas, each lengthwise thread is actually two thinner threads that have been twisted around each other and a single crosswise thread to produce a "locked" single mesh. The locked construction of the interlock mono canvas is more stable than the merely intersecting mesh of plain mono canvas. All needlepoint stitches can be formed successfully on an interlock mono canvas; plain mono canvas, however, is not suitable for use with certain needlepoint stitches, such as the half-cross stitch (see p. 120). Both the plain and interlock mono canvases are available in a wide range of gauges.

Penelope canvas has a double-mesh construction. The double mesh is formed by the intersection of pairs of lengthwise threads with pairs of crosswise threads. Besides being strong, a double mesh has a second advantage—it can be adjusted so that stitches of different sizes can be worked on the same piece of canvas (see photo below). Used as is, a double mesh can accept one size of stitch; when the

pairs of threads are separated, four plain mono meshes are formed that are capable of receiving four smaller stitches. Penelope's double-mesh adaptability is advantageous when your design calls for

finely stitched areas. The gauge of a penelope canvas is given as two numbers separated by a line, for example, 10/20. The smaller number designates the number of double meshes per inch; the larger number, the meshes per inch if threads are separated. Penelope canvas is readily available in 5/10 to 14/28 gauges.

In another type, **rug canvas,** each mesh is formed by two lengthwise threads that are twisted around each other and a pair of crosswise threads. Threads cannot be separated. Rug canvas comes in 3 to 5 gauges; is used primarily for rugs.

Patterned canvas supplies a design to follow, woven in so it appears on both sides. Darks and lights are reversed on the two sides, permitting a choice of impressions. Available in several patterns; worked with plain stitches.

Plastic canvas is molded rather than woven into a stiff, medium-gauge canvas-like form. Sold in cut pieces; used for items like tote bags and coasters.

Plain mono canvas

Penelope canvas

Patterned canvas

Interlock mono canvas

Rug canvas

Plastic canvas

114

Yarns

Yarns for needlepoint come in several fibers, weights, and textures, as well as many lovely colors. Shown below are the types of yarns most often used.

One of the most important criteria of yarn selection is weight or thickness. The weight of yarn varies with the type: tapestry yarn, for example, is thinner than rug yarn. The yarn should be thin enough to slide through the holes of the canvas easily and without distortion, but thick enough to cover the canvas in stitch form. In general, the larger the canvas gauge, the heavier or thicker the yarn should be. Appropriate yarn weight depends also on the stitch that is being

formed (p. 118). *Strand* and *ply* are two terms relating to yarn structure that need to be understood. A strand is the unit; a ply is a part of a strand. For example, Persian yarn is made up of three strands of yarn, but each of these strands consists of two plies. Strands are easily separated, which allows you to decrease or increase the number of strands as necessary to produce yarn of a particular thickness. Plies are not easily separated.

Needlepoint yarns are made of several different fibers, such as wool, cotton, silk, acrylic, rayon, and metallic. Wool is used most often. This is because it is an inherently strong fiber that has proven

very durable for needlepoint. A yarn selected for use in needlepoint should have the capacity to withstand abrasion both while the stitch is being worked and when the finished item is in use. If the needlepoint item will not get hard use, less sturdy fibers, such as rayon and metallic, can be used. Another strength factor is the length of the fibers used in manufacturing the yarn. The wool fibers in needlepoint yarns are longer, and therefore stronger, than those that are used in the yarns made especially for knitting. That is why knitting yarns are not recommended as substitutes for needlepoint yarns.

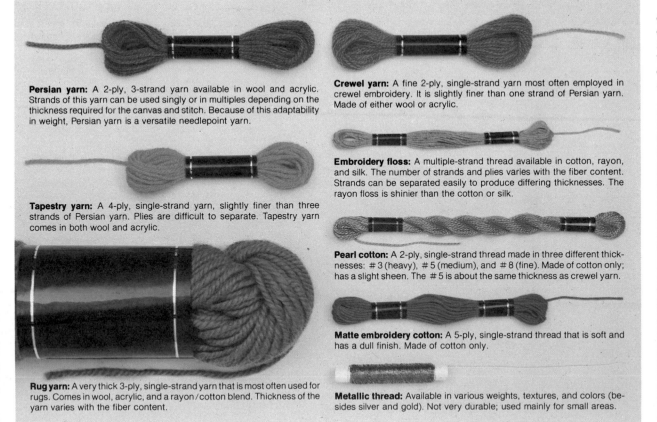

Persian yarn: A 2-ply, 3-strand yarn available in wool and acrylic. Strands of this yarn can be used singly or in multiples depending on the thickness required for the canvas and stitch. Because of this adaptability in weight, Persian yarn is a versatile needlepoint yarn.

Tapestry yarn: A 4-ply, single-strand yarn, slightly finer than three strands of Persian yarn. Plies are difficult to separate. Tapestry yarn comes in both wool and acrylic.

Rug yarn: A very thick 3-ply, single-strand yarn that is most often used for rugs. Comes in wool, acrylic, and a rayon/cotton blend. Thickness of the yarn varies with the fiber content.

Crewel yarn: A fine 2-ply, single-strand yarn most often employed in crewel embroidery. It is slightly finer than one strand of Persian yarn. Made of either wool or acrylic.

Embroidery floss: A multiple-strand thread available in cotton, rayon, and silk. The number of strands and plies varies with the fiber content. Strands can be separated easily to produce differing thicknesses. The rayon floss is shinier than the cotton or silk.

Pearl cotton: A 2-ply, single-strand thread made in three different thicknesses: #3 (heavy), #5 (medium), and #8 (fine). Made of cotton only; has a slight sheen. The #5 is about the same thickness as crewel yarn.

Matte embroidery cotton: A 5-ply, single-strand thread that is soft and has a dull finish. Made of cotton only.

Metallic thread: Available in various weights, textures, and colors (besides silver and gold). Not very durable; used mainly for small areas.

Needles

The needle type recommended for use in needlepoint is the tapestry needle. It has a large eye that allows for easy threading of yarn, and a blunt point that prevents the needle from piercing the canvas threads. Tapestry needles are available in a range of sizes from #13, the heaviest, to #26, the finest. The finer the size, the shorter the needle and the smaller its eye. Select the needle size according to the gauge of the canvas that is being worked on. The needle should be thin enough to be passed easily through the holes of the canvas without distorting them. The #18 needle is used most often, since it is suitable for the highly popular 10- and 12-gauge canvases. Needles from #20 to #26 are used on the finer-gauge canvases; those from #13 to #16, on heavier canvases. Test any needle to make sure it is the correct size. Tapestry needles are usually sold in packages of several needles; they may be one size only or an assortment of sizes.

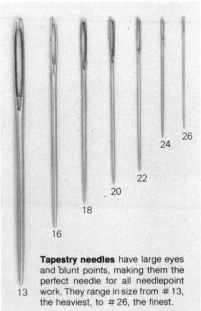

Tapestry needles have large eyes and blunt points, making them the perfect needle for all needlepoint work. They range in size from #13, the heaviest, to #26, the finest.

115

Frames and holders

In working needlepoint, use of a frame or some other kind of canvas holder can be a great help. Such devices help to keep the canvas neat and to allow the yarn of the stitches to be properly laid onto the canvas. They also prevent the canvas from being severely distorted by the stitches. The best device to use is a frame; a frame attached to a stand will free both your hands for stitching. Most needlepoint frames work on a scroll principle. The top and bottom edges of the canvas are first sewed to tapes on rods. Then the canvas is rolled onto the rods and the rods are fastened to the side arms of the frame. The canvas can be narrower but not wider than the tapes. In length, the canvas should not be too much shorter than the side arms; it can be longer, however, since excess length can be rolled onto the rods. Another device that can serve as a frame is a canvas stretcher. It must be large enough to accommodate the entire piece of canvas. Once the canvas is tacked in place, it should not be re-positioned. A needlepoint rod holds canvas in a compact, manageable roll; you roll the canvas out flat, a few inches at a time, as you work. A hoop is best reserved for finer-gauge, softer canvases, which are less likely to be creased by the pressure of the rings.

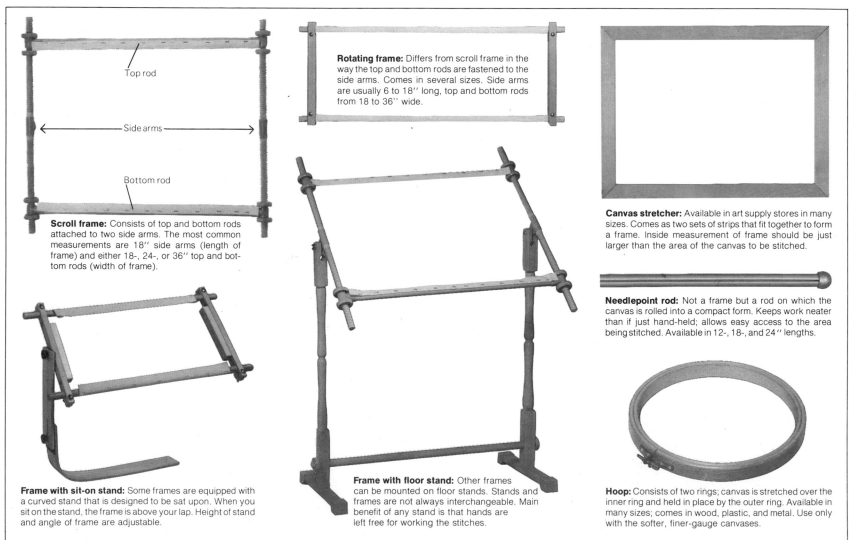

Top rod

Side arms

Bottom rod

Rotating frame: Differs from scroll frame in the way the top and bottom rods are fastened to the side arms. Comes in several sizes. Side arms are usually 6 to 18″ long, top and bottom rods from 18 to 36″ wide.

Scroll frame: Consists of top and bottom rods attached to two side arms. The most common measurements are 18″ side arms (length of frame) and either 18-, 24-, or 36″ top and bottom rods (width of frame).

Canvas stretcher: Available in art supply stores in many sizes. Comes as two sets of strips that fit together to form a frame. Inside measurement of frame should be just larger than the area of the canvas to be stitched.

Needlepoint rod: Not a frame but a rod on which the canvas is rolled into a compact form. Keeps work neater than if just hand-held; allows easy access to the area being stitched. Available in 12-, 18-, and 24″ lengths.

Frame with sit-on stand: Some frames are equipped with a curved stand that is designed to be sat upon. When you sit on the stand, the frame is above your lap. Height of stand and angle of frame are adjustable.

Frame with floor stand: Other frames can be mounted on floor stands. Stands and frames are not always interchangeable. Main benefit of any stand is that hands are left free for working the stitches.

Hoop: Consists of two rings; canvas is stretched over the inner ring and held in place by the outer ring. Available in many sizes; comes in wood, plastic, and metal. Use only with the softer, finer-gauge canvases.

Design transfer needs

If you intend to design your own needlepoint, certain tools will be essential, others will make the job easier and more professional. The most necessary tools, of course, are the papers and marking devices. If you are copying a design from a book, tracing paper is helpful. Graph paper is needed for charting a design; see-through graph paper, for tracing a chart or design. When a design is being colored on paper, the marking device need not be waterproof; it must be, however, when you want to color a design on canvas. To paint on a canvas, choose the acrylic type, thinned with water. When dry, acrylic paints are permanent.

Miscellaneous equipment

Shown below are some pieces of equipment that you will find yourself needing or wanting at different points in the needlepoint process. Some you may already have, others you may have to buy. The blocking board and rustproof tacks will be necessary for stretching the stitched needlepoint back into its original shape. The large scissors are for cutting the canvas, the embroidery scissors for cutting yarn. Masking tape is ideal for binding canvas edges. A yarn-sized needle threader will make it easier to thread yarn; a magnifier will help you do a better job with fine details. A tape measure will be useful many times as you work.

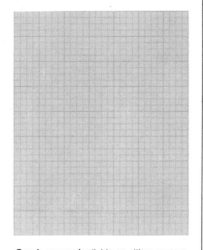

Graph paper: Available as either opaque or see-through paper with from 4 to 20 squares per inch (10 squares per inch is the most common).

Tracing paper: Useful for tracing designs from a book or other sources. Comes in many sizes; is usually sold by the pad.

T-square: A ruler-like device that has a head at right angles to its body. It is used for drawing straight lines and perfect 90° angles, and for marking centers. (Also used in blocking.) T-squares are available with or without ruler markings in wood, plastic, or metal.

Paints and brushes are needed if you paint a design. Acrylic paints, diluted with water, work well on canvas.

Felt-tipped markers are available with either a fine or a broad tip.

Tacks (rustproof) will be needed for blocking. Large-headed tacks are easiest to handle.

Tape measures are flexible; come 60″ long and have easy-to-read markings on both sides of the tape.

Masking tape is used for binding the raw edges of a canvas. Available in several widths; 1″ works well.

Blocking board is a piece of soft wood large enough to contain the canvas while it is being blocked. It can be purchased at a lumber yard.

Dressmaker's shears are needed to cut out the canvas. A left-handed model is also available.

Embroidery scissors are small and have sharp points, making them ideal for close, fine work.

Needle threader for yarn facilitates threading.

A magnifier can help to reduce eye strain, especially when you work on very fine canvas.

Needlepoint stitches

General information
Stitch tension and yarn coverage
General stitching techniques
Diagonal stitches
Straight stitches
Crossing stitches
Composite stitches
Pile stitches
Additional stitching techniques

General information

The most familiar needlepoint stitch is the small, slanted stitch known as the tent stitch (see first sample below). It is also the most basic stitch, and one that every needlepointer should master and use. There are many other needlepoint stitches, each with its own application and charm, and having a working knowledge of a variety of stitches can add greatly to the scope and originality of your needlepoint projects. You will find a great many stitches illustrated and explained in the 40-page section that follows. For ease in learning, they have been grouped according to the direction that the yarn takes while the stitch is being worked. There are five stitch groups: the **diagonal** stitches, **straight** stitches, **crossing** stitches, **composite** stitches, **pile** stitches. An actual-size sample of each stitch accompanies a detailed step-by-step explanation of how that stitch is worked. The best way to learn the stitches, however, is to actually do them. Working the stitches yourself will show you, too, which ones work up quickly and how much yarn is taken up by each. Also, of course, this will give you your own stitch samples. Do this stitching in sampler form, and it will be a permanent and handy reference tool to help in selecting stitches for a particular project. On page 162, you will find additional tips on choosing stitches for the enhancement of a particular design. If you decide to make your own sampler, a 10-gauge interlock mono canvas and Persian yarn will be suitable for most of the stitches. There are only a few, as you will see, that should be done on penelope canvas. Yarn thickness will depend on the stitch that is being done. A discussion of proper stitch tension and yarn weight appears at the immediate right; general stitching techniques are explained on the facing page. The stitches contained in this section are geared to right-handed people. For guidance on how to work if you are left-handed, turn to page 161.

Stitch tension and yarn coverage

As you work needlepoint stitches, two things must be observed simultaneously: maintenance of a correct stitch tension and use of a weight of yarn that satisfactorily covers the canvas. A good stitch tension allows the yarn to be held tautly around the threads of the canvas; when the correct tension is maintained, all the stitches will be formed evenly. Tension that is too loose causes the yarn to stand out more than it should from the surface of the canvas. This affects the durability of the stitch; loose yarns are susceptible to snagging when needlepoint is in use. Tension that is too tight will distort the canvas threads, and stretch the yarn too thin as well. If yarn is too thin, the canvas will not be well covered. This result is illustrated by the second sample of tent stitches below. Proper yarn weight is determined by both the gauge of the canvas and the stitch being formed. In general, the larger the gauge and the longer the stitch, the heavier the yarn should be. To successfully combine different stitch sizes on the same piece of canvas, you will most likely have to use different weights of yarn. All of the stitches shown below were done on a 10-gauge, interlock mono canvas. The first two samples are of tent stitches, both worked with two strands of Persian yarn. Coverage is good in the first sample because the stitch tension was correct. In the second tent stitch sample, tension was too tight. The adjoining samples (below right) are of straight Gobelin stitches. Both were worked with the proper tension, but the two strands of Persian yarn used in the second sample were too thin for adequate coverage. The first sample was worked with four strands, which, as the result shows, is the proper weight of yarn for the stitch and the canvas.

Tent stitches, proper tension/weight

Straight Gobelin, proper tension/weight

Tent stitches with too-tight tension

Straight Gobelin with too-thin yarn

General stitching techniques

There are a few working techniques common to all needlepoint stitches. The most basic of these are separating strands of yarn and threading a needle; these are explained fully in the Embroidery chapter. Before threading the needle for any needlepoint stitch, cut the yarn to an 18-inch length. A yarn longer than that tends to become frayed as the stitches are being worked. The number of strands will depend on the stitch and the canvas (see facing page).

In needlepoint, there are special methods for **securing yarn ends.** When starting, allow one to two inches of yarn to remain at the back of the canvas. Hold this yarn end against the canvas and catch it with the first few stitches. When the end is secured, clip off the excess and continue to work the rest of the stitches. To end a yarn, bring needle and yarn to the back of the canvas; weave the yarn through the underside of the last few stitches, then clip it. Avoid starting and ending yarns in line with each other. Instead, stagger their positions; this will avoid the formation of a uniformly positioned ridge on the right side of the canvas.

What makes each needlepoint stitch different from the other is the way the yarn is laid onto the threads of the canvas. In order for the yarn to be properly laid, the **canvas must be held correctly** while the stitch is worked. Most of the needlepoint stitches are worked with the canvas held so that its lengthwise threads are perpendicular to your body, and one of the lengthwise edges is always recognized as the top edge of the canvas. The technique for some stitches requires the canvas to be turned while you are working. With several of the stitches, among them the continental stitch (as shown on p. 121), the canvas is turned around for each new row. When these are finished, however, all the stitches lie in the same direction. Sometimes the canvas is given only a quarter-turn. This may be done to produce a particular textural effect (see p. 163), but quite often the quarter-turn simply makes it easier to work a particular stitch. Examples are those stitches, like the triangle stitch (see p. 155), in which the yarn is laid in four opposing directions.

Almost all of the stitches included in this section are shown worked on plain mono canvas. It should not be assumed from this, however, that a stitch cannot be done on another type of canvas. Where it is necessary to use a particular canvas, this requirement is pointed out.

The illustrations also show the stitches being formed by the **sewing method,** in which the point of the needle is inserted and brought out in a single scooping movement. There is another method, the **stabbing method,** that involves two separate motions for each stitch. The stabbing method is recommended when the canvas is on a frame; it is difficult to scoop under the canvas threads when a canvas is stretched taut. Both stitch formation procedures are shown below. With either working method, there is a possibility that the yarn may become too twisted. Excessive twist causes yarn to kink and knot and to appear thinner than it would in its normal, relaxed state. To untwist the yarn, discontinue stitching and allow the needle and yarn to dangle freely. When the yarn has unwound itself, resume stitching.

SECURING YARN ENDS

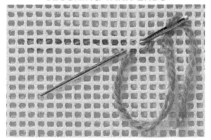

When starting, leave 1 to 2 inches of yarn at the back of the canvas. Catch the yarn end with the first few stitches; then trim off the excess.

When ending, bring the needle and yarn to the back of the canvas. Weave the yarn through the backs of the last few stitches; then cut it short.

HOLDING CANVAS WHILE WORKING

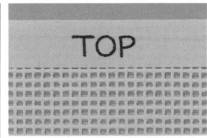

Canvas is held with the top edge at the top to work most needlepoint stitches. Before beginning, label the top edge of the canvas.

For some needlepoint stitches, the canvas is turned while you are working. With the continental stitch (p. 121), turn canvas for each new row.

METHODS OF STITCH FORMATION

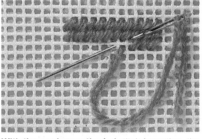

With the sewing method of stitch formation, the needle, in one motion, scoops in for the end of one stitch and out for the start of the next.

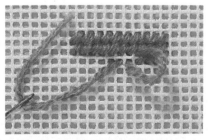

The needle and yarn are then pulled through the canvas and the yarn of the last stitch is positioned over the proper canvas threads or meshes.

The stabbing method requires two movements for each stitch. First, needle and yarn are pulled through to right side of the canvas.

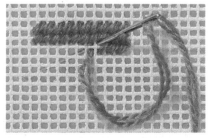

Then the needle and yarn are pulled through to the back side of the canvas. The yarn of the stitch is laid with the second motion.

119

Needlepoint stitches

Diagonal stitches

The needlepoint stitches in this first group are classified as diagonal stitches because all of them are worked to slant diagonally across the threads of the canvas. Included in the diagonal grouping are the tent stitches, the most familiar and frequently used of all needlepoint stitches. Tent stitches produce an even texture applicable to any type of needlepoint design. Each of the other diagonal stitches has its own distinctive texture or pattern. Whether you use any diagonal stitch will depend, first, on whether you find it appealing, and second, on how well its size and pattern meet the requirements of your needlepoint design.

TENT STITCHES

A tent stitch is a diagonal stitch formed over one canvas mesh. There are three methods of forming tent stitches, each with its own stitch name: the half-cross stitch, the continental stitch, and the basketweave stitch. The continental and basketweave methods form more durable stitches than the half-cross method. This is evidenced by the greater amount of yarn coverage on the back of the canvas. Half-cross stitches should not be done on plain mono canvas; the stitches tend to slip at the meshes of this canvas type.

Half-cross stitch (front and back views)

Continental stitch (front and back views)

Basketweave stitch (front and back views)

Half-cross stitch (done horizontally): Starting at the upper left, work each row of stitches from left to right. Form each stitch by bringing needle out at 1, then in at 2. At the end of each row of stitches, finish the last stitch and leave the needle at the back of the canvas. Then turn canvas completely around and form the new row in line with the stitches just completed.

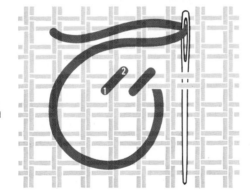

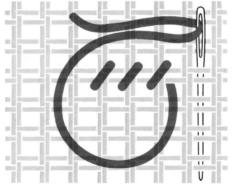

CANVAS TURNED

Half-cross stitch (done vertically): Begin at the lower right and work each row of stitches up the canvas. For each stitch, bring needle out at 1, then in at 2. At the end of each row, finish the last stitch and leave needle at back of canvas. Turn the canvas all the way around and form the new row of stitches next to those just done.

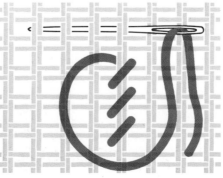

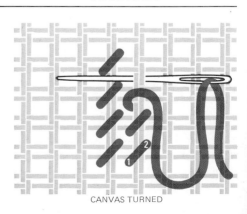

CANVAS TURNED

120

Continental stitch (done horizontally): Start at upper right and work each row of stitches from right to left. Form each stitch by bringing needle out at 1, then in at 2. At the end of each row of stitches, finish the last stitch and leave needle at back of canvas. Then turn the canvas completely around and work stitches of the new row directly in line with those in the row just completed.

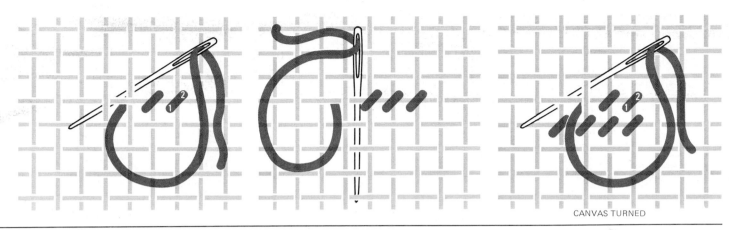

CANVAS TURNED

Continental stitch (done vertically): Start at the upper right and work each row of stitches down the canvas. To form each stitch, bring the needle out at 1, then in at 2. At each row's end, finish the last stitch and leave needle at back of canvas. Then turn the canvas completely around and form new row of stitches next to the row just completed.

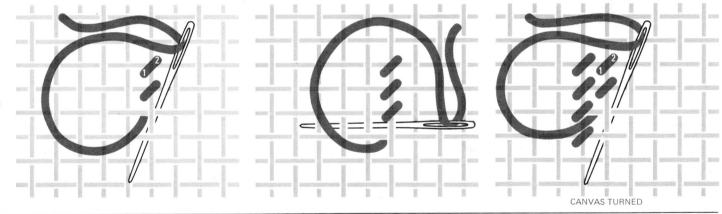

CANVAS TURNED

Basketweave stitch: Begin a few meshes from upper right and work rows alternately down, then up the canvas. For each stitch, bring needle out at 1, in at 2. Place stitches next to each other in a diagonal row; skip one canvas hole between. To work down, hold needle vertically to go from stitch to stitch. Below last stitch of a down row, form first stitch of an up row. To work up, hold needle horizontally between stitches. Form first stitch of down row next to last stitch of up row. Turn canvas to fill in corner above first row.

121

Needlepoint stitches

Diagonal stitches

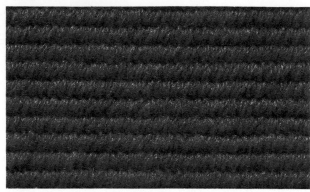

Slanted Gobelin stitch

Encroaching slanted Gobelin stitch

SLANTED GOBELIN STITCHES

Each of the individual slanted Gobelin and encroaching slanted Gobelin stitches is formed in the same way; each can vary in size to the same degree (see below). The visual difference between the two is caused by the way the rows of stitches are placed. The rows of slanted Gobelin stitches are kept separate, producing a definite, row-by-row configuration. Rows of encroaching slanted Gobelin stitches overlap, resulting in a single, uniform texture. Both stitches can be adapted in size to suit confined or background areas of a needlepoint design.

Slanted Gobelin stitch:
Start at upper right and work rows alternately right to left, then left to right. For each stitch, bring needle out at 1, pass it up over canvas, down into 2. Space between 1 and 2 can be from two to five crosswise canvas threads by one to two lengthwise threads. Spacing here is two crosswise by one lengthwise thread. At the end of each row, reverse working direction; place new stitches so their bases (1) are one stitch length below bases of stitches in preceding row.

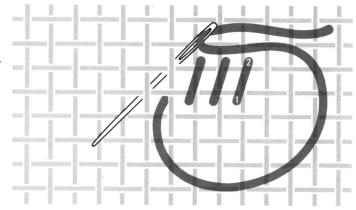

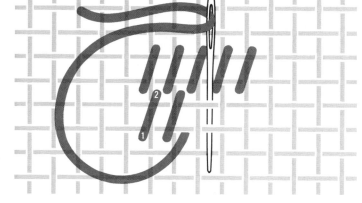

Encroaching slanted Gobelin stitch: Starting at upper right, work rows alternately right to left, then left to right. For each stitch, bring needle out at 1, up over canvas, and down into 2. Space between 1 and 2 can vary as for slanted Gobelin stitches. Space shown here is three crosswise by one lengthwise canvas thread. At end of each row, reverse the working direction. Position tops (2) of new stitches one canvas hole above and to the right of the bases of the stitches in the preceding row.

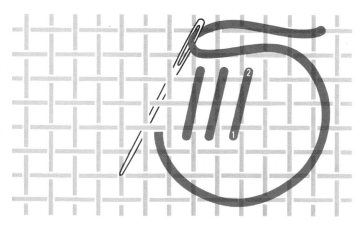

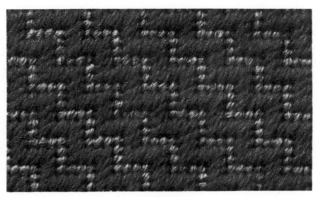

Byzantine stitch

Jacquard stitch

BYZANTINE STITCHES

The Byzantine stitch and its variation, the jacquard stitch, form striking patterns of diagonal, uniformly stepped rows of stitches. Each stitch in the Byzantine pattern is long and slanted; the jacquard pattern alternates rows of Byzantine stitches with rows of continental tent stitches. The size of both the long stitches and the steps can vary (see below). Both patterns are ideal for use as background in a needlepoint piece. A second color can be easily introduced into either pattern by alternating the color of yarn used for the rows.

Byzantine stitch: Start at upper left corner, work first row, in steps, diagonally down the canvas. Each row is a repetition of six or eight stitches (six here). Half are placed next to each other horizontally, the other half vertically, to form the steps. Form stitches consistently over two to four canvas meshes (two used here, 1 to 2). Subsequent rows are worked alternately up, then down the canvas to first fill in upper, then lower areas. Fit the steps of a new row into steps of preceding row (far right illustration).

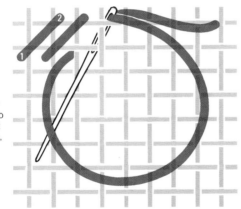

Jacquard stitch: Here too, canvas is covered with rows of Byzantine stitches, but rows are spaced one mesh apart, leaving stepped rows of blank meshes. On each row of exposed meshes, form continental stitches (p. 121). Work rows from bottom up, turning canvas completely for each new row. On horizontal steps, form stitches in the usual way, bringing needle out at base of stitch (1) and in at top of stitch (2). On vertical steps, reverse the direction of stitch formation, bringing needle out at top of stitch (A) and in at base (B).

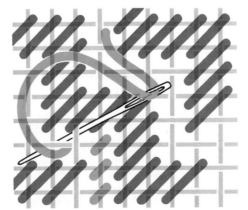
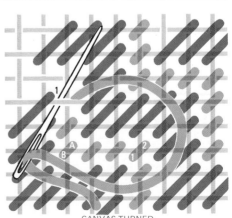

CANVAS TURNED

123

Needlepoint stitches

Diagonal stitches

Mosaic stitch

Condensed mosaic stitch

MOSAIC STITCHES
The mosaic stitch produces a block-like pattern through repetition of the same three stitches. Rows of these stitches can be worked either horizontally or diagonally across the canvas. When only one yarn color is used, both methods result in the same pattern; when two colors are used, because the colors are differently placed with each method, the resulting patterns will differ greatly (p. 160). The condensed mosaic stitch produces an overall texture by repeating the same two stitches. It is always worked diagonally. Use mosaic and condensed mosaic stitches in small or large areas.

Mosaic stitch (done horizontally): Begin at upper right; work rows right to left. Each is a repeated grouping of three stitches worked to form blocks. Form block as follows: Work one tent stitch, 1 to 2; next, a longer stitch across two canvas meshes, 3 to 4, then another tent stitch, 5 to 6. Begin next block one canvas hole to the left. At end of each row, leave needle at back of canvas, then turn canvas completely around. Align blocks of new row with blocks of preceding row.

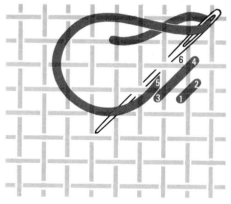

CANVAS TURNED

Mosaic stitch (done diagonally): Start at upper left and work first row diagonally down to lower right. Work successive rows alternately up, then down the canvas, filling in first the upper, then the lower areas. Each row is a repeated formation of mosaic stitch blocks (1 to 6), but blocks are placed diagonally next to each other, skipping one canvas hole between. At end of row, reverse working direction and fit new blocks between blocks of preceding row.

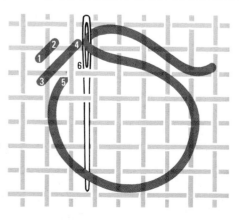

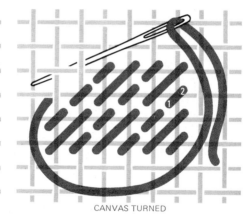

Condensed mosaic stitch:
Start at upper left; work first row diagonally to lower right. Work subsequent rows up, then down canvas; fill in first upper, then lower areas. For each row, alternately form a tent stitch, 1 to 2, then one stitch diagonally across two meshes, 3 to 4. Form the next tent stitch over the mesh opposite the center of the 3-4 stitch. At end of each row, change working direction; place new stitches so that the tent stitches are next to the long stitches of preceding row.

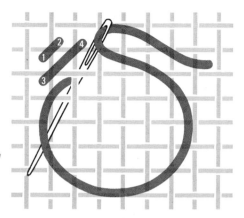  

Scotch stitch

Condensed Scotch stitch

Checker stitch

SCOTCH STITCHES

Like the mosaic stitch, the Scotch stitch can be worked horizontally or diagonally across the canvas to produce a block-like pattern. Blocks are formed, however, of five rather than three stitches. The condensed Scotch stitch is always worked diagonally: it repeats a group of four rather than five stitches. There is also a variation of the Scotch stitch called the checker stitch. It alternates blocks of Scotch stitches with same-size blocks of tent stitches (basketweave tent stitches here). Scotch stitches, being slightly larger than mosaic stitches, cannot fit into as small a canvas area.

Scotch stitch (done horizontally): Start at upper right; work each row from right to left. Each row is a repeated group of five stitches worked to form blocks. For each block: Form a tent stitch, 1 to 2, then a stitch over two meshes, 3 to 4, follow with stitch over three meshes, 5 to 6, another over two, 7 to 8, then a tent stitch, 9 to 10. Place next block to left of this. At each row's end, turn canvas around; place new blocks in line with those of preceding row.

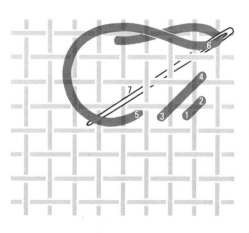 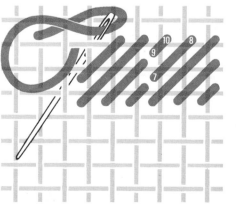 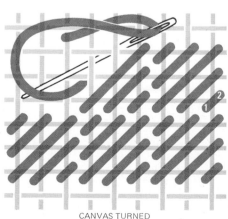

CANVAS TURNED

125

Needlepoint stitches

Diagonal stitches

Scotch stitch (done diagonally): Start at upper left and work first row diagonally to lower right. Work the remaining rows alternately up, then down canvas, first filling in upper right, then lower left. Each row consists of blocks of Scotch stitches (1 to 10). Place blocks diagonally next to each other with one canvas hole skipped between blocks. At the end of each row, reverse working direction and fit blocks of new row into indentations in preceding row.

Condensed Scotch stitch: Start at upper left and work first row diagonally to lower right. Work subsequent rows up, then down the canvas to fill in first the upper, then the lower halves. For each row, repeat the following four stitches: A tent stitch, 1 to 2, a stitch over two meshes, 3 to 4, another over three meshes, 5 to 6, a fourth over two meshes, 7 to 8. Start new repeat over mesh opposite center of last stitch. At end of each row, change working direction; form new tent stitches next to longest stitches of preceding row.

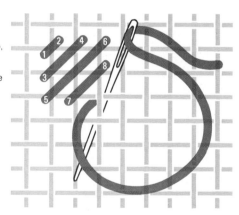

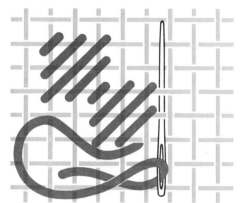

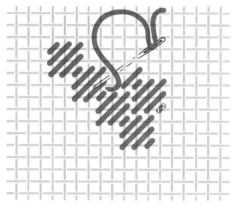

Checker stitch: Start at upper right; work each row right to left. Each row alternates a block of Scotch stitches with a block of tent stitches. Start with a block of Scotch stitches; next to it, work a block of tent stitches to cover same area (three by three meshes). Basketweave tent stitches (p. 121) used here are formed in the order indicated by the letters A through I. At the end of each checker-stitch row, turn the canvas around; align new tent-stitch blocks with the Scotch-stitch blocks of the preceding row.

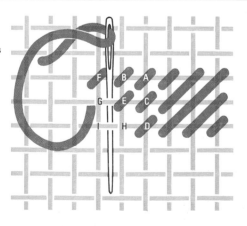

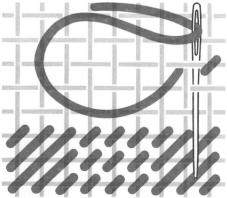

CANVAS TURNED

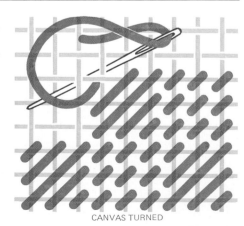

CANVAS TURNED

Cashmere stitch

Condensed cashmere stitch

CASHMERE STITCHES

Cashmere stitches, like the mosaic and Scotch stitches, form a block-like pattern on the canvas. The blocks in this case, however, are rectangular, not square like those formed with the other two stitch types. Each block of cashmere stitches consists of four stitches; rows of cashmere stitches can be worked either horizontally or diagonally across the canvas. In the condensed cashmere stitch, each repeat is three stitches; the rows are always worked diagonally. Cashmere stitches can be used in most parts of a needlepoint design but they are especially good for forming backgrounds.

Cashmere stitch (done horizontally): Start at upper right and work each row from right to left. Each row consists of rectangular blocks that are formed by identical groups of four stitches. Form each group of stitches as follows: Work a tent stitch, 1 to 2, two long stitches, each over two meshes, 3 to 4 and 5 to 6, then another tent stitch, 7 to 8. Place the next block to the left of this. At the end of each row, turn canvas around; align new rectangular blocks with those of the row just completed.

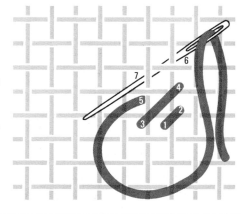

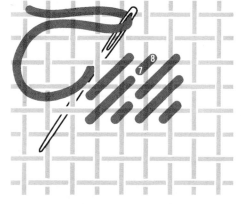

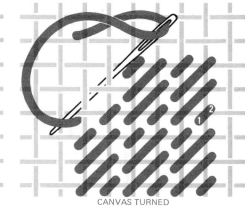

CANVAS TURNED

Cashmere stitch (done diagonally): Work first row of stitches from upper left corner diagonally down to lower right. Work subsequent rows alternately up, then down canvas, filling in first upper right, then lower left areas. Each row is made up of units of cashmere stitches (1 to 8). Each unit is placed diagonally next to the other, with one canvas hole skipped in between. At the end of each row, reverse the working direction and fit new units into indentations made by units of the preceding row.

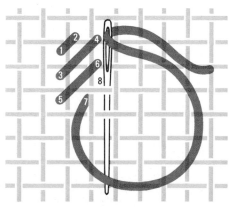

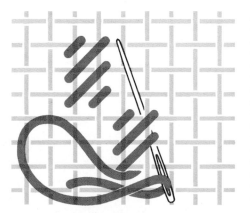

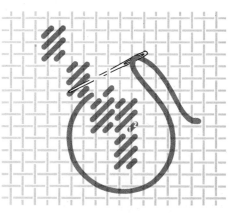

Needlepoint stitches

Diagonal stitches

Condensed cashmere stitch:
Start first row at upper left;
work to lower right. Successive
rows are worked alternately
up, then down the canvas to
first cover upper right, then
lower left areas of canvas.
Each row is a repeated series
of the same three-stitch unit:
One tent stitch, 1 to 2, then
two long stitches each over two
meshes, 3 to 4 and 5 to 6. Start
next unit over mesh that is
opposite last stitch. At end of
each row, change direction;
fit new units into indentations
formed by preceding row.

 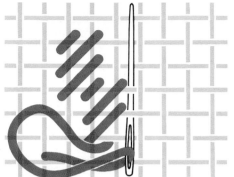 

Milanese stitch

Oriental stitch

MILANESE STITCHES

Both the Milanese stitch and its variation, the Oriental stitch, form large and
very dramatic patterns on the canvas.
Neither stitch is suitable for a small area.
The Milanese stitch is composed of rows
of triangular units of stitches. The Oriental stitch starts with rows of Milanese
stitches, but these rows are spaced to allow for the addition of groups of long
diagonal stitches. When all rows of the
Oriental stitch are done in one color, a
large, stepped pattern develops. But
when the rows are done in alternating
colors, as shown at left, the two different
stitch patterns frame one another.

Milanese stitch: Work first
row diagonally, upper left to
lower right. Do subsequent
rows up, then down canvas;
fill in upper, then lower areas.
Each row is a repetition of a
group of four stitches worked
to form triangular units. For
each unit, form one tent stitch,
1 to 2, then a stitch over two
meshes, 3 to 4, another over
three meshes, 5 to 6, the last
over four meshes, 7 to 8. Start
next unit over mesh opposite
center of last stitch. At each
row's end, change direction.
Form new tent stitches diagonally next to longest stitches
of previous row; reverse
direction of triangular units.

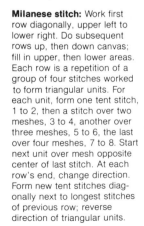 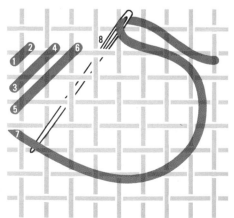 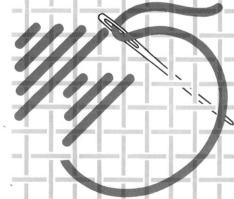 

Oriental stitch: Begin by laying down rows of Milanese stitches in the following manner: Starting at upper left, work rows down, then up the canvas, filling in first upper, then lower halves. Reverse direction of the triangular units with each row. Space these rows so that the longest stitches of all units lie next to each other diagonally. This particular row-to-row arrangement of the units leaves open rectangular areas of canvas between the rows; direction of the open areas alternates from vertical in one row to horizontal in the next.

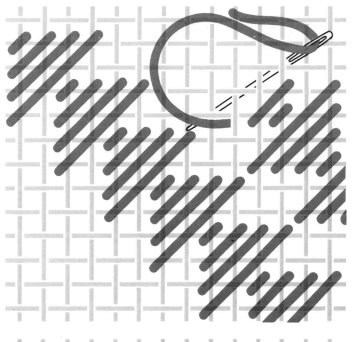

Fill in the open areas as follows: Starting with the first open space in the upper left corner, work the rows diagonally down, then up the canvas. Work the vertically shaped rows down the canvas; those that are horizontal, up the canvas. In every area, form three diagonal stitches, each over two meshes, 1 to 2. Form stitches in the vertical areas below one another; place the stitches in horizontal areas next to each other. All of the stitches should slant in the same direction, from lower left to upper right. All groups of stitches hug the edges of the Milanese stitches. When using compensating stitches (p. 161) to fill in the outer edges of the stitched area, maintain the pattern of separate rows of stitches.

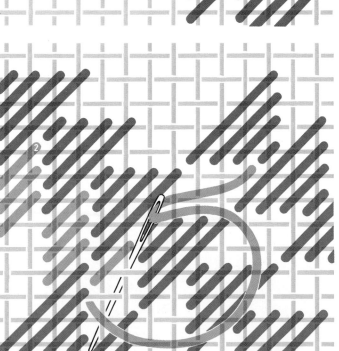

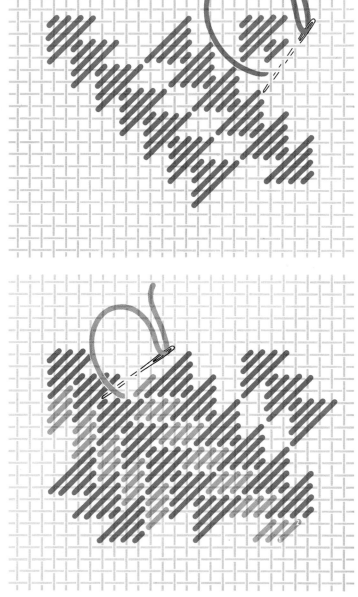

Needlepoint stitches

Diagonal stitches

Kalem stitch

Stem stitch

KALEM STITCHES

The Kalem stitch, and its variation, the stem stitch, form braid-like patterns on the canvas. The pattern that emerges from the Kalem stitch, as shown here, travels across the canvas; the stem stitch pattern goes up and down. Both patterns are composed of rows of diagonal stitches, with the stitches in each successive row slanted the opposite way from the stitches in the preceding row. The stem stitch also involves backstitches between paired rows of diagonal stitches. Both Kalem and stem stitches can be used for small or large design areas; the Kalem stitch is suitable for use in rugs.

Kalem stitch: Begin at upper right and work rows alternately from right to left, then left to right. Each stitch is taken over one crosswise by two lengthwise canvas threads. When working rows from right to left, bring needle out at base of stitch, 1, and in at top of stitch, 2. When working rows from left to right, reverse the slant of the stitches by bringing the needle out at top of stitch, 3, and in at base of stitch, 4. Rows of stitches are formed directly below one another.

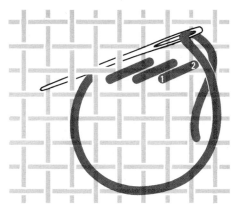
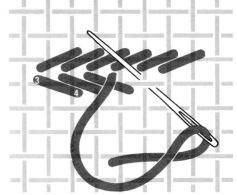
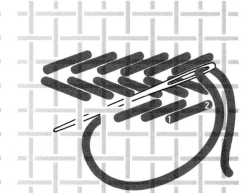

Stem stitch: Start at upper left and work in groups of three rows. One row of diagonal stitches is worked down the canvas, a second up; a third row, of backstitches (see p. 138), is worked down the canvas, between the first two rows. Form each diagonal stitch over two meshes. When working stitches down the canvas, slant them up to the left, 1 to 2; when going up the canvas, slant them up to the right, 3 to 4. Work a backstitch, A to B, over every crosswise thread between bases of diagonal stitches. Form next repeat to right.

130

Straight stitches

The stitches in this group are called straight stitches because all of them, except for the backstitch done diagonally, are formed to lie parallel to the threads of the canvas. In most instances, the stitches are parallel to the lengthwise canvas threads. Two exceptions are the darning stitch and the backstitch done horizontally; these lie parallel to the crosswise threads. The straight-stitch group also includes the Florentine stitch and its variations. These produce the familiar zigzag stitch patterns that are associated with Bargello. Bargello and its particular techniques are explained in more detail starting on page 173.

STRAIGHT GOBELIN STITCHES

The straight Gobelin and the encroaching straight Gobelin stitches are comparable in their formation, but not in the patterns they produce. The visual difference is caused by the way rows of stitches are placed in each case. Straight Gobelin stitches result in a definite row-by-row pattern because each row of stitches is separate from the other. Encroaching straight Gobelin stitches form a uniform texture because the rows overlap. Both stitches can be varied in length (see below) to suit canvas areas of any size.

Straight Gobelin stitch

Encroaching straight Gobelin stitch

Straight Gobelin stitch:
Start at upper right; work rows alternately right to left, then left to right. For each stitch, bring needle out at 1, pass it up over the canvas, down into 2. Space between 1 and 2 can be from two to five crosswise threads. Spacing here is two crosswise threads. At the end of each row, reverse working direction; place new stitches so their bases (1) are one stitch length below bases of stitches in preceding row.

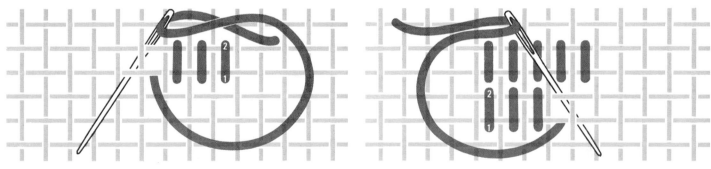

Encroaching straight Gobelin stitch: Start at upper right and work rows alternately right to left, then left to right. For each stitch, bring needle out at 1, pass it up over the canvas, down into 2. Space between 1 and 2 can vary as for straight Gobelin stitches. Space shown here is three crosswise canvas threads. At each row's end, reverse working direction. Position tops (2) of new stitches one crosswise thread above, but consistently to the left or right of the bases of the stitches in preceding row (tops here are to the left).

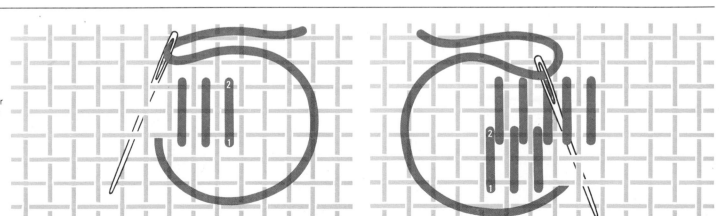

Needlepoint stitches

Straight stitches

Brick stitch

Gobelin filling stitch

BRICK STITCHES

The brick stitch and the Gobelin filling stitch are alike in that each produces a very similar pattern. Each individual brick stitch, however, is only two canvas threads long, whereas each Gobelin filling stitch is six threads long. Another similarity between the two is that the methods of row formation (shown below for both of the stitches) are interchangeable. The row method illustrated for the brick stitch produces single rows of stitches, each of which forms a zigzag pattern across the canvas. With the row method that is shown for the Gobelin filling stitch, this same zigzag effect is produced after two rows.

Brick stitch: Starting at upper right, work rows alternately right to left, then left to right. Each row makes use of three crosswise canvas threads, but each stitch spans only two of these threads. Placement of stitches alternates in each row, first being over the top two threads, then over the lower two threads. For each stitch, bring needle out at 1, insert at 2. At each row's end, reverse working direction. Position bases (1) of new stitches one stitch length below bases of stitches in preceding row.

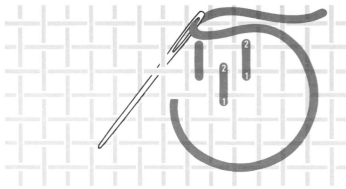

Gobelin filling stitch: Start at upper right and work rows alternately from right to left, then left to right. For each stitch, bring needle out at 1, up over six crosswise canvas threads, then down into 2. Position bases (1) of stitches one canvas hole apart. At the end of each row, reverse working direction. Position new stitches so that their top halves are between the stitches of the preceding row.

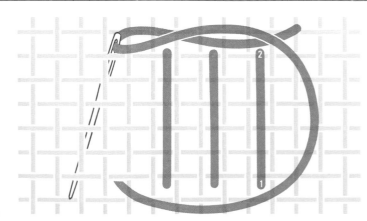

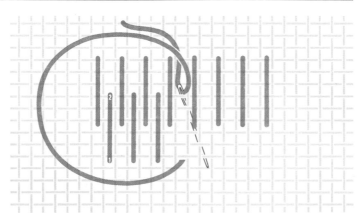

Florentine stitch

Two variations of the Florentine stitch

FLORENTINE STITCHES

The Florentine stitch and its variations form the zigzag patterns used so often in the type of needlepoint known as Bargello. The high points of the zigzag are referred to as peaks, the low points as valleys. Each row consists of straight stitches placed next to each other in a diagonal arrangement up and down the canvas. The diagonal effect results from the "step" between stitches. **Step** is the term for the number of crosswise canvas threads between the bases of neighboring stitches. A kind of shorthand is used to specify stitch length and step. Given as two numbers separated by a period, for example, 3.1, the first number means stitch length, the second number stands for the step between the stitches. The amount of step is always less than the length of the stitch. The pattern of a Florentine stitch is arrived at by manipulating the number, length, and steps of the stitches. In its basic form, the Florentine stitch has an even peak-and-valley pattern. This can be varied in many ways; two are shown here. For more on Florentine stitches, see page 173.

Florentine stitch: Work first row in two movements across horizontal center of canvas, from vertical center to left, then from center to right. Work subsequent rows in one movement, from right edge to left, or left to right. Place rows above or below first row, fitting stitches of each new row into jagged edge of preceding row. Overall pattern is usually a repeat of several rows; three-row repeat is shown here with second two above the first. In each row, there can be from three to eight stitches between valley and peaks (four shown). Stitches can be two to eight crosswise canvas threads long; step must be at least one less than the stitch-length number. Stitches in all of these rows are four threads long with step of two between stitches (4.2).

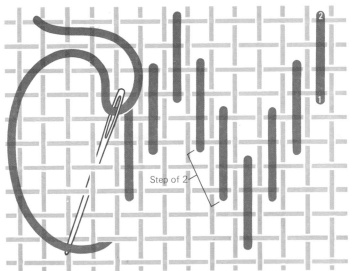

Step of 2

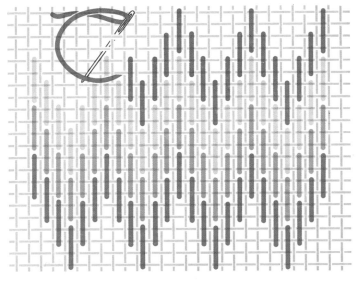

Needlepoint stitches

Straight stitches

One way to vary Florentine stitch is to work rows that form peaks and valleys of varying sizes. This general pattern of uneven points is called flame stitch. There is no set pattern; you can design your own. In general, the more stitches used between peak and valley, the longer those stitches, and the greater the step between stitches, the higher the point will be. Usually, the stitches of any one row are the same length; the step between them can vary to give an even more undulating look to the row. The stitch length used for each subsequent row can be different from the first, but the step plan established by the first row should be maintained. At the immediate right the first row is being done; in the compressed drawing, far right, the first row is the center row. Notice how the step change is maintained even though a different stitch length is used for each row.

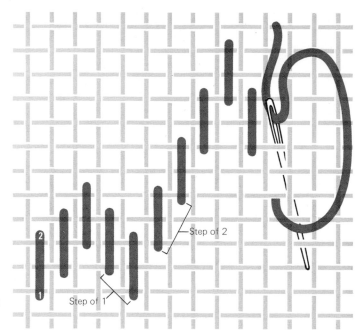

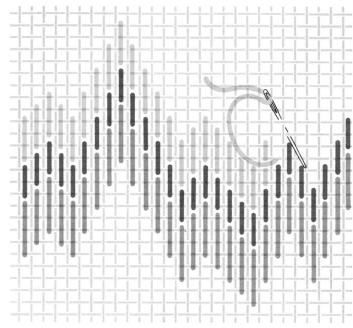

Another way to vary Florentine stitches is to round off the peaks (and valleys, not shown). This is achieved through the use of blocks of stitches. There can be two or more (usually up to six) in each block. The number of blocks used to round off the point can vary. In general, the more blocks used, and the more stitches in each block, the rounder the point will be. The stitches in each block are the same length; the step between blocks can vary with the length of stitch used. The row pattern can include pointed and rounded peaks and valleys. The block and step plan established by the first row (top row in compressed drawing) is maintained by the other two. It is not necessary, however, for the stitch length to be the same in each row.

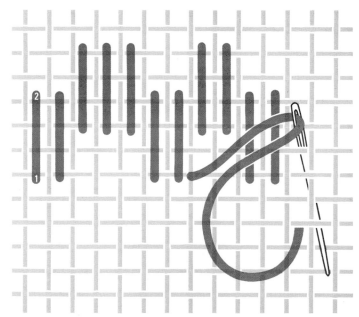

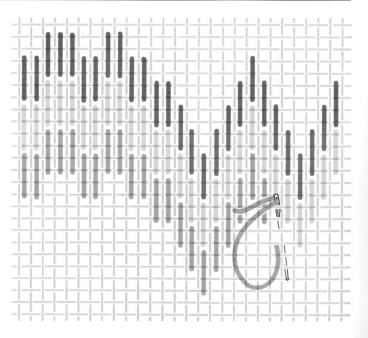

Hungarian stitch

Hungarian diamond stitch

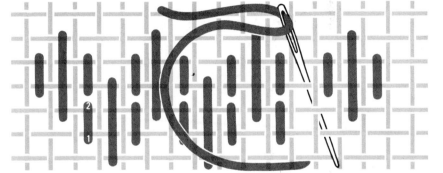

Hungarian grounding

HUNGARIAN STITCHES

Both the Hungarian stitch and the Hungarian diamond stitch produce patterns of diamond-shaped units across the canvas. Each of the diamond-shaped units of the Hungarian stitch is small and consists of three stitches. The diamonds of the Hungarian diamond stitch are larger because each unit consists of five stitches. The pattern of Hungarian grounding is achieved by alternating rows of Hungarian stitches with rows of Florentine stitches. Any of these stitches is excellent for filling in large or background areas of a needlepoint design.

Hungarian stitch: Start at upper right; work rows alternately right to left, left to right. Each row is a repeated grouping of three stitches to form diamond-shaped units. For each unit, work one stitch over two crosswise canvas threads, 1 to 2, next a stitch over four threads, 3 to 4, then another over two threads, 5 to 6. Skip one canvas hole to start next unit. At each row's end, reverse direction; work new units so tops of long stitches are between units of preceding row.

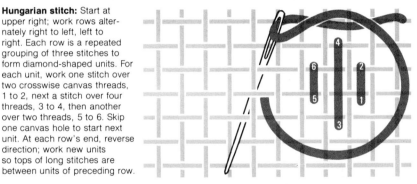

Hungarian diamond stitch: Begin at upper right and work rows alternately right to left, then left to right. Each row is a repeated grouping of five stitches to form large diamond-shaped units. Form each unit as follows: Work one straight stitch over two crosswise canvas threads, 1 to 2, a longer stitch over four threads, 3 to 4, another over six threads, 5 to 6, followed by a stitch over four threads, 7 to 8, then another over two threads, 9 to 10. Skip one canvas hole to start next unit. At end of each row, reverse working direction. Position new diamond units so that the tops of the longest stitches fall between the diamonds of the preceding row.

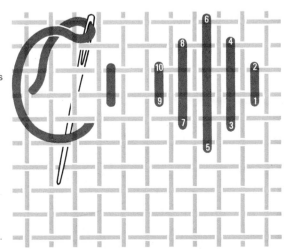

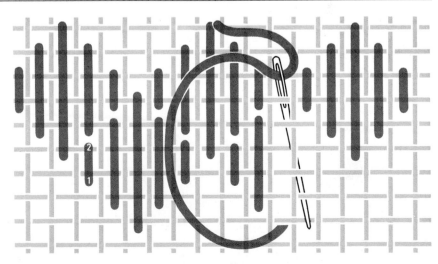

Needlepoint stitches

Straight stitches

Hungarian grounding: Start by working a row of Florentine stitches across center of canvas (p. 133). Form its even peaks and valleys three stitches deep, using stitches four threads long with a step of one between them. Then work a row of Hungarian stitches, placing longest stitches of each unit below the peaks of the Florentine. Below this, work a row of Florentine, placing its valleys below longest stitches of the Hungarian-stitch units. Continue alternating stitch rows; turn canvas to stitch open area of canvas in the same way.

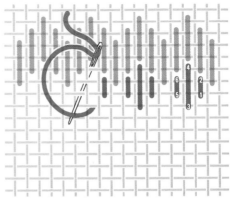
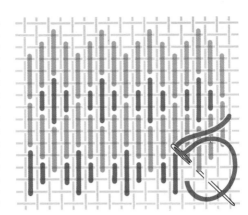

Parisian stitch

Old Florentine stitch

PARISIAN STITCHES

The Parisian stitch forms an irregular texture across the canvas; the old Florentine stitch produces a very large pattern resembling the surface of a woven basket. The size difference between these two patterns is caused by the size of the individual stitches, Parisian stitches being shorter than old Florentine. The row structure for both Parisian and old Florentine stitches is very similar (see below and facing page). Stitches in each row of Parisian alternate from one short to one long stitch; stitches in each row of old Florentine alternate two short stitches with two that are very long.

Parisian stitch: Start at upper right and work rows alternately right to left, then left to right. For each row, alternately form a short stitch over two crosswise canvas threads, 1 to 2, then a long stitch over four threads, 3 to 4. At end of each row, reverse working direction. Position new stitches so that the tops (2) of the short stitches are in the same canvas hole as the bases of the long stitches in the preceding row.

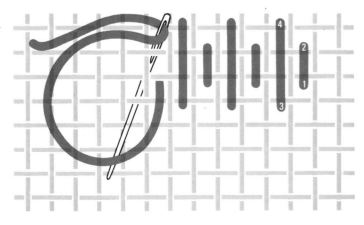
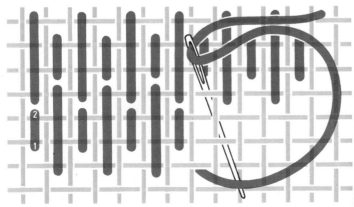

Old Florentine stitch:
Start at upper right; work rows alternately from right to left, then left to right. For each row, alternately form two short, then two long stitches. Work each short stitch over three crosswise canvas threads, 1 to 2 and 3 to 4; form each long stitch over nine threads, 5 to 6 and 7 to 8. At end of each row, reverse working direction. Position new stitches so that the tops of the short stitches (2 and 4) are in the same canvas holes as the bases of the long stitches of the preceding row.

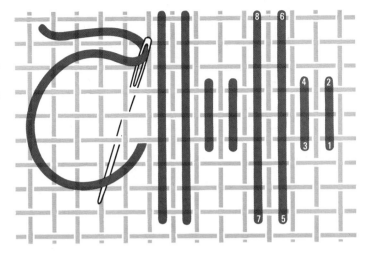
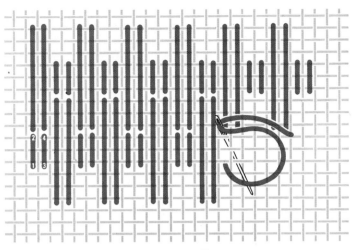

DARNING STITCH

The darning stitch produces a very tightly stitched surface on the canvas. For each row of darning stitches, the yarn is woven across the canvas in four journeys (complete spans) to form interlocking long and short stitches within the space of two crosswise canvas threads. The sample has been enlarged to make the stitches easier to see.

Darning stitch

Enlargement of darning stitch

Darning stitch: Work each row in four journeys (full spans) across the canvas, within the space of two crosswise canvas threads. Starting at upper left, work first journey to the right, forming long stitches as follows: Bring needle out at 1, over four lengthwise threads (1 to 2) then under two (2 to 1). At end of journey, reverse direction. Work second journey to the left, forming short stitches as follows: With needle out at 1, pass over two lengthwise threads (1 to 2) then under four (2 to 1). Work third journey like the first; work the fourth like the second. Form the next set of journeys between the next two crosswise canvas threads (1).

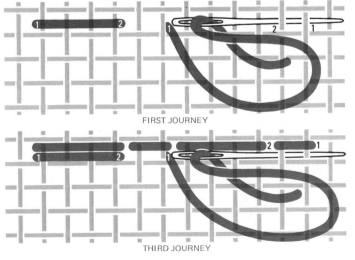

FIRST JOURNEY

SECOND JOURNEY

THIRD JOURNEY

FOURTH JOURNEY

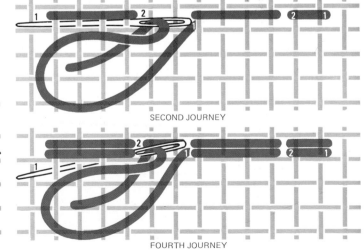

Needlepoint stitches

Straight stitches

Backstitch (done horizontally)

Backstitch (done vertically)

Backstitch (done diagonally)

BACKSTITCHES
In needlepoint, backstitches are never used to cover an entire area of blank canvas. Rather, they are used as single rows of stitches to outline a stitched area of a needlepoint design, or to cover the canvas threads left exposed by another needlepoint stitch (see diamond eyelet, p.153). They can be worked in all directions on the canvas.

Backstitch (done horizontally): Work rows either right to left or left to right. When working right to left, point needle to left; when working left to right, point needle to right. For each stitch, bring needle out at 1, pass it back over one lengthwise thread, into 2. To start next stitch, pass needle under two lengthwise threads.

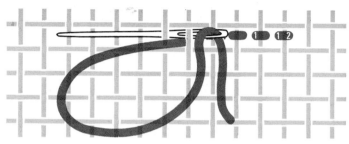

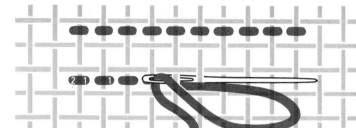

Backstitch (done vertically): Rows can be worked down or up the canvas. When working down, have needle pointing down; when working up, have needle pointing up. Form each stitch as follows: Bring needle out at 1, pass it back over one crosswise canvas thread, then into 2. Pass needle under two crosswise threads to start the next stitch.

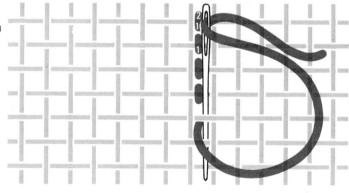

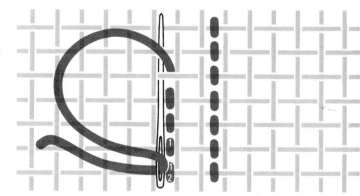

Backstitch (done diagonally): Rows can be worked diagonally up or down the canvas, to span canvas right to left, as shown, or left to right. When working down, have needle pointing down; when working up, have needle pointing up. For each stitch, bring needle out at 1, pass it back over one mesh, into 2. Pass needle under two meshes to start next stitch.

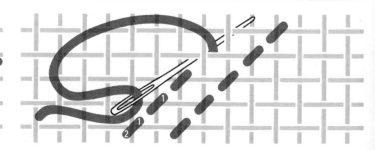

Crossing stitches

The stitches in this group are classified as crossing stitches because each of their patterns is achieved through the use of stitches that cross over each other. Some stitches are diagonal, some straight. Some of the stitches involve only two stitches for each unit; the cross stitch is an example. In others, there are more than two, eight in the double leviathan stitch, for instance. The crossing of the stitches occurs, for the most part, within each individual unit or within a row of units. Exceptions are the plaited and perspective stitches; in these two cases, the crossing takes place between two rows of diagonal stitches.

CROSS STITCHES

A cross stitch consists of two diagonal stitches crossing at the center. Generally a cross stitch spans only one canvas mesh and its upper stitch slants the same as a tent stitch. Cross stitches can be formed in two ways. Use either method to form any size cross stitch on interlock or penelope canvas; to form one-mesh cross stitches on plain mono canvas, use Method I below. To alter the slant of the upper stitch of any cross stitch, see the bottom of the next page.

Cross stitch with upper stitch slanting same as tent stitch

Cross stitch variation (upper stitch slanting opposite to tent stitch)

Cross stitch (Method I, done horizontally): Start at upper left; work rows alternately from left to right, then right to left. For each cross stitch, form the lower stitch first, coming out at 1 and going in at 2. Then form the upper stitch, bringing the needle out at 3, up over the 1-2 stitch, then inserting it at 4. At end of each row, reverse working direction and form the new stitch row directly below the stitches just completed.

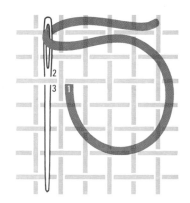

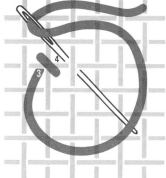
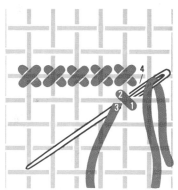

Cross stitch (Method I, done vertically): Start at upper left; work each row down the canvas. For each cross stitch, form the lower stitch first, coming out at 1, going in at 2. Then form the upper stitch over the lower, coming out at 3 and going in at 4. At end of each row, finish last stitch, but leave needle at back of canvas. Then turn the canvas completely around and form the new row of stitches next to those just completed.

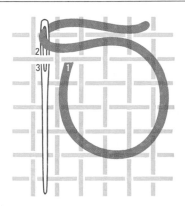
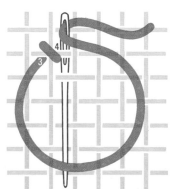

CANVAS TURNED

139

Needlepoint stitches

Crossing stitches

Cross stitch (Method II, done horizontally): Start at upper right; work each row of cross stitches in two spans—first from right to left, then left to right. When working from right to left, form lower stitches of the cross stitches by bringing needle out at 1, inserting at 2. At end of span, reverse work direction. Working from left to right, form the upper stitches of the cross stitches by bringing needle out at 3, over the 1-2 stitch, then in at 4. Work next row of cross stitches below those just completed.

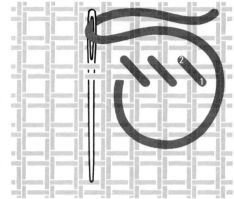 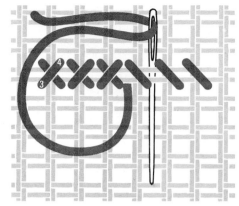 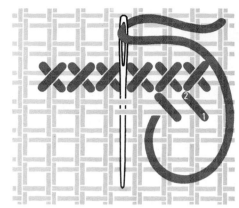

Cross stitch (Method II, done vertically): Start at upper right; work each row of cross stitches in two spans—first down, then up the canvas. When working down, form the lower stitches of the cross stitches by bringing needle out at 1 and inserting it at 2. At end of span, reverse working direction. Working upward, form the upper stitches of the cross stitches, bringing needle out at 3 and over 1-2 stitch, then inserting it at 4. Work next row of cross stitches to left of those just completed.

 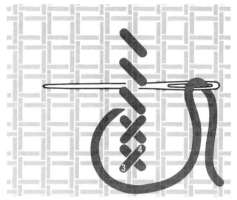 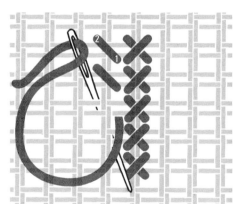

To reverse slant of upper stitch, change way of forming the upper and lower stitches of the cross. The easiest way to understand this is by comparing steps 1 to 2 (the lower stitch) and steps 3 to 4 (the upper stitch) at the right with the 1-2 and 3-4 steps shown above (Method II) and on preceding page (Method I). If you use Method I, the working direction of rows, whether horizontal or vertical, stays the same. With Method II, reverse directions, starting at upper left to work rows horizontally; at lower left to work rows vertically.

 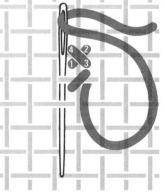 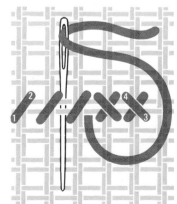 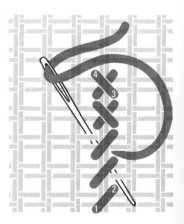

Oblong cross stitch

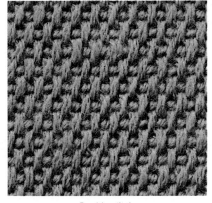

Oblong cross stitch with backstitch

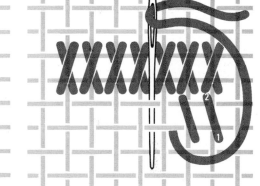

Double stitch

OBLONG CROSS STITCHES

The oblong cross stitch is an elongated cross stitch consisting of two diagonal stitches that cross each other to span a rectangular area of the canvas. All three of the stitch samples shown here use oblong cross stitches either by themselves or in combination with other stitches. First sample is of plain oblong cross stitches. The middle sample is of oblong cross stitches each of which has a backstitch across its center. The last sample is of the double stitch, in which oblong cross stitches alternate with one-mesh cross stitches. For a two-color version of the double stitch, see page 160.

Oblong cross stitch: Starting at upper right, work each row in two spans across the canvas. First work from right to left, forming lower stitches of each oblong cross stitch, 1 to 2. Space between 1 and 2 is two crosswise by one lengthwise canvas thread. Then, at end of span, work row back to right, forming upper stitches of each oblong cross stitch, 3 to 4. Space between 3 and 4 is same as between 1 and 2. With each new row, position bases of new stitches (1 and 3) one stitch length below the stitches of the preceding row.

Oblong cross stitch with backstitch: Start at upper right; work rows alternately from right to left, then left to right. For each stitch, form an oblong cross stitch, 1 to 2 and 3 to 4, then work a backstitch over the center of the cross stitch, 5 to 6. Size of oblong cross stitch is same as above; 5-6 stitch is over one lengthwise canvas thread. At each row's end, change work direction. Place bases of new stitches (1 and 3) one stitch length below stitches just done; reverse direction of 5 to 6 so a backstitch is formed.

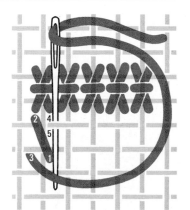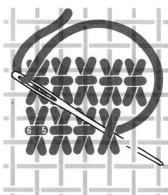

Needlepoint stitches

Crossing stitches

Double stitch: Start at upper left and work rows alternately left to right, then right to left. For each row, alternately form oblong and regular cross stitches. Work each oblong cross stitch over three crosswise by one lengthwise canvas thread, 1 to 2, 3 to 4; work each regular cross stitch over one mesh, 5 to 6, 7 to 8. At end of each row, reverse working direction. Place new stitches so that tops of oblong cross stitches (2 and 4) are in same canvas holes as bases of the regular cross stitches of the preceding row.

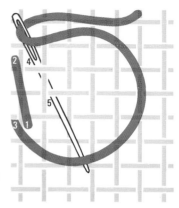 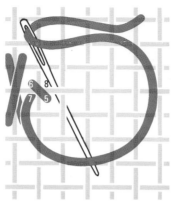  

Upright cross stitch

Double cross stitch

UPRIGHT CROSS STITCHES

Each upright cross stitch is composed of two straight stitches that cross at their centers. The lower stitch lies parallel to the lengthwise threads of the canvas; the upper stitch is parallel to the crosswise canvas threads. By themselves, upright cross stitches produce a pebbly texture on the canvas. Used in combination with large regular cross stitches, they become the double cross stitch pattern. The double cross stitch creates a lovely latticework pattern, which can be made even more dramatic and striking by working it in two yarn colors. For two-color working techniques, see page 160.

Upright cross stitch: Start at upper left and work rows alternately from left to right, then right to left. For each upright cross stitch, bring needle out at 1, in at 2, then out at 3 and in at 4. Each upright cross stitch can span two or four lengthwise by crosswise canvas threads (span of two is shown). At each row's end, reverse working direction. Place new stitches so their tops (2) share a canvas hole with neighboring horizontal stitches in the preceding row.

 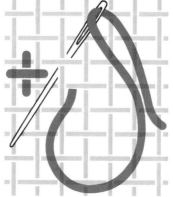  

Double cross stitch: Start at upper left; work rows left to right, then right to left. For each row, alternately form a large cross stitch to span four by four canvas threads, 1 to 2 and 3 to 4; then form an upright cross stitch over two by two threads, 5 to 6 and 7 to 8. At each row's end, change work direction. Place tops of new large cross stitches (2 and 4) in canvas holes of bases of large cross stitches in preceding row. Cover canvas with double cross stitch; form upright cross stitches between rows (A to B and C to D).

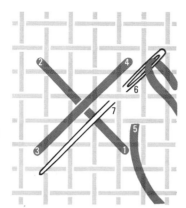 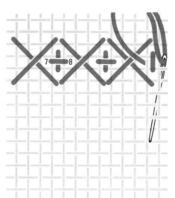 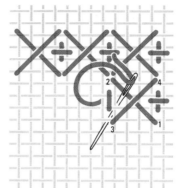 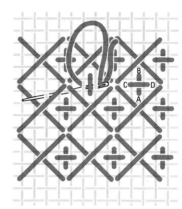

Double straight cross stitch

Leviathan stitch

Double leviathan stitch

DOUBLE STRAIGHT CROSS STITCH / LEVIATHAN STITCHES

All three of the patterns in this group form large, raised stitch units, each consisting of multiple layers of crossing stitches and spanning four crosswise by four lengthwise canvas threads. The resulting units, however, are different in shape. Units of the double straight cross stitch are diamond-shaped; those of both the leviathan and double leviathan stitches are square. A note of caution: These are very precise stitches, and to achieve their neat layering and distinctive look, you must follow the sequence of steps with great care.

Double straight cross stitch: Start at upper left and work rows left to right, then right to left. Form each stitch as follows: First, a large upright cross stitch that spans four by four canvas threads, 1 to 2 and 3 to 4; then, a large cross stitch, over center of upright cross stitch, spanning two by two threads, 5 to 6 and 7 to 8. Skip three canvas holes between bases (1) of stitches. At each row's end, change work direction. Place new stitches so tops (2) share canvas hole with neighboring horizontal stitches in row above.

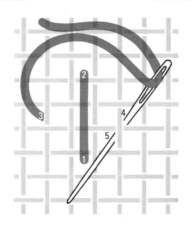 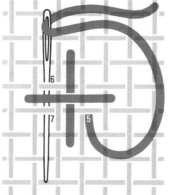  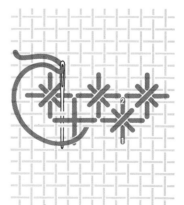

143

Needlepoint stitches

Crossing stitches

Leviathan stitch: Start at upper left and work rows from left to right, then right to left. Form each stitch as follows: First, a large cross stitch that spans four by four canvas threads, 1 to 2 and 3 to 4; then, a large upright cross stitch, over center of large cross stitch, that spans four by four threads, 5 to 6 and 7 to 8. At end of each row, reverse work direction. Place new stitches so tops (2, 6, and 4) share canvas holes with bases of stitches in row above.

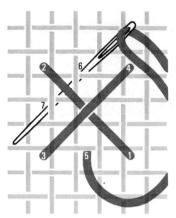
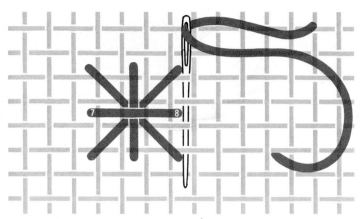
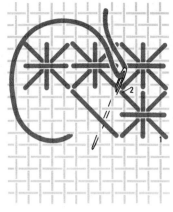

Double leviathan stitch: Start at upper left; work rows alternately left to right, then right to left. For each stitch, first form a large cross stitch over four by four canvas threads, 1 to 2 and 3 to 4. Then bring needle out at 5, up over the cross stitch and in at 6, out at 7. Pass needle down over cross stitch, in at 8, out at 9. Bring needle up over cross stitch, in at 10, out at 11. Pass needle down over cross stitch, in at 12, out at 13.

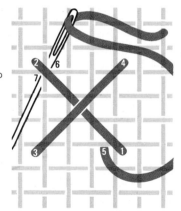
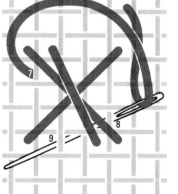
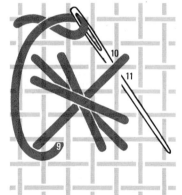
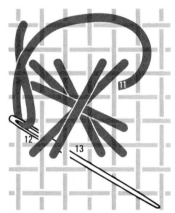

To complete the stitch, form a large upright cross stitch as follows: Bring needle from 13 up over the stitch and in at 14; then, out at 15, across the stitch, and in at 16. At the end of each row, reverse the working direction. Position stitches of new row so their tops (2, 6, 14, 10, and 4) share canvas holes with the bases of the stitches in the row just completed.

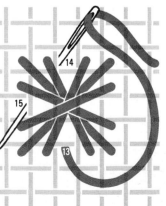
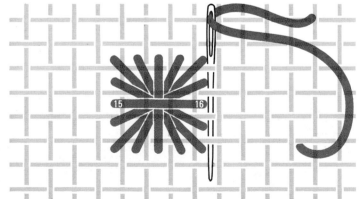

Knotted stitch

French stitch

Rococo stitch

KNOTTED STITCHES

These three patterns—the knotted stitch, French stitch, and rococo stitch—all involve long stitches that are held down to the canvas by short crossing stitches. In the knotted stitch, both the long and the short stitches cross diagonally over each other and over the canvas. In the French and rococo stitch patterns, long straight stitches are crossed by short straight stitches, but the long straight stitches become bowed in shape when the short crossing stitches have anchored them to the canvas. Of the three knotted types, the rococo stitch pattern is the largest and most dramatic.

Knotted stitch: Start at upper right; work rows alternately right to left, left to right. For each stitch, bring needle out at 1, over three crosswise and one lengthwise canvas thread, in at 2. Bring needle out at 3, over the 1-2 stitch, and in at 4. When working rows from right to left, work 3-4 stitch down over 1-2 stitch; working left to right, work 3-4 stitch up over 1-2 stitch. At each row's end, change working direction. Place tops of new stitches (2) one canvas hole above and to the right of bases of stitches just done.

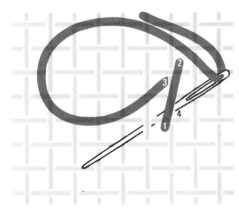
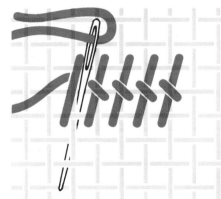
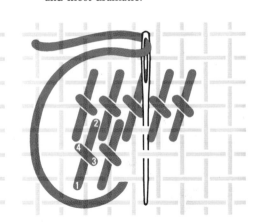

French stitch: Begin at upper right; work rows from right to left, then left to right. For each French stitch, form two tied-down straight stitches, both within the space of two lengthwise canvas threads. Work first stitch, 1 to 2 and 3 to 4; then second, 5 to 6 and 7 to 8. Start next stitch in second canvas hole from base of stitch just done. At each row's end, reverse working direction for rows and for horizontal stitches. Place new stitches between those of row above so their tops share canvas hole of neighboring horizontal stitches.

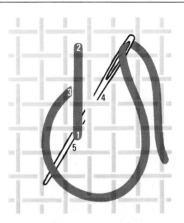
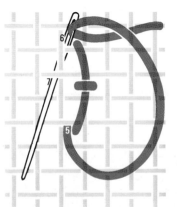
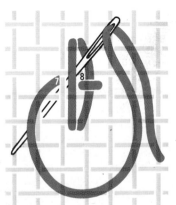
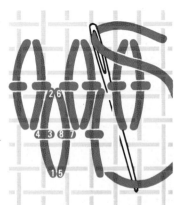

Needlepoint stitches

Crossing stitches

Rococo stitch: Begin upper right; work rows from right to left, then left to right. For each rococo stitch, form four tied-down straight stitches, all within the space of two lengthwise canvas threads, but fanned to span four threads. Work as shown, starting with the first stitch, 1 to 2 and 3 to 4, then the second, 5 to 6, 7 to 8, the third, 9 to 10, 11 to 12, then the fourth, 13 to 14, 15 to 16. Start next stitch in fourth canvas hole from base of stitch just done. Work new rows as shown (explained in French stitch, p. 145).

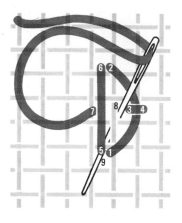  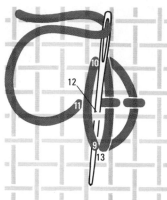 

Rice stitch

Enlargement of rice stitch

RICE STITCH
The rice stitch produces a very tightly stitched, well-covered canvas area. Each stitch unit consists of one large regular cross stitch and four additional small stitches, each of which crosses a corner of the larger base cross stitch. The sample at the far left shows rice stitches actual size; in the sample at the immediate left, an area of those stitches has been enlarged to show the pattern more clearly. If you wish, the rice stitch can be worked in two colors, the large cross stitches first in one yarn color, then the smaller crossing stitches in the other (see p. 160 for two-color techniques).

Rice stitch: Start at upper right; work rows alternately right to left, then left to right. For each rice stitch, first work a large cross stitch over two crosswise by two lengthwise canvas threads, 1 to 2 and 3 to 4. Form four small crossing stitches, each over a corner of the large cross stitch, 5 to 6, 7 to 8, 9 to 10, and 11 to 12. At end of each row, reverse working direction. Place new stitch units directly below those just completed.

 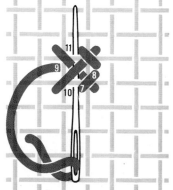  

FISHBONE STITCH / FERN STITCH

Though these stitch patterns are different in result—the fishbone stitch produces a wavy pattern across the canvas, the fern stitch up-and-down stripes—they are quite similar in technique. Both are worked in vertical rows; stitches in each row are crossed, this time off center. The rows of fishbone stitching are worked alternately down and then up the canvas; all fern stitch rows are worked down. Each fishbone stitch consists of a long diagonal stitch crossed at one end by a short crossing stitch. The fern stitch is made up of two stitches that cross one another at their lower ends.

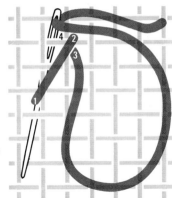
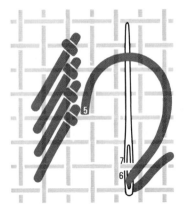
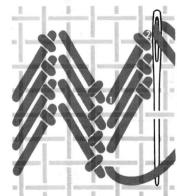

Fishbone stitch

Fern stitch

Fishbone stitch: Start at upper left and work rows down, then up the canvas. Each fishbone stitch consists of a long diagonal stitch that is crossed at one end by a short diagonal stitch. Each long stitch is over three crosswise and two lengthwise canvas threads; each short stitch is over one mesh. When working row down, work long stitch up, 1 to 2, and cross its top, 3 to 4. When working up a row, work long stitch down, 5 to 6, and cross its bottom, 7 to 8. Rows of stitches are formed next to each other.

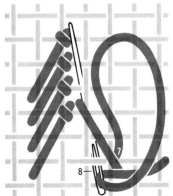

Fern stitch: Start at upper left; work all rows down the canvas. For each stitch, bring needle out at 1, down over two canvas meshes and in at 2; pass under one lengthwise thread, out at 3, up over two meshes and in at 4. Begin next stitch in canvas hole below the start of the stitch above (1). Form next row of stitches to the right of those just done.

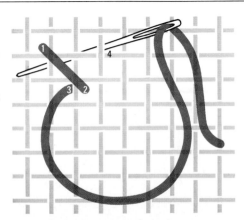

Needlepoint stitches

Crossing stitches

Herringbone stitch

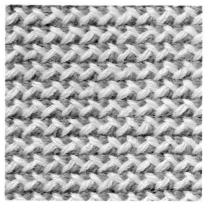

Double herringbone stitch

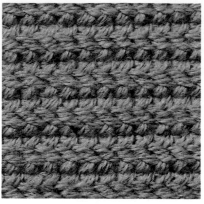

Greek stitch

HERRINGBONE STITCHES / GREEK STITCH

Both the herringbone stitch and its variation, the double herringbone stitch, form a tightly woven texture on the canvas. The Greek stitch produces a braid-like pattern. All three of these stitch patterns are worked in rows across the canvas; all rows consist of stitches that cross off center. Both of the herringbone stitches are strong enough to be suitable choices for rugmaking. The Greek stitch, however, is not as durable. The double herringbone stitch is usually worked in two contrasting yarn colors as shown at the left and explained below.

Herringbone stitch: Start at upper left; work all rows left to right. Consistently form stitches as follows: Bring needle out at 1, down over two canvas meshes and in at 2; then under one lengthwise thread, out at 3, up over two meshes and in at 4. Pass needle back under one lengthwise thread to start next stitch. Begin each new row of stitches in the canvas hole below the start of the stitches in the row above.

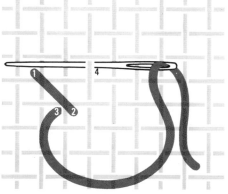

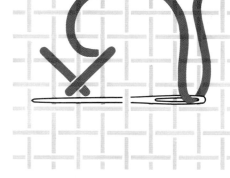

Double herringbone stitch: Begin at upper left; work all rows left to right. Cover the entire canvas area with rows of herringbone stitches (above) but space them by beginning each new row in second canvas hole below the start of the row above. Then go back and cover each of these rows with rows of "upside-down" herringbone stitches. Bring needle out at A, up over two canvas meshes, in at B; then back under one lengthwise thread, out at C, down over two meshes, in at D. Pass needle under a lengthwise thread to start next stitch.

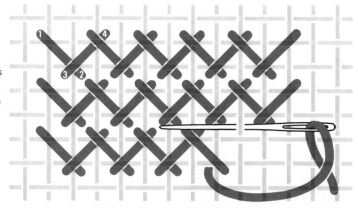

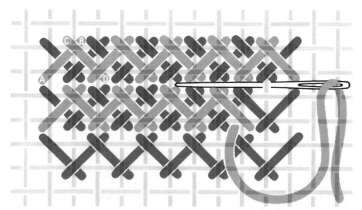

Greek stitch: Begin at upper left; work all rows from left to right. Form each stitch as follows: Bring needle out at 1, up over two canvas meshes and in at 2; then under two lengthwise threads, out at 3, and down into 4, the fourth canvas hole from start of stitch. Pass needle under two lengthwise threads to begin next stitch. End each row with a 1-2 stitch, then turn canvas completely around to work the next row of stitches. Start each row with a 1-2 stitch.

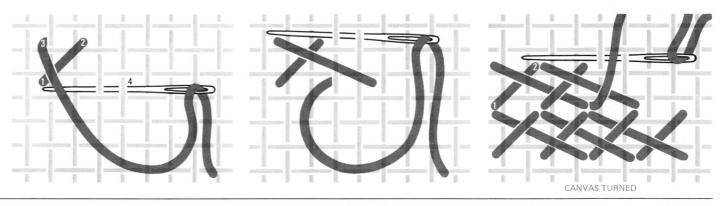

CANVAS TURNED

Plaited stitch

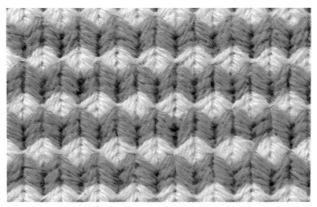

Perspective stitch

PLAITED STITCH / PERSPECTIVE STITCH

The plaited and perspective stitches are unique in the way that their individual stitches cross each other. With these two stitch patterns, the crossing of the stitches does not occur within single rows of stitches. Instead, the stitches of one row become crossed by the formation of the stitches in the next row. The plaited stitch produces the texture of a thick, woven fabric; the perspective stitch results in a pattern of three-dimensional boxes. The three-dimensional effect is strongest if the rows are done in varying shades of a single color as at the left.

Plaited stitch: Start at upper right and work rows right to left, then left to right. For each stitch, bring needle out at 1, up over four crosswise and two lengthwise canvas threads, then in at 2. Start next stitch in second canvas hole from base (1) of stitch just done. When working rows right to left, slant stitches back toward the right; when working left to right, slant stitches to the left. At each row's end, change working direction. Position new stitches so their tops (2) are in second canvas hole above bases of stitches just done.

Needlepoint stitches

Crossing stitches

Perspective stitch: Worked in series of four rows, each consisting of vertical groups of three diagonal stitches. Each stitch is over two canvas meshes; the working direction, and the slant of the stitches, alternate from group to group. Usually worked in contrasting colors as shown. Overall effect is best if the yarn colors alternate with each row.

For first row, start at 1 to 2 and work a group of three stitches, down the canvas, slanting each stitch from lower left to upper right. Then, at 3 to 4, work up the canvas, forming three stitches that slant from lower right to upper left. Continue to work across canvas, alternately working 1-2 and 3-4 stitch groups. At end of row, leave needle at back of canvas and turn canvas around.

Begin second row with a group of stitches slanted in a direction opposite to last group of preceding row. Start with a 1-2 or a 3-4 group, as needed; place all stitches of all groups to overlap groups of preceding row as shown. At end of row, turn canvas around.

Start third row with a group of stitches slanting the same way as the last group of row just completed. Start with a 3-4 or 1-2 group, as needed; position all stitches of all groups to "nest" below those of the preceding row. At end of row, turn canvas around.

For fourth row, begin with a group slanting in the opposite direction to that of the last group of the row just completed (3-4 or 1-2, as required). Overlap all stitches in this row with those in the preceding row (see far right). At end of fourth row, turn canvas. Following the same four-row procedure just described, cover the entire canvas area with perspective stitches.

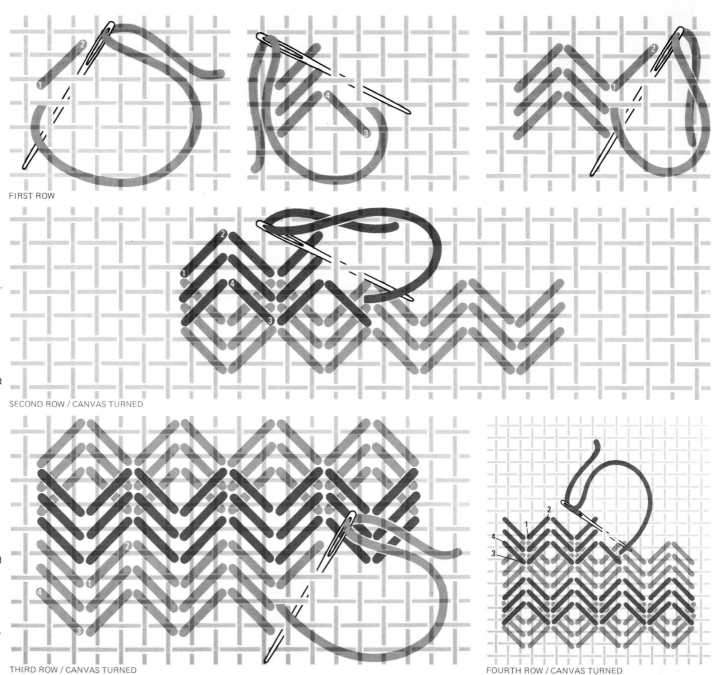

FIRST ROW

SECOND ROW / CANVAS TURNED

THIRD ROW / CANVAS TURNED

FOURTH ROW / CANVAS TURNED

Composite stitches

The stitches in this group are classified as composite stitches because each uses more than one of the other types of needlepoint stitches. For example, the Algerian eye stitch (below) makes use of straight and diagonal stitches; the triangle stitch (p. 155) contains straight and cross stitches. Except for the regular-size Algerian eye stitch, all the composite stitches are large, and produce definite shapes rather than overall textures. As can occur with any large stitch, the yarn may not completely cover the canvas threads. To help minimize the amount of canvas exposure, do not pull the yarn too tight while forming the stitches.

ALGERIAN EYE STITCHES

The Algerian eye stitches form star-like units on the canvas. Each unit, whether regular size or the enlarged version, consists of eight small stitches worked around a common canvas hole. When selecting yarn for this stitch, be sure that the yarn will be able to pass through the common canvas hole eight times without distortion. If the selected yarn does not adequately cover the canvas threads, form backstitches around each unit as shown at left and below.

Algerian eye stitch

Large Algerian eye stitch with backstitch

Algerian eye stitch: Begin at upper right and work rows alternately right to left, left to right. For each stitch unit, form eight small stitches, in a 1 to 8 sequence, around a center hole, A. Bring needle out at a number, over one mesh or thread, then in at center. When working rows right to left, work the eight stitches in a clockwise direction; when working rows from left to right, work them counterclockwise. Place the stitches of each new row below those of the preceding row.

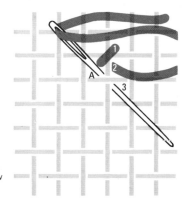

Large Algerian eye stitch:
This is a large version of the Algerian eye stitch (above). Row formation and stitch unit construction are the same; the difference is that each of the eight stitches is now taken over two canvas threads or meshes. With a large Algerian eye stitch, it can be difficult to cover the canvas completely. To cover canvas threads still exposed, form backstitches (see p. 138) around the stitch units. Use either the same or a contrasting color yarn (contrasting color used here).

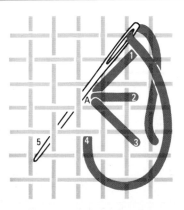
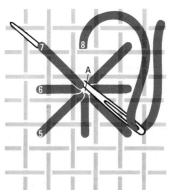
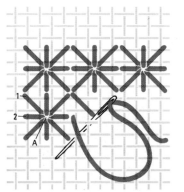
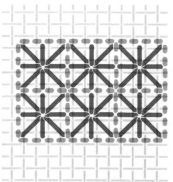

151

Needlepoint stitches

Composite stitches

Ray stitch

Expanded ray stitch

RAY STITCHES

Each ray stitch and expanded ray stitch consists of several stitches that radiate from a common canvas hole. The ray stitch consists of seven stitches that form a square; an expanded ray stitch comprises thirteen stitches that produce a rectangle. When selecting yarn for either of these stitches, choose one that is thin enough that the yarn of the multiple stitches will fit through the common canvas hole without distortion. While working either of these stitches, do not pull the yarn tight. For additional variety, alternate the yarn color with each unit or row of units.

Ray stitch: Begin at upper left and work rows alternately left to right, then right to left. Each ray stitch consists of seven stitches, fanned out around a common canvas hole, to cover a canvas area of three lengthwise by three crosswise canvas threads. Working counterclockwise and following a 1 to 7 sequence, begin each stitch at a number, end each in the common canvas hole, A. Fan each of the units as shown in the illustrations. At each row's end, reverse working direction; place new stitch units below those just done.

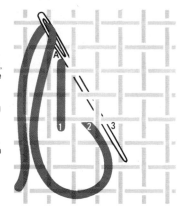
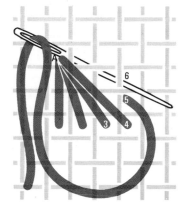
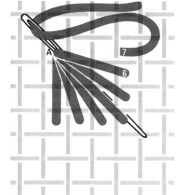
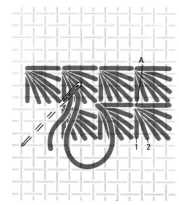

Expanded ray stitch: Start at upper left and work rows alternately left to right, then right to left. Each stitch unit consists of thirteen stitches, fanned out around a common canvas hole, to cover six lengthwise by three crosswise canvas threads. Work stitches in a 1 to 13 sequence. For each stitch, bring needle out at a number, in at A. When working row from left to right, work counterclockwise; when working row from right to left, work clockwise. Place stitch units of each new row below those of preceding row.

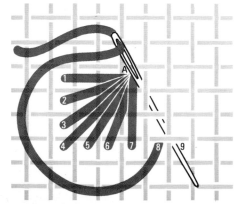
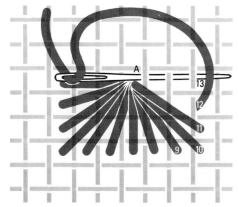

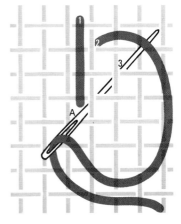

Diamond eyelet stitch

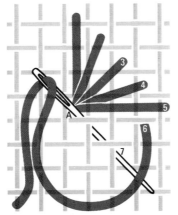

Diamond eyelet stitch with backstitch

DIAMOND EYELET STITCH

The diamond eyelet stitch is a pretty but large stitch. In fact, one diamond eyelet stitch can be used alone as a detail in a needlepoint design. Each unit is composed of sixteen stitches all emanating from one center canvas hole. Select yarn weight carefully so that it will pass through the same canvas hole sixteen times with no distortion. If the stitches do not adequately cover the canvas threads, backstitches can be worked over them (see left and below). Because of its long stitches, the diamond eyelet stitch is not recommended for items that will be subject to abrasion.

Diamond eyelet stitch: Begin at upper left and work rows alternately left to right, then right to left. Each diamond eyelet stitch consists of sixteen stitches that form a diamond-shaped unit over eight lengthwise by eight crosswise canvas threads. Start first stitch, 1, in the fifth canvas hole from the corner. Then, working clockwise, form the other stitches, 2 to 16, as shown. Begin each stitch at a number; end each in the center canvas hole, A. Start each new stitch unit in the eighth canvas hole from the start (1) of the unit just completed.

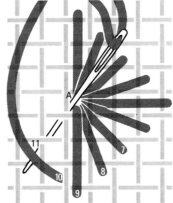

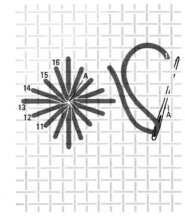

With each new row, reverse the working direction. Place new stitch units so that the first stitch, 1, shares a canvas hole with the horizontal stitches of the units in the preceding row. If desired, add backstitches (see p. 138) to cover the exposed canvas threads between the stitch units. Use the same or a contrasting color yarn.

153

Needlepoint stitches

Composite stitches

Leaf stitch

Leaf stitch with backstitch

LEAF STITCH

The leaf stitch is another relatively large stitch that can be used alone or in groups. Each leaf stitch uses eleven stitches to form a leaf shape. Five stitches are fanned to form the top of the leaf shape and there are three stitches, in a vertical row, on each side of the unit. If you want to make the leaf shape longer, increase equally the number of stitches in each vertical (side) row; the five stitches at the top remain the same. To give the leaf shape some additional detail, work backstitches in center of each unit; use the same or a contrasting color of yarn.

Leaf stitch: Start in upper left corner (at 1); work rows alternately left to right, then right to left. Each leaf stitch unit shown here consists of eleven stitches—three side stitches; five fanned out to form the top of the leaf; then three stitches for the second side. (Units can be made longer by working more but equal numbers of stitches on each side.) Work side stitches first, 1 to 6, then top stitches, 7 to 16, then other side stitches, 17 to 22. For each stitch, bring needle out at an odd number, in at an even number. When working rows from left to right, work stitches clockwise; when working right to left, work counterclockwise. Begin each new unit in the sixth canvas hole from the start (1) of the unit just completed.

With each new row, reverse direction for working rows and units. Position new units so their top parts are nested as shown along the lower edges of the units in the preceding row. For extra detail, backstitches (see p. 138) can be formed up or down the center of each leaf stitch unit. Color of yarn for the backstitches can be the same as or a contrast to the color used for leaf stitches.

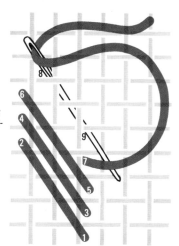

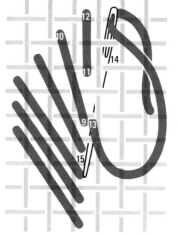

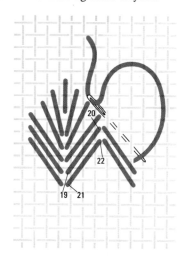

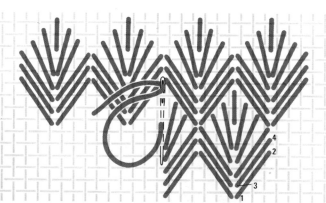

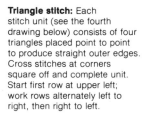

Triangle stitch (one color of yarn used)

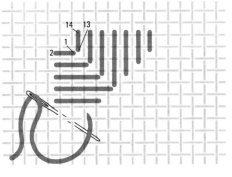

Triangle stitch (two colors of yarn used)

TRIANGLE STITCH

The triangle stitch, which is square in its overall shape, is made up of four triangular shapes placed point to point. A large cross stitch in each corner completes the unit and squares off its shape. The patterns produced by a grouping of several triangle stitches can be very interesting. When all the stitches are worked in the same color, the basic square shape of a unit will sometimes recede visually, while neighboring groups of triangles advance to form secondary patterns. Use of a second color increases the range of possible patterns.

Triangle stitch: Each stitch unit (see the fourth drawing below) consists of four triangles placed point to point to produce straight outer edges. Cross stitches at corners square off and complete unit. Start first row at upper left; work rows alternately left to right, then right to left.

For each inner triangular unit, work seven stitches, 1 to 14 as shown, bringing needle out at an odd number, in at an even number. Stitch top triangular unit first; work all units and stitches in a counterclockwise direction. Place triangles as shown, bringing needle out the same canvas hole for each of the four 7's. Although not shown, canvas can be turned a quarter to work each triangle.

Complete triangle stitch unit by working a large cross stitch (see p. 139), over two by two canvas meshes, in each of the four corners. Start in upper right corner and work cross stitches as shown, A to D. (Note: Working order of first cross stitch is different from other three.) Begin next triangle stitch in tenth canvas hole from start of stitch unit just done. With each new row, reverse direction for working row. Place new stitch units below those just completed.

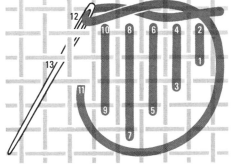

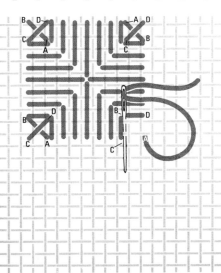

Needlepoint stitches

Composite stitches

Brighton stitch (one color of yarn used)

Brighton stitch (two colors of yarn used)

BRIGHTON STITCH

The Brighton stitch is produced by rows of diagonal stitches; these are worked in blocks and the slant of the stitches alternates from block to block. Each new row of stitches is a mirror image of the row above; sets of rows form a pattern of diamond shapes. An upright cross stitch in the center of each diamond completes the Brighton unit. The upright cross stitches can be worked in the same or a contrasting color of yarn, as shown in the samples at the left.

Brighton stitch: Rows consist of blocks of diagonal stitches. Each block has five stitches; the slant alternates with each block. Sets of rows form diamond-shaped units. An upright cross stitch is worked in center of each diamond.

Start at upper left; work all rows from left to right. Begin first row with a block of five stitches that slant from lower left to upper right, 1 to 10. Then work the next block of five stitches, slanting them from lower right to upper left, 11 to 20. Continue to work across the canvas, alternately forming 1-10 and 11-20 stitch blocks. At end of each row, leave needle at back of canvas and turn canvas around.

Begin each new row with a block of stitches that slant in a direction opposite to the slant of the last block in the row just completed. Start with either a 1-10 or an 11-20 block as required.

Cover entire canvas area with rows of stitches. Then, form an upright cross stitch in the center of each diamond, A to D, as explained on page 142.

FIRST ROW

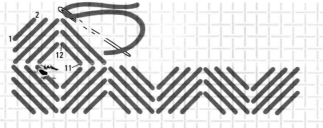

SECOND ROW / CANVAS TURNED

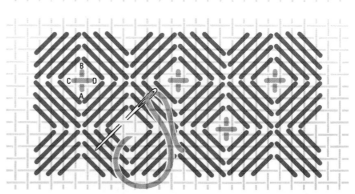

THIRD ROW / CANVAS TURNED

Pile stitches

There are only three stitches in this needlepoint stitch group. They are all alike in that each produces a texture that extends out from the surface of the canvas. This extended surface, referred to as a pile, is produced by the loops of yarn formed with the stitches. These loops may remain in their uncut form or they can be cut. The loop-cutting technique is explained on the next page with the velvet stitch; it can be used, however, for any of the three stitches in this group.

The pile stitches are most commonly used for rugs but they are suitable for any type of needlepoint item that calls for a pile surface.

RYA STITCH / VELVET STITCH / SURREY STITCH

Though these three stitches are alike in forming a pile surface, they differ in individual construction. Additional differences, pertaining to placement, can occur with each of the three. These stem from the type of canvas (mono, rug, or penelope) the stitch is being worked on, and are explained as they arise. For more about canvases, see page 114.

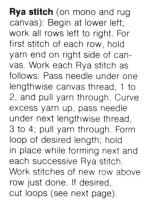
Rya stitch

Velvet stitch

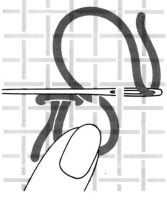
Surrey stitch

Rya stitch (on mono and rug canvas): Begin at lower left; work all rows left to right. For first stitch of each row, hold yarn end on right side of canvas. Work each Rya stitch as follows: Pass needle under one lengthwise canvas thread, 1 to 2, and pull yarn through. Curve excess yarn up, pass needle under next lengthwise thread, 3 to 4; pull yarn through. Form loop of desired length; hold in place while forming next and each successive Rya stitch. Work stitches of new row above row just done. If desired, cut loops (see next page).

  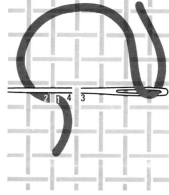 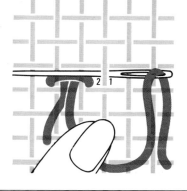  

Rya stitch (on penelope canvas): Stitch and row construction are same as above, but the placement of the stitch can vary. When using penelope canvas, each Rya stitch can be formed above two canvas meshes, like stitches above, or one mesh, as shown at right. To work a Rya stitch above one mesh of penelope canvas, spread double set of lengthwise threads and treat as single threads while forming the stitch. Pass needle under one thread, 1 to 2, then under the next thread, 3 to 4.

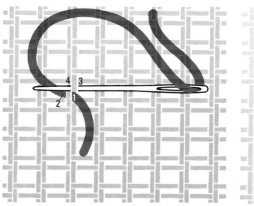  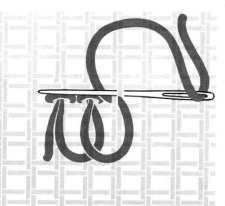

Needlepoint stitches

Pile stitches

Velvet stitch (on mono and rug canvas): Begin at lower left; work rows left to right. Work each velvet stitch as follows: Bring needle out at 1, up over two canvas meshes, in at 2, then out at 3 (same hole as 1). Form a loop of desired length; hold in place. Insert needle at 4 (same hole as 2), under two crosswise threads (or two sets of threads if using rug canvas), and out at 5 with point of needle under loop. Then pass needle back over two meshes and in at 6. Begin next stitch in same canvas hole as the 5 of the stitch just done.

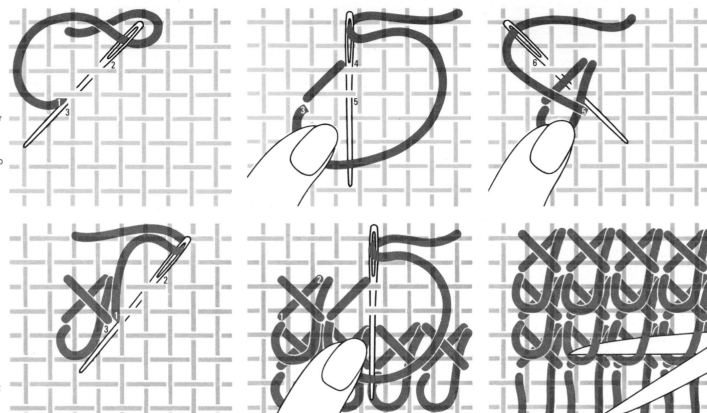

Work velvet stitches across the canvas, placing them next to each other. For each new row, begin at the left; place new stitches above those in the row just done. When all rows are completed, the loops can be cut, if so desired.

To cut the loops, open scissors and slide blade through a few loops (illustration at the far right). Cut the loops while slightly tugging on them with the scissors blade. Proceed to the next group of loops and cut them in the same manner.

Velvet stitch (on penelope canvas): Both row and stitch formation are the same as above. The only difference is another stitch-placement possibility permitted by the double-mesh canvas. Each velvet stitch can be worked over two meshes, as on mono canvas above; or over only one mesh, as at the right, following this procedure: Bring needle out at 1, over one double mesh, in at 2; out at 3, over the same mesh, and in at 4. Then under a set of crosswise threads, and out at 5; back over the double mesh, and in at 6.

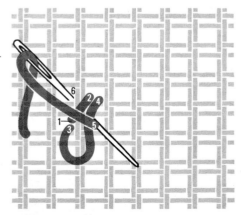

Surrey stitch (on mono and rug canvas): Start at lower left; work all rows left to right. For first stitch of each row, hold yarn end on right side of canvas. Work each Surrey stitch as follows: Insert needle at 1, pass under two crosswise threads (two sets of threads if using rug canvas), bring out at 2. Pull excess yarn through and curve up as in the second illustration. Bring needle over two meshes, in at 3, under two lengthwise threads, then out at 4 with point of needle over excess curved yarn. Pull yarn through. Form a loop of desired length; hold in place while forming the next and each successive Surrey stitch. For each new stitch, start in the same canvas hole as the 3 of stitch just done; make sure that when needle is brought out at 2, its point passes over the loop of yarn.

With each new row, start again at the left and place the new stitches above those in the row just done. When all rows are finished, the loops may be cut if so desired. Cutting of loops is explained on opposite page.

Surrey stitch (on penelope canvas): Row and stitch formation are the same as above. The only difference that can occur is in the placement of stitches. With penelope canvas, each Surrey stitch can be done over two meshes, as above, or over only one mesh, as are the stitches at right. When working a Surrey stitch over only one mesh of penelope canvas, consider the pairs of threads as single units and work stitch as shown, 1 to 2, then 3 to 4.

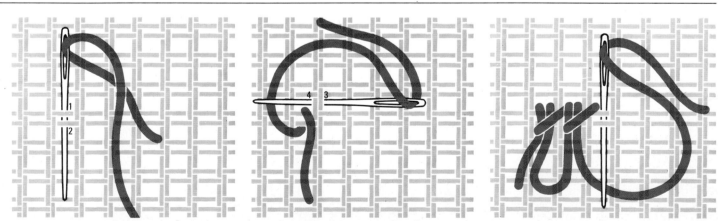

Needlepoint stitches

Additional stitching techniques

The technique discussed below, **multiple-color** stitching, is a process of forming a color pattern while working a needlepoint stitch pattern. The color designs can be formed by changing the yarn color with each row or by placing the various colors within the same row. The technique at the top of the opposite page, **compensating stitches,** concerns the formation of partial stitch patterns along the edge of an area. The last technique, **left-handed** stitching, is at the bottom of the facing page. It explains how the instructions and illustrations given for the stitches in this section can be adapted for use by a left-handed person.

MULTIPLE-COLOR STITCHING

The use of more than one yarn color to work an area of stitches actually produces two patterns. One is the pattern created by the stitch itself, the other results from the arrangement of the various colors. There are two different ways of introducing multiple yarn colors: row by row (Method I) or within a row (Method II). With both methods, the individual stitches are formed in their usual way but the procedure for working the rows of stitches is altered.

In **Method I,** the new yarn color is introduced with each row of stitches and the rows are worked in row-units, with each unit consisting of as many rows as there are colors. When rows are being worked normally, the working direction is reversed or the canvas is turned at the end of each row. When you are working with row-units, this change occurs with the first row of each new unit. With Method I, each color is threaded into a separate needle. If there is excess yarn at the end of a row, it is brought up to the right side of the canvas and secured away from the working area. When you are ready to work a new row in that color, the excess yarn is brought to the wrong side of the canvas to the point where the new row begins.

Method II places the multiple colors within a row of stitches. It works best when only two yarn colors are used for a stitch pattern that contains two stitch types. One such pattern is the double stitch, in which oblong cross stitches alternate with one-mesh cross stitches. First, all the rows of one stitch type and color are worked, leaving spaces for the other stitch type. Then, the other stitch type is worked in the spaces left, with the second color.

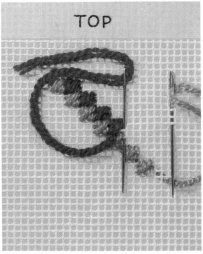

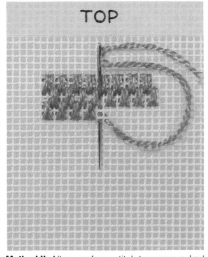

Method I: Stitch is worked as usual; colors change with each new row; rows are worked in units. The examples (both mosaic stitches) are worked in two colors so that two rows constitute a unit. Both rows in left sample are worked right to left; both in right sample are worked diagonally down.

Method II: All rows of one stitch type are worked as usual, leaving spaces for the second. Base stitches here are oblong cross stitches.

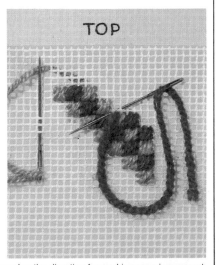

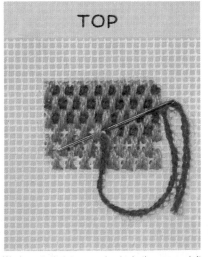

With first row of each new unit, canvas is turned around or the direction for working rows is reversed. Which it is depends on the way the rows of the stitch are usually done. Left sample was turned to work new unit; working direction was reversed in right sample.

Work next stitch type and color in the spaces left by first stitches. One-mesh cross stitches here complete the double stitch pattern.

160

COMPENSATING STITCHES

The photos below, details of the novelty stitch barn shown on page 113, illustrate compensating stitches in use. Compensating stitches are partial stitch patterns worked along the edge of a design area. They cover the open spans of canvas that are too small to hold full stitches of the pattern in that area. Their purpose is to maintain the effect of the area's stitch pattern (and color pattern) all the way out to its edges. They are formed along with the full stitches, and the length of each compensating stitch is equal to the span of canvas left between the edge and a full-size stitch.

LEFT-HANDED STITCHING

All of the stitches in this section are illustrated and explained for the use of a right-handed person. If you are left-handed, these illustrations and explanations can be adapted for your use.

To begin with, read and familiarize yourself with the way the stitch is done by a right-handed person. Then, when you are ready to work, turn the book and your canvas upside down. Begin working your stitches in the same corner that now appears in the upside-down illustration and work the row in the direction that it shows. Read the upside-down numbers in numerical order and follow that sequence for forming the stitch. If the instructions say to turn the canvas or reverse the working direction with each row of stitches, do so. If they indicate that all the rows are to be worked in one direction, work all your rows in the one direction that now appears in the upside-down illustration. Shown at the right are three needlepoint stitches. The top three illustrations show the stitches in the right-handed working order. The lower three show these same illustrations but turned to an upside-down position for left-handed use.

Continental stitches, done horizontally: Work from right to left; turn canvas with each row.

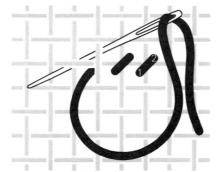

If left-handed, turn canvas upside down. Work from left to right; turn canvas with each row.

Mosaic stitches, done diagonally: Work first row down; reverse direction with each row.

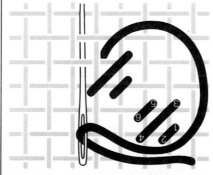

If left-handed, turn canvas upside down. Work first row up; reverse direction with each row.

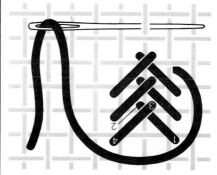

Fern stitches: Start at upper left and work all rows down the canvas.

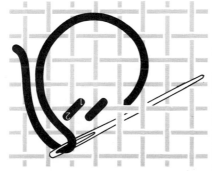

If left-handed, turn canvas, start in lower right corner and work all rows up the canvas.

161

Designing and working needlepoint

Design elements
Changing the direction of a stitch
Selecting working techniques
Basic preparations for working
Placing design on canvas
Understanding charts
Full design charts
Partial design charts
Half-charts
Quarter-charts
Multiple-repeat design charts
Charting a design

Design elements

The design used for any needlepoint is affected by several elements. With a kit, these elements have already been correlated so that all you have to do is stitch the design according to the instructions. When you are creating your own design, you must be aware of many things. First, you should know about the three different looks that needlepoint stitches can achieve (see p. 113). Also important is a familiarity with the primary tools of needlepoint, which are the canvases and yarns (pp. 114-115), and with the stitches (pp. 118-161). The more you know about these, the easier it will be for you to combine the design elements discussed on these two pages. (The elements described here do not pertain to the design of Florentine Bargello; for information about Florentine Bargello, see page 173.)

The most important element is the **design** itself. It should complement and be in proportion to the size and shape of the finished item. A design can consist of one motif on a plain background, or it can be a composition that fills the entire space. (Many compositions are repeats of a single motif; see pp. 170-171.) Most needlepoint designs are asymmetrical, that is, their components are different from area to area (barn design on p. 113 is asymmetrical). Some needlepoint designs are symmetrical in that their parts (halves or quarters) are mirror-images of each other (pp. 168-169). If you are good

at drawing, you can create a design. If you are not, trace the design from an existing source, such as a book, a plate, or a piece of fabric. While you are still working out the design, keep your drawing to a manageable size. It can be enlarged or reduced later, when you are ready to transfer it to canvas. (See Embroidery chapter for more on composing designs and on enlarging and reducing.)

The amount of detail in the design must also be considered; this determines the **gauge of canvas** you should use. A design with simple shapes or large masses of color can be carried out on a large-gauge canvas (under 10). A simple shape with moderate curves and some detail and color shadings can be done on medium-gauge canvas (from 10 to 14). Whether simple or complex, a design with strong curves, small details, and considerable shading will require a fine-gauge (16 to 20). An extremely delicate or small design could require a canvas even finer (over 20 gauge). The gauge of your canvas will affect the amount of time you spend stitching and the durability of the finished item. In general, the finer the gauge, the more time spent in stitching, but the more durable the final result. If you do not want to use the recommended gauge, you can either select another design better suited to the canvas you prefer, or adapt the design you have to the limitations of that canvas gauge.

For example, a very fine design can be re-drawn with larger details and less definite curves so that it will be suitable to a medium-gauge canvas.

How much detail your stitched design has will depend on the size and texture of the **stitches** you select. There are basically only two stitch categories, tent stitches and novelty stitches. Tent stitches are the smallest of the needlepoint stitches, and so do the best job of translating drawn lines or details. If you plan to use tent stitches, your design can be as detailed as the intended canvas gauge will allow. The novelty stitches (except for the one-mesh cross stitch) are larger than tent stitches and therefore less adapted to rendering drawn lines and small details. The beauty of the novelty stitches, however, is in the texture that each produces, and the way that these textures interpret design motifs. When drawing a design for novelty stitches, keep the lines simple and eliminate small details. How simplified these should be depends on the space needs of a particular stitch. Some of the smaller novelty stitches are capable of creating simple color shadings. The samples and illustrations in the stitch section will help you to determine the space requirements of particular stitches. Remember also that you can mix tent and novelty stitches in the same design. When drawing any design, place the lines and details as best you can;

Drawing of a leaf

Tent stitches on 18-gauge canvas

Tent stitches on 12-gauge canvas

they can be refined further as you work the stitches onto the canvas. If you want to be very accurate in your placement, the design can be charted (see p. 172). If your design is symmetrical or a multiple repeat, it should be charted.

Shown below is a leaf shape stitched onto four different gauges of canvas. The first three are worked with tent stitches, the fourth with the Byzantine stitch, a novelty stitch. All four were based on the same drawing, and each spans the same linear amount of canvas. The first tent-stitch leaf is on an 18-gauge canvas, the second on a 12-gauge, the third on a 7-gauge; the novelty-stitch leaf is on a 10-gauge canvas. Notice how the leaf shape becomes less detailed and its lines simpler as the gauge and the stitches grow larger. For another example of the change stitches can make in design lines and areas, compare the differences in the two stitched barns that are shown on page 113. Both samples were based on the same drawing of a barn scene.

With any needlepoint stitch, a portion of the textural effect comes from the way light strikes the yarn on the canvas. If you alter the direction the yarn (stitch) takes on the canvas, you also change the way the light hits the yarns. Changing the direction of a stitch is a simple working procedure, explained at the far right. This technique will affect any stitch except those, like the diamond eyelet, in

which the yarn is laid in all directions. It will also change the direction of some stitch patterns. For example, when the fern stitch is worked normally (p. 147), it produces a pattern of up-and-down stripes. When the fern stitch is worked with the method explained at the right, the stripes go across the canvas.

The type of **yarn** used to work a stitch will also affect its texture. Fuzzy, loosely twisted types, such as Persian yarn, produce a softer surface than do those that are more tightly twisted, such as tapestry yarn. Those that are inherently shiny, such as pearl cottons and the metallics, will add a bit of sparkle to the stitches. When deciding on the type of yarn to use, also consider its durability. Yarns that are made of wool, cotton, or acrylic are stronger than those made of rayon or metallic.

When selecting the **colors** for your design, choose a scheme that you like and that will enhance the design. Color schemes and their effects are discussed in the Embroidery chapter. When you have selected your colors, color in the drawing so that you can see how they look together. If you do not like the combination, experiment until you come up with one that pleases you. When you go to shop for yarns, use the colors in the drawing as a general guide. Yarns come in many shades, many more than most people have in paints or crayons.

Tent stitches on 7-gauge canvas

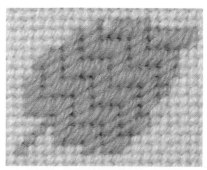
Byzantine stitch on 10-gauge canvas

Changing the direction of a stitch

To change the direction of a stitch or of its pattern on the canvas, work the stitch as usual, but hold the canvas so that its top edge is at the side. If the canvas needs to be turned around to work each new row of stitches, do so, but turn it so that the top edge alternates from right to left sides. The finished leaf at the left shows tent stitches slanting in opposite directions. The first illustration below shows the canvas with its top edge in the normal position to produce tent stitches with a normal slant (for the lower half of leaf). The second shows the canvas with its top at the side to produce tent stitches with the opposing slant (for the upper half of leaf). To avoid confusion while using this technique, label the top edge of the canvas.

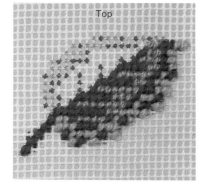

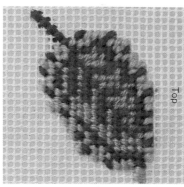

Selecting working techniques

There are many different working techniques in needlepoint; it is up to you to select the ones you will need to use. Many of the techniques pertain to the way the design is transferred to the canvas. These can be divided into methods for transferring uncharted designs (pp. 164-165) and charted designs (pp. 166-171). Techniques pertaining to Bargello, another class of charted designs, begin on page 173. Read all of these pages and choose the technique recommended for the type of design you are using. Before any design can be transferred to the canvas, the canvas must be prepared (p.164).

General working techniques that can be used with any type of design are described on the last few instructional pages of this chapter. The information on estimating yarn amounts enables you to calculate the quantities of yarns needed to stitch any design, especially one that you designed yourself. The other techniques—setting canvas into a frame, removing stitches, repairing canvas, blocking—will help you to make your needlepoint as perfect as possible. For ideas on needlepoint items and finishing techniques, see the projects at the end of the chapter.

Designing and working needlepoint

Design transfer needs 117
Miscellaneous equipment 117

Calculating yarn amounts 183
Blocking 185

Basic preparations

To work a needlepoint, you must first prepare a piece of canvas large enough to receive the design. "Large enough" means the finished size of the design plus a margin of at least 2 inches along each edge. When you are working with an uncharted design, finished size equals the dimensions of the drawing you will follow. When a design is charted, finished size depends upon the number of canvas threads called for by the chart in relation to the threads-per-inch in the canvas. If the canvas is too narrow, lengths can be joined to get the necessary width (center right). Before transferring the design, make a pattern of the prepared canvas (far right); it will be needed when it is time to block the worked canvas.

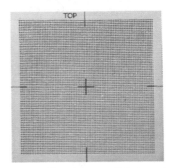

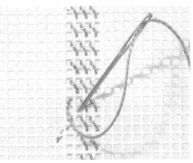

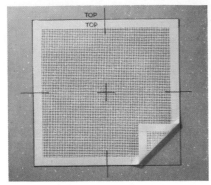

Basic preparation of canvas: Cut canvas to finished size of design plus a margin (2″ minimum) along each edge. Bind edges with tape; label top edge. Mark lengthwise and crosswise centers. If centers are on threads, mark at middle of canvas and on each side as above. If centers are between threads, yarn-baste (see p. 167).

To join lengths of canvas to produce necessary width: Cut two pieces to required length. Place side by side and cut off neighboring selvages. Overlap cut edges by 3 to 4 lengthwise threads and match all threads and meshes. Using strong thread, work down each row of matched threads, whipstitching around every other matched mesh.

To make a pattern of prepared canvas: Place canvas on a piece of brown paper and trace its outlines. Indicate top edge on paper and mark center of each edge. Keep pattern; it will be needed to block the worked canvas.

Placing the design on canvas/Method I

This design transfer method places both the shapes and the colors of the design on the canvas. The stitches are then worked right over the painted design. This method is recommended for use with any uncharted design, especially one that uses tent stitches only. Before a design of this type can be transferred, both the drawing and the finished size of the canvas must be equal to the finished size of the item for which the needlepoint is being done. To transfer the design to the canvas, use only waterproof coloring devices. If you are not absolutely sure about any coloring, do not use it; colors that are not waterproof might bleed while the worked canvas is being blocked. Use the painted canvas as a guide to calculate the amount of yarn that will be needed to stitch the design.

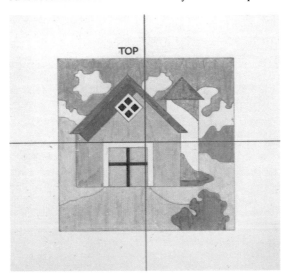

1. Draw a line down and another line across the center of the drawing. If necessary, label top edge and establish outer lines of design area. Prepare canvas as explained at top of page.

2. Place prepared canvas over drawing; match its center lines to those in drawing. Tack layers together and paint design onto canvas. Mimic shapes in drawing; use matching or similar colors.

3. When canvas is dry, work stitches right over the design. Work an area or a color at a time. Place stitches at the edges of an area as close as you can to its painted edges.

164

Placing the design on canvas/Method II

This method of transfer puts the lines of a design, but not its colors, on the canvas. It is recommended for use with any uncharted design, particularly one calling for some novelty stitches. Both the canvas and the drawing of the design are prepared as for Method I; if novelty stitches are being used, the name of the stitch is noted in appropriate areas on the drawing. To transfer the lines to the canvas, use markers that are waterproof and light and neutral in color. As you work a novelty stitch area, modify the size or shape of the area to conform to the space needs of the selected stitch. If you would prefer to check and perhaps adjust a novelty stitch area before transferring its lines to the canvas, chart the area and the stitch it involves as explained at the bottom of this page.

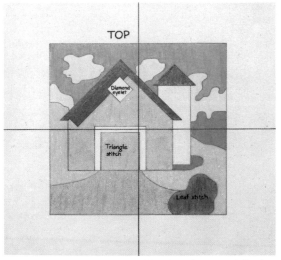

1. Draw a horizontal and a vertical line through center of drawing. Label each novelty stitch area with its name. Prepare the canvas as explained at the top of the preceding page.

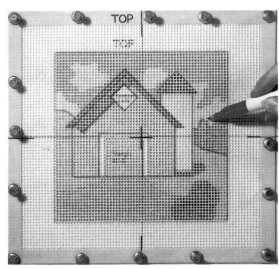

2. Place canvas on top of drawing and match center markings. Tack layers together and transfer lines of design to canvas. To chart an area before transferring its lines, see below.

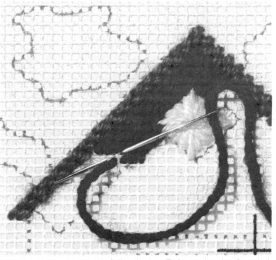

3. When canvas is dry, stitch the design. Refer to drawing for stitch and color placement. When you work novelty stitches, use compensating stitches to fill gaps, or alter area to fit stitch.

TO CHART AN AREA

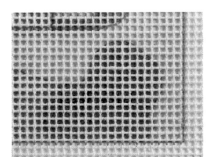

1. With the design area in position under the canvas, count out, at its widest points, the number of canvas threads that the area spans across and up and down. The area being checked here is the bush in the lower right corner of the full design. Leaf stitches are intended.

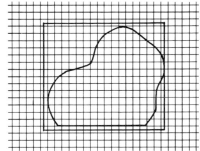

2. On a piece of graph paper (any gauge), count out these same totals in graphed lines and draw a box to enclose them. Then, referring to the area under the canvas, sketch its shape on the graph paper, crossing its lines in the same way as the lines cross the canvas threads.

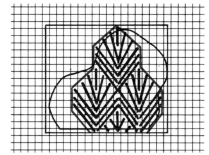

3. Sketch stitch pattern in outlined area. For help, see illustration in stitch section. If stitches nearly fill area, gaps can be filled with compensating stitches. If they cover too much or too little, adjust lines to fit stitch (above) or use a stitch better suited to the area.

4. Referring to the graph paper, transfer the area's outline (with changes, if any) to the canvas. Make sure that the lines cross the canvas threads the same way they cross the graph paper lines. When stitching this area, refer to its chart for guidance in placement.

165

Designing and working needlepoint

Understanding charts

Some needlepoint designs are rendered in chart form, that is, the placement of each stitch in the design is recorded on graph paper. Graph paper is used for charting because it is structurally similar to canvas. Its lengthwise and crosswise lines correspond to the canvas threads; the squares and intersections made by the crossing lines are like the holes and meshes of the canvas. Both come in several gauges, related to the number of subdivisions (squares with graph paper; threads with canvas) to the inch. There are two ways to make use of these similarities, and each produces a different type of chart.

With a **box chart,** the squares on the graph paper represent the threads and/or meshes of the canvas. For a tent stitch, one square means one mesh. With straight or novelty stitches, a square means one thread or mesh of the stitch's total span. The total span is represented by the requisite number of squares, heavily outlined. For example, a straight Gobelin stitch, four threads long, is represented by an outlined row of four squares. A large Algerian eye stitch, which spans four by four meshes, is represented by a group of four by four squares with a heavy outline.

Line charts are an exact duplication of how the stitches will be laid over the canvas threads and meshes. A tent stitch

is a slanted line over one intersection of a pair of lines. A straight Gobelin stitch, four threads long, is a straight line over four lines. A large Algerian eye stitch is represented by eight lines drawn over a group of intersections and lines and converging in a center square.

In either type of chart, the color of the stitch is indicated with actual colors or with symbols in black and shades of gray. With a box chart, the square is filled with either the color or the symbol. With a line chart, the indications are incorporated into the drawn line. If the chart is in colors, the line is drawn in the color. If symbols are being used, the symbol is made a part of the drawn line. Since there is no standardization of the character and meaning of symbols, they will differ from chart to chart. Sometimes the color symbols also indicate a type of yarn. With other charts, letters or numbers represent colors, stitches, or yarns.

An integral companion to a chart is a listing, or key, that translates the meanings of the symbols in the chart. There can be one or more keys. In addition to a key, some charted designs also include a simplified line drawing (schematic) to explain some aspect of the design that is not covered by the chart or key. For typical examples of symbols and keys used with box and line charts, see the symbol chart at the right.

In order to work a charted design on canvas, you will need a piece of canvas that contains at least the total number of threads needed to stitch the entire design. This thread number is based on the number of threads the chart calls for across and up and down, and the number of times the chart must be followed to produce the complete design. If the chart depicts a *full design* (see next page), it will be followed only once, and the total number of threads needed is just the amount contained in the chart. If it is a *partial design chart,* of which there are several types, it must be followed more

than once to produce the total design, and the total thread requirements will therefore be a multiple of the number called for by the chart (see pp. 168-171).

After total thread requirements have been calculated, cut and prepare canvas. Be sure to add a minimum 2-inch margin along each edge before cutting the canvas. The measurements of the prepared canvas will of course vary according to the gauge of the canvas, since it is by the number of threads per inch that canvas gauges differ. For example, 30 threads span 3 inches of a 10-gauge canvas but only 2½ inches of a 12-gauge canvas.

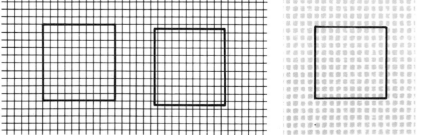

To calculate canvas thread requirements of a charted design, first count the threads across and up and down that the chart calls for. Then match these numbers with same number of canvas threads across and up and down. First chart area above represents 10 by 10 threads on a box chart; the second represents 10 by 10 threads on a line chart. Area of canvas at right has 10 by 10 threads.

TYPES OF CHARTING SYMBOLS

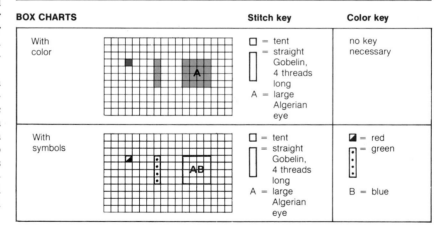

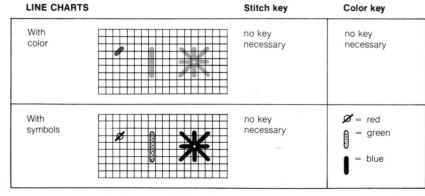

Full design charts

A full design chart is one in which all areas of the total design are represented. A partial design chart (pp. 168-171) lays out only one area; this one area, repeated, makes up the total design. The need for a full charting comes from the asymmetrical structure of a design, that is, from all of its areas being different. When you are using a full chart, the number of canvas threads necessary to stitch the design is the same as the number of threads in the chart. With a kit or chart that does not supply the canvas, you will need to determine the span of canvas that is required by the design. To do this, first determine whether the chart is a box or a line chart, and then notice how each represents threads (see preceding page) so that you will understand how to interpret yours. Once this is understood, count the threads across and up and down called for by the chart. Then calculate the quantity of canvas that will be needed to supply these same numbers of threads across and up and down, and add to this a minimum 2-inch margin along each of the edges. The overall dimensions of the canvas will vary according to its gauge; the finer the gauge being used, the smaller the finished size will be. The gauge of canvas should also be suitable to the design (see pp. 162-163) as well as to the size of the item it is intended for. If the chosen gauge of canvas will produce too small or too large a finished size, you have several options. You could change to a different gauge of canvas that would give you a more suitable finished size. If the design has a background area, it can be enlarged or reduced by using more or fewer stitches in the background. If a design needs enlarging and has no background area, one can be added if this would be appropriate to the design's character. There is no way to reduce such a design except to change the canvas gauge; if you don't want to do that, you will have to select another chart.

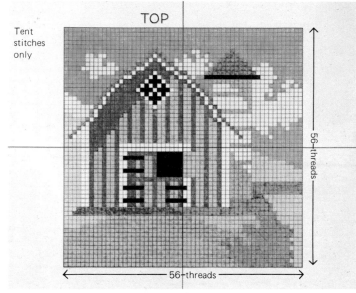

Tent stitches only

56 threads

56 threads

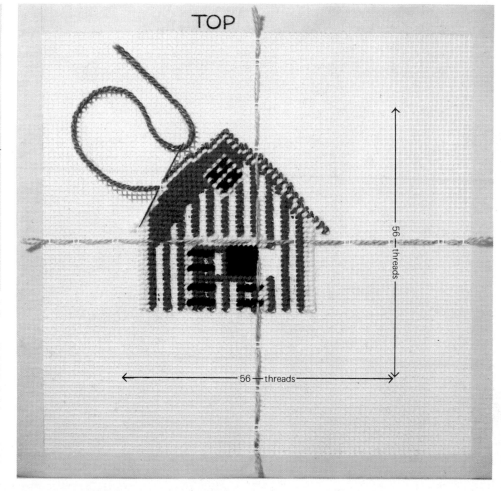

TOP

56 threads

56 threads

1. First locate and then draw horizontal and vertical center lines on the chart. If necessary, also label the top edge of the charted design. Count the number of threads across and up and down that are called for by the chart.

2. Prepare canvas for work: Calculate its measurements to be sure it contains the same number of threads across and up and down as called for by the chart. To this add a margin (minimum 2'') along each edge. Cut canvas to these overall measurements. Bind the edges with tape and label the top edge. Locate and mark the vertical and horizontal centers of the canvas. If the chart calls for an uneven number of threads, the center falls on a thread, as shown on page 164. If the chart involves an even number of threads, the center is between threads and is marked with yarn-bastings (see right). Use a pale color for bastings; stitch over or remove them as you work.

3. Stitch the design on the canvas. Refer to chart (and to keys, if necessary) for the stitch type, placement, and color. Use the center markings on chart and canvas as reference points for locating areas. Work design from the center out, an area or color at a time. If there is a background, work this part last.

Designing and working needlepoint

Partial design charts

A partial design chart presents only a portion of the total design. The reason for the partial representation is that the total design consists of repeats of that portion. There are several types of partial design charts. One type is used to form a multiple-repeat design (p. 170); another is the row chart used to work Florentine Bargello (p. 173). The two partial design charts that are discussed here are half- and quarter-charts; it is these that are used to form symmetrical designs.

A symmetrical design consists of two or four repeats that meet and mirror each other at the design's center. If there are two repeats, one on each side of a center line, the design has two-way symmetry. A half-chart, followed twice, will produce a two-way symmetrical design. If the parts are on each side of a horizontal center line, as in the fish design at the right, the chart used is a **horizontal half-chart**. If they are on each side of a vertical center line, as is the butterfly shown below, the chart used is a **vertical half-chart**. When there are four repeats that are arranged around horizontal and vertical center lines, the design has a four-way symmetry (see the tile design on the opposite page). A **quarter-chart**, followed four times, will produce a four-way symmetrical design.

The total number of canvas threads required to work a symmetrical design is a multiple of the number called for by the chart. These calculations are explained with the individual charts. When working the half or quarter represented by the chart, place its areas in the same positions as shown on the chart. When working the non-charted halves or quarters, place their areas so they mirror the comparable areas on the other side of the center. It is not necessary to start and stop stitching at the center lines. An exception to this: when you are alternating the direction of the stitches in each repeat (see bottom of opposite page).

Horizontal half-charts

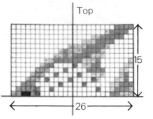

1. Label top of chart. Draw a line down the vertical center of the design, another line across its horizontal center. The total number of canvas threads required for the entire design is the *same* as the number of threads that the chart calls for across the design but *double* the number of threads indicated on the chart from the horizontal center to the design's edge. Prepare canvas for work. Label its top edge and mark its vertical and horizontal centers as well (p. 167).

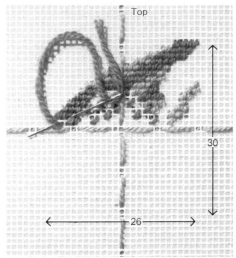

2. Work the top half of the design on canvas. Use the center markings on the chart to locate areas and work them in the exact same positions on the canvas, using its center markings as guides.

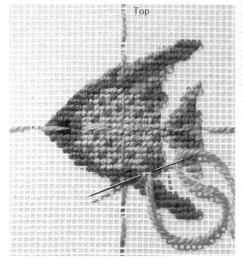

3. To work the lower half, use the chart to locate areas; place them on the canvas in the same relation to the vertical center of the canvas but in the reverse position in relation to its horizontal center.

Vertical half-charts

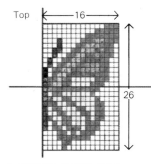

1. Label top of chart. Draw a line across the horizontal center of design, another line down its vertical center. Total number of threads needed for the entire design *equals* the number of threads the chart calls for from top to bottom of the design but *is double* the number from the design's vertical center to its edge. Prepare canvas. Label its top edge and mark its vertical and horizontal centers (p. 167).

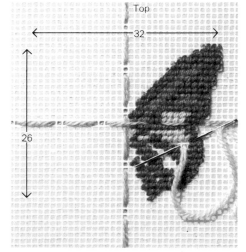

2. Work the right half of the design on the canvas. Use the center markings on the chart to locate areas and place these areas in the same positions on the canvas, using its center lines as guides.

3. To work the left half, use the chart to locate areas. Place the areas on the canvas in the same relation to the horizontal center but in the reverse relation to the vertical center.

Quarter-charts

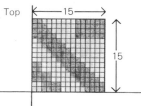

Top ← 15 → 15

1. Label top of chart. Draw a line down the vertical center of the design, another line across its horizontal center. The total number of canvas threads necessary for the entire design is *double* the number of threads that the chart calls for from the vertical center to the edge and from the horizontal center to the edge. Prepare the canvas. Label its top edge; mark its vertical and horizontal centers (p. 167). To work the upper quarters, hold chart with its top edge up and use it to locate areas.

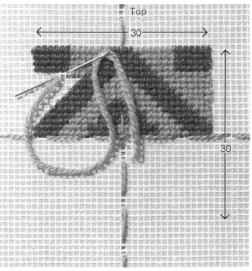

Top ← 30 → 30

2. Place areas in the right quarter as charted. Place areas in the left quarter in the same relation to the horizontal center, but in the reverse relation to the vertical center.

3. To work the lower quarters, hold the chart upside down (as it is shown in the illustration below) as you use it to locate the areas at the bottom.

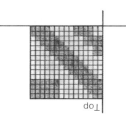

Top

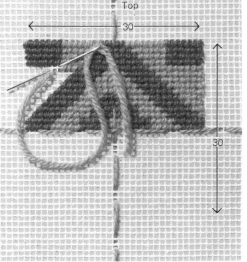

Top

4. Place areas in the left quarter as charted. Place areas in the right quarter in the same relation to the horizontal center, but in the reverse relation to the vertical center.

TO ALTERNATE STITCH DIRECTION WITH EACH QUARTER

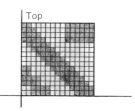

Top

1. Work the upper right quarter with top edge of chart at top. Locate areas on chart; work them in same positions on canvas.

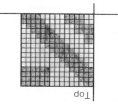

Top

2. To work lower left quarter, turn chart upside down. Find areas on chart; work them as they are positioned on upside-down chart.

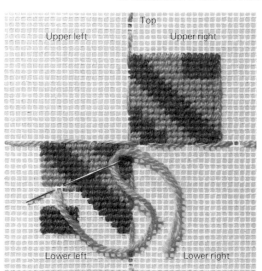

Upper left   Top   Upper right

Lower left   Lower right

3. To work the upper left quarter, hold the canvas with its top edge at the side. Read the worked upper right quarter to locate areas, and place them in the upper left quarter in the same relation to the horizontal center of the canvas but in the reverse relation to its vertical center.

4. To work the lower right quarter, hold the canvas with its top edge at the side. Read the worked lower left quarter to locate the areas, and place them in the lower right quarter in the same relation to the horizontal center of the canvas but in the reverse relation to its vertical center.

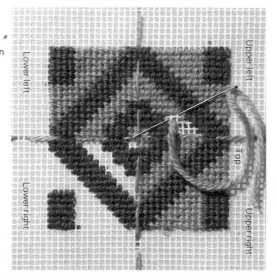

Lower left   Upper left   Top   Upper right   Lower right

169

Designing and working needlepoint

Multiple-repeat designs

A motif repeated a number of times according to a planned arrangement is a multiple-repeat design. The motif can be anything you like that makes an attractive pattern when it is repeated systematically. Before a design is worked, the arrangement must be planned and the basic motif charted. The chart must have a thread count that, when multiplied, permits the arrangement to fit a finished canvas size. To calculate repeat size for charting, see opposite page.

The motif can be your own design or a tracing from an existing source, perhaps a ready-made chart. If the source is a chart, it may turn out that its thread count will fit or can be altered to fit the arrangement. If it is a half- or quarter-chart, follow the procedures at the right to obtain a complete shape. Make several copies of the motif, either by re-tracing it or using a photocopying machine. Trim away excess paper, leaving a border if you want a background. Position the copies different ways until you find a satisfactory arrangement.

Although many repeat arrangements are possible, the three at the bottom of the page are the most common. In the first, a **continual** arrangement, the repeats in the rows line up horizontally and vertically. In the second and third arrangements, repeats are staggered. To achieve a **horizontally staggered** arrangement, line up the vertical centers of the repeats in every horizontal row with the ends of the repeats in the row above. For a **vertically staggered** arrangement, line up the horizontal centers of the repeats in every vertical row with the ends of the repeats in the row to the left. Be prepared to encounter partial motifs, which can occur with any arrangement, particularly those that are staggered.

When you have an arrangement you like, place tracing paper over it and trace all motifs and lines. Use this tracing when calculating the size of the motif and working the arrangement on canvas.

Producing the single motif

A complete motif can be your own original drawing, or a motif traced from a book, a piece of fabric, or even a ready-made full design chart.

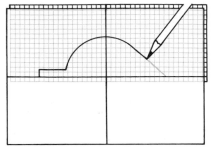

If motif is in half-chart form, draw a set of perpendiculars on tracing paper and align them with center lines on chart. Trace charted half.

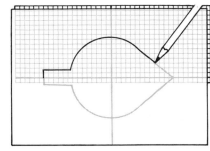

To form second half, flip tracing paper, positioning unmarked half over chart. Match lines on tracing paper and chart; re-trace chart.

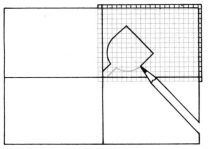

If motif is in quarter-chart form, draw a set of perpendiculars on tracing paper and match them with lines on chart. Trace charted quarter.

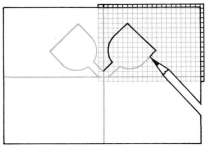

To trace second quarter, flip tracing paper so unmarked quarter is over chart. Match lines on tracing paper and chart; re-trace quarter.

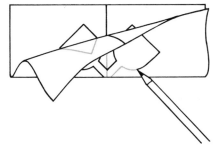

To form second half, fold tracing paper in half so unmarked half is over drawn half of design. Re-trace design half; open tracing paper.

Types of arrangements

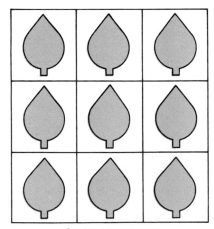

Continual arrangement

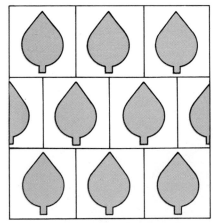

Horizontally staggered arrangement

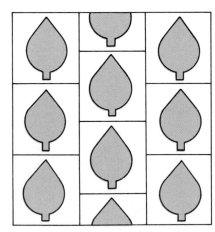

Vertically staggered arrangement

170

Calculating repeat size; working multiple repeats

To chart an original motif for a multiple-repeat design, you must first determine its linear measurement in the arrangement, then its thread size. Linear measurement is the length and width of one repeat; thread size is the number of canvas threads spanned by this linear measurement. To calculate the length of a repeat, divide the finished length of the canvas by the number of repeat rows up and down. To determine the width, divide the finished width of the canvas by the number of rows across. To find the thread size of the repeat, multiply its length and width by the gauge of the canvas. Canvas gauge should be suitable to the needs of the design and to the durability requirements of the finished item (pp. 112, 162-163). Once thread size is known, the motif can be charted (next page). Example A is a lesson in simple calculation. If you have traced an existing chart to obtain your motif, its thread size may fit exactly into the finished size of the arrangement. If it does not, perhaps the thread count of the finished size or of the chart can be altered. If the

charted motif has no background, try changing the arrangement's finished size or select a different gauge of canvas (Example B) to provide the number of threads needed for the chart's repetition. For a chart that has a background area, try increasing or decreasing the number of background threads to arrive at a new thread size that will fit the finished thread count (Example C, background area was increased). Sometimes, no matter what you do, the ready-made chart will not fit. If you find yourself in this situation, choose another motif.

To prepare to work a multiple-repeat design, cut canvas to contain the total number of threads needed for the arrangement plus a minimum 2-inch margin at each edge. Tape all edges; label the top edge. Also mark the horizontal and vertical lines of the arrangement; repeats are worked within their boundaries. Use the chart to work at least the first repeat; to work the others, follow either the chart or a worked repeat. For partial repeats, work just the portion required by the arrangement (Example B).

EXAMPLE B

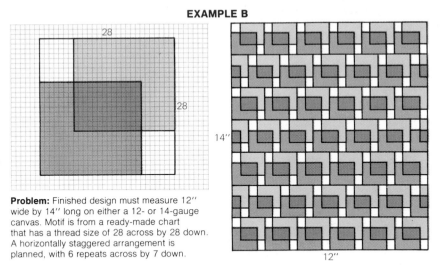

Problem: Finished design must measure 12″ wide by 14″ long on either a 12- or 14-gauge canvas. Motif is from a ready-made chart that has a thread size of 28 across by 28 down. A horizontally staggered arrangement is planned, with 6 repeats across by 7 down.

Solution: Since each of the repeats as charted requires 28 threads by 28 threads, the planned arrangement of 6 repeats across by 7 down will need a total of 168 threads across by 196 up and down. A piece of 12-gauge canvas measuring 12″ wide by 14″ long (size of finished design) contains 144 threads across by 168 up and down; this is not enough threads for the repeats as charted and planned. A piece of 14-gauge canvas 12″ wide by 14″ long contains 168 threads across by 196 up and down; this is the exact number of threads needed for the repeats as charted and planned. It makes sense, therefore, to use the motif as charted and work the arrangement as planned on a 14-gauge canvas. When working the partial repeats in the staggered rows, be sure to work the chart's right half at the left end of the row and the chart's left half at the right end of the row.

EXAMPLE A

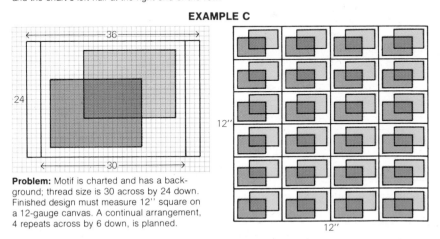

Problem: Finished item must measure 16″ wide by 12″ long on a 10- or 12-gauge canvas. Motif is original and in a continual arrangement of 8 repeats across by 6 down.

Solution: In order for a planned continual arrangement of 8 repeats across by 6 down to fit a finished linear measurement of 16″ wide and 12″ long , each repeat must measure 2″ by 2″. If a 10-gauge canvas is used for the entire design, each repeat will span 20 by 20 threads; if canvas is 12-gauge, each repeat will span 24 by 24 threads. Chart motif according to the gauge of canvas that the entire arrangement will be worked on. For instructions on charting, see next page.

EXAMPLE C

Problem: Motif is charted and has a background; thread size is 30 across by 24 down. Finished design must measure 12″ square on a 12-gauge canvas. A continual arrangement, 4 repeats across by 6 down, is planned.

Solution: A 12″ square of 12-gauge canvas contains 144 by 144 threads. If the chart (thread size of 30 across by 24 down) is used to work the arrangement as planned (4 repeats across by 6 down), it will span 120 threads across by 144 down (24 threads short of the finished width; correct number for length). If 6 threads of background are added to the width of each of the 4 repeats (3 on each end of each repeat), the 144 threads will be spanned. Add 3 threads to each side of chart.

171

Designing and working needlepoint

Charting a design

Before charting your own design, you should familiarize yourself with the types of designs and how they are presented in chart form. You should also understand the two ways canvas threads are represented in charts and how symbols and keys are used to indicate the stitch and color. All of this information is on pages 166 to 171.

To chart your own design, first decide on its finished size and then determine the number of canvas threads that will be required to carry out the full design or the repeated part. This procedure has already been explained for a multiple-repeat design (p. 171). Single-motif designs usually must be enlarged or reduced to fit the finished size (see Embroidery chapter). Draw one line across and another line down the center of the re-sized drawing; label its top edge. Decide what gauge of canvas is suitable for the needs of the design (pp. 162-163) and cut a piece to the finished size plus a minimum 2-inch margin on each edge. Bind its edges with tape; label the top edge; mark vertical and horizontal centers (p. 167).

Center the prepared drawing under the prepared canvas, then count the canvas threads spanned by the entire design or the repeated part. If the design is *asymmetrical*, count the number of threads across and up and down the entire design. For a *horizontal two-way symmetrical* design, count only the top half from side to side and from the center up. For a *vertical two-way symmetrical* design, count the right half from top to bottom and from the center out. For a *four-way symmetrical* design, count threads only for the top right quarter of the design, from its horizontal center to the top and from its vertical center out to the right edge.

When the thread size of the design or the appropriate part is established, you duplicate it within the same number of squares or lines on graph paper. If you are charting the motif for a multiple-repeat design, place a finished-size drawing of it under its prepared canvas and proceed with Step 2, below.

1. Center finished size drawing of design under prepared canvas. Tack layers in place; count canvas threads spanned by design or design part across and down.

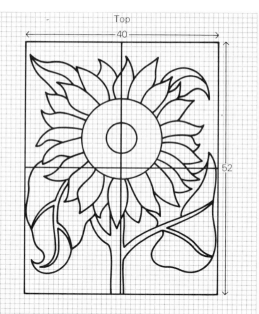

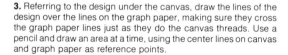

2. On graph paper (any gauge), count the threads called for by design or part being charted. On a box chart, a square is a "thread"; on a line chart, a line is a "thread." Draw box around threads; draw center lines for design or part being charted: both lines for full design, as above; for horizontal half, a vertical center line from bottom of box; for vertical half, a horizontal center line from left side of box. For a quarter design, left and bottom lines of box are the centers.

3. Referring to the design under the canvas, draw the lines of the design over the lines on the graph paper, making sure they cross the graph paper lines just as they do the canvas threads. Use a pencil and draw an area at a time, using the center lines on canvas and graph paper as reference points.

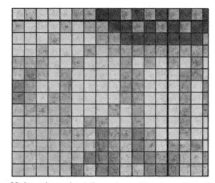

Make a box chart if you intend to use only tent stitches. Re-draw the lines in steps along the nearest squares. Fill squares with intended colors or use symbols and make a color key.

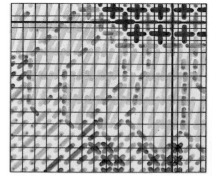

Make a line chart if you will use novelty stitches. Sketch intended stitch in design area, then modify the area's lines to fit the stitches (p. 165). Draw stitches in actual colors or use symbols to denote color and make a color key.

172

Designing and working Bargello

Types of Bargello
Florentine stitch patterns
Color
Equipment
Row designs
Motif designs
Four-way designs

Types of Bargello

Bargello is defined, in the most general terms, as any design worked on canvas with straight needlepoint stitches. By this broad definition, any design, even the sunflower opposite, becomes Bargello needlepoint if straight stitches are employed to work it onto the canvas. Traditionally, however, the name Bargello signifies a unique form of needlepoint in which the Florentine stitch or one of its variations is used to produce dramatic patterns on canvas. It is this traditional kind of Bargello that is described on the following pages.

There are three fundamental types of Florentine-based Bargello designs, represented by the three examples at the right. Each of the three overall designs is formed through the repetitious working of a single unit (for clarity, the repeated unit is outlined in each example). To ensure that the unit is the same each time it is worked, the unit is charted; such a chart is called a *row chart*. The three designs differ mainly in the character of their repeat units. In a **row design** (first example), the repeat consists of several rows of Florentine stitches that mimic the pattern established by the top row. For a more detailed explanation of designing and working a row design, see pages 176-177. In a **motif design** (second example), the top and bottom rows of the repeat mirror each other and together form an enclosed intervening area. This area is filled with Florentine stitches or other straight stitches that conform to the area's shape. Motif designs are explained on pages 178-179. The third type is a **four-way design,** in which the overall design is produced by working each triangular quarter of the design at right angles to the others. Although a row design repeat is the basic unit in the four-way design shown, a motif design unit can also be used to form this type of Bargello. The design and working of four-way Bargello designs are dealt with on pages 180-182.

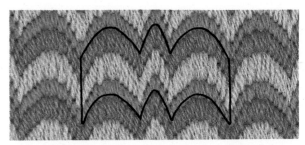

Row designs are the easiest of the Bargello types to design and work. The repeat unit consists of several rows of Florentine stitches that mimic the pattern of the top row of the repeat. The overall effect is bands of mirror-imaging repeats across the canvas.

Motif designs form medallion-like repeats across the canvas. The repeat consists of a top and bottom row that mirror each other and form an enclosed area. This area is filled with Florentine or other straight stitches.

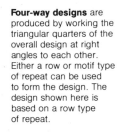

Four-way designs are produced by working the triangular quarters of the overall design at right angles to each other. Either a row or motif type of repeat can be used to form the design. The design shown here is based on a row type of repeat.

Designing and working Bargello

Forming Florentine stitch patterns

Even though there are only three fundamental types of Florentine-based Bargello designs, the number of possible patterns among them is almost limitless. This is because the span of Florentine stitches on which a repeat unit is based can be varied in many ways. Some knowledge of how these variations are achieved will help you to design your own Bargello, or to more easily understand and work a design from a ready-made row chart.

The zigzag pattern of any Florentine stitch is formed by combining two elements: straight Gobelin stitches and a stitch placement device known as *step*. Step allows the stitches to be placed diagonally next to each other so that the stitches can rise to form the peaks or descend to form the valleys of the zigzag pattern. The illustrations below show the effects of stitch length and step on the

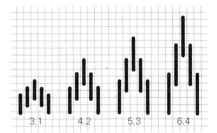

Effects of stitch length and step on peak height.

height of a peak. Under each example is a set of numbers. The first number denotes stitch length; the second, the amount of step between stitches. Stitches can be from two to eight threads long. Step, which is the number of threads between the bases of neighboring stitches, must be at least one less than the stitch length number. As the examples show, the greater the stitch length and step, the higher the peak (or lower the valley). The extremes would be even greater if more than three stitches were used between peak and valley.

The row pattern of a Florentine stitch is formed by combining peaks and valleys. If peaks and valleys are all the same size, the result is an even zigzag pattern, which is the Florentine stitch at its most basic. When pointed peaks and valleys of different sizes are combined, a variation of the Florentine stitch, known as the flame stitch, is produced. Additional variation can be achieved in a zigzag pattern by rounding the points. This is done by using blocks of straight Gobelin stitches. There can be from two to six stitches in a block; the blocks can be placed at the tip of a peak or valley or between the two.

The basic Florentine stitch produces an even zigzag pattern. This is achieved by combining peaks and valleys of the same size. To form a deep zigzag pattern, use high, same-size peaks and valleys; for a shallow zigzag, use short, same-size peaks and valleys.

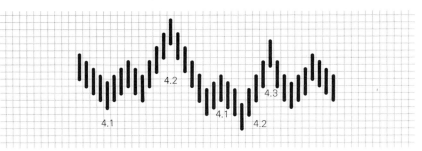

To form an uneven zigzag pattern, combine peaks and valleys of different sizes. Stitches in example above are all four threads long, but heights of peaks and valleys are varied by using different numbers of stitches between them, and changing the amount of step between the stitches.

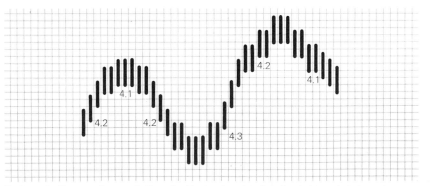

Peaks and valleys can be rounded by using blocks of straight Gobelin stitches at their tips or between them. Step is retained between blocks but not between the individual stitches of a block.

Color

Color's most basic role in Bargello is identifying rows or areas in the repeat, a natural result of each row or area usually being assigned its own color. Properly selected and placed in the repeat, however, color can also add depth or movement to the overall design. Colors cause different visual responses; you can control these by assigning color to a row or area according to how much you want it to stand out in the design. To select colors so that they will perform to your satisfaction, it helps to know something about color theory.

There are six basic colors in a color wheel—red, yellow, orange, blue, green, and violet. The first three, (red, yellow, and orange) tend to advance optically; the last three, (blue, green, and violet) tend to recede. Each of these colors has a range of values, that is, degrees of lightness and darkness. A light value, or *tint*, is achieved by adding white to the color. To produce a dark value, or *shade*, black is added to the color. As a general rule, tints advance and shades recede. How much a tint advances or a shade recedes will depend on the intensity of the pure color from which it was derived. For example, pink, which is a tint of red (an advancing color), will advance more than will pale blue, which is a tint of blue (a receding color).

The power of any color or value is affected by colors and values around it. A harmonious combination is one in which colors are close, producing a relaxed visual response. A contrasting combination, in which the colors are not close, produces an active response. Most harmonious of all is a combination involving variations of a single color with moderate value differences among its shades and tints. Also harmonious is a scheme of related colors, such as blue with blue-green and green. Contrasting schemes may consist of contrasts in value (very light against very dark) or in color (e.g., violet, green, and orange).

SHADES AND TINTS

Shades (darker values), formed by adding black.

Pure red   Pure blue

Tints (lighter values), formed by adding white.

KINDS OF COLOR SCHEMES

Harmonious color schemes: To form a monochromatic harmony, combine several close values of one color as was done in the first sample above. To create an analogous harmony, combine several related colors as in the second example above.

Contrasting color schemes may be produced by combining distant values of one color as shown by the example at the left. Or, to get a complementary contrasting scheme, combine unrelated colors as was done in the example at the right.

RELATED/UNRELATED COLORS

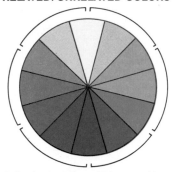

Related colors are those that are next to each other on the color wheel—red, red-orange, and orange; blue, blue-violet, and violet.

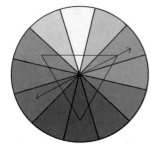

Unrelated colors are those that are opposite or separated on the wheel. Red and green are unrelated; so are green, orange, and violet.

Equipment

To work a Bargello, you will require a chart of the design and enough canvas and yarn to work it. Since Bargello is a type of multiple-repeat design, the amount of canvas needed will be a multiple of the number of threads called for by the chart. The procedures for estimating canvas amounts are explained on the next few pages. If you are designing your own Bargello, you will need graph paper and coloring devices for charting. A very handy designing tool is a set of projection mirrors. You can make a set yourself (see right) with felt, glue, and two identical purse-size mirrors.

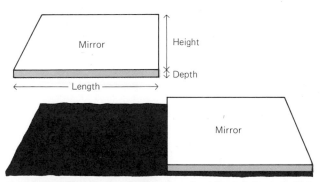

To make a set of projection mirrors, proceed as follows: Cut a piece of felt that is as wide as the mirror is high and equal in length to twice the mirror's combined length and depth (thickness).

Spread glue on wrong side of both mirrors. Position a mirror at each end of the felt, glued side down. Press both of the mirrors in place and wipe off any excess glue. Let dry before using.

Designing and working Bargello

Row design charts

The first step in designing any of the three types of Florentine-based Bargello designs is to establish the row pattern on which the repeat unit will be based. The easiest way to find a row pattern is to slide projection mirrors (see p. 175) along a predetermined row of Florentine stitches. Though any row of Florentine stitches can serve this purpose (even a photograph of a finished sample), you can improve your chances of discovering a unique pattern by experimenting with a stitch row that you designed (p. 174). The way the mirrors should be held to reflect the kind of establishing row pattern you need will depend on the type of repeat you are designing. The plotting of row design repeats is explained here; for motif and four-way design repeats, refer to pages 178, 180, and 181.

To plan a row design unit, you need to establish a side-to-side pattern for the top row. You can find one by sliding a mirror along a charted row of stitches (Steps 2 and 3 below). Slide it from right to left and from left to right; patterns will differ each way. More patterns can be produced by turning the row upside-down. When you have found a satisfactory top row, make a line chart of it (p. 166) on a new piece of graph paper; then chart the other rows of the repeat under the first (Steps 4, 5, and 6). Each new row can have a different stitch length so long as the length used will maintain the step arrangement established by the top row.

When charting, use a different color for each row. Colors need not match those in which the design will be worked on the canvas; once the actual color arrangement is decided, however, it should be indicated on the chart.

When designing your own repeat, it is recommended that you chart the entire side-to-side pattern of all the rows of the repeat; this lets you see the actual pattern. Many ready-made charts depict only half of the side-to-side pattern.

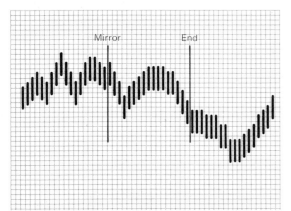

1. Begin by charting a row of Florentine stitches. Make the row long enough to include peaks and valleys of several different sizes and shapes. The red lines indicate position of mirror and end of side-to-side pattern established in Step 3.

2. Position one mirror parallel to the charted stitches. Slowly slide the mirror along the row, looking, as you do, at the charted stitches and their mirrored images. Stop when you come to a section that forms a pleasing pattern on each side of the mirror.

3. Holding the mirror in place and still looking at the charted stitches and their images, slide your finger along charted stitches until you come to a suitable end to the side-to-side pattern. Mark the end with a line; make another line along edge of mirror.

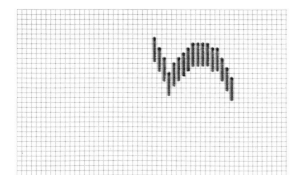

4. On a new piece of graph paper, chart the stitches that lie between the marks drawn in Step 3. When making the new chart, be sure to draw the stitches to the same length and step, and in the same positions, as they were on the original chart.

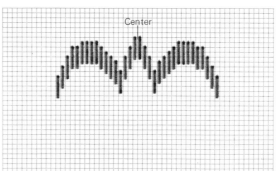

5. Then chart the mirror images of the stitches. These are charted in the opposite direction from those in Step 4 but in the same order. Make sure that you also chart them to the same stitch length and step. Mark the center of the side-to-side charted pattern.

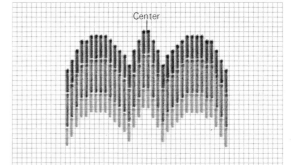

6. Using a different color for each, chart the other rows of the repeat under the first. For each row, use a stitch length that will maintain the step arrangement established by the top row (e.g., a 3-stitch length is too short for the 3-step in center peak).

Preparing for and working a row design

Bargello designs look best with repeats centered on the canvas. You can center a row design by centering the top row at the vertical center of the canvas (drawing A), or by placing a top row on each side (drawing B). Because of unevenness in heights, most row patterns will cross the horizontal center irregularly.

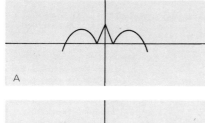

With the center placement determined, decide on the number of repeats you want across and up and down for the total design; then calculate the canvas threads needed to work the design. To find the number of threads needed across, multiply the number of repeats across by the number of threads across a repeat unit. To find the number needed for length, multiply the number of row repeats up and down the design by the number of threads needed for each repeat of rows. Divide these totals by your canvas gauge; the resulting numbers are the measurements of the finished canvas. If the arrangement and gauge produce too small a finished size, add full or partial repeats to enlarge it. If they produce too large a size, reduce the number of repeats or select a finer canvas gauge. Prepare canvas for work by cutting it to finished size plus a minimum 2-inch margin along each edge; tape all edges and label the top; mark centers (p. 167).

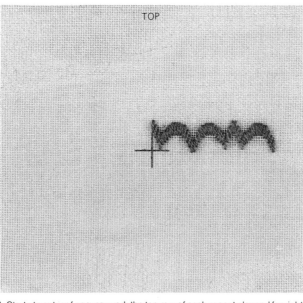

1. Start at center of canvas; work the top row of each repeat planned for right half of design. Refer to chart for color and stitch placement.

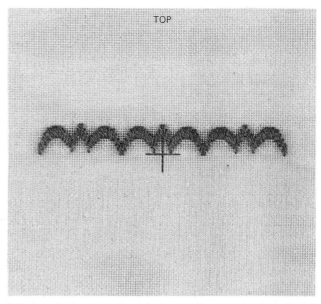

2. Begin again at center and work the top row of each repeat planned for left half of design. Check entire span for accuracy of stitch placement.

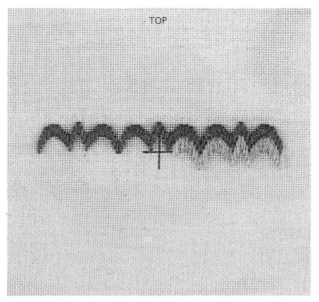

3. Using the row just completed as a guide, work the second row of all repeats in one journey across the canvas. Refer to chart for row color.

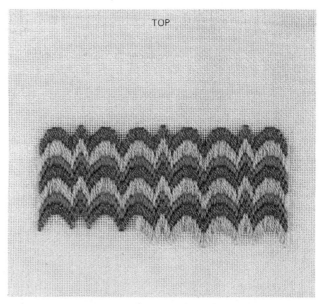

4. Work remaining rows of lower, then upper half of design. Begin each row at right or left edge; refer to chart for its correct color.

Designing and working Bargello

Motif design charts

To design a repeat unit of the motif type, you need to establish patterns for both top and bottom rows. The rows are identical, and are found simultaneously by holding projection mirrors (p. 175) at right angles to each other and to a row of Florentine stitches. As shown in Step 2 below, a side-to-side pattern is formed on each side of the vertical mirror and this same row pattern is also seen upside-down in both mirrors. When top and bottom rows are in this relationship, an open area is formed between them. This area is filled with Florentine or other straight stitches. With many of the motif patterns, open areas between rows will themselves form secondary motifs. When designing your own motif, it is recommended that you chart several motifs, as shown in Step 4, so that you can see and plan the design of the secondary motifs. Many ready-made charts show only half of both primary and secondary motifs.

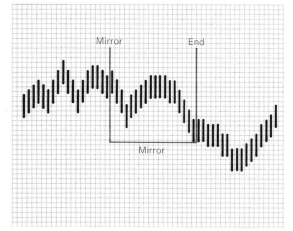

1. Chart a row of Florentine stitches long enough to include various sizes and shapes of peaks and valleys (p. 174). Red lines indicate the positions of the mirrors and the end of the side-to-side pattern established in the next step.

2. With mirrors at right angles to each other and stitches, slide them along row until you find a suitable motif pattern. To adjust motif depth, slide mirrors up and down. Mark end of side-to-side pattern; trace right angle formed by edges of both mirrors.

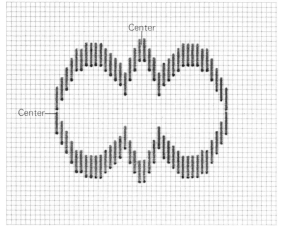

3. Re-chart stitches between marks; draw stitches intersected by horizontal line to the length above the intersection. Chart other half of side-to-side pattern and mark center (p. 176). Chart bottom row to mirror top row; mark horizontal center of motif.

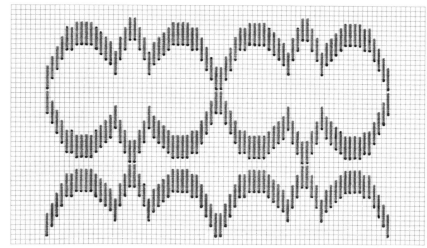

4. To determine if open areas between rows of motifs will form secondary motifs, chart another motif next to the first; under these, chart the top row of two corresponding motifs, aligning their vertical centers with centers of motifs above, and abutting highest points below with lowest points above.

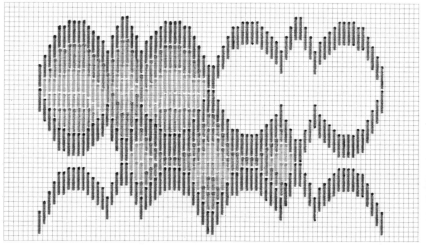

5. Fill in on your chart the open areas of the primary and secondary motifs with Florentine stitches or other straight stitches that make interesting patterns and conform to the shapes of the open areas. Use a different color for each row or area.

Preparing and working a motif design

The centering of motif design repeats is usually achieved either by centering a motif at the exact center of the canvas (drawing A), or by placing full motifs at each side of the centers (drawing B).

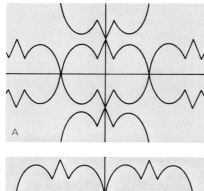

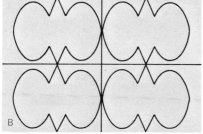

Some motif designs, however, combine these two placements. For example, the design at the right centers the motifs horizontally, but places full motifs on each side of the vertical center. When the centering is determined, decide how many repeats you want across and up and down to form the total design. Then calculate the amount of canvas needed, and prepare it for working (see p. 177).

As shown in Step 1 at the right, the first row to be worked is the top row of the motifs that run across the center. If you want the centers of the motifs to be at the horizontal center of the canvas, then work this top row along the horizontal center. If you prefer to have whole motifs above the horizontal center, you will need to work the top row a full motif above that center line.

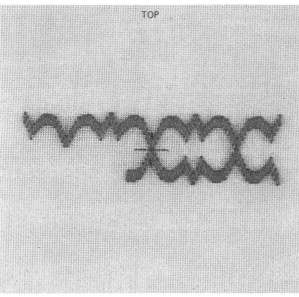

1. Work top row of motifs from vertical center out to each edge; work bottom row in one journey across. Placement depends on repeat centering plan.

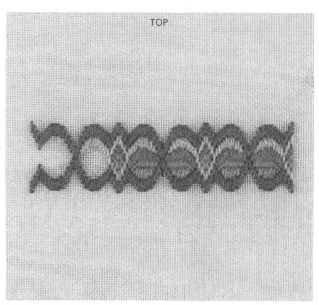

2. Referring to chart for color and stitch placement, work middle areas of motifs—either one at a time or parts of all progressively.

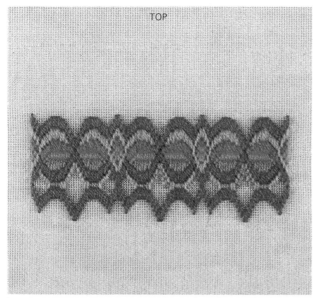

3. Work top row of next span of motifs in one journey across canvas. Work the middle areas of secondary motifs one at a time or progressively.

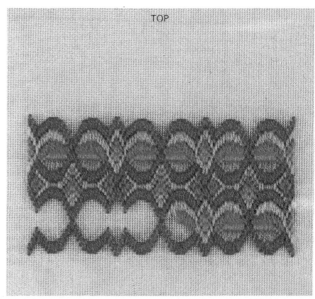

4. Continue to work this way—that is, work a row, then the middle areas—until lower half of the design, then upper half, are completed.

179

Designing and working Bargello

Four-way row design charts

Four-way Bargello consists of four identical triangular quarters that meet and change direction along diagonal lines. Because of this structure, it is also known as mitered Bargello. To design your own four-way Bargello, you need only chart one whole quarter; you then follow it four times to work the design. The design of the quarter can be based on a row design repeat, as on this page, or a motif design (opposite page). The main difference between the charting of the two types is the way the row or motif is established and centered in the triangular quarter. To work either type of four-way design, see page 182.

1. Design a row of Florentine stitches (row above is the same as on p. 176). Hold one mirror parallel to stitches; other at a 45° angle to first. Move mirrors along stitches to find a four-way side-to-side row pattern; up and down to alter length of pattern and its distance from center of design. Trace 45° angle along mirrors to mark first half of row pattern and its distance from center.

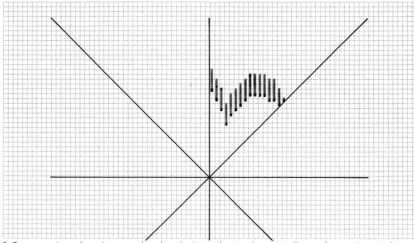

2. On a new piece of graph paper, draw lengthwise and crosswise center lines; miter quarters as shown. If row pattern has one stitch at center, draw lines *between* graph lines; if row has same number of stitches on each side of center, draw lines *on* graph lines. Chart first half of row same distance above center as marked; draw stitches intersected by diagonal mark to length above intersection.

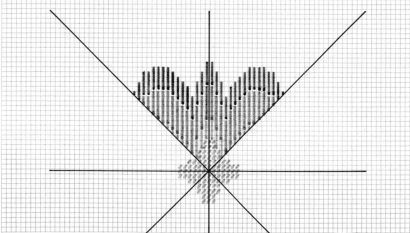

3. Chart second half of row to mirror first half (p. 176). Maintaining pattern set by the first row, chart progressively shorter rows toward center of design. If space between diagonals becomes too short to chart an acceptable row pattern, design an arrangement of tent or novelty stitches to fill rest of center area. Chart all quarters of center design; for another treatment, see next page.

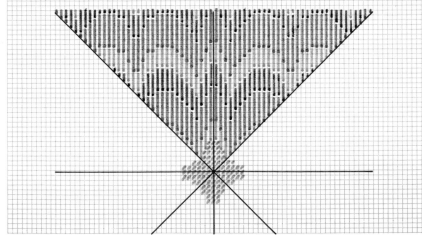

4. Design wide end of triangle to form a straight outer edge. Novelty or tent stitches can be used (see next page), or you can chart increasingly longer side-to-side row patterns as shown here. If charting rows, maintain pattern set by first; make rows longer by charting stitches to mirror the ends of the row patterns. Use compensating stitches and parts of rows to form straight edge.

Four-way motif design charts

The primary consideration, in charting a four-way design, is that the establishing row or motif be centered in a triangle. A row design is automatically centered in the process of designing four-way row patterns (Step 1, facing page). When a motif is used for a four-way design, design the top and bottom rows of the motif first (Step 1 below) and then establish its center placement in the triangle (Step 2). This must be done in two stages because there is no way to hold projection mirrors so that they simultaneously reflect both the top and bottom rows of a motif and the motif's arrangement in a four-way pattern.

1. Design a row of Florentine stitches (the row used above is different from the one on pp. 176 and 178). With mirrors at right angles to each other and to the stitches, slide them along the stitches until you find a suitable motif. Slide mirrors up and down if you wish to alter motif depth. Mark the end of the side-to-side pattern; trace the right angle formed by the mirrors.

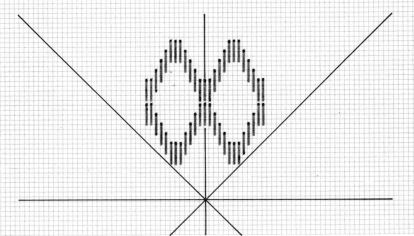

2. Chart top and bottom rows of motif (see p. 178); draw a line down vertical center of motif. Directly under motif, draw diagonal miter lines. Miter lines should meet at the vertical center line and form a 45° angle on each side of that line; they should not intersect any stitches of the motif. Draw a horizontal center line through point where diagonals meet vertical center line.

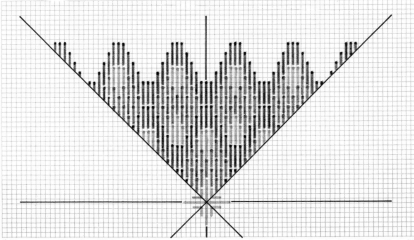

3. If upper portion of motif does not fully span the distance between diagonals, chart partial motifs to fill spaces. Chart middle of each motif, then chart rows and a center treatment to fill the space (if any) between motif and center of design. Chart all four quarters of the center treatment (novelty stitches are used here; design on facing page has tent stitches at its center).

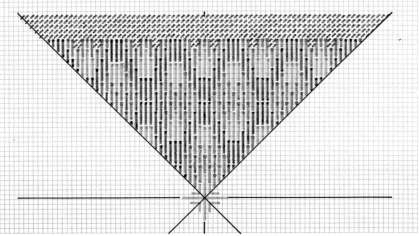

4. Design the wide end of the triangle, making its outer edge straight. Depending on the effect you want, either chart full, then partial rows above motif (as was done above establishing row in Step 4, opposite page), or plan to fill the space above the motif with tent or novelty stitches, or use a combination of partial rows and other stitches, as was done here.

Designing and working Bargello

Preparing for and working a four-way design

The centering of the repeats in a four-way Bargello design is established in its chart and should be maintained in all four quarters of the design as you work them. To work the full design, you have to determine the amount of canvas needed to contain it. To do this, first calculate the number of threads at the outer edge of the triangle, then divide this number by the gauge of your canvas. This one measurement is all that is needed because the outer edges of the triangles are the same on all four sides of the finished design. Some ready-made charts depict neighboring halves of triangles separated by a miter line (see the illustration of such a chart below). If you are using this type of chart, calculate the total number of threads for the outer edge of a whole

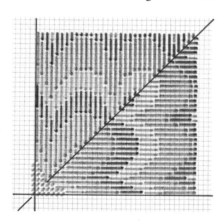

triangle by doubling the number of threads charted for the outer edge of one of the halves.

Cut a piece of canvas to measure the finished length and width plus a minimum 2-inch margin along each edge. Tape all edges and label the top edge. Mark the centers of the canvas (see p. 167). Use yarn-basting to mark the miter lines of the design. Although a row design is being worked at right, the same procedures apply for a four-way motif design.

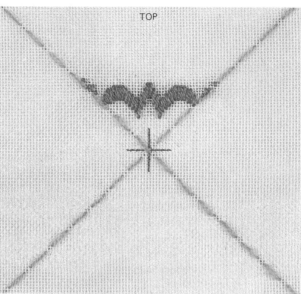

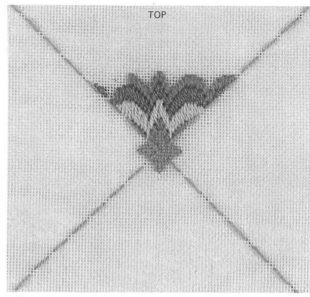

1. Begin with top quarter and work its middle row from vertical center out to each miter line. Refer to chart for color and stitch placement.

2. Work remaining rows from miter to miter: first those from middle row down; then entire center treatment; finally top rows to outer edge.

3. Turn canvas clockwise and work rows of next quarter in any convenient sequence. Be sure rows match their counterparts along the miter.

4. Work third and fourth quarters as the second quarter was done. Refer to chart or a worked quarter for color and stitch placement.

General working techniques

Calculating yarn amounts
Removing stitches
Repairing ripped canvas
Setting canvas into a frame
Blocking needlepoint

Calculating yarn amounts

The amount of yarn needed to work a particular design will depend on the stitches and the gauge of the canvas as well as the planned finished size of the design. In order to calculate the total yarn requirements, you have to determine the amount of yarn each stitch uses to cover one square inch of canvas. If you plan to use only one stitch, only one test is necessary; if several stitches are being used, you must test them all. All stitch tests must be done on the same gauge of canvas as the design will be worked on.

You must also use the proper weight of yarn for the stitch and the canvas gauge (see p. 118).

To do a stitch test, cut your yarn into several 18-inch (half-yard) lengths. Using the premeasured lengths, work one square inch of the stitch. Record how many lengths were used and convert this number into yards; if a partial length was used, count it as a full length. Use the test result yardage to calculate the total amount of yarn needed for that particular stitch over the entire design. Estimate how many square inches of that stitch will be worked in the design and multiply that number by the test result yardage. Apportion this total yardage among the different colors in which the test stitch will be worked.

Apply the test result yardage of each stitch test in the same way. Add the amounts for individual colors to arrive at the total yardage needed for each. To allow for mistakes in calculation or during work on the design, increase each color's yardage by ten to fifteen percent.

Removing stitches

Stitching mistakes are likely to happen, and are no cause for alarm. If you catch the error while you are stitching and it involves only two or three stitches, the correction is easy. Unthread the needle, pull out the incorrect stitches, and re-stitch them with the same yarn. If the mistake involves more than just a few simple stitches, or if you discover it after the area is finished, the procedure is different. In this case, you have to carefully cut the incorrect stitches from the canvas, as shown and explained at the right, then, with new yarn, re-stitch the area where stitches were cut.

1. From right side, slip scissors blade under a few incorrect stitches; pull yarn up from canvas and cut. Clip a few at a time until all are cut.

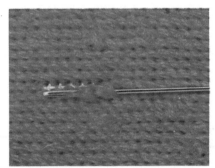

2. From wrong side, with eye end of needle, pull out cut yarn. To secure intact stitches, unstitch a few; catch yarn into backs of new stitches.

Repairing ripped canvas

You may discover that in the process of removing stitches you have accidentally cut the threads of the canvas. If this happens, you can easily repair the cut with a patch of the same canvas type and gauge. To prepare the area for the repair, pull out enough stitches around the cut to allow ample space for the patch. A patch needs to be a few meshes larger each way than the cut; the space for the patch must be slightly larger than the patch. When the area is ready, apply the patch as shown and explained at the right. Re-stitch the area through both canvas layers; trim canvas threads that protrude.

1. Position canvas patch under the cut. Align the threads of both canvases; baste patch in place.

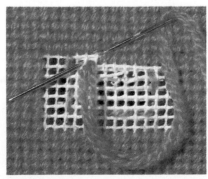

2. Re-stitch area through both layers of canvas. Carefully trim any protruding canvas threads.

General working techniques

Setting canvas into a frame

It is best to work a needlepoint on a frame or other holding device. Work that is done this way will stay neat and be less distorted when it is finished. As explained on page 116, there are different types of frames and holding devices, each with its own use and limitations. Basic instructions for setting canvas into most of the devices are given below. A fine-gauge canvas can be set into a hoop if you prefer; for instructions, see the Embroidery chapter. Because there will be slight variations among different brands of frames, you should use these instructions as guides, adapting them if necessary to your needs. If your frame is equipped with a stand, you should attach it before starting to work.

Scroll and rotating types are the most versatile of all the needlepoint frames. Each consists of top and bottom rods and two side arms (see the illustrations below). The canvas is attached to fabric tapes on the rods and the rods are then inserted into the side arms. If your scroll or rotating frame does not have fabric tapes, you should add them.

To add fabric tapes, cut two lengths of rug binding or 1-inch twill tape, each slightly longer than rod after insertion into side arms. Center tape on rod with one edge lapped and the other extending; turn raw edges of tape under flush with working ends of rod. Secure lapped edge with staples or masking tape. Attach the second tape the same way.

SCROLL FRAME

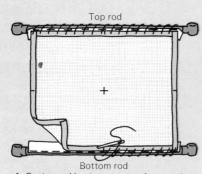

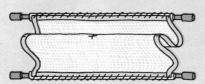

1. Center and lap top canvas edge over tape on top rod; hold in place. Sew canvas to tape by continuously bringing needle and thread through tape and canvas, around rod, then back into tape and canvas. Knot thread end at beginning; form several backstitches in fabric tape to secure ending. Sew bottom edge of canvas to bottom rod in the same way.

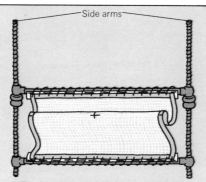

2. To attach side arms, distance between rods must be less than the side arms' length but no less than half that length. If necessary to achieve this, roll canvas onto one or both rods. Place a locking nut on each end of each side arm; bring to centers. Insert top ends of arms into ends of top rod; slip arms through and insert other ends into bottom rod.

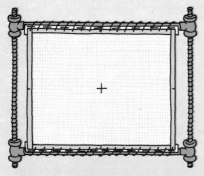

3. Slide rods along arms to center canvas in frame; bring centered nuts out to hold rods in place. Attach a nut to each end of each arm; bring toward rods. Tighten all locking nuts.

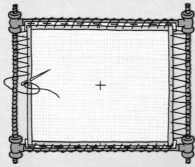

4. To hold canvas taut, whipstitch each side to an arm; begin and end by wrapping thread between nut and rod. To re-position canvas, remove whipstitches and repeat Steps 2 to 4.

ROTATING FRAME

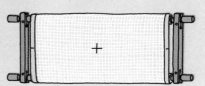

1. Secure top and bottom edges of canvas to top and bottom rods as explained in Step 1 of scroll frame instructions (see left). Loosen wing nuts at ends of side arms and slip the rods through openings in the arms.

2. Turn rods to take up slack canvas; secure by tightening nuts. Edges can be whipstitched to side arms (Step 4 at left). To re-position canvas, remove whipstitches and loosen nuts; re-roll canvas and tighten nuts.

CANVAS STRETCHER

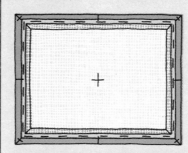

Arrange the four strips as they will be set together, each with its shorter edge toward the inside of the frame. At each of the four corners, fit ends of neighboring strips together and staple across each join to secure it. Mark center of each strip. Center canvas over frame, making sure that the entire working area is clear of the frame's inner edges. Staple or tack each edge of the canvas to the frame. Canvas should not be re-positioned after work has begun. This would mean stapling or tacking through some of the worked area.

NEEDLEPOINT ROD

1. Insert corner of canvas into slit at open end of rod. Then pull canvas along slit toward closed end of rod.

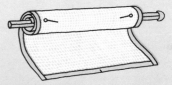

2. Roll canvas firmly onto the rod, letting the area to be worked extend from the rod. To secure rolled canvas, insert two hat pins through the rolled canvas into slit in rod. To re-position working area, remove the pins, re-roll the canvas, and secure again with pins.

Blocking needlepoint

Blocking is the process that brings the stitched needlepoint back to its original size and alignment. It is made necessary by the almost unavoidable distortion that occurs as the canvas is worked. The primary cause of distortion is the stitches themselves, with the diagonal and crossing stitches generally distorting the work more than straight stitches. Stitch distortion can be compounded by using too tight a stitch tension or too thick a yarn for the canvas gauge; it can be minimized by working the canvas on a frame. There are three methods of blocking; which one you use will depend on how misshapen your canvas is. Before blocking any needlepoint, check for any missed stitches.

Use Method I, below, for canvases with little or no distortion. For these, all that is needed is a light steam-pressing to stabilize the shape and even out the stitch surface. Method II, top right, is for can-

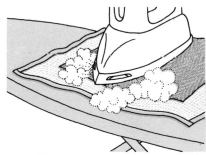

Method I: Lightly steam-press the needlepoint from the wrong side; let it dry thoroughly.

vases that show noticeable distortion; Method III, at the immediate right, is for those that are extremely distorted. With either of these last two methods, the canvas is stretched to match the pattern made of it before it was worked (p. 164). With any method, it is important to let the canvas dry thoroughly before it is moved. If it is still out of shape after drying is complete, block it again, using the same or another method.

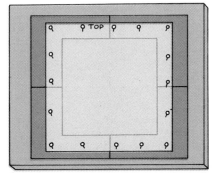

Method II: 1. Place pattern of prepared canvas right side up on blocking board; cover it with a sheet of tissue paper. Tack both to board.

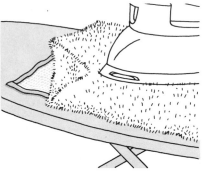

2. Place needlepoint face down on ironing board. Dampen a Turkish towel and use it to steam-press and dampen the needlepoint.

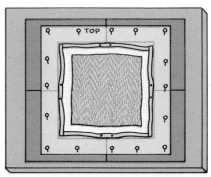

3. Place needlepoint face down on the pattern and stretch so that its centers and edges match those on pattern. Tack every 1″ to 2″; let dry.

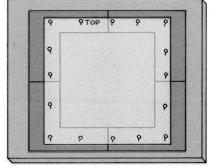

Method III: 1. Place pattern of prepared canvas right side up on blocking board; cover it with a sheet of tissue paper. Tack both to board.

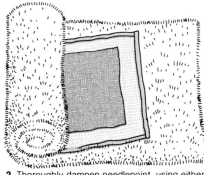

2. Thoroughly dampen needlepoint, using either of the following methods: Roll needlepoint in a damp Turkish towel and leave it rolled until moisture has penetrated both the yarn and the canvas (above left); or sprinkle or sponge the needlepoint with enough warm water to dampen it (above right).

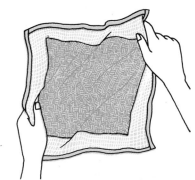

3. Stretch canvas in the direction opposite to the distortion. Begin by pulling at opposite corners; then pull along opposite edges.

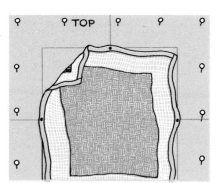

4. Place the needlepoint face down on the pattern. Stretch canvas so that the center markings at its edges match those on pattern. Tack in place.

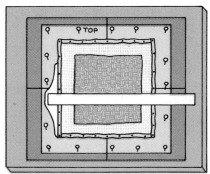

5. Stretch canvas to align its edges with those on pattern; tack in place every 1″ to 2″. Use a T-square to check straightness of canvas threads.

185

Initialed eyeglass case/Bargello

Personalize this case with initial of your choice.

A row-repeat Bargello (pp. 176-177) and tent stitches create a colorful eyeglass case in an unusually generous size.

Materials needed

14-gauge canvas, 11″ long by 11½″ wide
8″ of soft lining fabric
Persian yarn: 35 yds. light aqua; 21 yds. medium blue; 19 yds. royal blue; 17 yds. gold; 3 yds. burnt sienna
#20 tapestry needle
Sewing thread to match lining
Hand-sewing needle

Preparation

Cut canvas piece to the required size. Tape edges; label top. Mark centers of canvas between threads (p. 167). Vertical center is foldline between front and back of case. Mark boundaries of case. For top and bottom edges, draw a line on the fiftieth thread above and below the horizontal center. For each side of case, draw a line on the fifty-third thread on each side of vertical center.

The needlepoint

Following row chart on facing page, form two consecutive peaks across front of case. Begin at vertical center and place base of first stitch over the twentieth thread above horizontal center. Then, working from vertical center out to left, form two peaks across back of case. *Note:* There is a single stitch at each peak and valley. Referring to chart, work as many row repeats as necessary for the length of the case; form a straight edge along bottom. Using tent stitches and following appropriate chart, work chosen initial between the two peaks on front of case. The outlined square area on row chart locates center area between peaks; center your letter in that area. Fill unstitched areas between all peaks with tent stitches (refer to chart for color). Block the needlepoint (p. 185).

Finishing the case

Trim each edge of canvas to ½ inch. Turn back top edge along tent stitches; turn back the other three edges along the canvas thread next to the Bargello stitches. Miter corners (see right). With wrong sides of needlepoint together, fold case along vertical center; match threads along bottom and side edges. Sew together with whipstitches, first across bottom, then along side of the eyeglass case. Reinforce the top corner by forming three whipstitches in the same hole, fanning them around the corner.

Cut lining piece 8½ inches wide by 8 inches long. With right sides together, fold lining in half along vertical center. Form a ⅜-inch seam; trim. Turn top edge back ⅜ inch. Slip lining into case; align seams of lining and case. Stitch lining to case along top edge.

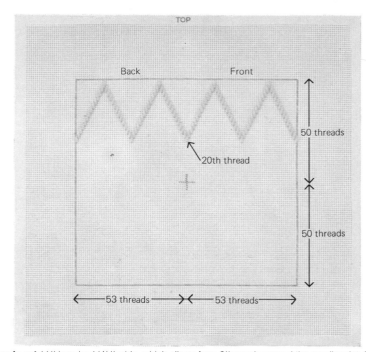

Canvas is cut 11″ long by 11½″ wide, which allows for a 2″ margin around the needlepoint. Dimensions of the case, and the starting point for the Bargello, are determined by counting threads.

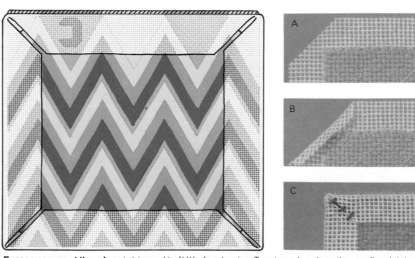

Excess canvas at the edges is trimmed to ½″ before turning. Turn top edge along the needlepoint; turn other three along thread next to the stitches. **To miter corners,** trim canvas diagonally across corner (A); fold back across corner (B); turn back edges on each side of corner and tack (C).

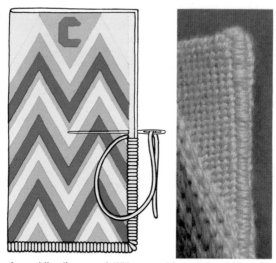

Assembling the case: 1. With wrong sides together, fold needle-point along its vertical center. Align edges and match threads along bottom and sides; stitch together with whipstitches. Begin stitching at fold and work first across bottom, then along side. Reinforce top corner by forming 3 whipstitches through the same hole, fanning them around the hole.

2. With right sides together, fold lining along vertical center. Stitch ⅝'' seam along bottom and side; trim. Turn top edge back ⅜''. Slip lining into case; sew to case at top edge.

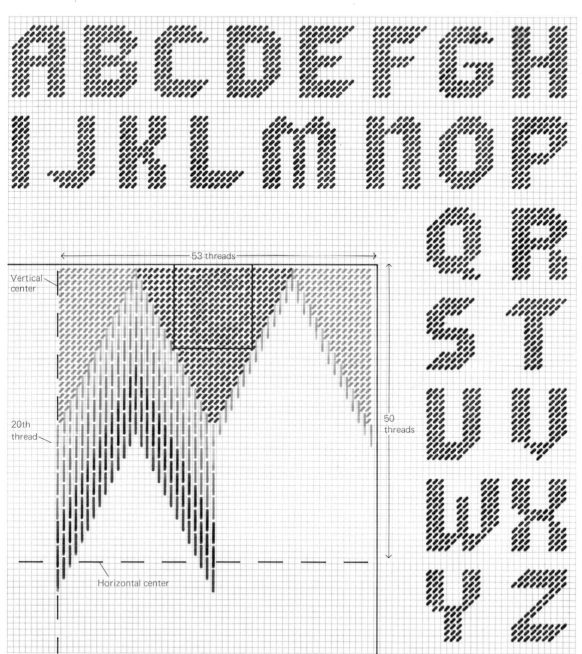

Line charts are used here (p. 166); the color of the drawn stitches represents the color of yarn in which they should be worked.

Oriental-design footstool cover

This Oriental design was first painted on the canvas and then worked in tent stitches.

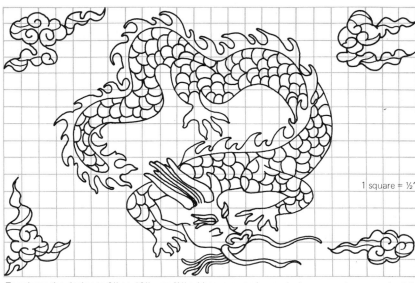

1 square = ½″

To enlarge the design to 8″ × 12″, use ½″ grid squares and copy design square for square (p. 14).

To make a needlepoint footstool like the one shown here, the stool must have a removable slip-seat top; footstools of this type are available in many needlework departments. Both instructions and materials are based on a 9 × 14 × 2-inch slip seat and on the design being worked in continental or basketweave tent stitches. The instructions can be used for covering any slip seat; if measurements differ, canvas and yarn needs must be recalculated (at right and p. 183).

Materials needed

Footstool with 9″ × 14″ × 2″ slip seat
⅔ yard 14-gauge canvas (for the footstool shown here)
Persian yarn: 140 yds. light gray; 10 yds. light mustard; 16 yds. rust red; 9 yds. dark green; 6 yds. each of turquoise and dark mustard
#22 tapestry needle
Staple gun
Paper, pencils, coloring devices to draw and transfer design
Unbleached muslin, batting, and masking tape if slip seat needs re-padding

Preparation

Remove slip seat (usually attached with screws on underside of footstool). If it needs to be re-padded, first remove old padding from mounting board. Then, lay several layers of batting over board and staple in place to underside of board; trim excess at corners or curves. Cover with muslin and staple in place to underside of board, gathering excess at corners or curves. Measure slip seat—length plus depth at each end and width plus depth at each end. Add 1 inch to each of these measurements to achieve the total area needed for design and background, plus a ½-inch turn-under along each edge. Cut canvas to these measurements plus a 3-inch margin on each edge. For a 9 × 14 × 2-inch slip seat, cut canvas to 20 × 25 inches. To determine the placement of the design and its dimensions, measure top surface of slip seat. Enlarge design (p. 14), using gridded drawing above as a guide. To produce an enlarged drawing of 8 × 12 inches, a size suitable for a 9 × 14-inch top, use ½-inch grid

squares. To make it significantly smaller or larger, assign a different measurement to the grid squares. To adapt the design for a square or circular area, either reposition corner motifs or eliminate them. Place design on canvas (pp. 164-165).

The needlepoint

Stitch design on canvas, using continental or basketweave tent stitches (p. 121). Two strands of Persian yarn should provide a suitable yarn coverage (p. 118).

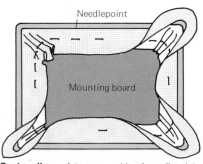

To re-pad slip seat: Layer batting over mounting board; staple to underside; trim excess. Cover with muslin; staple to underside; gather excess.

Block the canvas (p. 185); remove while it is still slightly damp.

Mounting the needlepoint

Center right side of slip seat to wrong side of needlepoint. Working opposite edges at the same time, wrap needlepoint to underside of slip seat, stretch taut and staple in place. Gather fullness at corners and curves. Trim excess canvas. Allow needlepoint to dry. Attach slip seat to footstool.

Center slip seat to wrong side of needlepoint. Bring edges of needlepoint to underside; staple in place; gather fullness at corners or curves.

Man's belt

Needlepoint belt makes a great gift for any man.

The overall design of this needlepoint belt is formed by the repetition of a single charted motif. The number of repeats will depend on the waist size of the man for whom it is being made; the belt here is made for a 33-inch waist.

Materials needed

Strip of 14-gauge canvas, 5½″ long (belt depth) by waist measurement plus 10″ (belt width)

Grosgrain ribbon, 1½″ wide by waist measurement plus 6″

Persian yarn (for sizes 33-34): 38 yds. each of rust and olive; 20 yds. light olive; 25 yds. camel

#22 tapestry needle

Sewing thread to match grosgrain

Hand-sewing needle

1½″ center-bar buckle

Awl

Metal eyelets and eyelet pliers

Preparation

Cut canvas to measure 5½ inches long by a width equal to the waist measurement plus 10 inches. If necessary, join lengths (p. 164) or cut along selvage to produce desired width. Tape edges of canvas.

Draw one line across canvas 2 inches below top edge, another line parallel to and 20 threads below the first line. These mark top and bottom of belt. To mark right end of belt, draw a vertical line 2 inches in from right end of canvas. To mark left end, draw a line that is the waist measurement plus 6½ inches away from the right-end mark. Next mark several points along horizontal center of belt: Place first mark 1½ inches in from left end—this marks place where buckle prong will be set. Place next mark, for center eyelet, the waist measurement minus the length of the prong away from the prong mark. Make additional marks, for more eyelets, to right and left of center eyelet, spaced about 1 inch apart.

The needlepoint

Following the chart for Example A on page 171 and using tent stitches, stitch design onto canvas. A two-strand weight of Persian yarn should provide suitable yarn coverage (see p. 118). Work first repeat to right of prong mark, then work repeats toward right end of belt, leaving four meshes unworked around each eye-

let marking. Work last repeat to left of prong mark; leave four meshes unworked around prong mark. (All unworked meshes should align with each other.) Block the needlepoint as described on page 185.

Finishing the belt

Trim each edge of canvas to ½ inch. Turn edges back along needlepoint; miter corners (p. 186). To attach buckle: Using an awl, spread unworked meshes at prong mark. Slip end of belt over bar of buckle; push prong through hole. Fold belt end back over bar of buckle. Align outer edges of fold-back to outer edges of front of belt; stitch together along edges. Cut grosgrain same length as belt; turn ends under ½ inch. Lay grosgrain onto wrong side of belt and match one folded end to right end of belt; lap other end over end of fold-back at left end. Pin in place; using small stitches, sew along all edges. From right side and using an awl, push apart the four unworked meshes at each eyelet marking; then, push the awl through the grosgrain at each mark. Using an eyelet pliers, attach the eyelets.

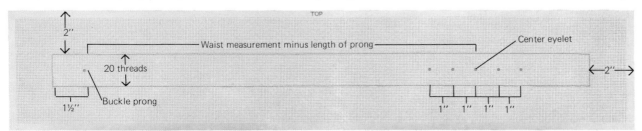

Strip of canvas should measure 5½″ by the waist measurement plus 10″. Markings include, besides edges of belt, points for buckle prong and eyelets.

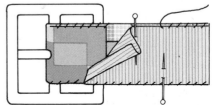

Grosgrain is same length as belt; ends are turned under ½″. One end aligns with belt's right end; other laps over fold-back at left end.

Repeats are worked with tent stitches, from prong mark to right, then final repeat to its left. Four meshes are left unworked at prong and eyelet marks.

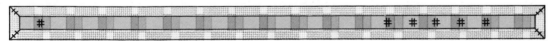

After stitching is completed, excess canvas at edges is turned back along the last row of stitches; corners are mitered as explained on page 186.

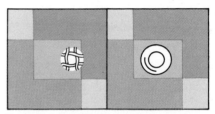

To prepare for eyelets, unworked meshes are spread and grosgrain is pierced with an awl. Eyelets can then be attached with eyelet pliers.

189

Address book cover

Barn is charming motif for an address book.

Charted barn is 56 threads square—about 5½ inches on 10-gauge canvas.

Materials needed

Binder (one shown is 9″ long by 7″ wide with a 1¾″-wide spine)

10-gauge canvas (length of binder plus 6″ by twice width of binder plus width of spine plus 6″)

Persian yarn: 160 yds. taupe; 12 yds. medium blue; 11 yds. pale orange; 10 yds. dark red; 9 yds. salmon; 7 yds. each of light blue and light green; 6 yds. white; 5 yds. each of dark green and yellow-brown; 4 yds. each of black, medium green, blue-green, cream

#18 tapestry needle

Lining fabric (length of binder plus 1″ by twice the width of binder plus width of spine plus 2½″)

Sewing thread to match lining

Hand-sewing needle

Preparation

Cut canvas the length of the binder plus 6 inches, by twice the width of the binder plus the width of the spine plus 6 inches. For a 9 × 7 × 1¾-inch binder, cut canvas 15 inches long by 21¾ inches wide. Tape the edges of the canvas; label the top. Open the binder and center it on the canvas. Mark canvas as follows: Draw a line ¼ inch above and below the binder; then draw a line along each side of the binder. Mark the width of the spine at both top and bottom. Remove binder and mark front edge of spine from top to bottom marks. Mark the center of the front cover (see right).

Cut one strip of lining fabric that is the length of the binder plus 1 inch, by the width of the spine plus 2½ inches. This strip will be used to face the spine area; for the binder shown, facing is 10 inches long by 4¼ inches wide. Cut two strips of lining fabric, each measuring 1 inch more than the length of the binder but the same as the binder in width. These pieces will be used to face the front and back covers; for the binder shown, each of these pieces measures 10 inches long by 7 inches wide. Turn under all of the edges of all three of the facing pieces ¼ inch. Machine-topstitch the folded edges in place.

The needlepoint

Stitch the barn onto the center of the front cover. Follow the chart on page 167; use tent stitches and a 3-strand thickness of yarn. Cover the remaining area with a novelty stitch (Hungarian stitch is used here); change the yarn weight if necessary for adequate coverage (p. 118). Block needlepoint (p. 185).

Finishing the cover

Trim the excess canvas to 1 inch. Turn back each edge along the needlepoint; miter the corners (p. 186). Apply facings as shown at right. To insert binder into finished cover, fold covers of binder and needlepoint back, then slip each binder cover under a cover facing.

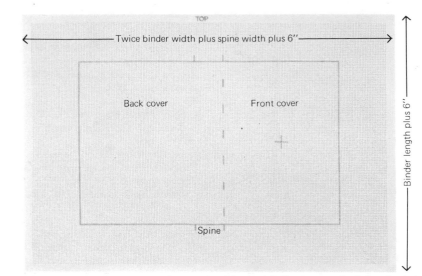

Canvas is cut and prepared as shown above and explained at left. Front cover extends from front of spine to right edge of needlepoint, back cover from back of spine to left edge of needlepoint.

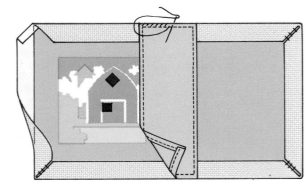

Attaching facings: With wrong sides together, center spine facing over spine area of cover. Align its top and bottom edges with top and bottom edges of needlepoint. Stitch the two together along these edges.

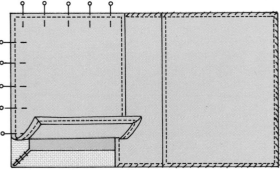

With wrong sides together, place a cover facing to the front cover area of the needlepoint. Align its top, side, and bottom edges with those of the needlepoint. Stitch the two together along those three edges. Apply a facing to the back cover area the same way.

Appliqué

192 Appliqué basics
Tools and supplies
Design ideas
193 Making templates
Transferring designs
Other design possibilities
194 Cutting appliqués
Handling curves and corners
195 Securing appliqués by hand
Methods of sewing appliqué
196 Securing appliqués by machine
Straight-stitch method
Zigzag method
197 Zigzagging around corners
and curves
Securing by fusing
198 Planning appliqué layering
order
199 Using bias strips in appliqué
Interfacing an appliqué
Stuffing an appliqué
200 Decorating appliqués
201 Reverse appliqué
General introduction
202 Reverse appliqué/San Blas
Basic technique
Using two fabric layers
203 Using three fabric layers
Using slits
204 Using colored patches
Using shaped patches
205 Reverse appliqué/cut-through
General introduction
Basic technique
Special techniques
206 Basic machine technique
Special machine techniques

Appliqué projects
263 Boy's coveralls/machine appliqué
264 Baby quilt
266 Cut-through appliqué wall hanging

Appliquéd wall hanging/"Landscape with Mountain"/Size: 36" x 46"/© Madge Huntington 1976

Appliqué basics

Tools and supplies
Designing appliqué
Making templates
Transferring designs
Cutting appliqués
Handling curves and corners
Securing appliqués by hand
Securing appliqués by machine
Securing appliqués by fusing
Planning appliqué layering order
Using bias strips in appliqué
Interfacing an appliqué
Stuffing an appliqué
Decorating appliqués

Tools and supplies

Appliqué work is basically a sewing craft, and so it calls for much the same tools and supplies. **Fabrics** are of course essential, but not necessarily in great quantities; scraps and pieces are usually adequate for a small project. Easiest to handle are smooth-surfaced fabrics in a light- to medium-weight. Be sure that all the fabrics used are compatible if they are to be laundered. Try to avoid loosely woven or extremely bulky fabrics; they can be very difficult to manage. If, despite this limitation, you still want to use a particular loose weave, back it with iron-on interfacing (see p. 199). Before using any fabrics, press out all wrinkles and creases.

To stitch an appliqué in place, use an all-purpose (size 50) sewing **thread.** For additional decorative stitching, you can go to embroidery floss or pearl cotton. Sharps are a type of medium-length **needle** excellent for hand stitching. They come in different sizes to accommodate different fabric weights. Other needle types, such as embroidery and chenille, have larger eyes, permitting thicker threads and yarns to be used.

Another essential tool in appliqué work is a sharp pair of **scissors.** Ideally, you should have two pairs, a medium-size dressmaker's shears for general cutting and a small, pointed embroidery scissors for close trimming jobs.

Other useful sewing supplies include fine **straight pins** for holding appliqués in place, and a dressmaker's **marking pencil** or hard lead pencil for marking fabrics. **Thimbles** are handy if you are accustomed to using them. **Frames** and **hoops** are optional and should be used only if they will make your work easier. **Heavy tracing paper** and **colored construction paper** are helpful to have for copying or cutting out designs.

As an alternative to stitching appliqué down, you can use **fusible webs,** purchasable by the yard or in precut lengths. See page 197 for the fusing technique.

Design ideas

Inspiration for appliqué designs can be found in many sources, among them coloring books, greeting cards, and everyday objects. Traditionally the designs are quite primitive and childlike rather than precise works of art. A typically simple design can consist of a central motif cut from a single piece, or perhaps made up of two or more pieces. A composition, in contrast, is somewhat more difficult and consists of many motifs that together form a complete picture. If you are a beginner, start with designs consisting of one or a few large pieces.

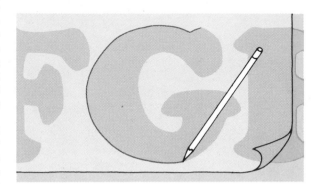

The monogram letter is a typical one-piece design. It is being *traced,* which is the simplest method for obtaining a design. If traced drawing is not the desired size, enlarge or reduce it to your liking by the methods described in the Embroidery chapter.

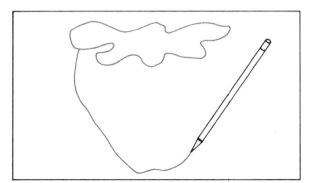

The single strawberry exemplifies a simple design of two main pieces. It is being *free-drawn,* which is another way to obtain a design. Free-drawn designs can come from your imagination or from a model. Drawings need not be precise; in fact, simplified lines and details work best.

This sheep design is a composition created by first *cutting free shapes* of construction paper, then arranging them to form a pastoral scene.

Making templates

If you have cut out shapes from construction paper to arrive at a design, or if you have cut out pattern pieces from a book or pattern, those pieces become the actual templates. If, however, you have traced or free-drawn a design, you will have to make templates for each separate shape in the design (see below). When appliqué is employed in patchwork, a single design may be duplicated many times over, which means the patterns are used again and again. In such instances, it is wise to re-cut the patterns from very heavy paper so that the templates will not become too worn to use (see Patchwork).

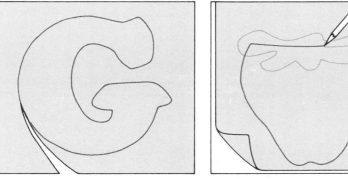

To make a template from a tracing or drawing, simply cut along the drawn outline of the appliqué piece. If the template is to be used many times, re-cut it from heavy paper.

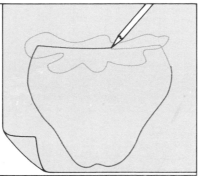

If your design consists of two or more pieces, re-trace each piece separately. Straighten out edges that will be covered by another piece instead of trying to jigsaw the two pieces together.

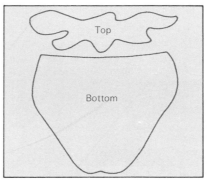

Cut out each separate piece along the drawn outlines. To avoid any errors when cutting the actual appliqué, mark the right side of each pattern piece with an identifying word or symbol.

Transferring designs

Before transferring a design, cut background fabric, which may be a patchwork block or even a garment section, to desired size. In order to center the design accurately, mark lengthwise and crosswise center lines through the background piece. The center lines are especially helpful in patchwork because they enable you to position the appliqué in exactly the same spot for each of the blocks involved.

The placement of single appliqués is not always marked on the background if the center lines will serve adequately as guides. For greater accuracy, however, placement marking is recommended.

To determine center lines, fold and crease background fabric in half, then in quarters. Open fabric out, and if necessary for a firm guideline, baste along lengthwise and crosswise creases.

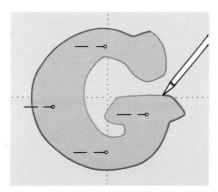

To transfer your design, position template, right side up, on background fabric and pin in place. Trace around template, using either a sharp dressmaker's pencil or a hard lead pencil.

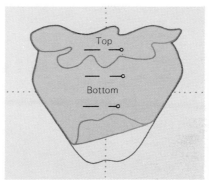

If a design has two or more pieces, carefully assemble all pieces into their correct positions, then pin them to the background fabric. Trace around design formed by the combined templates.

Other design possibilities

Paper cutouts are another good source of designs. This kind of snowflake is often seen in traditional Hawaiian quilts. Because of its intricacies, hand stitching is advised and is usually accompanied by echo quilting (see p. 200).

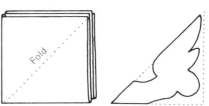

To make paper cutout, fold square sheet of paper in quarters, then in half diagonally. Cut out pieces through all thicknesses, then open out.

Using a fabric print is a quick and easy way to obtain an appliqué design. Simply cut ½″ to 1″ outside design silhouette and machine-stitch appliqué print to background fabric (see p. 196).

193

Appliqué basics

Cutting appliqués

The first step, if you will be cutting several appliqués, is to assemble your fabric scraps and decide which ones will be used for each piece. Try to achieve a balance of colors as well as a balance of prints, solids, and textures. If the fabrics you have selected have a dominant print or weave, consider carefully how you want that print or weave placed on each appliqué piece. For example, if a fabric is striped, it can be cut so that the stripes run vertically, horizontally, or diagonally, or a combination of these. In making each decision, consider the surrounding fabrics as well.

Another consideration is the compatibility of the appliqué fabric and the background fabric in terms of care. Generally speaking, if the appliquéd article will not be laundered, almost any combination of fabrics is acceptable. If it will be laundered, be sure that all of the fabrics you plan to combine can take the same kind of washing and drying.

To cut out an appliqué, follow the step-by-step instructions given at the right. Note that staystitching is recommended to make it easier to turn edges under. If an appliqué has curves or corners, the seam allowances need to be clipped or notched to facilitate turning.

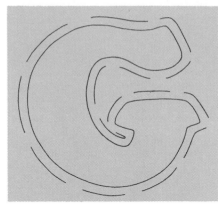

1. Pin template to right side of fabric. Trace around pattern with dressmaker's pencil. Remove template. Mark a ⅛'' to ¼'' seam allowance outside the drawn seamline. Use the wider seam allowance on fabrics that are loosely woven.

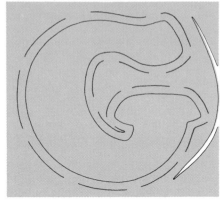

2. Cut appliqué outside of marked lines so that an ample fabric width is left. This wider margin will make it easier for you to staystitch in the next step.

3. To facilitate turning under of edges, staystitch a hair outside inner marked seamline. Set sewing machine to 12-15 stitches per inch.

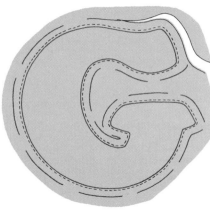

4. Trim margin by cutting appliqué on outer marked lines as shown. Clip seam allowances around curves and corners so edges can be properly turned (see below).

Handling curves and corners

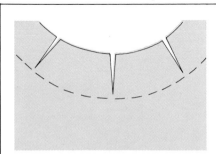

Along inner curves, clip seam allowance to staystitching to aid turning. Space the clips closer together along deeper curves.

Along outer curves, notch out pieces along seam allowances to keep bulky pleats from forming when edges are turned under.

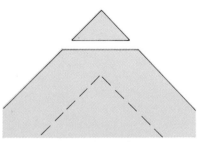

At outside corners, blunt seam allowance as shown to help reduce bulk in the point when the edges are mitered (see opposite page).

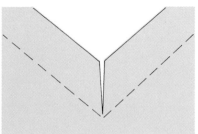

At inside corners, make a single clip into the point of the corner (up to staystitching) so the edges can be turned under.

194

Securing appliqués by hand

An appliqué can be hand-stitched in place by either of the two methods shown below. The first method, though somewhat more time-consuming, is recommended for beginners. It calls for an additional basting step that holds the turned-under seam allowance in position, making it less awkward to secure the appliqué to the background. The second method skips the initial basting of edges; instead the appliqué is pinned in place, and the edges turned and stitched.

To secure the appliqué, a fine slipstitch is recommended; it holds the appliqué dependably and is almost invisible

when carefully worked. An overhand stitch, though not invisible, should be used in small areas that tend to fray; these little straight stitches can keep the short fabric threads from popping out (see below). Embroidery stitches such as the running stitch and the cross stitch can also be used to fasten down an appliqué. Remember that these are decorative stitches, meant to be seen; they will become part of the design (see p. 200).

The use of a hoop or frame is optional. Some find stitching easier without one, while others find it a necessity. Try working both ways, then judge for yourself.

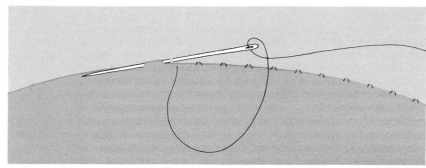

To slipstitch, work from right to left. Bring needle and thread through folded edge of appliqué. Pick up a thread or two from background fabric just opposite, then insert needle back into folded edge and slip it through fold about ⅛"; bring needle out and pull thread through. Continue this way to end.

Methods of sewing appliqué

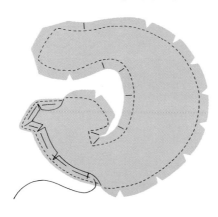

Method 1: Along marked seamline of appliqué, fold and finger-press seam allowance to wrong side; hand-baste folded edge as you finger-press. Keep staystitching within the seam allowance width.

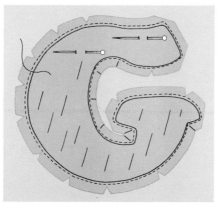

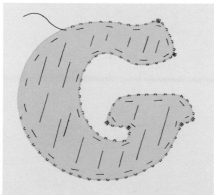

Pin appliqué to background, and if necessary, hold in place with vertical bastings. Secure appliqué with a fine slipstitch along folded edges. Remove all bastings.

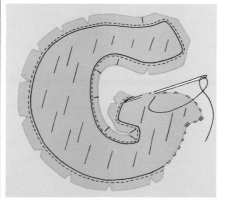

Method 2: Pin cut appliqué to the background (edges are not yet turned under). If needed, hold appliqué in place with vertical bastings. Be sure that bastings do not extend into seam allowance; edges must still be turned under.

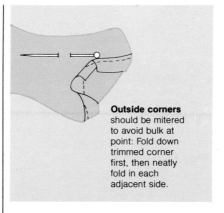

Using point of needle to roll seam allowance under, slipstitch turned edges in place. Be sure staystitching is turned in with seam allowance. Continue to turn and stitch in this way until appliqué is fully secured. Remove all bastings.

Outside corners should be mitered to avoid bulk at point: Fold down trimmed corner first, then neatly fold in each adjacent side.

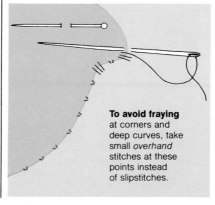

To avoid fraying at corners and deep curves, take small *overhand* stitches at these points instead of slipstitches.

Appliqué basics

Securing appliqués by machine

The sewing machine is used extensively in appliqué work today because it makes it possible to complete a project in less than half the time it would take to do a similar project by hand. A decision to stitch an appliqué by machine instead of by hand can depend upon several factors.

First, if the fabrics you are working with are relatively substantial rather than fine and delicate, they will be easier to handle with the sewing machine. Another consideration is the ultimate use of the appliquéd article. If it is likely to get a great deal of wear (a child's coverall, for exam-

ple), a machine application is undoubtedly more practical.

There are basically two methods of machine appliqué. One is done entirely by means of straight stitching; the other, which is considerably faster, uses a combination of straight and zigzag.

Before starting, test and adjust the machine so its tension is balanced and the pressure is correct for the fabrics being used. The stitch length for straight stitching is generally 10-12 stitches per inch. Zigzag stitching is usually narrow, with a short stitch length.

Straight-stitch method

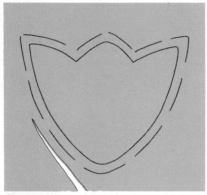 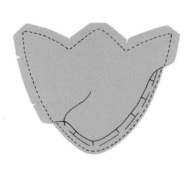  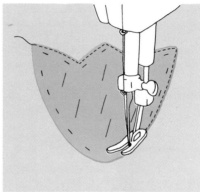

Pin template to right side of appliqué fabric. Trace around pattern and remove it. Mark ¼" seam allowance outside marked line. Cut outside marked lines, leaving ample fabric width.

Staystitch just outside inner marked seamline. Trim excess margin by cutting on outer marked lines. Clip and notch curves and corners. Fold seam allowance to wrong side; baste in place.

Position and pin appliqué to right side of background fabric; if necessary, baste appliqué down with vertical bastings as shown to keep appliqué from shifting during stitching.

Set sewing machine to medium stitch length (about 10-12 stitches per inch). Carefully stitch along folded edges of appliqué. Pull thread ends to wrong side and knot. Remove bastings.

Zigzag method

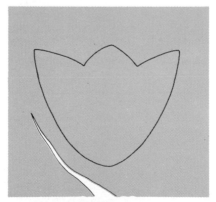 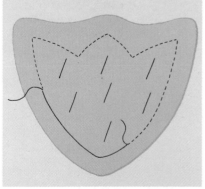 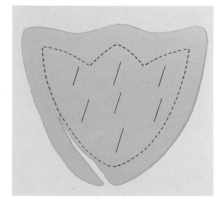 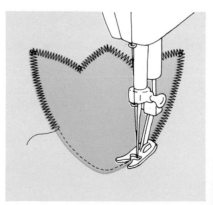

Pin template to right side of appliqué fabric and trace around it. Remove pattern. Cut out appliqué outside marked lines, leaving an ample seam allowance (approximately ½" to 1" wide).

Position and pin appliqué to right side of background fabric; if necessary, baste appliqué down with vertical bastings as shown. Straight stitch directly over the marked seamline.

Using a sharp pair of pointed embroidery scissors, trim away seam allowance, cutting as close to stitching line as possible; be careful not to cut the stitches or the background fabric.

Sew narrow, short zigzag (satin stitch) over raw edges and straight stitching. Pull thread ends to wrong side; knot. Remove bastings. To zigzag around corners and curves, see opposite page.

Zigzagging around corners and curves

Right-angle corners:
Zigzag down one side of corner and stop at point shown by dot. For *outside* corner, position needle outside of point. For *inside* corner, position needle inside of point. Pivot and zigzag down other side of corner.

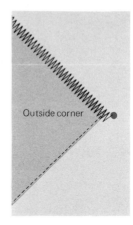

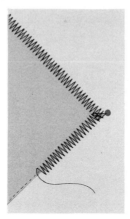
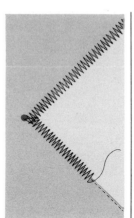

Wide-angle corners:
Imagine a line running through center of corner. Zigzag down one side of corner and stop when needle hits imaginary line at dot. For *outside* corner, position needle on dot outside of corner. For *inside* corner, position needle on dot inside of corner. Pivot and zigzag down the other side.

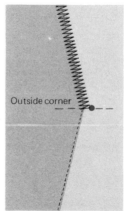
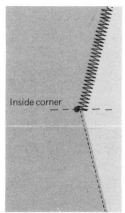
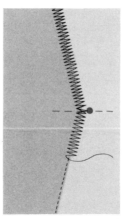
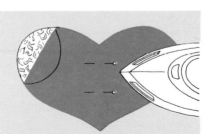

Sharp-angle corners:
Zigzag down one side of corner. Shortly before reaching point, start narrowing zigzag width. Continue stitching to just beyond corner (zigzag by then will be very narrow). Pivot and zigzag down the other side, gradually widening zigzag back to original width. Technique is the same for both outside and inside sharp corners.

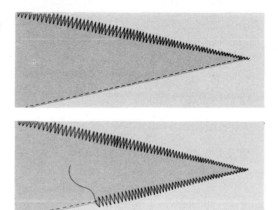

Tight curves: Zigzag down one side toward curve. To get around curve, stop and pivot work often, positioning needle on the narrower side of the curve each time work is turned. The technique is the same for both outside and inside curves.

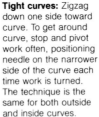
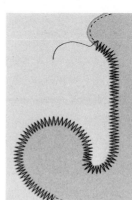

Securing by fusing

Appliqués can be secured with a fusing web, a bonding agent that holds two fabrics together when it is melted between them. Fusing works best on large appliqué pieces; alignment of appliqué and web becomes difficult with small or intricate shapes. Follow manufacturer's instructions carefully for a bond that will hold through normal cleaning.

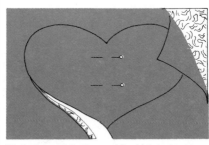

Pin fusing web to wrong side of fabric; treat two as one layer. Pin template to right side of fabric; trace around. Cut out appliqué on marked line.

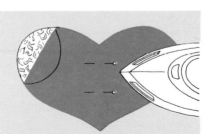

Pin appliqué and web to right side of background; be sure they are perfectly aligned. Heat-baste appliqué by pressing between pins with tip of iron.

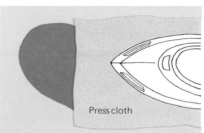
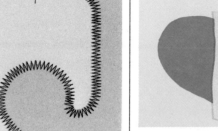

Remove pins. Place damp press cloth over appliqué. Hold iron on cloth until area is dry. Lift iron and move to next area; do not glide iron.

Appliqué basics

Planning appliqué layering order

If the design of your appliqué is made up of two or more pieces, a certain amount of planning must be done to work out a numerical *order of layering*. This plan of action establishes the order in which the appliqué pieces will be laid down so that elements that should appear below others are properly positioned to do so. This type of planning is especially important if the design consists of many pieces (see example below at right).

Use a drawing of your design as a map for your layering plan. Number each piece in the order in which it should be laid down. The elements that lie lowest are number 1 and subsequent layers building upward are numbered 2, 3, etc. When layering order is established, each piece is stitched down in numbered sequence: All the pieces numbered 1 are stitched first, then pieces numbered 2, 3, etc., until the design is completed.

An exception can be made to sequential stitching if you are making several such appliqués. With this method, all pieces are pinned in layering order, then stitched at random. The result is not as neat as with sequential stitching, nor as secure, since hidden edges are not finished. But it is faster, and, if the item is quilted, this will compensate for the incomplete stitching.

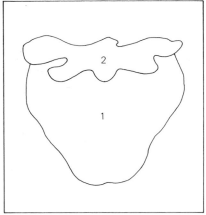

1. Make a layering plan on your drawn design by numbering each piece from lowest layer up. Following numbered plan, lay out actual appliqué pieces on marked background fabric as a check.

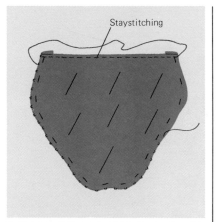

2. Remove all pieces except those numbered 1. Secure layer 1 in position, leaving unturned the edges that will be completely covered by another piece (top edge in the example above).

A layering plan is especially important in intricate compositions such as the sheep design shown here. As the numbering shows, four separate layers have been established in this design.

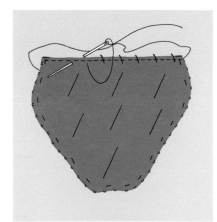

3. After the turned edges have been secured, use an overhand stitch along the unturned edge of the appliqué as shown; this will prevent a bulky ridge showing through at the overlap.

4. Pin and stitch layer 2 in position, covering the raw edges of layer 1. If the design has more layers, continue layering and stitching this way until the composition is completed.

This illustration shows the composition being built from the bottom layer up. Layers numbered 1 (cloud, mountain, sheeps' feet) have been appliquéd to the background; layer 2 (bodies) is being pinned.

Using bias strips in appliqué

When a design calls for a thin, gently curved strip of fabric (for example, a stem), use a length of bias strip instead of cutting a thin, curved appliqué piece that can be difficult to manage. The bias strip has some stretch and can be shaped to the curve. Commercially packaged bias tapes are convenient; come in a wide range of colors.

To make your own bias strip, find the true bias of the fabric by folding it diagonally so a straight edge on crosswise grain is parallel to lengthwise grain (1). Press fabric on diagonal fold, then open it out and use crease as a guide to mark parallel lines that are as wide as the desired width of the strip plus ½″ for seam allowances (2).

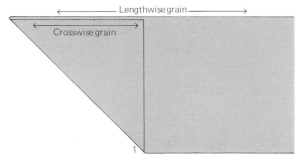

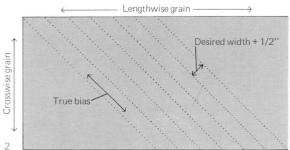

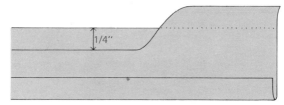

Cut bias strips along marked lines. Press under ¼″ seam allowance along both long edges of the cut bias strips.

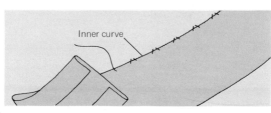

To secure, pin bias strip to background fabric, stretching it as necessary to conform to the desired curve. Secure the inner curve of the strip first.

Gently stretch outer edge of bias strip to shape to the curve; secure in place. Press bias strip after it is secured.

Interfacing an appliqué

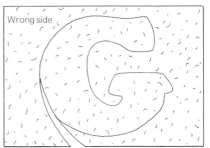

Appliqué fabrics that are limp or loosely woven usually need interfacing to give them stability and body for easier handling. Lightweight iron-on interfacings are usually the most convenient and can be purchased by the yard. The wrong side of the interfacing is covered with a special bonding agent that will melt and adhere to another fabric when a hot iron is applied.

To interface appliqué, cut out appliqué as usual (see p. 194). Place template on *wrong* side of interfacing and trace. Cut out interfacing along marked line; do not leave any seam allowances.

Center the interfacing over the appliqué so that wrong sides are touching, then press interfacing in place following the manufacturer's instructions. The appliqué is now interfaced and can be handled as you would a regular appliqué piece.

Stuffing an appliqué

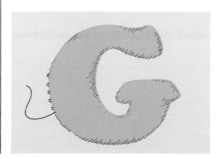

To add dimension to some appliqué designs, you can stuff the appliqué or parts of it with a soft batting, thereby bringing the appliqué into relief. Either cotton or polyester batting is suitable for this type of work.

To stuff an appliqué, first cut and secure it in place as described on pages 194-195; instead of completely fastening the appliqué down, leave a small opening in a strategic area, and carefully stuff batting through opening with a blunt needle or stick. Distribute the stuffing equally, but do not overstuff; this might distort the appliqué.

When you have finished stuffing the appliqué, stitch the opening down. Manipulate stuffing in this area if it has become flattened.

Appliqué basics.

Decorating appliqués

Decorating with embroidery or quilting can greatly enhance the overall look of any appliqué design. Even though you may not deliberately plan on any such embellishment, possibilities may occur to you after your appliqué is completed. There is a vast array of **embroidery** stitches to choose from; you can use them to work out original details or special effects, or simply as a decorative means of securing the appliqué in place.

Quilting is another decorative device that can add immeasurably to appliqué; it is especially favored for patchwork ap-

pliqué. Before quilting is begun, a layer of batting and one of muslin are placed under the appliqué background and all three are basted together. The simplest form of quilting is called *outline quilting*—a single row of running stitches sewed around the entire design, or parts of it, to emphasize its silhouette. Several quilting lines stitched in a radiating fashion are known as *echo quilting*. These can add a whole new dimension to a design. Quilting stitches can even be introduced as part of a composition (see the sheep picture at the lower right).

Embroidered details add a touch of realism to the simple appliquéd strawberry.

Embroidered cluster of grapes gives originality and charm to the appliquéd block initial.

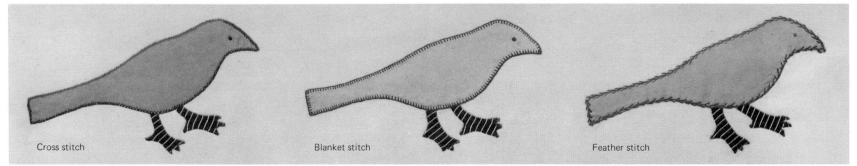

Cross stitch

Blanket stitch

Feather stitch

A different embroidery stitch is used to edge each of these appliquéd birds. The decorative stitches not only hold the appliqués in place, but also contribute color and texture to the individual designs.

Outline quilting, stitched just outside motif, silhouettes and emphasizes appliqué cut from fabric print.

Echo quilting radiates from an appliquéd motif. Technique is popular in Hawaiian quilts.

Quilting stitches are sometimes introduced as a part of the design itself. Here lines of quilting have been stitched to simulate falling rain.

Reverse appliqué

General introduction
Basic San Blas technique
Using two fabric layers
Using three fabric layers
Using slits in San Blas design
Using colored patches
Using shaped patches
Introduction to cut-through appliqué
Basic cut-through technique
Special cut-through techniques
Basic machine cut-through technique
Special machine cut-through techniques

General introduction

Reverse appliqué, like surface appliqué, involves multiple fabric layers, but they are differently handled. In the reverse technique, layers are stacked, and shapes cut away to expose the fabric layers beneath. The areas left on top are then secured at the cut edges to those below.

Reverse appliqué is known, in its traditional form, as **San Blas appliqué,** in honor of its best-known practitioners, the Cuna Indians from the San Blas Islands off the Panama coast. Even today, their colorful primitive designs decorate the blouses, or *molas,* of the San Blas women. Their motifs are usually radiating, silhouetted shapes of people, plants, and small creatures. These, plus slits that add strokes of color, give this intriguing appliqué form its unique look.

Aspects of this traditional technique have been adapted to create a modern form of reverse appliqué that is known as **cut-through appliqué.** This technique gives an almost sculptured look to the bolder and larger designs generally used.

The basic difference between the traditional and modern forms of reverse appliqué is the order in which layers are cut and stitched, and the relative complexity of technique that this imposes. To produce the intricate channels of San Blas appliqué, you must work from the bottom up, cutting and stitching as each layer is added. Simpler cut-through designs require far less exacting techniques than those of the traditional method. For cut-through work, all fabric layers are basted together at once, and shapes are cut out from the top layer down, producing larger to smaller "shaped holes." Special color effects are made possible by variations on each technique; these are explained on the following pages.

Fabrics for either technique, ideally, should be tightly woven, lightweight, and opaque. When you have chosen a pleasing combination of solid colors to carry out your design, find a matching thread for each fabric color.

San Blas appliqué is distinguished by the radiating shapes and free-form slits. Surface appliqué and embroidery can also be used. This animal design was worked from the bottom layer up.

Cut-through appliqué is stencil-like and almost sculptured in appearance. The fanciful sun design was systematically stitched and cut from the top layer down.

201

Reverse appliqué/San Blas

Basic technique

San Blas appliqué can be improvised, but to do this without losing the characteristic look, you must understand the basic technique, and the equal importance of the areas both *inside* and *outside* the drawn shape. When you work with only two layers of fabric, the drawn shape is cut from the top layer; at this point, depending on how the cutting was done, three different effects can occur (see the variations at right). Simply by interchanging these three effects, you can get a variety of linear images, whether you stay with two layers, or decide to add a third. The total is rarely more than three even in the most seemingly complex designs.

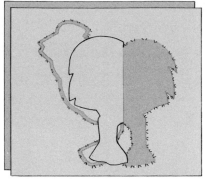

When a drawn shape is cut on the top layer, **the area inside can be removed,** and cut edges of outside area turned and stitched to bottom layer.

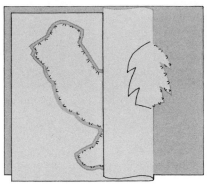

Or the area outside the drawn line can be removed. This time the cut edges of the inside area are turned and stitched to the bottom layer.

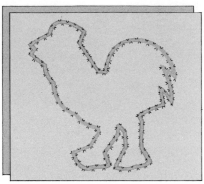

As a third alternative, **both inside and outside areas can be kept,** and cut edges on each side turned and stitched to create a channel.

Using two fabric layers

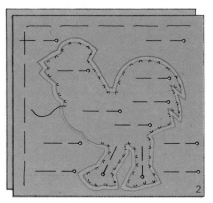

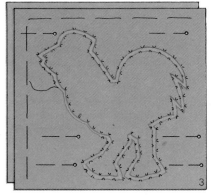

Using a total of only two fabric layers, you can still achieve the distinctive linear effect typical of San Blas appliqué.
1. Lay second fabric layer on first layer and baste them together around two edges. Draw or trace the main shape onto the top layer, and pin the two layers of fabric together inside and outside the drawn line.
2. Cut along the marked line, being careful not to cut layer below. Using point of needle, turn under the cut edges of the inside shape and slipstitch it to the layer below; clip curves as necessary as you work around. Remove pins from the inside area.
3. Now turn and stitch the cut edge of the outside area the same way to produce the colored channel that defines the shape. Remove pins.

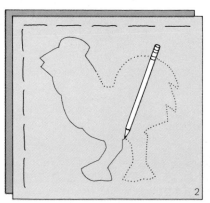

As a variation, a *third color* can be added without adding a full third layer of fabric. This new color can cover either the inside or outside areas of the drawn shape. In the example, the third color covers the outside area.
1. Follow Steps 1 and 2 in instructions above. Remove bastings and take away portions of the top layer that are not stitched down.
2. Lay the third fabric over the first pair and baste fabrics together around two edges. With a sharp pencil, feel edges of main shape below and trace around it. Pin the layers of fabric together outside the traced line.
3. Cut along line of top layer only. Remove inside area to expose second color below. Turn and stitch cut edges to bottom layer. Result is three colors, but only two full fabric layers.

Using three fabric layers

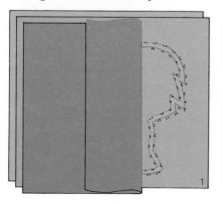 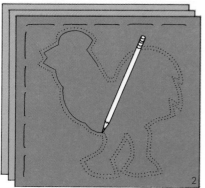 

Using a total of three fabric layers, you can achieve more elaborate linear effects.
1. After working first two layers (see opposite page), place third fabric layer over them, and baste all three together around two edges.
2. Using a sharp pencil, feel edges of finished channel below and trace around it. Pin all three layers of fabric together inside and outside the drawn channel lines. Now you must decide which part of the layer will be cut away and which part will remain (see Basic technique). Example shown is just one way to handle this third layer.
3. Cut along the inner marked line first. Turn under cut edges of the inside shape and stitch to layer below. Cut along outer marked line; turn and stitch the cut edges, turning enough to expose a total of three different channels.

Using slits in San Blas designs

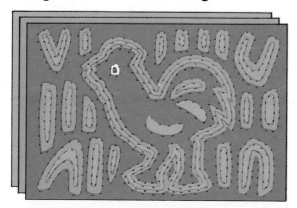

The series of elongated slits within the main motif and in the background is a typical feature of all San Blas appliqué. The slits are either *straight, angular,* or *curved,* and are used at random according to the design's configuration. Slits can be worked on the second layer as well as the third.

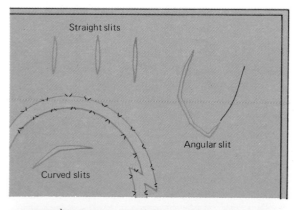

Straight slits

Angular slit

Curved slits

1. Draw desired slit lines on the uppermost fabric layer. Slits can be positioned in any direction. Cut on marked line through top layer only.

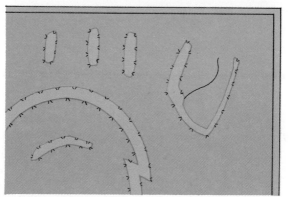

2. Using point of needle, turn cut edges under and stitch to the layer below, clipping as necessary to get around the curves and corners.

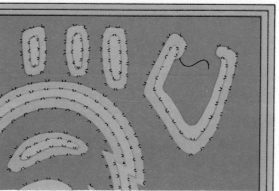

If third layer of fabric is added to piece already worked with slits, proceed first with the channeling of the main shape as described above. With a sharp pencil, feel edges of slits and trace around them. Cut along marked lines, then turn under and stitch cut edges to fabric layer below. An additional channel of color will be revealed around the original slits as shown. New slits can be added to the top of the third layer as well.

Reverse appliqué/San Blas

Using colored patches

Colored fabric patches are still another way of getting more color into your San Blas piece without adding whole layers of fabric. This technique, like most of the San Blas methods, is intended to be improvised and can be introduced whenever you would like a touch or two of new color. Merely baste fabric patches of desired colors and sizes between any two layers of fabric; then cut away small shapes and slits to expose the additional patch color below. In the examples shown, patches are applied to both the first and second layers. Be sure to select colors that will give you a strong contrast.

1. Cut and secure main motif (bottom left, p. 202). Position patches as desired; baste in place.

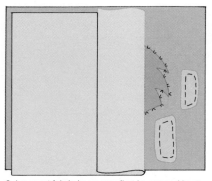

2. Lay next fabric layer over first layers and baste together around two edges.

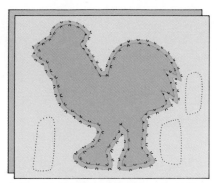

3. Complete the channeling of the main motif as described on page 202.

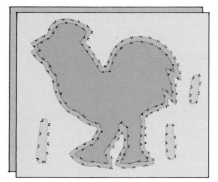

4. Feel patched areas below; cut and stitch slits or shapes over them to reveal their color.

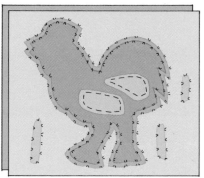

5. Position more patches over the top layer of fabric and baste around each.

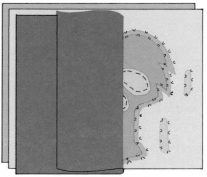

6. Lay another fabric layer over the first group and baste together around two edges.

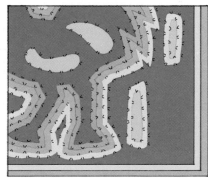

7. Complete channeling of main motif, then of the slits and smaller shapes over patched areas.

Using shaped patches

Another patch possibility in San Blas appliqué is a shaped patch, like the standard patch except that its edges are meant to produce a predetermined contour, and are revealed to achieve that. This requires the patch to be cut to a definite shape and its edges finished neatly before the next layer is put down. Shaped patches, like standard patches, can be used between any two layers. A shaped patch along the edge of a major motif will change its overall silhouette (see example). The patch in the example is added to the first layer, with the main motif already stitched down (see p. 202).

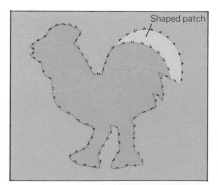

Shaped patch

1. Cut patch to appropriate shape. Position over desired area; turn and stitch edges in place.

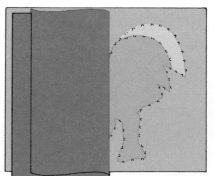

2. Lay next fabric layer over first layers and baste together around two edges.

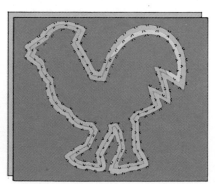

3. Trace around motif, and complete channeling as desired to reveal edges of shaped patch.

Reverse appliqué/Cut-through

General introduction

Cut-through appliqué is worked with all layers basted together first, then shapes cut away to expose the layer below; five layers are the maximum number used.

The first shape that is cut from the uppermost layer must be large enough to accommodate each subsequent shape to be cut within it. Cut-through designs are usually loose and bold, and have an almost sculptured look. Because of the bolder designs, this technique can also be done by machine (see next page).

Sometimes a layer can be exposed out of sequence by cutting through one or two layers above it. Additional colored patches can also be added if desired.

Basic technique

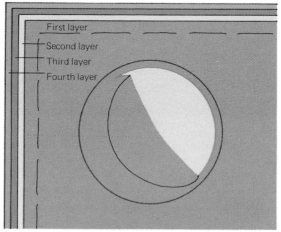

Cut desired number of layers to same size and stack them; baste together around outer edges. Trace or draw main shape (face) on top layer. Cut ⅛″ inside marked line; do not cut layer below.

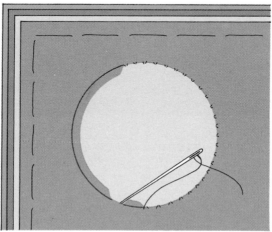

Using point of needle, turn under cut edge, clipping seam allowance as necessary to turn it under. Slipstitch turned edge to fabric layer below, letting a few stitches go through all layers.

Draw smaller parts of design that float within the main shape. Decide which shape or shapes will expose third layer (in this instance, the mouth). Cut and stitch shape the same way as before.

Special cut-through techniques

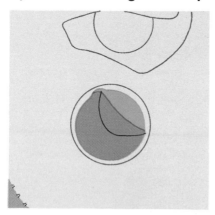

To skip a layer, cut away shape (cheeks) from *two* top layers; cut lower one slightly deeper so its edges lie under upper layer. Turn and stitch edges of upper layer to newly exposed layer below.

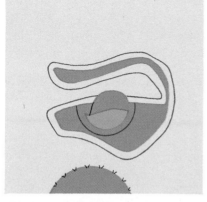

With this multiple layer procedure, you can work a detailed area so that two shapes abut one another (rather than one floating inside the other). First cut away the larger shape (eye unit) from top

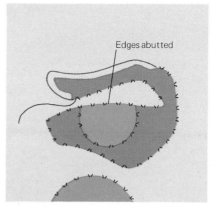

layer; do not secure edges yet. Draw and cut the smaller shape (eyeball) from newly exposed layer. Turn and stitch edges first of the smaller shape, then of the larger shape.

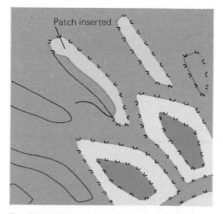

To add another color, draw and cut shape (sun ray) from top layer. Cut a patch ¼″ larger than cut piece. Insert patch under upper layer, then turn and stitch cut edges to patch below.

Reverse appliqué/Cut-through

Basic machine technique

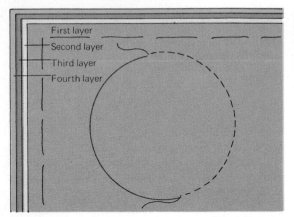

First layer
Second layer
Third layer
Fourth layer

Cut desired number of layers to same size and stack; baste together around outer edges. Draw main shape (face) on top layer. Set stitch length at 12-15; straight-stitch on marked line.

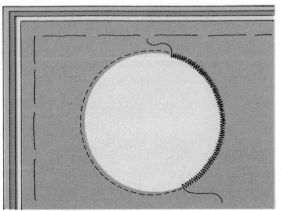

Cut top layer just inside stitched line. Adjust sewing machine for a narrow, short zigzag (satin stitch), then sew around cut shape to cover the raw edges and straight stitching.

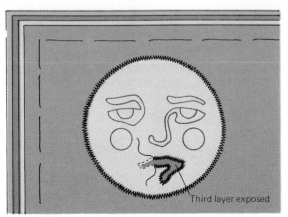

Third layer exposed

Draw smaller parts of design that float within the main shape. Decide which shape or shapes will expose third layer (in this case, the mouth). Stitch and cut as described for larger shape.

Special machine cut-through techniques

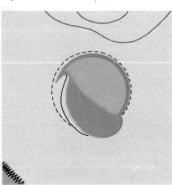

To skip a layer, straight-stitch around drawn shape. Cut away the shape (cheeks) from the two uppermost layers to expose the fourth layer below.

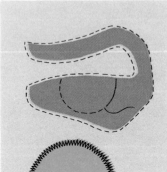

Zigzag over the cut shape to cover the raw edges and the straight stitching.

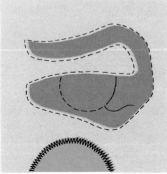

To work multiple layer procedure so two shapes abut, straight-stitch along larger marked shape (eye unit). Cut away shape just inside stitching line. Mark and straight-stitch the smaller shape (eyeball) on newly exposed layer.

Edges abutted

Cut away small shape inside stitching line. Zigzag over cut edges of both large and small shapes.

To add patch for extra color, draw shape (sun ray) on top layer. Cut ⅛" inside the marked line. Cut a patch that is ¼" larger than the cut-out piece.

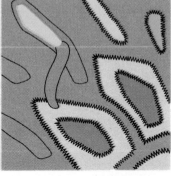

Patch inserted

Insert patch under cut edges of upper layer. Straight-stitch on marked line. Trim seam allowance even closer to stitching line. Zigzag over the raw edges.

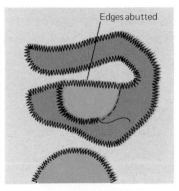

206

Patchwork

208 Patchwork basics
       Types of patchwork
 209   General considerations
       Fabrics and equipment
 210   Designing patchwork
 216   How color can influence
       a patchwork design
 217   Charting a patchwork
**218 Preparing and sewing a block-
       unit patchwork**
       Making and using templates
 220   General sewing techniques
 221   Straight seams
 222   Cornered seams
 223   Curved seams
 224   Seams through a base fabric
 226   General techniques for
       appliqués
 228   Single-layer appliqués
       Multiple-layer appliqués
 229   Pieced appliqués
       Appliqué-pieced block units
 230   Joining blocks, dividers, and
       borders
**232 Preparing and sewing a one-
       shape patchwork**
       Preparatory steps
       Shell
 233   Baby Blocks
 234   Grandmother's Flower Garden

Patchwork projects
 262   Man's patchwork vest
 264   Baby quilt
 267   Patchwork floor pillow

Patchwork basics

Types of patchwork
General considerations
Fabrics and equipment
Designing with squares and
diagonal lines
Designing with circles and parts
of circles
Designing appliqués
Crazy patchwork
Dividers and borders
How colors can influence
a patchwork design
Charting a patchwork

Types of patchwork

Patchwork is the joining of pieces of fabric to form a larger unit of fabric. The most interesting characteristic of any patchwork is the design that the joined fabric pieces produce. Some patchwork designs are simple and easy to analyze, others are so intricate that it is hard to tell how they were achieved.

The easiest type of patchwork to understand is the **one-shape** patchwork, in which all the pieces are the same shape and size. A one-shape patchwork can have great charm in a single color; two or more, carefully arranged, can produce an attractive overall design. An example of the one-shape patchwork is the Shell design (first illustration below).

All other patchwork can be classified as **block-unit** patchwork, so called because the fabric pieces are first joined into a block that itself becomes the basic shape. There are two kinds of block units, pieced and appliquéd. Most pieced block units consist of precisely shaped pieces that form a definite design within a square; when several such units are joined, a secondary overall design can be formed. An example is the Simple Star (second illustration). Also a pieced block patchwork, but an exception to the rule about precision, is the Crazy patchwork (see below). In it the pieces are random, rather than precise, shapes and colors. An appliquéd block unit consists of an appliqué and the base fabric to which it is stitched. Appliqués tend to be stylized versions of realistic objects (see the Rose, below); base fabric is usually square. For additional examples of patchwork designs, and instructions for producing the geometric shapes of which they are composed, refer to pages 210-215.

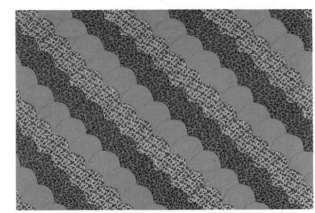
Shell design, a one-shape patchwork

Simple Star, a block patchwork of precisely shaped pieces

Crazy patchwork, a random-pieced block patchwork

Rose design, an appliquéd block patchwork

General considerations

Before any patchwork is started, two decisions need to be made simultaneously: the purpose of the patchwork, that is, whether it will be used for a skirt, a pillow, a quilt, etc.; and the patchwork design. Certain considerations can influence both choices. One is your level of expertise. If you are a beginner, it is best to start with a comparatively small project, and a simple design that does not have too many pieces. Also, you might find it easier to copy an existing design than it would be to create one.

Another influential factor is the construction techniques advised for different types of patchwork. There are basically only two methods of construction, both explained briefly at the right. The first is recommended mainly for one-shape patchworks because the shapes associated with them are difficult to join accurately by any other sewing method. Hand sewing here is preferable to machine; it adapts better to the variations involved in preparing and joining the pieces (see pp. 232-234). The second method is used for block-unit patchworks; in this case, joining may be done either by hand or by machine. Shapes that can be joined with straight seams will be easier to sew than those requiring cornered or curved seams. For more details on sewing block-unit patchwork, see pages 220-231.

Also to be considered are the size and number of pieces that will be needed to produce the finished patchwork. Both of these are determined in the course of charting the entire patchwork (p. 217). In general, the more pieces a design involves, the longer it will take to make the patchwork. It should not be assumed that a large finished size necessarily means a great many pieces. A single block of Simple Star (facing page), for example, can be made quilt- or pillow-top size. Regardless of its size, each block would take the same number of pieces; in this particular case the number required to finish each block is seventeen.

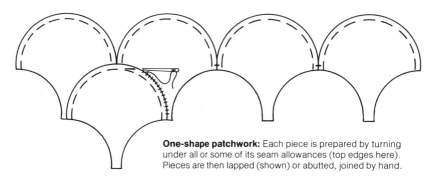

One-shape patchwork: Each piece is prepared by turning under all or some of its seam allowances (top edges here). Pieces are then lapped (shown) or abutted, joined by hand.

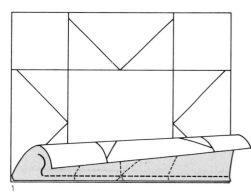

Block-unit patchwork: This type of patchwork can be sewn by hand or machine. First, the pieces are joined to form the individual block units (illustration 1). If it is a pieced block, the pieces are seamed to each other; for an appliquéd block, the appliqué is stitched to the base fabric. Next, the blocks are sewed together into strips of blocks (illustration 2). Finally, the strips are joined to complete the patchwork (illustration 3).

1

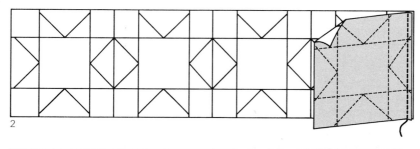

2

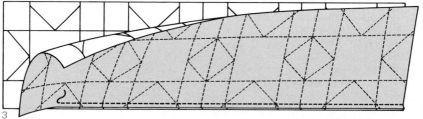

3

Fabrics and equipment

The fabrics for a patchwork should be compatible in weight, construction, and care requirements. Similar weight and construction makes them easier to join and assures that, when the fabrics are joined, one will not overpower and weaken the other. Medium-weight, evenly woven fabrics work best. When fabrics have common care requirements, they can all be cleaned in one way, either laundering or dry cleaning, with no fear of some being ruined.

Before buying any fabrics, chart the entire patchwork (p. 217). A chart gives you a preview of the finished patchwork design, and it becomes the basis for experimenting with and deciding on suitable color and print combinations. With a chart, you can also determine the exact size of each piece and then make templates (patterns) for cutting them out. Templates are also used to calculate how much of each fabric is needed to carry out the patchwork (p. 219). When you buy fabrics, try to find colors and prints that match or come close to those on the chart. If you are not sure how the fabric colors and prints will work together, buy a small amount of each and make a test patchwork. If you like the result, you can then buy the necessary quantities.

Besides the fabric, certain drawing and sewing tools are necessary. For designing and charting, you will need pencils, graph paper, an eraser, a ruler, and coloring devices. A compass will help you to draw curves and circles; a protractor is used to divide a circle. Have heavy paper or fine sandpaper on hand for making the templates. Scissors, pins, hand or machine sewing needles, and thread will be needed for cutting and sewing. Thread should be either white or a color that blends with the fabric colors. To mark fabric shapes and their seamlines, use a dressmaker's pencil. A white pencil is recommended for marking dark fabrics; a medium-shade pencil is best for marking light-colored fabrics.

Patchwork basics

Designing with squares and diagonal lines

Of all the shapes used in patchwork, the most frequent is the **square.** It is possible to draw a very accurate square on graph paper, using its lines as guides.

During the designing of a pieced block, the square can be any size, but before templates are made, it must be drawn to finished size (p. 218). In both design and template stages, the square is divided into smaller squares equal in size and number across and up and down. These inner squares form the grid used to produce the shapes of the pieced design. The simplest division of a square is two squares across by two down, or a 2 × 2 grid, but other and finer divisions are possible (see below). The more squares in a grid, the greater the number and the variety of potential shapes. The pieced block designs on these two pages run a typical gamut from simple to complex. To make it easier to "see" the basic structure, the underlying grid of each has been emphasized in the drawings.

Some pieced block designs consist of just the grid squares, for example, the Checkerboard (1). In other designs, grid squares are grouped to form rectangles or larger squares; one such block design is Patience Corner (9).

Diagonal lines are introduced to form more intricate shapes. A diagonal may be drawn through a square or a rectangle; in either case, it is a straight line drawn from one corner to the diagonally opposite corner. When a diagonal line is drawn through a square, two half-square triangles are formed; when drawn through a rectangle, it produces two half-rectangle triangles. The triangles may be used as they are, or grouped with other triangles, squares, or rectangles to create shapes. Half-square triangles are the basis of the Windmill (2). Pairs of half-square triangles with their diagonal edges in opposing directions form the four larger triangles along the edges of the Simple Star (4). Pairs of half-square triangles with their diagonal lines parallel produce the rhomboid shapes that represent the "scraps" in the Basket of Scraps (6). The center piece of the Crazy Ann block (14) results from joining two half-rectangle triangles to a grid square. The unusual shape in each corner of Lincoln's Platform (15) is a grouping of three grid squares and two half-square triangles.

Much of the effectiveness of pieced block designs hinges on the assignment of colors to shapes. For guidance in this, turn to page 216.

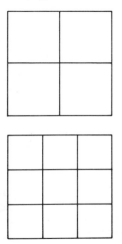

A grid is formed by dividing a square into smaller but equal squares. To do this, measure, then divide equally each side of the square; mark each dividing point. Draw grid by connecting sets of marks with straight lines from top to bottom, side to side. Shown at left are a 2 × 2 grid (top) and a 3 × 3 grid (bottom). At right are a 4 × 4 grid (top) and a 5 × 5 grid (bottom).

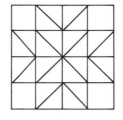
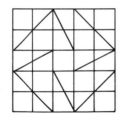

A diagonal line drawn between two diagonally opposite corners of a square or rectangle will form two triangles. Triangles can be used as is for the shapes of a design or grouped with other triangles, rectangles, or squares to create other shapes. First illustration shows diagonals for Eight Point Star shapes (p. 222); the second, diagonals for shapes of Crazy Ann (14, next page).

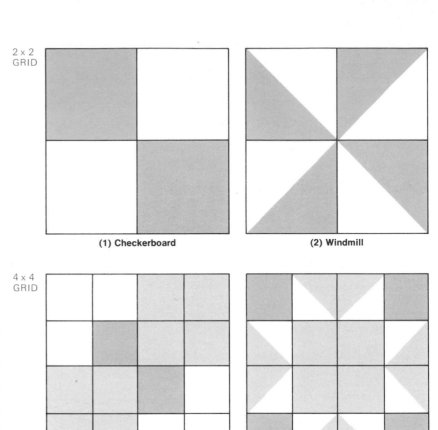

(1) Checkerboard

2 × 2 GRID

(2) Windmill

4 × 4 GRID

(3) Tam's Patch

(4) Simple Star

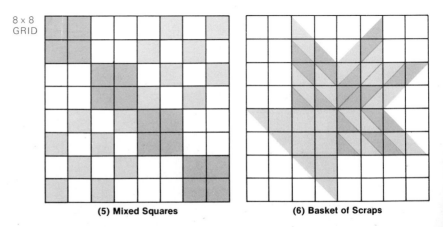

8 × 8 GRID

(5) Mixed Squares

(6) Basket of Scraps

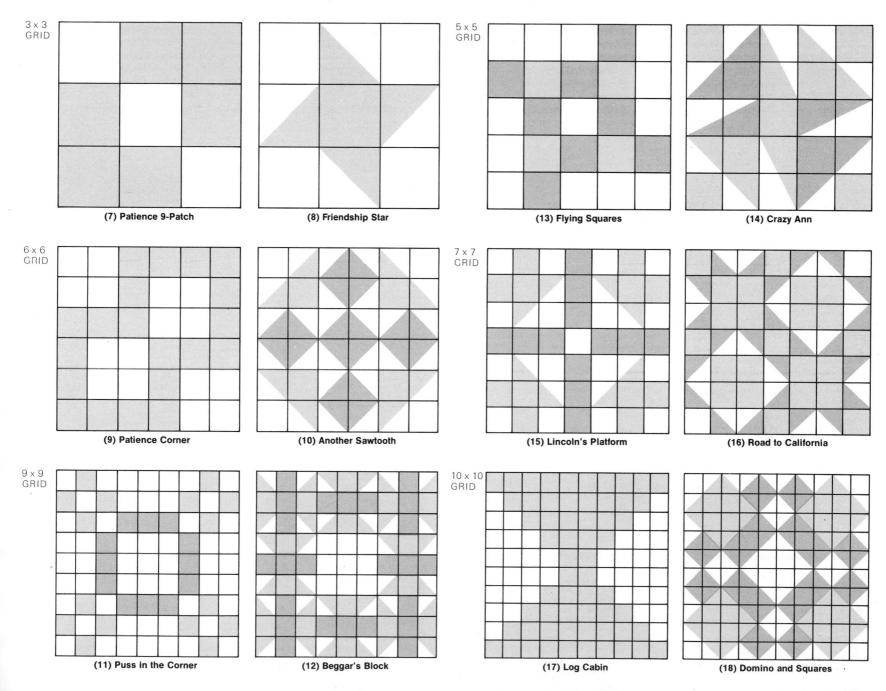

3 x 3 GRID

(7) Patience 9-Patch

(8) Friendship Star

5 x 5 GRID

(13) Flying Squares

(14) Crazy Ann

6 x 6 GRID

(9) Patience Corner

(10) Another Sawtooth

7 x 7 GRID

(15) Lincoln's Platform

(16) Road to California

9 x 9 GRID

(11) Puss in the Corner

(12) Beggar's Block

10 x 10 GRID

(17) Log Cabin

(18) Domino and Squares

Patchwork basics

Designing with circles and parts of circles

The use of circles and their parts to produce shapes is demonstrated by the patchwork designs on these pages. The techniques for forming the shapes accompany each design and are based on certain basic facts about circles.

A *circle* is a closed curve, of which all points are equidistant from a center. Its perimeter is called the *circumference*. The distance from the center of a circle to one edge is a *radius*, and equals one-half the circle's width. The *diameter* is the distance from edge to edge through the circle's center (in effect, two radii); it equals the width of the circle. Any circle contains 360°.

A compass is used to draw a circle. Formation of a circle to a certain size is best accomplished by drawing it within a square. The size of the square and of the circle within it depend on the design (see

Dresden Plate; Grandmother's Flower Garden). Their common center is located with perpendicular lines that also act as diameters and radii.

A portion of the circumference, called an *arc*, is also used to form shapes. A six-part division, with straight lines between division points, produces a hexagon (top of next page). An arc bounded by two radii creates a *sector*. Its shape depends on the length of the arc; that is determined by the degrees between radii. An arc equal to half a circumference and bounded by a diameter is a semicircle, containing 180° (see Shell). An arc equaling one-fourth of a circumference and bounded by two radii at right angles is a quarter-circle, containing 90° (see Shell; Drunkard's Path). To form a sector containing less then 90°, use a protractor (see Dresden Plate).

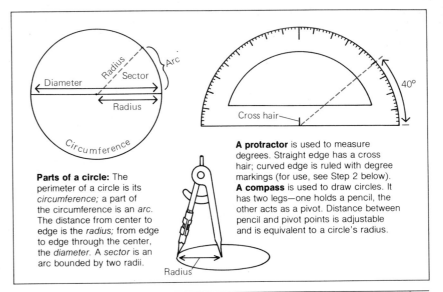

Parts of a circle: The perimeter of a circle is its *circumference;* a part of the circumference is an *arc*. The distance from center to edge is the *radius;* from edge to edge through the center, the *diameter*. A *sector* is an arc bounded by two radii.

A protractor is used to measure degrees. Straight edge has a cross hair; curved edge is ruled with degree markings (for use, see Step 2 below).
A compass is used to draw circles. It has two legs—one holds a pencil, the other acts as a pivot. Distance between pencil and pivot points is adjustable and is equivalent to a circle's radius.

Circles/Small sector

Dresden Plate

Concentric circles within a square supply the shapes for this appliquéd block design. The square determines the base block, also the large circle; from the large circle comes the **sector** for the wedge-shaped pieces. Small circle is the center piece.

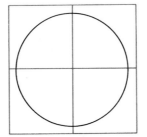

1. Draw a square (if you are making templates, draw it to finished size). Locate and mark the center of each side. Connect marks on top and bottom edges with a vertical line, those on the sides with a horizontal line. The point where these lines intersect is the exact center of the square. Place pivot point of compass on center of square. Extend pencil leg out horizontally to a point close to the side of the square (if you are drawing a template to finished size, point is about 1½" from side). Draw the circle.

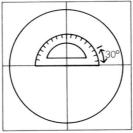

2. To determine the degrees in each wedge, first decide on number of wedges, then divide this number into 360 (circle contains 360°). Appliqué at left has 12 wedges; each wedge contains 30°. To form a sector with the desired number of degrees, proceed as follows: Align straight edge of protractor along horizontal center line; align its cross hair with vertical line. Find desired degree marking along curved edge of protractor and mark (30° in this case).

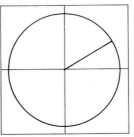

3. Remove protractor. Using a ruler, align the exact center point of square and the angle marking. Hold ruler in place and draw a radius from the center, through the angle measurement mark, to circumference of circle. Remove ruler. The horizontal center line of the square serves as the second radius for the sector.

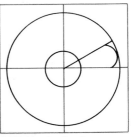

4. Working freehand, curve the outer edge of the sector as shown. Then place pivot point of compass on center of square, and spread pencil leg enough to draw a small circle. Small circle is the finished shape for the center piece of the appliqué. The sector, from its newly curved outer edge to the small circle, is the finished shape of each of the wedges in the appliqué. If making templates, only these two shapes need be drawn. If still in the design stage, roughly sketch in the other wedge shapes.

Circle/Small arcs

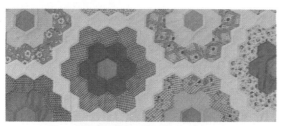

Grandmother's Flower Garden

Baby Blocks

A circle divided into six arcs underlies a **hexagon,** the six-sided figure repeated in both patchworks at the left. *Grandmother's Flower Garden,* the first example, consists simply of small hexagons; the hexagons in *Baby Blocks* are large, and each is composed of three same-size **diamonds.** The first step in constructing a hexagon is to draw a square with sides equal to the height of the desired hexagon. The finished hexagon will be the same height as the square, but narrower. In general, the hexagons for Grandmother's Garden are 1½″ high by slightly more than 1¼″ wide, and the hexagons for Baby Blocks are 6″ high by just over 5″ wide.

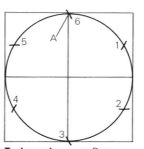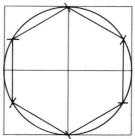

To draw a hexagon: Draw a square and find its center (Step 1, facing page). Draw a circle same width as square. With compass at same setting, divide circumference into six equal parts by means of six arcs, 1 to 6. Draw first arc with pivot of compass at point A; draw each new arc with pivot at point where arc just drawn intersects circumference.

Then draw the six sides of the hexagon. For each side, line up two neighboring arc intersection points along the edge of a ruler and draw a straight line from point to point.

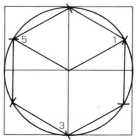

For Baby Blocks, start by drawing a hexagon. Then divide the hexagon into three equal diamonds as follows: Draw a straight line from intersection point 1 to the center; another line from intersection point 5 to the center. Bottom of vertical center line from center to intersection point 3 acts as the other dividing line.

Semicircle/Quarter-circles

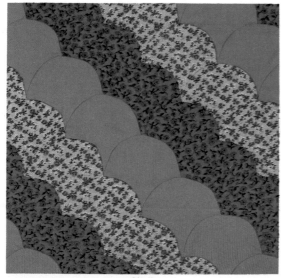

Shell

A semicircle and two quarter-circles produce the shape repeated in the *Shell* patchwork. To form the shell to a desired finished size, begin with a square the height and width of the shell (they are the same, the most common actual size being 3″).

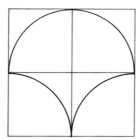

Draw a square and find its center (Step 1, facing page). With pivot point of compass on center, extend pencil leg along the horizontal center line to side of square; form a semicircle in upper half of square. With compass at same setting, place pivot on lower left corner and form a quarter-circle; move pivot to lower right corner and form another quarter-circle.

Drunkard's Path

A quarter-circle smaller than a square is what must be drawn to produce the repeat in this pieced block design. The block begins with a square divided into a 4 × 4 grid; identical quarter-circles are drawn with compass, guided by 16-square grid.

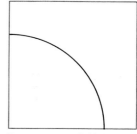

Draw a square; divide into a 4 × 4 grid (p. 210). With pivot of compass on corner of grid square, extend its pencil leg along one side of the square to a point about three-fourths the length of the side. Draw a quarter-circle by swinging the pencil to the opposite side. For templates, only one quarter-circle need be drawn. When designing, form a quarter-circle in each grid square, keeping the compass at a uniform setting; follow illustration at left for placement of quarter-circles.

213

Patchwork basics

Designing appliqués

The appliqué block units used most often consist of a **single-** or **multiple-layer** appliqué and a square of base fabric. As the names imply, the first appliqué type consists of one layer of fabric, the second of several layers. Because of the one fabric layer limitation, single-layer appliqués can have only one color and their shapes are usually those of simple, recognizable objects that you can trace or draw freehand. Maple Leaf is a single-layer appliqué. A more intricate design, such as the Snowflake, can be formed by cutting a design through a folded piece of paper (p. 193). Multiple-layer appliqués can have more than one color; their designs, which can be drawn or traced, can be more realistic than single-layer designs. The Rose and the flowers in the Basket of Flowers are examples.

When designing these appliqués, draw the base square and appliqué any size; at the template stage, draw them to finished size. The appliqué must fit within the square; some space can be left between the appliqué and the edges of the square as background. To draw designs to their proper size, see pages 14-15; for a folded-paper design, use a piece of paper the size of the appliqué.

There are two other types of appliqué block units. One consists of a **pieced** appliqué and a square of base fabric. The appliqué is designed to fit in the square; the area for the appliqué is subdivided to form the shapes of the appliqué. An example is the Dresden Plate; to design it, see page 212. The last type of appliqué block unit combines a single- or multiple-layer **appliqué** with a **pieced block.** An example is the Basket of Flowers. To design such a unit, draw a square, subdivide it into a grid, and form a pieced block design (pp. 210-211). Then design an appliqué to fit an area of the block. Basket of Flowers is based on a 6 × 6 grid; appliqué fits its upper part.

Maple Leaf

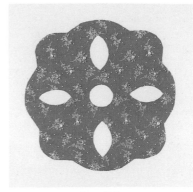

Snowflake

Rose

Dresden Plate

Basket of Flowers

Crazy patchwork

Crazy patchwork design is unique among pieced block patchworks in that the pieces that form the design are random sizes, shapes, and colors. Originally, crazy patchwork was worked as one large block unit. An easier way of working is to sew the pieces to form small block units, then sew these blocks together. The only element that has to be exact in size and shape is the block of base fabric to which the pieces are sewed; this is decided during charting (p. 217). For a method of determining the character of pieces that form the design, see suggestion at right.

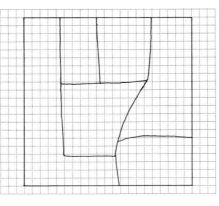

A sketch of an arrangement of shapes for one or all of the blocks can be helpful in designing and working a crazy patchwork. The most difficult aspect of crazy patchwork is imagining how random shapes will work together. By drawing an arrangement of shapes, you can see the design they form, and alter any of the shapes before they are cut out. You can even color in the sketch to see how colors will work in the design. A tinted sketch can serve as both a shape and a color guide when you are cutting out the pieces. If you like, you can make a finished-size replica of the sketch, cut it apart, and cut the fabric pieces from the paper pieces. Remember, if you do this, to add a ¼'' seam allowance along each edge of each piece.

Dividers and borders

Two other elements in patchwork are dividers and borders. Made of strips of fabric, they are joined to other patchwork units to become part of the overall patchwork fabric. Dividers are sewed between blocks and strips of blocks; borders are sewed to the outer edges of the joined patchwork units. The best time to plan for them is when you are charting the design (p. 217). It is then that you can see the needs of the overall patchwork design; you are also able to decide if the addition of a border or divider or both will produce a more desirable finished size for the patchwork. Although their main function is to "frame" other patchwork units, an interesting patchwork fabric can be formed by sewing these strips to each other. The resulting patchwork is known as a *strip quilt.*

Depending on the effect you want, the strips can be made of continuous fabric lengths or of pieced lengths. Strips made from continuous fabric lengths do not require finished-size templates; just calculate their length and width and add a ¼-inch seam allowance at each edge. If necessary, plan to join lengths to achieve the measurement you require. Additional decoration can be supplied by appliqués. If using appliqués, decide where they will be placed and design them to fit that area. Appliqués will need finished-size templates.

Pieced fabric strips are made up of small and relatively simple pieced block units. To design a pieced strip, decide on a suitable block design and plan to repeat it for the length of the strip. Some designs are shown at the right; for more information, turn to pages 210-211. While designing, pay attention to corners and other points where strips will meet. Some pieced designs will not match at these points; the easiest remedy is to use a plain square at corners or intersections. With other pieced designs, a different color arrangement in the block will make the design work.

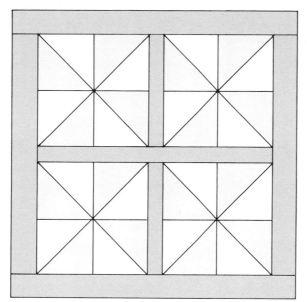

Continuous-strip dividers and borders are used in the patchwork above. They can be left plain (as above) or decorated with appliqués. Several examples of appliquéd strips are illustrated below.

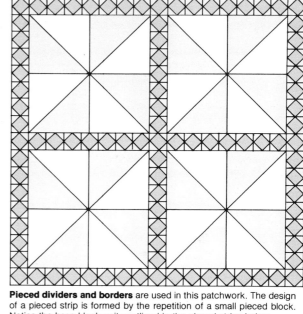

Pieced dividers and borders are used in this patchwork. The design of a pieced strip is formed by the repetition of a small pieced block. Notice the base block units outlined in the pieced strips below.

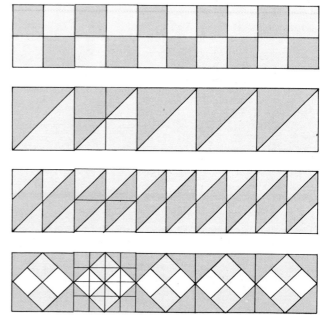

Patchwork basics

How color can influence a patchwork design

Color selection and placement are central to the overall design impression of a patchwork. It is simple to choose and arrange colors for a single pieced block, but for a multi-block patchwork, you must consider the effect of colors on one another when many blocks are joined.

The colors need only be ones you like. Their placement depends on the area you want emphasized—whether you want the design of the *individual units* to stand out, or prefer to develop a *secondary overall pattern* from the combined units.

Supposing you like the idea of a secondary pattern, should it have more impact than the individual units? Or would you like to create the illusion of an interplay between the two, with first one and then the other predominant?

Getting the effect you want calls for experimentation with colors and their arrangement. A good way is to try out color plans over a charted patchwork (see far right, opposite page). Bear in mind, as you do, these general color theories as they pertain to patchwork.

The dominant colors—reds, yellows, and oranges—stand out more than do blues, greens, and violets. Thus in combining, say, red and green, put red where you want emphasis.

Lighter shades, as a rule, advance more than darker ones. A qualification: the dominance of the color they come from. Pink, derived from red, will stand out more than a comparable value of blue.

The more space a color covers, the greater its strength will generally be.

Place emphasis in a patchwork *within* the units if you want their design more obvious; *at their edges* if you prefer to stress the secondary pattern. To equalize the two, balance color strength and quantity among all pieces of all units.

Placement of units, too, can affect a design's look. Notice below the dramatic result of setting blocks diagonally. On the facing page, plain blocks and dividers separate the pieced blocks, emphasizing their design but also creating another kind of secondary pattern.

Printed fabrics: For patchwork, the small patterns are best. Small prints change color quality very little and create an impression of dots. The prints with straight lines produce striping.

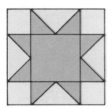

Concentration of one color over the entire star shape gives that area great impact, strong enough that the block unit remains dominant in the total design. The color itself, being moderate in value and having yellow and red as its major components, contributes to this emphasis.

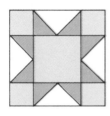

The colors here are balanced in mass and comparative impact, their weight evenly distributed over the patchwork piece. Glance at the design, letting your eye move naturally from shape to shape, and you will perceive the play back and forth from unit design to secondary pattern.

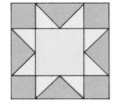

Blocks set on the diagonal, with strong color emphasis at their edges, show the striking difference unit placement can make. The eye is drawn diagonally, making the secondary pattern more prominent than the unit design. It takes effort, in fact, to find the block design in the pattern.

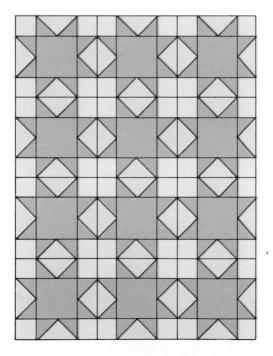

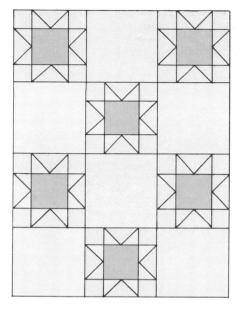

Alternating plain and pieced blocks is undoubtedly the surest and easiest way to make unit designs stand out, if that is your preference. In every sense of the words, the plain blocks set the pieced blocks apart, giving them great clarity and definition.
This idea is worth considering for a first try at color selection and placement because it avoids the extreme graphic changes that can occur when pieced blocks are set edge to edge. The plain blocks could be a totally different color than any in the unit design, but it is simpler and more effective to pick up one of the shades in the pieced block.

Dividers emphasize unit designs as a frame does a painting. These are made of continuous fabric strips, but they could also be pieced (see p. 215). Dividers are often introduced into patchwork to bring it up to a required size. If you preferred to place the pieced blocks edge to edge, you could use borders instead of dividers to increase the size. It is also possible to combine the two. For details about these and other possibilities offered by borders and dividers, see page 215. Techniques for joining them to blocks appear on pages 230-231.

Charting a patchwork

Before actually charting a patchwork design, assign measurements to all the different units and see how they will fit into the approximate finished measurement of the patchwork. Then, if the combined measurements do not total close to the desired finished size, alter the size and/ or number of the units. Suppose, for example, you want your finished patchwork to measure approximately 80 by 96 inches, and you plan to use five Simple Star blocks across by six down, with dividers between blocks and strips of blocks. If 12-inch blocks are used, they total 60 by 72 inches; if the dividers are 3 inches wide, the total is 72 by 87 inches, far smaller than the desired 80 by 96 inches. Add a 4-inch border, and the total measurement would be 80 by 95 inches, almost exactly the right size. Another plan, which would produce exactly 80 by 96 inches, is shown below. It uses larger (16-inch) but fewer blocks (4 across by 5 down) and an 8-inch border. The blocks total 64 by 80 inches; the border brings the total to 80 by 96 inches.

If the combined units produce a satisfactory design, chart them to scale on graph paper and record the finished size of each. Then determine the best color plan for the design. Place tissue over the chart and color in all pieces. Use a new piece of tissue for each color plan; leave the selected one on the chart. In buying fabrics, try to get as close a color match as possible. Refer to the chart and its listed information when making and using templates (pp. 218-219). The chart can also be used as a guide to follow as you sew the patchwork.

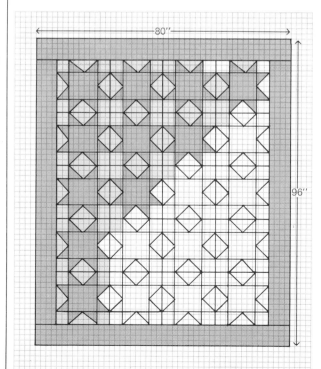

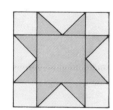

Finished size:
80″ wide by 96″ long
Units:
20 Simple Star blocks, each measuring 16″ square and colored as shown

4 brown border strips, each measuring 8½″ by 80½″ (measurement includes a ¼″ seam allowance along each edge)

Preparing and sewing a block-unit patchwork

Making and using templates
Choosing a joining sequence
General sewing techniques
Straight seams
Cornered seams
Curved seams
Seams through a base fabric
General techniques for appliqués
Single-layer appliqué block units
Multiple-layer appliqué block units
Pieced appliqué block units
Appliqué-pieced block units
Joining blocks, dividers,
and borders

Making templates

The first step in the construction of a patchwork is to make a cutting and a marking template (pattern) for the different shapes in the design. To make templates of the correct size and shape, first draw to finished size each of the units in the patchwork that require templates. (All but crazy patchwork and continuous strip dividers or borders, pages 214-215, will need templates.) For guidance in drawing patchwork units, see pages 210-215. When units are drawn to finished size, study each one to determine the combination of shapes that can be most easily joined to form the unit's design. For example, when a Simple Star block is colored as below, the first impression is of a one-piece star surrounded by separate triangles and corner squares. If you look more closely, you will see that the star, too, is composed of several pieces—namely, a large center square, with small triangles making the points. Though it may seem otherwise, the second of the two combinations will be easier to join. To understand why, see page 220 on choosing a joining sequence. When the shapes have been determined, make templates of them, using sturdy paper or fine sandpaper (see below).

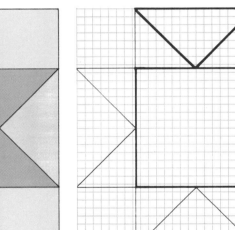

To make templates, proceed as follows:

1. On graph paper, draw the patchwork unit to its finished size.

2. Study the unit and determine the shapes that will need templates.

3. Carefully cut out one of each of the required shapes from the finished-size drawing. For example, the shapes needed for a Simple Star block are a large and a small square and a large and a small triangle. These shapes are indicated at left by heavy lines.

4. Place cut graph-paper shapes on sturdy paper or fine sandpaper; trace around each. Remove shapes and cut out new pieces along traced lines. These are your *marking* templates.

5. Place graph-paper shapes back on the heavy paper, leaving 1″- 2″ between them; tape in place. Mark several points ¼″ beyond each edge of each shape. Draw lines to connect marks; cut out new pieces along these lines. These are your *cutting* templates. The ¼″ between graph-paper shape and edge of template is the seam allowance needed to sew the pieces together.

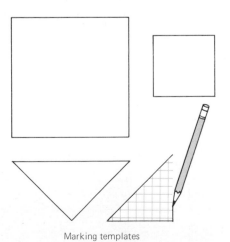

Marking templates

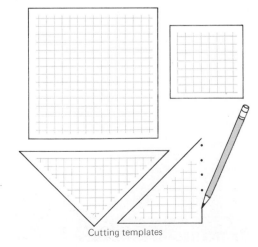

Cutting templates

Using cutting templates

Cutting templates are used first to determine the amount of fabric needed for a patchwork, then to cut out the pieces (see right). **To calculate yardages,** look at your charted patchwork and list the number of times each shape appears in each color. Then, using one of the templates, see how many times it can be repeated across a 45-inch width (usual fabric width). Divide this number into the number of times that shape appears in one color; multiply that answer by the depth of one row (actually of one shape) to get the total length needed. Repeat for each shape and color; add the totals for each color to determine the amount required of each. For 36-inch-wide fabric, buy one and one-quarter times these totals. To allow for mistakes, always buy a little extra of each color.

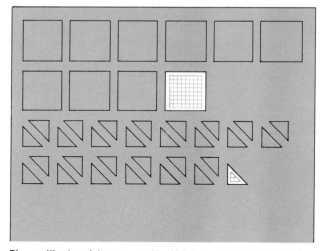
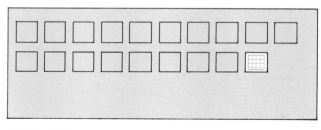
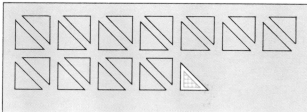

Place cutting template on wrong side of fabric and, using a dressmaker's pencil, draw its outline. Repeat until all of the pieces are drawn; be sure to draw the correct shape on the correct color of fabric. Cut out the pieces along the marked lines; keep the different cut shapes separate.

Special layout and cutting situations

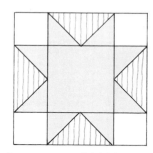
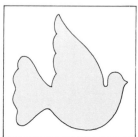
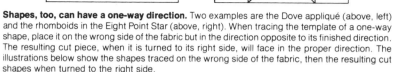

If using a one-way print fabric, such as a stripe, draw the shapes to reflect the direction you want the print to take in the finished block. Triangles were laid out as below so that the stripes would be as shown above in the finished block.

Shapes, too, can have a one-way direction. Two examples are the Dove appliqué (above, left) and the rhomboids in the Eight Point Star (above, right). When tracing the template of a one-way shape, place it on the wrong side of the fabric but in the direction opposite to its finished direction. The resulting cut piece, when it is turned to its right side, will face in the proper direction. The illustrations below show the shapes traced on the wrong side of the fabric, then the resulting cut shapes when turned to the right side.

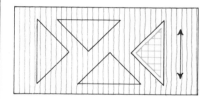

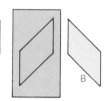
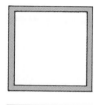

Using marking templates

Marking templates are used in preparing cut fabric pieces for sewing; how they are used depends on the method of joining the pieces. Since most are joined with plain seams, a marking template is used mainly to mark seamlines (below). In appliqué pieces, marked seamlines are used as guides for staystitching and for turning seam allowances under; sometimes the marking template itself is used as a guide for pressing seam allowances back (p. 227). The marking templates of some one-shape patchworks are used to make paper backing pieces (p. 233).

To mark seamlines, center marking template on wrong side of cut shape; hold it in place and, using a dressmaker's pencil, draw outline of marking template on fabric.

219

Preparing and sewing a block-unit patchwork

Choosing a joining sequence

Before doing any sewing, you must determine the best sequence to follow in putting the separate pieces together. With an appliqué block unit, you must decide on a layering sequence (p. 226). With a pieced block, you need a sequence for joining smaller pieces into progressively larger units. Look, first, for small units "built" by repetitious joinings of the same shapes. Then check the shapes adjoining these for another repetitious joining that will make those small units larger. The small units, with additions, form strips that, when joined, produce many blocks. Simple Star and Drunkard's Path, below, are examples. Some block designs are built from the center out (see the Eight Point Star, below).

Test the validity of your sequence by sewing one block. If it is not satisfactory, modify it until you find one that works, then follow it to sew all of the blocks simultaneously—that is, form all of the *smallest* units of all the blocks; then add the pieces that make them *progressively larger;* and finally, join the *larger strip units,* block by block, until all the blocks have been formed.

General sewing techniques

The pieces in block units may be joined with either hand or machine stitching. If it is an appliqué block, the appliqué is topstitched, usually by hand, to its base block (pp. 226-229). The pieces of pieced block units are generally joined with plain seams (exceptions: Log Cabin and Crazy blocks, pp. 224-225). **To form a plain seam,** place the pieces that are to be joined with right sides together and seamlines matched; pin and stitch through both layers on the seamline. Remove pins as you approach them; do not stitch over them. Hand-sew with a small running stitch (see below); set the machine for 10-12 stitches per inch. The thread color should blend with fabric colors. The character of a seam—that is, whether straight, cornered, or curved—will depend on the shapes of the pieces. (See straight seams below and on the facing page; cornered and curved seams on pages 222-223.) Press seam allowances to one side (except certain cornered seam allowances, which are pressed open). At cross seams, alternate the direction of the seam allowances; this will distribute the bulk more evenly.

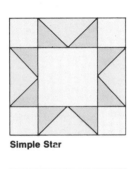

Simple Star

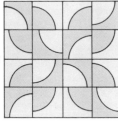

Drunkard's Path

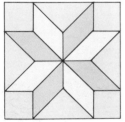

Eight Point Star

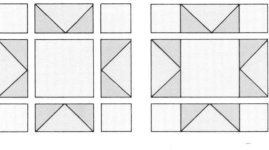

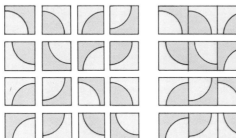

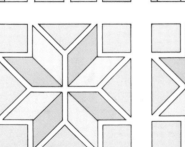

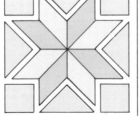

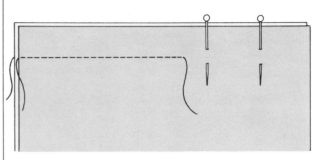

Machine sewing: Test stitch length (10-12 stitches per inch), tension, and pressure before starting to sew the blocks. Place stitches on seamline. Do not backstitch to secure stitches; tie thread ends if necessary (p. 222).

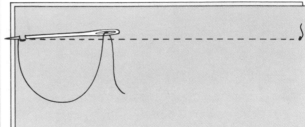

Hand sewing: Use running stitches. Weave needle in and out of fabric several times before pulling needle and thread through. Keep stitches and spaces between them short and even (about 9 stitches per inch). Knot thread end to secure the start of the seam.

To secure the end of a seam, form a few small backstitches on top of each other.

Straight seams

A large proportion of all the pieces in pieced block designs have straight edges and will therefore be joined with plain straight seams. An example of a block in which all of the pieces are joined with straight seams is the Simple Star. This block consists of 17 pieces—a large center square, four small corner squares, four large and eight small triangles. The pieces are joined to each other in the sequence shown at the right.

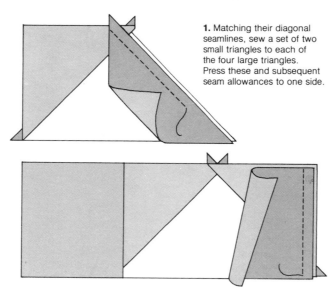

1. Matching their diagonal seamlines, sew a set of two small triangles to each of the four large triangles. Press these and subsequent seam allowances to one side.

2. To form the top and bottom strips of the Simple Star block, sew a small square to each end of two of the triangle units that were formed in Step 1 above.

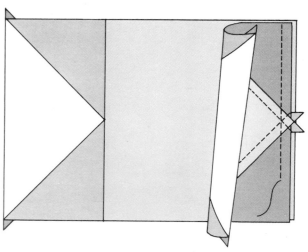

3. To form the center strip of the block, sew the two remaining triangle units made in Step 1 to opposite edges of the large square. Take care to position the point of the large triangle and stitch across it exactly as shown above. This will ensure that the point of the triangle will be visible and will face toward the center of the block when it is finished.

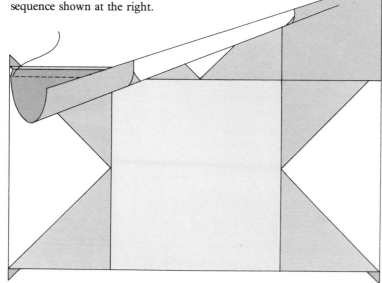

4. Sew the top strip to the center strip. Match all cross seamlines and position and stitch across the point of the large triangle as was done in Step 3.

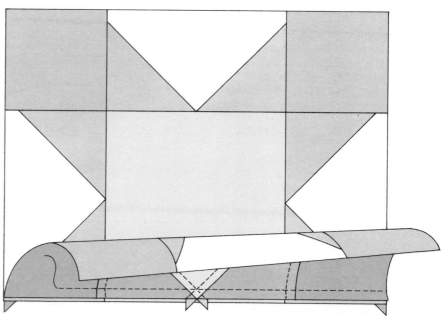

5. Complete the Simple Star block by sewing the bottom strip to the free edge of the center strip. Be sure to match all cross seamlines and carefully position and stitch across the point of the triangle.

Preparing and sewing a block-unit patchwork

Cornered seams

A cornered seam is used to join a piece having an outward-cornered edge to a piece with an inward-cornered edge. One will occur between each of the triangles and squares (outward corners) and the star unit (inward corners) of the Eight Point Star shown on this page. To prepare for a cornered seam, the inward corner is split; this allows the piece to be spread so its edges can be matched to the edges of the outward corner. If the inward-cornered piece is formed by the seaming of two pieces (as happens in the Eight Point Star), the split will automatically be formed by stopping the seaming of the two pieces at the inward-cornered seamline (Steps 1, 3, and 4). If a *continuous piece of fabric* forms the inward corner, the corner will need to be stay-stitched and clipped (see the first column of the next page).

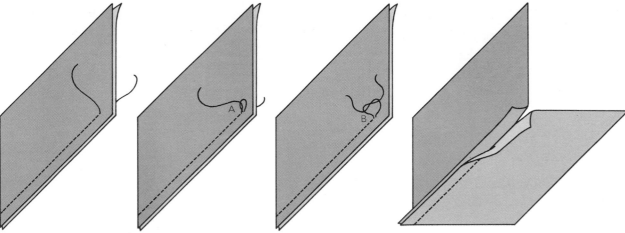

1. With long edges matched, sew a set of rhomboids together from edge of narrow corner to cross seam of wide corner. Pull top thread to bring up bobbin thread (A); tie together (B).

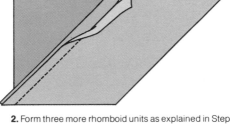

2. Form three more rhomboid units as explained in Step 1; press open the seam allowances of all four.

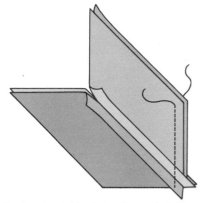

3. Sew two rhomboid units together; end stitching and tie threads as in Step 1. Press seam open. Sew remaining two units together the same way.

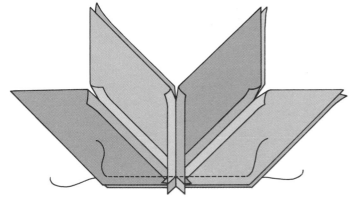

4. With right sides together, match seamlines and cross seams at lower edges of units made in Step 3; pin in place. Stitch units together, starting and stopping at the cross seamlines at each end of the matched units. Tie threads as in Step 1; press the seam open.

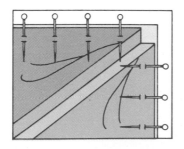

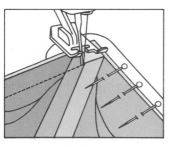

Squares and triangles are pinned and stitched to outer edges of star as follows: With right sides together and star uppermost, spread inward corner of star so its edges match those of piece being joined. Pin the two together, keeping seam allowances of star open.

To sew first half of seam, stitch from edge of seam to corner; leave needle in fabric at corner. Lift presser foot; pivot fabric on needle to bring it into position for sewing the second half of the seam.

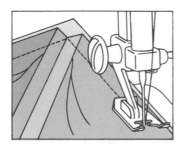

To sew second half of seam, lower presser foot and stitch from corner to end of seam.

Curved seams

If a continuous piece of fabric is used as the inward-cornered portion of a cornered seam, it must be reinforced with staystitching and clipped for flexibility as shown and explained below.

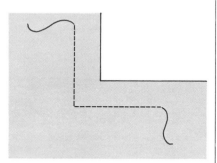

Reinforce the inward corner by placing a row of staystitching, just inside the seamline, for 1″ on each side of the corner.

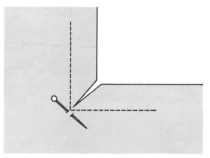

Clip the corner, being careful not to cut the staystitching. To avoid cutting these stitches, place a pin across the corner.

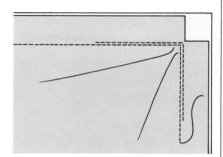

Spread clipped piece so its edges match those being joined to it. *Pin and stitch* through both layers as explained at bottom of facing page.

A curved seam is used when a piece with an outward-curved edge must be joined to one with an inward-curved edge. Such a seam forms each of the 16 small repeated units in the Drunkard's Path design illustrated here. To permit the oppositely curved edges to match, it is necessary first to staystitch and clip the inward-curved edge (Step 1). Then spread it to match the outward-curved edge and stitch through both layers on the seamline (see Step 2). To make the curved seams lie quite flat, press their seam allowances toward the inward curve. When all of the individual units have been stitched, they are joined to form four strips (Step 3); these strips are then joined with straight seams (Step 4).

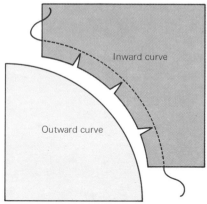

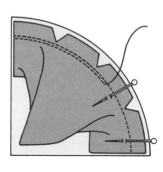

1. Prepare each inward-curved edge as follows: Place a row of staystitching just inside the seamline. Then clip the seam allowance in a few places without cutting into the staystitching.

2. With right sides together and clipped piece uppermost, spread clipped edge to fit the outward curve. Pin and stitch along the seamline. Do the same for remaining 15 sets of pieces.

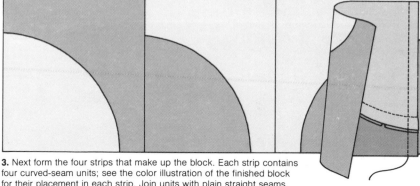

3. Next form the four strips that make up the block. Each strip contains four curved-seam units; see the color illustration of the finished block for their placement in each strip. Join units with plain straight seams.

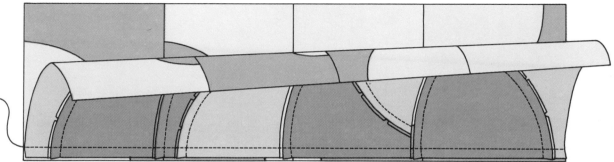

4. Sew the four strips to each other with plain straight seams, again referring to the colored block for the placement of individual strips. Be sure to match their cross seamlines exactly before stitching any of the strips together.

Preparing and sewing a block-unit patchwork

Seams through a base fabric/Log Cabin blocks

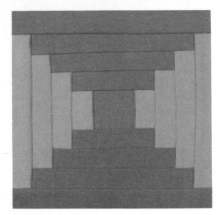

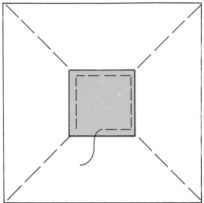

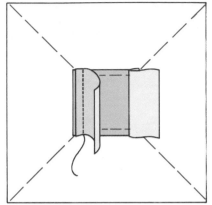

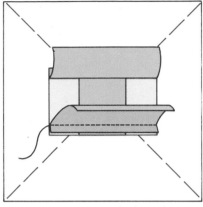

The pieces that make up Log Cabin blocks are seamed through a base fabric block as they are seamed to each other. Blocks are built from the center out; the sewing sequence for the pieces (strips) depends on the Log Cabin design. This design suggests an hourglass; the sequence for sewing its strips is at the right.

1. Fold block of base fabric diagonally in half, then into quarters; lightly press folds. Open up block, mark the folds with bastings, then press block flat. With its right side up, center the center square of the pieced design on the block; use the bastings as guides for placement. Pin and baste square to base block.

2. Sew the set of shortest strips to opposite edges of the center square. With right sides together, match, pin, and stitch one strip to the right edge of square. Then turn the strip back to its right side and press it flat. Sew the other short strip to the left edge of the center square. Turn it back to its right side and press it flat.

3. Sew the next larger set of strips to the top and bottom edges of the center square and the strips sewed to it in the preceding step. Turn each strip to its right side and press flat. Continue sewing progressively larger sets of strips to the block, alternating their placement from side to side, then to top and bottom. When all the strips have been sewed to the block, baste the free edges of the final strips to the base block of fabric.

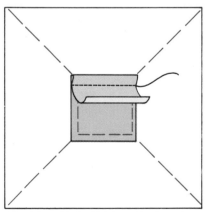

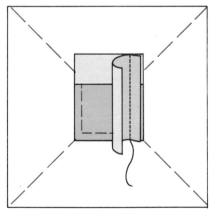

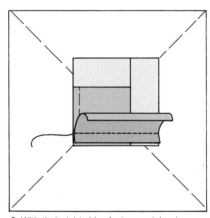

In another popular Log Cabin design, dark and light strips are grouped on opposite sides of a diagonal center. The design here differs from the one shown above mainly in the sequence used for sewing the strips to each other through the base block of fabric (see right).

1. Mark base block of fabric and baste center square in place as explained in Step 1 above. Then, with right sides together, match, pin, and stitch the shortest light-colored strip to the top edge of the center square. Turn the strip to its right side and press it flat.

2. With their right sides together, match, pin, and stitch the next longer light-colored strip to the right edge of the center square and the strip sewed to it in the preceding step. Turn the strip to its right side and press flat.

3. With their right sides facing, match, pin, and stitch the shortest dark strip to the bottom edge of the center square and the strip sewed to it in Step 2. Turn strip to its right side and press. Working clockwise, sew gradually longer sets of dark and light strips to block. End with the longest dark strip; turn and press each strip before sewing the next. Baste free edges of last round of strips to base block.

Seams through a base fabric/Crazy patchwork

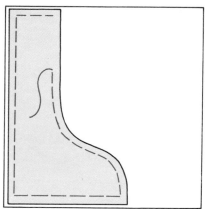

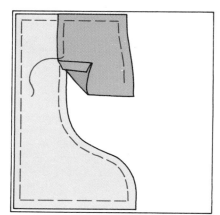

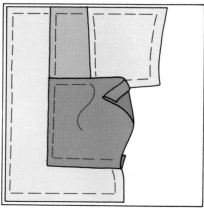

Crazy patchwork is different from other patchwork designs in that the only guide used for cutting the pieces is a sketch of the block's design (see p. 214). Also unique to crazy patchwork is the way in which the pieces are sewed to each other and to a base block of fabric (see the detailed instructions at the right).

1. Referring to your rough sketch of the block design (explained on p. 214), decide which piece should be laid down first. In general, it is best for the first piece to be laid along an edge of the block (left edge here). Cut a piece of fabric like the drawn shape, plus at least a ¼" seam allowance along each edge. Position the fabric piece, right side up, on base block of fabric; pin and baste it in place.

2. Decide which piece will be laid down next and cut a piece of fabric to that approximate shape, with a ¼" seam allowance along each edge. Position this piece, right side up, on the block, lapping it appropriately over the piece basted in Step 1. Turn under the seam allowance of any lapped edge that will be exposed in the finished block; baste the piece in place along all of its edges. To turn under curved or cornered edges, see page 227.

3. Continue to cut out and lap pieces one at a time and in the order of their relationship in the design. When cutting a piece, always remember to include a ¼" seam allowance along all of its edges; before basting any piece in place, turn under the seam allowance of edges that will be exposed when the block is finished. When all of the pieces have been basted in place, trim off any edges that extend beyond the edges of the base block.

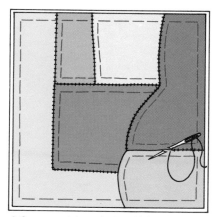

4. Secure each turned edge with hand stitches. If you want the stitches to be almost invisible, use either the slipstitch or the blindstitch, both shown and explained at the right. For a more decorative finish, use the featherstitch (bottom right) or any embroidery stitch that will span both sides of a seamline. Finally, remove all bastings except at edges of block.

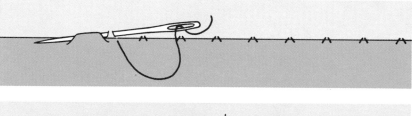

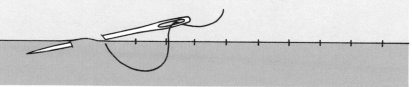

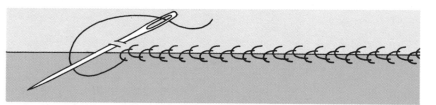

Slipstitch: Work stitches from right to left. Begin by bringing needle and thread out through fold of turned-under edge. Form the stitches as follows: Slightly ahead of point where thread comes out of fold, insert needle through block, catching only a few threads, then through the fold for about ¼". Pull the needle and thread through, and repeat.

Blindstitch: Work stitches from right to left. Begin by bringing needle and thread through turned-under edge, back to front. Form stitches as follows: Directly opposite point where thread comes out of folded edge, insert needle into block, take a small (about ¼") stitch, and bring needle out through turned-under edge. Pull needle and thread through, and repeat.

Featherstitch: Work stitches down the seamline. To begin, bring needle and thread up on one side of seamline. Pass to opposite side, then, holding thread in place, point the needle diagonally down toward seamline and take a small stitch; keep thread under needle point. Pull stitch through, letting thread under it curve slightly. Cross to opposite side; repeat.

Preparing and sewing a block-unit patchwork

General techniques for patchwork appliqués

The first step in constructing an appliqué block unit is to make finished size templates (p. 218) for all of the shapes in the appliqué as well as for the block if it is pieced (e.g., Basket of Flowers). If the base block is a continuous piece, no template is needed, only its finished measurement. Other elements, such as stems (in the Rose below) and the basket handle in the Basket of Flowers, can be made from bias fabric strips (p. 199). They are also exceptions and do not require templates; their finished measurements are sufficient.

Once all the pieces have been cut out and marked, the next step is to plan a **layering sequence,** that is, the order in which the pieces of the appliqué should be laid on top of each other. If it is a single-layer appliqué (for example, the Snowflake), no sequence is involved. For appliqués consisting of more than one layer, such as multiple-layer appliqués (Rose) or certain pieced appliqués (Dresden Plate), lay the pieces down in this order: the lowest layer first, and from the center of the block out. Notice the sequence planned for the Rose below.

More examples of layering sequences, as well as traditional construction techniques for appliqué block units, are given on pages 228-229. For other appliqué methods, see pages 192-206.

When planning a layering sequence, identify those edges that can be lapped under other pieces, and those that will be exposed and therefore must be turned under. The dotted lines in the schematic drawing of the Rose (below) signify lapped edges; all other edges will be turned under. It is usually easier to turn under the edges of the pieces before they

are positioned on the base block. When **turning an edge under,** turn it along its seamline and crease the seamline with either finger-pressing or an iron. If you have difficulty turning the edge, place a row of staystitching along the seamline or use the marking template as a pressing guide (next page). If the edge is cornered or curved, clip or notch it.

After all the pieces have been basted onto the block, hand-stitch the appliqué in place. Use either the slipstitch or blindstitch (p. 225) or, for a more decorative finish, an embroidery stitch.

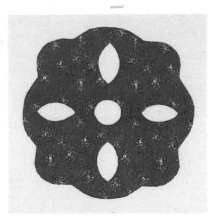

Snowflake

Rose

Dresden Plate

Basket of Flowers

Plan a layering sequence, that is, the order for laying down the pieces (indicated by numbers). Then determine which edges will be *lapped* (dotted lines) and which *turned under* (all other edges).

Turning edges

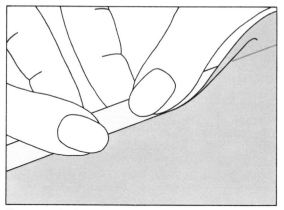

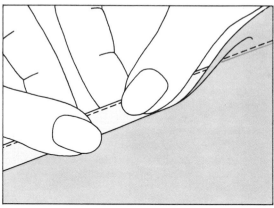

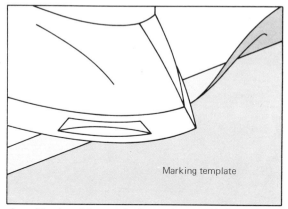

Marking template

Finger-pressing is one way of creasing a turned-under edge. Turn the edge under along its seamline, pressing the fold between your fingers as shown.

A row of staystitching placed just inside the seamline will make it easier to turn an edge under. While turning, use an iron or finger-pressing to crease the seamline.

A marking template can also be used as a guide for turning an edge under. Center template on wrong side of piece and hold it in place. Then, using an iron, press edge back onto template.

Handling curves and corners

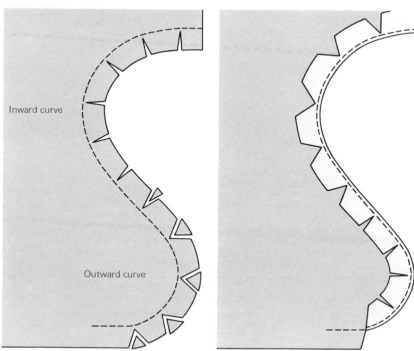

Inward curve

Outward curve

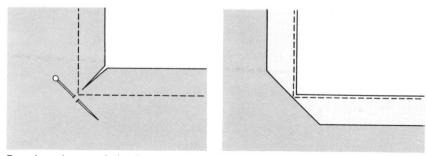

For an inward-cornered edge, first staystitch for at least 1'' on each side of corner. Place a pin through stitches at corner, then clip up to the stitches. Pin keeps you from cutting into the stitches; clipping lets seam allowances spread so they can be turned under.

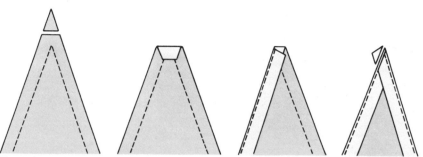

Curved edges will need to be either clipped or notched before they can be turned under; they should also be staystitched. If the edge has an *inward curve,* clip the seam allowance so it can be spread as the edge is turned. Notch an *outward curve* to reduce fullness and facilitate turning.

For an outward-cornered edge, first staystitch for at least 1'' on each side of corner. Trim half of the seam allowance across the corner; then turn the remainder back across point of corner. Then, one at a time, turn back the seam allowance on each side of the corner; trim any excess seam allowances.

227

Preparing and sewing a block-unit patchwork

Single-layer appliqué block units

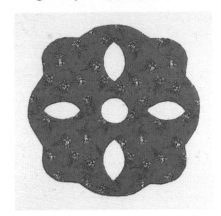

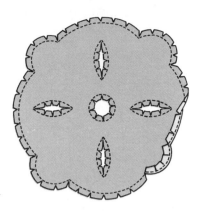

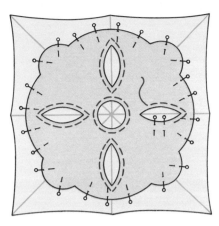

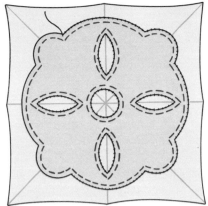

Appliqué block units involving a single-layer appliqué, such as the Snowflake above, are easy to construct. The only pieces called for are one fabric layer for the appliqué and one for the base block. All edges of such an appliqué will need to be turned under.

1. Using the methods described on page 227, turn under all the edges of the appliqué. Since all the edges of this appliqué are curved, they should all be staystitched; then edges that have inward curves should be clipped and those with outward curves should be notched.

2. Fold base block of fabric in half, then into quarters. If parts of the appliqué must be centered diagonally, as do the four "corners" of appliqué above, fold block into eighths as well. Lightly press all folded edges; open up block. Using foldlines as guides, center the appliqué on the block. Pin and baste appliqué in place from its center out. Be sure to catch the turned-under edges in the bastings.

3. Working from the center of the appliqué out, hand-sew the appliqué to the base block. If you want the stitches to be almost invisible, use either the slipstitch or blindstitch (p. 225) and a thread color that matches the appliqué. For a more decorative finish, use an embroidery stitch; thread color can match or contrast. Remove the bastings and press.

Multiple-layer appliqué block units

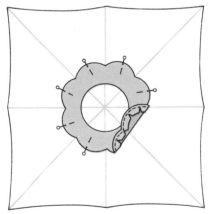

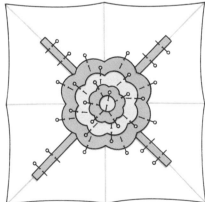

Before constructing a multiple-layer appliqué block unit, e.g., the Rose above, plan a layering sequence for the appliqué pieces. When the sequence has been determined, identify the edges that can be lapped under other pieces and those that will need to be turned under.

1. Prepare all the pieces of the appliqué. Referring to its planned layering sequence (p. 226) and using the methods on page 227, turn under only those edges that will be exposed. Form centering guidelines on the base block of fabric by folding it in quarters, and eighths if necessary (see Step 2 above). Begin to lay down and pin the pieces to the base block according to the planned sequence.

2. Continue to lay down the pieces of the appliqué according to the planned layering sequence, pinning each piece in place. If necessary, lift an edge so another can be lapped under it (as happens above with each stem at the edge of the center rose).

3. When all the pieces have been pinned to the block, baste them in place. Remove pins as you baste, and work the bastings from the center of the appliqué out to its edges. Then hand-sew the appliqué to the block as explained in Step 3 above.

Pieced appliqué block units

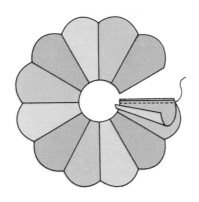

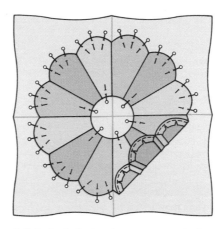

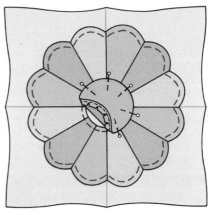

Some appliqué block units, such as the Dresden Plate, employ pieced block techniques to form all or part of the appliqué design. If more than one layer is involved, as is the case with the Dresden Plate, plan a layering sequence and determine which edges need turning.

1. Construct the pieced appliqué, using pieced block techniques (pp. 220-225). Choose those seaming techniques that are suited to the character of the pieces being joined; wherever possible, press seams open. The pieced portion of the Dresden Plate appliqué (above) is formed by means of plain straight seams; all of the seams are pressed open.

2. Referring to the layering sequence and using the techniques on page 227, turn under the necessary edges of the appliqué. For Dresden Plate, all edges of the center circle and outer edges of pieced portion need to be turned; before turning, each edge is staystitched, then clipped or notched. Form centering guides on the base block (Step 2, top of facing page). Begin to lay down and pin pieces to block.

3. When all of the pieces have been pinned to the base block of fabric, baste them in place, removing the pins as you baste. When basting, be sure that the turned-under edges are caught in the stitching. Then hand-sew the appliqué to the block as described in Step 3 at the top of the facing page. Remove all bastings and press.

Appliqué-pieced block units

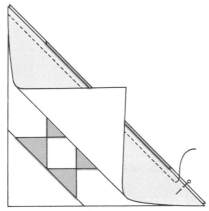

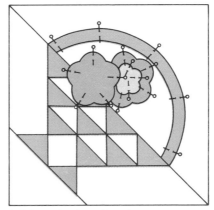

Certain appliqué block units combine a pieced block with a single- or multiple-layer appliqué. Basket of Flowers is an example. Base block, including bottom of basket, is pieced; flowers and basket handle in the upper half of the block are a multiple-layer appliqué.

1. Construct the pieced base block, using the appropriate pieced block techniques (see pp. 220-225). Plain straight seams are used to join all the pieces in the block above; pairs of triangles are its smallest repeated unit. The lower half of the block is pieced first, and is then sewed to the upper half, which is a large triangle.

2. Refer to the planned layering sequence (p. 226) and turn under the appropriate edges of the appliqué, using the methods on page 227. If necessary, fold the block to form centering guidelines (Step 2, top of facing page). Begin to lay down the pieces of the appliqué; pin each in place. The basket handle is a bias fabric strip that has been shaped into a curve (p. 199).

3. Finish laying down the appliqué pieces, pinning each in place. When all are pinned to block, baste each in place. Remove pins as you baste; be sure to catch the turned-under edges in the bastings. Then hand-stitch the appliqué to the block (see Step 3, top of facing page). Remove bastings and press.

229

Preparing and sewing a block-unit patchwork

Joining blocks, dividers, borders

In general, this is the progression for joining blocks, dividers, and borders to form a patchwork fabric: Sew the units to form strips; sew the strips to each other; add the borders last. To determine how a particular patchwork should be formed, study its chart and mentally group the units into strips. In most designs, the strips go *across* the patchwork (see examples, immediate right). If vertical dividers are included, strips will be vertical (facing page, top left); in a diagonal setting (facing page, right), they will be diagonal.

The elements in a strip will depend on the units to be used and their placement in the design. If a patchwork is blocks only, the strips will be the same. If only vertical or only horizontal dividers are used, there will be, in addition to the strips of blocks, strips for the dividers. If *both* vertical and horizontal dividers are included (facing page, bottom left), there will be strips composed of blocks and vertical dividers and also strips for horizontal dividers.

Finishing techniques for any patchwork will depend on the item being made; refer to the Quilting chapter and the projects that follow Quilting.

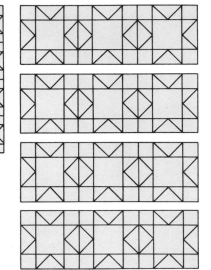
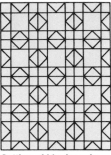

Setting of blocks only: Form strips of blocks to be set horizontally. Sew strips of blocks to each other. If setting contains *horizontal dividers* (not shown), sew block strips to divider strips—one divider between each pair of block strips.

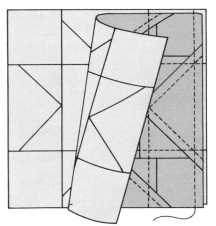
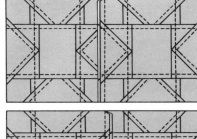
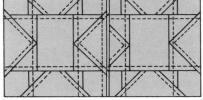

1. Join units to form strips. The number of units in a strip and the number of strips will depend on the planned patchwork. When joining units, use ¼" seams; match cross seamlines.

2. Press seam allowances between units to one side; alternate the direction from strip to strip. For example, press all in one strip to the left, all in the next strip to the right.

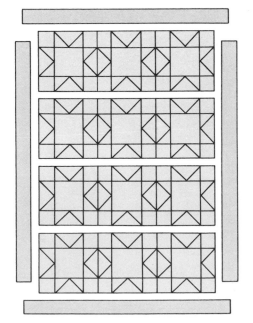

Borders are the last strips to be added to any patchwork. After all of the other units have been joined, sew a border strip to each edge of the patchwork—first to the right and left edges, then to the top and bottom.

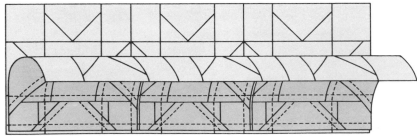

3. Join strips to each other according to the planned patchwork design. When joining the strips, use ¼" seams and be sure to match cross seamlines. Press these seam allowances down.

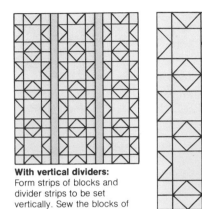

With vertical dividers:
Form strips of blocks and
divider strips to be set
vertically. Sew the blocks of
strips to the vertical
divider strips, with one
divider strip between each
pair of block strips.

Diagonal setting: Here units are joined to each
other to form strips that will be set diagonally.
The number of units in a strip will depend on
the location of that strip in the patchwork.
Partial units (necessary to permit all edges of the
patchwork to be straight when all the strips are
joined) are usually required at the ends of strips;
some strips contain nothing but partial units.
Shown below is the strip breakdown of the patchwork
at the right. Notice that each strip is different
from the others, and that the upper right corner
is formed by a quarter of a block and the lower left
corner by two diagonally halved blocks. The numbers
next to the strips indicate a suggested sequence
for joining the strips.

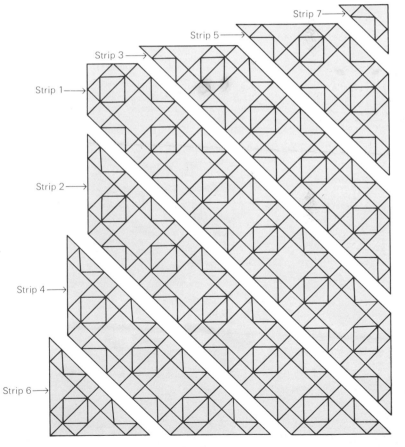

**With both vertical and
horizontal dividers:** Join
blocks and short vertical
dividers in such a way as to
form horizontal strips with
a vertical divider between
each pair of blocks. Next
form horizontal divider strips.
Sew the horizontal block
strips to the horizontal
dividers, with one divider
strip between each pair
of horizontal block strips.

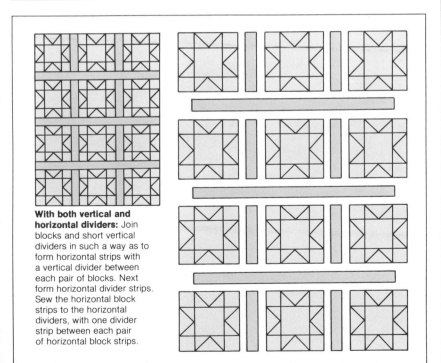

Preparing and sewing a one-shape patchwork

Preparatory steps
Shell
Baby Blocks
Grandmother's Flower Garden

Preparatory steps

The Shell, Baby Blocks, and Grandmother's Flower Garden are the three most popular one-shape patchworks; for instructions on how to draw their necessary shapes, see page 213. Many of the preparatory steps taken for a one-shape patchwork are the same as those taken for a block-unit patchwork. A one-shape patchwork should be charted and its color arrangement planned (pp. 216-217). Once charting is complete, finished-size marking and cutting templates can be made and the pieces cut out of the appropriate colors of fabric (pp. 218-219). If you are making the **Shell** patchwork (below), use its marking template to mark the seamlines of each shell shape. For **Baby Blocks** or **Grandmother's Flower Garden,** use the marking template as a pattern for cutting out finished-size paper shapes (pp. 233-234).

Shell

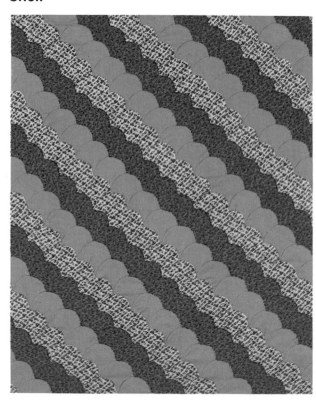

Many different color arrangements can be used with the Shell patchwork; the one above produces diagonal stripes. If you want the outer edges of the patchwork to be straight, place partial shell shapes at the edges. Make marking and cutting templates for them, and sew them as you would full shells. Turn under the seam allowances of the edges that form the patchwork's edges (see detail, Step 3).

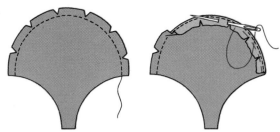

1. Staystitch and notch (p. 227) the upper seam of each shell shape. Turn each upper seam allowance to the wrong side and baste it in place.

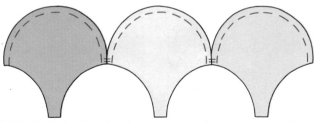

2. Referring to chart for color, place top row of shells next to each other. Tack shells to each other, forming tacks within lower seam allowances.

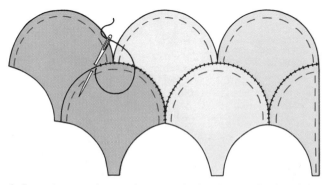

3. For each successive row, lap appropriately colored shells along lower curved seamlines of shells just positioned. Blindstitch (p. 225) in place.

Baby Blocks

When colors are appropriately chosen and placed, Baby Blocks patchwork produces the overall effect of three-dimensional blocks. The simplest way to achieve this effect is with three values of one color, placed in the same position in each block (Step 2). The Baby Blocks above combines three values of brown, with the lightest at the top of the block, the darkest at the left, and the medium tone to the right. If you want the patchwork to have straight edges, use partial shapes (see Shell, facing page).

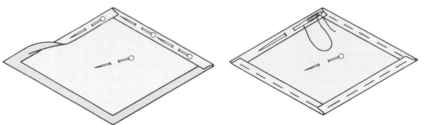

1. Using marking template as a pattern, cut out a paper diamond for each fabric diamond. Back each fabric diamond as follows: Center a paper diamond on wrong side of fabric diamond. Turn seam allowances under and baste in place.

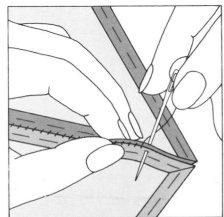

2. Form each Baby Block as follows: Position a set (3) of diamonds as shown in the far left illustration and sew them together, working from the center of the Baby Block out. When sewing, hold the diamonds with their right sides together and form small whipstitches over the matched edges as shown in illustration at the immediate left.

3. Again using small whipstitches (Step 2), sew Baby Blocks to each other to form strips. Check chart for number of strips and of blocks in a strip. Whipstitch the strips together to form the patchwork. When stitching is done, remove paper backing pieces.

Preparing and sewing a one-shape patchwork

Grandmother's Flower Garden

The most popular color arrangement for Grandmother's Flower Garden places colors to form "flower rounds" and white to form "paths" between the flowers. Each round consists of a center hexagon surrounded by six same-color hexagons, then twelve of another color. Colors for each round can be the same or different from round to round. If you want your patchwork to have straight outer edges, use partial shapes (Shell, p. 232).

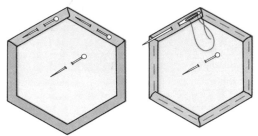

1. Using marking template as a pattern, cut a paper hexagon for each of the fabric hexagons; use to back the fabric pieces. Center a paper hexagon on wrong side of fabric hexagon; turn back seam allowances and baste in place.

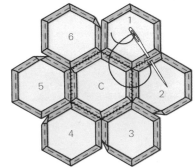

2. To make full flower rounds, first set six hexagons (of the correct color) around center hexagon. Using small whipstitches (Step 2, p. 233), sew each of the six hexagons to the center one; then sew the six to each other.

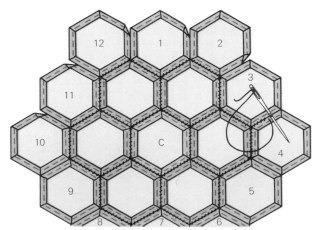

3. Complete each flower round with twelve hexagons (of correct color) around row sewed in Step 2. Sew the twelve in place, then to each other. If patchwork calls for *partial rounds*, use same general sequence for forming them.

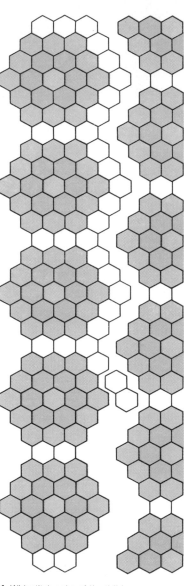

4. Whipstitch pairs of "path" hexagons together; make strips of rounds by sewing a pair of path hexagons between them. If plan calls for them, add path hexagons to ends of strips; use partial rounds where necessary. Join strips by sewing pairs of path hexagons between them. When all pieces are joined, remove paper backing.

Quilting

236 Quilting and quilts
Tools and supplies
237 Constructing a quilting frame
238 Quilting designs
Design aids
Planning a quilting design
239 Outline quilting designs
All-over patterns
240 Ornamental motifs
242 Border designs
244 Transferring and marking designs
246 Basic quilting techniques
Estimating quilt size and yardage
247 Cutting top and backing
Cutting filler
248 Assembling quilt
Setting quilt into frame
249 Setting quilt into hoop
No-frame method of quilting
250 Basic hand-quilting techniques
251 Machine quilting
252 Other quilting techniques
Tying a quilt
253 Padded quilting
254 Corded quilting
255 Sectional quilting
256 Pillow quilting
Puff quilting
257 Finishing edges
Extended binding
258 Slipstitched edges
Bound edges
260 Lining and underlining
261 Care of quilts

Quilting projects
264 Baby quilt
267 Patchwork floor pillow
268 Quilted evening bag

American quilt / Amish, Lancaster County, Pennsylvania / Circa 1890 / Source: America Hurrah Antiques

Quilting and quilts

Introduction to quilting
Tools and supplies
Constructing a quilting frame

Introduction

Quilting, like so many needlecraft techniques, is centuries old. Throughout history it has been valued as a source of warmth in such forms as clothing and bed quilts. The basic quilting technique involves simple running stitches used to anchor a soft filler between two layers of fabric. These stitches are usually worked in a systematic pattern to create a subtly textured fabric surface. The quilting patterns (see pp. 239-243) may be the primary or only source of decoration on a particular article, or they may be a secondary source that is introduced to enhance a completed design surface, such as patchwork or appliqué.

Although this basic quilting technique is usually associated with the making of a quilt (or bed covering), it is often decoratively applied today to sections of such garments as jackets, vests, and robes. Quilting is also suitable for decorating such accessories for the home as cushions and wall hangings.

Ornamental motif quilted on solid fabric is quilt's primary design source.

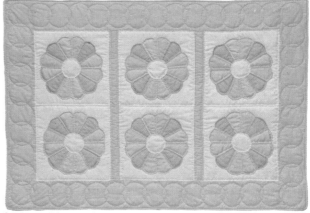

Outline quilting merely enhances the main patchwork design of this quilt.

Tools and supplies

Fabrics and fillers: The *top layer* or decorative side of a quilted project can be a printed or solid-colored fabric, or it can be a completed piece of patchwork, appliqué, or embroidery. Whatever it is, the fabrics used should be smooth, light- to medium-weight, and opaque. Broadcloth, percale, muslin, and chambray are popular choices, although fine linen-weave fabrics or flannels are also suitable. Rich fabrics, such as velvet, satin, and silk, can also be used for special quilted projects. For a delicate effect, use sheers (voile, organdy, organza) as an overlay on an opaque top fabric. Avoid heavy or stiff fabrics; they do not easily conform to quilted contours. Today bed sheets are convenient, coming as they do in a wide range of colors and prints, and in generous widths that make it possible

to have an amply large seamless piece.

The *bottom layer,* backing or lining, traditionally has been a utilitarian light-weight fabric such as muslin. Nowadays it, too, is likely to be decorative, and made from fabrics bright in pattern and color, and similar in type and style to the top fabric layer. If the backing will also be the binding (see p. 257), you will need to cut it larger than the quilt top. Before quilting, preshrink all fabrics, for both the top and the bottom.

The most common contemporary filler is cotton or polyester fiber batt manufactured in sheet form. Cotton batt, which was the original filler, is washable, lightweight, warm, and easy to quilt. Polyester batt, however, besides having those qualities, is more stable, and so less quilting is required in a given area to

keep it from separating. The polyester batt also creates a plumper quilted surface and is available in a variety of weights. A good quality polyester batt will be uniformly thick and dense, which eases handling when a project is assembled. Both cotton and polyester batts come in various sizes; try to purchase one that is large enough to be used as a single piece. If a batt is too small, you can join two pieces to produce one of the desired size (see p. 247). Other less popular but suitable fillers include wool or polyester fleece, blankets, and cotton flannel.

For some special quilting techniques (see pp. 253 and 256), a loose stuffing rather than a sheet of batt is needed as the filler. Again, cotton or polyester types are available. Kapok and shredded foam can also be used in these situations.

Needles, thread, hand-sewing aids: *Quilting needles,* which are also known as "betweens," are the usual choice. As a rule, the sizes are 8 or 9, but a heavier size 7 can be used on heavier quilt fabrics, and a finer number 10 can be used on fabrics that are delicate.

Thread for quilting must be strong. Cotton thread coated with a "glaze" is sometimes labeled *quilting thread* and does the job well. A good, all-purpose thread, number 50 or coarser number 40, can also be used; you may want to run each strand of thread through a cake of *beeswax* to help prevent tangles and fraying as you work. For a richer look, use a lustrous silk twist.

A *thimble* that fits your finger snugly is very helpful, as is a small *embroidery scissors* for cutting thread.

Frames and hoops: A quilting *frame* is a great convenience for quilting large expanses of fabric. It holds the three layers together securely to prevent any shifting, bunching, or wrinkling, and it frees both hands for work. All commercial frames work basically the same way, but they do differ in size and styling; check mail-order catalogs and needlecraft stores for a frame that suits your needs, or you can build your own (see below).

A large *hoop* holds the quilting layers securely and is adaptable for any size quilting project. To use a hoop on a large quilt, shift it from area to area. Hoop sizes vary; select one that is 18 inches or more in diameter to provide a practical working area. Some hoops also come with a stand, which leaves both of your hands conveniently free.

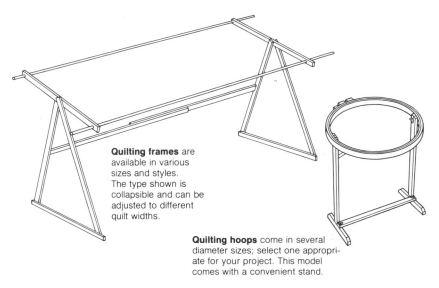

Quilting frames are available in various sizes and styles. The type shown is collapsible and can be adjusted to different quilt widths.

Quilting hoops come in several diameter sizes; select one appropriate for your project. This model comes with a convenient stand.

Constructing a quilting frame

A sturdy quilting frame can easily be constructed at home according to the instructions below. When not in use, it can be disassembled and stored.

Materials

To make the frame, you will need four 1 × 2-inch wooden boards that have been sanded smooth to prevent any snagging of the quilt fabric. Two of the boards will be used as *rails* around which the quilt will be rolled. Each rail should equal the width of the quilt, plus 12 inches to allow for clamping at corners. The two remaining boards will act as side *stretchers;* a length of approximately 2 to 3 feet, plus another 12 inches to allow for clamping, should be adequate for most projects. You will also need about eight 6-inch *C-clamps,* and two strips of *ticking* or other sturdy fabric about 2 to 3 inches wide and as long as the cut rails. *Staples* or *thumbtacks* are needed to hold the ticking to the rails. Support the frame with two *sawhorses* cut to a comfortable working height.

Assembly

To assemble the frame, first attach a strip of ticking to each rail as shown below. (Ends of quilt will be sewed to ticking when quilt is set into frame.) Position the four boards at right angles to each other with the rails resting on top of the stretchers. Secure boards together with a C-clamp at each outside corner. Raise the frame onto the sawhorses, placing it so that the stretcher bars lie directly on the sawhorses. Hold the frame steady with additional C-clamps. Set the quilt into the frame following the procedure described on pages 248-249.

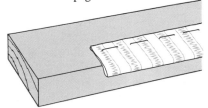

To attach fabric strip, fold in half lengthwise, staple or tack to long edge of rail.

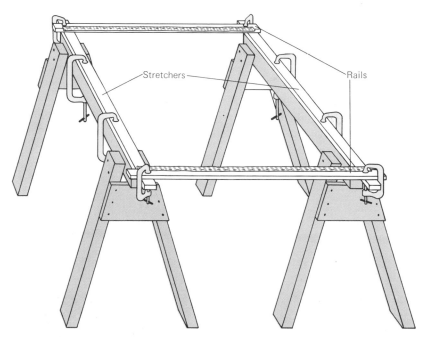

To assemble frame, clamp rails to stretchers at corners. Position frame so the stretchers rest on the sawhorses, then clamp sawhorses and stretchers together as shown.

Quilting designs

Design aids
Planning a quilting design
Types of quilting designs
  Outline quilting
  All-over patterns
  Ornamental motifs
  Borders
Transferring and marking designs
In-frame methods
Off-frame methods

Design aids

A wide range of accessories exists to help with designing, or with the transfer of designs, but not all of them will be needed for any single project. What you select depends upon your design, and the transfer method it requires.

A commercial *stencil, template,* or *perforated pattern* is a quick and easy way to get a quilt design; selection, however is limited. You can make your own if you need or wish to (see p. 245).

Planning a quilting design

There are many different kinds of quilting designs, each offering a particular look or effect (see pp. 239-243). In deciding which one (or ones) to use, you must first consider the top fabric layer. Then, with that in mind, plan the quilting design so that it both enhances the piece and maintains its original mood. In general, an already patterned top layer (such as patchwork or an appliquéd top) will be most appealing with simple, unobtrusive quilting. A common design practice is merely to quilt around the shapes that are already there. Elaborate quilting designs, on the other hand, stand out most attrac-

There are several kinds of paper that will help with planning and transfer. *Graph paper* is useful for planning or sketching a design to scale. For full-size quilting designs and perforated patterns, *tracing paper* is the best choice. Use a stiff, *sturdy paper,* such as oaktag or cardboard, to make durable templates and stencils. *Dressmaker's carbon* is handy for transferring markings.

A *ruler* or *yardstick* will double as a

tively against plain, solid colors. In fact, the most detailed quilting designs often appear on plain white quilts. A typical antique quilt of this sort may feature an ornate central motif surrounded closely by smaller motifs and an overall quilted background. Sometimes a single quilting project may combine both of these design approaches. For example, an intricately quilted solid-color border may be used around a patchwork top quilted in a starkly simple style.

The type of filler can also influence your quilting plans. Of the fillers previously mentioned (p. 236), cotton batt is

straight edge for marking straight-line designs and as a measuring device. A *compass* or a *round object* (such as a teacup) can be used for drawing curves. A single-edged *razor* or a *mat knife* will cut stencils and templates accurately.

To mark directly on fabric, use a hard lead *pencil* or *dressmaker's chalk.* A special powder called *pounce* is used for temporary markings with perforated patterns (check art supply stores).

the least stable, and requires close quilting to prevent the batt from shifting and separating into unsightly lumps after use and laundering; if this is the filler you prefer to use, no more than a 3-inch square area can be left unquilted. Far less quilting is needed to stabilize polyester batt, or any of the more stable fillers; with these, as much as a 10-inch square can be left unquilted. If you want a comparatively flat overall surface, plan on a closely quilted piece, whether the filler is cotton or polyester. Widely spaced quilting designs hold the filler down less, and so will result in a puffier surface.

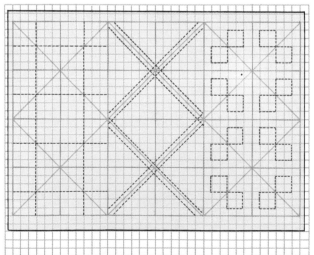

To plan a design for a quilt or any large expanse of fabric, sketch the proposed design on graph paper. **For patchwork,** first draw the completed patchwork design on graph paper, then lay a sheet of tracing paper on top and sketch a quilting plan over the drawing as shown. Try several quilting plans in this way, and select the one you feel most enhances the patchwork.

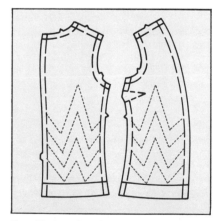

For odd-shaped projects, plan quilting design on traced pattern pieces. Match quilting at seamlines to quilting lines of adjoining sections. Do not let quilting lines cross darts.

Types of quilting designs/Outline quilting

Outline quilting follows the outlines of shapes already present on the top fabric layer. Patchwork and appliqué are the most common candidates for this type of quilting. Position quilting lines about ¼'' from the seamed edges of stitched-down shapes.

Each shape can be outlined as in the first illustration; every patch in design is quilted.

Selected areas can be quilted to emphasize certain aspects of a design. In the second illustration, 8-sided star is accentuated by quilting around the patches that form the star.

In echo quilting, the outline of a shape is repeated in concentric quilting lines. This technique is often used for appliquéd tops.

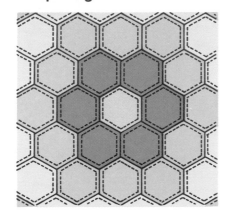 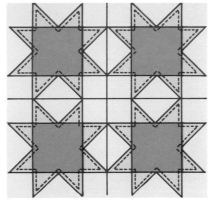 

Types of quilting designs/All-over patterns

All-over quilting produces a regular pattern by consistent repetition of one or more shapes. Designs can be adapted to any space, and so are widely used. They can be used to cover an entire surface with a simple, unobtrusive quilted background, or to fill open areas around or within other quilted motifs.

Straight-line designs are the easiest patterns to use; they can be drawn using just a yardstick or ruler. A simple vertical pattern is shown in the first illustration.

Criss-crossed diagonals produce a pattern of diamond shapes in the second illustration.

Diamond shapes surround and emphasize a central motif in the third illustration.

All-over curved patterns make interesting background designs. Templates of stiff paper are used over and over to create the patterns. Some patterns are formed by overlapping one or more templates; notches are cut along template curve to indicate overlapping points.

Shell pattern in first illustration calls for the simple repetition of a single template.

Overlapping circles in next illustration are marked with one round template, notched to indicate overlapping points of circles.

Crescent pattern is formed by using round templates in two sizes. A predetermined arc on each one is used to mark the top and bottom curves of the crescent shape.

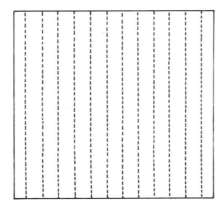 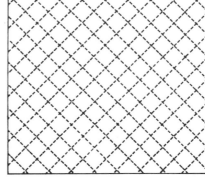 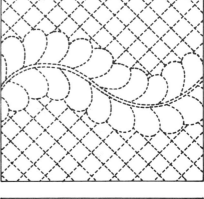

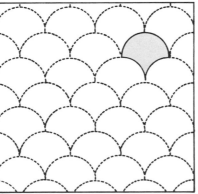 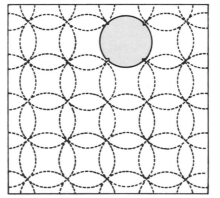 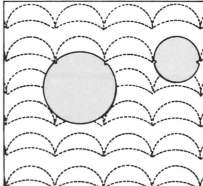

Quilting designs

Types of quilting designs/Ornamental motifs

Another type of quilting design is the ornamental motif, which pictures traditional subjects in a somewhat formal fashion. These motifs usually contain intricate details (see illustrated examples) that can best be seen and appreciated when they are worked on plain fabric surfaces. In many of the most elegant quilts from earlier periods, the larger, more elaborate designs act as a central motif; smaller motifs may surround the center design, perhaps decorate the corners as well. If you would prefer to combine two or more motifs in a single piece, work out your design ideas first on graph paper. A single ornamental motif is a dramatic way of decorating individual patchwork blocks or cushion covers.

Patterns for ornamental quilting designs can be purchased, or you can make your own perforated patterns (p. 245). Quilt with very fine stitches in order to get around the tight curves that are typical of so many of the designs.

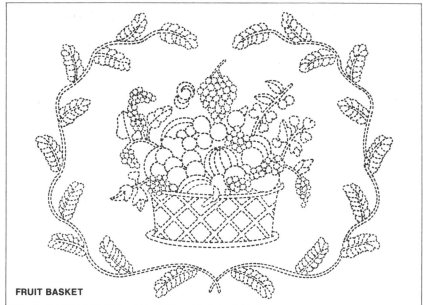

FRUIT BASKET

FLORAL

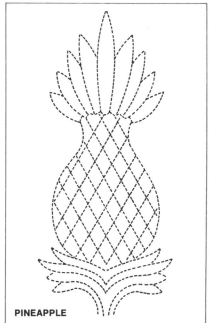

PINEAPPLE

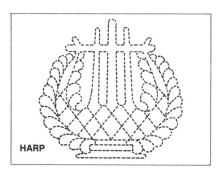

HARP

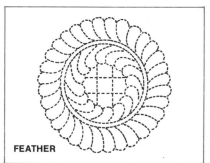

FEATHER

BUTTERFLY

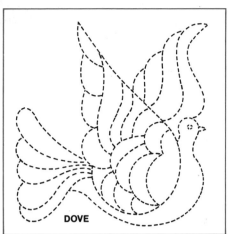

DOVE

TULIP

AMERICAN EAGLE

SNOWFLAKE

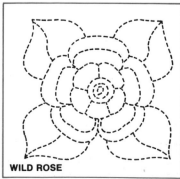

WILD ROSE

Quilting designs

Types of quilting designs/Borders

Border designs are made up of repeated patterns of motifs that frame and complement the main design (quilted or otherwise) on a quilt. To be effective, the border should relate to the overall mood of the other quilt decorations. Traditionally, flowing motifs, such as undulating feathers and gracefully twined cables, were drawn. Now, almost any design suited to long and narrow spaces can be used; even simple geometrics and some all-over patterns are appropriate. Some designs are quite rigid in structure and require special planning (see opposite page). When a border turns corners, plan the design so that it flows smoothly around the corner, and is balanced on either side (see below).

Plan any border design on graph paper. Select the design and corner treatment, then work out from each corner to centers of sides, adjusting design repeats in between. In example above, tulip motif is placed in each corner and at center of each side; graceful scroll design connects motifs.

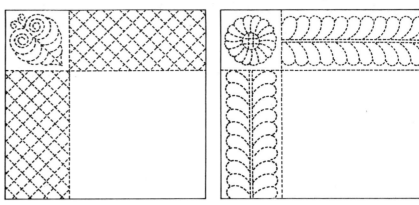

Corners can be filled with a *different motif* provided border design is balanced on either side.

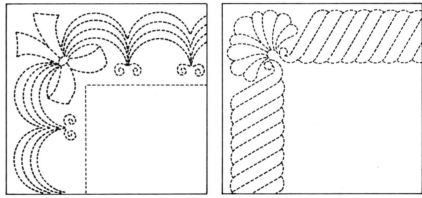

Or a *related motif can be introduced* at corners to bring the border to a conclusion.

Or the *border design itself might be modified* to fit corners in one continuous line.

The patterns of rigidly structured designs develop basically from a square, and must be laid out according to the measurements of that square. For such a design to be successful, the border must be made long enough and wide enough to accommodate full repeats; partial repeats spoil the continuity. To be sure of full repeats, work out your border design on graph paper, then adjust quilt dimensions as needed. Because each border will consist entirely of full repeats, the corners will usually work out satisfactorily. When repeats have different motifs or internal patterns (see the top two designs at the far right), you will want particular motifs to fall at the corners and will have to plan for this.

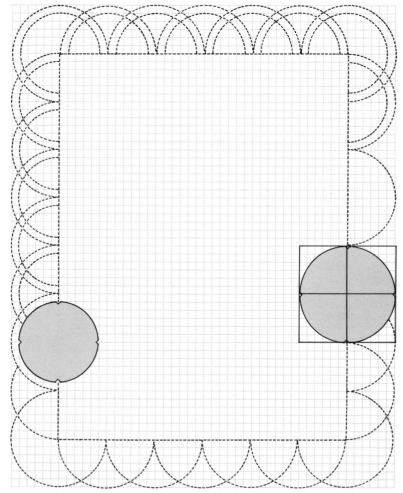

To graph a border design based on geometric repeats, divide the border into equal-size squares. The squares themselves may be the repeated shape (see top two designs, far right). In the design above, circles are developed from the square; templates are notched to show placement and intersecting points.

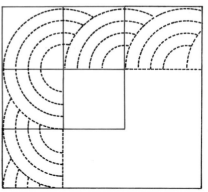

Design of concentric circles is like one at left, except overlaps are differently handled.

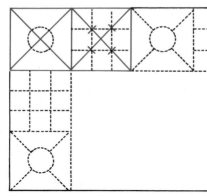

Alternating squares: Graph an *odd* number both ways to place crossed circle in corners.

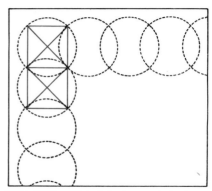

Wine glass design stems from a circle drawn *around* basic square and made into template.

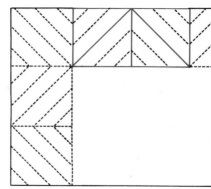

Squares of diagonals: Graph an *even* number to have lines at corners slant toward center.

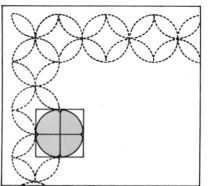

For petal-like motif, the template is made from a circle drawn *within* the square.

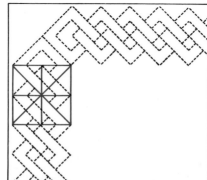

Interlocking links: Both their shape and placement evolve from a basic square as shown.

Quilting designs

Transferring and marking quilting designs

Quilt designs can be marked on fabric in a variety of ways. Which method you use will depend upon the type of design that is being marked and whether you will be marking it in or off the frame.

In-frame marking is done *after* the three quilting layers have been assembled and set into a frame or hoop. Designs must be marked a part at a time, as much as will fit within the exposed working area. In-frame markings are usually temporary, which allows the quilter to quilt each section right after marking, thereby avoiding smudges and smears.

Off-frame methods (see far right and opposite page) are used more often. With these, the quilting design is marked on the top fabric layer *before* it is assembled with the other layers and set into a frame or hoop. Marking off the frame permits the entire design to be done at one time, a real advantage with highly complex designs. Markings are intended to last through all subsequent handlings.

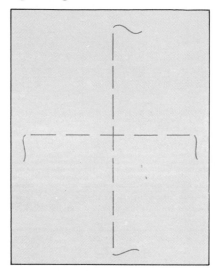

To prepare fabric for marking, press out any wrinkles or creases first. As a guide for proper placement of quilting designs, mark the center of the piece by connecting side-to-side and top-to-bottom midpoints with basting threads.

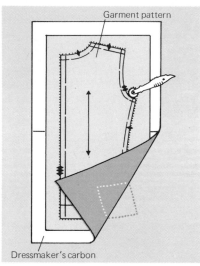

To mark odd shapes, such as parts of garments, lightly transfer the outline of each section onto the fabric, using dressmaker's carbon. Mark quilting design, but do not cut sections out until all quilting has been completed.

Off-frame methods

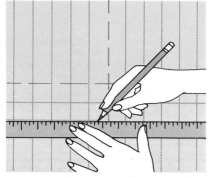

Straight-line designs begin with centering lines. *For a grid of squares,* use the basted lines; space subsequent lines equally from these.

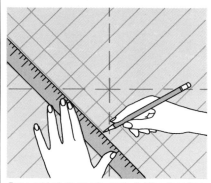

For a grid of diamonds, mark dividing lines from corner to corner; space the remaining lines evenly from these initial markings.

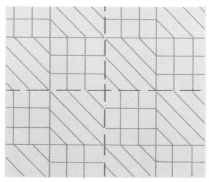

Design above combines both grid types. Notice the interesting pattern produced by having horizontal and vertical lines meet the diagonals.

In-frame methods

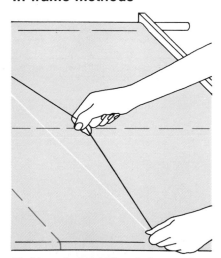

Chalking of straight-line designs such as squares, diagonals, and channels is easily accomplished by snapping a taut chalk-coated string across a stretched quilt. Two people are needed to hold each end of the string securely.

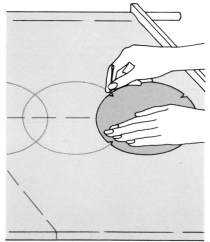

Needle marking, a useful though transitory method, usually follows a straight edge or yardstick, a template, or a stencil. Holding needle like a pencil, draw it firmly across the fabric surface to produce an indentation of the design.

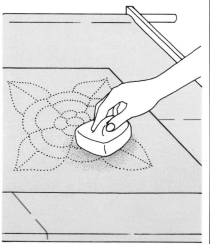

Perforated patterns are the usual choice for transferring intricate designs to top fabric. Make and use the perforated patterns as described for the off-frame method on the opposite page, but do not go over the dots with a pencil.

244

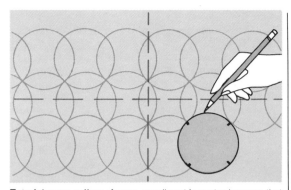

Templates are pattern shapes, usually cut from sturdy paper, that you simply trace around. Template for this design is notched on the edge to indicate where the shapes should overlap.

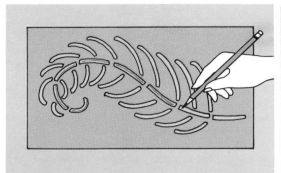

Stencils are marking patterns in which lines of simple quilting motifs appear as cut-out slots. With stencil on fabric and fabric on firm surface, draw lines through slots with hard pencil.

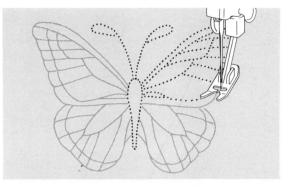

A perforated pattern is usually used to transfer intricate motifs. The design lines on the paper pattern may be pricked with a needle or stitched with an unthreaded sewing machine.

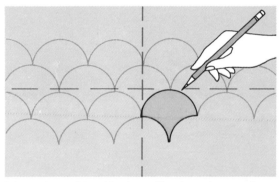

A frequent use of templates is repetition to produce an all-over pattern, such as this shell design. When you are using a template for such all-over marking, work from the center out.

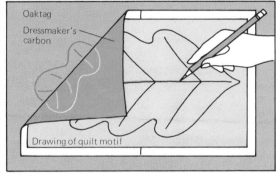

Oaktag

Dressmaker's carbon

Drawing of quilt motif

To make your own stencil, work out a line design on paper, keeping the details within the motif very simple. Using dressmaker's carbon, transfer the design to sturdy paper, such as oaktag.

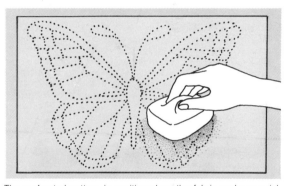

The perforated pattern is positioned on the fabric and a special powder called pounce is gently rubbed over the surface, leaving a dotted outline of the design on the fabric beneath.

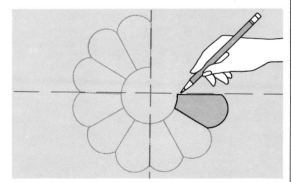

A template can also be the basis for forming a larger motif. The template used here is a wedge-shaped piece, called a *sector,* of a larger circle. Small center circle remains after tracing.

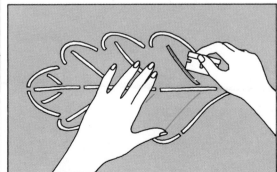

Cut out narrow channels along the drawn lines, using a single-edged razor blade or a mat knife. Be sure to leave connecting "bridges" where lines intersect so the stencil holds together.

To reinforce the powder markings so that they do not disappear or smudge with handling, go over the dotted lines with a hard lead pencil or a dressmaker's chalk pencil.

Basic quilting techniques

Estimating quilt size and yardage
Cutting top, backing, and filler
Assembling quilt
Setting quilt into frame
Setting quilt into hoop
No-frame method of quilting
Basic hand-quilting techniques
Hand-quilting tips
Machine quilting

Estimating quilt size and yardage

To determine the size of a quilt, first consider the size of the bed the quilt is intended for. Measure the bed, using a flexible tape measure, when it is fully made up, with sheet, blankets, and pillows in place (see below). Next, consider the way the quilt will be used; this will determine how much extra length is needed for the drop at the sides and at the foot of the bed, and whether or not a tuck-in allowance is desired for the pillows. For example, a quilt used as a bedspread will need a drop that falls to the floor and an extra allowance (about 15 inches) to tuck under the pillow. A short coverlet, on the other hand, need only hang down as far as the dust ruffle, and

may or may not be tucked in at the pillows. Many times, the depth of the drop is a matter of personal preference. If you are in doubt about what you prefer, drape a sheet over the bed, then fold and pin it in place until you arrive at a size of suitable and pleasing proportion. Remove the sheet and measure it. The overall size of a quilt is calculated from these basic measurements: Bed length plus depth of drop, plus tuck-in allowance (if any), equals finished quilt length; bed width plus depth of drop (times 2) equals finished quilt width.

To estimate the yardage needed for a quilt, first determine its overall cutting size (see opposite page) and work out

your estimates according to that. Yardage for a pieced top will depend, of course, on the patch design you select (see Patchwork). For a solid top, the amount of fabric required will depend upon the fabric width and its relation to the cutting size of the quilt width. For example, if the quilt width is narrower than the fabric width, only one length of fabric (a length equal to the quilt cutting length) is needed. If the quilt width is wider than one fabric width and anywhere up to twice as wide as the fabric width, two lengths of fabric are needed. You will want to add some more yardage to your estimate if you plan to use the same fabric as binding.

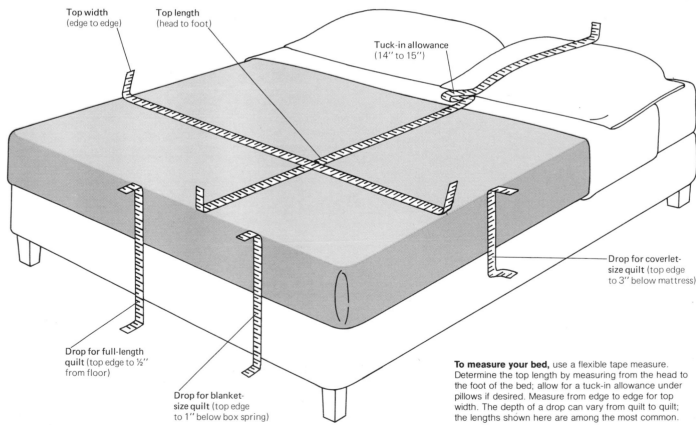

Top width (edge to edge)

Top length (head to foot)

Tuck-in allowance (14″ to 15″)

Drop for coverlet-size quilt (top edge to 3″ below mattress)

Drop for full-length quilt (top edge to ½″ from floor)

Drop for blanket-size quilt (top edge to 1″ below box spring)

To measure your bed, use a flexible tape measure. Determine the top length by measuring from the head to the foot of the bed; allow for a tuck-in allowance under pillows if desired. Measure from edge to edge for top width. The depth of a drop can vary from quilt to quilt; the lengths shown here are among the most common.

Cutting quilt top and backing

To calculate cutting dimensions of quilt top and backing, consider these variables along with your estimated quilt size: Depending on the edge finish that you select, you may only need an additional half-inch seam allowance all around; or you might have to add several inches to your calculations. To compensate for the "shrinkage" that usually results from quilting, add a few more inches to your overall figures as well. A quilt can be as much as three to six inches smaller after quilting; as a rule, the thicker the batting and heavier the quilting, the greater the reduction in size.

When proper sizes are determined, cut out the top and backing. Press out any wrinkles or creases. Mark the midpoints on each side of both pieces to simplify alignment when they are assembled.

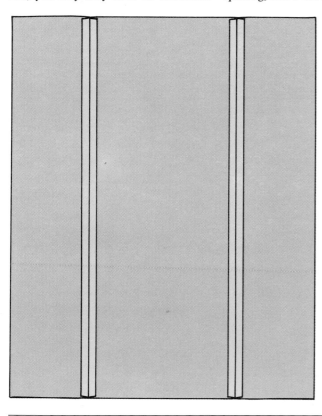

If the fabric is not wide enough for the top or backing, panels of appropriate widths can be joined to achieve the required measurement. When joining panels, avoid running a seam down the center of the quilt; instead, use one central panel, usually a full fabric width, and add matching panels to each side. Press seams open. Any quilt top, whether patchwork, appliquéd, or embroidered, can be enlarged to size if necessary by adding a border of the appropriate depth.

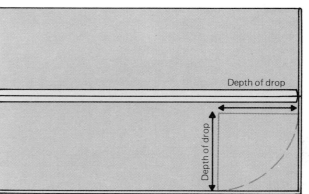

Rounding off corners for a quilted spread: On wrong side of quilt top, mark a square on corner of foot end; sides of square should equal depth of drop. Using a yardstick, measure from inner corner out, marking an arc as shown. Duplicate arc on opposite corner. Baste along arc to transfer curve to right side. Cut along arc after quilting has been completed.

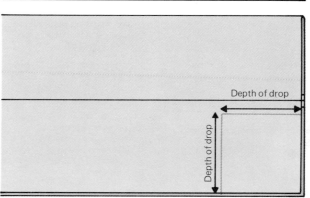

Cutting away corners to accommodate beds with foot posts: On right side of quilt top, mark a square on a corner of foot end; sides of square should equal depth of drop. Duplicate corner marking on opposite corner. Cut away corners along marked lines after quilting is completed.

Cutting quilt filler

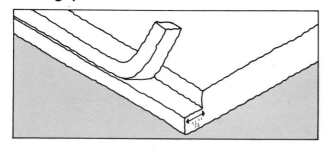

Cut batt to same size as quilt top. If batt must be pieced, separate it into two layers along one of the edges to be joined; cut a ½″ strip from one layer. Separate and cut off a similar strip from the adjoining edge.

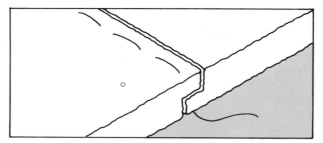

Overlap the cutaway edges as shown and baste the two together through both thicknesses. They are now joined with no telltale ridge.

Basic quilting techniques

Assembling quilt

When assembling any quilting project, stack the top, filler, and backing carefully, then baste them together securely so they remain smooth and wrinkle-free throughout the quilting process. Proceed slowly when basting; this can be the key to your quilting success. Even if you are using a frame or hoop, basting is an important step, especially when working a large quilt; the stitches hold the layers together to prevent any shifting and bunching. For small projects, such as cushion covers, pin-basting can be sufficient. If you are using the no-frame method (described at the lower right on the opposite page), or are quilting by machine (see p. 251), careful basting is even more essential.

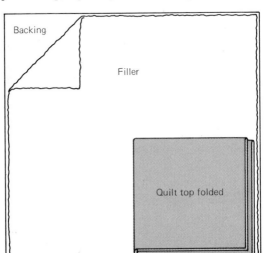

Backing

Filler

Quilt top folded

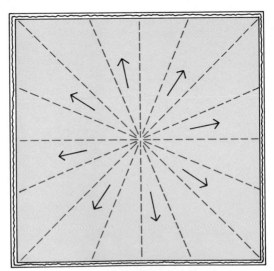

To assemble quilting layers, lay backing, wrong side up, on a hard, flat surface such as a table. Spread the batt or other filler over the backing, then lay the top piece, right side up, over all.

For large quilts, lay backing on floor. Spread batt over it, then stroke batt with a yardstick to help remove any wrinkles. Do not stretch the batt to fit, as it may tear. Fold quilt top into quarters with right side folded inside, and place it on one corner of the filler as shown; use the marked midpoints on backing and top piece for accurate alignment. Carefully unfold the top, and again use the yardstick to smooth it in place. Do not kneel or stand on the fabric to reach the center; this can cause hidden wrinkles in the filler and the backing.

Baste the three layers together in a sunburst pattern to avoid forming a lump of filler in the center: Using large running stitches, start from the center and work out toward the edges. Baste only from the top, being careful not to shift layers. As a general rule, there should be a basted line about every 6″ around the edges; baste more generously if the quilting will be done off a frame or hoop. Basting stitches may be cut and released as needed during the quilting process.

Setting quilt into frame

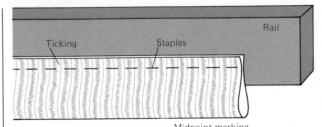

Rail

Ticking

Staples

Midpoint marking

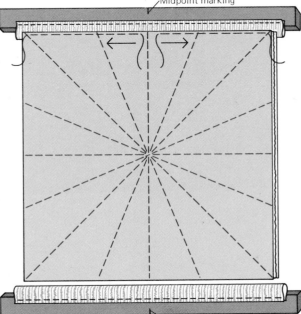

Midpoint marking

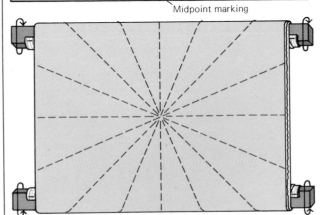

Staple ticking or other sturdy fabric to the rails as shown on page 237. Mark the midpoints of each rail for proper alignment when attaching the quilting project.

To attach quilt to rails, lay the basted quilt on the floor, and position the rails at each end, matching the midpoints of rails and quilt top. Baste the quilt to the ticking along each rail, working from midpoint out to each side.

Roll the quilt evenly and tightly onto each rail so a central area is exposed for quilting.

Attach the rails to the stretchers, adjusting them both so the quilt is held taut and straight, without sagging. Check for any wrinkles on the top and the backing of the exposed working area.

Secure the sides of the quilt by pinning twill tape to the edges, and looping it around the stretchers as shown; pin at about 3″ intervals. After completing the quilting within the exposed area, reveal a fresh section by unpinning the taped sides and rolling the completed part onto one of the rails. Secure the sides again as before.

Setting quilt into hoop

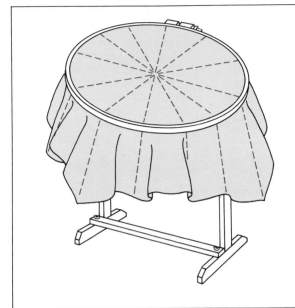

To set quilt or any other project into a hoop, place the center of the basted project over the inner hoop. Work out any fullness from the quilt by smoothing it over the edges of the hoop. Slide the outer ring in place and tighten the adjustment screw to keep the layers taut.

After quilting within this central area, remove the hoop and re-position the quilt to expose a fresh section; work from this central area out toward the edges. To quilt up to the edges, use a smaller hoop along the sides, or quilt without a hoop.

No-frame method

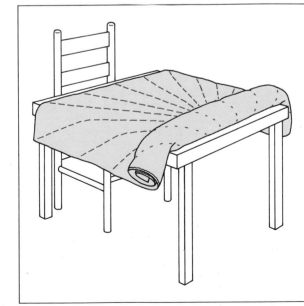

To quilt without a frame or hoop, place the basted project over a table or ironing board so its weight is fully supported. Do not allow large portions of the project to hang heavily over the sides of the table; this can cause pulling and some distortion. If necessary, roll or fold up the sides so they are properly supported. For small projects, you can simply spread the work over your lap.

Basic quilting techniques

Basic hand-quilting techniques

To quilt by hand, use an even *running stitch* that is short and closely spaced so as to give the illusion of an unbroken line (see below). Though white thread is the usual choice, a color that matches or contrasts with the fabric can also be used if you prefer. To avoid excessive tangling, use a single length of thread, no more than 18 inches long. Ideally, the quilting stitches should be fine (about 12 stitches to the inch), and even on both the top and backing. As you become more proficient with experience, you can increase your working speed by picking up several stitches on the needle before pushing it through; you will begin to develop a rhythm as your needle rocks back and forth, picking up the stitches. To facilitate this rhythmic motion, keep your quilting project slightly less than drum-tight when working in a frame or hoop.

You will also find stitching easier and more natural if you start an arm length away, and quilt toward yourself, changing your position as the quilting dictates. Extra-thick fillers can make quilting difficult, and so should be avoided, especially if you are working an intricate design.

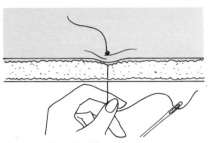

To start a line of quilting, knot end of thread, and insert needle from the top through all three layers. Gently but firmly pull the thread from underneath so knot slips through the top layer, and lodges in the filler. Cut off any thread end that may be visible at the surface.

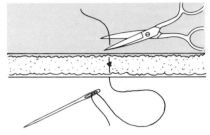

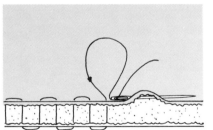

To end a line of quilting, make a knot on top of quilting surface. Insert needle a stitch length away and run needle through filler for a short distance; bring needle up, and gently pull the thread so knot slips through the top layer. Cut off thread end close to the surface.

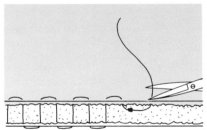

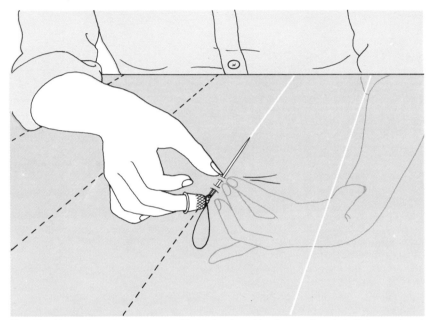

To quilt with running stitch, grasp needle with thumb and forefinger; take a few stitches, and push needle through with middle finger. To be sure needle penetrates all layers, hold other hand beneath the surface so tip of finger actually feels the needle point each time a stitch is taken.

Hand-quilting tips

For curved or circular motifs, use a double length of thread and start quilting at the 2 o'clock position; quilt in each direction from this starting point so that you are able to quilt toward yourself at all times.

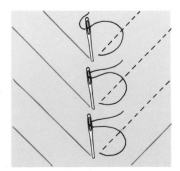

Keep several threaded needles in action. Quilt on a design line until it turns away from you or until you reach the end of an exposed quilting area. Leave needles on top layer and pick them up after you have shifted your position or have rolled a fresh area onto the frame.

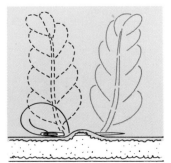

Avoid unnecessary starts and stops when quilting closely spaced motifs. Instead of knotting each time, simply run the needle from a completed motif through the filler and start again at next motif.

Machine quilting

Quilting with a sewing machine creates a durable and even stitching line that takes a fraction of the hand-quilting time. While it is possible to quilt almost any kind of project by machine, it is not always convenient to do so. Machine quilting is especially appropriate for small projects, such as crib quilts, garment sections, and home accessories, because they are easy to maneuver under the needle and can be made to fit under the arm of the machine when necessary. (It is also best for hard-to-quilt fabrics.) For such large projects as full-sized quilts and bedspreads, the sewing area must be modified and the sequence of quilting precisely planned to allow for the bulk as it passes through the sewing machine (see above right). If possible, avoid a single large piece by dividing the project into smaller sections—bedspread panels, for example, or quilt blocks. These can be quilted separately and joined later (see unit method of quilting on p. 255).

The sewing machine also limits the type of quilting design that is advisable. Avoid elaborate or curved designs that require cumbersome and frequent turnings under the machine needle; they are both awkward and time-consuming. Simple quilting designs composed of straight lines are better choices and can be worked up quickly and easily, especially if the lines of quilting extend from one edge of the project to the other. For this reason, all-over grid designs are highly suitable and frequently chosen (see lower right corner).

When preparing a project for machine quilting, be sure to baste generously so the layers do not shift as they are being fed through the machine. To avoid unsightly puckers, adjust the machine by loosening the tension and decreasing the pressure. Set the stitch length to about 10 to 12 stitches per inch, and test the settings on a complete sample, assembled of top, filler, and backing scraps that have been basted together.

To modify the sewing area for large projects, move the sewing machine out into an open space. Raise a large piece of cardboard or wood on sawhorses or chairs to the level of the sewing machine and place alongside the machine. This extension will supply the needed support for a large, heavy project, and so make it easier to maneuver.

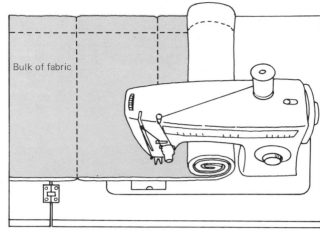

When quilting by machine, be sure to plan the direction and sequence of your stitching so that the bulk of the project always lies to the left of the needle. When working on a large project, such as a quilt, extend the working area as shown at left; roll the project up tightly enough to fit under the sewing machine arm as it becomes necessary.

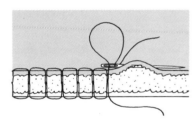

To secure thread ends that start or end away from raw edges, leave long thread ends on both top and bottom of quilted surface. Thread one of the ends through a needle and run needle through filler for a short distance.

Bring needle out, and cut off excess thread end close to the quilting surface. Run the other thread end through the filler the same way.

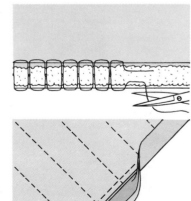

If quilting line starts or ends at the edges, the thread ends need not be secured; the final edge finish (such as a binding) will keep the stitches from pulling out.

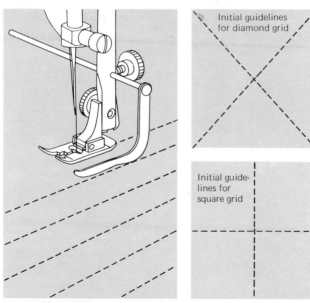

Use a quilter guide-bar attachment to quilt grid designs. Its adjustable bar extends out from the machine foot and falls along a guideline so that each quilting line can be equally spaced. Stitch initial guidelines as shown in the small drawings, then use the attachment to quilt lines on either side.

Other quilting techniques

Tying a quilt
Padded quilting
Corded quilting
Quilting in units
Sectional quilting
Pillow quilting
Puff quilting

Tying a quilt

Tying is a method of holding a quilt together without making lines of running stitches. To tie a quilt, you take a single stitch, at regular intervals, through all layers, leaving thread ends long enough to tie in a knot on the quilt top. Tying is faster than quilting with a running stitch, and more practical when the filler is thick or otherwise difficult to handle. Also, crazy quilts, which have no filler, are usually tied. This technique is not suitable when the filler is cotton batt, which tends to shift and so needs the control of stitching. For tying, you will need a large-eyed crewel needle and a strong decorative thread, such as embroidery floss, pearl cotton, narrow ribbon, or knitting yarn.

This quilt top is secured to the batting and backing with knots tied at regular intervals.

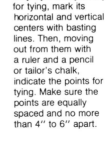

To prepare a quilt top for tying, mark its horizontal and vertical centers with basting lines. Then, moving out from them with a ruler and a pencil or tailor's chalk, indicate the points for tying. Make sure the points are equally spaced and no more than 4″ to 6″ apart.

On a patchwork top, you can follow the design of the quilt to place the points for tying. Keep spacing as uniform as possible, and try not to leave large areas untied.

After marking, baste the top, filler, and backing together as shown on page 248.

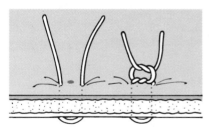

Make a tie at each of the marks on the top layer as follows: Take a stitch down through all three layers, then back up, leaving enough thread at ends to tie a square knot, as shown. Trim ends to a uniform length, usually about 1″.

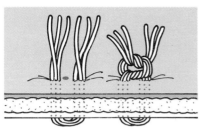

To make tufts, thread a needle with two or three lengths of yarn or floss. Take a stitch as above, and tie all of the ends in a square knot. Trim ends evenly.

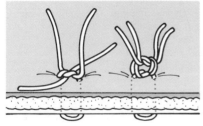

Another way of tufting, useful when a quilt is difficult to penetrate with multiple strands of thread, is to make the stitch with one length of yarn or floss and then add one or more lengths while tying the square knot, as illustrated.

Padded quilting

Padded or English quilting is a type of quilting in which only certain sections of the stitch design are padded, bringing them into relief and giving dimension to the design. It is especially effective on a solid-color fabric. To do this kind of quilting, you stitch the design through two layers of fabric (top and backing) and then insert the filler (polyester or cotton batting) between them by means of slits cut in the backing. The top layer is usually a tightly woven fabric, such as broadcloth or sateen. Because the filler is inserted through the backing, the best choice for this is a loosely woven fabric, such as lightweight muslin, voile, or cheesecloth. To protect the back of the quilt and conceal the ragged edges left

from the insertion of filler, the work should be lined or underlined with fabric of a type similar to that used for the top layer. For quilting stitches, use cotton quilting thread or a synthetic thread of a similar weight. Silk twist can be substituted for a richer look.

The designs best suited to this type of quilting include motifs and curved geometrics composed of many small sections, as shown in the photograph (right). It is difficult to stuff large areas uniformly. If you want to try a quick, modern approach to padded quilting, find a printed fabric with a distinct motif composed of small, curved areas, and use the techniques described below to put the motif in relief.

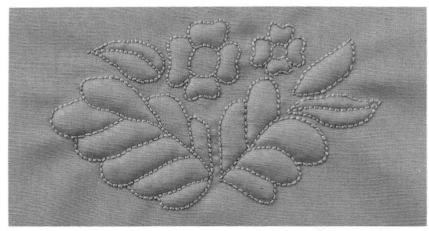

Leaves and flower petals above are padded with small pieces of batting inserted through backing.

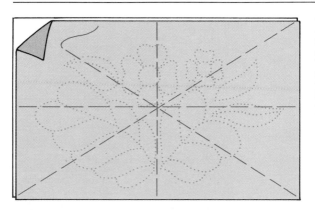

1. Transfer the quilt design to the fabric, using pounce, pricking, or other invisible method. Then, with raw edges and grainlines aligned, baste fabric to backing through horizontal and vertical centers, and diagonally from corner to corner, as shown.

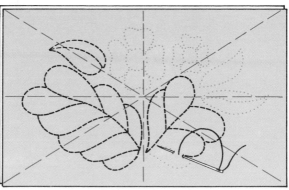

2. Hand-sew the fabric layers together along the design lines, using either a backstitch or an even running stitch. Or straight-stitch around the design by machine. Keep stitches as small as fabric thicknesses will permit. If you prefer a firmer marking line, transfer the design to the backing fabric, tracing the mirror image of the design. When stitching is complete, remove bastings.

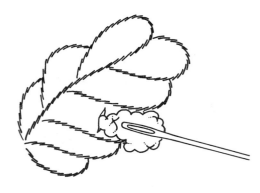

3. Cut a slit in center of one small section; make the slit slightly off-grain to avoid weakening the fabric. Stuff the section lightly with filler so the area is raised but not so packed as to distort the fabric.

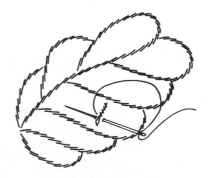

4. Close the slit with a whipstitch, as shown. Repeat the procedure of cutting a center slit, stuffing the section, and closing the slit, for each of the design areas that you want to pad.

Other quilting techniques

Corded quilting

Trapunto or corded quilting is a type of quilting in which linear designs are raised from the background with a cord or yarn filler. This kind of quilting is often combined with padded quilting to accentuate both the lines and shapes of the design. There are two ways to achieve the raised look. The first and most common method is to stitch the quilt design, in parallel lines, through two layers of fabric. The resulting tunnels are then threaded with yarn or other rope-like filler. Preshrink the filler to avoid puckering after laundering. The top fabric should be tightly woven, the back fabric a loose weave. Use cotton or

synthetic quilting thread or, for a richer look, stitch with silk twist. The piece must be lined to protect and conceal the filler insertions.

The second method involves only one layer of fabric. The cord is laid under the fabric and stitched in place at the same time. Since only one layer of fabric is used, this method is suitable for projects where a backing or lining is undesirable. For either method, use a soft cotton cable cord or yarn to fill the channels. Select the thickness according to the width between the parallel lines; the cord should fill the space so the channel is raised but not so tightly that it distorts the fabric.

METHOD I

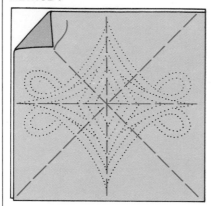

1. Transfer the quilt design to the fabric, using pounce, pricking, or other invisible method. Then, with raw edges and grainlines aligned, baste fabric to backing through horizontal and vertical centers, and diagonally from corner to corner, as shown.

2. Sew the two fabric layers together along marked lines, using a small running stitch or backstitch, or the straight stitch on your machine. Keep stitches small and even.

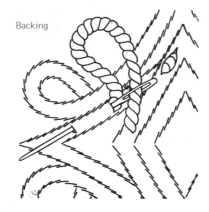

Backing

3. On the backing side, make a small slit in one of the tunnels formed by the parallel stitching. Using a blunt needle or bodkin, insert the yarn or cord filler a bit at a time: Run the needle through the tunnel for about 1″ and bring the needle out, pulling the cord taut; insert the needle in the same exit hole and repeat, taking care not to pierce the top fabric.

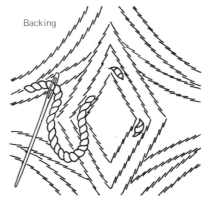

Backing

4. When filling a curve or corner, proceed as in Step 3, but do not pull the cord taut. Instead, leave a bit of slack at the turn to fill in the space, as shown. This will prevent puckering at these points on the top of the quilt.

METHOD II

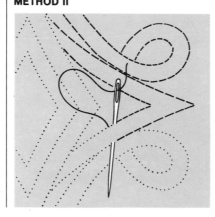

1. Transfer the quilt design to the right side of the fabric. Insert the fabric in a frame or hoop to leave both hands free for working. Use a sharp needle and embroidery floss. Holding the cord in position underneath the fabric with one hand, backstitch along the parallel lines, alternating stitches from side to side.

2. The crossed threads on the underside of the fabric hold the cord within the design lines and keep it flat against the fabric. As you work, keep the stitches even and the tension consistent.

Quilting in units/Sectional quilting

Quilting in units simplifies the making of large quilts or other quilted items by dividing the work into small, manageable units. **Sectional quilting** enables you to quilt one block or panel at a time. This technique, adapted from traditional quilting, is especially appropriate when you want a portable project or when you want to stitch by machine. **Pillow quilting** and **puff patchwork** (described on the next page) are contemporary techniques that also enable you to stitch and stuff one block at a time before assembling several of them.

Although these methods are generally limited to simple quilting designs and simple patchwork, they do offer several conveniences: they require little work space, they need no frame or hoop, and all or part of the stitching involved can be done by machine, which makes the work go considerably faster.

Sectional quilting, or dividing a quilt into sections for quilting, makes it easier to handle. Although adaptable to any size project, this technique is particularly helpful when it would be awkward to quilt a big project by machine. No matter how large the finished quilt is to be, it can be divided for quilting purposes into sections no bigger than one of its blocks.

To divide a project into sections, use the existing seams in the item. For example, a patchwork or appliqué quilt top can be quilted so that each block constitutes a section, or the quilt can be divided into groups of blocks. A border for such a quilt would be another separate section for quilting. These parts would be joined together after the quilting of all of the parts is completed as instructed below.

This seaming approach can also be used for quilting and assembling a garment. For example, the fronts and back of a vest can be quilted separately and then stitched together at the side seams. When choosing fabric for backing, remember that in this technique of sectional quilting, the backing fabric functions as a kind of lining because all of the raw edges are enclosed. No extra lining or underlining need be added for a finished look.

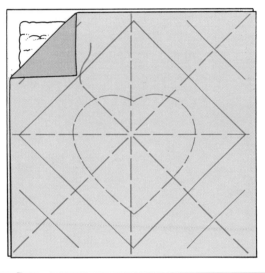
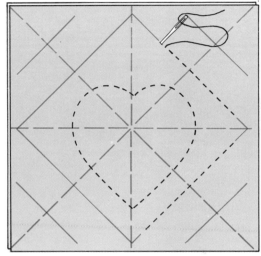

1. Cut the top and backing the same size for each section, allowing a ¼″ seam allowance on each side. Cut the filler for each section to the same size, but omit the seam allowances. Transfer the quilt design to the top fabric. Stack the layers and baste them together through the center, as shown.

2. Quilt the section, being careful to start and stop the quilting ½″ from the seamline so the seam allowances are left free for joining and turning back. Remove the bastings.

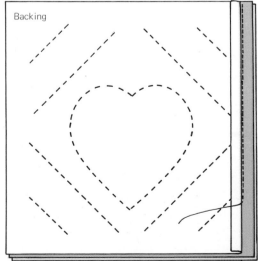
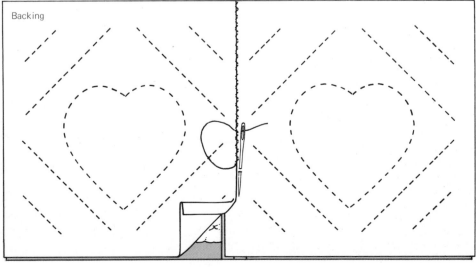

3. To assemble, place adjoining sections together, right sides facing, and join the *top fabrics only*, stitching the seam by hand or machine.

4. To finish the back, place the sections face down on a flat surface. Finger-press the seam open. The filler edges should abut; if they overlap, trim off excess. Turn under the seam allowance of one edge of the backing and slipstitch it securely to the backing of the adjoining section. Where necessary, go back and finish the quilting to the seamline.

255

Other quilting techniques

Quilting in units/Pillow quilting

In pillow quilting, each patchwork piece is backed, filled, and finished on all sides before the pieces are assembled. The effect of the finished quilt is similar to outline quilting in that the shape of each individually stuffed piece stands out. Any patchwork block or one-patch design that is a straight-edged geometric shape can be used. If the backing and top fabric are the same, the quilt will be identical on both sides; to create a reversible quilt with two different impressions, use a contrasting fabric for the backing. Or you could use up remnants by cutting each patch from a different fabric. For stuffing, use polyester or cotton batting.

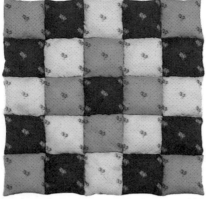

Pillows are sewed and stuffed before assembly.

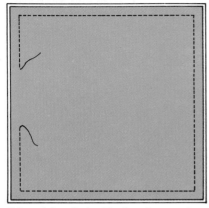

Cut a patch and a backing from the same template. Align them, right sides facing; stitch around edge, leaving an opening for turning.

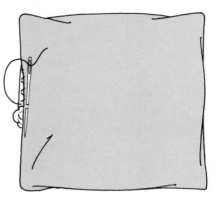

Carefully turn patch right side out. Add filler through the opening, stuffing lightly and evenly. Slipstitch the opening closed by hand.

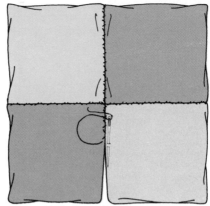

To assemble the finished patches, butt the edges and join them by hand with a slipstitch, or by machine with a fine zigzag stitch.

Quilting in units/Puff quilting

In puff quilting, a top patch is eased or tucked to fit a smaller backing so the top patch can be heavily stuffed to produce a puffy look. The edges are concealed after assembly with a lining, so the backing can be muslin or a similarly economical fabric. For stuffing, select polyester or cotton batting. Because of its puffiness, this style is confined to quilts and pillow covers. Although any one-patch design can be used, straight-sided shapes are easiest to work with. Two templates are needed: one for the patch, and another, which is the same basic shape but smaller, for the backing. The patch is usually 1½ times larger than the backing—for example, a 6-inch top fabric will be eased to fit a 4-inch backing. The greater the difference between the sizes, the puffier the finished unit will be.

Pieces in puff quilting are more heavily stuffed.

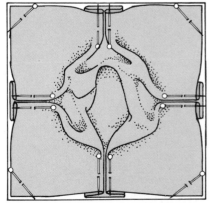

Wrong sides facing, pin patch to backing at corners. Match midpoints at sides and pin. Fold excess fabric in center into tucks as shown.

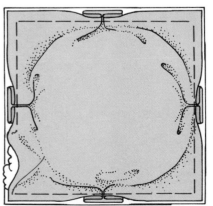

Baste around the edge by hand or machine, leaving an opening to one side of one tuck. Add filler, then baste the opening closed by hand.

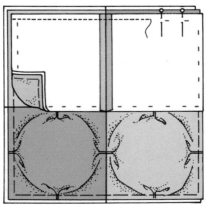

To assemble individual units, sew seams with right sides facing. To finish, line the entire piece or add a backing (for directions see p. 260).

Finishing edges

Self-finished edges
Extended binding
Slipstitched edges
Bound edges
Applying binding
Handling corners
Lining and underlining

Self-finished edges/Extended binding

When the quilting part of a project is completed, it is still necessary to finish the edges. Several methods are available to you; your choice depends upon the type of quilt you are making and its design. The first, called the self-finished edge, utilizes only the quilt top and backing. There are two kinds of self-finish: the **extended binding,** which can be used only if the backing fabric is of the same quality as the top fabric; and the **slipstitched edge** (explained on the next page). To make an extended binding, you must plan on it before you cut the main pieces; in order for the extra fabric to be folded up over the raw edges onto the quilt top, the backing must be cut larger than the top. This method can also be worked in reverse—that is, the top fabric can be cut larger and folded down over the backing.

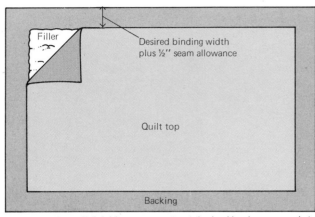

To prepare for self-finishing, you must cut the backing large enough to extend beyond the top piece by the desired binding width plus a ½" seam allowance on all four sides. Cut both top and filler to finished quilt size.

After quilting, press up the seam allowances of the backing. Then fold it over the edge to form the binding and slipstitch it to top fabric. Decide before you begin to stitch which corner treatment (below) you want to use.

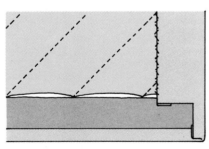

For a straight corner, slipstitch one side of the quilt. To reduce the bulk, trim away some of the corner fabric as shown.

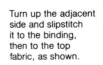

Turn up the adjacent side and slipstitch it to the binding, then to the top fabric, as shown.

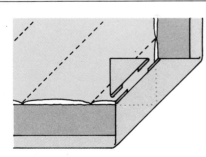

For a mitered corner, fold up the corner of the backing fabric so the diagonal fold lies at the corner point of the top fabric. Trim off the corner of the backing as shown.

Fold up one side of the binding and slipstitch it in place. Then fold up the adjacent side and slipstitch it in place. Slipstitch the miter—the diagonal line where the two edges of the binding meet—to close it.

257

Finishing edges

Self-finished edges/Slipstitched edges

The slipstitched method of finishing a quilt creates an inconspicuous finished edge, formed simply by folding under the seam allowances for both the top and backing fabrics, and slipstitching the folds together. This method requires no additional fabric, but trims, such as piping, rickrack, or ruffles, can be inserted between the folds if desired. When using the slipstitched method, be sure the quilting stitches stop about ½ inch from the edge so the seam allowances can be folded under. Do not stop the quilting too far from the edges, however, because this method does not secure the filler along the edges.

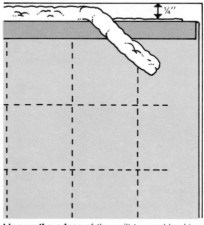

Line up the edges of the quilt top and backing. Trim the batting so it is about ¼″ shorter than the top and backing fabrics.

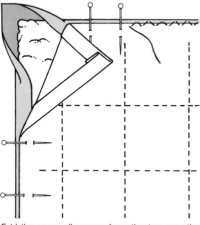

Fold the seam allowance from the top over the filler. Turn under the backing seam allowance. Align folds; pin, then slipstitch them together.

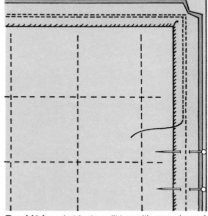

To add trim, pin trim to quilt top with raw edges of both trim and quilt facing in the same direction; stitch along the quilt seamline.

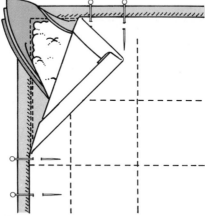

Fold top seam allowance over filler. Turn under backing seam allowance and pin. Slipstitch backing to trim along stitched line of trim.

Bound edges

Binding is a type of edge finish that calls for a separate strip of fabric to cover the raw edges of the quilt. It is neat, durable, and especially practical if the raw edges are worn and raveled from having been stretched in the quilting frame. Binding is also recommended for finishing a quilted garment in order to avoid a bulky hem. This edge finish should be planned from the beginning so you can purchase enough fabric. Finished bindings are traditionally narrow, about ⅜- to ½-inch wide. Cut from a contrasting fabric, binding becomes an attractive trim. Binding can be cut either from the straight grain or on the bias of the fabric. Curved edges require bias binding; either will do for straight and angular edges. There are both single and double bindings. Single is used most often for quilts; for greater durability, however, you can use a double binding.

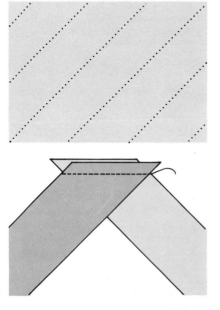

To make bias bindings, cut strips of fabric along the true bias of the fabric. For single binding, cut strips four times the desired finished width. For double binding, cut strips six times the desired finished width.

To join bias strips, place two together as shown and stitch on the straight grain of the fabric. Press the seam open.

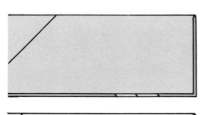

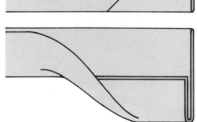

For a single binding, fold the strip in half lengthwise with wrong sides facing and press the fold lightly.

Open the pressed strip and fold the edges in so that they meet at the center; press.

For a double binding, fold the strip in half lengthwise and press. Then fold this halved strip in thirds and press.

Applying binding

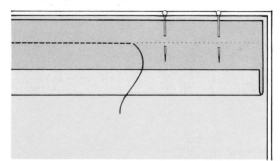

To apply single binding, open one folded edge. With right side of binding facing quilt top, pin binding to the edge of the quilt. Stitch along the fold-line of the binding.

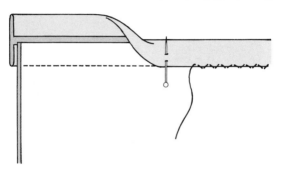

Press binding up. Turn it over raw edge so fold meets stitched line on the backing. Pin it in place and slipstitch to seamline by hand.

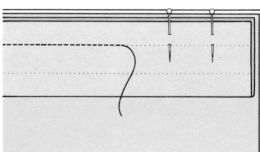

To apply double binding, open both folds. Pin binding to the quilt top with raw edges of binding and quilt aligned. Stitch binding to quilt along foldline nearest the edge.

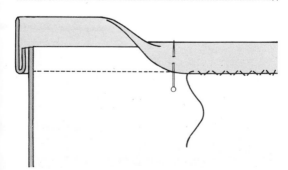

Press binding up. Turn it over the raw edge so fold meets stitched line on backing. Pin it in place and slipstitch to seamline by hand.

Handling corners

Corners in a binding application are handled in different ways, according to the situation. If a corner is curved, binding can be eased to fit around it. To do this, binding must be bias. If a corner is square, the binding can be applied so that corners are straight, as below, or mitered (see next page). The techniques for all three remain the same whether the binding is single or double.

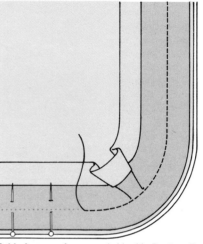

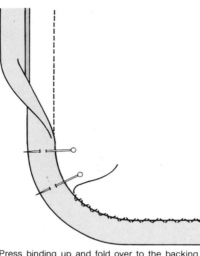

To bind a curved corner, pin bias binding to quilt edge as shown. Gently stretch the binding as you round the corner. Stitch along fold.

Press binding up and fold over to the backing. Binding will mold naturally over curved raw edge of quilt. Slipstitch to backing at stitch line.

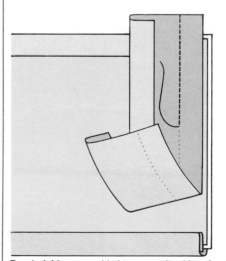

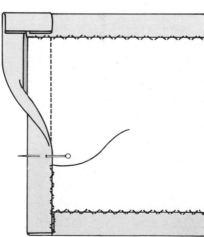

For straight corners, bind two opposite sides of the quilt. Then pin and stitch binding to one of the two remaining sides, letting the binding extend ½'' at both ends.

Turn the extended portion of the binding over the bound edge, then finish binding the raw edge in the usual way. Repeat the same procedure to bind the remaining raw edge.

Finishing edges

Handling corners/Mitering

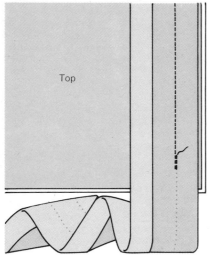

For mitered corner, pin binding to one raw edge of quilt. Stitch along binding fold nearest raw edge, stopping and securing stitches at point where adjacent seam will cross this seamline.

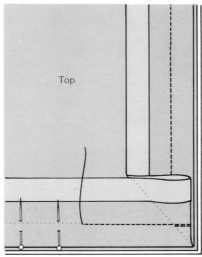

Fold free binding to right, perpendicular to stitched edge, forming diagonal fold. Press fold. Bring binding straight back, aligning right-hand fold with right edge. Stitch as shown.

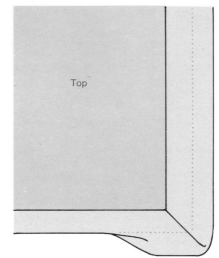

Press the binding away from the quilt top, then fold it over raw edge to backing. A miter will form on the quilt top. Another miter will be formed by manipulating binding on back.

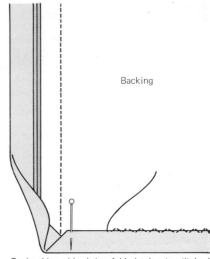

On backing side, bring folded edge to stitched line; pin. Fold excess binding under at corner, then bring adjacent binding together to form a miter. Slipstitch binding along fold and miter.

Lining and underlining

Some quilting methods, the raised quilting techniques and puff patchwork in particular, require a lining or underlining to protect the stitching on the backing and to hide any raw edges. A lining is appropriate if you want to finish an item—such as a quilt, place mat, or tablecloth—to the edge. You will want to use an underlining if you are working on a project, such as a garment, where the quilting will be seamed to adjoining sections, or where you want to finish the edge with a binding. A lining or underlining should be planned from the beginning so you can allow for the extra fabric that is needed.

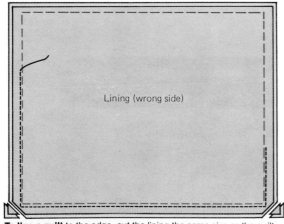

To line a quilt to the edge, cut the lining the same size as the quilt. Pin or baste the lining to the quilt with right sides facing. Stitch around the edge, leaving an opening for turning.

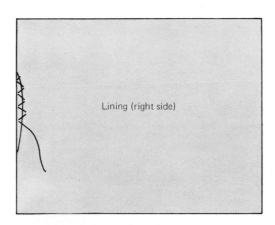

Remove the pins or basting stitches. Trim off the corners to reduce bulk and turn the quilt right side out. Turn under the seam allowances of the opening and slipstitch it closed.

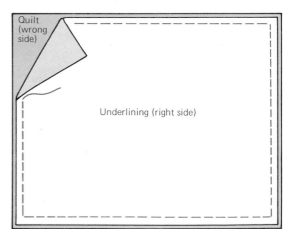

To underline, cut underlining the same size as quilt. With wrong sides facing, baste underlining to quilt along edges. Treat quilt and underlining as one layer during subsequent construction.

Care of quilts

Washing, drying,
pressing, storing
Repairing damages

Careful laundering, proper storage, and attention to repairs will prolong the life of quilts and quilted items.

To wash a quilt by machine, use a mild detergent and gentle agitation. Avoid bleach, harsh detergents, or too much detergent because these chemicals weaken textile fibers. Do not spin a quilt dry; this strains the quilting stitches and may break them. When washing by hand, use mild soap and do not twist or wring the quilt. Roll it in towels to remove as much moisture as possible.

To dry a quilt, tumble in a dryer or hang it on a clothesline. Or, if you have the space, dry the quilt by spreading it out flat on a clean sheet.

If a quilt is made from fabrics such as wool, silk, or velvet, which must be dry-cleaned, have this done as seldom as possible. Dry-cleaning chemicals wear out textile fabrics in time.

To press a quilt, pad the ironing board with a thick terry towel. Place the item quilted side down and steam-press lightly. Never press with the weight of the iron on the quilt.

Because textiles need to breathe, store a quilt by rolling it in a clean bed sheet. Do not use plastic because it prevents the air from circulating. Air a stored quilt at least once a year by hanging it on a clothesline, preferably on a breezy day, and launder it approximately every five years to prevent the fabric from yellowing. If a quilt is folded for storage in a chest, re-fold it yearly to avoid permanent creases.

Damages to quilts that occur during use can easily be repaired. Re-binding will renew a worn edge. Remove the original binding before applying the new one. To blend new with faded colors, prepare the new binding fabric by washing it repeatedly or by bleaching it in the sun. To mend broken quilting stitches, insert the damaged area in a small hoop, carefully pull out the broken threads, and re-stitch with matching thread.

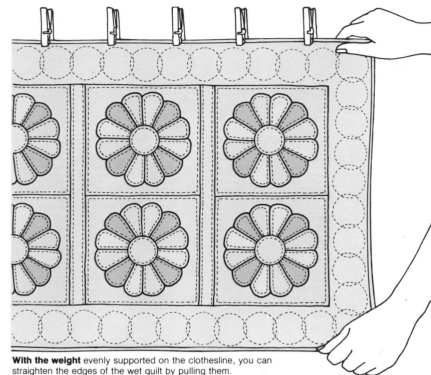

With the weight evenly supported on the clothesline, you can straighten the edges of the wet quilt by pulling them.

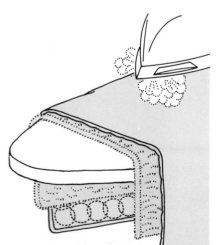
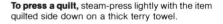

To press a quilt, steam-press lightly with the item quilted side down on a thick terry towel.

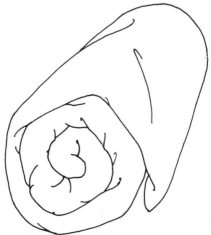

Store a quilt by rolling it up in a clean sheet. Do not use plastic; it does not breathe.

261

Man's patchwork vest

A patchwork vest is a handsome addition to any man's wardrobe. A one-shape design is preferable to a block because the vest shape will not distort it.

Materials needed
1 yard each of two different fabrics
Sewing thread
Fabric for vest back and lining as indicated on pattern envelope

Making a template
To determine what size template to use, decide how many shells you want to fit across the front of the vest and divide this number into the vest width. For example, the size 40 vest shown here measures 24 inches across. To fit 12 shells across the front, we used a 2-inch template. The template should not be smaller than 2 inches but it may be larger. To make the template, see pages 213 and 218.

Estimating fabric needs
To determine how large the pieced fabric must be, you need paper patterns for two vest fronts. To make the second, place the front pattern piece, flipped over, on a piece of paper; trace and cut it out, duplicating markings. Position the two pieces on graph paper; leave 2 inches between them for matching. The pieced fabric should equal at least the length and width of the combined vest fronts.

Draw the shell design over the area that is graphed; color it in. Count the shells in each color; you will need enough of each fabric for the shells in its color. To calculate the actual amount, see page 219. Here it was 1 yard of each fabric.

Stitching
Cut out the shells (see p. 219) and sew them together (p. 232). Press the pieced fabric. Lay it on a flat surface; place the pattern pieces on top. To match the design down the center front, place the markings for center front (which allow for an overlap for a button closure) at the edge of one row of shells. Cut out the pieces. Staystitch around the vest fronts ½ inch in from the edge, then continue constructing the vest, following pattern directions.

The shell design used for the man's patchwork vest was adapted from the one shown on page 213.

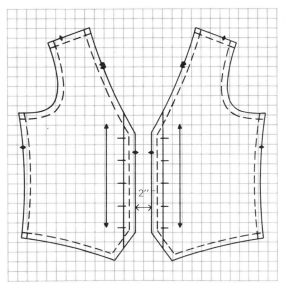

Place pattern piece and its mirror image on graph paper, leaving 2″ between the two for matching the design. Pieced fabric should equal at least the length and width of combined pattern pieces.

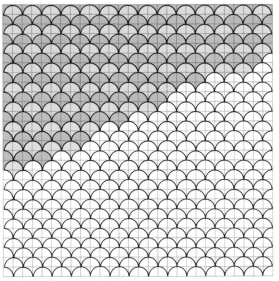

To determine amount of fabric needed, draw shell design on graph paper and color it in. Count number of shells in each color; you will need enough of each fabric for each quantity of shells.

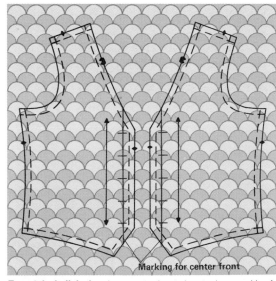

Marking for center front

To match shell design down center front of vest, place marking for center front (not seamline marking) at edge of one row of shells as if you were matching plaid or printed fabric.

Machine appliqué, sturdy enough for children's clothing, is easy to do on a zigzag machine.

Boy's coveralls/Machine appliqué

A child's name spelled out in bright calico letters and a polka dot turtle are machine-appliquéd to boy's coveralls. A name or initials could also be appliquéd to a dress or skirt.

Materials needed
Paper and pencil for enlarging design
4-inch-square pieces of various print or
    solid fabrics *or* ⅛ yard of each
Sewing thread

Enlarging the design
To enlarge the design, make a grid with ¼-inch squares and copy the appropriate letters and the turtle square for square (refer to p.14). The enlarged letters measure 1¼ inches high by approximately 1¼ inches wide, depending on the width of the specific letter. To see if the name you want to appliqué will fit the space you have, multiply the number of letters in the name by 1¼ inches. Allow a ⅛- to ¼-inch space between letters.

Cut out the letters and the separate parts of the turtle. Pin these pieces to the appropriate fabrics and trace around each one with a pencil. Cut out each piece outside the marked lines, leaving an ample seam allowance.

Stitching
Position letters on coverall bib and pin them in place. Here the name is placed 1 inch above top seam of waistband. The placement of both name and turtle will vary, depending on type and size of garment used. To position the parts of the turtle, pin the shell on the coveralls first. We placed it in the center of the bib, 1¼ inches down from top edge. Then pin head, legs, and tail pieces in position, lifting edge of shell so it overlaps the other pieces. (The extra allowance outside the marked lines will overlap still more.) Straight-stitch around the shell on the marked line. Then, with sharp, pointed embroidery scissors, trim away extra fabric around shell, cutting as close to the straight stitching as possible. Straight-stitch around the head, legs, and tail; straight-stitch also around each of the letters; trim the excess fabric from all these pieces. Satin stitch (close zigzag stitch) around each letter and parts of turtle to cover raw fabric edges and stitching (see p. 196). To zigzag around corners and curves, see page 197. Pull thread ends to inside, knot them, and trim excess.

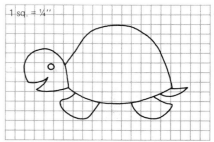

To enlarge turtle, make grid with ¼'' squares; copy design square for square (see p.14).

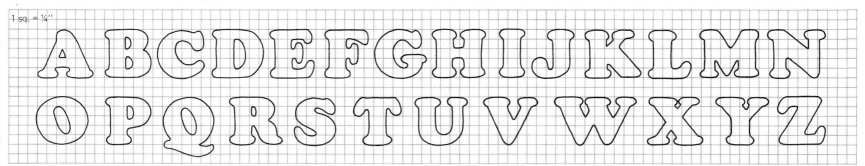

To enlarge the letters, make a grid with ¼'' squares and copy the desired letters square for square (see p. 14). Make sure the letters in the name you want to appliqué will fit the space you have.

Baby quilt

A quilt appliquéd with baby animals is a delightful addition to any child's room. The directions that follow are for making the quilt exactly as pictured at the right. To change the quilt to suit your needs, you can choose one favorite animal and appliqué it twelve times. Or you could select three or four animals, arranging them any way that pleases you.

Materials needed

Paper and pencil for enlarging designs

Sturdy paper for templates

¼ yard each of 10 different fabrics for animal appliqués

1 yard white fabric for base squares

2¾ yards fabric for strips, borders, and quilt backing

40½″ × 52½″ piece of batting

White quilting thread

Sharp needle

1 skein black embroidery floss

Crewel needle

Embroidery hoop

Sewing thread

The appliqués

To enlarge the animals, make a grid with 1-inch squares; copy the shapes square for square (see p. 14). Each animal appliqué is composed of two or more fabrics. The animal's body is made of one fabric; the head, tail, ear, and other body parts indicated in gray on the drawing (see facing page) are of a second fabric. You will need a template for each shape. Trace around each piece of each animal separately; follow the directions on pages 193-194 for making templates and cutting out each shape. We used ten different printed and solid fabrics in pink, yellow, light blue, and light green for the animals; you can use fabrics in colors of your choice.

On the white fabric, mark twelve 10½-inch squares (a 10-inch square plus a ¼-inch seam allowance on each side). Appliqué the animals to the squares by hand (see p. 195). To determine the layering order of the appliqué, see page 198. For most of the animals, the body is appliquéd first, with such separate parts as the head, tail, or ear applied as the second layer. Exceptions are the squirrel's tail, the elephant's leg, the ladybug's head, and the chick's back wing; these parts are appliquéd first. A third layer is used for the teddy bear's nose.

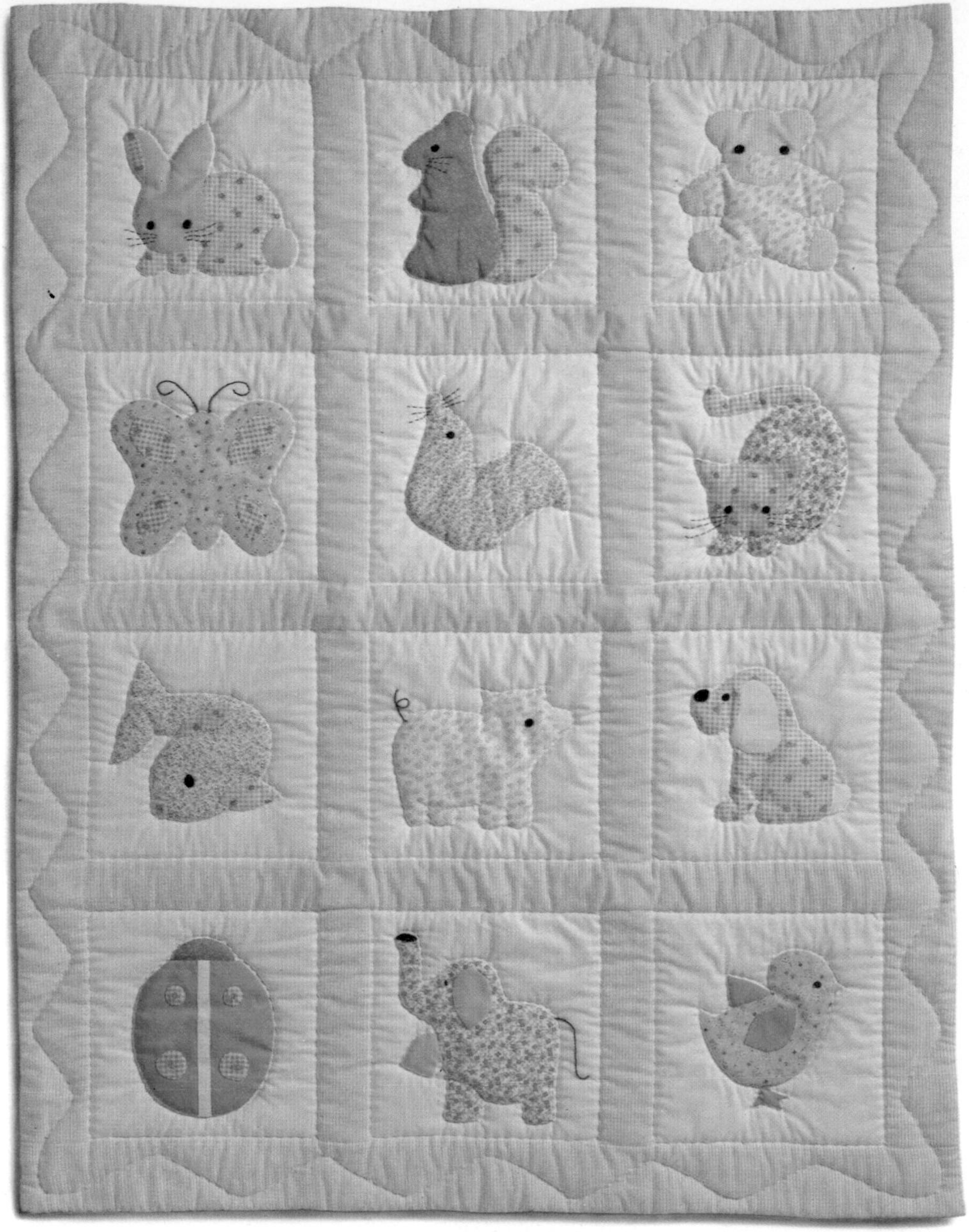

Embroidery

The animals' small features, those that are too small to be an appliqué, are embroidered. The eyes are satin stitched (see p. 48), the tails and antennae are backstitched (see p. 22), whiskers are worked in running stitch (p. 46). When appliqué and embroidery are complete, cut out the squares.

The quilt top

To complete the quilt top, cut out, from the backing fabric, three 2½ × 34½-inch strips for the horizontal dividers and eight 2½ × 10½-inch strips for the ver-

The baby quilt combines the techniques of appliqué, patchwork, and quilting. Animals are appliquéd; blocks, dividers, and borders are pieced; and the layers are quilted together. Each appliquéd block is also embellished with embroidery stitches. You can make the quilt exactly as pictured at left or you can change it to suit your needs. One animal could be appliquéd in twelve different fabrics. Or you could use three or four favorite animals in a pleasing arrangement. Or you could use fabrics in colors that are bolder than the pink, yellow, light blue, and light green that we used here.

tical dividers. For borders, cut two 3½ × 40½-inch rectangles for the top and bottom, and two 3½ × 46½-inch rectangles for the sides. These measurements allow a ¼-inch seam allowance on all edges. To sew the blocks, dividers, and borders, see pages 230-231. Join them in this order: Join the blocks and the vertical dividers to form horizontal strips; sew horizontal strips and horizontal dividers together; add the borders last. Follow the drawing (far right) for the placement of the individual blocks. Then press the seam allowances between blocks and vertical dividers to one side; alternate the direction from strip to strip. When all blocks and dividers have been joined, add the borders. Attach the side borders first, then stitch top and bottom borders, overlapping side borders. Press seams, then the entire quilt top.

Assembling the quilt

Cut a 40½ × 52½-inch rectangle of fabric for the backing and a piece of batting the same size. Place the backing right side down on a flat surface; put the batting on top. Smooth out any wrinkles. Fold the quilt top in quarters with right side inside (see p. 248). Place folded top on bottom quarter of batting, then unfold it, smoothing wrinkles. Pin and baste layers through the center.

Quilting

Each animal appliqué is outline-quilted (see p. 239). To do this kind of outlining, quilt around each animal and around the inside of each square. To quilt the border, enlarge the border quilting design (see p. 14) and transfer it to the fabric (see p. 244), following the drawing at right. Remove the bastings.

Finishing

The edges of the quilt are finished with a technique called self-finishing (see p. 258). Turn under ¼ inch on all four edges of both the quilt top and backing; trim away ¼ inch of batting on all sides. Slipstitch quilt top to backing, being careful not to catch batting in between.

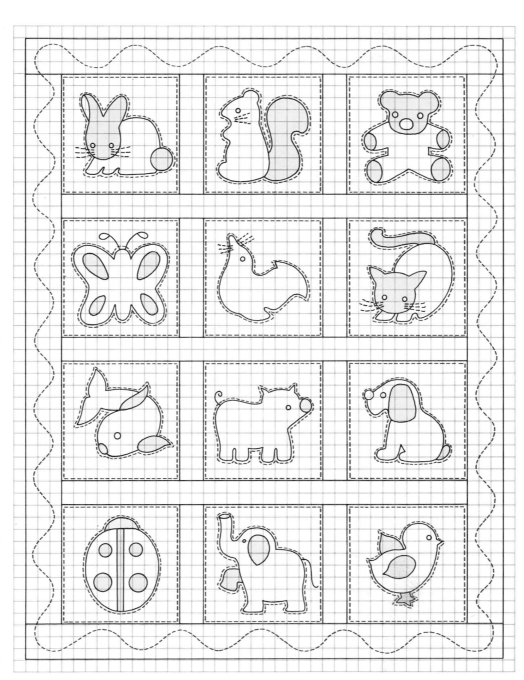

To enlarge the animals, make a grid with 1″ squares and copy the shapes square for square (see p. 14). The gray areas represent changes of appliqué fabric. The drawing shows placement of squares to make the quilt pictured opposite; you can place the animals in any positions you wish.

The sewing of blocks, dividers, and borders is done in a precise order. The vertical dividers are first sewed to the blocks; strips of blocks are sewed to horizontal dividers. Then borders are attached: side borders first, then top and bottom borders.

To quilt, outline each animal, then quilt around the inside of each block. To quilt the border, enlarge the border design by making a grid with 1″ squares and copy the quilting design square for square. Transfer the border design to the quilt (see p. 244).

Finished size of quilt:
40″ × 52″

Cut size of quilt parts:
Base squares, 10½″ square

Vertical dividers, 2½″ × 10½″

Horizontal dividers, 2½″ × 34½″

Top and bottom borders, 3½″ × 40½″

Side borders, 3½″ × 46½″

Cut-through appliqué wall hanging

The motif for this wall hanging is adapted from the cut-through appliqué design shown on page 201.

Cut-through appliqué gets its striking effects for very little money. Fabrics are all simple, inexpensive cottons.

Materials needed
½ yard each of unbleached muslin and green, beige, and rust cotton fabrics
¼ yard orange cotton fabric
Thread to match each fabric color
½ yard fabric for backing
½ yard interfacing
Crewel needles
Embroidery scissors
Two ½-inch-diameter cafe curtain rods that extend from 18″ to 28″

Cut-through appliqué
To enlarge the design, make a grid with ½-inch squares and copy design square for square (see p. 14). Cut 16 × 19-inch rectangles from the muslin and from the green, beige, and rust fabrics. Trace design on the green fabric. To assemble fabrics, place the rust face up, followed by the beige, the muslin, and the green. Baste layers together around the edges. Orange fabric is used to insert patches (see p. 205). To work the appliqué, follow the directions on page 205, using the diagram below to determine which shapes are cut from which layers.

Finishing
For the backing, cut a 16 × 19-inch rectangle of backing fabric and one of interfacing. Baste interfacing to wrong side of backing ¼ inch from the edge. To make hanging loops, cut six 6½ × 3½-inch rectangles. Fold them in half crosswise with right sides facing; stitch ¼ inch from the edge. Turn the resulting tube right side out; press tube with seam in center back. Fold tube so raw edges meet and seam is on the inside. To attach loops to backing fabric, pin one loop on each end and one in the center of the two 19-inch sides, aligning raw edges of loops and backing. Stitch ½ inch from raw edge; remove pins. Place appliqué face down on top; stitch around all four sides, leaving a 6-inch opening. Trim corners, turn right side out, and press. Stitch opening closed by hand.

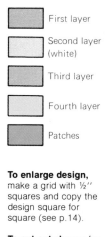

1 sq. = ½″

First layer

Second layer (white)

Third layer

Fourth layer

Patches

To enlarge design, make a grid with ½″ squares and copy the design square for square (see p.14).

To cut out shapes for reverse appliqué, follow directions on page 205, using the key above to determine which shapes are cut from which layers.

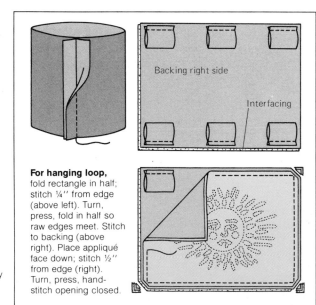

Backing right side

Interfacing

For hanging loop, fold rectangle in half; stitch ¼″ from edge (above left). Turn, press, fold in half so raw edges meet. Stitch to backing (above right). Place appliqué face down; stitch ½″ from edge (right). Turn, press, hand-stitch opening closed.

Patchwork floor pillow

Floor pillow adapts Drunkard's Path, a traditional design, to a modern setting.

Materials needed

Paper, pencil, cardboard for templates
½ yard each of two contrasting cottons
2 yards unbleached muslin (½ yard for patches, 1½ yards for pillow form)
1 yard fabric for backing
24½-inch-square piece of batting
Fiber fill for stuffing
Sewing thread
Quilting thread

The patchwork

The pillow top consists of four Drunkard's Path patchwork blocks. Each block is made up of sixteen 3-inch squares, which in turn are composed of two curved pieces. The cut size of the squares is 3½ inches; this allows for ¼-inch seams. To make the templates for the two curved pieces, see page 218. Use the drawing below, left, to determine how many pieces you will need to cut from each fabric. To stitch the pieces together for each block, see page 223. To join the blocks, follow the directions on page 230.

Quilting

Cut a 24½-inch square of muslin and one of batting. Place muslin on a flat surface; put the batting on top, followed by the patchwork right side up. Pin and baste these three layers together. The quilting outlines the shape formed by the red patches; the quilting stitches are placed ¼ inch inside the seamlines.

Assembling the pillow

To make a pillow form, cut two 25-inch squares of muslin. With right sides facing, stitch ½ inch from the edge around all four sides, leaving a 10-inch opening. Trim the corners, turn right side out, and fill with fiber fill. Stitch the opening closed by hand. To finish the pillow, cut a 24½-inch square of printed fabric. With right sides together, stitch the quilted pillow top to the backing along three sides ¼ inch from the edge. Trim the seams and turn pillow cover right side out. Insert the pillow form, then stitch the opening closed by hand.

The design for the floor pillow was adapted from the Drunkard's Path block shown on page 213.

The pillow top is composed of four blocks in the Drunkard's Path pattern. The patches that form the design are red; the background patches are off-white in the center and brown at the corners.

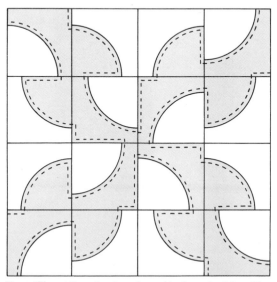

The quilting outlines the shape formed by the red patches. Place quilting stitches ¼″ inside the seamlines. The drawing shows stitching plan for one block; the others are quilted the same way.

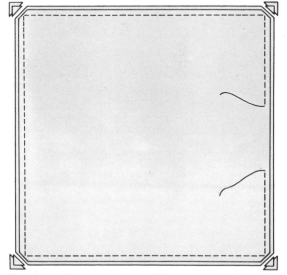

To make a pillow form, place two 25″ squares of muslin together. Stitch ½″ from the edge, leaving a 10″ opening. Clip corners, turn right side out, add fiber fill. Stitch opening closed by hand.

Quilted evening bag

Padded and all-over quilting decorate a stunning and original evening bag.

Materials needed

Paper and pencil for enlarging design
¾ yard satin
¾ yard unbleached muslin
Batting
1 yard rayon-covered cording
3 spools silk buttonhole twist
Sewing thread

The design

To enlarge the pattern for the bag, make a grid with ½-inch squares and copy the shape square for square (see p. 14). Put the pattern on the satin and trace around it; cut it out about 2 inches beyond the cutting lines. Transfer the oval and quilting lines to the fabric (see pp. 16-17). Enlarge the floral design by making a grid with ¼-inch squares; transfer the design to the fabric. Using the silk buttonhole twist, work the padded quilting first (see p. 253).

Trace the bag pattern on the muslin and the batting; cut out the shape about 2 inches beyond the cutting line. Put muslin face down, followed by batting. Place bag face up on top. Pin and baste the layers together. Quilt along marked lines with running stitch (see p. 250), using the silk buttonhole twist.

Assembling the bag

Trim the quilted bag along the cutting line. Use the pattern to cut the shape for the lining out of satin. Place lining and bag with right sides together. Stitch ½ inch from the edge, leaving a 6-inch opening. Trim corners; turn right side out. Stitch opening closed by hand. For the handle, cut a 26-inch length of cording, or any length that is comfortable for you. To finish the ends, cut two 1 × 2-inch rectangles of satin. Fold under ¼ inch on all sides, then fold the rectangles in half crosswise. Put a cording end inside each fold; stitch the top edges, catching cord securely; sew satin pieces to bag lining. To assemble, fold the bag, following diagram below right, and stitch the sides closed.

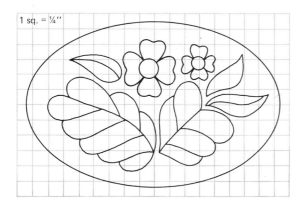

The floral motif on the flap of the evening bag is the padded quilting design shown on page 253.

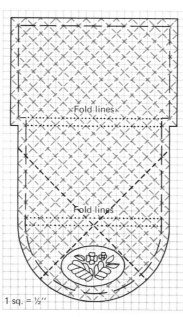

1 sq. = ¼″

To enlarge the design, make a grid of ¼″ squares and copy the design square for square (see p.14). Transfer design to the oval area on the bag. To work the padded quilting, follow the directions on page 253.

To enlarge pattern for bag, make a grid with ½″ squares and copy the shape square for square. Transfer oval motif and quilting lines, starting with black lines, to bag (see pp. 16-17). Work padded quilting first. Assemble bag, batting, and muslin; stitch quilting lines.

Fold lines

Fold lines

1 sq. = ½″

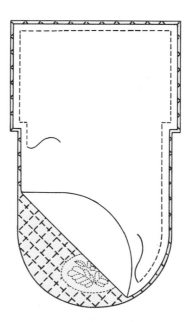

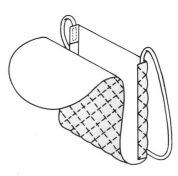

Place lining on bag with right sides facing. Stitch ½″ from the edge, leaving a 6″ opening for turning. Trim seam; turn right side out. Sew opening closed.

To assemble bag, fold as shown. Stitch sides to body of bag along bottom and back. Sew one satin-covered cord end to lining at each side.

Knitting

270 Knitting supplies
Yarns
271 Buying and winding yarn
272 Needles
273 Knitting aids
274 Knitting basics
Casting on
276 Forming the knit stitch
278 Forming the purl stitch
280 Elementary stitch patterns
281 Yarn tension
282 Binding off
284 Side selvages
285 Scarf to knit
Attaching new yarn
286 Following knitting instructions
Knitting terminology
287 Multiples and repeats
Checking the gauge
288 Elongating stitches
289 Increasing
292 Decreasing
294 Crossing stitches
297 Picking up stitches
298 Circular knitting
300 Knitting stitches
Using a pattern stitch
Textures
302 Ribs
303 Diagonals
304 Laces
308 Crossed stitches
310 Cable stitches
312 Novelty stitches
313 Smocks
314 Knotted stitches
315 Aran-pattern pullover to knit
316 Multicolor stitches/techniques
322 Charted stitches

324 Knitting a garment
Taking and using measurements
325 Designing
Determining yarn needs
326 Charting
Man's pullover to knit
328 Shaping diagonals
329 Pleats
330 Shaping necklines and collars
332 Shaping armholes and sleeves
334 Long-sleeve finishes
335 Borders
336 Hems and facings
338 Pockets
341 Buttonholes
342 Assembling and finishing
Blocking
344 Joining sections
346 Inserting a zipper
Adding tape
347 Adjusting fit
348 Adding embroidery
Making a duplicate stitch
349 Alphabet to embroider

Knitting projects
285 Scarf
315 Aran-pattern pullover
326 Man's pullover
350 Children's sweaters and hats
352 Sport socks
353 Mittens and hat
354 Evening skirt, top and shawl
356 Knitted trims for sheets and
pillowcases

Knitting supplies

Yarn descriptions
Yarn selection
Tips for buying yarn
Winding yarn
Knitting needles
Knitting aids

Yarns

Many yarns are suitable for use in knitting. Choices differ in fiber content, texture, weight, and ply. The chart below gives characteristics and uses of wool and synthetic yarns that are widely available and frequently chosen for knitting. (Cotton yarns are used also for knitting, but more often for crochet, and so are described in that chapter.) In addition to basic types included in the chart, most yarn manufacturers produce synthetic and blended yarns of their own design, labeled with their trade names. These will become familiar to you after a few visits to local yarn stores.

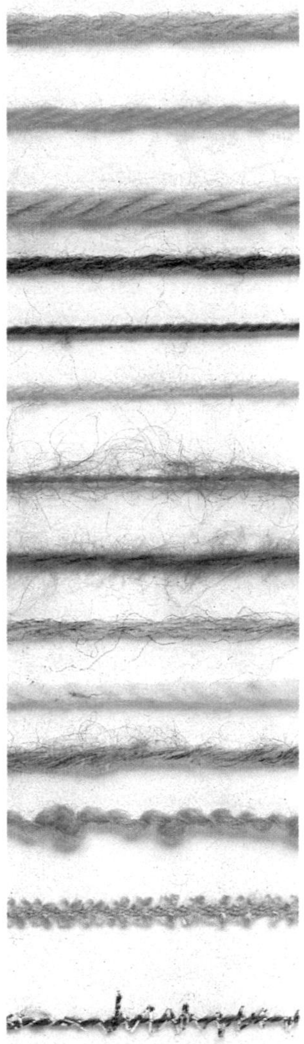

NAME	DESCRIPTION	WEIGHT	USES
Knitting worsted	Wool, usually 4-ply, the most versatile of wool yarns	Heavy	Any article for which bulk and warmth are desired, such as a hat, sweater, suit, or afghan
Knitting worsted weight	Acrylic with same weight and bulk as the wool version	Heavy	Same as knitting worsted
Rug	Wool or acrylic	Very heavy	Rug, pillow cover, tote, boutique items
Sport	Wool or acrylic, usually 4-ply	Medium	Hat, shawl, sweater, gloves, socks, vest
Fingering	Wool or acrylic, usually 3-ply	Light	Shawl, bed jacket, baby garments
Baby	Similar to fingering yarn but slightly bulkier; pastels only	Light	Baby garments, baby blanket
Mohair	Fluffy hair of the Angora goat; sometimes blended with other fibers	Light to medium	Hat, sweater, shawl, suit
Angora	Very soft and fluffy hair of the Angora rabbit	Light	Same as mohair
Shetland	Loosely twisted wool from Shetland sheep	Medium	Sweater, hat, mittens
Fisherman	Unbleached wool, usually a worsted weight	Heavy	Aran-style garments
Icelandic	Homespun wool from mountain sheep of Iceland	Very heavy	Sweater, poncho, blanket
Bouclé	Novelty, any fiber type, usually one thin and one thick yarn twisted together	Light to heavy	Sweater, suit, dress, hat
Chenille	Novelty, usually cotton or a synthetic fiber, short and fluffy tufts entwined with long, thin strands	Light to heavy	Sweater, suit, dress, hat
Lurex	Novelty, blend of metallic strands with wool or synthetic fiber	Light to medium	Evening garments

Selecting yarn

A knitting yarn should be appropriate for both style and intended purpose. To reach a satisfactory decision, consider the differences in yarn characteristics and weigh the advantages and disadvantages for each situation.

The most significant factor in yarn performance is fiber content. *Wool* and *acrylic* are warm yarns, the most versatile because they can be spun in many weights and types. Their resiliency makes them especially desirable for garments. Most experts agree that wool gives the best results, but its short supply and increasing price are causing acrylics to be produced in greater variety. *Linen* and *cotton* are cool yarns, used mostly for summer garments and household items. *Rayon* and *nylon* are incorporated into some blends, mostly for textural interest.

A yarn's construction is crucial to its suitability for a purpose. Highly twisted yarns are smooth, easy to work with, generally durable, and suitable for any stitch pattern. Loosely twisted or homespun yarns are less durable, but have an ap-

pealing texture and give great warmth due to their high loft (fluffiness). Novelty yarns, in which plies of different thicknesses or fibers are twisted together, are exciting in texture, but less durable than smooth yarns and suited only to simple stitch patterns.

The number of yarn plies (units twisted together) is not a significant factor in yarn selection, though the information is usually included on the label. It can indicate strength (four plies might be tougher than two), but never thickness, as plies can vary in diameter.

Yarn thickness is usually expressed as a weight—light, medium, or heavy. Suggestions for suitable articles in each weight are in the chart, opposite.

In selecting a garment yarn, good elasticity (stretch capacity) and recovery (return to original size) are desirable qualities. Both comfort and fit retention depend on them. In a yarn for the home, ability to withstand many washings may be more important. Check yarn labels for the care requirements.

Tips for buying yarn

Most knitting projects represent a substantial investment in time and money. It pays to be an informed consumer when purchasing yarns.

1. Check yarn labels for the dye lot number and purchase all yarn of one color from the same dye lot. Each number represents a different dye bath and may differ slightly from another.

2. Buy enough yarn of the same dye lot to complete the article. This is an instance where too much is better than not enough. Some stores will accept the return of unused skeins within a reasonable time. You can check this possibility at the time of purchase.

3. Check the yarn label for washability and other care information. If none is given, you should wash and block your gauge swatch to see how the yarn responds to these procedures.

4. If a yarn label gives gauge information, the needle size mentioned is the one recommended for that particular yarn. It is wise to stay within two sizes of the recommendation.

5. To duplicate the appearance and fit of your chosen pattern, you should always buy the yarn recommended for it, though you can of course choose a color other than the one shown.

6. If you choose to substitute another yarn for the one recommended, select yarn as close as possible to the original in weight and type. It is a good idea to buy a single skein first and knit a swatch to see how the gauge and appearance compare with those of the pattern.

7. To calculate yarn needs for a substitution or your own design, see Designing a garment.

8. Should you need to convert ounces to grams or vice versa, use this formula: 100 grams = 3.52 ounces. For example, if 16 ounces of yarn are called for, and you are substituting a yarn weighed in grams, divide 16 by 3.52 and multiply times 100. The quantity is 454 grams.

9. Before each purchase, check a yarn's recovery. Stretch and release a 6″ length. If it does not return to its original size, you cannot expect the knitted article to hold its shape.

Winding yarn

The most convenient way to use yarn is from a ball or skein that can be pulled out from the center. In this form it is less likely to tangle or to unwind too quickly. Yarn is often sold this way; if yours is not, it should be re-wound before you use it. Directions are given below for re-winding a skein. Before you begin, slip it over the back of a chair and cut the an- choring string. Take care to wind the ball loosely. If yarn is pulled too tight, it will stretch and may lose some elasticity.

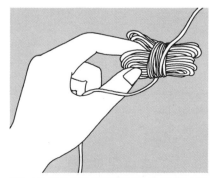

Grasp a loose end of yarn firmly between back fingers and palm of left hand, about 12″ from the end. Wind yarn 6 or 8 times around thumb and index finger in figure eight fashion.

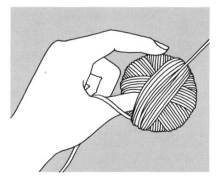

Slip yarn off fingers and fold it in half, end to end. Holding the folded bunch between thumb and index finger, wind the yarn loosely around both yarn and fingers about a dozen times.

Keeping thumb in center, continue to wind yarn, turning the ball constantly so it will be round. When it is 3″ across, remove your thumb, but be careful not to wind over the center yarn.

Continue winding *loosely* until all the yarn is taken up, then tuck the final end into the ball. Use the ball by drawing yarn out from the center, as shown in the illustration.

Knitting supplies

Needles

There are three basic types of knitting needles—*single-pointed,* *double-pointed,* and *circular.* Examples are shown below; chart at right describes available materials, lengths, and sizes.

Needle thickness is signified by number. The higher a number, the thicker the needle and the larger the stitch. While there are no precise rules for needle and yarn relationship, generally, thicker yarns should be worked with large needles, thinner yarns with small ones. If a needle is too large for the yarn, knit structure will be flimsy; if too small, texture will be too compact and inelastic. Yarn labels often include a recommended needle size; a safe approach is to stay within two sizes of this number.

Needle length should be chosen according to a project's dimensions, and only has to be sufficient to hold all stitches comfortably. In general, shorter ones are easier to manipulate. A circular needle should be at least two inches less than the circumference of the knitting.

Choice of needle material—plastic, metal, or wood—is largely a matter of personal preference and availability. Plastic is quieter and somewhat easier for a beginner to manage. Metal is noisier but stitches slide more readily, an advantage for the fast knitter. Wood is esthetically pleasing, but wood needles are scarce and more trouble to maintain.

In caring for needles, it is best to store them flat with their points protected. An occasional rub with waxed paper helps retain a slick surface.

Needle types and sizes

Needle information below is a compilation of what was available, at time of this printing, from three major manufacturers of knitting equipment. (Wood needles are not included, but are available some places. They are usually hand-produced in a limited size range.) The number sequence for American sizes is regular from 0 to 10, and irregular from 10½ to 50. These are the available sizes and their diameters in millimeters: **0** (2.1), **1** (2.4), **2** (2.8), **3** (3.2), **4** (3.5), **5** (3.8), **6** (4.2), **7** (4.6), **8** (5.0), **9** (5.3), **10** (5.8), **10½** (6.6), **11** (8.0), **13** (9.2), **15** (10.2), **17** (12.7), **18** (14.3), **19** (16.0), **35** (19.0), **50** (25.4).

NEEDLE TYPE	MATERIAL	LENGTH	SIZE (American)	SIZE (mm)
Single-point	Aluminum	10″	0 to 15	2.1 to 10.2
		14″	0 to 15	2.1 to 10.2
	Plastic	10″	2 to 15	2.8 to 10.2
		14″	17 to 50	12.7 to 25.4
Double-point	Plastic	7″	2 to 8	2.8 to 5.0
		10″	6 to 15	4.2 to 10.2
	Aluminum	7″	0 to 8	2.1 to 5.0
		10″	0 to 15	2.1 to 10.2
Circular	All nylon	16″	3 to 10½	3.2 to 6.6
		24″	1 to 10½	2.4 to 6.6
		29″	1 to 15	2.4 to 10.2
		36″	5 to 15	3.8 to 10.2
	Nylon body with aluminum tips	16″	0 to 10½	2.1 to 6.6
		24″	0 to 10½	2.1 to 6.6
		29″	0 to 15	2.1 to 10.2
		36″	9 to 15	5.3 to 10.2

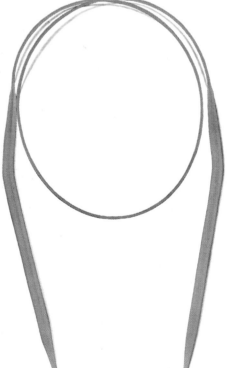

A circular needle is used to knit round, seamless garments and also large, flat pieces for which straight needles might not be long enough. It consists of two nylon or aluminum tips connected by a flexible nylon cord.

Single-point needles are used in pairs to knit flat pieces. Straight and rigid, they are used more frequently than other types, and are considered the standard needles. In fact, knitting instructions usually do not specify them by type, simply indicating what size to use. The jumbo sizes (# 17 and larger) are sometimes referred to as *jiffy* needles. Work proceeds rapidly with jiffy needles and the fabric is quite thick and loosely structured.

Double-point needles are used in sets of 4 or more to knit seamless, circular items, such as socks or mittens. In some instructions, they are abbreviated as dp needles.

Knitting aids

There are many knitting aids available, each one designed to make a certain task easier. A sampling of such aids is shown below. Besides those items specifically meant for knitting, a few other craft supplies are indispensable. Examples are the crochet hook and tapestry needle shown below, also scissors for cutting yarn, and straight pins and tape measure for blocking. In addition, graph paper and a notebook are useful for charting and keeping track of patterns, and a totable basket or bag will help to keep your work organized and close at hand. The type with a foldable stand is particularly useful and convenient.

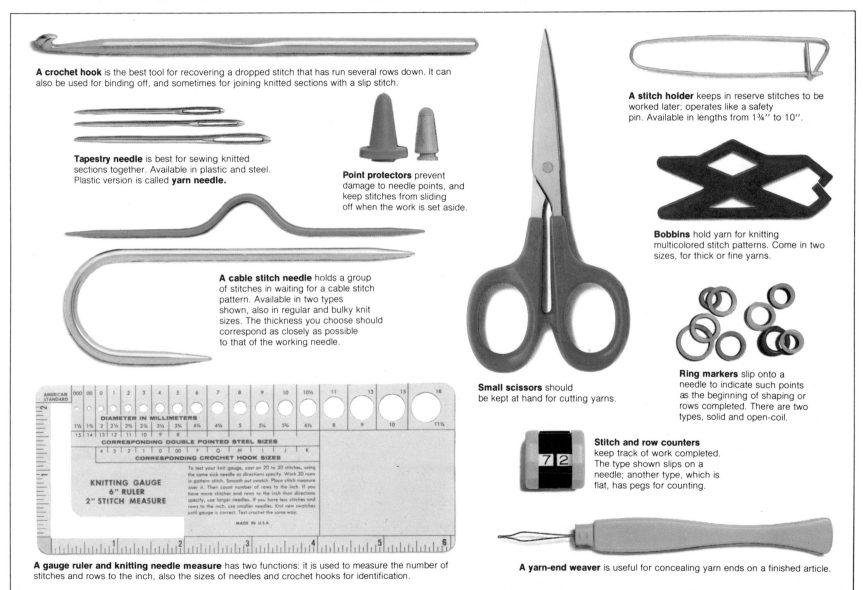

A crochet hook is the best tool for recovering a dropped stitch that has run several rows down. It can also be used for binding off, and sometimes for joining knitted sections with a slip stitch.

Tapestry needle is best for sewing knitted sections together. Available in plastic and steel. Plastic version is called **yarn needle.**

Point protectors prevent damage to needle points, and keep stitches from sliding off when the work is set aside.

A cable stitch needle holds a group of stitches in waiting for a cable stitch pattern. Available in two types shown, also in regular and bulky knit sizes. The thickness you choose should correspond as closely as possible to that of the working needle.

A gauge ruler and knitting needle measure has two functions: it is used to measure the number of stitches and rows to the inch, also the sizes of needles and crochet hooks for identification.

A stitch holder keeps in reserve stitches to be worked later; operates like a safety pin. Available in lengths from 1¾″ to 10″.

Bobbins hold yarn for knitting multicolored stitch patterns. Come in two sizes, for thick or fine yarns.

Ring markers slip onto a needle to indicate such points as the beginning of shaping or rows completed. There are two types, solid and open-coil.

Small scissors should be kept at hand for cutting yarns.

Stitch and row counters keep track of work completed. The type shown slips on a needle; another type, which is flat, has pegs for counting.

A yarn-end weaver is useful for concealing yarn ends on a finished article.

273

Knitting basics

Casting on
Forming the knit stitch
Forming the purl stitch
Elementary stitch patterns
Variations on elementary
stitches
Yarn tension
Binding off
Side selvages

Casting on

Casting on is the first step in knitting. It forms the first row of stitches and one selvage of the finished article, usually the bottom, or hem edge.

There are many methods for casting on; five of the most representative are shown here. Each is best suited to a particular type of knit or situation, depending on the elasticity or firmness required, and the simplicity or elaborateness of the appearance desired.

The character of a cast-on edge is determined not only by the way in which stitches are put on the needle, but also by the way they are worked off. Knitting into the stitch fronts produces a looser edge, into the backs, a firmer edge.

Stitches of the cast-on row should be uniform in size or the edge will be untidy. It is worth the time to re-do them if the first attempt is unsatisfactory. The cast-on stitches should also be moderately loose so they will be easy to work off. If yours tend to be snug, try working over two needles, using one of the methods on the opposite page.

When you are casting on a large number of stitches, keeping count is easier if you slip a coil ring marker or yarn loop on the needle every 10 or 20 stitches.

To form slip knot for first stitch, make a loop 6″ from yarn end; insert needle under short length, draw through a loop and tighten it.

Two-needle methods of casting on

KNITTING ON

Knitting on employs two needles and one yarn length. Each new stitch is formed as in knitting, then transferred to the left needle. A versatile selvage, it is soft when worked through loop fronts, firm if worked through loop backs. Suitable also for increasing stitches at one side or completing a buttonhole.

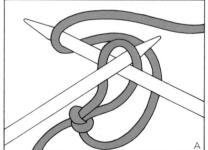

Hold needle with slip knot in left hand. Insert right needle and take yarn around it as for knitting (**A**); draw yarn through to form a new stitch, but do not

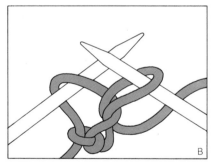

drop first loop from left needle (**B**). Instead, transfer new stitch to left needle and knit into it to form the next new stitch.

CABLE CAST-ON

Cable cast-on is produced the same way as knitting on, but for each new stitch, the needle is inserted between the two previous stitches. The resulting edge is decorative and elastic, nicely suited to ribbing and attractive for the edges of socks or hats. Stitches should be knitted off through the loop fronts only.

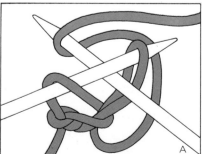

Make slip knot and first stitch as in knitting on (above). For each new stitch after that, insert the right needle between 2 stitches; take yarn around

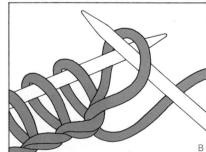

needle as for knitting (**A**). Draw through a new stitch, then transfer it to left needle (**B**). Continue forming new stitches between 2 loops.

One-needle methods of casting on

SINGLE CAST-ON

Single cast-on is done with one needle and one length of yarn. It forms a delicate selvage that is particularly good for a hem edge or for lace. This is a very easy cast-on method, but somewhat difficult to work off the needle evenly in the first row. For a beginner, the double cast-on is easier to control.

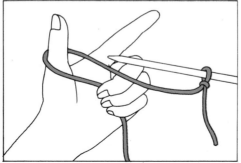

1. Make slip knot on needle held in the right hand. Wrap yarn from the ball around left thumb, as shown, then grasp yarn firmly between the palm and back fingers.

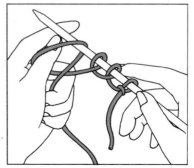

2. Turn thumb so the back of it is facing you; insert needle front to back through the loop that is formed by twisting the thumb.

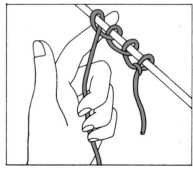

3. Slip thumb out of loop, at same time pulling yarn downward to close the loop around the needle. Repeat Steps 2 and 3.

DOUBLE CAST-ON

Double cast-on employs one needle and a double length of yarn; it is started a measured distance from the yarn end, allowing 1 inch per stitch. Firm, yet elastic, this method is suitable for any pattern that does not require a delicate edge. It is especially recommended for beginners, since no experience is needed.

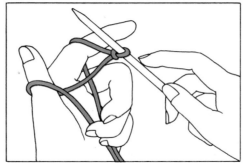

1. Make slip knot a measured distance from yarn end. Wrap short end over left thumb, yarn from ball over left index finger; hold both ends between palm and back fingers.

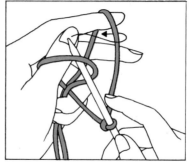

2. Slip needle up through the thumb loop, then scoop yarn from the index finger (see arrow) and draw a loop onto the needle.

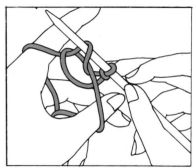

3. Release thumb loop; tighten loop on the needle by drawing the short yarn forward with the thumb. Repeat Steps 2 and 3.

LOOPED CAST-ON

A **looped cast-on** employs one needle and two yarn lengths; one yarn forms a foundation, the other is wrapped around it. Left intact, the edge is very flexible, especially suited to cotton yarns, which have limited elasticity. If the foundation yarn is removed, stitches can be picked up for knitting or grafting.

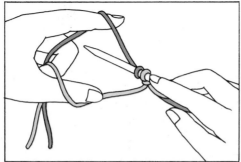

1. Make slip knot in foundation yarn (light), then casting yarn (dark). Take foundation yarn over thumb, and casting yarn over index finger; grasp both yarn ends against palm.

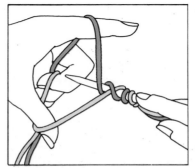

2. Wrap casting yarn around needle, front to back; foundation yarn around needle, back to front (yarns should cross as shown).

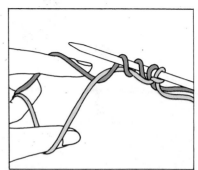

3. Wrap casting yarn around needle again, front to back. Pull downward so that yarns are under needle. Repeat Steps 2 and 3.

Knitting basics

Forming the knit stitch/English (right-handed) method

The **knit stitch** is one of two fundamental movements in knitting; it forms a flat vertical loop on the fabric face.

Knitting methods vary from one place to another; two widely used ones are shown below and opposite. In both, the stitches are worked off the left needle onto the right, but in one, yarn is controlled with the right hand, in the other, with the left. Whatever your natural hand preference, you should be able to master either method, because the nature of knitting is basically ambidextrous.

The right-handed technique prevails in English-speaking countries. In this approach, yarn is drawn around the right needle with the right index finger. Tension (control of yarn released with each stitch) is maintained between the two end fingers by wrapping yarn around the last, as shown. There are other correct ways to wrap yarn. The main thing is to feel comfortable with the method and be able to achieve even tension and speed.

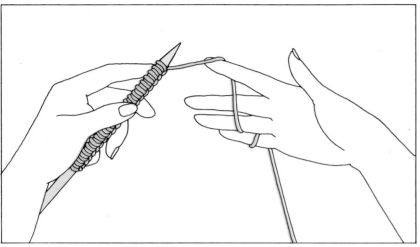

1. Grasp the needle with cast-on stitches in the left hand. The first stitch should be about 1″ from the tip. Take yarn around little finger of right hand, under the next two fingers, and over the top of the index finger, extending it about 2″ from the first stitch on the needle.

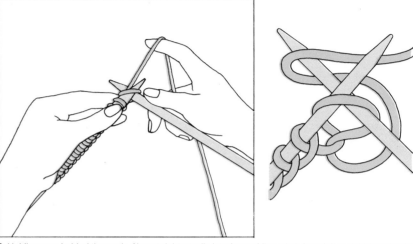

2. Holding yarn behind the work, *insert right needle into front of first stitch from left to right (needle tip points toward the back). With the right index finger, take yarn forward *under* the right needle, then backward *over* the top (see detail above right).

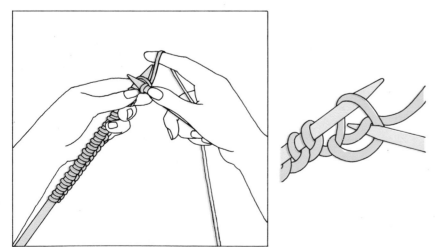

3. Draw the loop on the right needle forward through the stitch, at the same time pushing the stitch on the left needle toward the tip. (With the deftness that comes with practice, these two movements will become smoothly coordinated. When they do, your speed will increase.)

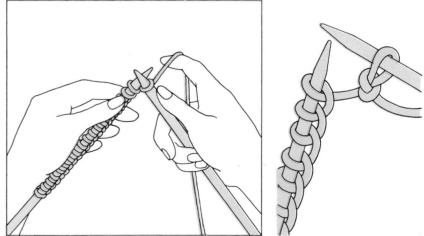

4. Allow first stitch to slide off left needle. New stitch (the loop just made) remains on right needle.* Repeat steps between asterisks, pushing stitches forward on left needle with thumb, index, and middle fingers, moving stitches back on right needle with the thumb.

Forming the knit stitch / Continental (left-handed) method

Controlling yarn with the left hand is the customary knitting practice in many European and Eastern countries. In this method, familiarly known as Continental, the fundamental action is to scoop yarn from the left index finger onto the right needle. There are several popular ways to position yarn. In the one shown, tension is controlled partly with the last two fingers, and partly with the index finger, extending it to tighten yarn after the needle passes underneath.

Many experts feel that greater speed can be attained with the Continental than with the English method. Whatever your own choice, you will find that speed is developed by holding the needles lightly and minimizing all movements. For the right-handed method, nimble finger action is required; for the left-handed, the key is flexible wrist movement. If you learn both methods, you will be able to knit certain two-color patterns more quickly and smoothly.

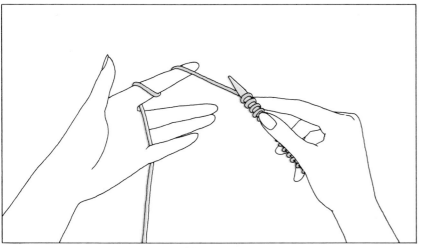

1. Hold the needle with cast-on stitches in the right hand and wrap yarn over the left, taking it between the 4th and 5th fingers, under the next two fingers, over the top of the index finger, then around it once more. The yarn should extend about 2″ from the first stitch.

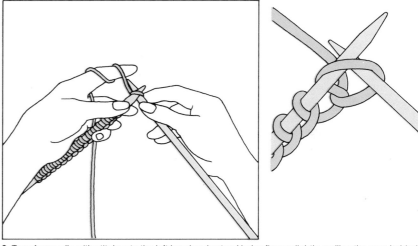

2. Transfer needle with stitches to the left hand and extend index finger slightly, pulling the yarn behind the needle. Push the first stitch up near the tip. *Insert right needle into front of first stitch from left to right (needle tip points toward the back).

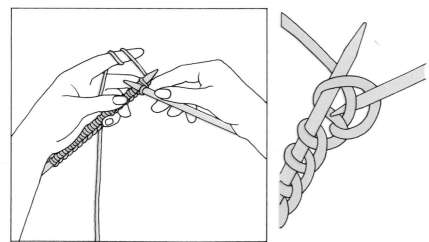

3. Twist the right needle and pull the tip *under* the yarn to draw a loop through the stitch. At the same time, push the stitch on the left needle toward the tip. (With the deftness that comes with practice, these two movements will become smoothly coordinated.)

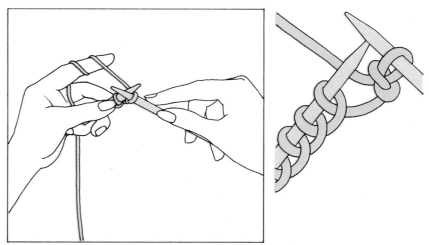

4. Allow first stitch to slide off left needle. New stitch (the loop just made) remains on the right needle.* Repeat steps between asterisks, pushing stitches forward on the left needle with thumb and middle finger, moving stitches back on right needle with the thumb.

Knitting basics

Forming the purl stitch/English (right-handed) method

A **purl stitch** is the reverse side of a knit stitch. Its loop structure is a horizontal semicircle, whereas the knit loop is vertical and flat (see preceding page).

In forming a purl stitch, the movements are the reverse of those used for knitting. The needle enters the front of the stitch from right to left, and the yarn, held in front of the work, is cast over the needle back to front.

When yarn is controlled with the right hand (as shown below), purl stitches tend to be looser than the knitted ones. This is because the yarn must be cast farther to form a purl stitch than is required for the knit movements. With experience, a natural compensation is usually developed, especially if the index finger is kept close to the work. Should the difficulty persist, a good practice exercise is to work a 1 × 1 rib (see p. 280 for directions) until an even tension is established and the stitches have the same appearance on both sides of the fabric.

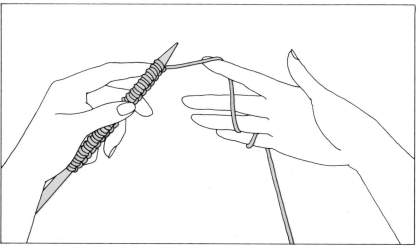

1. Grasp the needle with cast-on stitches in the left hand. First stitch should be about 1″ from tip. Take yarn around little finger of the right hand, under the next two fingers, and over the top of the index finger, extending it about 2″ from first stitch on needle.

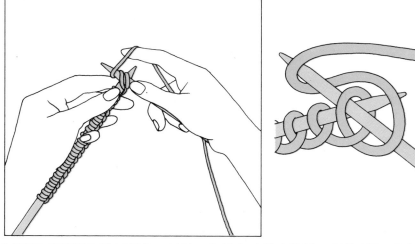

2. Holding yarn in front of the work,*insert right needle into front of first stitch from right to left (needle tip points upward slightly). With the right index finger, take yarn backward *over* the right needle, then forward and *under* it (see detail above right).

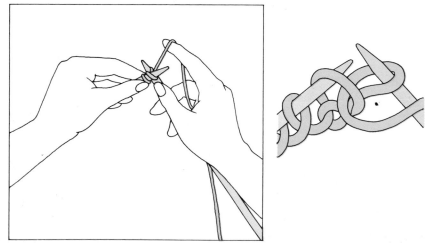

3. Draw the loop on the right needle backward through the stitch, at the same time pushing the stitch on the left needle toward the tip. (With the deftness that comes with practice, these two movements will become smoothly coordinated.)

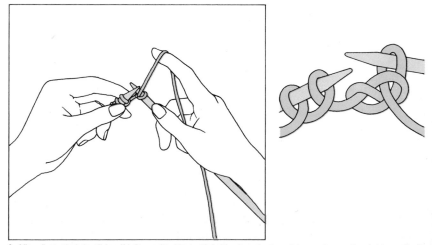

4. Allow first stitch to slide off left needle. New stitch (the loop just made) remains on the right needle.* Repeat steps between asterisks, pushing stitches forward on left needle with thumb, index, and middle fingers, moving stitches back on right needle with thumb.

Forming the purl stitch/Continental (left-handed) method

To form a purl stitch in the Continental style, yarn is held taut with the left index finger while a new loop is scooped up with the right needle. This action is facilitated by a forward twist of the wrist to release yarn, and by anchoring the working stitch with the thumb as the new stitch is drawn through it.

Shifting yarn from knit to purl position, and vice versa, can slow your working speed unless the maneuver is part of the working rhythm, and minimal effort is required for it. With yarn held in the left hand, a shift is made by swinging yarn forward between needle tips to the purl position, and back again, the same way, to resume the knit position. Yarn in the right hand must be wrapped around the right needle, back to front, to work a purl stitch, then front to back again for the knit stitch. Less speed will be lost if you keep the index finger close to the work and the working stitches as close as possible to the needle tips.

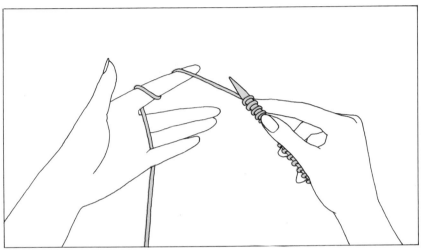

1. Hold the needle with cast-on stitches in the right hand and wrap yarn over the left, taking it between the 4th and 5th fingers, under the next two fingers, over the top of the index finger, then around it once more. Yarn should extend about 2" from the first stitch.

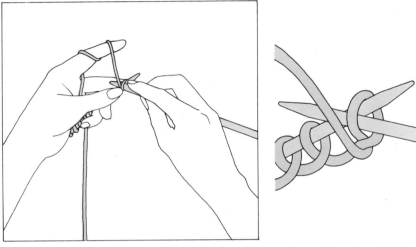

2. Transfer needle with stitches to left hand and extend index finger, pulling yarn in front of needle. Using thumb and middle finger, push first stitch up near tip. *Insert right needle into front of first stitch, right to left (tip points upward slightly).

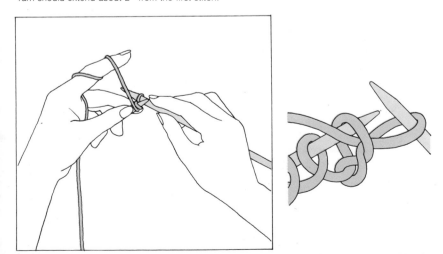

3. Turn left wrist so that yarn on index finger comes toward you, then push back and down with right needle to draw a loop back through the stitch. At the same time, push stitch on left needle toward tip. (With practice, these movements become smoothly coordinated.)

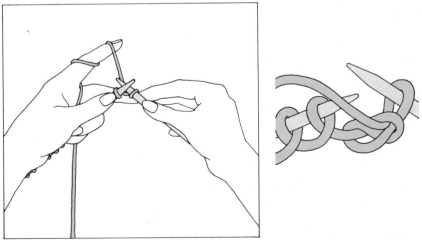

4. Allow first stitch to slide off left needle and straighten left index finger to tighten new stitch on right needle.* Repeat steps between asterisks, pushing stitches forward on left needle with thumb and middle finger, moving stitches back on right needle with the thumb.

Knitting basics

Elementary stitch patterns

The elementary stitch patterns, shown below, are the most versatile and the easiest patterns to produce, ideal for a beginner. To practice these patterns, use knitting worsted and a #8 needle, and cast on 20 to 24 stitches. (**Note:** Each pattern has a *multiple,* which is the least number of stitches needed to complete one pattern unit. If the multiple is four,

for example, the number of stitches cast on must be divisible by four.) Work the first pattern row, then turn the needle and work the next row. As you knit, pay special attention to developing moderate and even tension (see opposite page for clarification), and always complete a row before setting the work down. Each time you try a new pattern or check a

gauge, you can proceed this way. Eventually, if you like, squares can be joined to make something useful such as a pillow top or soft tote bag.

Each elementary pattern is produced with plain knit and/or purl stitches—the techniques demonstrated on pages 276 to 279—in which the stitch loop is positioned with the left side (thread) to the

back of the needle, and the right side to the front. Plain stitch methods can be modified to produce the twisted variations illustrated opposite. If you are aware of these distinctions, you can avoid twisting stitches accidentally, a not unusual occurrence when a dropped stitch has been retrieved or work put down with a row in progress.

The garter stitch is normally produced by knitting every stitch of every row, though purling every stitch will give the same results.
The simplest of all stitch patterns, it has a pebbly surface that is identical on both sides, and a somewhat loose structure that stretches equally in both directions. Use for sweaters, blankets, and accessories.
Multiple is any number of stitches
Every row: K

Stockinette

The stockinette stitch is produced by knitting one row and purling the next. The most versatile of the basic stitch patterns, it is smooth on one (the knitted) side and pebbly on the other (the purled) side. The knit side is usually considered to be the right side, but the purled side can be used for this purpose if desired; it is then referred to as **reverse stockinette** (below left). This fabric stretches more in the crosswise than the lengthwise direction. Use it for sweaters and dresses, also for knitted accessories such as hats, gloves, and socks. See pages 318-321 for the way stockinette is employed in jacquard patterns.
Multiple is any number of stitches
Row 1: K
Row 2: P

Reverse stockinette

The seed stitch is produced by alternating one knit and one purl stitch within a row, then knitting the knit stitches and purling the purl stitches on the return row. The texture of this pattern is similar to that of the garter stitch, but the fabric is firmer. Use it for blankets and garments, also as a contrasting texture for another pattern stitch.
Multiple of 2 sts plus 1
Every row: *K 1, P 1*, K 1

1 x 1 rib

2 x 2 rib

The rib stitch is produced by alternating knit and purl stitches on one row, then purling the knit stitches and knitting the purl stitches on the return row. The result is a pattern of vertical ridges that is identical on both sides when knit and purl stitches are interchanged in equal numbers, with no variations in technique. The ratio of knit to purl stitches may be even or uneven. It is frequently indicated by numbers. Examples are 1 × 1 and 2 × 2, shown left. These are the classic rib patterns often referred to as ribbing. They have considerable elasticity in the crosswise direction and are especially suitable for garment edges, where they provide a snug fit. For this purpose, ribbing is usually worked with needles a size or two smaller than those that are used for the garment.
For 1 × 1 rib, multiple of 2 sts
Every row: *K 1, P 1*
For 2 × 2 rib, multiple of 4 sts
Every row: *K 2, P 2*

Variations on elementary stitch patterns

The performance and appearance of basic stitch patterns can be altered by entering the stitch or wrapping yarn contrary to the usual way. These variations were common in other eras; some are the familiar practice today in certain parts of the world. The resulting fabrics (examples shown below) are somewhat firmer and more elastic than those shown on the opposite page. You can knit swatches and compare the difference.

One variation is the **twisted stitch,** formed by entering the back instead of the front of a loop. This action twists the loop a half turn at the base so that it does not lie as flat as the regular stitch. Either knit or purl stitches can be twisted in a pattern, but rarely both. For *twisted stockinette* stitch, you work into the back loop of all stitches on the knit row and work all purl stitches normally. For a *1 × 1 twisted rib*, work into the back loop of all knit stitches and work all purl stitches normally.

Another variation is **plaited stitch,** produced by wrapping yarn the reverse of the usual way, that is, *over* the needle for a knit stitch, *under* the needle for a purl stitch. Stitches formed this way are continually twisted and the resulting fabric is exceptionally firm. In the *plaited stockinette* stitch, both knit and purl stitches are worked with the techniques shown below right. On the right side, vertical rows resemble 3-ply braid. For *1 × 1 plaited rib*, plaited knit stitch is alternated with plaited purl.

The plaited methods are convenient for working with beads or sequins. They are also practical for knitting with large needles and heavy yarns because the fabric is firmer. Tension for these stitches must be kept looser than normal because of the twist in the stitch.

Twisted stockinette

1 x 1 twisted rib

Plaited stockinette

Plaited rib

To form a twisted knit stitch, enter *back* of loop, take yarn under needle as for regular knit stitch. On the return row, purl normally.

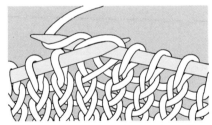

To form a twisted purl stitch, enter *back* of loop, take yarn over needle as for regular purl stitch. On the return row, knit normally.

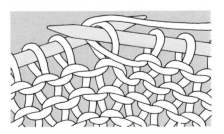

To form a plaited knit stitch, enter front of loop as for regular knit stitch, then take yarn *over* the needle to produce the new stitch.

To form a plaited purl stitch, enter front of loop as for regular purl stitch, then take yarn *under* the needle to produce the new stitch.

Yarn tension

Tension is resistance on the yarn as it passes through the fingers that are controlling it. Moderate, consistent, correct, and exact tension are the accomplishments of the expert knitter. They should be among the skills for which a beginner is striving.

Moderate tension is evident when stitches can be worked easily, yet no space is visible between the loops and the needle. If stitches are too tight, inserting the right needle is difficult and knitting speed will probably be slowed; also, the yarn can become weakened by being overworked. If loops are too loose, they tend to slip off the left needle too soon; also, the knitted fabric holds its shape poorly.

Consistent tension results in an even fabric, that is, one in which stitches are the same size throughout. Achieving this requires practice, but the suggestions that follow may help. If your purl stitches tend to be looser than your knit stitches, or vice versa, work a practice swatch of 1 × 1 rib stitch until you see a balance. If your tension varies from one day to the next, keep a practice swatch handy and work a few rows on it before proceeding with your work. This warm-up period should bring you to your habitual tension level.

Correct tension is exhibited in a fabric that is supple but not flimsy, firm but not stiff. It is the result of using a tension that suits both the yarn and the pattern stitch, and working with the proper needle size. Some understanding of yarn characteristics and experience with different pattern stitches help to achieve proper tension. Here are some general guidelines: Loosely spun or thick yarns should have an easy tension. Firmly spun and inelastic yarns (cotton is an example of the latter) require a firm tension. Twisted stitches (examples at the left), also crossed and cable stitches, need a little looseness in the tension, or they are difficult to work. Open and lacy stitches need to be tensioned more firmly.

Exact tension is the duplication of a specified gauge in a knitting pattern. In this case, it is best to adjust by changing needle size rather than attempting to alter control of the yarn.

Knitting basics

Shaping: armholes, shoulders 330-331
Horizontal buttonhole 338

Binding off

Binding off (also called **casting off**) is the removal of stitches from a needle in such a way that they will not ravel. It forms the last row of finished work and sometimes is used to begin the shaping of an armhole, or to produce one side of a horizontal buttonhole. As in casting on, this procedure forms a selvage, and should be suitable for the type of knit and the purpose it must serve.

Of several binding-off methods, the most versatile are plain and suspended, shown below. Unless instructions say otherwise, these stitches are worked from the right side and in the same sequence in which they were formed (that is, knitting the knit and purling the purl stitch). On the bound-off row, stitches should be moderately loose and uniform, or the edge may draw in or look distorted. If your stitches tend to be tight, bind off on a needle one size larger than the size that was used for knitting.

The three techniques illustrated on the opposite page have limited uses. One should know them, however, to obtain the best results in those situations for which they are suitable.

To secure yarn end after binding off, slip it through last stitch, pull to tighten loop.

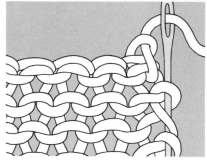

Thread yarn end in a tapestry needle and weave it into a seam edge for 2″ to 3″. Cut remainder.

Binding-off techniques

PLAIN BIND-OFF

Plain bind-off is the simplest, most frequently used method. It is suitable for any situation where an unadorned, firm selvage is required, for example a shoulder seam or buttonhole.

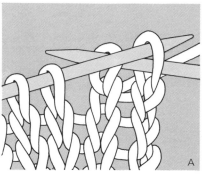

Work 2 stitches at beginning of row. *Holding yarn behind work, insert left needle in first

stitch (**A**). Pull the first stitch over the second one (**B**), and off the needle (**C**). Work the next

stitch.* Repeat instructions between the asterisks until desired number of stitches are bound off.

SUSPENDED BIND-OFF

Suspended bind-off is similar to plain bind-off (above), but more flexible. Use this method to finish ribbing, or as a substitute for the plain technique if your selvages tend to be tight.

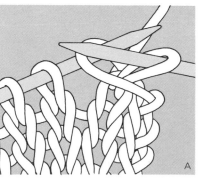

Work 2 stitches. *Pull first stitch over the second as for plain bind-off, but keep pulled stitch

on left needle (**A**). Work the next stitch (**B**); drop both stitches off the left needle at the same

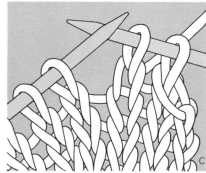

time (**C**).* Repeat instructions between asterisks until 2 stitches remain; knit these together.

INVISIBLE BIND-OFF

Invisible bind-off makes an inconspicuous finish for 1 × 1 ribbing, ideal for a cuff or turtleneck. To begin, cut yarn, leaving an end four times the knitting width; thread yarn in a tapestry needle.

*Insert tapestry needle knitwise in knit stitch at end of needle; drop stitch off (**A**). Skip next purl stitch; insert needle purlwise in the next knit

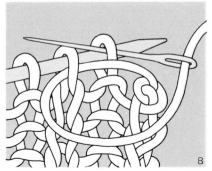

stitch; draw yarn through. Insert needle purlwise in purl stitch at end of needle (**B**); draw yarn through; drop stitch off. Take needle behind the

knit stitch and insert it knitwise in next purl stitch (bring yarn forward between stitches first) (**C**); draw yarn through.* Repeat from first asterisk.

CROCHETED BIND-OFF

In **crocheted bind-off,** the stitches are worked off in a chain stitch. The result is a firm and decorative edging appropriate for a blanket or afghan, also a pretty finish for a hat or booties.

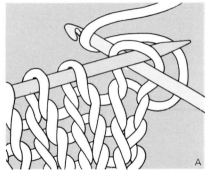

*Holding crochet hook in your hand as if it were a needle, insert it knitwise in first stitch; take

yarn around hook (**A**). Draw through a loop and let first stitch drop off needle. Draw a loop through

next stitch in same way (**B**). Draw a loop through 2 loops on hook (**C**).* Repeat from first asterisk.

PLAIN BIND-OFF OF TWO PIECES

Plain bind-off of two pieces forms a neat, seamless joining. It can be used for two straight edges having an equal number of stitches, or for shoulder edges that have been shaped by turning.

*With right sides together and both pieces held in the left hand, work the first stitch on each

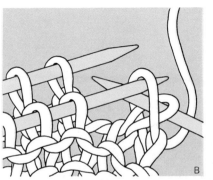

needle simultaneously (**A**). Work next 2 stitches together the same way. Slip first stitch over

second one (**B**).* Repeat from first asterisk. Ridge produced will be wrong side of seam (**C**).

Knitting basics

Side selvages

A side edge, whether it is exposed or in a seam, should be neat and suited to its purpose. Usually, greater precision is attained by working a narrow border, called a *selvage*, in addition to the pattern stitches. Six ways to form selvages are shown below. For each one, you must add two or four stitches to the total when casting on; instructions do not normally include selvage stitches.

One-stitch methods are used for edges to be seamed, or along which stitches will be picked up. Two-stitch methods are more decorative, and also prevent curling. They are especially suitable where no other finish will be applied, for example, the edge of a facing. If appropriate, different selvages might be used on the same piece—one type for the left side, another for the right.

Single chain edge I: Use for stockinette stitch and pattern stitches when seams are to be joined edge to edge or stitches are to be picked up later.

On *right side,* slip first stitch knitwise; knit the last stitch. On *wrong side,* slip first stitch purlwise; purl the last stitch.

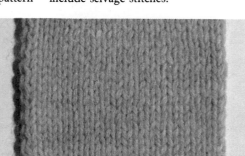

Double picot edge: A decorative and delicate edging; very pretty for baby things. See page 289 for the way to make a yarn over at the beginning of a row.

On the *right* side, bring yarn in front of right needle (yarn over), insert needle knitwise in first stitch and slip it, knit the next stitch, pass the slipped stitch over the knitted one. On the *wrong* side, take yarn behind right needle (yarn over), purl first two stitches together.

Single chain edge II: Forms a neat and flat edge for the garter stitch.

Holding yarn at the front of the work, slip the first stitch of each row purlwise, then take yarn behind the work for knitting.

Double chain edge: Use when a decorative as well as firm edging is required.

On the *right* side, slip first stitch knitwise, purl the second stitch. At the end of the row, purl 1, slip the last stitch knitwise. On the *wrong* side, purl the first two and the last two stitches.

Single garter edge: A firm border, especially good for a stockinette stitch or a pattern stitch where edges tend to be loose. Use also for seam edges that are to be backstitched or overcast.

Knit the first and last stitches of every row.

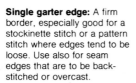

Double garter edge: A firm and even edge; will not curl.

On every row, slip the first stitch knitwise and knit the second stitch; knit the last two stitches.

Mohair scarf measures approximately 6½″ by 60″ plus 7″ of tasseled fringe at each end.

Scarf to knit

Casting on 274-275
Binding off 283
Knitting terminology 286

A beginner can knit this warm scarf. It is worked in simple garter stitch and progresses rapidly on number 8 needles. If gauge is accurate, the scarf should measure 6½ inches wide. Because of mohair's softness, and the natural stretchiness of garter stitch, your finished scarf may be slightly wider.

Materials
120 grams or 5 ounces of mohair yarn, 1 pair #8 needles, 1 crochet hook, medium to large, for fringe

Gauge
4 sts = 1 inch

Pattern stitch
Garter stitch

Selvage stitch
Single chain edge II

Instructions
Cast on 26 stitches loosely. Knit until scarf measures 60 inches; bind off loosely. When you finish one ball of yarn, attach a new one at the beginning of a row (see explanation above, right). Weave in the yarn ends later.

Finishing
Prepare fringe as directed below. Insert yarn groups in first and last stitches at each end of scarf, then every 5th stitch in between.

ATTACHING NEW YARN

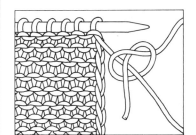

At beginning of row, tie yarn on as shown, then slide it close to the needle. Weave the end into the edge later.

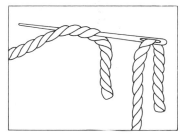

In middle of a row, thread new yarn in a tapestry needle; weave it into the old yarn for 1″ to 2″. Trim rough ends later.

Making tasseled fringe

A tasseled fringe is a handsome edge for a scarf or stole, and easy to make. On the scarf above, yarn groups have 10 strands spaced 5 stitches apart. For another project, you can experiment with dimensions to see what looks best.

To make this fringe, wind yarn 60 times around a cardboard 8 inches long. Cut through the yarn at one end, and divide it into groups of 5 strands each. Fold each group in half and, with a crochet hook, draw the folded end through one stitch in the scarf edge. Draw yarn ends through the loop and pull to tighten it. The finished length is 7 inches because 1 inch is taken up by the knot.

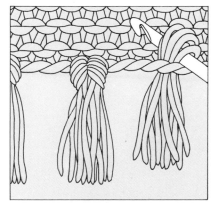

Draw folded end of yarn group into a stitch.

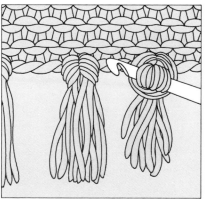

Draw the ends through the loop and tighten it.

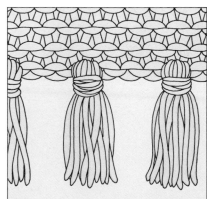

The fringe looks like this on the reverse side.

285

Following knitting instructions

Knitting terminology
Multiples and repeats
Checking the gauge
Elongating stitches
Increasing
Decreasing
Crossing stitches
Correcting errors
Picking up new stitches
Circular knitting

Knitting terminology

For written knitting instructions there is a special vocabulary, much of it expressed in abbreviated or symbolic form. Listed below are abbreviations, symbols, and terms used in this book, with their definitions alongside. Also included are the numbers of pages on which illustrations of techniques can be found.

These abbreviations or their facsimiles are in common use elsewhere. You may encounter terms that are expressed differently, or which are not included here, but an explanatory key for them will usually be provided.

An alternative to written instructions is a chart. For this purpose, different symbols are used. Examples of chart symbols can be found on page 322.

K	knit
P	purl
K-wise	insert needle as though to knit
P-wise	insert needle as though to purl
KP, KPK, etc.	knit and purl, or knit, purl, knit into same stitch as many times as there are letters
K 2 (3) tog	knit 2 (or 3) stitches together *p.293*
P 2 (3) tog	purl 2 (or 3) stitches together *p.293*
tbl	into back of loop (enter stitch from the back instead of the front) *p.281*
blw	below (work into the loop below the next stitch) *p.288*
alt	alternate
beg	beginning
dec	decrease *pp.292-293*
inc	increase *pp.289-291*
patt	pattern
rep	repeat
rnd	round
sl	slip a stitch, without working it, from the left needle to the right one *p.288*
st	stitch
psso	pass the slipped stitch over *p.292*
sl 1, K 1, psso	slip 1 stitch, knit 1 stitch, pass the slipped stitch over the knitted one *p.292*
dp	double-pointed (needles) *p.272*
ybk	yarn back (take yarn to back of work)
yfwd	yarn forward (bring yarn to front of work)

yo	yarn over *p.289*
R	right
L	left
cross 2 R K	cross 2 stitches to the right, knitting *p.294*
cross 2 L K	cross 2 stitches to the left, knitting *p.294*
cross 2 RP	cross 2 stitches to the right, purling *p.294*
cross 2 LP	cross 2 stitches to the left, purling *p.294*
C4F	cable 4 front *pp.294, 310-311*
C4B	cable 4 back *pp.294, 311*
CC	contrasting color
MC	main color
* *	instructions between asterisks should be repeated as many times as there are stitches to accommodate them
( )	instructions enclosed by parentheses should be repeated the number of times indicated after the parentheses
[ ]	*for stitch patterns,* instructions within brackets explain the method of working a particular stitch or technique *in garment directions,* numbers between brackets are for additional sizes
" or in.	inches
00,000	wind yarn around the needle as many times as there are zeros *p.288*
gauge	number of stitches and rows per inch that should be obtained using designated yarn and needles
multiple	the number of stitches required to work one motif horizontally in a pattern stitch
place marker on needle	slip ring marker or a loop of contrasting yarn on the needle
selvage	a finished edge *pp.274-275, 282-284*
work even	continue work without increasing or decreasing

Multiples and repeats

In knitting terminology, a **multiple** is the number of stitches needed to complete one segment of a pattern stitch horizontally; it appears as a sequence of stitches between two asterisks. Here is a typical example of how it works:

Multiple of 6 sts plus 3
Row 1: *K 3, P 3*, K 3
Row 2: P 3, *K 3, P 3*

The six stitches between asterisks comprise the multiple. The three stitches fol-lowing or preceding an asterisk are added to balance the pattern, or permit moving it left or right for a diagonal.

The number of stitches on the needle should be divisible by the multiple. For instance, if a multiple is 8 sts plus 3, the number to be cast on would be 16 plus 3, or 64 plus 3, or 128 plus 3, and so forth. In following a pattern, the multiple is then repeated as many times as there are stitches to be worked.

As a rule, a multiple remains constant throughout a pattern. If a change does occur, as happens in some lace stitches, it is always temporary, and the count is restored eventually to the original.

If you should want to substitute one pattern for another, the relation of the multiple to cast-on stitches must be considered. For instance, if instructions are to cast on 126 stitches and the pattern multiple is 6, you could substitute a stitch with a multiple of 7, because it divides evenly into 126. If you chose one with a multiple of 8, which does not divide evenly into 126, you would have to adjust the stitch total and probably the gauge, too (see gauge information below).

The term **repeat** is sometimes used as a synonym for multiple. It can also denote the number of rows needed to complete one pattern motif vertically; the second meaning is used in this book.

Checking the gauge

Knitting instructions always specify a **gauge**—the number of stitches and rows per inch that should be obtained using the designated yarn and needles. The size of a finished article is based on the gauge, so to achieve the correct size, you must duplicate the gauge precisely. Before beginning each new project, try the gauge by working a swatch 4 inches square, using the recommended yarn and needles. Here is the procedure. Using the gauge as a guide, cast on four times the number of stitches that should equal one inch, then knit four times the number of rows in an inch. For example, if the gauge is 5 stitches and 7 rows to the inch, cast on 20 stitches and work in the pattern for 28 rows. Place the completed swatch right side up on a flat surface and pin the corners, taking care not to stretch it. (The ironing board is a good place to work.) Using a ruler, knitting gauge, or tape measure, count the number of stitches and rows that fall within a 1-inch span (see the photographs below). If your results do not match those of the pattern, knit another sample using needles one size smaller or larger as needed. The time will be well spent, because even half a stitch per inch multiplies to a big size difference over a wide area, and results could be very disappointing.

To prepare a gauge swatch for accurate measuring, pin it to a flat surface, using enough pins to hold it flat, and taking care not to stretch it.

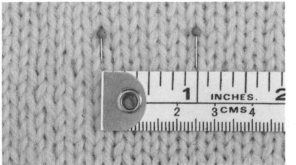

To measure the gauge vertically, place 2 pins an inch apart and count the rows between them. It is easier to count rows on the purl side of stockinette, where every two ridges equal one row; gauge in the sample shows that 7 rows = 1 inch. In counting rows for garter stitch, every ridge equals one row and every furrow equals another.

To measure the gauge horizontally, place 2 pins an inch apart and count the stitches between them. It is easier to count stitches on the knit side of stockinette stitch, where each loop represents one stitch; gauge in the photo, left, shows that 5 stitches = 1 inch. In counting stitches for garter stitch, count the loops in one row only.

Following knitting instructions

Elongating stitches

Unusual textures can be produced by making certain stitches in a knitting sequence longer than others. Three methods for elongating are shown below.

A **slipped stitch** is a lengthened loop made by moving a stitch from the left needle to the right one without working it. Slipping forms a long vertical loop on one side of the work, a loose horizontal ridge on the reverse side. Unless the instructions say otherwise, stitches are slipped *purlwise* when working a pattern stitch, and the yarn is held in the working position of the preceding stitch. In making a decrease, the stitch is usually slipped *knitwise* (see p. 292).

A **double stitch** is a knit stitch that is twice as long as a regular one. It is produced by knitting into the loop below the stitch on the needle. This should not be confused with lifted increase, for which you knit into the loop below, then the one above. A double stitch is knitted just once, the upper and lower loops dropped off simultaneously. This method is limited to every other stitch in a row.

A **simple elongated stitch** is made by wrapping yarn more than once around the needle, then dropping the extra loop(s) on the next row. As a rule, this technique is used for an entire row and it results in a band of openwork.

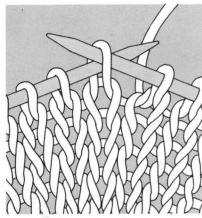

To slip one purlwise (sl 1 P-wise) in a knit row, hold yarn behind the work; insert needle into front of next stitch from right to left and slide the stitch onto the right needle.

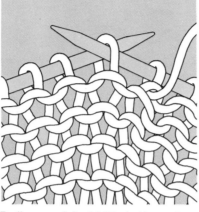

To slip one purlwise (sl 1 P-wise) in a purl row, hold yarn in front of work; insert needle into front of next stitch from right to left and slide the stitch onto the right needle.

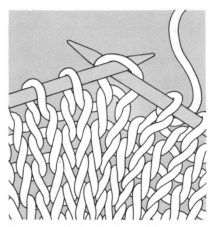

To slip one knitwise (sl 1 K-wise) in a knit row, hold yarn behind the work; insert needle into front of next stitch from left to right and slide the stitch onto the right needle.

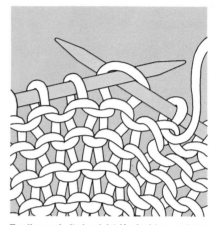

To slip one knitwise (sl 1 K-wise) in a purl row, hold yarn in front of work; insert needle into front of next stitch from left to right and slide the stitch onto the right needle.

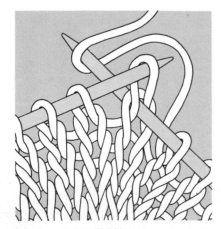

To knit one below (K 1 blw), also called double stitch, insert right needle front to back in center of the loop just below next stitch. Take yarn around needle to make a knit stitch.

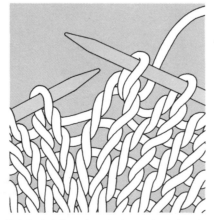

Pull the knit loop through the stitch, then slide stitch off the needle, at the same time pulling gently upward to elongate the stitch. Always work a normal stitch between 2 double stitches.

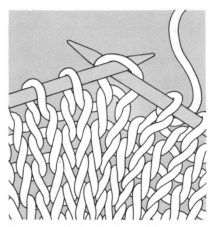

For a simple elongated stitch (K 00 or K 000), take yarn two or three times around the needle as you work the stitch. The number of wraps is indicated by the number of zeros.

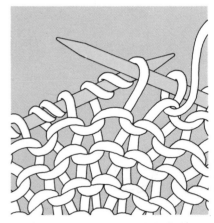

On the next row, let the extra loop(s) drop off the needle as you work each elongated stitch. Long stitches formed in this way are generally used as lacy bands between solid areas (see p. 307).

Increasing

An **increase** (inc) in knitting is the addition of a stitch, and is sometimes referred to as a *made* stitch. Its main function is to shape work by enlarging certain areas, but it is also used to produce fancy stitch patterns such as laces and bobbles. For pattern purposes it is combined with a decrease, in the same or a subsequent row, so the stitch total remains constant.

There are four basic increase methods: **yarn over** (right), **raised** (p. 290), **lifted** (p. 290), and **bar** (p. 291). **Casting on** (pp. 274-275) is also used for increasing, principally to add three or more stitches at either side of the work. Knitting instructions do not always say what type of increase to use. If you familiarize yourself with all methods, you can then choose the most appropriate method for each situation.

Choice of an increase method is based largely on the appearance desired, and sometimes on location of the increase. The yarn-over increase, which forms a hole in the fabric, is used only for a decorative effect, most often, in fact, to form lace stitches. A bar increase is also decorative. It is a desirable choice when increases must be made in steps, because it is readily seen and easily counted. A lifted increase is nearly invisible. It is especially suitable for shaping a dart or any area where a subtle enlargement would be called for. A raised increase can be decorative or inconspicuous, depending on how it is made. This last is the most versatile of all the increase methods.

When increasing gradually, to shape a sleeve, for example, the seam edge will be smoother if you place the additions two or three stitches in from the edge. With a complicated stitch, however, it is better to increase at the edges so as not to disrupt the pattern sequence.

When increasing rapidly, or shaping a chevron, **double increases** (p. 291) are used. These are paired additions made on either side of a center or axial stitch, and are more conspicuous than singles.

YARN-OVER INCREASE

A yarn-over increase (yo) is made by taking yarn around the needle between two stitches. Because a hole is formed, this method is used for knitting laces and for shaping work when a lacy effect is desired. The basic technique is to wind yarn once around the needle, making a loop to be knitted or purled on the next row. The direction in which the yarn is wound depends on the type of stitch that precedes and follows the yarn over.

Occasionally directions specify a multiple yarn over. This is wound as for an elongated stitch (opposite page), but all loops are worked on the return row.

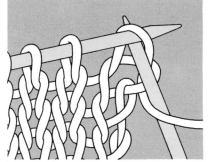

yo—before first knit stitch (for picot selvage, some laces): Holding yarn *in front of* right needle, insert needle knitwise in first stitch and knit it. The made stitch can then be seen.

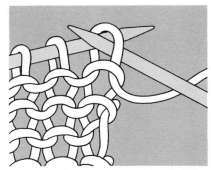

yo—before first purl stitch (for picot selvage, some laces): Holding yarn *behind* right needle, insert needle purlwise in first stitch and purl it. The made stitch can then be seen.

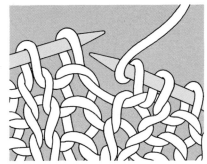

yo—after knit stitch, before purl stitch (for rib patterns): Bring yarn forward between needles, then back over right needle and forward under it into position for next purl stitch.

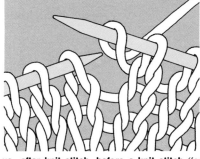

yo—after knit stitch, before a knit stitch (for stockinette and lace stitches): Bring yarn forward *under* the right needle, then back *over* it into position for the next knit stitch.

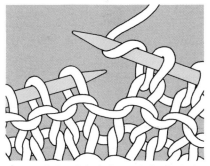

yo—after knit stitch, before a knit stitch (for garter stitch): Bring yarn forward *over* the right needle, then back *under* it again, into position for the next knit stitch.

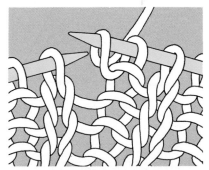

yo—after purl stitch, before a knit stitch (for rib patterns): Take yarn over right needle from front to back. The made stitch can be seen after the next knit stitch is completed.

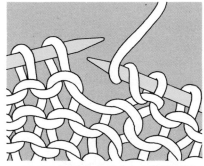

yo—after purl stitch, before a purl stitch (for reverse stockinette and lace stitches): Take yarn back *over* right needle, then forward *under* it into position for the next purl stitch.

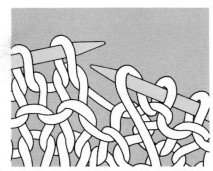

yo—after purl stitch, before a purl stitch (for garter stitch): Take yarn back *under* right needle, then forward *over* it. The made stitch can be seen after purl stitch is completed.

Following knitting instructions

Increasing

RAISED INCREASE

A raised increase is made by picking up a horizontal strand between two stitches and working it as if it were a stitch. There are two ways to work the strand; each gives a very different result. If you knit or purl into the front of it, a hole is left beneath, a suitable approach for a lace stitch or wherever a decorative effect is desired. If you work into the back of the strand, the stitch thus made is twisted and the increase is nearly invisible. This last is a subtle increase method, and can be used effectively where you want the shaping to be inconspicuous, for instance, when shaping a dart.

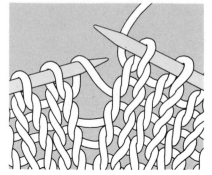

First step for a raised increase is to insert left needle front to back under the horizontal strand that lies between 2 stitches.

LIFTED INCREASE

A lifted increase is made by working into the loop below a stitch as well as into the stitch itself. The result is basically inconspicuous, but there is a definite slant to the stitches, which makes them particularly suitable for paired increases to each side of a center area (see illustration, at the immediate right).

Because the lifted increase is not clearly visible, it can be used where several increases must be made at intervals along one row, as above ribbing on a sleeve. It should be worked with a loose tension when repeated vertically, as it tends to draw in the fabric.

To pair lifted increases on either side of a center area, work a *left* increase as you approach the center; work a *right* increase after it.

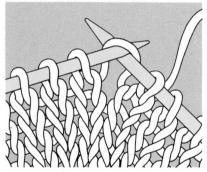

For a decorative raised increase on a knit row, knit into the front of the strand (a hole is formed under the stitch).

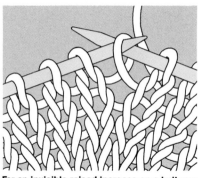

For an invisible raised increase on a knit row, knit into the back of the strand (the stitch is thus twisted; the result is inconspicuous).

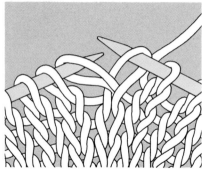

For lifted knit increase, right, insert *right* needle in top of loop just below next stitch; knit the loop, then knit stitch on needle.

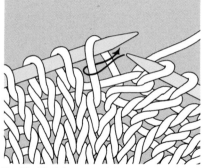

For lifted knit increase, left, insert *left* needle in top of loop below last completed stitch; pull back gently; knit into front of the loop.

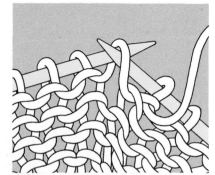

For a decorative raised increase on a purl row, purl into the front of the strand (a hole is formed under the stitch).

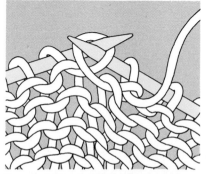

For an invisible raised increase on a purl row, purl into the back of the strand (the stitch is thus twisted; the result is inconspicuous).

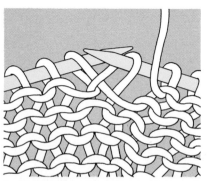

For lifted purl increase, right, insert *right* needle under loop just below next stitch; purl the loop, then purl the stitch on the needle.

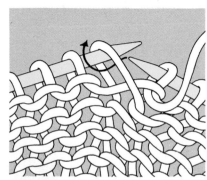

For lifted purl increase, left, insert *left* needle under loop below last completed stitch; pull back gently; purl into front of the loop.

BAR AND MOSS INCREASES

Bar and moss increases are produced by working into the same stitch twice. For a bar increase, you knit into the front and back of a stitch; for a moss increase, you knit and purl into the front. In both cases, the result is decorative, either a bar or nub, and it is easy to keep track of the increases over several rows.

The bar always follows the stitch on which an increase is made, a fact that must be allowed for in paired increases. For example, when an increase is worked three stitches from the end on the right edge, it must be made four stitches from the end on the left edge.

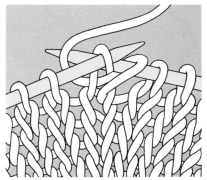

For a bar increase on a knit row, knit a stitch, but do not drop it off the needle; instead, knit again into the back of the same stitch.

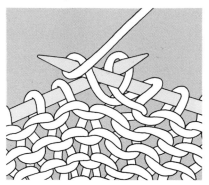

For a bar increase on a purl row, purl a stitch, but do not drop it off the needle; instead, purl again into the back of the same stitch.

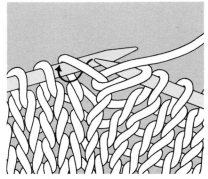

For a moss increase on a knit row, knit a stitch but do not drop it off the needle; instead, purl into the front of the same stitch.

Double increasing

Double raised increase: Knit into back of horizontal strand before center; knit center stitch; knit into back of next strand.

Double lifted increase: In stitch before center, make lifted increase left; knit center stitch; make a lifted increase right.

Double lifted increase into 1 stitch: Knit loop below center stitch; knit into back of center stitch; knit again into loop below center.

Double bar increase: Knit into front and back of stitch before center stitch; knit into front and back of center stitch.

Double moss increase: Knit and purl the stitch before center stitch; knit center stitch; knit and purl the next stitch.

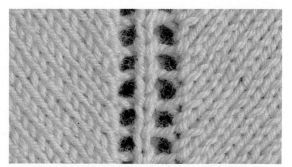

Double lace increase: Make a yarn over just before the center stitch; make another yarn over immediately following it.

Following knitting instructions

Decreasing

A **decrease (dec)** in knitting is the reduction of one or more stitches. Its purpose, generally, is to shape work by making it narrower, but it is used also, combined with increasing, to form stitch patterns such as laces and bobbles.

Two basic methods are shown below and at the top of the opposite page. There is little difference in the way they look, but the slip stitch method (below) draws in less snugly than two stitches worked together (above opposite), and is easier to work when tension is snug.

Each decrease method pulls stitches on a diagonal to the right or the left. If decreases are worked randomly, or at the edge of a garment, the direction of this slant is not significant. It *is* important for symmetrical shaping, such as a raglan or a V-neck where a line will be seen. The rule for this situation is to slant decreases to the right at the left side of the center,

slant them to the left at the right of it. On stockinette, for instance, you would sl 1, K 1, psso to decrease at the beginning of a row, K 2 tog at the end.

To use decreases for gradual shaping, stitches are reduced one at a time on the right side, which means that you work them every other row. If stitches must be reduced every row, then decreases can be worked on the wrong side, but care must be taken to keep direction of the slant (as

viewed from the right side) consistent.

To shape a chevron or mitered corner, **double decreases** are used. These are paired decreases, worked on each side of a center or axial stitch. They form a rather thick nub or ridge.

To decrease three or more stitches in succession, a plain bind-off is preferable (see p. 282). This would be used, for example, at the beginning of an armhole, or the center of a neckline.

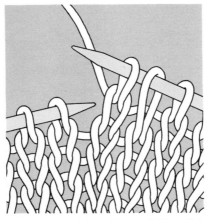

Knit decrease, left (sl 1, K 1, psso): Slip a stitch knitwise; knit the next stitch.

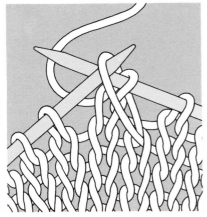

Insert left needle into the front of the slipped stitch and pull it over the knitted one.

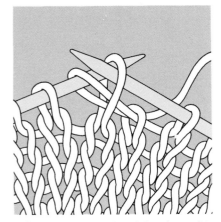

Knit decrease, right: Knit a stitch and return it to the left needle. Pass the next stitch over it.

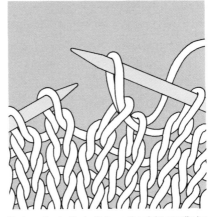

Replace the knitted stitch on the right needle by slipping it purlwise.

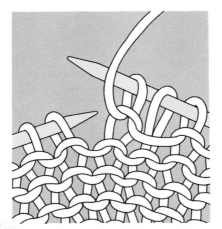

Purl decrease, right (sl 1, P 1, psso): Slip a stitch knitwise; purl the next stitch.

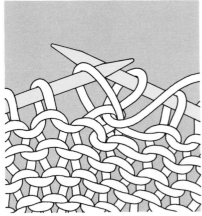

Insert left needle into the front of the slipped stitch and pass it over the purled one.

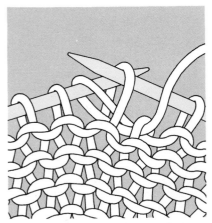

Purl decrease, left: Purl a stitch and return it to the left needle. Pass the next stitch over it.

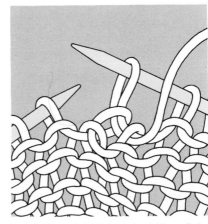

Replace the purled stitch on the right needle by slipping it purlwise.

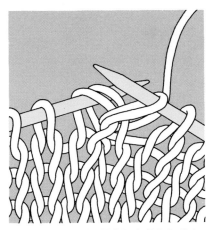

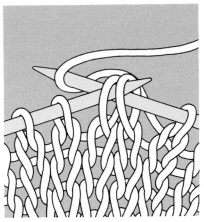

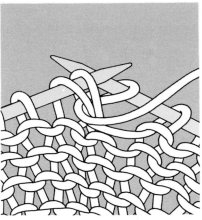

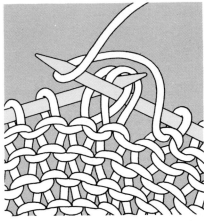

Knit decrease, right (K 2 tog): Knit 2 stitches together through the front of both loops.

Knit decrease, left (K 2 tog tbl): Knit 2 stitches together through the back of both loops.

Purl decrease, right (P 2 tog): Purl 2 stitches together through the front of both loops.

Purl decrease, left (P 2 tog tbl): Purl 2 stitches together through the back of both loops.

Double decreasing

Double decrease, left (K 3 tog tbl): Knit 3 stitches together through the back of all 3 loops. The result is a thick ridge with sharply slanted stitches on either side.

Double decrease, right (K 3 tog): Knit 3 stitches together through the front of all 3 loops. The result is a rather thick ridge with sharply slanted stitches on either side.

Double decrease, left (sl 1, K 2 tog, psso): Slip a stitch knitwise, knit the next 2 stitches together, pass the slipped stitch over the knitted ones. This decrease is similar in appearance to the one above, but draws in a little less snugly. It is also a bit easier to work.

Double decrease, vertical: Slip 2 stitches knitwise, inserting the needle into the second stitch, then the first one; knit the next stitch, then pass the 2 slipped stitches over the knitted one. This is an attractive decrease, especially suitable for a V-neckline.

Following knitting instructions

Cable needle 273

Crossed stitches 308-309
Cable stitches 310-311

Crossing stitches

Crossing stitches is a way to produce certain decorative effects, such as a braid, basket weave, or honeycomb pattern. The crossed stitches appear to be twisted because they are pulled diagonally right or left. The twist direction is determined by the way stitches are worked—to the front or the back.

To cross two stitches, you work the second stitch on the left needle, then the first. Three stitches can also be exchanged this way, working the third stitch, then the first stitch, and finally the second one. The crossovers are easier to manipulate and yarn is less strained if you keep overall tension somewhat loose.

A variation of the above method is crossing through two stitches, as illustrated at the top of the opposite page. The results are subtly different from crossing two stitches, but close enough in appearance that you could substitute the variation for the regular crossing technique, if you preferred.

Crossing more than three stitches is called **cabling.** This technique requires a double-pointed or cable needle to hold the first stitches out of the way until needed. The holding needle should be the same size or smaller than the working needle; a larger one might stretch the stitches. It is correct to work cable stitches from the holding needle, as illustrated opposite, but some people find it easier to slip them back onto the left needle and work them from that position.

The look of a cable is varied by the number of stitches exchanged (this number can be even or uneven), the number of rows worked between twists, and the direction of the twist itself. If stitches are held to the front, a cable twists to the left; if held to the back, the twist is to the right. Because of the complexities, most cable instructions are written out rather than abbreviated. An exception is the common cable exchange of two pairs, abbreviated C4F and C4B.

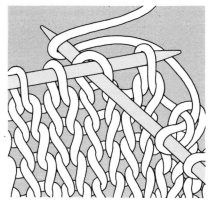

Cross 2 stitches right, knitting (cross 2 RK): Knit into the front of second stitch on the left needle, but do not drop the stitch off.

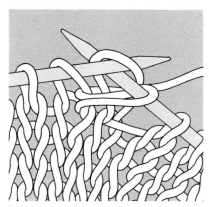

Knit into the front of the first stitch (the one that was skipped); allow both first and second stitches to drop off the needle together.

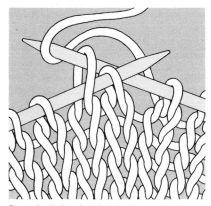

Cross 2 stitches left, knitting (cross 2 LK): Knit into the back of second stitch on the left needle, but do not drop the stitch off.

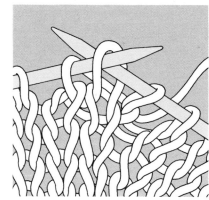

Knit into the back of the first stitch (the one that was skipped); allow both first and second stitches to drop off the needle together.

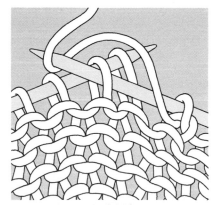

Cross 2 stitches right, purling (cross 2 RP): Purl into the front of second stitch on the left needle, but do not drop the stitch off.

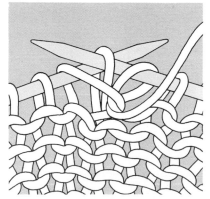

Purl into the front of the first stitch (the one that was skipped); allow both first and second stitches to drop off the needle together.

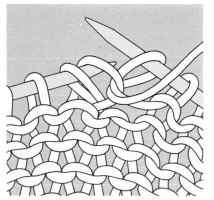

Cross 2 stitches left, purling (cross 2 LP): Purl into the front of second stitch on the left needle; pass it over the first stitch and off the needle.

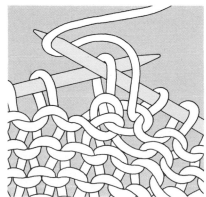

Purl into the front of the first stitch (the one that was skipped), then allow this first stitch to drop off the left needle.

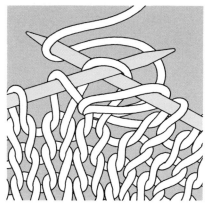

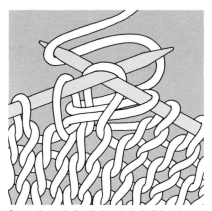

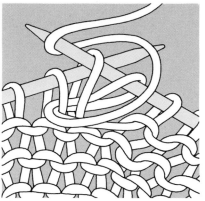

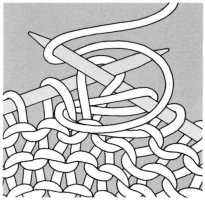

Cross through 2 stitches right, knitting (cross through 2 RK): Knit 2 stitches together through the *front;* knit the first stitch again, then drop both stitches off the left needle together.

Cross through 2 stitches left, knitting (cross through 2 LK): Knit 2 stitches together through the *back;* knit the first stitch again, but through the *front;* drop both stitches off together.

Cross through 2 stitches right, purling (cross through 2 RP): Purl 2 stitches together through the *front;* purl the first stitch again, then drop both stitches off the left needle together.

Cross through 2 stitches left, purling (cross through 2 LP): Purl 2 stitches together through the *front;* purl the first stitch again, but through the *back;* drop both stitches off together.

Crossing stitches with a cable needle

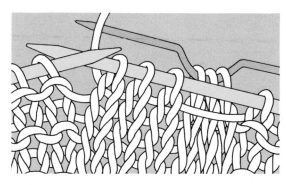

For a cable twisted right, slip the cable stitches onto a cable needle, or any double-pointed needle, and hold these at the back of the work while you knit the remaining stitches of the cable section.

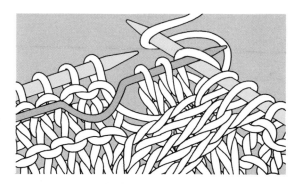

Knit the stitches from the cable needle, as shown, or if you prefer, slip them back onto the left needle and knit them from there. Continue with the rest of the pattern according to instructions.

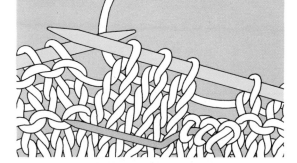

For a cable twisted left, slip the cable stitches onto a cable needle, or any double-pointed needle, and hold these at the front of the work while you knit the remaining stitches of the cable section.

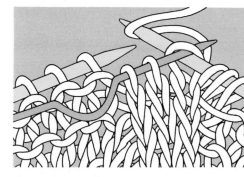

Knit the stitches from the cable needle, as shown, or if you prefer, slip them back onto the left needle and knit them from there. Continue with the rest of the pattern according to instructions.

Following knitting instructions

Correcting errors

Sometimes it is necessary to correct a mistake in your knitting. The methods given here will help you to correct in the easiest and most suitable way. If an error is one row down, drop the stitch off the needle directly above it, then retrieve it by the appropriate method of the two shown below. When it is a few rows down, let that stitch run, and pick it up with a crochet hook, as shown right. Use these same methods to pick up a stitch that has dropped or run accidentally. When the error is several rows down, or if for any reason you wish to unravel a portion of work, follow the directions at the top of the opposite page.

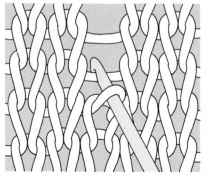

To retrieve a run in stockinette, insert a crochet hook front to back, hook it *over* the horizontal thread and draw through a loop.

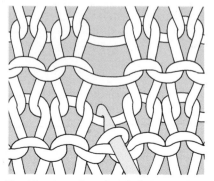

To retrieve a run in garter stitch, insert crochet hook front to back in each knit loop; pull through a loop as for stockinette.

For a purl loop in garter stitch, insert the crochet hook back to front, hooking it *under* the horizontal thread; draw through a loop.

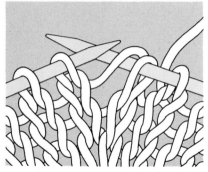

To retrieve a dropped knit stitch, insert the right needle through the loop and under the strand, as shown in the illustration.

Insert the left needle from back to front through the top of the loop only, then pull gently upward and forward on it.

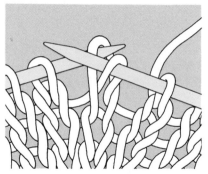

Pull the loop over the strand and off the needle. The stitch (which was the strand) remains on the right needle and is facing the wrong way.

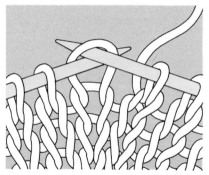

To transfer the stitch, insert the left needle from front to back and slip the stitch onto it. It will be in the correct position to knit.

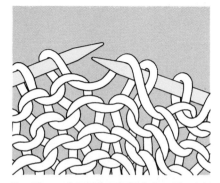

To retrieve a dropped purl stitch, insert the right needle through the loop and under the strand, as shown in the illustration.

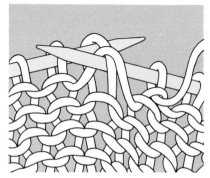

Insert the left needle from front to back through the top of the loop only, then pull gently upward and forward on it.

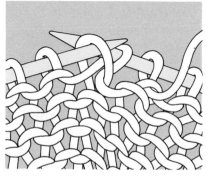

Pull the loop over the strand and off the needle. The stitch (which was the strand) remains on the right needle and must be transferred.

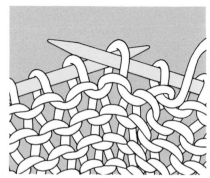

To transfer the stitch, insert the left needle from front to back and slip the stitch onto it. It will be in the correct position to purl.

To correct an error several rows down, mark the row in which the error occurs, using a yarn loop or a coil ring marker.

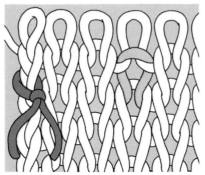

Unravel the stitches to within one row of the mark. Position the knitting so that the working yarn is on the left side (right side of the work faces you).

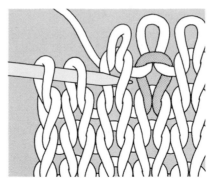

For each knit stitch, hold the yarn behind the work; insert the *left* needle front to back, then pull out the stitch.

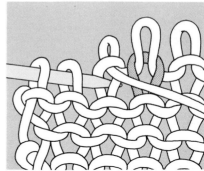

For each purl stitch, hold the yarn in front of the work, insert the *left* needle front to back, then pull out the stitch.

Picking up new stitches

By picking up stitches along a finished edge (usually written pick up and K in instructions), you can add a collar, cuff, trim, even sleeves, without sewing sections together. Two methods for picking up stitches are shown here. Results are the same with both, but Method II is easier to manage when the shape is a deep curve. Ideally, one loop should be picked up in each stitch, but this is not always possible. Before beginning, divide the edge in sections, marking with pins or yarn, calculate how many stitches will fit in each section, and decide how they should be spaced for even distribution.

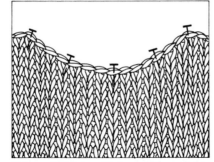

Before picking up stitches, divide work into equal sections, using pins or scraps of yarn. Tie on working yarn where stitches will begin.

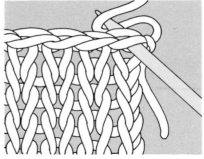

Method I: Hold work in left hand, right side facing you. *Insert right needle under the edge stitch; take yarn around needle as for knitting.

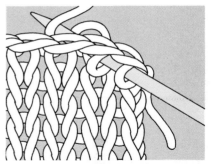

Bring stitch through to the right side.* Repeat from asterisk. Work proceeds from right to left; first row is knitted on the wrong side.

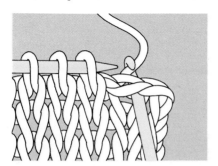

Method II (right-handed): Hold the yarn, needle, and work in left hand, right side facing you, needle just above the edge. *Insert hook under stitch.

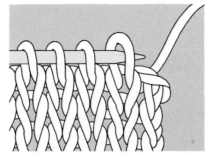

Pull through a loop, place on needle, pull it snug.* Repeat from asterisk. Work proceeds left to right; first row is knitted on the right side.

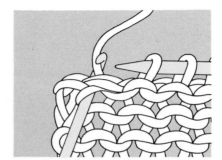

Method II (left-handed): Hold yarn, needle, and work in right hand, wrong side facing you, needle just above edge. *Insert hook under stitch.

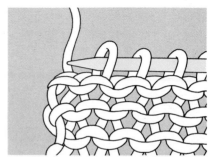

Pull through a loop, place on needle, pull it snug.* Repeat from asterisk, proceeding right to left; first row is knitted on the right side.

297

Following knitting instructions

Circular knitting

Circular knitting is the way of making a seamless tube or a flat piece worked from the center out. There are two ways of working, with a circular needle or with a set of double-pointed needles.

The **circular needle** is practical for any large item, tubular or flat. It holds a great many stitches and permits most of the weight to be supported in the lap, thus lessening strain on the arms. To knit a tube or flat circle, the circumference of the knit piece must be at least 2 inches larger than that of the needle for stitches to fit comfortably and without stretching. Available needle lengths are 16, 29, and 36 inches, so the smallest tube possible would be 18 inches. Anything smaller must be knitted on double-pointed needles.

A circular needle can also be used to knit a large, flat item that would normally

be worked on straight needles, an afghan, for instance. For this purpose, the stitches are worked back and forth as in regular knitting (see method below right).

Double-pointed needles are used most often for small items, such as mittens, socks, or a turtleneck. A large work is possible, however, if the needles are long enough, and there are enough of them, that stitches will not slide off. As a rule, double-pointed needles are sold in sets of four. You will have to buy an extra set when five or more needles are required (the knitted square, opposite page, is an example).

When casting on for double-pointed needles, the stitches are divided evenly among the total number of needles in use. (One needle is always left free for working.) Some adjustment may be necessary to allow for the pattern multiple.

For example, to knit a 2 × 2 rib, each needle would have to carry a multiple of 4 stitches. The cast-on method at the top of the opposite page is best for most purposes. The cast-on method below it is more convenient to use when the center area is very small.

Almost any stitch can be knitted in the round, but an adjustment must be made in the row sequence because the right side always faces you. Knitting every row, for example, produces a stockinette stitch; alternating knit and purl rows produces a garter stitch. Certain laces and jacquards are easier to knit in the round because the pattern sequence becomes less complicated.

While there are some differences in the handling of double-pointed and circular needles, the fundamental approach for knitting is the same with both.

Important points to remember:

1. As you start the first round, the bottom edge of all stitches must face the *center;* twisted stitches cannot be adjusted without unravelling the work.

2. A marker should be placed after the last cast-on stitch, and slipped before the first stitch of each round. Pattern changes, for example, a switch from knit to purl stitches, will occur at this point, and progression will be uneven if rounds are not clearly marked. (To mark other key points, such as locations of increases, without confusion, use markers of a different color.)

3. Every joining stitch (the first one on a needle or round) must be pulled extra firmly to avoid a ladder effect.

4. The right side of a tube or flat motif always faces you, and the stitch pattern must be adjusted accordingly.

Knitting with a circular needle

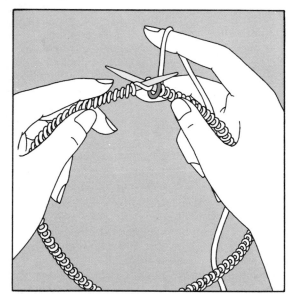

To knit a tubular fabric, hold needle tip with the *last* cast-on stitch (the one attached to ball of yarn) in your *right* hand, the tip with *first* cast-on stitch in your *left.* Knit the first stitch, pulling yarn firmly to avoid a gap where the tube is joined.

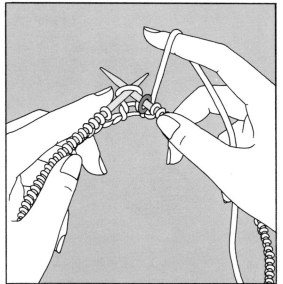

Knit around the circle until you reach the marker, then slip the marker and start the next round. At this point, check for twisted stitches; if you find any, unravel the work and start again. A twisted edge cannot be corrected in any other way.

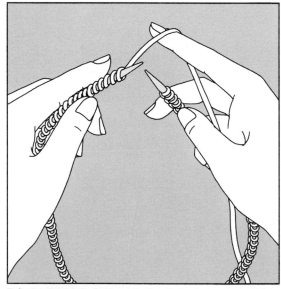

To knit a flat fabric, hold needle tip with the *last* cast-on stitch in your *left* hand, the tip with *first* cast-on stitch in your *right.* Knit to the last stitch, then flip needle around so that wrong side faces you. Continue to turn work with each round.

Knitting with double-pointed needles

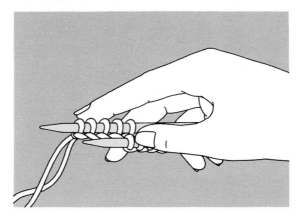

1. To knit a tube with 4 dp needles, cast 1/3 the total number of stitches on each of 3 needles. As you complete one needle, place the next one parallel and directly above it, with the point a little bit forward of the lower one. (To knit with 5 or more needles, use the same approach, dividing stitches evenly among the total, minus 1 needle for working.)

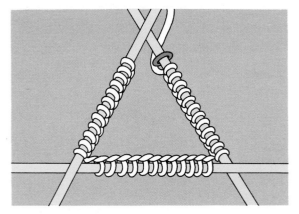

2. Lay the 3 needles in a triangle, with the bottom edges of all stitches facing the center. Place a ring marker after the last stitch (where the ball end of the yarn is).

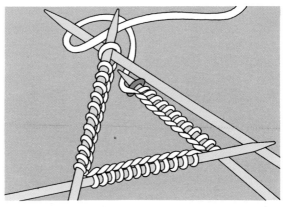

3. Using the fourth needle, knit into the first cast-on stitch, thus closing the triangle. Pull extra firmly on the yarn for this stitch, so there will not be a gap. When you have knitted all stitches off the first needle, use that one for the working needle, placing it behind the others as you knit the first stitch in the next group.

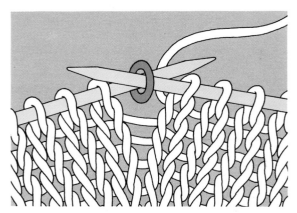

4. Knit each section of the circle until you reach the marker, then slip it and start the next round. Continue to slip the marker with each round; it marks regular progression of rows.

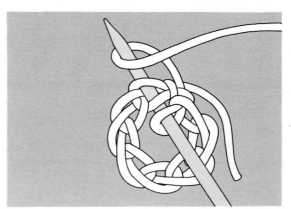

To knit a flat item, started at the center (a tablecloth, for example, or a patchwork motif), cast on the stitches by this method: Crochet a chain, having one loop for each stitch that is needed; join it in a ring. Transfer the loop that remains on the hook to one dp needle, then pick up stitches around the ring, setting the correct number on each needle. For a small center area, this method is easier to manage than the one shown above, left.

To knit a square from the center out, crochet 8 chains, join in a ring, and pick up 2 stitches on each of 4 needles. On first round, increase 1 stitch between each 2-stitch group. On the next and subsequent rounds, increase 2 stitches at the center of each section. A triangle is worked in the same way, but with 6 stitches in 3 sections. A circle is made similarly, but started with 10 stitches on 5 needles; 1 increase is made in each section every round, moving its location 1 stitch forward each round.

Knitting stitches

Using a pattern stitch
Textures
Ribs
Diagonals
Laces
Crossed stitches
Cables
Novelty stitches
Knotted stitches
Aran knitting
Directions for Aran sweater
Multicolor knitting
Changing colors at the end
of a row
Twisting yarns to change colors
Stranding method
Jacquard patterns using stranding
Weaving method
Jacquard patterns using weaving
Charting a pattern stitch

Using a pattern stitch

A **pattern stitch** (often called pattern for short) is the sequence of knitting techniques, repeated continuously, that forms knitted fabric. It consists of a *multiple,* the stitches needed for one horizontal motif, and a *repeat,* the rows required to form one vertical unit.

Knitters are highly inventive, so there are more pattern stitches than anyone can count. Most have fanciful names that often suggest what the stitches look like. These designations vary, however, from one region to another, so do not be surprised if you encounter a familiar stitch with an unfamiliar name.

Most pattern stitches can be classified according to structure. Familiarity with basic structures will permit you to knit almost anything as your skill increases, even to invent your own stitch if you do not find one to suit your needs.

Patterns in this section are grouped according to type, though in a few cases a stitch may fit more than one category. The first group, *Textures,* comprises those compact knits that are sometimes called fabric stitches. The first eight stitches in this group are ideal for beginners, since they require limited skill.

In choosing a pattern stitch, you will naturally be influenced by its appearance, but other things should be considered, too. Is it suitable for the yarn? A highly textured yarn and a busy pattern, for instance, do not mix. Is it appropriate for the intended use? Few lace stitches would make a warm winter garment.

To knit a pattern, cast on a number of stitches that can be divided by the multiple; add any additional stitches indicated, plus selvage stitches. Follow instructions through the last row, then begin again at Row 1. Unless stated otherwise, the first row is the right side. The word *reversible* appears whenever a pattern is identical on both sides, a desirable quality if both sides will be seen, as in an afghan. For a reminder of what abbreviations mean, see page 286.

Textures

Simple seed: A stockinette stitch interspersed with purl stitches; a nice pattern for baby garments.
Multiple of 4 sts
Row 1: *K 3, P 1*
Row 2 and alt rows: purl
Rows 3 and 7: knit
Row 5: K 1, *P 1, K 3*, P 1, K 2

Tracks: Streaks of purl stitches on a face of stockinette pattern.
Multiple of 10 sts
Row 1: *K 4, P 6*
Row 2 and alt rows: purl
Rows 3 and 7: knit
Row 5: *P 5, K 4, P 1*

Chevron seed: Zigzags of purl stitches on stockinette background.
Multiple of 8 sts
Row 1: *P 1, K 3*
Row 2: *K 1, P 5, K 1, P 1*
Row 3: *K 2, P 1, K 3, P 1, K 1*
Row 4: *P 2, K 1, P 1, K 1, P 3*

Diamond seed: Purl stitches tracing diamonds on a stockinette face.
Multiple of 8 sts
Row 1: *P 1, K 7*
Rows 2 and 8: *K 1, P 5, K 1, P 1*
Rows 3 and 7: *K 2, P 1, K 3, P 1, K 1*
Rows 4 and 6: *P 2, K 1, P 1, K 1, P 3*
Row 5: *K 4, P 1, K 3*

Basket stitch (reversible):
Checkerboard squares of stockinette and reverse stockinette stitches.
Multiple of 10 sts
Rows 1 through 6: *K 5, P 5*
Rows 7 through 12: *P 5, K 5*

Gathered stitch: Shirred sections are created by doubling stitches, working even, then decreasing stitches to the original number. The section depths can be varied, also stockinette substituted for garter stitch if desired.
Multiple is any number of sts
Rows 1 through 6: knit
Row 7: K into front and back of each st
Rows 8, 10, 12: purl
Rows 9 and 11: knit
Row 13: K 2 tog all along the row
Rep from Row 2

Quilted diamonds (reversible): The diamonds of reverse stockinette appear to be embossed on a background of stockinette. This pattern pulls inward slightly in much the same manner as a rib (see p. 302 for rib characteristics).
Multiple of 10 sts
Row 1: *K 9, P 1*
Rows 2 and 8: K 2, *P 7, K 3*, P 7, K 1
Rows 3 and 7: P 2, *K 5, P 5*, K 5, P 3
Rows 4 and 6: K 4, *P 3, K 7*, P 3, K 3
Row 5: P 4, *K 1, P 9*, K 1, P 5

Linen stitch: The appearance and firmness of a woven fabric; especially well suited to tailored garments.
Multiple of 2 sts
Row 1: *K 1, yfwd, sl 1, ybk*
Row 2: *P 1, ybk, sl 1, yfwd*

Ridge stitch: Horizontal ridges stand out in strong relief against stockinette.
Multiple of 2 sts
Row 1: knit
Row 2: *K 2 tog all across the row*
Row 3: K into front and back of each st
Row 4: purl

Herringbone: Very firm stitch, similar to a woven in appearance and elasticity. Tension must be kept fairly loose.
Multiple of 2 sts
Row 1: K 2 tog tbl dropping only first loop off left needle, *K 2 tog tbl (the remaining stitch and next stitch), again dropping only the first loop off the needle*, K 1 tbl
Row 2: P 2 tog dropping only the first loop off left needle, *P 2 tog (the remaining stitch and next stitch), again dropping only first loop off needle*, P 1

Waved welt (reversible): Undulating rows of stockinette and reverse stockinette. The emphatic horizontals give a strong feeling of width to the fabric.
Multiple of 8 sts plus 1
Row 1: *P 1, K 7*, P 1
Row 2: K 2, *P 5, K 3*, P 5, K 2
Row 3: P 3, *K 3, P 5*, K 3, P 3
Row 4: K 4, *P 1, K 7*, P 1, K 4
Row 5: *K 1, P 7*, K 1
Row 6: P 2, *K 5, P 3*, K 5, P 2
Row 7: K 3, *P 3, K 5*, P 3, K 3
Row 8: P 4, *K 1, P 7*, K 1, P 4

Waffle: A heavy, 3-dimensional stitch; done in knitting worsted, it is suitable for a jacket, coat, or afghan.
Multiple of 2 sts
Rows 1 and 2: knit
Row 3: *K 1, K 1 blw* (see p. 288)
Row 4: *pick up the long (top) yarn produced by the K 1 blw and K it along with the st on the needle, K 1*
Row 5: *K 1 blw, K 1*
Row 6: *K 1, K the next st tog with the long yarn as for Row 4*
Rep Rows 3 through 6 for the pattern

301

Knitting stitches

Introduction to rib stitches

Rib stitches are characterized by vertical ridges and great elasticity in the crosswise direction. The classical rib patterns are 1 × 1 and 2 × 2 ribs, shown on page 280; the examples here are meant to give you an idea of the many interesting variations that are possible.

A typical rib is formed by alternating knit and purl stitches in the same row. The ratio of knit to purl stitches may be even or uneven. The larger the numbers, the less elastic the fabric.

Because of its exceptional elasticity, a rib stitch is often used at garment edges. In this use, it is called *ribbing*. To assure a snug fit, ribbing is usually worked with needles a size or two smaller than those used for the garment body. In selecting a ribbing, take care that it complements the fabric stitch.

Ribs

7 × 3 flat rib: Less elastic than narrower rib patterns; can be used successfully for a garment fabric.
Multiple of 10 sts
Row 1: *K 7, P 3*
Row 2: *K 3, P 7*

Tweed stitch rib: A nubby texture produced by slipping stitches on the knit portions; best suited to plain yarns.
Multiple of 6 sts
Row 1: *P 3, yfwd, sl 1 P-wise, ybk, K 1, yfwd, sl 1 P-wise*
Rows 2 and 4: *P 3, K 3*
Row 3: *P 3, K 1, yfwd, sl 1 P-wise, ybk, K 1*

Moss stitch rib: An attractive variation on a 5 × 6 rib pattern.
Multiple of 11 sts plus 5
Row 1: K 5, *(K 1, P 1) 3 times, K 5*
Row 2: *P 5, (P 1, K 1) 3 times*, P 5

Stocking heel stitch: Not a true rib structure, but has appearance and nearly the elasticity of one; often used for sock heels, as it withstands heavy wear.
Multiple of 2 sts plus 1
Row 1: *K 1, sl 1 *, K 1
Row 2: purl

Broken ribbing: An interesting texture produced by fragmenting the rib stitches; especially suitable as a fabric stitch for sweaters.
Multiple of 12 sts
Rows 1 and 3: K 2, *P 2, K 4*, P 2, K 2
Rows 2 and 4: P 2, *K 2, P 4*, K 2, P 2
Rows 5 and 7: K 1, *P 4, K 2*, P 4, K 1
Rows 6 and 8: P 1, *K 4, P 2*, K 4, P 1

Changing rib: A pretty variation on a 1 × 3 rib; suitable for an all-over pattern as well as a rib trim.
Multiple of 8 sts
Rows 1 and 3 (wrong side): *K 3, yfwd, sl 1 P-wise, K 3, P 1*
Row 2: *K 1, P 3, ybk, sl 1 P-wise tbl, P 3*
Row 4: *K 1, P 3, K 1, P 3*

Ribbed cables: Not a true cable rib but similar in appearance.
Multiple of 5 sts plus 4
Row 1: *P 4, K into the front, back, and front again of next st*, P 4
Row 2: K 4, *P 3, K 4*
Row 3: *P 4, K 3 tog*, P 4
Row 4: K 4, *P 1, K 4*

Precautions in the use of diagonal stitches

Diagonals are patterns in which the stitch progression slants to the right, the left, or alternately right and left, produced by moving the repeat one stitch left or right on successive rows.

One-way diagonals, though dynamic looking, have limited uses because they tend to stretch on the bias. This can be overcome to some degree by taking these precautions: (1) Choose firmly twisted, yarns; avoid soft ones. (2) Use needles one size smaller than is normally recommended for the yarn choice. (3) Take special care in blocking and washing; do not wring, twist, or tug.

The two-way diagonals (herringbone twill, for example) resemble their woven counterparts in both looks and performance. They have limited stretchability and are suitable for tailored garments.

Diagonals

Oblique seed stitch: An interesting texture, a super simple technique.
Multiple of 5 sts
Row 1: *K 4, P 1*
Row 2: *P 1, K 1, P 3*
Row 3: *K 2, P 1, K 2*
Row 4: *P 3, K 1, P 1*
Row 5: *P 1, K 4*
Row 6: *K 1, P 4*
Row 7: *K 3, P 1, K 1*
Row 8: *P 2, K 1, P 2*
Row 9: *K 1, P 1, K 3*
Row 10: *P 4, K 1*

Ripple: A very subtle diagonal with the knit stitches twisted to the right on a stockinette face.
Multiple of 3 sts
Row 1: *K 2 tog, then K the first st again before slipping both sts off left needle, K 1*
Rows 2 and 4: purl
Row 3: *K 1, K 2 tog, K the first st again*

Diagonal rib: Typical of diagonals produced by moving the pattern one stitch to the right on alternate rows.
Multiple of 4 sts
Row 1: *K 2, P 2*
Row 2 and alt rows: knit the purl sts and purl the knit sts of previous row
Row 3: *K 1, P 2, K 1*
Row 5: *P 2, K 2*
Row 7: *P 1, K 2, P 1*

Steps: Small knots on stockinette face.
Multiple of 5 sts
Row 1 (wrong side): *P 2, (K front and back) 3 times*
Row 2: *(K 2 tog tbl) 3 times, K 2*
Row 3: *P 1, (K front and back) 3 times, P 1*
Row 4: *K 1, (K 2 tog tbl) 3 times, K 1*
Row 5: *(K front and back) 3 times, P 2*
Row 6: *K 2 (K 2 tog tbl) 3 times*
Continue moving pattern 1 stitch to the right every odd-numbered row. After 10 rows, pattern repeats from Row 1.

Herringbone twill: Side-to-side zigzag.
Multiple of 4 sts
Rows 1 and 5: *K 2, yfwd, sl 2, ybk*
Rows 2 and 6: sl 1, *yfwd, P 2, ybk, sl 2*, P 3
Rows 3 and 7: *yfwd, sl 2, ybk, K 2*
Rows 4 and 8: P 1, *ybk, sl 2, yfwd, P 2*, ybk, sl 2, yfwd, P 1
Rows 9 and 13: *yfwd, sl 2, ybk, K 2*
Rows 10 and 14: sl 1, *yfwd, P 2, ybk, sl 2*, yfwd, P 2, sl 1
Rows 11 and 15: *ybk, K 2, yfwd, sl 2*
Rows 12 and 16: P 1, *ybk, sl 2, yfwd, P 2*, ybk, sl 2, yfwd, P 1

Chevron rib: An up-and-down pattern to the zigzag, rather than side-to-side as in the herringbone twill above.
Multiple of 12 sts
Row 1: *P 2, K 2, P 2, K 1, P 2, K 2, P 1*
Rows 2, 4, 6, 8: knit the purl sts and purl the knit sts of previous row
Row 3: *P 1, K 2, P 2, K 3, P 2, K 2*
Row 5: *K 2, P 2, K 2, P 1, K 2, P 2, K 1*
Row 7: *K 1, P 2, K 2, P 3, K 2, P 2*

Diagonal couching stitch: The slant is produced by pulling an extra knit loop across two stitches on the knit row. Each increase is compensated for by a decrease in the purl row.
Multiple of 2 sts plus 1
Row 1: K 1, *insert right needle between next 2 sts, draw through a loop; keeping this loop on right needle, sl the first st k-wise, K the second st*
Row 2: P 1, *P 1, P 2 tog*
Row 3: K 2, *proceed as for Row 1*, K 1
Row 4: P 2, *P 1, P 2 tog*, P 1

Knitting stitches

Introduction to laces

A **lace stitch** is basically any pattern with openwork. Its forms are numerous, ranging from eyelet bands in stockinette background to the most delicate lace networks. The structuring also varies, and includes some of the simplest and some of the most complex of patterns. Those shown here and on the next three pages are just a sampling of possibilities.

You can usually recognize a lace pattern by the frequent appearance of a yarn-over increase. This technique creates a hole. Elsewhere in the sequence, each increase is offset by a decrease to keep the stitch total constant. Another lace technique is the elongated stitch (see drop stitch lace, p. 307), which forms more of a slit than a hole.

The casting on is important in lace knitting; it should be flexible and inconspicuous. Either the single or looped method is appropriate (p. 275).

Lace stitches, especially the airy ones, look best knitted with fine yarns and needles. Medium-weight yarns can be used when a more tailored product is desired. For this purpose, suitable stitches are those with fewer openings.

Laces

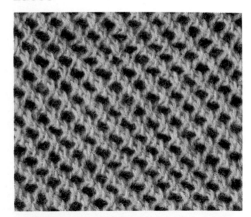

Oblique openwork: A stitch formation typical of many lace stitches, it is a combination of yo increase (which forms a hole) and K 2 tog decrease (which keeps the number of stitches constant). Has a tendency to slant on the bias.
Multiple of 2 sts
Row 1: K 1, *yo, K 2 tog*, K 1
Rows 2 and 4: purl
Row 3: K 2, *yo, K 2 tog*

Turkish stitch: Openwork similar to that in stitch above, but more delicate. Here the yo increase is combined with a decrease of sl 1, K 1, psso. (See p. 292 to review this last method.)
Multiple of 2 sts
All rows: *yo, sl 1, K 1, psso*

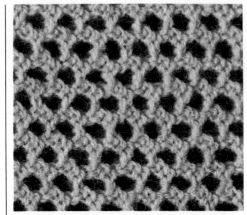

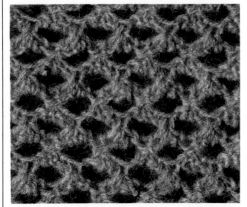

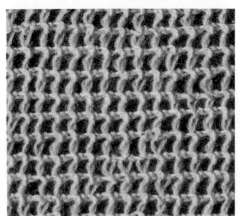

Eyelet stitch: Large holes formed by taking yarn twice around the needle for the increases. Yarn overs at the beginning and end of Row 3 produce a delicate selvage. For a firmer edge, add one selvage stitch at each end.
Multiple of 4 sts
Row 1: *K 2, yo 00 (wind yarn twice around the needle), K 2*
Row 2: *P 2 tog, K 1, P 1, P 2 tog*
Row 3: *yo, K 4, yo*
Row 4: *P 1, (P 2 tog) twice, K 1*

Network (reversible): Chunky texture interspersed with large holes. Worked with fine yarn and medium needles, this is a very good stitch for a shawl. Tension should be kept fairly loose, in order to work the P 4 together.
Multiple of 4 sts
Row 1: P 2, *yo, P 4 tog*, P 2
Row 2: K 2, *K 1, KPK into the yo of the previous row*, K 2
Row 3: knit

Cellular stitch: An airy pattern resembling a type of crochet; very light and easy to execute; suitable for a baby blanket or shawl. For best results, work this stitch with medium or large needles and block carefully, as it has a tendency to stretch on the bias.
Multiple is any number of sts
Row 1 (wrong side): purl
Row 2: K 1, *K under the horizontal strand before the next st, K 1, pass the made st over the K 1*

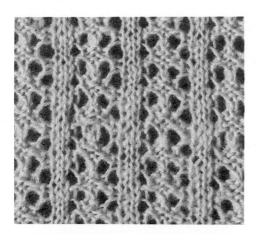

Lace rib: A combination of openwork and stockinette. The right side is shown, but the reverse side is just as pretty.
Multiple of 7 sts plus 2
Row 1 (wrong side): P 2, *yo, sl 1, K 1, psso, K 1, K 2 tog, yo, P 2*
Rows 2 and 4: *K 2, P 5*, K 2
Row 3: P 2, *K 1, yo, sl 1, K 2 tog, psso, yo, K 1, P 2*

Bluebells: A delicate pattern suitable for a shawl or baby garments.
Multiple of 8 sts plus 5
Rows 1 and 3: K 1, *yo, 1 double dec [K 2 tog tbl, return st obtained to left needle, pass the next st over it, then put st back on right needle], yo, K 5*, yo, 1 double dec, yo, K 1
Row 2 and alt rows: purl
Row 5: K 1, *K 3, yo, sl 1, K 1, psso, K 1, K 2 tog, yo*, K 4
Row 7: K 1, *yo, 1 double dec, yo, K 1*, yo, 1 double dec, yo, K 1

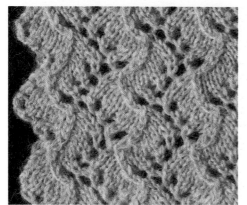

Traveling vine: Left edge is scalloped.
Multiple of 8 sts
Row 1: *yo, K 1 tbl, yo, sl 1, K 1, psso, K 5*
Row 2: *P 4, P 2 tog tbl, P 3*
Row 3: *yo, K 1 tbl, yo, K 2, sl 1, K 1, psso, K 3*
Row 4: *P 2, P 2 tog tbl, P 5*
Row 5: *K 1 tbl, yo, K 4, sl 1, K 1, psso, K 1, yo*
Row 6: *P 1, P 2 tog tbl, P 6*
Row 7: *K 5, K 2 tog, yo, K 1 tbl, yo*
Row 8: *P 3, P 2 tog, P 4*
Row 9: *K 3, K 2 tog, K 2, yo, K 1 tbl, yo*
Row 10: *P 5, P 2 tog, P 2*
Row 11: *yo, K 1, K 2 tog, K 4, yo, K 1 tbl*
Row 12: *P 6, P 2 tog, P 1*

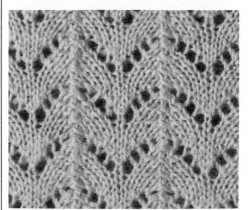

Horseshoes: One of many beautiful stitches that originated in the Shetland Islands in the nineteenth century, when gossamer laces were a favorite form of knitting.
Multiple of 10 sts plus 1
Row 1: K 1, *yo, K 3, sl 1, K 2 tog, psso, K 3, yo, K 1*
Row 2 and alt rows: purl
Row 3: K 1, *K 1, yo, K 2, sl 1, K 2 tog, psso, K 2, yo, K 2*
Row 5: K 1, *K 2, yo, K 1, sl 1, K 2 tog, psso, K 1, yo, K 3*
Row 7: K 1, *K 3, yo, sl 1, K 2 tog, psso, yo, K 4*

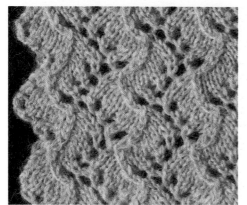

Lace zigzag: Both side edges are scalloped. Suitable for a shawl or afghan.
Multiple of 2 sts
Row 1: K 1, P 1, *yo, K 1, P 1*
Rows 2, 4, 6, 8, 10: *K 1, P 2 tog, yo*, K 1, P 1
Rows 3, 5, 7, 9: K 1, P 1, *yo, K 2 tog, P 1*
Rows 11, 13, 15, 17, 19: K 1, P 1, *sl 1, K 1, psso, yo, P 1*
Rows 12, 14, 16, 18, 20: *K 1, yo, P 2 tog tbl*, K 1, P 1
Row 21: K 1, P 1, *yo, sl 1, K 1, psso, P 1*
Rep pattern from Row 2

Hyacinths: Soft, bell-like clusters in an openwork background. This is a delicate stitch, especially suitable for a shawl. For best results, keep the tension fairly loose when working.
Multiple of 6 sts plus 2
Row 1 (wrong side): K 1, *P 5 tog, KPKPK into next st*, K 1
Rows 2 and 4: purl
Row 3: K 1, *KPKPK into next st, P 5 tog*, K 1
Row 5: K 000 (winding thread 3 times around the needle for each st)
Row 6: purl, letting extra loops drop off the needle

305

Knitting stitches

Yarn tension 281
Yarn-over increase 289

Knitting front and back of loop 291
Decreasing methods 292-293

Laces

Chevron lace: Horizontal zigzags. Multiple is increased one stitch in Row 9, reduced one stitch in Row 11.
Multiple of 8 sts plus 1
Row 1: *K 5, yo, K 2 tog, K 1*, K 1
Row 2 and alt rows: purl
Row 3: *K 3, K 2 tog tbl, yo, K 1, yo, K 2 tog*, K 1
Row 5: K 1, *K 1, K 2 tog tbl, yo, K 3, yo, K 2 tog*
Row 7: *yo, K 2 tog tbl, return st to left needle, pass next st over it and put st back on right needle, yo, K 5*, K 1
Row 9: *K 1, K into front and back of next st, K 6*, K 1
Row 11: *K 2 tog, K 4, yo, K 2 tog, K 1*, K 1
Rep from Row 3

Diagonal lace stripe: A rib stitch pattern with diagonal bands of openwork.
Multiple of 10 sts plus 3
Row 1: *P 3, yo, sl 1, K 1, psso, K 5*, P 3
Row 2: *K 3, P 4, P 2 tog tbl, yo, P 1*, K 3
Row 3: *P 3, K 2, yo, sl 1, K 1, psso, K 3*, P 3
Row 4: *K 3, P 2, P 2 tog tbl, yo, P 3*, K 3
Row 5: *P 3, K 4, yo, sl 1, K 1, psso, K 1*, P 3
Row 6: *K 3, P 2 tog tbl, yo, P 5*, K 3
Row 7: *P 3, K 7*, P 3
Row 8: *K 3, P 7*, K 3

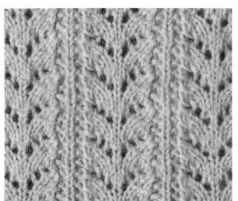

Baby fern: A very elegant lace pattern with the cast-on edge slightly scalloped. Suitable for baby clothing, a dress, or an afghan; use medium-weight yarn.
Multiple of 12 sts
Row 1 and alt rows (wrong side): purl
Row 2: *K 2 tog, K 2, yo, K 1, yo, K 2, sl 1, K 1, psso, P 1, K 1, P 1*
Row 4: *K 2 tog, K 1, yo, K 3, yo, K 1, sl 1, K 1, psso, P 1, K 1, P 1*
Row 6: *K 2 tog, yo, K 5, yo, sl 1, K 1, psso, P 1, K 1, P 1*

Fancy trellis: Crossbars in relief; suitable for a pullover or cardigan.
Multiple of 7 sts
Row 1: *K 2, K 2 tog, yo, K 3*
Row 2: *P 1, P 2 tog tbl, yo, P 1, yo, P 2 tog, P 1*
Row 3: *K 2 tog, yo, K 3, yo, sl 1, K 1, psso*
Rows 4 and 8: purl
Row 5: *yo, sl 1, K 1, psso, K 5*
Row 6: *yo, P 2 tog, P 2, P 2 tog tbl, yo, P 1*
Row 7: *K 2, yo, sl 1, K 1, psso, K 2 tog, yo, K 1*

Fern stitch: Like baby fern but larger.
Multiple of 29 sts
Row 1: *K 1, sl 1, K 2 tog, psso, K 9, yo, K 1, yo, P 2, yo, K 1, yo, K 9, sl 1, K 2 tog, psso*
Row 2 and alt rows: *P 13, K 2, P 14*
Row 3: *K 1, sl 1, K 2 tog, psso, K 8, (yo, K 1) twice, P 2, (K 1, yo) twice, K 8, sl 1, K 2 tog, psso*
Row 5: *K 1, sl 1, K 2 tog, psso, K 7, yo, K 1, yo, K 2, P 2, K 2, yo, K 1, yo, K 7, sl 1, K 2 tog, psso*
Row 7: *K 1, sl 1, K 2 tog, psso, K 6, yo, K 1, yo, K 3, P 2, K 3, yo, K 1, yo, K 6, sl 1, K 2 tog, psso*
Row 9: *K 1, sl 1, K 2 tog, psso, K 5, yo, K 1, yo, K 4, P 2, K 4, yo, K 1, yo, K 5, sl 1, K 2 tog, psso*

Vandyke stitch: V-shaped openwork in a stockinette background. An attractive stitch for a sweater.
Multiple of 10 sts
Row 1: *yo, sl 1, K 1, psso, K 8*
Row 2 and alt rows: purl
Row 3: *K 1, yo, sl 1, K 1, psso, K 5, K 2 tog, yo*
Row 5: *K 2, yo, sl 1, K 1, psso, K 3, K 2 tog, yo, K 1*
Row 7: *K 5, yo, sl 1, K 1, psso, K 3*
Row 9: *K 3, K 2 tog, yo, K 1, yo, sl 1, K 1, psso, K 2*
Row 11: *K 2, K 2 tog, yo, K 3, yo, sl 1, K 1, psso, K 1*

Horizontal openwork: Lacy bands set at intervals in a stockinette stitch. In the example, lace stitches occur every ten rows; they could be set closer together or farther apart, or just one band used for a decorative touch.
Multiple of 2 sts
Rows 1, 3, 5, 7, 9, 10: knit
Rows 2, 4, 6, 8: purl
Row 11: *yo, P 2 tog*
Row 12: knit

Lace insert: A double band of openwork alternating with strips of garter stitch (or seed or stockinette). Can be used effectively for trim or an entire fabric.
Multiple of 2 sts
Rows 1 to 6: knit
Rows 7 and 9: *yo, K 2 tog*
Rows 8 and 10: *yo, P 2 tog*

Striped fagoting: Openwork ribs combined with reverse stockinette. This stitch can be worked as shown, or one multiple of the lace might be used for a lacy insertion.
Multiple of 8 sts plus 4
Row 1: *P 4, K 2 tog, yo, K 2*, P 4
Row 2: *K 4, P 2 tog, yo, P 2*, K 4

Drop stitch lace: Bands of elongated stitches alternating with bands of garter (or seed or stockinette). The open bands can be set close together or far apart, depending on the effect desired.
Multiple is any number of sts
Rows 1 to 4: knit
Row 5: K 00 (winding thread twice around the needle)
Row 6: K, letting extra loop drop

Butterfly: A very pretty stitch for a child's sweater.
Multiple of 10 sts plus 5
Rows 1 and 3: K 5, *K 2 tog, yo, K 1, yo, sl 1, K 1, psso, K 5*
Rows 2 and 4: *P 7, sl 1 P-wise, P 2*, P 5
Rows 5 and 11: knit
Rows 6 and 12: purl
Rows 7 and 9: *K 2 tog, yo, K 1, yo, sl 1, K 1, psso, K 5*, K 2 tog, yo, K 1, yo, sl 1, K 1, psso
Rows 8 and 10: *P 2, sl 1 P-wise, P 7*, P 2, sl 1 P-wise, P 2

Double drop stitch: Two rows of elongated stitches, back to back, make an attractive lacy insert.
Use one row as a trim, or several for an airy fabric, as shown here.
Multiple is any number of sts
Rows 1, 3, 5, 7: knit
Rows 2, 4, 6: purl
Row 8 (wrong side): K 00 (winding thread twice around the needle)
Row 9: rep Row 8, letting the extra loop drop
Row 10: K, letting extra loop drop

307

Knitting stitches

Introduction to crossed stitches

Richly embossed **crossed-stitch patterns** are produced by switching the working order of two or three stitches, which pulls knitted loops on a diagonal. Some of these patterns are actually cables in miniature (see pp. 310-311 for cable stitches), but are easier and faster to work because there are fewer steps. Other crossed-stitch patterns resemble woven fabrics, in both appearance and performance. Basket weave, right, is an example. In this case, crossing locks the stitches, limiting their stretchability somewhat.

To cross two stitches, you work the second stitch on the left needle, then the first one, slipping both stitches off the needle together. To do this comfortably and without stretching the yarn, tension should be kept fairly loose.

After stitches are crossed, they slant either to the left or right. The direction depends on the way in which loops are worked—to the front or back. A review of crossed-stitch methods may be advisable before starting (pp. 294-295).

Because the technique provides so much textural interest, these patterns are best carried out with smooth yarns.

Basket weave: Stitches crossed left and right to form a sturdy fabric that is similar to a woven structure.
Multiple of 2 sts
Row 1: *cross 2 LK*
Row 2: P 1, *cross 2 RP*, P 1

Crossed stitches

Wasps nest: A 3-dimensional texture produced by crossing knit stitches alternately to the right and the left. It looks very much like smocking.
Multiple of 4 sts
Row 1: *cross 2 RK, cross 2 LK*
Row 2 and alt rows: purl
Row 3: *cross 2 LK, cross 2 RK*

Basket weave rib: A very wide decorative pattern, more suitable for a fabric than for ribbing, or one panel of the rib might be used as a decorative insert on a garment worked in stockinette or reverse stockinette.
Multiple of 12 sts plus 5
Row 1: *P 5, K 1, (cross 2 LK) 3 times*, P 5
Row 2: K 5, *P 1, (cross 2 RP) 3 times, K 5*

Knotted cross stitch: The crossed stitches slipped over two increases form a moderate-sized nub on a stockinette background.
Multiple of 4 sts plus 2
Rows 1 and 3: knit
Row 2 and alt rows: purl
Row 5: *K 2, cross 2 LK, (yo, pass the second st on right needle over the first st and the yo) twice*, K 2

Crossed-stitch ribbing: Forms a very elastic fabric that retains its springiness through many washings.
Multiple of 3 sts plus 1
Row 1: P 1, *cross 2 RK, P 1*
Row 2: K 1, *P 2, K 1*

Chain stitch: Resembles a cable rib, but is much easier to execute.
Multiple of 8 sts plus 4
Row 1: *P 4, cross 2 LK, cross 2 RK*, P 4
Row 2: *K 4, P 4*, K 4
Rows 3 and 5: *P 4, K 1, P 2, K 1*, P 4
Rows 4 and 6: *K 4, P 1, K 2, P 1*, K 4

Small diamonds: A lattice pattern in a scale small enough for a child's sweater.
Multiple of 6 sts plus 2
Row 1: K 3, *cross 2 RK, K 4*, cross 2 RK, K 3
Row 2 and alt rows: purl
Row 3: *K 2, cross 2 RK, cross 2 LK*, K 2
Row 5: K 1, *cross 2 RK, K 2, cross 2 LK*, K 1
Row 7: *cross 2 RK, K 4*, cross 2 RK
Row 9: K 1, *cross 2 LK, K 2, cross 2 RK*, K 1
Row 11: *K 2, cross 2 LK, cross 2 RK*, K 2

Double rickrack: Can be used effectively as an all-over pattern (shown), or one rickrack panel would make an interesting accent or trim.
Multiple of 9 sts plus 5
Row 1: *P 5, cross 2 RK, cross 2 LK*, P 5
Rows 2 and 4: K the P sts and P the K sts of the previous row
Row 3: *P 5, cross 2 LK, cross 2 RK*, P 5

Twigs: Delicate branches traced on a stockinette background.
Multiple of 13 sts plus 2
Row 1: *K 1, cross 2 RK, K 2, cross 2 RK, K 1, cross 2 LK, K 3*, K 2
Row 2 and alt rows: purl
Row 3: *K 4, cross 2 RK, K 3, cross 2 LK, K 2*, K 2
Row 5: *K 3, cross 2 RK, K 1, cross 2 LK, K 2, cross 2 LK, K 1*, K 2
Row 7: *K 2, cross 2 RK, K 3, cross 2 LK, K 4*, K 2

Twill rib: A very elastic as well as an attractive stitch, produced by crossing through two stitches (p. 295).
Multiple of 9 sts plus 3
Row 1: *P 3, (cross through 2 RK) 3 times*, P 3
Row 2 and alt rows: *K 3, P 6*, K 3
Row 3: *P 3, K 1, (cross through 2 RK) twice, K 1*, P 3

Palm fronds: Leaves appear to be embossed on the stockinette background.
Multiple of 14 sts plus 6
Rows 1 and 5: K 6, *K 2, cross 2 RK, cross 2 LK, K 8*
Row 2 and alt rows: purl
Row 3: K 6, *K 1, cross 2 RK, K 2, cross 2 LK, K 7*
Row 7: K 6, *K 3, sl 1, K 1, psso and K it before dropping off the needle, K 9*
Row 9: knit
Rows 11 and 15: *K 1, cross 2 RK, cross 2 LK, K 9*, cross 2 RK, cross LK, K 1
Row 13: *cross 2 RK, K 2, cross 2 LK, K 8*, cross 2 RK, K2, cross 2 LK
Row 17: K 2, *sl 1, K 1, psso and K, K 12*, sl 1, K 1, psso and K, K 2
Row 19: knit

Knitting stitches

Introduction to cables

A **cable** is one of the handsomest of the pattern stitches. Coordinating its technique requires some knitting experience, but once that is mastered, the applications are numerous and fascinating.

Like a crossed stitch, a cable results from an exchange of stitch positions, usually four or more. A double-pointed or cable needle is used to hold the first stitches in waiting while working the next group. Holding stitches to the front produces a cable twist left; to the back, a cable twist right. To make it sharper, the raised portion of a cable is usually knitted, the stitches on each side of it purled. Exceptions are the pattern types, shown below, in which cables are continuous.

Though cables can be worked strikingly in fine yarn, their main use is for sportswear in heavier yarns.

Cables

Simple cable rib: The classic cable on a background of reverse stockinette.
Multiple of 7 sts plus 3
Rows 1 and 3: *P 3, K 4*, P 3
Rows 2, 4, 6: *K 3, P 4*, K 3
Row 5: *P 3, C 4F [sl 2 sts on cable needle and leave at front of work, K 2 sts, K 2 sts from cable needle]*, P 3

Lattice stitch: Embossed crisscrosses, produced by cabling right and left on alternate rows.
Multiple of 4 sts
Row 1: knit
Row 2 and alt rows: purl
Row 3: K 2, *sl 2 sts on cable needle and leave at back of work, K 2, K 2 sts from cable needle*, k 2
Row 5: *sl 2 sts on cable needle and leave at front of work, K 2, K 2 sts from cable needle °
Rep from Row 2

Coiled rope: A spiral, the result of twisting the cable continuously to the right.
Multiple of 9 sts plus 3
Rows 1 and 3: *P 3, K 6*, P 3
Rows 2, 4, 6: *K 3, P 6*, K 3
Row 5: *P 3, sl 3 sts on cable needle and leave at back of work, K 3, K 3 sts from cable needle*, P 3

Sand tracks: Continuous cables form a deeply waved allover pattern.
Multiple of 12 sts
Rows 1, 5, 9: knit
Row 2 and alt rows: purl
Row 3: *sl next 3 sts on cable needle and leave at front of work, K 3, K 3 sts from cable needle, K 6*
Row 7: *K 6, sl next 3 sts on cable needle and leave at back of work, K 3, K 3 sts from cable needle*
Rep from Row 3

Minaret stitch: Slender cabled towers.
Multiple of 12 sts plus 4
Rows 1, 3, 5: P 4, *K 2, P 4*
Rows 2 and 4: K 4, *P 2, K 4*
Row 6: K 4, *yfwd, sl 2 P-wise, ybk, K 4*
Row 7: P 4, *sl 2 sts on cable needle and leave at front of work, P 2, yo, K 2 tog tbl from cable needle, put 2 sts on cable needle and leave at back of work, K 2 tog, yo, P 2 from cable needle, P 4*
Row 8: K 4, *P 2, K 1 tbl, P 2, K 1 tbl, P 2, K 4*

Wild oats: A softly contoured pattern in low relief.
Multiple of 4 sts plus 1
Rows 1 and 5: *K 2, sl 1 P-wise, K 1*, K 1
Rows 2 and 6: P 1, *P 1, sl 1 P-wise, P 2*
Row 3: *sl 2 sts on cable needle and leave at back of work, K the sl st of 2 rows previous, K 2 sts from cable needle, K 1*, K 1
Rows 4 and 8: purl
Row 7: K 1, *K 1, put the sl st on cable needle and leave at front of work, K 2, K st from cable needle*

Braided cable: A very wide pattern, suitable where a bold accent is desired.
Multiple of 23 sts plus 5
Rows 1 and 5: *P 5, K 18*, P 5
Row 2 and alt rows: *K 5, P 18*, K 5
Row 3: *P 5, (sl 3 sts on cable needle and leave at back of work, K 3, K 3 sts from cable needle) 3 times*, P 5
Row 7: *P 5, K 3, (sl 3 sts on cable needle and leave at front of work, K 3, K 3 sts from cable needle) twice, K 3*, P 5

Crossed ribs: A bold, rather large pattern.
Multiple of 16 sts plus 2
Row 1 and alt rows (wrong side): *K 2, P 2*, K 2
Rows 2, 4, 6, 8: *P 2, K 2*, P 2
Row 10: P 2, *sl 4 sts on cable needle and leave at front of work, K 2, slip the 2 P sts from cable needle to left needle and purl them, K last 2 sts from cable needle, (P 2, K 2) twice, P 2*
Rows 12, 14, 16, 18: *P 2, K 2*, P 2
Row 20: *(P 2, K 2) twice, P 2, sl 4 sts on cable needle and leave at back of work, K 2, slip the 2 P sts from cable needle to left needle and purl them, K last 2 sts from cable needle*, P 2

Crossed ribs with fagoting: Cable combined with openwork: suitable for lightweight or medium-weight yarns.
Multiple of 6 sts plus 2
Rows 1, 3, 5, 7, 9, 11 (wrong side): K 2, *P 2 tog, yo, P 2, K 2*
Rows 2, 4, 6, 8, 10: P 2, *sl 1, K 1, psso, yo, K 2, P 2*
Row 12: P 2, *sl 2 sts on cable needle and leave at front of work, sl 1, K 1, psso, yo, K 2 sts from cable needle, P 2*

Crossed cables: Elongated cable ribs in an allover pattern.
Multiple of 8 sts plus 6
Row 1 and alt rows (wrong side): *K 2, P 2*, K 2
Rows 2, 4, 6: *P 2, K 2*, P 2
Row 8: *P 2, sl 3 sts on cable needle and leave at front of work, K 3, K 3 sts from cable needle*, P 2, K 2, P 2
Rows 10, 12, 14: *P 2, K 2*, P 2
Row 16: P 2, K 2, P 2, *sl 3 sts on cable needle and leave at back of work, K 3, K 3 sts from cable needle, P 2*

Honeycomb: A popular stitch for Aran knitting.
Multiple of 8 sts
Row 1: *C 4B (sl 2 sts on cable needle and leave at back of work, K 2, K 2 sts from cable needle), C 4F (sl 2 sts on cable needle and leave at front of work, K 2, K 2 sts from cable needle)*
Rows 2, 4, 6, 8: purl
Rows 3 and 7: knit
Row 5: *C 4F, C 4B (see above)*

Trellis stitch: Example of a cable worked with an uneven number of stitches.
Multiple of 6 sts
Rows 1 and 3: *P 2, K 2, P 2*
Row 2 and alt rows: K the P sts and P the K sts of previous row
Row 5: *sl 2 sts on cable needle and leave at back of work, K 1, P 2 sts from cable needle, sl 1 st on cable needle and leave at front of work, P 2, K 1 st from cable needle*
Rows 7 and 9: *K 1, P 4, K 1*
Row 11: *sl 1 st on cable needle and leave at front of work, P 2, K 1 st from cable needle, sl 2 sts on cable needle and leave at back of work, K 1, P 2 from cable needle*

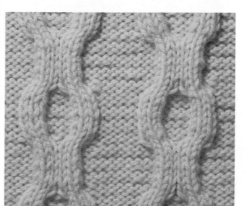

Chain cable: A large and bold stitch.
Multiple of 18 sts plus 6
Rows 1, 3, 5, 7 (wrong side): *K 6, P 3*, K 6
Rows 2, 4, 6: *P 6, K 3*, P 6
Row 8: *P 6, sl 3 sts on cable needle and leave at front of work, P 3, K 3 sts from cable needle, sl 3 sts on cable needle and leave at back of work, K 3, P 3 sts from cable needle*, P 6
Rows 9, 11, 13, 15: K 9, *P 6, K 12*, K 9
Rows 10, 12, 14: P 9, *K 6, P 12*, P 9
Row 16: *P 6, sl 3 sts on cable needle and leave at back of work, K 3, P 3 sts from cable needle, sl 3 sts on cable needle and leave at front of work, P 3, K 3 sts from cable needle*, P 6

Knitting stitches

Slipping a stitch 288
Crocheted loop stitch (boucle) 388

Novelty stitches

Daisy stitch: Elongated petal loops.
Multiple of 10 sts plus 8
Rows 1, 3, 5: knit
Rows 2, 4, 6: purl
Row 7: K 2, make daisy [insert needle in loop 3 rows below the 2nd st on left needle, draw up a loop, K 2, draw 2nd loop through same st, K 2, draw 3rd loop through same st], *K 6, make daisy*, K 2
Row 8: P 2, *(P 2 tog, P 1) twice, P 2 tog, P 5*, (P 2 tog, P 1) twice, P 2 tog, P 1
Rows 9, 11, 13: knit
Rows 10, 12, 14: purl
Row 15: K 7, *make daisy, K 6*, K 1
Row 16: P 2, *P 5, (P 2 tog, P 1) twice, P 2 tog*, P 6

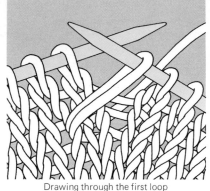

Drawing through the first loop

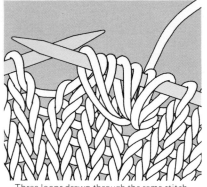

Three loops drawn through the same stitch

Bowknot: Yarn strands carried *loosely* across the knitted face, caught together at a designated point to form a bow.
Multiple of 10 sts plus 7
Rows 1 and 3 (wrong side): purl
Rows 2, 4, 6, 8: knit
Rows 5, 7, 9: P 6, *ybk, sl 5 sts, yfwd, P 5*, P 1
Row 10: K 8, *make bowknot [slip right needle under 3 strands, knit next st, pulling the loop through under the strands], K 9*, make bowknot, K 8
Rows 11 and 13: purl
Rows 12, 14, 16, 18: knit
Rows 15, 17, 19: P 1, *ybk, sl 5 sts, yfwd, P 5*, ybk, sl 5 sts, P 1
Row 20: K 3, *bowknot, K 9*, bowknot, K 3

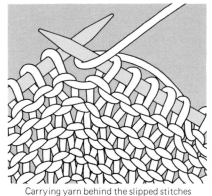

Carrying yarn behind the slipped stitches

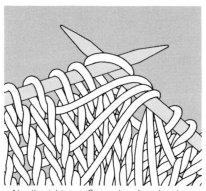

Needle picking up 3 strands to form bowknot

Loop stitch: Shaggy texture suitable for a rug, pillow cover, or trim. The right-handed method is given here since it yields the firmest stitch. If desired, loop length can be adjusted by winding yarn over 1 or 3 fingers instead of 2. A loop stitch can also be crocheted.
Multiple of 2 sts plus 1
Rows 1 and 3: knit
Row 2: K 1, *make 1 loop [insert needle in next st, wind yarn over needle point, then over 2 fingers of left hand, then over needle point again; draw 2 loops through the st and place them back on left needle; knit the 2 loops together through the back], K 1*
Row 4: K 2, *make 1 loop, K 1*, K 1

Winding yarn over 2 fingers of left hand

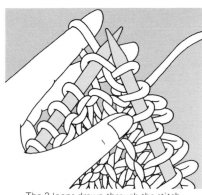

The 2 loops drawn through the stitch

Smocks

Smocked ribbing I: A 2 × 2 rib pattern with groups of stitches tied together at intervals to form honeycomb smocking. One double-pointed needle or a cable needle is required.
Multiple of 8 sts plus 10
Row 1 and alt rows (wrong side): *K 2, P 2*, K 2
Rows 2 and 4: *P 2, K 2*, P 2
Row 6: *P 2, tie 6 sts [sl 6 sts on dp needle and hold at front of work, wind the working yarn around the 6 sts twice, then K 2, P 2, K 2 off the dp needle]*, P 2, tie 6 sts, P 2
Rows 8 and 10: *P 2, K 2*, P 2
Row 12: P 2, tie 2 K sts, P 2, *tie 6 sts, P 2*, tie 2 k sts, P 2

Winding yarn around stitches on the dp needle

Knitting the stitches off the dp needle

Smocked ribbing II: Knitted ribs sewed together at intervals to form honeycomb smocking. Fabric should be twice the finished width that is desired.
Multiple of 4 sts plus 1
Row 1: *K 1, P 3*, K 1
Row 2: *P 1, K 3*, P 1
Thread a tapestry needle with matching or contrasting yarn. Starting at upper right corner, sew first 2 ribs together. Taking yarn behind work, bring needle out 3 rows down, next to 2nd rib; sew 2nd and 3rd ribs together. Taking yarn behind work, return to upper row and join the 3rd and 4th ribs. Continue to join alternate pairs of ribs on each row. Repeat these 2 rows for desired depth.

The rib pattern ready to be embroidered

Working 2 rows of honeycomb smocking

Smocked stockinette: Honeycomb smocking on stockinette. Other smocking stitches would be suitable, too.
Multiple is 4, 5, or 6 sts depending on the spacing of smocking sts
Work stockinette stitch twice the finished width that is desired. Thread tapestry needle with heavy-duty thread. Starting at upper right corner, baste parallel lines across fabric, picking up same vertical stitches on each row. Space basting 4 (5 or 6) stitches and 4 (5 or 6) rows apart (closer for heavy knit, wider for a fine one). Draw up threads, gathering fabric to desired width; fasten. Make honeycomb stitches on the ''raised'' ribs; remove basting.

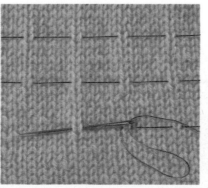

Basting rows over which smocking will be worked

Working 2 rows of honeycomb smocking

Knitting stitches

Knotted stitches

Popcorn: A medium-size knot made by knitting several times into the same stitch, then slipping all extra loops over the first one. Knot size can be varied by working fewer or more times into a stitch. The number and spacing of popcorns in a pattern can also be varied according to the effect desired.
Multiple of 6 sts plus 3
Rows 1 and 5: knit
Row 2 and alt rows: purl
Row 3: K 1, *make popcorn in next st [(K front and back of loop) twice, then slip the 2nd, 3rd, and 4th sts over the lst], K 5*, make popcorn, K 1
Row 7: K 4, *make popcorn, K 5*, make popcorn, K 4

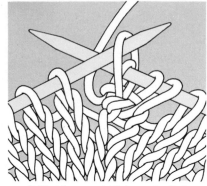

Pulling the second stitch over the first

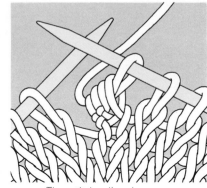
Three stitches slipped over one

Bobble: A dramatic-looking knot made by working several times into the same stitch, knitting back and forth on the increases, and finally slipping the extra stitches off the needle in the same way as for a popcorn (above). The bobble size can be varied, but it is essentially a large knot, suitable for a trim or accent, or to be used sparingly in an all-over pattern.
Multiple is any number of stitches
On stockinette or other background, work bobble as follows: (K front and back of same st) twice, (turn work and P these 4 sts, turn work and K them) twice, slip the 2nd, 3rd, and 4th sts over the lst. Space bobbles as shown or as desired.

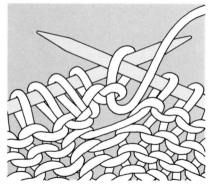
Purling the made stitches

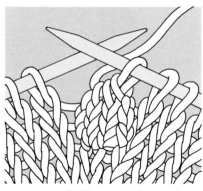
Bobble completed

Trinity stitch: A smaller, less complicated knot than either a popcorn or bobble. It is formed by making a double increase in one stitch followed by a double decrease in the next. Trinity (also called blackberry) is a popular choice for one panel in an Aran motif. Note that at the end of Row 2 there are 2 stitches fewer than you started with. At the end of Row 4, the pattern normalizes to the starting number.
Multiple of 4 sts plus 3
Rows 1 and 3: purl
Row 2: *P 3 tog, KPK into next st*, P 3 tog
Row 4: *KPK into first st, P 3 tog*, KPK into last st

Hazelnut stitch: A flatter and broader knot than either a popcorn or a bobble; it looks embossed. The knot is produced by making a double increase and working it even for two more rows.
Multiple of 4 sts
Row 1: *P 3, (K 1, yo, K 1) in next st*
Rows 2 and 3: *P 3, K 3*
Row 4: *P 3 tog, K 3*
Rows 5 and 11: purl
Rows 6 and 12: knit
Row 7: *P , (K 1, yo, K 1) in next st, P 2*
Row 8: K 2, *P 3, K 3*, P 3, K 1
Row 9: P 1, *K 3, P 3*, K 3, P 2
Row 10: K 2, *P 3 tog, K 3*, P 3 tog, K 1

Aran-pattern pullover to knit

Aran knitting is the combining of several stitches to form a richly patterned surface. This style, which originated in the Aran Isles, is traditionally worked in off-white wool, using stitches that, to the islanders, symbolize married life and a fisherman's trade.

Cables are always included in Aran knits. Other popular patterns are popcorns or bobbles, traveling stitches, such as tree of life (see panel below), and nubby textures like seed stitch.

A typical Aran sweater has a wide center panel flanked by narrower bands repeated identically on both sides. Three to four different motifs are used, each set on a background of reverse stockinette and often separated by two crossed stitches or one slipped stitch. Sleeves repeat two or three of the motifs.

Panel motifs, from right to left: **1.** Tree of life, **2.** Coiled cable, **3.** Popcorn, **4.** Honeycomb

Directions for Aran sweater

An Aran pullover in chest sizes 32, 34, 36, and 38. The style is suitable for a woman, a man (size small), or a teen-ager.

Materials
5 (6:6:7) 4-oz skeins of off-white knitting worsted, 1 pair #5 needles, 1 pair #6 needles, 1 set #5 dp needles, 1 cable needle (optional)
Gauge
6 sts and 6 rows = 1 inch
Panel motifs

PATTERN 1: Tree of life
Multiple of 11 sts
Row 1: P 5, K 1, P 5
Row 2: K 5, P 1, K 5
Row 3: P 3, C 2B (sl 1 st on cable needle and leave at back of work, K 1, P 1 st from cable needle), K 1, C 2F (sl 1 st on cable needle and leave at front of work, P 1, K 1 st from cable needle), P 3
Row 4: K 3, yfwd, sl 1, ybk, K 1, P 1, K 1, yfwd, sl 1, ybk, K 3
Row 5: P 2, C 2B, P 1, K 1, P 1, C 2F, P 2
Row 6: K 2, yfwd, sl 1, ybk, K 2, P 1, K 2, yfwd, sl 1, ybk, K 2
Row 7: P 1, C 2B, P 2, K 1, P 2, C 2F, P 1
Row 8: K 1, yfwd, sl 1, ybk, K 3, P 1, K 3, yfwd, sl 1, ybk, K 1

PATTERN 2: Coiled cable
Multiple of 14 sts

Row 1: ybk, sl 1, yfwd, P 2, sl 4 sts on cable needle and leave at front of work, K 4, K 4 sts from dp needle, P 2, ybk, sl 1
Rows 2, 4, 6, 8: P 1, K 2, P 8, K 2, P 1
Rows 3, 5, 7: ybk, sl 1, yfwd, P 2, K 8, P 2, ybk, sl 1

PATTERN 3: Popcorn variation
Multiple of 3 sts
Row 1: P 1, K into front and back of next st 5 times, then slip the 2nd, 3rd, 4th, and 5th sts over the 1st one, P 1
Rows 2, 4, 6, 8: knit
Rows 3, 5, 7: purl

PATTERN 4: Honeycomb (center panel)
Multiple of 38 sts
Row 1: ybk, sl 1, yfwd, P 2, *C 4B [sl 2 sts on dp needle and leave at back of work, K 2, K 2 sts from dp needle]; C 4F [sl 2 sts on dp needle and leave at front of work, K 2, K 2 sts from dp needle]*, rep from * 3 times, P 2, ybk, sl 1
Rows 2, 4, 6, 8: P 1, K 2, P 32, K 2, P 1
Rows 3 and 7: ybk, sl 1, yfwd, P 2, K 32, P 2, ybk, sl 1
Row 5: ybk, sl 1, yfwd, P 2, *C 4F, C 4B*, rep from * 3 times, P 2, ybk, sl 1

SWEATER BACK: Using #5 needles, cast on 98 (104:110:116) sts. Work 1 × 1 ribbing for 3", ending with a right-side row.
Purl across the wrong side.

Change to #6 needles.
Patt row 1: K 2 (5:8:11), over next 94 sts establish Patterns 1, 2, 3, 4, 3, 2, and 1, K 2 (5:8:11)
Patt row 2: P 2 (5:8:11), over next 94 sts work in patt, P 2 (5:8:11). Continue working in patt until piece measures 16 (16½:17:17) inches.
Shaping raglan: Bind off 5 (6:7:8) sts at beg of next 2 rows.
Next row: K 2, K 2 tog tbl, work in patt to last 4 sts, K 2 tog, K 2
Following row: P 3, work in patt to last 3 sts, P 3. Rep last 2 rows 19 (21:23:25) times.
Next row: K 2, K 3 tog tbl, work in patt to last 5 sts, K 3 tog, K 2. Dec same way every other row 2 times more. Place remaining 36 sts on holder. Armhole measures 7½ (8¼:9:9½) inches.
FRONT: Work as for back until 62 (64:66:68) sts remain, ending with a wrong-side row.
Shaping neck: K 2, K 2 tog tbl, work in patt for next 17 (18:19:20) sts; turn. Bind off 2 sts, work to end. Dec 1 st at neck edge every other row 4 times; at same time, dec 1 st at armhole every other row 6 (7:8:9) times, ending with a wrong-side row; turn. K 2, K 3 tog tbl, work to end. Dec same way every other row twice more. Bind off rem 2 sts. Put center 20 sts on holder. Join yarn to next st; work left front to correspond.
SLEEVES: Using #5 needles, cast on 44 (46:48:50) sts; work in ribbing for 3", ending with right-side row. Purl across wrong side increasing 4

(6:8:8) sts evenly across the row. You should have 48 (52:56:58) sts. Change to #6 needles.
Patt row 1: K 1 (3:1:2), P 2, cable 8 sts as in *Pattern 2*, P 2, ybk, sl 1, yfwd, P 2, cable 16 (16:24:24) sts as in *Pattern 4*, P 2, ybk, sl 1, yfwd, P 2, cable 8, P 2, K 1 (3:1:2). Continue in patt, increasing 1 st (in stockinette) at both ends every 1½'' until you have 62 (68:74:80) sts. Work these sts until piece measures 17½ (18:18:18½) inches, ending with wrong-side row.
Shaping raglan: Bind off 5 (6:7:8) sts at beg of next 2 rows.
Next row: K 2, K 2 tog tbl, work in patt to last 4 sts, K 2 tog, K 2. Dec the same way every other row 21 (23:25:27) more times.
Place rem 8 sts on holder.
NECKBAND: Sew raglans together. Right side facing you, using dp needles, K the 36 sts from back holder, decreasing 6 (6:4:4) sts evenly across; 30 (30:32:32) sts remain. K 8 sts of one sleeve, decreasing 1 st at beg and end; 6 sts remain. Pick up and K 11 (12:13:14) sts along one neck edge, K the 20 center sts, pick up and K 11 (12:13:14) sts along other side of neck; you should have 42 (44:46:48) sts for the front neck. K 8 sts of other sleeve, decreasing 1 st at beg and end; total of 84 (86:90:92) sts for neck. Work in 1 × 1 ribbing for 2½''. Bind off.
FINISHING: Sew side and sleeve seams.
Fold neckband in half and sew to inside of neck.

315

Knitting stitches/multicolor

Selvage stitches 284 Lifted increases 290
Joining in a new yarn 285 Duplicate stitching 348

Introduction

There are several methods for knitting with colors. The choice of any one depends on its suitability to the pattern and to the end use of the article.

When knitting horizontal or chevron stripes and certain all-over patterns (examples below), you change colors at the end of a row. If a color is repeated after two or four rows, yarns not in use can be carried loosely up the side. Otherwise, the yarn is cut and joined with the new color, with enough length left to weave into the edge later.

In wide vertical stripes, an inset motif, or a plaid, color changes occur within a row. Such patterns are usually worked in stockinette with the changeovers made on the purl side. One color is dropped, the next one picked up, and the yarns *twisted* to prevent gaps in the work.

For patterns in which two colors must be interchanged often, the yarn not in use is usually carried across the back by either *stranding* (p. 318) or *weaving* (p. 320). The advantage of these methods is that knitting progresses quickly and evenly, especially if work is done with both hands, as recommended. More yarn is used, however, which adds both thickness and warmth. Typical uses for stranding and weaving are the Fair Isle and similar designs in which a motif (also called a jacquard pattern) is repeated to form a larger design or band.

An alternative to multicolored knitting is embroidery, in which contrasts are worked on stockinette with duplicate stitches. These correspond exactly to the stitches they cover, but stand out slightly, so the effect is somewhat different.

Changing colors at the end of a row

Horizontal stripes: Crosswise bands of color in stockinette stitch.
Any number of rows can be worked in each color, but the minimum, usually, is two rows. The example shown here has a sequence of 10 rows dark green, 2 rows rust, and 4 rows light green. Each color change is made at the end of a row; a yarn not in use is carried loosely up the side, and caught periodically in the selvage stitch on very long spans.

Star stitch: Chunky texture like that of certain crochet stitches. Produced by knitting 3 times into a group of 3 stitches. Tension must be kept loose.
Multiple of 4 sts plus 3
Row 1: Light, purl
Row 2: Light, *make 1 star [insert needle into group of 3 sts as if to K 3 tog but instead K into front, back, and front again of all 3 sts], K 1*, make 1 star
Row 3: Dark, purl
Row 4: Dark, K 2, *make 1 star, K 1*, K 1

Chevron stripes: Zigzag bands of color alternating in any proportions that suit. In the example, 4 rows of rust color are inserted between 8 rows each of green. The cast-on edge of a chevron pattern is scalloped.
Multiple of 14 sts
Row 1: *K 1, make 1 lifted inc L, K 4, sl 1, K 2 tog, psso, K 4, make 1 lifted inc R*
Row 2: purl

Woven stitch: Slipped stitches appear to be interlaced with knitted ones. Double-pointed needles are used to work two rows on the same side before turning.
Multiple of 2 sts
Row 1: Dark, purl, return to beg of row
Row 2: Light, *P 1, sl 1 P-wise*
Row 3: Dark, knit, return to beg of row
Row 4: Light, *K 1, sl 1 P-wise*

Sand stitch: A striped effect that is vertical, though color changes occur at the end of a row.
Multiple of 2 sts plus 1
Row 1: Light, knit
Row 2: Light, purl
Row 3: Dark, K 1, *sl 1 P-wise, K 1*
Row 4: Dark, *K 1, yfwd, sl 1 P-wise, ybk*, K 1

Ladders: A very simple pattern with a distinctive optical effect.
Multiple of 6 sts plus 5
Row 1: Light, K 2, *sl 1 P-wise, K 5*, sl 1 P-wise, K 2
Row 2: Light, P 2, sl 1 P-wise, *P 5, sl 1 P-wise*, P 2
Row 3: Dark, *K 5, sl 1 P-wise*, K 5
Row 4: Dark, *K 5, yfwd, sl 1 P-wise, ybk*, K 5

Twisting yarns to change color

Wide vertical stripes: Broad bands or similar large color areas in which colors are changed mid-row. A separate ball of yarn is used for each stripe, and with each color change, one yarn is dropped and the next one picked up from underneath it, thus crossing the yarns. This technique, called **twisting**, prevents a gap in the work. The near right illustration shows how twisting works on a knit row; illustration at far right shows twisting on purl side.

Inset design: A motif, in one or more colors, set into a plain background. The working method is similar to that used for wide stripes (above). A separate ball of yarn is introduced for each color change, and yarns are twisted at each changeover. When a motif is complete, you cut the contrast yarns, also the extra strands of main color, leaving enough length to weave into the back later. If you prefer, the motif can be embroidered on the background once the knitting is finished. For this method, see Duplicate stitching, page 348.

Argyle plaid: Diamond blocks overlaid with stripes in two or more colors. Adapted from the tartan of the clan Campbell of Argyll. This and similar multicolored patterns are worked more easily using yarn bobbins as pictured. Each bobbin holds a different color, keeping yarn snugly wound until you release the quantity needed. As with the patterns above, yarns should be twisted with each color change. Instructions for multicolored patterns are usually given in charted form. See box, far right, for the way to read such a chart (and incidentally, the chart for working this particular plaid pattern).

Working from a chart

Often a chart is substituted for written instructions when a pattern is to be worked in two or more colors. This is usually the case for plaids, jacquards, and inset motifs, as such patterns are easier to follow in visual form.

The chart is a graph with each square equal to one stitch, each line equal to a row. Plain squares usually represent the background color, filled-in squares the contrast. If a design has more than two colors, each one is depicted by a symbol, such as a dot, and its equivalent noted in a color key (example below).

A chart is easy to follow; starting at the bottom, you read from right to left for a knit row, from left to right for a purl row. A ruler placed below the working row is a helpful guide.

Still easier to follow is a chart colored with facsimiles of yarn colors to be used; the squares, however, must still be discernible. A colored-in chart also serves as a preview of the color relationships in the finished article.

Charts for multicolored knitting are similar to those used for cross stitch, needlepoint, and some other needle crafts. Following the guiding principles above, you can convert another chart for knitting. The success of such a project will depend on how well the design proportions adapt to the knitted scale. A sample swatch will show this very quickly.

Color key

△ = rust   ● = dark green

317

Knitting stitches/multicolor

Stranding technique

When two colors are interchanged often in the same row, it is practical to carry each color that is not in use across the back (purl side). Fabric will be thick, but work will progress more smoothly than with separate balls of yarn. One method for doing this is **stranding,** the results of which are shown at the right.

Stranding is best accomplished by working one color with the right hand (English style), the second color with the left (continental style), as shown below. One hand can do the work, if you switch with each color, but progress will be slower and tension less even. With either method, the unused yarn must be carried *loosely,* or the fabric will pucker.

Stranding is suitable for color changes that occur over one to five stitches. For a broader pattern, twisting (p. 317) or weaving (p. 320) is preferable.

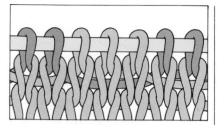
Stranded yarns are carried loosely on wrong side

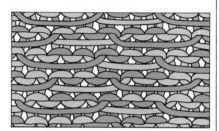
Back of knitted fabric with stranded yarns

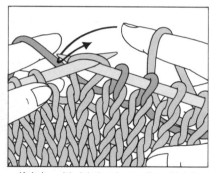
Knitting with right hand, stranding with left

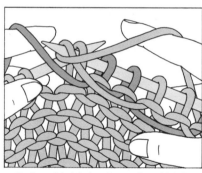
Purling with right hand, stranding with left

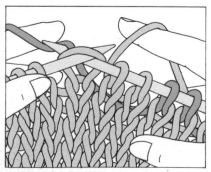
Knitting with left hand, stranding with right

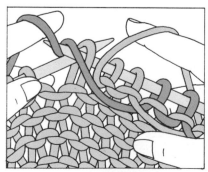
Purling with left hand, stranding with right

Bicolor stitches worked with stranding

Striped ribbing: A classic rib pattern in two colors. To maintain the natural rib flexibility, carry yarn very loosely across the back of the work.
Multiple of 4 sts
Row 1: *P 2 light, K 2 dark*
Row 2: *P 2 dark, K 2 light*

Checkerboard: A simple pattern in which colors alternate in two stitches and two rows. For larger checks, you can change the colors every three, four, or five stitches and increase the number of rows to match.
Multiple of 4 sts plus 2
Row 1: K 2 light, *2 dark, 2 light*
Row 2: P 2 light, *2 dark, 2 light*
Row 3: K 2 dark, *2 light, 2 dark*
Row 4: P 2 dark, *2 light, 2 dark*

Houndstooth check: A traditional pattern stitch that is easy to execute.
Multiple of 4 sts
Row 1: K 2 light, *1 dark, 3 light*, 1 dark, 1 light
Row 2: purl *1 light, 3 dark*
Row 3: knit *1 light, 3 dark*
Row 4: P 2 light, *1 dark, 3 light*, 1 dark, 1 light

Fleur-de-lis: Charming small lilies. Their size is just right for a hat or other small garment.
Multiple of 6 sts plus 3
Rows 1 and 3: K 3 dark, *1 light, 5 dark*
Row 2: P 1 light, *3 dark, 3 light*, 2 dark
Rows 4 and 6: P 2 dark, *1 light, 5 dark*, 1 light
Row 5: K 2 light, *3 dark, 3 light*, 1 dark

Jacquards worked with stranding

Abstract diamond: A lively pattern, somewhat dramatic; can be equally attractive in subtle or bold color combinations.

Flower border: Traditional motif in the Fair Isle style; typical use would be along the bottom of a plain sweater.

Geometric border: Fascinating theme of triangles and diamonds; suitable for a man's or a woman's garment.

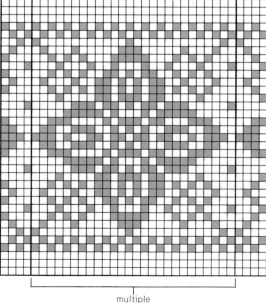

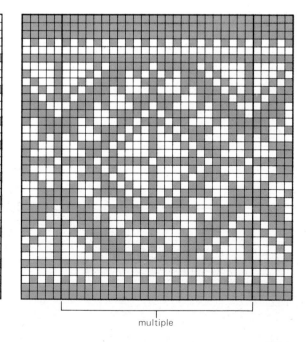

multiple

multiple

multiple

Weaving technique

Weaving is a way of working unused yarn into the fabric back when colors must be carried over more than a five-stitch span. The procedure is similar to stranding (p. 318), but the carried yarn is brought alternately above and below each stitch, in effect, weaving it in. The result is a thick fabric, sturdy on both right and wrong sides. (The carried yarns cannot be snagged as they might with stranding.) Weaving is practical for a heavy outer garment or blanket.

This method, like stranding, is easier to work using two hands simultaneously. The movements may seem awkward at first, but work will go more smoothly as rhythm is established. If a pattern has a mixture of long spans and shorter ones (as in the Greek key, opposite), you can weave the longer yarns and carry the short ones by stranding.

Weaving is a Fair Isle technique, traditionally worked in the round. With this approach, only the *knit* weaving movements must be learned, because the knit side will always be facing you.

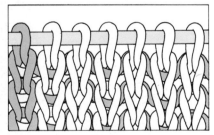

Woven yarns carried above and below stitches

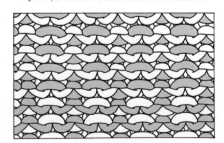

The back of a fabric with woven yarns

WITH KNIT STITCHES

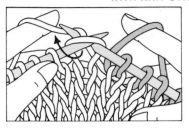

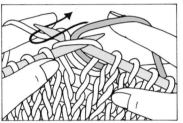

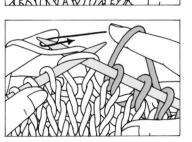

To weave right yarn above a knit stitch, simply hold yarn away from the work with the right index finger, then knit with the left yarn.

To weave right yarn below a knit stitch, two movements are necessary: (1) Make a knit movement with the right yarn, followed by a knit movement with the left yarn (top illustration). (2) Reverse the right yarn, taking it back around and beneath the right needle, at the same time drawing the left knit stitch through the loop (result shown in lower illustration).

To weave left yarn above a knit stitch, bring it over (but not around) the right needle, as shown, then make your knit stitch with the right yarn.

To weave left yarn below a knit stitch, hold it away from the work with the left index finger, then make the knit stitch with the right yarn.

WITH PURL STITCHES

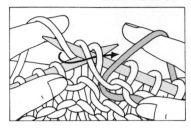

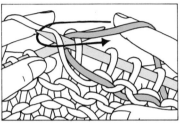

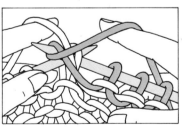

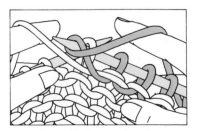

To weave right yarn above a purl stitch, pull it up with the right index finger, then make the purl stitch with the left yarn.

To weave right yarn below a purl stitch, two movements are necessary: (1) Make a purl movement with the right yarn, followed by a purl movement with the left yarn (top illustration). (2) Reverse the right yarn, taking it back around and beneath the stitch made with the left yarn (bottom illustration), then draw the purl stitch through the loop.

To weave left yarn above a purl stitch, bring it over (but not around) the right needle, as shown, then make your purl stitch with the right yarn.

To weave left yarn below a purl stitch, hold it taut with the left index finger, as you make the purl stitch with the right yarn.

Jacquards worked with weaving

Greek key: Perfect accent for a classic sweater; adaptable also for a blanket, pillow cover, or other household item.

Diamond jacquard: Pleasing choice for a boy's or man's sweater; could be used effectively for just the front.

Norwegian tile: Elaborate yet delicate, this design is suitable for a border or an all-over pattern.

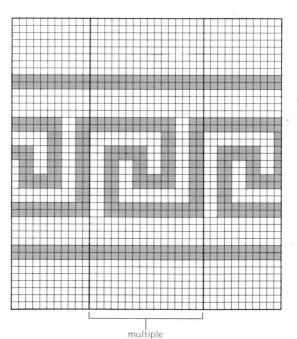

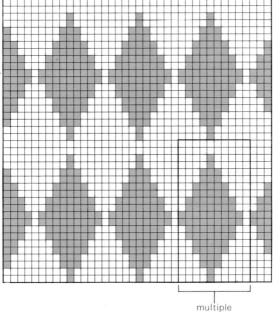

multiple

multiple

multiple

Knitting stitches/charted

Shorthand symbols

Knitting techniques can be represented by symbols, the symbols used to chart a pattern stitch visually. Because a chart resembles the actual look of a pattern, it aids in visualizing an unfamiliar stitch and facilitates keeping track of a complicated pattern. An added plus, no adjustment is needed for circular knitting because a chart represents each technique as viewed from the right side.

Though they are used in many countries, knitting symbols are not standardized. The ones given here are typical, but not universal, examples. If different pictures would have more meaning for you, or if you should need a symbol not included here, you can invent your own.

Listed at the right are symbols, their definitions, and the numbers of the pages on which illustrations of the techniques can be found. As a rule, no more than a few symbols are used in one pattern, so it is necessary to remember only those for which you have immediate use.

A comparison of charted and written directions is given below. For the stitches opposite, written forms can be found elsewhere (see top of page).

Reminders about charted patterns
1. Each row is represented as it appears on the right side. For example, a dot (.), which stands for a purl stitch, would be purled on a right-side row, but knitted on a wrong-side row.
2. A chart is read from bottom to top, starting at the lower right corner.
3. To keep track of rows worked, it is helpful to place a ruler on the chart, and move it upward as work progresses.
4. The multiple in a chart is enclosed by heavy parallel lines, the equivalent of asterisks in written directions.
5. Rows are numbered to either side of a chart; when the odd numbers appear to the left, they represent wrong-side rows, to the right, right-side rows.
6. A chart can show as many multiples or repeats as desirable for giving an accurate picture of the pattern stitch.

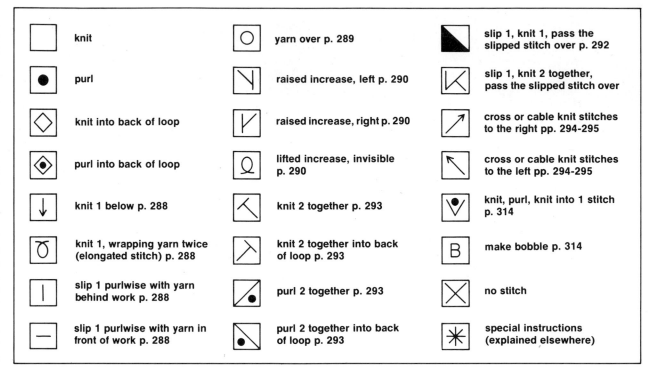

	symbol		symbol		symbol
	knit		yarn over p. 289		slip 1, knit 1, pass the slipped stitch over p. 292
	purl		raised increase, left p. 290		slip 1, knit 2 together, pass the slipped stitch over
	knit into back of loop		raised increase, right p. 290		cross or cable knit stitches to the right pp. 294-295
	purl into back of loop		lifted increase, invisible p. 290		cross or cable knit stitches to the left pp. 294-295
	knit 1 below p. 288		knit 2 together p. 293		knit, purl, knit into 1 stitch p. 314
	knit 1, wrapping yarn twice (elongated stitch) p. 288		knit 2 together into back of loop p. 293		make bobble p. 314
	slip 1 purlwise with yarn behind work p. 288		purl 2 together p. 293		no stitch
	slip 1 purlwise with yarn in front of work p. 288		purl 2 together into back of loop p. 293		special instructions (explained elsewhere)

Charted patterns

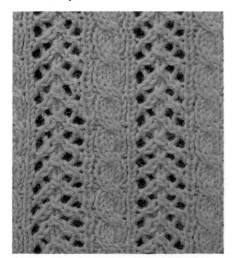

Lace and cable pattern: A richly textured surface that makes an interesting sweater fabric. The directions are given here in both written and charted form.
Multiple of 13 sts
Rows 1 and 5: *K 1, yo, sl 1, K 1, psso, K 1, K 2 tog, yo, K1, P 1, K 4, P 1*
Row 2 and alt rows: *K 1, P 4, K 1, P 7*
Row 3: *K 2, yo, sl l, K 2 tog, psso, yo, K 2, P 1, C 4F [slip 2 sts on cable needle and leave at front of work, K 2, K 2 from cable needle], P 1*
Rows 7 and 11: *K 2, yo, sl 1, K 2 tog, psso, yo, K 2, P 1, K 4, P 1*
Row 9: *K 1, yo, sl 1, K 1, psso, K 1, K 2 tog, yo, K 1, P 1, C 4F, P 1*

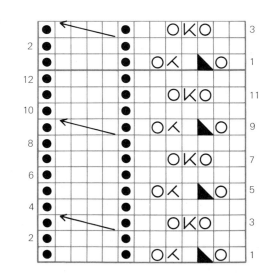

WAVED WELT

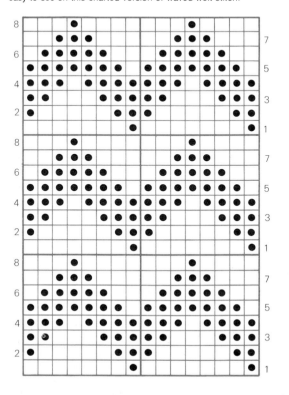

The configuration of purl stitches, as viewed from the right side, is easy to see on this charted version of waved welt stitch.

TRAVELING VINE

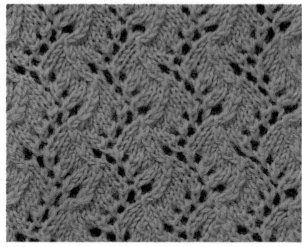

The basic multiple here is 8, but increases to 9 on the odd rows because of an extra yarn over. An X balances the chart on the even rows.

SMALL DIAMONDS

The number of stitches to cross, also their direction and position, can be followed readily on a chart.

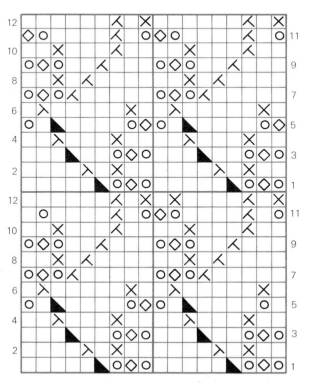

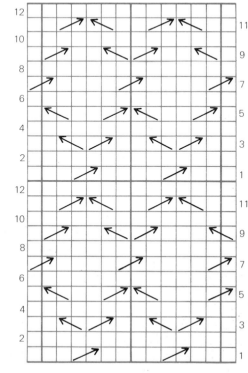

Knitting a garment

Introduction
Taking and using measurements
Designing a knitted garment
Determining yarn needs
Charting a man's sweater
Shaping diagonals
Pleats
Shaping necklines and collars
Shaping armholes and sleeves
Long-sleeve finishes
Borders
Hems and facings
Pockets
Buttonholes

Introduction

Time-honored formulas are used to knit garments. The purpose of this section is to familiarize you with the basic procedures so you can better understand pattern directions, and if you would like to, even design your own garments.

Before knitting a garment you should always do the following: (1) Compare its measurements with those of the person for whom it is intended. If measurements are not specified, you can determine them by dividing a stitch or row total by the gauge. For example, if the shoulder has 25 stitches, and the gauge is 5 stitches to the inch, the shoulder should measure 5 inches. (2) Check the gauge. Planned garment dimensions can be obtained only by duplicating the one specified.

Taking and using measurements

Garment dimensions are based on body measurements plus ease. To achieve good fit, you should know what these are.

The body measurements described at the right are all the ones you might need, but not, of course, for every garment. Waist and hip measurements, for example, are used only for a fitted style, usually a woman's; head circumference is needed only for a hat. To be accurate, measurements should be taken over undergarments and with someone's help.

Ease must be added to measurements of circumference, chest and upper arm for example. Ease allowances range from ½ to 4 inches and are determined by: **the garment's purpose**—a cardigan, for instance, would have more ease than a pullover; **garment style**—a dolman sleeve is fitted more loosely than a set-in sleeve; **the garment area**—more ease is needed for the bust than the wrist; **yarn type**—a garment of bulky yarn requires more ease than one of fine yarn; **personal preference**—a closer or a looser fit.

If you do not have body measurements to work with, there are two other alternatives for sizing a garment. One way is to measure a similar garment (see below right), bearing in mind that ease is included. The other is to work from measurement charts, like the ones opposite, which designers use to plan a garment in a certain size. Such charts are useful as guidelines, especially for determining proportions of a sweater or blouse. It should be remembered, though, that these are merely average measurements. A person's measurements are always more reliable for obtaining perfect fit.

Chest or bust: Straight across back, under the arms, and across fullest part of chest or bust.
Shoulder width: Across back between outside edges of shoulder bones (about 3″ below neck base on a toddler, 4″ on a child, 5″ on a woman, 6″ on a man).
Shoulder length: From base of neck to tip of shoulder.
Neck: Around the neck just above the collarbone.
Armhole depth: From top of shoulder bone, straight down to 1″ below the armpit.
Underarm to waist: From 1″ below armpit to waist indentation.
Sleeve upper arm: Around the top portion of the arm, just below the armpit.
Sleeve seam length: From 1″ below armpit, straight down inside of arm to wristbone.
Wrist: Just above wristbone.
Waist: At natural indentation.
Hip: Around the fullest part (about 4″ to 6″ below waist for a child, 7″ to 9″ for an adult).
Head: Around the crown at mid-forehead level.

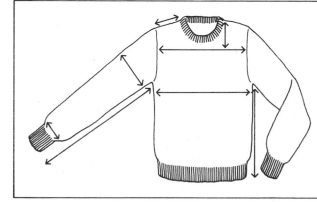

When taking measurements from a garment, lay it flat, and as you measure, pull each seam or area comfortably (that is, without distortion) to its fullest dimension. Take all measurements as indicated by arrows: double the upper arm and wrist measurements for the sleeve width.

BABIES/TODDLERS

Size	6 mos.	12 mos.	18 mos.	2	4
Chest	19	20	21	22	23
Shoulder width	7¾	8	8½	9¼	9¾
Shoulder length	2¼	2¼	2½	2¾	3
Back of neck*	3¼	3½	3½	3¾	3¾
Armhole depth	3¾	4	4¼	4½	4¾
Bottom to underarm*	6½	7	7½	8	8½
Sleeve upper arm	6	6½	7	7½	8
Sleeve seam length	6½	7½	8½	9½	10½
Crotch length*	6½	7	7½	8	8½

CHILDREN

Size	4	6	8	10	12
Chest	24	25	26	28	30
Shoulder width	9¾	10½	11	11¾	12¼
Shoulder length	3	3¼	3½	3¾	4
Back of neck*	3¾	4	4	4¼	4¼
Armhole depth	5	5¼	5½	6	6½
Bottom to underarm*	9½	10	10½	11	11½
Sleeve upper arm	8½	9	9½	10½	11
Sleeve seam length	11½	12	13	14	15

TEEN GIRLS/MISSES

Size	6	8	10	12	14	16
Bust	30½	31½	32½	34	36	38
Shoulder width	12¼	12½	13	13¼	14	14¾
Shoulder length	4	4⅛	4¼	4¼	4½	4¾
Back of neck*	4¼	4¼	4½	4¾	5	5¼
Armhole depth	6½	6¾	7	7¼	7½	7¾
Underarm to waist	7	7¼	7½	7¾	8	8¼
Sleeve upper arm	11¼	11½	12	12½	13	13½
Sleeve seam length	16½	16¾	17	17¼	17½	18

WOMEN

Size	18	20	40	42	44	46
Bust	40	42	44	46	48	50
Shoulder width	15½	16	16¾	17¼	18¼	18½
Shoulder length	5	5⅛	5¼	5¼	5½	5½
Back of neck*	5½	5¾	6¼	6¾	7¼	7½
Armhole depth	8	8¼	8½	9	9¼	9½
Underarm to waist	8¼	8½	8½	8¾	8¾	9
Sleeve upper arm	14	14½	15	15½	16	16½
Sleeve seam length	18	18¼	18¼	18½	18½	18½

TEEN BOYS/MEN

Size	30-32	32-34	36-38	40-42	44-46	48-50
Chest	31	33	37	41	45	49
Shoulder width	13	14	16	17	18¼	19¼
Shoulder length	4¼	4½	5¼	5½	6	6¼
Back of neck*	4½	5	5½	6	6¼	6¾
Armhole depth	7½	8	8½	9	9½	10
Bottom to underarm*	13½	14	15½	16	16½	17
Sleeve upper arm	12½	13	14½	15½	16½	17½
Sleeve seam length	16	17½	19	19½	20	20½

*This is a garment, not a body measurement.

Designing a knitted garment

There are two ways of designing a knitted garment. One is to alter an existing pattern to suit your needs; the other is to originate a pattern of your own. With either approach, you need to make a plan, for which you must have the following:
1. An accurate list of body or garment measurements (see the facing page).
2. A test swatch to determine gauge and, if necessary, to calculate yarn needs.
3. Familiarity with the way to structure each garment area (see pp. 328-341).
4. Paper to outline or chart a pattern.

The first step is to write down width and length dimensions for each section of the garment you are planning. If your plan is based on body measurements, you must add ease, using for guidance other patterns and/or the general criteria explained opposite. You also need to add ¼ inch for seams and plan the overall length, for example, from the underarm to the bottom edge of a sweater.

Next choose a yarn and a stitch pattern, knit a swatch or several, if necessary, until you like the appearance of the stitch, then measure gauge.

To translate garment width dimensions into stitches, multiply stitch gauge by number of inches. For instance, if you are planning a jacket that measures 17 inches at the bottom edge of the back, and the stitch gauge is 5 stitches to the inch, you would need to cast on 85 stitches plus 2 stitches for seams.

To translate garment length dimensions into rows, multiply row gauge by inches. If the jacket measures 14 inches from bottom edge to underarm, and row gauge is 7 rows per inch, there would be 98 rows from starting point to underarm.

To determine the number and distribution of increases or decreases for shaping, follow the guidelines on pages 328-333. To plan garment details, see pages 334-341. Prepare a chart or outline (see pp. 326-327 for the method), determine the quantity of yarn that is needed, and you are ready to begin knitting.

Determining yarn needs

To estimate how much yarn you need for your own design, you can use the amount specified for a similar pattern that is structured of the same yarn and stitch. (For this purpose, it is useful to keep a notebook of patterns you like.) This quantity may not be precisely what you need, so it is wise to buy extra yarn.

Another approach is to consult with a salesperson in a yarn shop. Salespeople will usually have the experience and/or pattern files from which to make an estimate of your project's yarn needs.

If you cannot find either an appropriate pattern or an able consultant, here is a way to make your own estimate: Buy a skein or ball and make a gauge swatch. Weigh it (a postal or kitchen scale will do) and record the weight. It might be, say, 0.4 ounce. Also record the swatch area; if the swatch is 4 inches square, its area would be 16 inches.

Next, calculate the approximate area for each garment section by multiplying widest dimension times overall length. Add these figures together, then divide the sum by the swatch area and multiply this number by the swatch weight. Here is an example of such a calculation:

Sweater back

across the chest	18 in.
length, neck to bottom	20 in.
total area (roughly)	360 sq. in.

Sweater front

area, same as the back	360 sq. in.

Sweater sleeve

width at upper arm	12 in.
overall length	23 in.
total area, both sleeves	552 sq. in.
Total area for sweater	1272 sq. in.
Sweater area divided by swatch area (16)	79

The number 79 represents the number of 4-inch swatches needed to knit this sweater. Multiply 0.4 ounce (swatch weight) times 79 to determine the approximate yarn needed—32 ounces. Deduct 10% of 32 to allow for shaping decreases; 29 ounces is the estimate.

Knitting a garment

Charting a man's sweater

This classic crew neck sweater is presented in both written and charted form so you can compare the two methods. It is a man's size medium (40-42). Though the front and back block to the same size, the front has 6 additional stitches to allow for the pulling-in of the cable.

Materials

5 4-oz. skeins of knitting worsted, 1 pair #5 needles, 1 pair #7 needles, 1 cable needle or dp needle

Gauge

5 sts and 7 rows = 1 inch

Cable pattern

Rows 1, 3, 5, 7 (wrong side): K 2, P 8, K 2

Rows 2, 4, 8: P 2, K 8, P 2

Row 6: P2, C 8F [sl 4 sts on cable needle and leave at front of work, K 4, K 4 sts from cable needle], P 2

SWEATER BACK: Using #5 needles, cast on 105 sts. Work 1 × 1 ribbing for 3", ending with a right-side row. Change to #7 needles and work in stockinette stitch until piece measures 15½ inches.

Armholes: Bind off 6 sts at beg of next 2 rows; dec 1 st at each end every other row 4 times. Work even on rem 85 sts until armholes measure 9 inches.

Shoulders: Bind off 9 sts at beg of next 6 rows; place rem 31 sts on a holder.

FRONT: Using #5 needles, cast on 111 sts. Work 1 × 1 ribbing for 3", ending with a right-side row. Change to #7 needles and work as follows:

Wrong side, P 18, K 2, P 8, K 2, P 51, K 2, P 8, K 2, P 18.

Right side, K 18, P 2, C 8F, P 2, K 51, P 2, C 8F, P 2, K 18. Continue in stockinette, inserting cable pattern as indicated, working it over 12 sts and 8 rows.

Armholes: Shape as for back; work even on rem 91 sts until armholes measure 5"; end with a wrong-side row.

Shaping neck: Work across 34 sts, turn. Bind off 2 sts at beg of next row; thereafter, dec 1 st at the neck edge every other row 5 times. Work even on 27 sts until armhole measures 9"; end at armhole edge; bind off for shoulder 9 sts at beg of every other row; fasten off. Place center 23 sts on holder; attach yarn to next st; work other neck half to correspond.

SLEEVES: Using #5 needles, cast on 47 sts. Work 1 × 1 ribbing for 3". Change to #7 needles and stockinette; inc 1 st at each end every 6th row 15 times. Work even on 77 sts until piece measures 19 inches. Bind off 6 sts at beg of next 2 rows; decrease 1 st at each end every other row 15 times. Bind off 2 sts beg of next 4 rows. Bind off rem 27 sts.

NECKBAND: Sew the right shoulder seam. Starting at left shoulder with right side of front facing you, use #5 needles to pick up and knit 26 sts along neck edge; then knit 23 sts from holder; pick up and knit 26 sts on right half of front; knit 31 sts from back holder. Knit 1 × 1 ribbing on 106 sts for 15 rows; bind off.

FINISHING: Sew left shoulder, neckband, side and sleeve seams; sew in the sleeves. Fold neckband in half and whipstitch loosely to inside of neck.

A man's handsome pullover has crew neck and one cable pattern inserted on each side of the front.

How to make a garment chart

A garment chart is a visual representation of written instructions. There are two different chart forms—**outline** and **graph.** Either can be used when designing or adjusting a pattern.

An outline is a drawing of the exact dimensions of each main garment section, with shaping information written on it. This form gives you a realistic view

of garment shape; can be used later, if desired, for blocking. To make an outline, use sturdy wrapping paper and start by drawing a straight line on it equal to the widest dimension (usually the underarm) of the garment back. Then draw a second line perpendicular to and through the center of the first. Using these as reference points, measure other areas.

Draw the sleeve and any other garment sections in the same way. (Note: If the front differs from the back only in neck shaping, you can draw an alternate line for the front neck on your back pattern, instead of making a second outline.)

A graph is worked on paper that is marked off into squares. Each square represents a stitch, each line of squares a

row. To chart this way, the gauge must already have been determined. You can graph an entire garment section or just the areas that are shaped (as shown opposite); only half need really be graphed. A graph gives a less realistic view of garment shape than an outline, but it is somewhat easier to follow, especially if you use a ruler to keep track of progress.

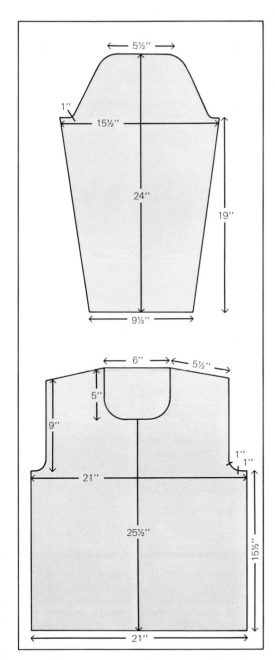

5½"

1"

15½"

24"

19"

9½"

6" **5½"**

5"

9"

1"
1"

21"

25½"

15½"

21"

An **outline** is an exact duplicate of garment dimensions.

½ back

63 rows

38 stitches

½ sleeve

52 stitches

Center stitch

133 rows

Center stitch

½ front

63 rows

35 rows

23 stitches

55 stitches

In a **graph,** each square represents a stitch, each line of squares a row. Only half of each shaped area need be represented.

327

Knitting a garment

Shaping

Shaping a knitted garment is a matter of working increases or decreases where fabric is to conform to body contours.

There are formulas for shaping major garment areas. In this section we have dealt with those for flat pieces (knitted on two needles) and, for uniformity of concept, have presented examples in stockinette stitch. Most flat knits are contoured along outside edges only. Certain dress or skirt styles may require darts for a closer fit, but such shaping is suited mainly to garments worked in fine yarns and smooth textures.

If this is your first experience with shaping a garment, it may help to think of each piece initially as a rectangle, as wide and long as the widest and longest dimensions of that garment portion. From the wide points, you subtract stitches gradually to obtain the narrower and shorter measurements.

These shaping guidelines can be used to design your own garment or alter an existing pattern to suit your needs, keeping these points in mind:

1. After making calculations, you should chart your design before knitting it.
2. Except for necklines, shapings are usually the same for both front and back.
3. Changes in shape are made on the right side and as gradually as possible.

Shaping diagonals

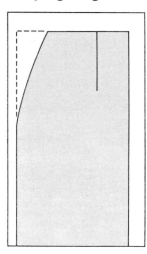

Forming a diagonal by decreasing is the way to shape an A-line; contour a skirt from hipline to waist, a sleeve cap, or a hat crown worked from the bottom up.
Side seam decreases are calculated by subtracting the number of stitches at the waist from the number at the starting point (skirt bottom or hipline), allotting half to each side and distributing them evenly over the rows to be knitted.
Skirt darts are calculated the same way and should end 4″ to 6″ from the side seam at the waist. Average depth is ¾″ to 1″, length 5″.
Hat darts are distributed evenly around the crown.

To shape side seams on a skirt, first calculate the number and distribution of decreases, then work them in pairs. For example, if you are decreasing 30 stitches (15 on each side) over 90 rows, you would decrease at the beginning and end of every sixth row.

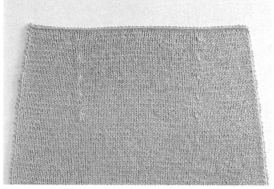

To make paired darts on a skirt, place a marker at the beginning of each dart (approximately 5″ to 7″ from each side). For the first dart, knit to the marked stitch and decrease left (sl 1, K 1, psso); for the second dart, decrease right (K 2 tog).

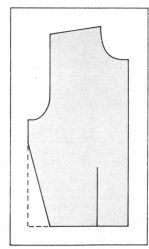

Forming a diagonal by increasing is the way to contour a bodice from waist to armhole, or a hat that is started at the crown. It is also the way to shape the sleeve underarm.
Side seam increases are calculated by subtracting the stitches at the waist from the number required at the bustline, then allotting half the increases to each side and distributing them evenly over the rows to be knitted.
Bodice darts are calculated the same way and increases are begun 4″ to 6″ from the side seam. Average depth is ¾″ to 1″, length 5″ to 6″.
Hat darts are distributed evenly around the crown.

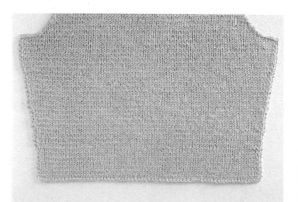

To shape side seams on a bodice, first calculate the number and distribution of increases, then work them in pairs. For example, if you are increasing 20 stitches (10 on each side) over 40 rows, you would increase at the beginning and end of every fourth row.

To make paired vertical darts on a bodice, place a marker at beginning of each dart. For the first dart, increase right (lifted increase is especially suitable); for the second dart, increase left, using the same type of increase as for the first dart.

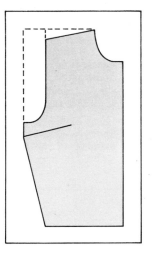

Forming a diagonal by turning is a way to shape a shoulder seam, horizontal dart, or sock heel.

Turning is the working of short rows in graduated lengths, with the steepness of the angle controlled by the number of stitches worked in each stage.

A shoulder is usually worked in 2, 3, or 4 steps.

A bustline dart averages 3'' to 4'' long, ¾'' to 1'' deep; its shaping ends 1'' below armhole. To determine the number of stitches left unworked in each step, divide the stitch total (dart length) by half the number of rows (dart depth).

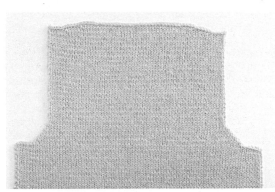

To turn a right shoulder, for example, in 3 steps on 24 stitches, *work to within 6 stitches at end of the knit row, turn, slip 1 stitch, purl to neck edge, turn.* Repeat from * twice, leaving 6 more stitches unworked each time; bind off. **To turn left shoulder,** work as for right shoulder, but start with a purl row.

To make paired horizontal darts, for example, on 20 stitches over 10 rows, *work to within 4 stitches at end of the purl row, turn, slip 1 stitch, work to within 4 stitches at end of knit row, turn, slip 1 stitch.* Repeat from * 3 times, each time leaving 4 more stitches unworked, then knit across all stitches in the row.

Pleats

Pleats add fullness to the bottom of a skirt and, in some instances, additional thickness at the waist. There are two basic pleat types, **regular** and **mock**; examples of each are shown below. Both look best in finer yarns and are most suited to slender figures.

Regular pleats have a *face, turn-back,* and *underside.* When knitting is complete, pleat tops can be knitted together by putting the turn-back and underside on spare needles and working three stitches together across pleat width; they can also be sewed. Finished dimensions should equal waist size.

Mock pleats do not have true folds but the effect of them is created by knitting in a broad rib pattern, such as K 7, P 4, or in a textured stitch with one stockinette rib to suggest a fold.

Knife pleats: All folds face in the same direction; face, turn-back, and underside are the same width. This pattern has a multiple of 26 and is knitted so that the seam can be placed at a backfold. **Right side,** *K 16, sl 1, K 8, P 1.* **Wrong side,** *K 1, P 25.*

Box pleats: The two outer folds face away from each other and the backfolds meet at the center. Pattern shown has a multiple of 58 and is worked as follows: **Right side,** *K 9, sl 1, K 18, sl 1, K 9, P 1, K 18, P 1.* **Wrong side,** *K 1, P 18, K 1, P 38.*

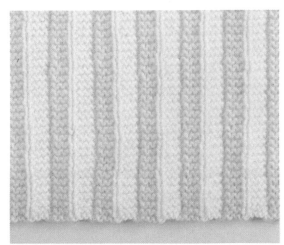

Mock pleats: The impression of folds is created in this instance by regularly inserting a stockinette rib on the face of garter stitch. This pattern has a multiple of 8 and is knitted as follows: **Right side,** *K 7, P 1.* **Wrong side,** K 3, *P 1, K 7,* P 1, K 4.

329

Knitting a garment

Shaping necklines and collars

Special care should be taken in knitting a neckline, as this part of a garment is particularly noticeable. In general, the fit should be smooth, with no gaping or wrinkling; in the case of a pullover, the opening must be large enough for the head to pass through comfortably. For a child's sweater, you may have to provide an additional opening, along one shoulder for instance, because a child's head is large in proportion to his neck size.

The neck width calculation is based on shoulder width and equals about one-third of it, or the number of stitches that remain after subtracting the two shoulder lengths. Front neck depth is figured in relation to armhole depth, and varies according to style (see below and opposite). With few exceptions, a back neck is bound off straight across. If a front is oval or square, the back may be shaped the same way, but would be less deep.

In shaping a neckline, work is usually divided, each half knitted separately, and all decreases made on the right side.

A neckline is finished with a band, a facing, or a collar that is knitted by picking up stitches along the neck edge, or worked as a separate piece and sewed in place. For the first method, a general rule is to pick up 1 stitch for each stitch and 3 stitches for every 4 rows. A more precise approach is to pick up a number of stitches that will yield the required measurement in the gauge of your finishing stitch (a test swatch of the border stitch may be needed to determine this).

Basic neck shapings and suitable finishes for them are given here. These represent typical but not all possibilities.

Square neckline

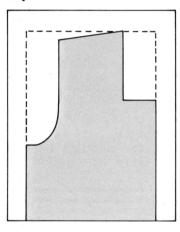

Square neckline shaping is begun 4″ to 6″ below the start of shoulder shaping with the binding off of all stitches allotted for the neckline. (Reminder: The number of stitches for the neck is what remains after subtracting stitches for each shoulder.) There is no decreasing for this style: after binding off the center, you work straight up the sides. When adding a border, as shown right, you can bind off 1″ more of stitches on each side to maintain the full width after a band is added.

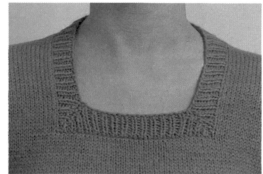

Ribbed band: Pick up stitches across front; work 1 × 1 ribbing for 1″, decreasing 1 stitch at beginning and end of every right-side row. Repeat for other sections; sew sections at corners.

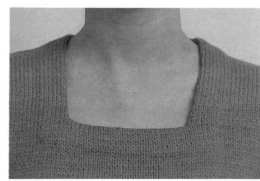

Facing: Pick up and knit each section separately as for a ribbed band, but work in stockinette and increase at each corner; fold facing to wrong side; whipstitch it to garment.

V-neckline

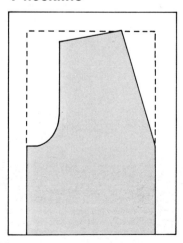

A V-neckline is usually started 7″ to 9″ below the shoulder, or just after binding off to begin armhole shaping. Work is divided at the center and each side is knitted separately, with decreases evenly spaced over the number of rows to be worked to the top of the shoulder. Decreases can be made either at the neck edge, or 3 to 4 stitches from the edge, in which case they must be paired. If you have an odd number of stitches across the front, decrease the center stitch before dividing the work.

Ribbed band: Pick up stitches on 3 dp needles; knit 1 × 1 ribbing, making double decrease at the point every round; or work rows on circular needle, decreasing at each end; sew V edges.

Overlapping band: Work a strip of 1 × 1 ribbing, 1″ wide and long enough to fit around neckline. Sew strip to neck edge with a whipstitch, overlapping two ends at front, as shown.

Round necklines

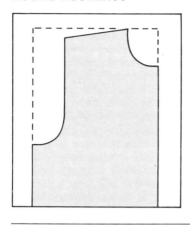

A high round neckline is the classic shaping in the same sense as the set-in sleeve. Shaping is begun 2″ below the shoulder tip for an adult garment, 1½″ for a child's. Half the total of stitches to be decreased are either placed on a holder or bound off; the remaining stitches are decreased at each neck edge every other row. The rest of the neckline is then worked even until the shoulder shaping is complete.

Turtleneck: Pick up stitches on 3 dp needles; work 1 × 1 ribbing (or another rib pattern if preferred) for 6″ to 9″. Bind off loosely. Fold collar to the right side.

Polo collar: Pick up stitches on straight or circular needle and work 1 × 1 ribbing in rows, increasing just inside each edge every other row; work chain selvage on both edges for a neat finish.

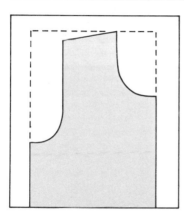

A lower round neckline can vary in depth from 3″ to 4″ below the shoulder tip. The 3″ depth is ideal for a crew neck (right); the 4″ depth is suitable for a summer blouse or evening wear. To shape the 3″ neckline, bind off and decrease just as for a high round neck. To shape a lower neckline, subtract a few stitches from each shoulder and work them into the neckline so that the neck is proportionately wider as well as deeper.

Crew neck: Pick up stitches on 3 dp needles; work 1 × 1 ribbing for 2″ to 3″. Bind off (invisible bind-off recommended). Fold ribbing in half and sew loosely to wrong side of neck edge.

Crocheted edging: Using a hook 1 or 2 sizes smaller than the needles used for garment, work ½″ of single crochet around neck edge, decreasing as necessary to keep the edge flat.

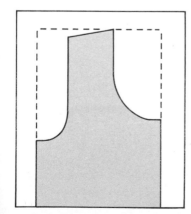

A low oval or U-shaped neckline is begun 6″ to 7″ below the shoulder tip; its overall depth is usually greater than its width. When calculating the division for shoulders and neck opening, be sure to include the width of the band, if you are using one. For example, if the finished neckline width is to be 7″, and the band will measure 1″, the neck opening should be 9″ when you shape it.

Ribbed band: Pick up stitches on 3 dp needles; work 1 × 1 ribbing for 1″. On the bind-off row, work several decreases along the deep part of the curve at the center front.

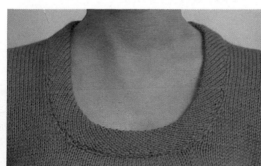

Bias border: Knit a bias strip in stockinette, twice the desired width and long enough to go around neck. Sew one edge to garment; fold in half; sew other edge to inside of neck edge.

Knitting a garment

Shaping armholes and sleeves

The armhole and sleeve shapings are an important part of knitting a well-fitted garment. Five basic styles are described here. The **classic** armhole with a set-in sleeve is the type used most often, and is suited to any garment style. A **saddle yoke** is generally chosen for a sportier style. It is especially attractive with a pattern insert, such as a cable braid, running the length of sleeve and yoke. The **raglan** is a comfortable shaping. It can also become a decorative part of the garment design if the decreases are worked two to three stitches in from the selvage. A **semi-raglan** combines the comfort and decorative possibilities of a raglan with the classic look of a set-in sleeve. A **dolman** is an extension of the garment body and with its deep armhole is the most comfortable of all the sleeve styles.

To chart an armhole with the formulas given here, you need the measurements for *shoulder width* (distance across the back between the armholes), the *chest* or underarm across half the garment, plus standard *shoulder length* and *armhole depth* for your garment size, and for a raglan only, the *neck circumference*. To chart a sleeve, you need *wrist, underarm length,* and *upper-arm* measurements.

The usual way of knitting a sleeve is from the bottom edge up, shaping the underarm seam as a diagonal, increasing symmetrically between wrist and underarm. For comfort, you may want to add 1 inch of ease at the wrist, 2 inches at the upper-arm area. Armhole and sleeve caps are shaped with decreases; if you wish these decreases to be decorative, they must be paired, slanting to the left at the beginning of a row and slanting to the right at the end of a row.

There are two ways to shape a standard shoulder seam. The most common method is to bind off in steps (see sweater, pp. 326-327), which produces a slightly jagged edge. The other approach is to shape by turning (p. 329), which makes a smooth line that can be grafted.

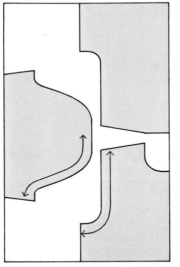

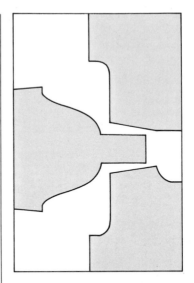

A classic armhole shape is formulated by subtracting the number of stitches for shoulder width from the number at underarm. This figure is then halved and the result is the number of stitches to decrease for each armhole. At start of shaping, bind off half these stitches (the equivalent usually of 1″ to 1½″); decrease the remainder over the next few rows, then work even until correct depth is reached. To start sleeve cap, bind off the same number of stitches as at the beginning of the armhole. Work decreases symmetrically until curve of cap matches that of armhole and measures 2″ to 5″ across. Bind off the remaining stitches.

A saddle yoke armhole is shaped just like the classic style but is 1″ to 1½″ shorter to accommodate the yoke width. The set-in sleeve cap is also shaped the same, but instead of binding off the shoulder stitches, you continue to work on them until the yoke section equals the shoulder length. To fit well, the top of the sleeve cap and the yoke should be no less than 2″ and no more than 3″ across. Keep in mind that the bound-off edge of yoke becomes part of the neckline.

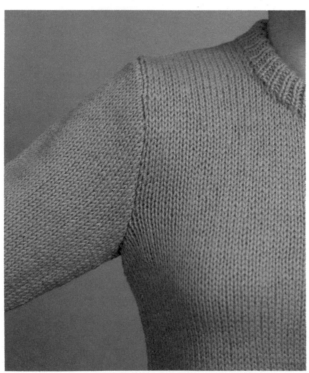

A set-in sleeve has a symmetrically curved cap that fits a classic armhole.

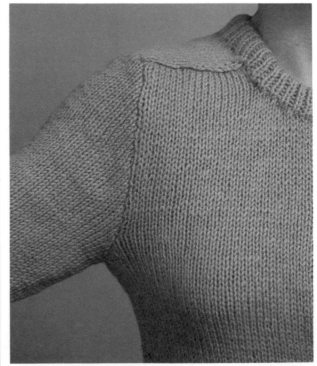

A saddle yoke sleeve combines a classic sleeve with yoke extension.

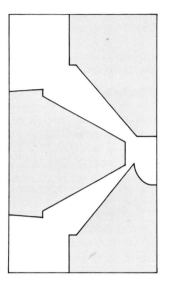

A raglan armhole ends at the neckline and must be planned in relation to it. To calculate decreases, subtract stitches for half the neck circumference from the number of stitches at the underarm. Take off another 2″ of stitches (these will go at the top of sleeves); this figure is the total of decreases for two armholes. Start raglan shaping with a bind-off of ½″ to ¾″ on each side; distribute the remaining decreases symmetrically and evenly over rows to be knitted (armhole depth plus 1″). Work sleeves with the same number of rows and a 2″ width at neckline.

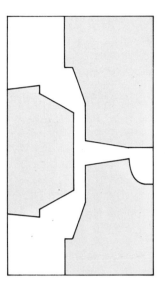

A semi-raglan armhole is shaped like a raglan on the lower half, like a classic armhole on the upper half and shoulder. Calculate the decreases as for a classic armhole, but instead of distributing them in the first 4 to 5 rows, space them in a sloped line over half the armhole depth; work evenly for remaining depth and shape the shoulder by the standard method. For the sleeve, decrease symmetrically for the same number of rows as for the armhole, bind off remaining stitches straight across.

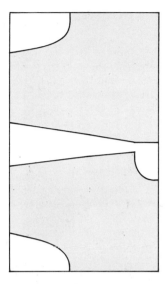

A dolman sleeve is formed by adding stitches to the garment body. Begin shaping 2″ to 3″ below normal armhole depth, increasing 2 stitches at each side over several rows to form an underarm curve. For the sleeve, cast on 1″ to 2″ of stitches at beginning and end of each right side row until you have the total sleeve length. Continue to work even until sleeve depth is half the wrist measurement plus 1″ to 2″ for ease. Shape the top edge by binding off in the same stitch sequence as when casting on. Shape shoulder the standard way.

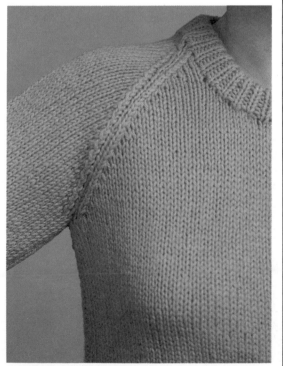

A raglan sleeve is shaped in a continuous slope to the neckline.

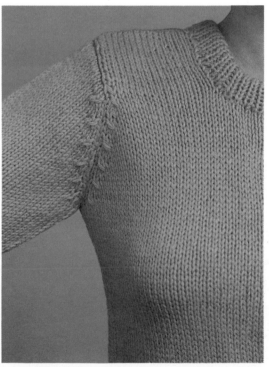

A semi-raglan sleeve has raglan slope combined with a wide cap.

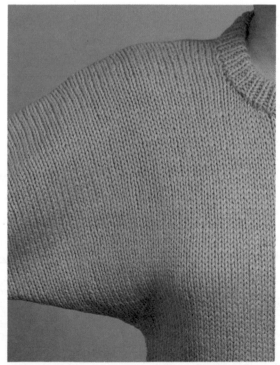

A dolman sleeve is wide at the armhole, narrow at the wrist.

333

Knitting a garment

Seed, garter, rib stitches 280
Picking up stitches 297

Horizontal buttonholes 341
Seam joining techniques 344-345

Long-sleeve finishes

A *ribbed cuff* is the typical finish for a long sweater sleeve. It is usually knitted to the wrist size plus 1 inch so the hand can pass through easily, and is worked on needles a size or two smaller than those used for the sleeves so it will fit snugly. The usual stitch choices are 1 × 1 or 2 × 2 ribbing because these have good elasticity and trim appearance.

A *bracelet cuff* is the type of sleeve finish that might be used for a blouse, novelty sweater, or jacket. It is usually worked in a firmer stitch, such as seed or garter, and so must be combined with a sleeve opening and some kind of closure. (Typical examples are shown below.)

A *border or hem* is a suitable finish for a full sleeve that is wide at the wrist (a kimono sleeve, for instance). See pages 335-337 for these finishes.

Cuff in single ribbing: This neat and inconspicuous style is used more often than any other. Average depth is 2″ to 4″; the fuller the sleeve, the longer the cuff should be.

Cast on an even number of stitches and work in 1 × 1 ribbing for the desired length. When sewing the cuff, use a backstitch, taking in one stitch (1 knit and 1 purl) from each side. The join should be nearly invisible.

Cuff in double ribbing: A bolder style than single ribbing, more suitable for sporty than tailored garments.

Cast on a multiple of 4 stitches plus 2; work in 2 × 2 ribbing, beginning and ending each right side row with K 2. Sew the cuff seam with a backstitch, taking in one knit stitch from each side. The finished cuff will appear to have continuous ribbing.

Turn-back cuff in ribbing: Either single or double ribbing can be used; overall length is 4″ to 5″. This cuff is a particularly good choice for a child's sweater, as it gives some adjustability to the sleeve length.

Following the directions above for either single or double ribbing, knit to within 4 rows of half the cuff length; bind off 1 stitch at beginning of next 2 rows, then cast on 1 stitch at beginning of next 2 rows (there will be a notch at each edge). Complete the cuff. When joining the cuff seam, sew the lower half with wrong sides together; reverse seam edges at the notch; sew the upper half with right sides together.

Bracelet cuff with slit opening: Especially suitable for a knitted blouse with full sleeve. The opening should be 2″ to 3″ long and the cuff ¾″ to 1″ deep in a stitch that does not curl.

To make the opening, divide the bottom of the sleeve into two parts— ⅓ for the back, ⅔ for the front. Work the parts separately, casting on 2 extra stitches at each opening edge for a facing, binding off these stitches again before joining the sections. When the sleeve is finished, sew the seam, turn the facings to the inside and whipstitch them in place. *To knit the cuff,* pick up stitches along the sleeve bottom equal to the wrist measurement plus ½″ for ease. If the sleeve is exceptionally full, pick up more stitches than you need and decrease along the first row to obtain the wrist measurement. When cuff is finished, make a crocheted button loop on the edge that faces the sleeve back; sew a button on opposite edge.

Bracelet cuff with banded opening: This is appropriate for a sweater, jacket, or coat sleeve fitted snugly at the wrist. It could also be used for decorative or novelty styling on a wider sleeve; in this use you would not need buttonholes. Opening should be 3″ to 4″ long, the cuff ¾″ to 1″ deep.

To make the opening, divide and work the sleeve as directed above for a slit but do not add facing stitches. Instead, make a double selvage along the back edge of the opening; leave the front edge plain. Complete the sleeve and sew the underarm seam. *To knit the band and cuff,* pick up stitches along the bottom edge of the sleeve and front edge of the slit. Mark the corner stitch and work a double increase at this point every other row. Make two horizontal buttonholes in the band. When completed, sew top edge of band to sleeve; attach buttons.

Borders

A border or band is an extension of a knitted edge that makes a decorative finish and helps to retain shape. There are two basic types—single, which should be worked in a non-curling pattern, such as seed, garter, or ribbing; and double, which is usually done in stockinette. Finished width ranges from ¼'' to 1½''. If necessary, work a border with needles of a size different from size used for garment so gauges match.

Border knitted with garment body: Direction of the garment and border stitch are the same.
For horizontal border, work bottom of garment in border stitch, then change to garment pattern.
For vertical border, knit the border stitches alongside the garment pattern.
Combine horizontal and vertical borders to edge a cardigan. The effect is similar to a mitered border (bottom right) but easier to work.

Horizontal border

Vertical border

Combined borders

Border knitted on picked-up stitches: This type needs no seam if you sew garment sections together before picking up the stitches.
For a single straight border, pick up the number of stitches needed to match the garment edge. For example, if edge measures 20 inches, and border stitch gauge is 5 stitches per inch, pick up 100 stitches, spacing them evenly along the edge. The finished border should lie flat.
For a single curved border, follow the same procedure as for straight border, but decrease or increase as needed to shape the curve.
For a double border, work in stockinette for 1'' to 2''; purl 1 row on the right side for a turning ridge; continue in stockinette for another 1'' to 2''; bind off loosely. Fold border in half and whipstitch free edge to inside of garment.

Single straight border

Single curved border

Double border

Border knitted separately and sewed on: This method takes more time than either of the two above, but size and shape are easier to control.
For a straight border, cast on stitches needed for length of garment edge; knit desired width; bind off loosely. Lay garment and border edge side by side; whipstitch together on wrong side.
For a bias border, cast on enough stitches to fit garment edge; work in stockinette for twice the desired width, decreasing 1 stitch at beginning of every knit row, increasing 1 stitch at end. With right sides together, backstitch one edge of band to garment; fold strip in half; whipstitch free edge to garment edge on the wrong side.
For a mitered border, cast on stitches needed and mark corner stitch; work a double increase at the marked stitch every other row; bind off and whipstitch in place as for straight border.

Straight border, sewed-on

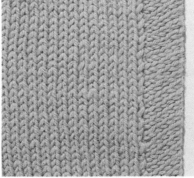

Bias border

Mitered border

335

Knitting a garment

Slipping a stitch 288
Picot edging 338

Hems and facings

A hem is a turned-up finish for the lower edge of a garment; a facing is a turned-in finish for any other edge, such as an armhole. In general, these are functional rather than decorative finishes that help keep an edge from curling or stretching.

To make a flat edge where a facing or hem is to be folded, a turning ridge is usually worked into the pattern. Depending on the desired effect, this can be a slipped stitch, purl ridge on a knit face, or lacy picot ridge (see examples below).

To prevent buckling, a hem or facing allowance is knitted in stockinette on needles one to three sizes smaller than needles used for the garment. Average hem allowance is ½ to 1 inch for an adult; a deeper hem can be worked on a child's

garment to provide for child's growth.

To keep the stitch line inconspicuous, the hem or facing should be sewed with matching yarn, the stitches pulled firmly but not too tight. If yarn is thick, separate one or two plies for sewing.

Making a hem foldline

Purl ridge: Suitable for tailored garments in stockinette stitch.

On smaller needles (one to three sizes smaller) than those used for the garment, cast on the stitches needed for the bottom edge. Work in stockinette stitch until the hem is the desired length, ending with a wrong-side row. On the next (right-side) row, purl to form a ridge. Change to larger needles and continue in stockinette stitch. When garment is completed, fold up hem along the purled ridge.

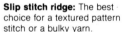

Slip stitch ridge: The best choice for a textured pattern stitch or a bulky yarn.

On smaller needles, work hem in stockinette stitch for desired length, ending with a wrong-side row. On the next (right-side) row, *K 1, yfwd, sl 1, ybk, K 1.* At end of this row, change to larger needles and pattern stitch.

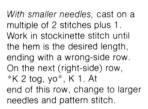

Picot ridge: Attractive for babies' and children's clothing and for dressy garments.

With smaller needles, cast on a multiple of 2 stitches plus 1. Work in stockinette stitch until the hem is the desired length, ending with a wrong-side row. On the next (right-side) row, *K 2 tog, yo*, K 1. At end of this row, change to larger needles and pattern stitch.

Sewing the hem edge

The whipstitch is a neat and firm way to sew the hem on a medium- or lightweight knit.

Using matching yarn, insert needle at a right angle, taking it through the back of one stitch on the garment and a corresponding stitch on the hem edge. Pull stitches firmly but not too tight; otherwise the sewing line may pucker.

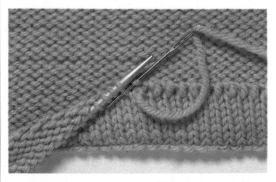

The stitch-by-stitch sewing method is a better choice for thick knits because the ridge on the edge is eliminated. This technique can be used either when a hem is formed at the end of work or is started with the looped cast-on (see p. 275).

For hem at end of work, sew each stitch directly from the needle to a corresponding one on the wrong side (as shown). *For looped cast-on,* sew stitches in place; remove foundation yarn.

A blind-hemming stitch is the best choice for a heavy or bulky knit that has a bound-off edge, because the hem edge is not pressed against the garment. Stitches are taken inside between hem and garment.

Turn hem edge back ¼″ to ½″. Working from right to left, take 1 stitch in the garment, then 1 stitch in the hem, placing each stitch just to the left of the previous one. Do not pull yarn too tight.

Knitting a hem edge to the garment

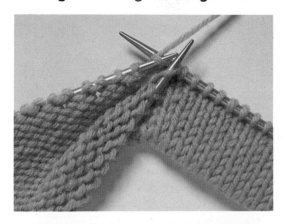

Knitted-in hem on stockinette:
A trim finish for a jacket or sweater for which limited stretch but a moderate fit is desired at the bottom edge. Usually worked without a turning ridge, but you could add one if you preferred. It is very important to use smaller needles for the hem allowance, or the edge will fan outward at the bottom.

On smaller needles (two to three sizes smaller) than those used for the garment, make a looped cast-on with contrasting yarn for the foundation. Work in stockinette until you have twice the desired hem depth, ending with a purl row. Slip a spare needle through the stitches of the cast-on row and remove the foundation yarn. Fold hem in half, purl sides together. Knit together 1 stitch from each needle across the row. Change to larger needles and continue in stockinette stitch.

Knitted-in hem on ribbing:
A firm edge that can be used when a hem is desired on a ribbed border, or for a garment worked entirely in ribbing.

On larger needles (one size larger) than those used for the ribbing, cast on half the required stitches, using the looped cast-on method with contrasting foundation yarn. Work in stockinette for 1″, ending with a purl row. Slip the cast-on edge onto a spare needle and remove foundation yarn. Fold hem in half, purl sides together; change to smaller needles and ribbing, working stitches alternately from front and back needles. Continue in ribbing.

Hemming corners and curves

Hem and facing for mitered corner: Cast on stitches needed for hem, less 1″; work in stockinette, increasing 1 stitch at front edge every other row until 1″ has been added. Work turning ridge.

Continue in stockinette, adding 1 stitch at front edge every other row until 1″ has been added for facing. For facing foldline, slip a stitch purlwise, where garment and facing meet, every knit row.

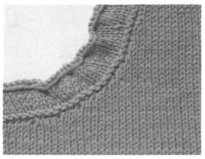

Facing for inside curve: Edge is enlarged to provide for the fact that it is an outside curve when folded to wrong side. Using needles one or two sizes smaller than for garment, pick up stitches

with right side facing you, then *knit* a row (for turning ridge) on wrong side. Continue in stockinette for 1″, making several increases along the deep part of the curve. Bind off loosely.

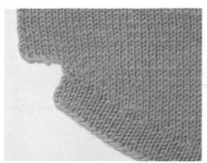

Hem and facing for outside curve: Curve is formed at the lower front edge by working turned rows on about ¼ of the garment stitches and for about 2½ times the hem depth. Cast on stitches required for the hem and knit 1″. Next, work the curve, decreasing the turning stages gradually.

For example, if garment has 78 stitches, you might leave 20 stitches unworked to start, then add on 4 stitches once, 3 stitches twice, 2 stitches 3 times, and 1 stitch 4 times, every other row; adjust numbers to keep work flat. After curve is shaped, cast on stitches needed for front facing.

Knitting a garment

Pockets

Pockets are both decorative and functional additions to a knitted garment. The basic types are inside and patch.

Patch pockets (p. 340) are easiest to produce. Any stitch is suitable for them, including crochet patterns. If stockinette is used, facings or a non-curling border must be added to make edges neat.

Inside pockets vary in style, but all are basically worked the same way, and each must be lined. A knitted lining is best, but a fabric lining plus knitted extension may be preferable for bulky yarns. Directions opposite are for a right pocket; reverse shaping for a left one.

A general rule for pocket placement is to set the center of it about one-third of the distance from the side seam. Average pocket size is 4 to 5 inches square; 1 to 1½ inches is allowed for a border.

Horizontal inside pockets

Horizontal pocket with ribbed border:
Knit the garment front to within 1″ of the pocket opening. Place a marker at the beginning of the opening and another at the end. Continue up the front, working the stitches between markers in a rib pattern (1 × 1 ribbing shown here). When you have 1″ of ribbing, bind off the pocket stitches loosely on a right-side row and complete the row (A).
To knit a lining,
cast onto a spare needle the same number of stitches as for the pocket opening, plus 4 stitches for selvages. Work in stockinette stitch for 4″ to 5″, ending with a knit row, binding off 2 stitches at the beginning and end of it; cut yarn. Work purl stitches across the garment to the pocket opening, purl across the lining (B), then continue with garment on the other side of the opening. The pocket lining is now part of the garment front. Continue to work on all stitches until garment front is complete. Whipstitch the 3 sides of the pocket lining to the wrong side of the garment.

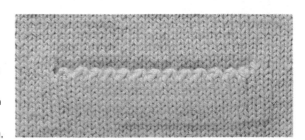

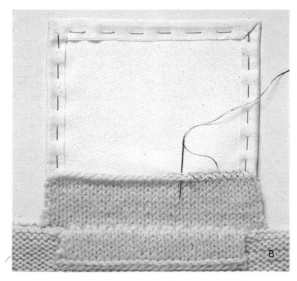

Horizontal pocket with picot edging:
Knit the garment front up to the pocket opening, ending with a purl row. Count off an odd number of stitches for the pocket opening and place markers at each end of it. On the knit row, work to the first marker, then work the pocket edge and facing as follows: slip first marker, K 1, *yo, K 2 tog*, repeat instructions between asterisks to the second marker, turn; change to smaller needles and work ¾″ in stockinette stitch; bind off and fasten off yarn (A), leaving a 12″ end. Thread yarn end in a tapestry needle; fold facing to wrong side and whipstitch it to the garment.
To knit a lining extension,
follow the directions for knitting a lining (far left), but work in stockinette stitch for only 1½″; cut yarn; join extension with garment front as directed.
To make a fabric lining,
cut a rectangle of lightweight fabric 1″ wider than the pocket opening and 3″ to 4″ deep. Press edges under ½″ all around and baste them. With wrong side of garment facing you, fold back edge of pocket extension and whipstitch it to pocket lining along one edge (B). Lay the lining against the garment and slipstitch it all around (see photo, upper right corner of facing page). If you prefer a pouch lining, cut 2 pieces of fabric, sew them together on 3 sides, then attach 1 open edge to the pocket extension and the other to the pocket facing.

Vertical inside pockets

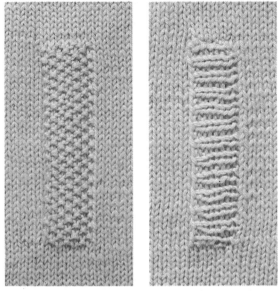

Seed stitch border is knitted on; ribbed border is picked up.

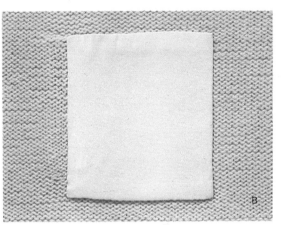

Vertical pocket with knitted-on border: Knit from center front to pocket position; place remaining stitches on a holder. Work front stitch group with 1¼'' of stitches at the pocket edge in border pattern. At top of pocket opening, end with a knit row; fasten off; place these stitches on a spare needle. Attach yarn to second stitch group and cast on 1'' of stitches for lining extension. Work until this side is the same length as the first, ending with a purl row. On the next (knit) row, bind off extension stitches, then re-join the two sections (A), and complete the front. Cut lining fabric 4'' wide and length of pocket opening plus 2''; sew to pocket extension (see facing page, lower right) and garment (B).

Vertical pocket with picked-up border: Knit two sides of pocket opening as a plain slit, without border stitches or pocket extension. When completed, pick up stitches along the front pocket edge and work in border stitch (ribbing shown left) for 1¼''; bind off. Attach lining. Sew top and bottom edges of border to garment.

Slanted inside pockets

Seed stitch border is knitted as an extension of pocket opening.

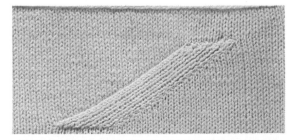

Ribbed border is knitted separately, then sewed to pocket edge.

Slanted pocket with knitted-on border: Work to lower end of pocket opening; place remaining stitches (those close to side seam) on a holder. Working on first group, knit 2 to 3 stitches less at lower end of pocket every other row until 1 stitch of pocket opening remains; fasten off yarn; place pocket stitches on spare needle, leave front stitches on another. Knit a lining extension as for picot pocket (opposite), ending with a purl row. Next row, knit across both extension and side group of stitches (A); continue until this portion is the same length as front section, then join these two groups and complete the garment front. *For the border,* work pocket edge in a non-curling pattern, increasing 1 stitch at the top (front) end, decreasing 1 stitch at the lower (side) end, every other row. Attach lining as for horizontal pocket.

Slanted pocket with separate border: Work pocket opening in steps as directed at left, but bind off stitches with each turning instead of leaving them unworked (B). *For border,* cast on 1 stitch and place marker in it. Increase 1 stitch every other row until border is 1¼'' wide; continue in pattern until border measures ½'' less than pocket opening. Decrease 1 stitch every other row at marked edge until 1 stitch remains. Fasten off. Sew in place.

339

Knitting a garment

Patch pockets

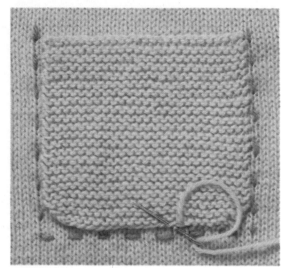

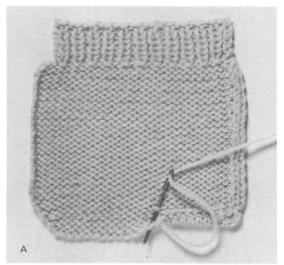

Patch pocket in garter stitch: Cast on the number of stitches for width, less 4. Work in garter stitch (or other non-curling pattern such as seed stitch), increasing 1 stitch at each end of rows 2 and 4. When pocket is desired depth, bind off. Mark placement lines on garment with contrasting yarn; sew pocket with whipstitch.

Patch pocket in stockinette with ribbed border: Cast on the number of stitches for the width, less 2. Purl the first row; continue in stockinette, increasing 1 stitch at each end of first 3 knit rows. You now have pocket width plus a 3-row facing at bottom and a 2-stitch facing at each side. Work to within 1¼" of finished depth, then bind

off 2 stitches at beginning of next 2 rows. Change to needles one size larger; work 1 × 1 ribbing for 1"; bind off. Fold facings to wrong side; whipstitch to pocket (A). Slipstitch pocket to garment. To make sewing easier, insert a needle through stitches along the placement line; sew through the raised loops (B).

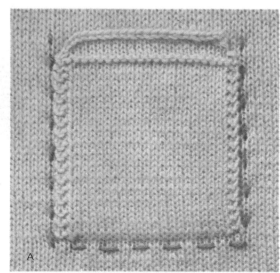

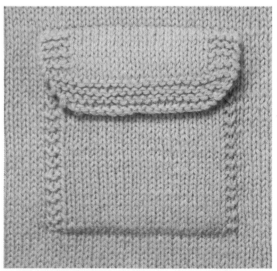

Patch pocket in stockinette worked on picked-up stitches: Mark pocket placement with contrasting yarn. With right side of work facing you and yarn behind it, pick up stitches along bottom placement line, taking up 1 stitch through each garment stitch; fasten off yarn and secure. Turn work, fasten on new yarn and work in stock-

inette with a double garter selvage until pocket is desired depth; work a purl ridge for a foldline. To knit a facing, change to smaller needles and work 4 rows of stockinette, decreasing 1 stitch at each end of knit row; bind off (A). Fold facing to wrong side; whipstitch in place. Whipstitch pocket sides to garment (B).

To add a flap, mark a row ½" above top edge of pocket. Pick up stitches along marked row to equal pocket width. Work toward the pocket in stockinette, with ¾" of garter stitch at each side, until flap is ¼ of pocket depth; change to garter stitch and work for ¾", decreasing 1 stitch at each end, every other row.

Buttonholes

There are three basic buttonhole types— *round,* used for baby garments and eyelets; *vertical,* usually centered on a vertical band; and *horizontal,* suitable for jackets, coats, and cardigan sweaters.

Buttonholes are always placed in relation to button placement. A round hole aligns with the button exactly; the top of a vertical style extends 1 row above it; the front end of a horizontal type extends 1 stitch beyond it. Three key placement points are the neck, the fullest part of the bust, and the bottom just above the hem or border. All others are evenly spaced between these points.

Buttonhole finish is optional; you can leave it as formed, or hand-work the edges as shown below. A ply or two of matching yarn is most attractive, but buttonhole twist is suitable, too.

Round buttonhole
(also used for eyelet):
Right side row, for each buttonhole, make a yarn over, then knit 2 together.
Wrong side row, work all stitches in pattern, including the yarn over.

Vertical buttonhole:
Divide work at base of buttonhole and knit each part separately for the desired depth, then re-join the sections. The last row for both sections must be worked in the same direction. That is, if the first section ends with a right-side row, so must the second.

Horizontal buttonhole:
Right side row, bind off the number of stitches that equals the button diameter.
Wrong side row, work to within 1 stitch of buttonhole opening; increase by working into front and back of this stitch. Using the single cast-on method, cast onto right needle the same number of stitches that were bound off, less 1; continue in pattern.

Finishing a buttonhole

Overcast stitch is the simplest finish for a buttonhole. It reinforces the edge without diminishing its flexibility.
To overcast, take diagonal stitches over the edge, spacing them an even distance apart and at a uniform depth.

Buttonhole stitch is a firm finish. It is the better stitch to use if you have a tape or ribbon facing, as it covers a cut edge more effectively than overcasting.
To buttonhole, work right to left with needle pointed away from the opening, thread looped as shown. Space stitches close together.

Cut-in buttonhole

A

B

C

Cut-in buttonhole technique can be used if you want to add a buttonhole after work is finished.
To make the buttonhole, mark its placement by basting above and below the row where it is to be made and at each end of opening. With small scissors, snip a stitch at the center and carefully

pick out the yarn to each end (A), then tie knots on the wrong side to prevent further raveling.
For a simple finish, draw matching yarn through each loop of the opening (B); fasten off.
For a crocheted finish, make a slip knot and place on hook. Working on wrong side, insert hook in loop

of 2nd stitch at right of buttonhole, make 1 slip stitch, then another in next loop; make 1 slip stitch in each open loop of buttonhole, inserting hook from right to wrong side, then 2 more slip stitches at top left of opening. Turn work; repeat along opposite edge (C); fasten off.

341

Assembling and finishing

Blocking
Washing hand-knitted articles
Joining sections edge to edge
Grafting
Joining sections with seam allowances
Setting in a sleeve
Joining an edge to a section
Inserting a zipper
Adding tape
Adjusting fit
Embroidering on a knit
Alphabet to embroider

Blocking

Blocking is the shaping of knitted pieces to specific dimensions. It can serve, at the same time, to smooth stitch irregularities and flatten curling edges.

Knitting directions usually give blocking measurements. If they do not, or if only some are given, you can calculate the ones you need, using the gauge. For example, if there are 28 stitches on the shoulder, and gauge is 7 stitches per inch, the shoulder should be blocked to 4 inches. If an underarm seam has 98 rows, and gauge is 8 rows per inch, this seam should be blocked to 12¼ inches.

There are two basic blocking methods—*steam* and *wet*—illustrated below and opposite. The first employs moisture plus heat, and is most suitable for wool and other natural yarns. The second relies on moisture only and is preferred for some synthetic yarns and highly textured stitches in any yarn type. Yarn manufacturers sometimes recommend the proper blocking method. If there are no instructions, or if you have doubts about which procedure to follow, use the wet method. It takes more time, but the yarn will not be subjected unsuitably to heat.

Some yarn labels say "do not block." Always heed this recommendation, as certain yarns do not respond well to blocking and may, in fact, be altered unfavorably by it. Most acrylic yarns and some blends are in this category.

Because blocking works on the principle that damp yarn can be molded, it can be used, if necessary, to alter garment size. The amount of adjustment possible will depend on fiber type, how tightly spun the yarn is, and how close or open the pattern. Natural yarns—wool, linen, cotton, and silk—are more responsive to this process than most synthetics; an open stitch expands more than a closed one. Whatever the yarn or stitch type, alteration is usually limited to enlarging a garment one size; it is difficult to block to smaller dimensions.

In steam blocking, a combination of moisture and heat is used to mold a knit to desired shape and dimensions. A steam iron is the best source of steam for this purpose; if unavailable, a dry iron and damp cloth can be substituted. To produce steam, the dry iron should be held lightly against the cloth without applying pressure. *To block a section* as shown here, lay it wrong side up on a padded surface (as described above); adjust measurements. Pin the corners, then pin along the edges as it seems advisable. Fewer pins are usually better, but not if the edges become scalloped. Apply steam until knit is uniformly damp. Leave it pinned until thoroughly dry. Remove the pins and press the piece lightly, if necessary.

A basic blocking need is a flat surface large enough to lay out items to their full dimensions. A padded board is ideal for this purpose. There are directions on page 55 for making a blocking board for embroidery. This would serve nicely for knitting and crochet too, but a larger size, about 24″ × 36″, would be more versatile. A suitable substitute is a dressmaker's cutting board, or a carpeted floor area. With either of these, a layer of plastic should be laid down to protect the surface from moisture. In addition to a padded surface, you will need a towel and a large cloth for wet blocking, an iron for steam blocking, and rustproof pins (the rustproof pins are optional).

A garment is usually blocked before sections are joined; they are more easily adjusted in this state, and assembling is easier to do after blocking. To prepare the pieces, weave in all loose yarn ends, as illustrated at the far right. Block the back first, then the front (s), matching the armholes, and the shoulder and side seams. Next, do the sleeves, matching one to the other so that the dimensions are the same. Do not block ribbing, as it may lose its elasticity.

Pressing is sometimes done after blocking to remove wrinkles or smooth the surface of the knit, or to open seams.

The decision to press or not depends on yarn type, pattern stitch, and personal preference. Most synthetic yarns should not be pressed—heat and pressure have an adverse effect on them. Stockinette and similarly smooth stitches can be pressed and are often improved by this measure, but a deeply textured pattern, such as an Aran knit, would be unsuitable flattened. Pressing tends to even out the natural irregularities of a hand knit, and some people do not press because they prefer to keep this look. If you choose to press, use a damp press cloth and apply the iron with light pressure. Press seams with just the tip of the iron.

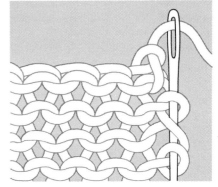

Weave loose yarn ends into a seam edge for about 2″, using a tapestry needle; cut excess.

Washing hand-knits

HAND WASHING
Suitable for any yarn type, but especially recommended for wool.
Wash in lukewarm to cool water, using soap flakes or a mild detergent. Work lather through the fabric by pressing the article up and down; do not twist it. If using liquid detergent, you can pour a little of it directly onto a soiled area, such as a cuff, then rub gently until dirt is removed.
Rinse several times, using the same water temperature as for washing. After final rinse, drain water, then lift the article and, supporting it with both hands, gently squeeze out excess water. Roll it in a towel and squeeze again to remove as much moisture as possible.
Dry article on a flat surface, molding it into shape (see method, left); allow to dry completely before moving it.

MACHINE WASHING
Use only when indicated by yarn label. Turn garment wrong side out first.
Wash with setting on "delicate synthetic" or "gentle" cycle and warm or cold water.
Rinse with cold water, adding fabric softener to the final rinse if possible.
Dry in automatic dryer with low setting (no hotter than 120 degrees), removing article when it is just dry. Check its condition every few minutes during the drying process, as the required time may be less than a full machine cycle.

In wet blocking, moisture alone is used to mold a knit. *To block a section* (as shown opposite), lay it on a wet towel and adjust measurements, pinning if necessary. Lay a damp cloth over the knit; leave knit undisturbed until dry. *To block a finished piece* (one that is wet from washing), squeeze out excess moisture, then lay knit on a dry towel. Push or "bunch" knit into shape; check measurements if necessary; let dry thoroughly before moving.

Assembling and finishing

Joining sections edge to edge

The joining of knitted sections edge to edge makes a smooth, bulkless seam that is nearly invisible. There are two ways to do this: **weaving** finished edges (see directly below); and **grafting** stitches (bottom of page). Both methods are especially recommended for heavy yarns.

Four weaving methods are illustrated below. All are worked basically the same way, that is, yarn is woven under alternate loops on each edge so that a row of stitches is formed between the sections. One strand of the knitting yarn is best for this purpose, unless it is nubbly; then a matching smooth yarn might be substituted. A tapestry needle is advisable because it will not split yarn. Edges to be joined must be neat and have equal numbers of stitches; otherwise use methods at top of the facing page.

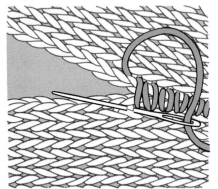

Stockinette—side seams: Lay sections right side up, corresponding stitches aligned. Attach yarn at right end. *Insert needle under next horizontal loop adjacent to edge stitch on one section, then under corresponding loop on the other.*

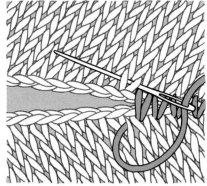

Stockinette—shoulder seams: Lay sections right side up, corresponding stitches aligned. Attach yarn at right end. *Take needle under next knit stitch adjacent to bind off on one section, then under next knit stitch on the other.*

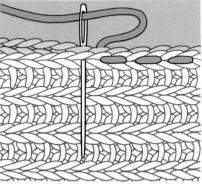

Ribbing—side seams: Hold sections right sides together, corresponding stitches aligned. Attach yarn at right end. *Bring needle up through centers of next 2 corresponding edge stitches, then down through centers of next 2 stitches.*

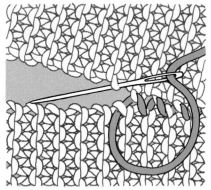

Garter stitch—side seams: Lay sections right side up, corresponding stitches aligned. Attach yarn at right end. *Insert the tapestry needle through lower loop on one edge, then through corresponding upper loop on the other edge.*

Grafting

Grafting, also called kitchener stitch, is a way of joining sections horizontally so that the seam is smooth and elastic. It is accomplished by weaving stitches together, directly from the needles.

To graft, both edges must have the same number of stitches. Grafting is always used to join the side of a sock heel to the body; it is also suitable for joining shoulders that were shaped by turning.

There are two ways to position the work for grafting; use whichever feels most comfortable. **(1)** Hold both needles in the left hand with wrong sides of the work facing each other. **(2)** Lay the two sections faceup on a table, as illustrated below. To sew, use a tapestry needle and one strand of matching yarn, removing each stitch from the needle after yarn has been pulled through.

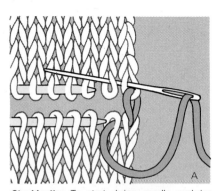

Stockinette: To start, bring needle *purlwise* through bottom and top end stitches; re-insert *knitwise* in bottom stitch, *purlwise* through next stitch on needle. *Insert needle *knitwise* in top

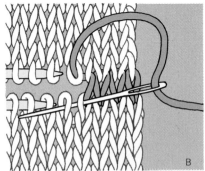

stitch where thread emerges, *purlwise* through next stitch on needle (A). Insert needle *knitwise* through bottom stitch where thread emerges, *purlwise* through next stitch on needle (B).*

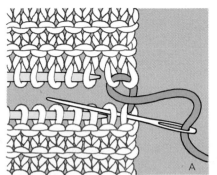

Garter stitch: To start, bring tapestry needle *purlwise* through bottom and top end stitches, then insert *knitwise* through next top stitch. *Insert needle *knitwise* in bottom stitch where

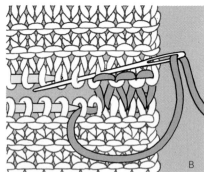

thread emerges, then *purlwise* through next stitch on needle (A). Insert needle *purlwise* through top stitch where thread emerges, then *knitwise* through next stitch on needle (B).*

Joining sections with seam allowances

Joining with seam allowances is ideal for sections on which edges are uneven, such as a shoulder that has been bound off in steps. It is also suitable for taking in a garment or shaping curved seams, as the stitches can be made any distance from the edge. Two methods are shown below. Both make sturdy and neat joinings with any yarn type, but are best suited to fine or medium weights.

Setting in a sleeve

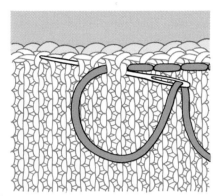

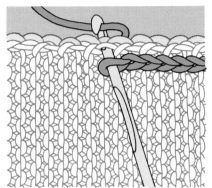

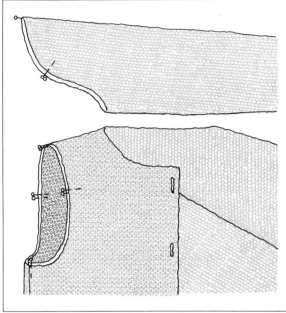

A sleeve cap is curved differently than the armhole and is sometimes slightly larger. Follow these steps to ensure a smooth joining. First, join garment side and shoulder seams and the sleeve underarm seam. Fold sleeve in half; place a pin in center of cap. Set two more pins on each side halfway between center of cap and underarm seam. On the garment, place pins at shoulder and halfway between shoulder and underarm seams. With sleeve and garment right sides together, pin sleeve to armhole, matching pins and underarm seams. Insert more pins if needed. Sew seam inside sleeve with backstitch.

Backstitch: Using tapestry needle and matching yarn, bring needle up 2 stitches ahead of edge, *Insert it 2 stitches back (within row, at the point where thread emerged for previous stitch); bring it out 2 stitches ahead of emerging thread.

Slip stitch: Using a crochet hook of appropriate size and matching yarn, draw a loop through a corresponding stitch on each section; *insert hook through next 2 stitches; draw a loop through both stitches and the loop on the hook.*

Joining an edge to a section

The joining of an edge with a section should be as inconspicuous as possible. Choose a suitable method from those below; as you work, stretch the knit gently now and then to prevent puckering.

The **whipstitch** is used for most flat edges; it makes a firm joining and, at the same time, keeps the edge from curling. A **slipstitch** is suitable only for a folded edge. You would use it, for example, to sew on a patch pocket that has turned-under facings. A **stitch-by-stitch** method is an inconspicuous joining for heavy yarns. It is used primarily when the hem or facing is formed at the end of work, but could be used with a looped cast-on. Stitches can be sewed in the same way as a whipstitch, or by the technique shown below, in which the knit and purl stitches are duplicated.

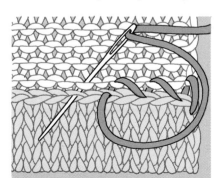

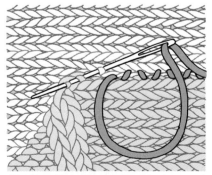

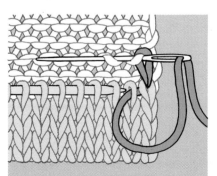

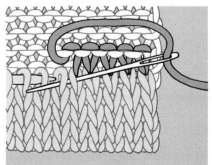

Whipstitch: *Insert needle at a right angle under 1 loop (purl stitch) on the garment, then under 1 strand of a corresponding stitch on the hem or facing edge; pull yarn through.*

Slipstitch: *Insert the needle under 1 garment stitch (preferably a purl stitch if the fabric is stockinette), then under 1 or 2 stitches of the folded edge; pull yarn through.*

Stitch-by-stitch: To start, insert needle purlwise in 1st stitch on knitting needle, up through 1st purl stitch on garment and down through next purl stitch. *Insert the needle knitwise through knit stitch where thread emerges, then purlwise through next stitch on knitting needle. Insert the needle up through purl stitch where thread emerges, down through next purl stitch.*

Assembling and finishing

Knitted buttonholes 341   Whipstitch 345
Backstitch 345   Crocheted slip stitch 363

Inserting a zipper

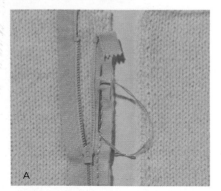

Sewing first half of zipper with the backstitch

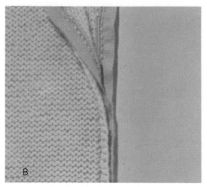

Second half of zipper sewed in place

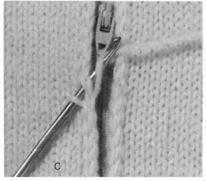

Finishing the edge with crocheted slip stitches

For a garment of fine or medium-weight yarn, adding crochet to the edges of the zipper opening makes them flat, neat, and firm.
To face the zipper opening, work 1 or 2 rows of single crochet along each side.
To attach zipper, open it and place half of zipper face down against right side of garment, having edge of tape face edge of garment. Sew tape to garment with a backstitch, placing stitches along the line where crochet meets the edge of the knitting (A). Fold garment right sides together with opening edges aligned so that second half of the zipper can be sewed exactly as first half was (B). Close zipper; press zipper opening lightly from right side. Work a row of crocheted slip stitches along both edges of the zipper opening (C).

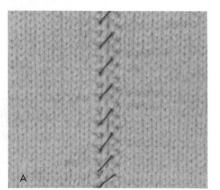

Garment edges basted

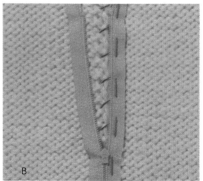

Basting zipper to the inside of the garment

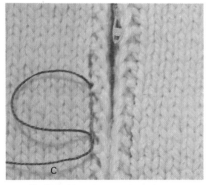

Backstitching zipper to the garment

For a garment of heavy or tweedy yarn, a two-stitch selvage makes a neat and firm finish for the edge of the zipper opening.
To border the zipper opening, substitute a selvage for 2 stitches of the pattern. Double chain edge or double garter edge is suitable (see p. 284 for the methods). With large overcast stitches, baste the border edges together on the right side (A).
To attach zipper, baste it to wrong side of the garment, teeth aligned with center of the opening (B). On the right side, sew zipper to the garment with a backstitch, placing stitches along the line where border meets edge of the pattern stitch (C). Use buttonhole twist or a double strand of heavy-duty thread in a matching color.

Adding tape

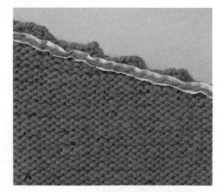

Twill tape added to a seam

Ribbon backing for buttonholes on a cardigan

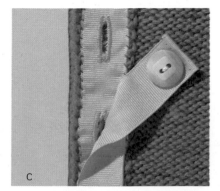

Tape with buttons, inserted in buttonholes

A seam can be taped when extra stability is needed, for example, on a jacket shoulder. Twill tape ⅜″ or ½″ wide is suitable.
To attach tape, center it over the seam on one section; baste in place. Backstitch seam (A).
Buttonhole and button edges are often backed to prevent sagging; twill tape and grosgrain are suitable. Cut 2 pieces to fit; whipstitch one to edge on which buttons will be sewed; baste other to buttonhole edge and mark buttonhole placements. Remove tape; work buttonholes in it by machine or hand. Re-baste tape, aligning buttonholes; whipstitch edges (B). On right side, finish buttonholes.
Buttons can be sewed to tape to make a child's cardigan suitable for a girl or a boy. Work buttonholes on both sides of cardigan; button the tape onto whichever side is suitable (C).

Adjusting fit

ADDING ELASTIC

Elastic thread woven into back of ribbing

Elastic thread inserted through ribbing back

Elastic inserted through a casing stitch

Elastic stitched with machine zigzag

TAKING IN WIDTH

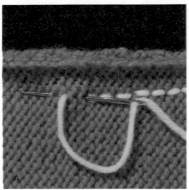

A seam taken in with a backstitch

Seam allowances trimmed and overcast

A snugger fit for a cap or socks is obtained by adding elastic thread to the ribbing, either weaving or threading it. **Weave in elastic** as you knit, carrying it on the wrong side as if it were a second color (see p. 320 for weaving technique). **Thread the elastic** after ribbing is completed, using tapestry needle and inserting it under the vertical knit ribs along each row on the wrong side. **A close yet flexible fit at the waist** is achieved by drawing elastic through a band or casing stitch, or stitching it in place; the last two methods are shown. **For casing stitch,** use a crochet hook to form zigzag chain that is anchored to garment with slip stitches, fits snugly over elastic. **For stitched elastic,** cut elastic to fit waist; join ends. With pins, divide elastic and waistline in 8 sections; pin them together, matching divisions. With machine zigzag, stitch top and bottom edges of elastic, stretching to fit garment.

A garment can be made smaller, if necessary, or a curve can be shaped in a straight seam, by sewing a new seam with a backstitch (A). Such an adjustment may result in a bulky or unsightly seam allowance that can be eliminated as follows: Trim the seam allowance to within ¼" of the seam; then overcast the trimmed edges (B).

SHORTENING OR LENGTHENING

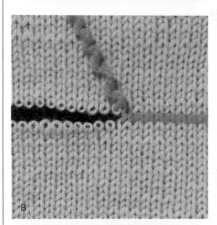

If necessary, a garment can be shortened after it is finished by separating the unwanted length from the garment. This can be done, however, only with a simple pattern, such as stockinette or garter stitch. Before beginning, open the seams to the cut-off point. Snip a yarn at one edge and start to draw it out (A). Snip the other end of the yarn at the opposite edge; draw yarn out completely. Both sections are now completely separated (B). Insert a needle through stitches along garment edge and knit a border or hem as desired.

If necessary, a garment can be lengthened after it is finished by removing the foundation yarn of the cast-on row (C), inserting a needle through the stitches, and knitting on the needed length. This procedure is suitable for any pattern stitch. Since lengthening might be required for a child's garment, you can plan for it in several ways:
(1) Buy extra yarn; knit it into a large swatch and wash it each time you wash the garment. When it is time to lengthen the garment, ravel the swatch and use the yarn to knit the extra length; it should match perfectly.
(2) Cast on the garment stitches using the looped cast-on, as its foundation yarn is easily removed; or
(3) knit the garment sections from the top down, as a bound-off row is easy to undo.

347

Assembling and finishing

Embroidery yarns 8   Tapestry needles 273   Jacquard techniques 318, 320

Embroidering on a knit

Simple knitted patterns, such as garter, seed, and stockinette, can be enhanced with embroidery. This is a particularly nice touch on a child's garment.

Embroidery techniques that work well on knitted fabric are chain stitches (pp. 28-32), in particular a lazy daisy; detached filling stitches (pp. 42-43), especially bullions; and raised needle-weaving (p. 52), which permits the making of a solid motif without stretching the fabric. Basic cross stitch and its variations are also suitable, because a knitted structure lends itself naturally to any counted thread technique.

Duplicate stitch, also called Swiss darning, is another suitable embroidery form and one that is unique to knitting. It is a way of working over stockinette stitches so that they are outlined precisely. Using duplicate stitch, you can, if you prefer, work a jacquard pattern over plain fabric instead of working in the additional color(s) as you knit. Use it also to embroider motifs, such as the letters graphed opposite.

Transfer of a design should not be attempted with hand-knitted fabric. It is helpful, however, to mark the area to be embroidered by basting around it with contrasting yarn. If a design has several parts, you could mark each with a different color. When working from a graph (on which each stitch is represented by a square), remember that knit stitches are wider than they are tall and adjust proportions, if necessary, making them taller and narrower to compensate for this widening. To preview results, use the charting method below.

The most appropriate yarn for embroidering on a knit is one that matches the knitting yarn in type and thickness. If yarn is thinner, it tends to sink into the fabric; yarn that is thicker could stretch the knit. If you have no yarn leftovers suitable for this purpose, you can buy small skeins of embroidery or needle-point yarns, such as crewel, tapestry, Persian, pearl cotton, or embroidery floss, and use the number of strands that matches the knitting yarn weight.

To start the embroidery, thread yarn in a tapestry needle (this type will not split the stitches) and bring it through from the wrong side, leaving an end long enough to weave into the back later. For the basic cross stitch or the duplicate stitch, follow directions on this page; for other stitches, see appropriate embroidery pages. Take special care not to pull stitches too tight. After completion, a light steam blocking may be needed; do not press the embroidered area.

CROSS STITCHING ON STOCKINETTE

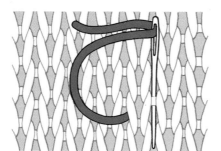

To form a basic cross stitch, bring needle up under a purl strand connecting 2 knit stitches; *cross right, take needle down behind the purl strand that lies between next 2 knit stitches.

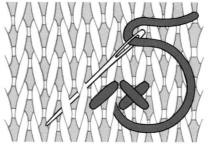

Cross left, insert needle above purl strand between the 2 stitches where thread emerges, then take it diagonally behind next knit stitch, and bring it out again under the next purl stitch.*

DUPLICATE STITCHING ON STOCKINETTE

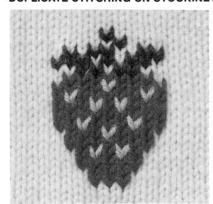

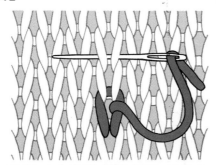

To form a duplicate stitch, *bring needle up under the connecting strand at the bottom of a knit stitch (where strands lie close together), then right to left behind knit stitch above.

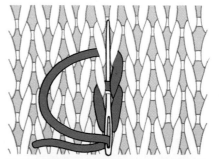

Insert needle bottom to top under same strand where thread emerges for 1st half of stitch.* As you work, take care to match the tension of the knitting, otherwise the fabric may pucker.

MAKING A CHART FOR EMBROIDERY

A charted embroidery design is usually represented on a graph in which one square equals one stitch. If you use such a chart to embroider on a knit, the design will flatten out because knit stitches are always wider than they are tall. To be sure that a design will work on a knit fabric, you can first adapt it to a rectangular chart like the one shown below. These rectangles are 1/8" high by 3/16" wide, and nearly duplicate the proportions of most knit stitches. (Compare the chart with the embroidered samples to the left).

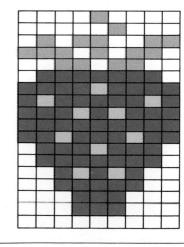

Alphabet to embroider

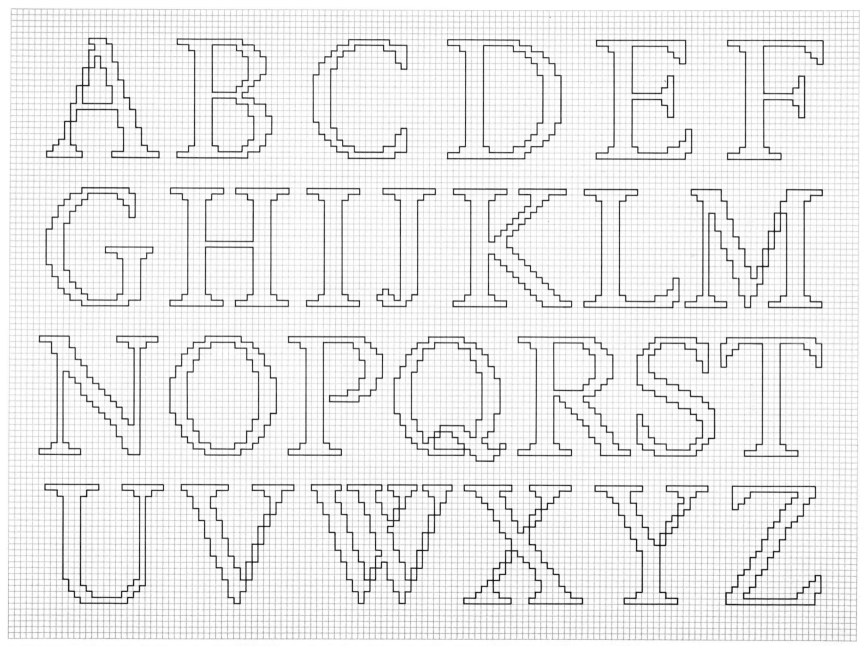

An initial or monogram can be added to your hand-knitted project, using the duplicate stitch and the letters above (see the sock, p. 352, for an example).

Children's sweaters and hats

ALL-OVER-STRIPE SET

Size

Directions are for size 4 (24½″ chest); changes for size 6 (26″) in parentheses.

Materials needed

Acrylic yarn in knitting worsted weight: 5 (6) ozs. blue, 5 (6) ozs. white, 2 (3) ozs. bright yellow, 1 (1) oz. each green and turquoise; knitting needles, 1 pair #5, 1 pair #7; crochet hooks sizes F and G; seven ⅜″ buttons; tapestry needle

Gauge

9 sts and 13 rows = 2″ in stockinette st

Sweater back

Using #5 needles, cast on 56 (60) sts with blue yarn. Work 1 × 1 ribbing for 1 row. Attach white, leaving blue at the side. Work 2 rows of ribbing with white, 2 rows blue, 2 rows white, 2 rows blue. Change to #7 needles and work in stockinette st, alternating 2 rows white, 2 rows blue until piece measures 8¼″ (9½″), ending with P row in blue; fasten off. Attach green and K 2 rows; attach turquoise and K 2 rows; K 2 more rows each of green, turquoise, green; fasten off. Attach yellow; K 1 row, P 1 row.

Shaping armholes: Attach white and continue in stockinette, binding off 3 sts at beg of next 2 rows; then alternate 2 rows yellow with 2 rows white, dec 1 st at each end every other row. Work even on rem 44 (48) sts until armholes measure 4″ (4¼″), ending with a K row. P next row, binding off center 18 (20) sts.

Shaping neck: Working one half of neck [13 (14) sts], dec 1 st at neck edge every other row twice; work even until armhole measures 5″ (5¼″). **Shoulders:** At armhole edge, bind off 6 (6) sts at beg of next row, 5 (6) sts at beg of next row; fasten off. Work the other half of the neck and shoulder to correspond.

Right front

Using #5 needles, cast on 28 (30) sts with blue yarn. Work as for back until armhole measures 3½″ (3¾″). **Shaping neck:** At neck edge, bind off 9 (10) sts. Dec 1 st at neck edge every other row twice. Work even until front is same

Children's sweaters and hats shown at left are knitted from the same pattern. The all-over-stripe sweater and matching hat (left) and the stripe-trimmed sweater and matching hat (right) vary in the use of color. You could knit the sweater and hat in any colors you wish. Directions are for size 4; changes for size 6 are given in parentheses.

Baby sweater and matching hat in photograph at right will fit a 6- to 9-month-old baby. Design of sweater yoke and hat is alternating bands of stockinette and garter stitch. The sweater and hat may be knitted in baby yarn as was done here, or in 3-ply sock and sweater yarn.

length as back. Shape shoulder as for back.

Left front
Work the same as right front, reversing the shaping.

Sleeves
Using #5 needles, cast on 36 sts with blue yarn and work 1 × 1 ribbing in stripes as for back. Change to #7 needles and continue in stockinette stripes until sleeve measures 2″; inc 1 st at each end of next row, then inc 1 st at each end every 2″ (1¾″) until there are 44 (46) sts. Work even until sleeve measures 9¼″ (10¼″). Fasten off blue and white yarns. Work garter stitch stripes with green and turquoise as for back. Attach yellow, K 1 row, P 1 row. **Shaping cap:** Attach white; bind off 3 sts at beg of next 2 rows. Continue with yellow and white stripes, dec 1 st at each end every other row 8 (9) times. Bind off 2 sts at beg of next 4 rows, 3 sts at beg of next 2 rows; bind off rem 8 sts.

Finishing
Sew shoulder seams; sew in sleeves; join the side and sleeve seams. With right side facing you, using G hook and blue yarn, begin at lower right front and *loosely* sl st along front and neck edges (for crochet abbreviations, see p. 366). With F hook, work second row in sc, making 3 sc in each corner st. With yarn scraps, mark 7 buttonhole positions on right front for girls, left front for boys. **Next round,** with F hook and white, work 1 sc in each sc, making a ch-2 buttonhole at each marking and 3 sc in each corner st. Work 1 more row with blue, decreasing a few stitches around the neck for a closer fit; fasten off. Attach buttons. Weave in yarn ends.

Hat
Using #5 needles, cast on loosely 86 (90) sts with blue yarn. Work alternate blue and white stripes in ribbing as for sweater; fasten off. Change to #7 needles and garter stitch; work rows of green and turquoise stripes as for sweater; fas-

ten off. Attach yellow and white; work stripes in stockinette until hat measures 4½″ (5″). *For size 4 only:* When hat measures 4″, K 2 tog at one edge only (85 sts). **Dec row 1:** *K 3, K 2 tog* across row; P 1 row, K 1 row, P 1 row. **Dec row 2:** *K 2, K 2 tog* across row; P 1 row, K 1 row, P 1 row. **Dec row 3:** *K 1, K 2 tog* across row; P 1 row. **Dec row 4:** *K 2 tog* across row; P 1 row. **Dec row 5:** K 2 (K 3 tog), *K 3 tog* across row. 7 (6) sts remain; fasten off, leaving an 18″ end. With tapestry needle, thread yarn through each st, then draw it up tightly; fasten securely. Sew back seam. Make a pompon with white yarn (see p. 353 for instructions).

STRIPE-TRIMMED SET
Yarn amounts
Acrylic yarn in knitting worsted weight, both sizes: 9 ozs. white, 3 ozs. blue, 2 ozs. green, 1 oz. each yellow and orange

Sweater back
Using #5 needles, cast on 56 (60) sts with blue yarn. Work 1 × 1 ribbing for 7 rows. Attach white; work 2 rows of ribbing. Change to #7 needles and work in stockinette stitch: 6 rows of green, 2 rows white, 4 rows yellow, 2 rows white, 2 rows orange. Continue in white until back measures 9½″ (10¾″). Shape underarm and neck same as for other sweater.

Sweater fronts
Work the same as for other sweater, using stripe design given above.

Sleeve
Work stripes same as described above. Work in white until sleeve measure 10½″ (11½″); shape the sleeve cap same as for other sweater.

Finishing
Finish same as for other sweater, but work all three rows of trim in blue.

Hat
Work same as for other hat, using stripe design given above.

BABY SET
Size
6- to 9-month-old baby; 19″ chest

Materials needed
4 ozs. acrylic baby yarn; #4 knitting needles; size D crochet hook; tapestry needle

Gauge
7 sts and 10 rows = 1″ in stockinette st on #4 needles

Pattern stitch: Row 1: K. **Row 2:** P. **Row 3:** K. **Row 4:** P. **Rows 5-12:** K. This pattern is 4 rows of stockinette stitch followed by 8 rows of garter stitch.

Sweater back
On #4 needles, loosely cast on 124 sts. K 7 rows. Work in stockinette st (K 1 row, P 1 row) until piece measures 6″, ending with a P row. **Next row:** K 8,*K 2 tog* across to within last 8 sts, K 8 (70 sts). K 7 rows. **To shape raglan armholes:** Starting with Row 1 of the pattern stitch, dec 1 st each side every other row until 24 sts remain. Complete garter st band, loosely binding off all sts on Row 12 of pattern.

Sleeves
Cast on 46 sts. K 7 rows. Work in stockinette st, inc 1 st at beg and end of row every inch 5 times (56 sts). Work even until piece measures 6″; end with purl row. K 8 rows. **To shape raglan cap:** Starting with Row 1 of pattern, dec 1 st each side every other row until 10 sts remain. Complete garter st band, loosely binding off all sts on Row 12 of pattern.

Left front
Cast on 62 sts. K 8 rows. **Next row:** K 4, P to end. (Front border is garter st.) Work in stockinette st with first 4 sts in garter until piece measures 6″, ending with a purl row. **Next row:** K 8, *K 2 tog* across to within last 4 sts, K 4 (37 sts). K 7 rows. **To shape raglan armhole:** Starting with Row 1 of pattern, dec 1 st at *beginning* of Row 1 (to dec at beg of a row, sl 1, K 1, psso) and every other row thereafter until 14 sts remain. At same time, to work front border, knit *first* 4 sts of the purl rows. Complete the garter st band, loosely binding off all sts on Row 12 of pattern.

Right front
Cast on 62 sts. K 9 rows. **Next row:** P across to within last 4 sts, K 4. Work in stockinette st with last 4 sts in garter until piece measures 6″, ending with a purl row. **Next row:** K 4, K 2 tog to within last 8 sts, K 8 (37 sts). K 7 rows.

To shape raglan armhole: Starting with Row 1 of pattern, dec 1 st at *end* of row 1 (to dec at end of a row, K 2 tog) and every other row thereafter until 14 sts remain. At same time, to work front border, knit *last* 4 sts of the purl rows. Complete the garter st band, loosely binding off all sts on Row 12 of pattern.

Finishing
Join raglan seam, then side and sleeve seams, with backstitch or crocheted slip stitch (p. 345). For ties, make six 6″ double chains (p. 365); sew to yoke front.

Hat
With #4 needles, cast on 100 sts. K 7 rows. Starting with Row 1 of pattern, work Rows 1-12 four times. Piece should measure 4½″ from beg to last knit row. Bind off 35 sts at each edge, leaving center 30 sts on needle. Fasten off. Attach yarn to center sts, and begin with Row 1 of pattern. Continue in pattern until piece measures 9½″ from beginning, ending with Row 10 of pattern. To sew cap to itself, see drawing below. For ties, make two 10″ double chains (see p. 365) and sew to cap at bottom edges.

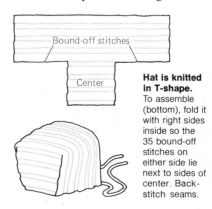

Hat is knitted in T-shape.
To assemble (bottom), fold it with right sides inside so the 35 bound-off stitches on either side lie next to sides of center. Backstitch seams.

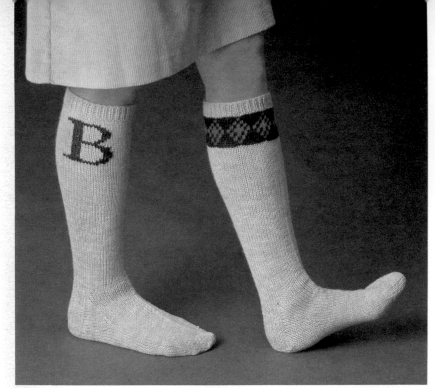

Sock pattern can be made with diamond band knitted in or with duplicate-stitch initial added later.

Sport socks

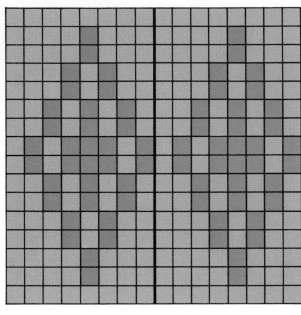

Follow this chart for the decorative band on the geometric sock. One square on the graph equals one knit stitch. See page 317 for working from a chart. Because the sock is knitted in the round, the chart is read from right to left for each row. Diamond-shape motif is repeated eight times around the top of the sock.

The same pattern offers you socks with a geometric trim knitted in or an initial added in duplicate stitch after the sock is completed. Instructions for working from a chart are on page 317. Directions for duplicate stitch appear on page 348.

Size

Adjustable (see foot instructions)

Materials needed

6 ozs. beige wool sport yarn for one pair of socks in either design; for geometric design, 1 oz. each green and red wool sport yarn; for initials, 2 yds. green wool sport yarn; 1 set #2 double-pointed knitting needles; tapestry needle

Gauge

7 sts and 10 rows = 1″

Ribbing

With beige, cast on 64 sts, dividing the stitches onto 3 needles (see p. 299). Work in 1 × 1 ribbing for 1″. Change to garter st. **Geometric design:** Working in garter st, knit the next 16 rows in the color pattern, following the chart given above. For directions on working with two col-

ors of yarn, see pages 317 and 318. **Initialed design:** Work 16 rows of beige in garter st. **For either sock:** With beige, continue to knit around until the sock measures 5″ from the cast-on row. **Next round:** Dec 1 st at beg of 1st needle and end of 3rd needle. Repeat this dec every inch, 7 more times. Work even on 48 sts until piece measures 13″.

Divide for heel and foot

At beg of next rnd, K 12, sl 24 sts in center onto a holder, turn

Heel

P across 12 heel sts, then P across next 12 heel sts (24 sts on 1 needle), turn.

Row 1: *K 1, sl 1*. Repeat between * across row.

Row 2: Purl. Repeat these 2 rows for 2½″, ending with Row 1.

Turn heel

Turning is the working of short rows in graduated lengths (see p. 329).

Row 1: P 9, P 2 tog, P 3, P 2 tog, P 1, turn

Row 2: sl 1, K 4, sl 1, K 1, psso, K 1, turn

Row 3: sl 1, P 5, P 2 tog, P 1, turn

Row 4: sl 1, K 6, sl 1, K 1, psso, K 1, turn

Row 5: sl 1, P 7, P 2 tog, P 1, turn

Row 6: sl 1, K 8, sl 1, K 1, psso, K 1, turn

Row 7: sl 1, P 9, P 2 tog, P 1, turn

Row 8: sl 1, K 10, sl 1, K 1, psso, K 1, turn

Row 9: sl 1, P 11, P 2 tog, P 1 (14 sts). Break off. Divide heel sts between 2 needles, 7 sts on each. With right side facing you, join yarn at top left of heel ribbing. Pick up and K 14 sts along ribbing side, placing sts on left heel needle; onto a 2nd needle, K 24 sts from holder; onto 3rd needle, pick up and K 14 sts along other side of heel plus 7 sts of other heel needle (21 sts on each heel needle).

Shape heel gusset

Start at center of heel to shape gusset.

Round 1: On 1st needle, K to within last 3 sts, K 2 tog, K 1; on 2nd needle, K instep sts; on 3rd needle, K 1, sl 1, K 1, psso, K to end of rnd. **Round 2:** Knit.

Repeat these 2 rnds until there are 12 sts on 1st and 3rd needles.

Foot

Knit around until piece is 2″ less than desired finished length from back of heel. For example, for a size 10 sock, work until piece measures 8″.

Shape toe

Round 1: On 1st needle, K to within last 3 sts, K 2 tog, K 1; on 2nd needle, K 1, sl 1, K 1, psso, K to within last 3 sts, K 2 tog, K 1; on 3rd needle, K 1, sl 1, K 1, psso, K to end of needle. **Round 2:** Knit. Repeat these 2 rnds until there are 5 sts on each heel needle, then put all heel sts on one needle. Break off yarn, leaving 12″ tail. Weave toe sts tog.

Finishing

Block the socks lightly (pp. 342-343). For the initialed sock, use the duplicate stitch to add the desired initial (see p. 349). For a snugger fit, you can weave a length of elastic into the ribbing at the top of the sock. To do this, see instructions on page 347.

Mittens and hat

MITTENS

Size
Woman's medium or man's small (or equivalent in teen sizes)

Materials needed
Wool sport yarn, 3 ozs. beige, 1 oz. each green and red; knitting needles, 1 pair #1, 1 pair #2; tapestry needle

Gauge
7 sts and 10 rows = 1"

Cuff
With beige and #1 needles, cast on 48 sts; work in 1 × 1 ribbing for 2½".

Hand
Change to #2 needles and work in stockinette st for 6 rows, ending with a purl row. K 23, put marker on needle, inc in each of next 2 sts, put marker on needle; work to end of row. **Next row:** Purl. **Next row:** K to marker, slip marker, inc in next st, K 2, inc in next st, slip marker, K to end of row. **Next row:** Purl. **Next row:** K to marker, slip marker, inc in next st, K 4, inc in next st, slip marker, K to end of row. Continue in this manner, increasing 1 st after 1st marker and 1 st before 2nd marker on every knit row until you have 22 sts between markers and 68 sts on needle. Work even on all sts until you have 3" of stockinette, ending with a purl row. **Next row:** K 43, turn. **Next row:** P 18. Work back and forth on these 18 sts *only* for 2¼" to make thumb. End with purl row.

Thumb shaping
Row 1: *K 1, K 2 tog*. Repeat between * across row (12 sts). **Row 2:** Purl. **Row 3:** K 2 tog across row (6 sts); break off yarn, leaving 12" tail. Thread tapestry needle with tail end of yarn and run needle through sts. Fasten off.

To complete hand
Attach beige to base of thumb and work to end of row. Continuing in stockinette st on all sts, work 2 rows beige, 2 rows green, 2 rows beige, 4 rows red, 2 rows beige, 2 rows green. Work even in beige until piece measures 8¼" from cast-on row, ending with a purl row.

Top shaping
Row 1: K 1, K 2 tog, K 19, K 2 tog, K 2, K 2 tog, K to within last 3 sts, K 2 tog, K 1. **Row 2:** Purl. **Row 3:** K 1, K 2 tog, K 17, K 2 tog, K 2, K 2 tog, K to within last 3 sts, K 2 tog, K 1. **Row 4:** Purl. Continue to decrease in this manner until 18 sts remain. Break off yarn, leaving 12" tail. Thread tapestry needle with yarn end and run through sts; fasten off. To sew side seam, weave cuff seam (p. 344) and backstitch hand seam (p. 345). Make second mitten the same way.

HAT

Size
Adjustable

Materials needed
Wool sport yarn, 2 ozs. beige, 1 oz. each green and red; #2 knitting needles; tapestry needle; cardboard for making pompon

Gauge
7 sts and 14 rows = 1"

With beige, cast on 60 sts. K 2 rows. Hat is made in garter stitch in following color pattern: 2 rows green, 6 rows beige, 4 rows red, 6 rows beige. Repeat until piece fits snugly around head; end with 2 more beige rows. Bind off; work in yarn ends. Sew cast-on row to bound-off row with backstitch. Thread separate yarn through one side edge; gather up tightly (see below). To hem other edge, turn under ½" and sew. Make a pompon (see below); sew to top of hat.

Mittens and matching hat are knitted in wool sport yarn; you could choose any colors you wish.

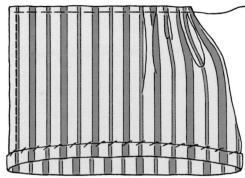

To assemble hat, sew cast-on row to bound-off row with backstitch. Thread separate length of yarn through one side edge; gather up tightly. To hem other edge, turn under ½" and sew.

To make a pompon, wrap yarn around a 2" piece of cardboard 180 times. Slip separate piece of yarn under wraps at one edge and tie securely. Cut yarn at other edge. Shake the pompon vigorously; then trim yarn ends so pompon is rounded.

Evening skirt, top, and shawl

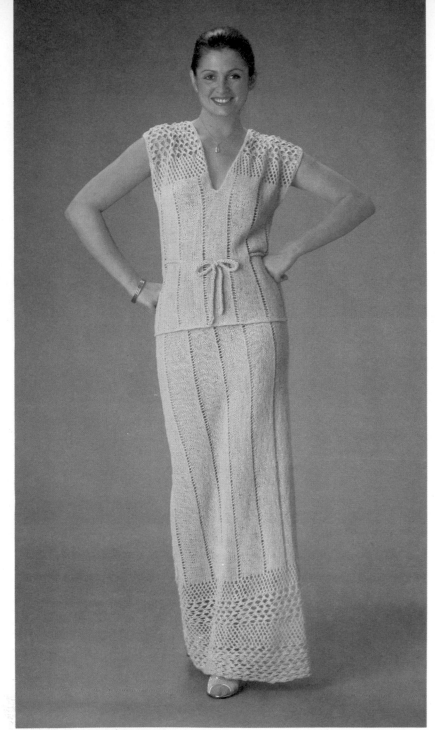

Evening skirt and matching top can be worn as a dress as shown, or over a blouse as a jumper.

Coordinating shawl is worked in the same three knitted lace patterns as the skirt and top at left.

The skirt, top, and shawl are knitted in a combination of three stitches: network and oblique openwork lace stitches are on page 304; stockinette stitch with rows of eyelet stitches is described in the instructions below. The skirt may be knitted floor length (about 40 inches long) with a double border of network and oblique openwork stitches as shown in the photograph at the left. Or it can be knitted in a shorter version (about 33½ inches long) that reaches to approximately the middle of the average calf and has a single border of the two open lace stitches. The top has a center front slit that is formed into a V-neckline by gathering the front shoulders to the back. The side seams may be sewed up to the armhole or, for a tabard style, tacked together only at the waist. A drawstring belt is threaded through eyelets at the waistline. The shawl is made with the same yarn type used for the skirt and top. You could choose a contrasting color for the shawl as was done here (see photograph opposite), or you could use the same yarn color for all three pieces. The shawl is square with a square center and four flounce sections with mitered ends. The top edge of each flounce section is eased slightly to fit the sides of the center square; sections are attached with single crochet (see p. 362) so the shawl has a finished look on both the right and wrong sides.

SKIRT AND TOP
Size
Directions are for size 8/10; changes for size 12/14 are in parentheses.
Materials needed for skirt and top
Parfait yarn, 1 oz. balls: 8 balls for the skirt, 5 balls for the top; pair of #5 knitting needles; size H crochet hook; stitch holder; ring stitch markers; yarn needle; 1 yd. 1"-wide elastic; ½ yd. ¼"-wide twill tape or satin ribbon; sewing needle, and thread to match the yarn color; for lining (optional), 2½ yds. lining fabric for long skirt, 2 yds. for shorter version
Gauge
5 sts and 7 rows = 1" in stockinette st
Skirt border
Cast on 116 sts (124). For the floor length skirt, work 4" in network, 2½" in oblique openwork, *3" in network, 2" in oblique openwork. Start work at * for the shorter skirt. (Additional length adjustments can be made at the top before working the waistband.)
Body of skirt
Change to stockinette st with eyelets.
Row 1: K 8 (12), 1 eyelet (to work eyelet: yo, K 2 tog), *K 12, 1 eyelet*. Repeat between * 6 more times, then end with K 8 (12). **Row 2:** Purl. Repeat these two rows, dec 1 st at beg and end of every 10th row until there are 88 sts (96). Then work straight until the skirt measures 39½", or length desired. For the waist-

band, work in 1 × 1 ribbing for 1"; bind off. Make a second skirt piece the same as the first. Sew pieces together with weaving stitch (p. 344).
Finishing
If you want to line the skirt, fold it in half and pin it to the fold of the lining fabric. Trace around the skirt, allowing ½ inch for seam allowances and 2 inches for hem. Cut out lining; stitch side seams. Fold up and sew the hem. Fold under ½ inch at top edge; put lining inside skirt with wrong sides facing. Stitch together at top edge; then stitch again 1 inch from top, leaving 2 inches open. Thread the elastic through the casing formed by the lining and the knitted waistband. Stitch ends of elastic together; then stitch opening closed. If you are not lining the skirt, insert the elastic by sewing it to wrong side of waistband with a zigzag stitch or anchor it with a crocheted casing (see p. 347).
Back of matching top
Cast on 84 sts (90). Work stockinette st with eyelets. **Row 1:** K 6 (10), 1 eyelet, *K 12, 1 eyelet*. Repeat between * 4 more times, then K 6 (10). **Row 2:** Purl. Repeat these 2 rows for 13½"; put markers at each side for armholes. Continue stockinette st with eyelets as above for 2½". Change to oblique openwork for 2½", then network for 4". Bind off.
Front of matching top
Work same as for back but after armhole markers, form a slit in center front as follows: work to center, place remaining unworked sts in row on stitch holder, turn and continue up first half to shoulder. On other half, attach yarn at center and continue to shoulder.
Finishing the top
Block the pieces. With an extra length of yarn and a yarn needle, run a basting stitch along each shoulder front on right side. Gather the knitting along the basted thread until each piece measures 6½"; pin to back shoulder, matching armhole edges. Sew the shoulder seams with a

weaving stitch, working from the wrong side, catching more than one stitch from the front to accommodate the gathers. Remove the basting thread. Hand-stitch the ¼" twill tape or satin ribbon to the front edge of the seam, using sewing thread. Sew side seams together, working from the bottom up for 13½", leaving armholes open. Or, for a tabard, sew sides together for 1" at the waistline. To finish the edges, work single crochet (p. 362) around neckline, armholes, and bottom edge. For a belt, make a 50"-long double chain (p. 356), using two strands of yarn, and thread it through the row of eyelets nearest your waist.

SHAWL
Size
48" square
Materials needed
Parfait yarn, 11 balls (1 oz. each); #5 knitting needles; size H crochet hook; yarn needle

Center section
Cast on 160 sts. Work in oblique openwork pattern stitch (see p. 304) for 36". Bind off.
Flounce
Make four pieces. Cast on 212 sts. Work in the network pattern stitch (see p. 304), dec 1 st at beg and end of every other row until you have 200 sts (piece measures 2½"). Change to stockinette st with rows of eyelets (directions above), dec 1 st at beg and end of every row until you have 168 sts (the piece measures 6"). Bind off.
Finishing
Block the pieces lightly. Pin mitered edges of flounce sections together; join them with single crochet (p. 362). With an extra length of yarn, run a basting stitch along the inner edge of the flounce. Ease the flounce slightly to conform to the sides of the center square. Pin the flounce to the square and attach the two with single crochet.

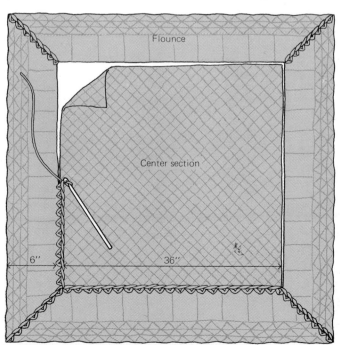

To assemble the shawl, pin the mitered ends of the four flounce pieces together; join with a single crochet stitch (p.362). With an extra length of yarn, baste along inner edge of flounce sections. Ease the flounce slightly to fit sides of center square. Pin together and attach with single crochet.

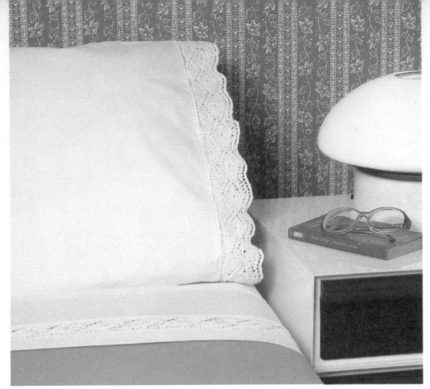

A knitted lace border is added to a pillowcase; a knitted lace insertion decorates a plain sheet.

Knitted trims for sheets and pillowcases

One band of knitted lace decorates the edge of a pillowcase; another lace band is inserted below top hem of a sheet.

Materials needed
Knit cro-sheen, 4½ yds. per inch (including crocheted edge) for the border, 5 yds. per inch for the insertion; pair of #2 knitting needles

Gauge
Pillowcase border: one repeat = 2″
Sheet insertion: one repeat = 1¾″

Measuring the linens
To determine how long a border to knit, measure around the pillowcase edge. To determine insertion length, measure the width of the top sheet. Add 1 inch to both measurements to allow for any take-up in the knitting. To determine how much cotton crochet thread you will need, multiply the length you will be knitting by the yardage per inch above. Block both pieces before sewing them to the linens.

BORDER
Cast on 20 stitches
Row 1: sl 1, K 2, yo, K 2 tog, yo, sl 1, K 1, psso, K 3, K 2 tog, yo twice, sl 1, K 1, psso, K 2 tog, yo, K 1, yo, K 2 tog, K 1
Rows 2, 4, 6, 8, 10: yo, P to within last 5 sts, K 2, yo, K 2 tog, K 1
Row 3: sl 1, K 2, yo, K 2 tog, K 4, K 2 tog, yo, K 1, K 2 tog, yo twice, sl 1, K 1, psso, K 2, yo, K 2 tog, K 1
Row 5: sl 1, K 2, yo, K 2 tog, K 3, K 2 tog, yo, K 1, K 2 tog, yo, K 2, yo, sl 1, K 1, psso, K 2, yo, K 2 tog, K 1
Row 7: sl 1, K 2, yo, K 2 tog, K 2, K 2 tog, yo, K 1, K 2 tog, yo, K 4, yo, sl 1, K 1, psso, K 2, yo, K 2 tog, K 1
Row 9: sl 1, K 2, yo, K 2 tog, K 1, K 2 tog, yo, K 1, K 2 tog, yo, K 6, yo, sl 1, K 1, psso, K 2, yo, K 2 tog, K 1
Row 11: sl 1, K 2, yo, (K 2 tog) twice, yo, (yo, sl 1, K 1, psso, K 3, K 2 tog, yo) twice, K 1, yo, K 2 tog, K 1
Rows 12, 14, 16, 18, 20: yo, (P 2 tog) twice, P to within last 5 sts, K 2, yo, K 2 tog, K 1
Row 13: sl 1, K 2, yo, K 2 tog, yo, sl 1, K 1, psso, sl 1, K 1, psso, K 8, K 2 tog, yo, K 1, yo, K 2 tog, K 1

Row 15: sl 1, K 2, yo, K 2 tog, K 1, yo, sl 1, K 1, psso, K 1, yo, sl 1, K 1, psso, K 6, K 2 tog, yo, K 1, yo, K 2 tog, K 1
Row 17: sl 1, K 2, yo, K 2 tog, K 2, yo, sl 1, K 1, psso, K 1, yo, sl 1, K 1, psso, K 4, K 2 tog, yo, K 1, yo, K 2 tog, K 1
Row 19: sl 1, K 2, yo, K 2 tog, K 3, yo, sl 1, K 1, psso, K 1, yo, sl 1, K 1, psso, K 2, K 2 tog, yo, K 1, yo, K 2 tog, K 1

Finishing
To finish border edge, work a crochet edging (p. 362) in picot loops on zigzag side of strip. To do this, attach new strand of thread in picot loop at one end of strip as follows: Holding thread at back of work, yo hook, then insert hook under loop and end of thread, yo and draw up loop, yo and through both loops on hook; one sc made. Work 1 more sc in same loop, work 2 sc in each loop to the end. Fasten off. Sew short ends of strip together. Pin straight edge of border to pillowcase; stitch in place with sewing thread and needle, making the stitches as inconspicuous as possible.

INSERTION
Cast on 24 sts
Row 1: sl 1, K 2, yo, K 2 tog, K 1, 1 popcorn [(K into front and back of st) twice, then slip 3rd, 2nd, and 1st sts over 4th one], K 3, yo, sl 1, K 1, psso, K 2 tog, yo, K 3, 1 popcorn, K 3, yo, K 2 tog, K 1
Rows 2, 4, 6, 8, 12, 14, 16: sl 1, K 2, yo, K 2 tog, P 14, K 2, yo, K 2 tog, K 1
Row 3: sl 1, K 2, yo, K 2 tog, K 3, K 2 tog, yo, K 4, yo, sl 1, K 1, psso, K 5, yo, K 2 tog, K 1
Row 5: sl 1, K 2, yo, K 2 tog, K 2, K 2 tog, yo, K 6, yo, sl 1, K 1, psso, K 4, yo, K 2 tog, K 1
Row 7: sl 1, K 2, yo, K 2 tog, K 1, K 2 tog, yo, K 8, yo, sl 1, K 1, psso, K 3, yo, K 2 tog, K 1
Row 9: sl 1, K 2, yo, (K 2 tog) twice, yo, K 3, K 2 tog, yo twice, sl 1, K 1, psso, K 3, yo, sl 1, K 1, psso, K 2, yo, K 2 tog, K 1
Row 10: sl 1, K 2, yo, K 2 tog, P 6, K 1, P 7, K 2, yo, K 2 tog, K 1
Row 11: sl 1, K 2, yo, K 2 tog, K 2, yo, sl 1, K 1, psso, K 6, K 2 tog, yo, K 4, yo, K 2 tog, K 1
Row 13: sl 1, K 2, yo, K 2 tog, K 3, yo, sl 1, K 1, psso, K 4, K 2 tog, yo, K 5, yo, K 2 tog, K 1
Row 15: sl 1, K 2, yo, K 2 tog, K 4, yo, sl 1, K 1, psso, K 2, K 2 tog, yo, K 6, yo, K 2 tog, K 1

Finishing
To attach the knitted insertion to the sheet, follow the directions given with the drawing below.

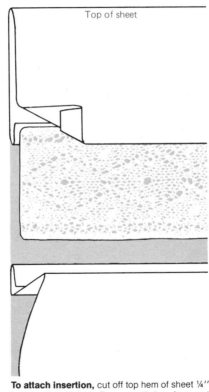

Top of sheet

To attach insertion, cut off top hem of sheet ¼″ below stitched fold. Remove stitches from cut piece; press raw edge up ¼″. Fold lace and hem in quarters; mark with pins; unfold both pieces. Insert one edge of lace into open hem edge (top); match markings; stitch in place. On cut edge of sheet, press ¼″ to right side twice; fold doubled edge to wrong side (bottom) and press. Fold and mark sheet edge in quarters. Insert other lace edge between folds; match markings; stitch.

Crochet

358 Crochet basics
        Yarns, hooks, other equipment
360 Introduction to crocheting
        Holding the hook/right-handed
        Making the chain stitch/
        right-handed
361 Holding the hook/left-handed
        Making the chain stitch/
        left-handed
362 Forming the elementary stitches
364 Variations on elementary
        techniques
366 Following crochet instructions
        Testing the gauge
367 Tote bag to crochet
        Joining and securing yarns
368 Increasing and decreasing
369 Geometric shapes
371 Hats to crochet
372 Crochet stitches
        Using a pattern stitch
        Textures
374 Shells
376 Clusters
377 Motifs
378 Motifs/patchwork
380 Meshes
381 Shaping mesh ground
382 Filet crochet
383 Overlaid meshes
384 Irish crochet
385 Irish crochet pillow top
386 Tunisian crochet
388 Loops
390 Multicolor stitches
        Working with a color chart
        Jacquard techniques
392 Charted stitches

393 Crocheting a garment
        Introduction
        Designing a crocheted garment
394 Charting a woman's cardigan
        How to make a garment chart
396 Shaping necklines
397 Shaping armholes and sleeves
398 Ribbing
        Buttons
399 Buttonholes
400 Assembling and finishing
401 Crocheted edgings and
        insertions

Crochet projects
367 Tote bag
371 Three hats
385 Irish crochet pillow top
394 Woman's cardigan
402 Afghan

Crochet basics

Yarns
Hooks and supplementary
equipment
Holding the hook/right-handed
Making the chain stitch/
right-handed
Holding the hook/left-handed
Making the chain stitch/
left-handed
Forming the elementary stitches
Variations on elementary
techniques

Yarns

Crocheting can be done with any stringy material from finest tatting cotton to raffia, leather cords, or fabric strips. Your choice only has to suit the purpose and be worked with an appropriate hook (see opposite page for selection).

For convenience in comparing similar yarn types, a chart of wools and synthetics appears on the opening page of the Knitting chapter; below is a chart of cotton yarns. A significant difference between these two groups: yarns in the first are sold by weight, those in the second by length, which is specified on the label in yards, meters, or both.

Most cotton yarns are *mercerized;* this means they have undergone a process that strengthens and gives them greater luster. Some also are *boilfast,* a term that signifies colors will not run or fade in hot water. If applicable, these terms appear on the label, along with other descriptive information, such as number of *plies* or *cords*—single units—that have been twisted together, and sometimes a number (usually between 10 and 70) that signifies thickness of the ply. The higher the number, the finer the yarn. If yarn comes in a skein, it is best to wind it in a ball to prevent its tangling in use.

NAME	DESCRIPTION	THICKNESS	USES
Knit-cro-sheen cotton	4-ply, firmly twisted, large color selection including shaded tones	Approximately size 5	Shawl, blouse, dress, bedspread, curtains, trim
Metallic Knit-cro-sheen cotton	4-ply cotton plus 1 ply of Mylar, available in white plus a few colors	Approximately size 5	Sweater, blouse, fashion accessories
Glo-tone cotton	4-ply, firmly twisted, large color selection	Approximately size 5	Shawl, blouse, dress, bedspread, curtains, trim
Speed-cro-sheen cotton	8-ply, firmly twisted, large color selection	Approximately size 3	Bedspread, tablecloth, place mat, fashion accessories
Bedspread cotton	4-ply, very firmly twisted, available in white and ecru only	Approximately size 5	Bedspread, tablecloth, place mat, trim
Pearl cotton	2-ply, loosely twisted, very high sheen, large color selection including shaded tones	Size 5	Vest, blouse, trim, fashion accessories
Tatting-crochet cotton	3-ply, very firmly twisted, large color selection	Size 70	Lace, trim
Bouclé	4-ply, slubbed novelty, loosely twisted, soft	Varied	Sweater, dress, fashion accessories
Six-cord cotton	6-ply, very firmly twisted, available in ecru and white only	Sizes 20, 30	Tablecloth, trim, lace
Three-cord cotton	3-ply, very firmly twisted, white and ecru (sizes 10, 20, 30), colors and shaded colors (size 30 only)	Sizes 10, 20, 30	Tablecloth, trim, lace

Hooks and supplementary equipment

Crochet hooks are made in many sizes and materials. Thickness of most hooks is indicated by both letter and number (the number corresponds to the same size in a knitting needle); the larger the number, the larger the size. Steel hooks are an exception; they are measured by a reverse scale in which 14 is the smallest size, 00 the largest. When selecting a hook, the thicker your yarn, the larger your hook should be for ease in working.

There are supplementary knitting aids that can be useful for crochet. Among these are flat row counters, coiled ring markers, and a ruler for measuring gauge and hook sizes (see Knitting, p. 273).

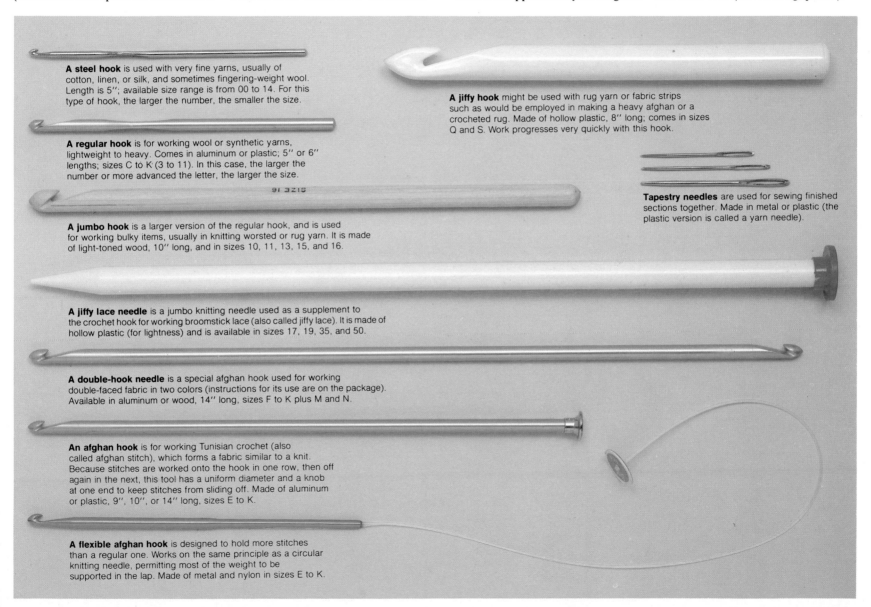

A **steel hook** is used with very fine yarns, usually of cotton, linen, or silk, and sometimes fingering-weight wool. Length is 5″; available size range is from 00 to 14. For this type of hook, the larger the number, the smaller the size.

A **regular hook** is for working wool or synthetic yarns, lightweight to heavy. Comes in aluminum or plastic; 5″ or 6″ lengths; sizes C to K (3 to 11). In this case, the larger the number or more advanced the letter, the larger the size.

A **jumbo hook** is a larger version of the regular hook, and is used for working bulky items, usually in knitting worsted or rug yarn. It is made of light-toned wood, 10″ long, and in sizes 10, 11, 13, 15, and 16.

A **jiffy lace needle** is a jumbo knitting needle used as a supplement to the crochet hook for working broomstick lace (also called jiffy lace). It is made of hollow plastic (for lightness) and is available in sizes 17, 19, 35, and 50.

A **double-hook needle** is a special afghan hook used for working double-faced fabric in two colors (instructions for its use are on the package). Available in aluminum or wood, 14″ long, sizes F to K plus M and N.

An **afghan hook** is for working Tunisian crochet (also called afghan stitch), which forms a fabric similar to a knit. Because stitches are worked onto the hook in one row, then off again in the next, this tool has a uniform diameter and a knob at one end to keep stitches from sliding off. Made of aluminum or plastic, 9″, 10″, or 14″ long, sizes E to K.

A **flexible afghan hook** is designed to hold more stitches than a regular one. Works on the same principle as a circular knitting needle, permitting most of the weight to be supported in the lap. Made of metal and nylon in sizes E to K.

A **jiffy hook** might be used with rug yarn or fabric strips such as would be employed in making a heavy afghan or a crocheted rug. Made of hollow plastic, 8″ long; comes in sizes Q and S. Work progresses very quickly with this hook.

Tapestry needles are used for sewing finished sections together. Made in metal or plastic (the plastic version is called a yarn needle).

Crochet basics

Introduction to crocheting

All crochet stitches are formations of interlocking loops, the simplest of which is the chain stitch, shown below. To work these loops, the hook is held in one hand and yarn is tensioned in the other, while the hand holding the yarn also supports the work where the hook enters it.

Two common ways to hold a hook with the right hand are shown at the immediate right. Use whichever feels more comfortable. There are several correct methods of holding yarn; one popular technique is illustrated below. The basic idea is to keep yarn taut over your index finger so you can manipulate yarn easily and with even tension around the hook.

Holding the hook/Right-handed

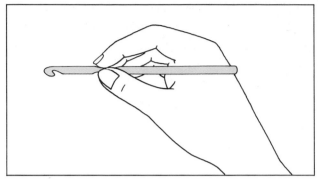
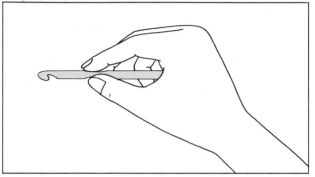

Method I: With hook facing down, grasp tool in the right hand, holding it almost as you would a knife, with thumb and index finger on either side of the flat portion, middle finger resting against the thumb.

Method II: With hook facing down, grasp tool in the right hand, holding it as you would a pencil, with thumb and index finger on either side of the flat portion, middle finger resting against the thumb.

Making the chain stitch/Right-handed

The chain stitch (ch st) is used to form the first row of crochet, and is an integral part of many pattern stitches as well. As the foundation, it should be formed loosely enough that the hook can enter each chain easily, and the edge of the work will not draw in.

1. To start chain, make a slip knot about 6″ from the yarn end; insert hook right to left.

2. Pulling both yarn ends, draw in the loop until it is close to hook, but not too tight.

3. Wrap ball end of yarn around little finger of left hand, take it under fourth and third fingers, then over top of index finger, leaving about 2″ of yarn between finger and hook.

4. Holding the slip knot between thumb and middle finger of left hand, and keeping yarn taut over index finger, push hook forward, at the same time twisting it, so yarn passes over it back to front and is caught in the slot.

5. Draw yarn through the loop, thus forming a new loop on the hook. The newly formed loop should be loose enough that the next chain can be drawn through it easily.

6. Holding chain nearest the hook with thumb and middle finger, repeat Steps 4 and 5 until you have desired number of chains (loop on hook does not count as part of the total). All chains should be the same size. If they are not, it is best to pull them out and start again.

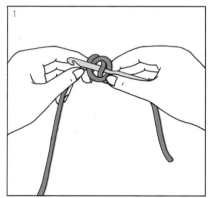
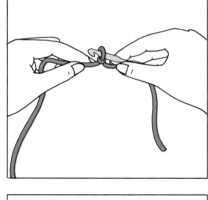
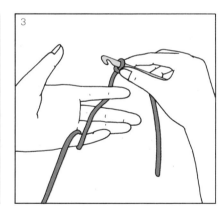
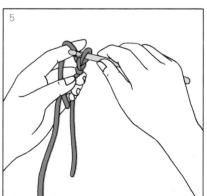
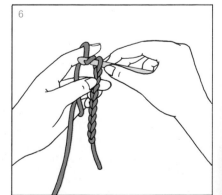

Holding the hook/Left-handed

Crocheting with the left hand is exactly the same as with the right, but with the hook and yarn position reversed. Because starting a new technique can be difficult if you have to mirror illustrations, instructions on this page are provided to orient the left-handed person.

Two common ways to hold a hook with the left hand are shown at the immediate right. Use whichever feels more comfortable. There are several correct methods of holding yarn; one popular technique is illustrated below. The basic idea is to keep yarn taut over your index finger so you can manipulate yarn easily and with even tension around the hook.

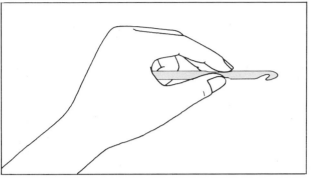

Method I: With hook facing down, grasp tool in the left hand, holding it almost as you would a knife, with thumb and index finger on either side of the flat portion, middle finger resting against the thumb.

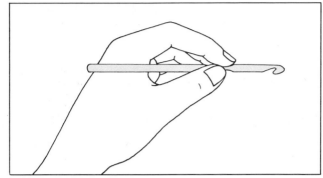

Method II: With hook facing down, grasp tool in the left hand, holding it as you would a pencil, with thumb and index finger on either side of the flat portion, middle finger resting against the thumb.

Making the chain stitch/Left-handed

The chain stitch (ch st) is used to form the first row of crochet, and is an integral part of many pattern stitches as well. As the foundation, it should be formed loosely enough that the hook can enter each chain easily, and the edge of the work will not draw in.

1. To start chain, make a slip knot about 6″ from the yarn end; insert hook left to right.

2. Pulling both yarn ends, draw in the loop until it is close to hook, but not too tight.

3. Wrap ball end of yarn around little finger of right hand, take it under fourth and third fingers, then over top of index finger, leaving about 2″ of yarn between finger and hook.

4. Holding the slip knot between thumb and middle finger of right hand, and keeping yarn taut over the index finger, push hook forward, at the same time twisting it, so yarn passes over it back to front and is caught in the slot.

5. Draw yarn through the loop, thus forming a new loop on the hook. The newly formed loop should be loose enough that the next chain can be drawn through it easily.

6. Holding chain nearest the hook with thumb and middle finger, repeat Steps 4 and 5 until you have desired number of chains (loop on hook does not count as part of the total). All chains should be the same size. If they are not, it is best to pull them out and start again.

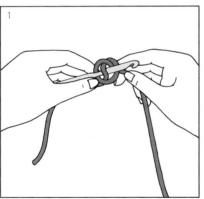
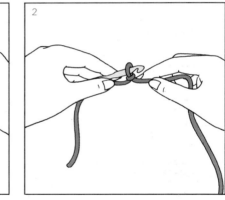
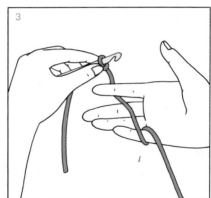
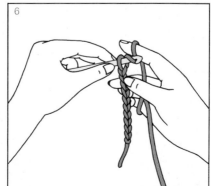
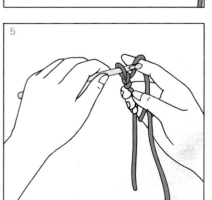

Crochet basics

Forming the elementary stitches

Single crochet (sc): Shortest of the basic stitches, it makes a firm, flat fabric. Often used to finish edges of other stitch patterns, and sometimes to join two finished sections.

Insert hook in *2nd* chain from hook, catch yarn (A), and draw a loop through the chain (2 loops on hook), yarn over hook and draw through 2 loops to complete stitch (B). Make 1 single crochet in each chain across row. After last stitch, chain 1 and turn; insert hook in 1st stitch to start next row (C).

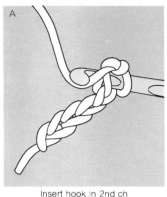

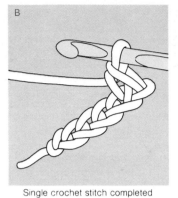

Insert hook in 2nd ch

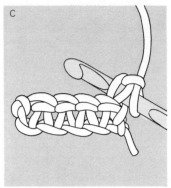

Single crochet stitch completed

Ch 1 to turn, insert hook in 1st st

Half double crochet (hdc): Slightly taller than single crochet, this stitch has a pronounced ridge in its texture, makes a firm, attractive fabric.

Yarn over and insert hook in *3rd* chain from hook, catch yarn (A), and draw a loop through the chain (3 loops on hook), yarn over hook and draw a loop through 3 loops to complete stitch (B). Make 1 half double crochet in each chain across the row. After last stitch, chain 2 and turn; yarn over, insert hook in 1st stitch to start next row (C).

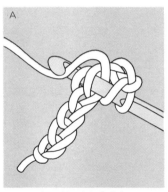

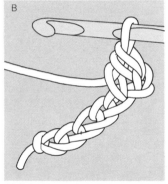

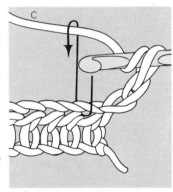

Insert hook in 3rd ch

Half double crochet stitch completed

Ch 2 to turn, insert hook in 1st st

Double crochet (dc): Twice as tall as single crochet and less compact. Forms the basis of many pattern stitches.

Yarn over and insert hook in *4th* chain from hook, catch yarn (A), and draw a loop through the chain (3 loops on hook), yarn over hook and draw through 2 loops, yarn over and draw through last 2 loops to complete stitch (B). Make 1 double crochet in each chain across the row. After last stitch, chain 3 and turn, yarn over, insert hook in 2nd stitch to start next row (C).

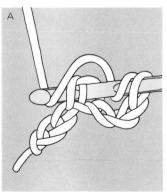

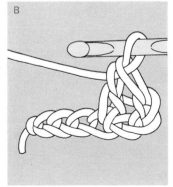

Yarn over, insert hook in 4th ch

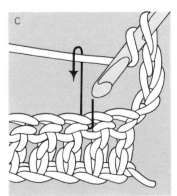

Double crochet stitch completed

Ch 3 to turn, insert hook in 2nd st

Triple crochet (tr): A tall stitch, more open than double crochet and used less frequently. Sometimes called treble crochet.

Yarn over twice, insert hook in *5th* chain from hook, catch yarn (A), draw a loop through the chain (4 loops on hook), yarn over, draw through 2 loops, yarn over, draw through 2 more loops, yarn over and draw through last 2 loops to complete stitch (B). Make 1 triple crochet in each chain across row, chain 4, turn; yarn over twice, insert hook in 2nd stitch to start next row (C).

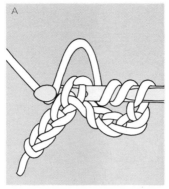

Yarn over twice, insert hook in 5th ch

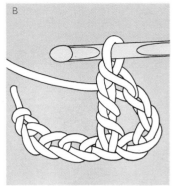

Triple crochet stitch completed

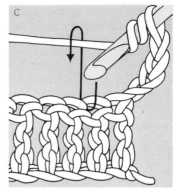

Ch 4 to turn, insert hook in 2nd st

Double triple crochet (dtr): Essentially the same as triple crochet but taller. You can make an even taller stitch, *triple triple crochet,* by adding yet another yarn over at beginning.

Yarn over 3 times, insert hook in *6th* chain from hook, catch yarn (A), draw a loop through chain (5 loops on hook), °yarn over, draw through 2 loops°, repeat the instructions between asterisks 3 more times to complete stitch (B). Make 1 double triple crochet in each chain across row, chain 5, turn; yarn over 3 times, insert hook in 2nd stitch to start next row (C).

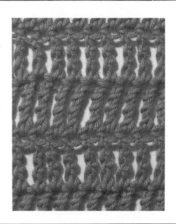

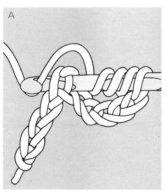

Yarn over 3 times, insert hook in 6th ch

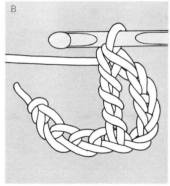

Double triple crochet stitch completed

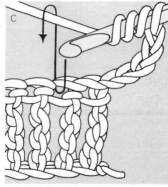

Ch 5 to turn, insert hook in 2nd st

Slip stitch (sl st): A very short stitch used principally for joining, as in the closing of a ring or motif round, or the seaming of two finished pieces. Though not used to produce fabric, it is sometimes worked along an edge to strengthen it and to minimize stretching.

Insert hook in chain (or stitch), catch yarn (A), draw a loop through both the chain and the loop on the hook (B).

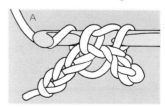

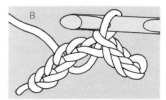

BASIC CROCHET RULES

1. The chain on the hook is never counted as part of a foundation row. For example, if directions say chain 18, you should have 18 in addition to one on the hook.
2. Always insert hook into a chain or stitch from front to back.°
3. Always insert hook under the two top loops of a chain or stitch.°
4. There should be just one loop left on the hook at completion of a stitch or sequence.

°unless directions say otherwise

TURNING CHAINS

At the beginning of each row (including the first one), a certain number of chains are needed to bring work up to the level of the stitch that is to be formed. The exact number of chains depends on the height of the stitch (see below), and in the case of tall stitches — double, triple, and so on — this chain usually replaces the first stitch of each row. When instructions place the turning chain at the end of a row, you should turn work right to left to avoid twisting the chain, then insert hook in the stitch that is specified.

Single crochet	chain 1 to turn, insert hook in 1st stitch
Half double crochet	chain 2 to turn, insert hook in 1st stitch
Double crochet	chain 3 to turn, insert hook in 2nd stitch
Triple crochet	chain 4 to turn, insert hook in 2nd stitch
Double triple crochet	chain 5 to turn, insert hook in 2nd stitch
Triple triple crochet	chain 6 to turn, insert hook in 2nd stitch

Crochet basics

Variations on elementary techniques

Working under one loop produces a ribbed effect and a more open pattern than is achieved with the usual technique (that is, inserting the hook under two loops).
To work the back loop only, insert hook front to back with a downward motion, catch the yarn (A), draw up a loop and complete the stitch.
To work the front loop only, insert hook front to back with an upward motion, catch the yarn (B), draw up a loop and complete the stitch.

Working a stitch in back loop only

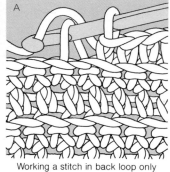

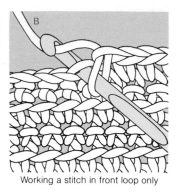

Working a stitch in front loop only

Working between stitches is a technique used in many patterns, meshes (p. 380), for example. One or more chains are made between stitches in one row; in the next row, you crochet into the *chain* or *chain space*. Always note which method is specified, because results are different for each.
To work chain between stitches, insert hook under the 2 top loops; make stitch *through* the chain (A).
To work a chain space between stitches, insert hook under the chain and make a stitch or group of stitches *over* the chain (B).

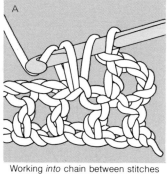

Working *into* chain between stitches

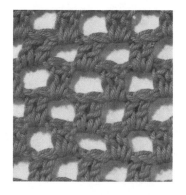

Working *over* chain between stitches

Working around the post (vertical shaft of a stitch) is a technique that creates a three-dimensional effect. Though it is shown here applied to double crochet, the method is suitable also for single or triple crochet. The post stitches can be worked to either the front or the back, or alternately front and back, depending on the desired results. See page 373 for patterns in which this technique is employed; page 398 for a ribbing that can be produced by it.

To work a post dc around the back, take yarn over hook, insert hook front to back between next 2 stitches, then bring it forward between the stitch being worked and the one after it; hook is now positioned horizontally in back of stitch. Complete the double crochet.

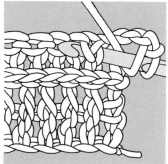

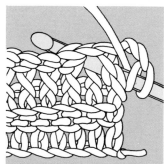

To work a post dc around the front, take yarn over hook, insert hook back to front between next 2 stitches, then back again between the stitch being worked and the one after it; hook is now positioned horizontally in front of stitch. Complete the double crochet.

A double chain stitch makes a sturdier foundation than a simple chain. It can also be used alone for a narrow trim or cord.

Make a slip knot and chain 2, work 1 single crochet in 2nd chain from hook, *insert hook under the left loop of the single crochet, catch yarn (A) and draw up a loop (B), yarn over, draw through 2 loops (C)*. Repeat instructions between asterisks until chain is the desired length.

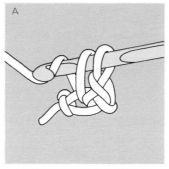

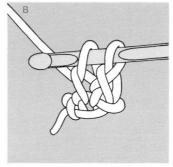

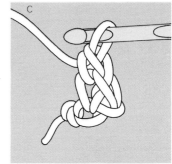

Working under left loop of the sc	Two loops on the hook	Loop drawn through the 2 loops

Double-faced double crochet makes a sturdy, very thick fabric. *Multiple is any number of chains*
Row 1: *1 double crochet in each chain*, chain 3, turn
Row 2: With fabric sideways, skip 1st stitch, *yarn over, insert hook in back loop of next stitch and back loop of foundation chain, catch yarn (A), draw a loop through 2 back loops, then complete double crochet (B)*, repeat from asterisk to end of row, chain 3, turn. Repeat Row 2, working into back of each double crochet and double crochet of previous row (C).

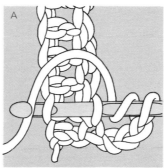

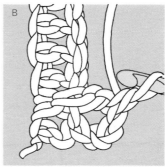

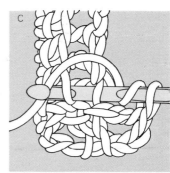

Working under 2 back loops of Row 1	A double crochet completed in Row 2	Starting the 1st stitch of Row 3

A double knot stitch is a formation of elongated loops interlocked in such a way that they produce a mesh fabric similar to netting. Though ½'' is the typical recommendation for loop length in many instructions, any length is suitable as long as it is consistent. A general rule is to make a longer loop for a thick yarn, a shorter loop for a fine one. As you follow the directions, right, for forming a single knot, pay close attention to where the hook is inserted after a chain is drawn through the long loop (illustration A); correct insertion of the hook in this step is important to obtaining the desired result.

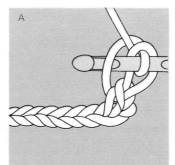

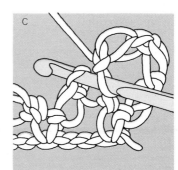

Work 1 single crochet in the 2nd chain from the hook, *lengthen loop on hook to ½'', draw up a new loop, then take hook across the front of the elongated loop and insert it under the yarn that was drawn up for the new loop (A), work 1 single crochet* to complete single knot.

Repeat instructions between asterisks and you will have made a *double knot*. *Skip 3 chains, work 1 single crochet in next chain (B), make 1 double knot.* Repeat instructions between these last 2 asterisks across the row, ending with 3 single knot stitches.

Turn, *work 1 single crochet in center of next double knot (C), make 1 double knot.* Repeat instructions between the last 2 asterisks across the row, ending with 1 single knot. This row is repeated to form a pattern (see p. 381 for an example of the finished stitch).

365

Following crochet instructions

Crochet terminology
Testing the gauge
Tote bag project
Joining and finishing yarn ends
Increasing
Decreasing
Geometric shapes worked in rows
Working in rounds
Three hats to crochet

Crochet terminology

For written crochet instructions, there is a special vocabulary, much of it expressed in abbreviated or symbolic form. The forms used in this book are listed below with their definitions alongside. Also included are the numbers of pages on which techniques are illustrated. You may encounter slight variations of the terms given here, but these are common American forms. Before using new instructions, you should find out whether they are American or British, because British terms have different meanings. English double crochet, for example, is the same as American single crochet.

An alternative to written instructions is a chart. For this purpose, different symbols are used (see pp. 390 and 392).

ch	chain p. 360		**sl st**	slip stitch p. 363
dc	double crochet p. 362		**sp**	space
dtr	double triple crochet p. 363		**yo**	yarn over
hdc	half double crochet p. 362		* *	Instructions between asterisks should be repeated as many times as there are stitches to accommodate them.
sc	single crochet p. 362			
tr	triple crochet p. 363		( )	A series of steps within parentheses should be worked according to instructions that follow the parentheses. Such a series is either worked into one stitch, or repeated a specified number of times.
tr tr	triple triple crochet p. 363			
alt	alternate			
beg	begin, beginning			
dec	decrease pp. 368-369		[ ]	Instructions within brackets explain the method for working a particular stitch or technique.
inc	increase p. 368			
patt	pattern		**gauge**	the number of stitches and rows per inch p. 366
rep	repeat		**mark the stitch**	tie on a contrasting yarn or slip a coil ring marker on the stitch indicated
rnd	round p. 370			
tog	together		**multiple**	the number of stitches required to work one repeat of a pattern stitch
sk	skip		**work even**	continue to work in pattern without increasing or decreasing

Testing the gauge

All crochet instructions have a specified gauge—the number of stitches that equals one inch. Some also include a row gauge—the number of rows to an inch. Because the size of a finished piece is based on these mathematics, it is important to duplicate the gauge before proceeding with any new project.

For a test swatch, make a chain four times the stitch gauge in length, using the specified yarn and hook size. Work in pattern until the piece measures 4 inches; fasten off. Measure the gauge as directed at right. If an adjustment is necessary, make a new swatch using a hook either one size larger or smaller.

To measure stitch gauge, place swatch on flat surface; insert 2 pins, 1″ apart; count stitches between them. If pin falls in center of a stitch, gauge may be the number of stitches per 2″.

To measure row gauge, insert 2 pins, 1″ apart (as shown) and count the number of rows between them. In measuring a swatch, always take care to keep it flat and avoid stretching it.

Tote bag is approximately 15" wide by 14" deep and measures 6" across the bottom.

Tote bag to crochet

Backstitch 344
Whipstitch 345

Handsome tote, easy enough for a first try at following a crochet pattern.

Materials

Wool rug or quickpoint yarn, five 8-oz. skeins (1 red, 2 gray, 2 camel); size J hook; 2 dowels, each 14" × ¾"; sturdy cardboard 6" × 14" (optional)

Gauge

5 sc = 2 inches, 2 rows = ¾ inch

1st handle: ch 11 with gray

Row 1: sk 1 ch, 10 sc, ch 1, turn

Row 2: 1 sc in each st, ch 1, turn

Rep Row 2, 15 more times, fasten off. Make 2nd handle the same way.

Top edge: ch 8, 10 sc across 1st handle, ch 17, 10 sc across 2nd handle, ch 9, turn

Body: sk 1 ch, 1 sc in each ch and each st across row (total of 53 sc), ch 1, turn. Work 7 more rows in gray, attach red on last loop of last sc (see illustrations, top right), ch 1, turn. Continue with red for 2 rows, then work 4 rows camel, 4 rows red, 8 rows gray, 2 rows red, 38 rows camel, 2 rows red, 8 rows gray, 4 rows red, 4 rows camel, 2 rows red, 8 rows gray, fasten off.

3rd handle: sk 8 sc, attach gray, work 10 sc, turn, work 17 rows, fasten off

4th handle: sk 17 center sc, attach gray, work 10 sc for 18 rows, fasten off. Sew sides, bottom, and handles as directed below. Slip dowels into the handles. Set cardboard in bottom, if desired.

JOINING AND SECURING YARNS

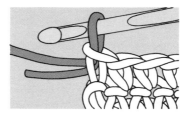

To join a new yarn at the end of a row, work last stitch with first yarn to final 2 loops; draw up last loop with new yarn.

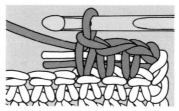

Cut first yarn to 2". Make a chain; turn. Pull up 2 short yarns and lay over previous row; work over them for 4-5 stitches.

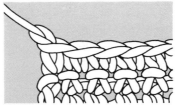

To secure yarn end (fasten off) on finished work, cut yarn to a 6" length; pull end through the last loop and tighten it.

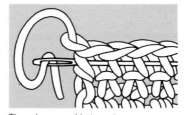

Thread yarn end in tapestry or yarn needle; weave into back of work for 1" to 2", below top row of stitches. Cut remainder.

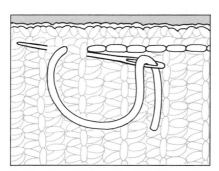

To join sides, fold bag with right sides together and top edges aligned. Working from bottom to top, backstitch each side seam 1 stitch in from edge (see Knitting for backstitch method).

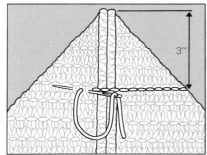

To sew bottom corners, lay bag flat with one side seam centered over the bottom, forming an angle. Measure 3" up from bottom of seam; backstitch across base of triangle at this point.

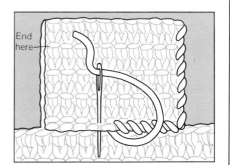

To sew handles, fold in half, wrong sides together, top edge and top of bag aligned. Whipstitch side edges together, top edge to the bag, center edges together, ending 2 rows from top fold.

367

Following crochet instructions

Shaping

Shaping in crochet is accomplished with increases and decreases. Once mastered, these techniques permit you to crochet any shape or form. Three examples are shown opposite, more on pages 370-371.

A single increase is made by working twice into the same stitch. If made within a row, and repeated over several rows, the increase positions move right or left. To keep the progression orderly, place a marker (contrasting yarn or a plastic coil ring) where increasing begins. For shaping to the right, increase before the marker; to the left, after the marker. On the next row, reverse this order to maintain consistency of the direction.

A single decrease is made by working two successive stitches that share one final loop. Repeated over several rows, progression is the same as for increasing.

Increasing

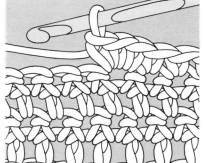

To make a single increase, work 2 stitches in 1 stitch. Single crochet is shown in the example; all other stitches are increased the same way.

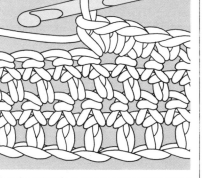

To make a double increase, work 3 stitches in 1 stitch. Single crochet is shown in the example; all other stitches are increased the same way.

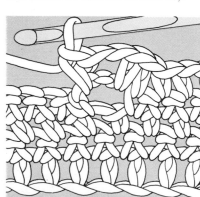

To make a decorative double increase (lacy chevron), work 2 chains at increase location. On next and subsequent rows, work (1 stitch, 2 chains, 1 stitch) in 2-chain space of previous row.

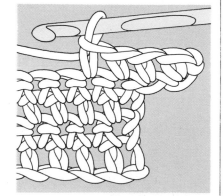

To increase several stitches at one edge, as when a sleeve is made in one piece with the garment, extend a chain from the side edge, then work back along the chain on the next row.

Decreasing

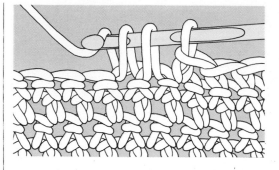

To decrease 1 stitch in single or half double crochet, insert hook in stitch, draw up a loop, insert hook in next stitch, draw up a loop (3 loops on hook), yarn over, draw through the 3 loops.

If a decrease occurs at the beginning of a row, you can, if you prefer, skip the first stitch instead of working 2 stitches together. If a decrease is designated for the end of a row, skip the next to last stitch.

To decrease 2 stitches in single or half double crochet, insert hook in stitch, draw up a loop, skip next stitch, insert hook in next stitch, draw up a loop (there are 3 loops on the hook, as shown), yarn over, draw through the 3 loops.

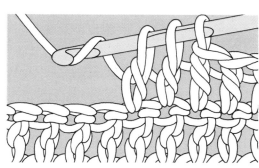

To decrease 1 stitch in double crochet, yarn over, insert hook in stitch, draw up a loop, yarn over, draw through 2 loops, yarn over, insert hook in next stitch, draw up a loop, yarn over, draw through 2 loops (3 loops on hook), yarn over, draw through 3 loops. .

If a decrease occurs at beginning of a row, you can skip the first stitch instead of working 2 stitches together; if at end of a row, skip next to last stitch.

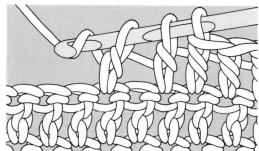

To decrease 2 stitches in double crochet, yarn over, insert hook in stitch, draw up a loop, yarn over, draw through 2 loops, skip next stitch, yarn over, insert hook in next stitch, draw up a loop, yarn over, draw through 2 loops (there are 3 loops on the hook, as shown), yarn over, draw through 3 loops.

To decrease 1 stitch in triple crochet, yarn over twice, insert hook in stitch, draw up a loop, yarn over, draw through 2 loops, yarn over, draw through 2 loops (2 loops remain on hook); yarn over twice, insert hook in next stitch, draw up a loop, yarn over, draw through 2 loops, yarn over, draw through 2 loops (there are 3 loops on the hook, as shown), yarn over, draw through last 3 loops.

To decrease 2 stitches in triple crochet, follow the method for decreasing 1 stitch, but skip a stitch between the 2 stitches that are worked together.

To decrease several stitches at the beginning of a row without an abrupt change in stitch heights, omit turning chain and work slip stitches for the number of decreases, make 1 single crochet in next stitch, then continue in pattern. Do not work the slip stitches on return row.

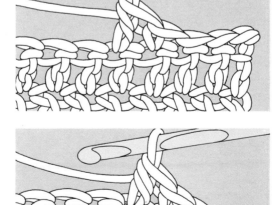

To decrease several stitches at the end of a row without an abrupt change in stitch heights, leave unworked the number of stitches to be decreased, work 1 slip stitch at end of row, chain 1 and turn. Skip the slip stitch, work 1 single crochet in the next stitch, then continue in pattern.

Geometric shapes/Worked in rows

Oval: Stitches worked around the chain instead of back and forth.
Ch 6
Row 1: sk 1 ch, 1 sc in each of next 4 ch, 3 sc in last ch, turn work so bottom of ch is on top
Row 2: 1 sc in each of next 5 ch (working into single loop that remains after working Row 1), 3 sc into ch that was skipped in Row 1, continue around, working next row in sts of Row 1
Row 3: *1 sc in each st*, 2 sc in last st, 2 sc in end st, 2 sc in st that begins row on opposite side Continue as in Row 3, increasing stitches at ends as needed.

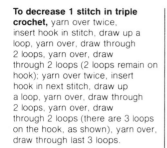

Triangle: Formed by increasing the first and last stitches every other row. The triangle becomes a diamond if, after reaching the desired width, you continue in pattern, decreasing the first and last stitches on alternate rows.
Ch 2
Row 1: 1 sc, turn
Row 2: 3 sc in the 1 sc, ch 1, turn
Row 3: 2 sc in 1st sc, 1 sc in each of next 2 sc, 2 sc in last sc, ch 1, turn
Row 4: *1 sc in each sc*, ch 1, turn
Row 5: 2 sc in 1st sc, *1 sc in next sc*, 2 sc in last sc, ch 1, turn
Rep Rows 4 and 5 as many times as necessary to obtain the desired size; fasten off.

Square: Formed by working increases in the center stitch of each row. An attractive variation on the usual approach, which is to work a square in straight rows.
Ch 2
Row 1: 3 sc in 2nd ch from hook, ch 1, turn
Row 2: 1 sc in 1st st, 3 sc in next st, 1 sc in last st, ch 1, turn
Row 3: 1 sc in each of 1st 2 sts, 3 sc in next st, 1 sc in each of last 2 sts, ch 1, turn
Row 4: 1 sc in each of 1st 3 sts, 3 sc in next st, 1 sc in each of last 3 sts, ch 1, turn
Continue as in Row 4, working 1 sc in each st except the center one, in which you work 3 sc.

Following crochet instructions

Geometric shapes/Worked in rounds

Crocheting in rounds is an alternative to working in rows. Flat geometrics, also bowl and tube shapes, are formed this way. Each is started with a ring (see method below), and is then developed in either concentric or spiral rounds, always working from the right side.

For concentric shaping, each round is started with a chain, which substitutes for the first stitch, and ended with a slip stitch into the starting chain (see illustration D, below). Examples of a concentric approach are the geometric shapes, right, and patchwork motifs, pages 378–379. Angles on such motifs are formed with increases of either two or four stitches placed directly above one another.

In spiral shaping, each round continues out of the previous one, with no starting chain or closing slip stitch. For this method, you should place a marker at the end of Round 1, then move it up with each new round to keep track of the rounds completed. For smooth shaping, the position of increases or decreases is usually moved forward by one stitch on each round. The hats, opposite, are typical examples of this technique.

A tube is also made in spiral fashion. To form a tube, you start with a ring of the desired diameter, then keep working around it (usually with single crochet), neither increasing nor decreasing, until the tube is as long as you wish.

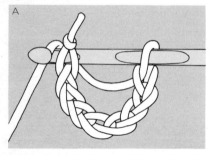

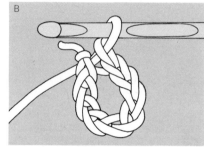

To form ring, make a chain; join last chain to first with a slip stitch (A and B). Depending on how

large you want the center space to be, allow 1 chain for every 2 to 4 stitches of first round.

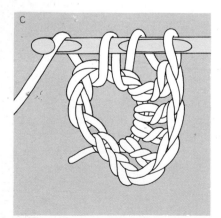

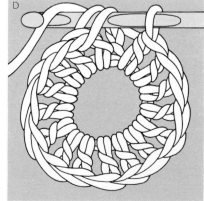

To work the first (center) round, start with a chain or stitch, as directed, and work stitches over

the ring (C); for concentric rounds, close with a slip stitch in top of beginning chain (D).

Circle: Concentric rounds worked with enough increases to keep edges from curling. The number and placement of increases may have to be adjusted for a particular yarn, hook size, or stitch that is used, but a general formula is to increase each round by the number of stitches that you started with.
Ch 6 and join in a ring with sl st
Round 1: ch 3, 11 dc in ring, sl st in top of beg ch (total of 12 sts)
Round 2: ch 3, 1 dc in sl st, 2 dc in each dc of Round 1, sl st in top of beg ch (24 sts)
Round 3: ch 3, 2 dc in next dc, (1 dc in next dc, 2 dc in next dc) 11 times, sl st in top of beg ch (total of 36 sts)
To continue, increase every 3rd st on next round, every 4th st on next round, and so on, increasing a total of 12 stitches every round.

Square: Sample (left) is in double crochet, but any stitch is suitable, as long as number of stitches in Round 1 is divisible by four.
Ch 6 and join in a ring with sl st
Round 1: ch 3, 2 dc in ring, ch 1, (3 dc in ring, ch 1) 3 times, sl st in top of beg ch (total of 12 sts)
Round 2: ch 3, 1 dc in each of next 2 sts, *(2 dc, ch 1, 2 dc) in ch sp, 1 dc in each of next 3 sts*, (2 dc, ch 1, 2 dc) in last ch sp, sl st in top of beg ch (total of 28 sts)
Round 3: ch 3, 1 dc in each of next 4 sts, *(2 dc, ch 1, 2 dc) in ch sp, 1 dc in each of next 7 sts*, (2 dc, ch 1, 2 dc) in last ch sp, 1 dc in each of next 2 sts, sl st in top of beg ch (total of 44 sts)
To continue, work evenly along each side, and put (2 dc, ch 1, 2 dc) in the ch sp at each corner, increasing 16 sts on each round.

Octagon: Structured the same as a square, but with two increases at each angle instead of four (to keep it flat). Number of stitches in Round 1 is divisible by number of sides.
Ch 4 and join in a ring with sl st
Round 1: ch 2, 1 hdc in ring, ch 1, (2 hdc in ring, ch 1) 7 times, sl st in top of beg ch (total of 16 sts)
Round 2: ch 2, 1 hdc in next st, *(1 hdc, ch 1, 1 hdc) in ch sp, 1 hdc in each of next 2 sts*, (1 hdc, ch 1, 1 hdc) in last ch sp, sl st in top of beg ch (total of 32 sts)
Round 3: ch 2, 1 hdc in each of next 3 sts, *(1 hdc, ch 1, 1 hdc) in ch sp, 1 hdc in each of next 4 sts*, (1 hdc, ch 1, 1 hdc) in last ch sp, sl st in top of beg ch (total of 48 sts)
To continue, work evenly along each side and put (1 hdc, ch 1, 1 hdc) at each angle, increasing a total of 16 sts on each round.

Hats to crochet

A trio of hats to crochet for yourself or a favorite child. The women's hats fit small to average head sizes; the cap is for a child 4 to 8 years old.

BERET
A classic style for any season.
Materials
4 ozs. knitting worsted, hook size F
Gauge: 7 hdc = 2 inches
Crown: ch 4, join in ring with sl st
Round 1: 8 hdc in ring, attach marker; move it up with each new round
Round 2: 2 hdc in each st
Round 3: *1 hdc in next st, 2 hdc in next st* (total of 24 hdc)
Round 4: *1 hdc in each of next 2 sts, 2 hdc in next st* (total of 32 hdc)
Round 5: increase 8 hdc, placing the increases every 4th st (40 hdc)
Rounds 6 and 7: increase 10 hdc in each round (60 hdc at end of Round 7)
Rounds 8, 9, 10, 11, 12: increase 6 hdc in each round (total of 90 hdc)
Rounds 13 and 14: increase 10 hdc in each round (110 hdc at end of Round 14)
Rounds 15, 16, 17: work evenly
Rounds 18, 19, 20, 21: decrease 10 sts in each round (70 hdc at end of 21)
Band: work in sc for 6 rounds; join last round with sl st to 1st sc; fasten off. Weave yarn end under edge for 1 inch.

HAT WITH BRIM
Of two-tone yarn for a tweed effect: fits heads 21-23 inches.
Materials
4 ozs. knitting worsted, hook size F
Gauge: 9 sc = 2 inches
Crown: ch 3, join in ring with sl st
Round 1: ch 1, 9 sc in ring, mark end of round with yarn or coil ring; continue to move marker with each new round
Round 2: 2 sc in each st of Round 1 (total of 18 sc)
Round 3: *1 sc in next sc, 2 sc in next sc* (total of 27 sc)
Round 4: *1 sc in each of next 2 sc, 2 sc in next sc* (total of 36 sc)

Round 5: *1 sc in each of next 3 sc, 2 sc in next sc* (total of 45 sc)
Round 6: 1 sc in each st (no increase)
Work 7 more rounds, increasing 9 sc on every other round. You will have 81 sc at end of Round 13. Increase 9 sc in both Rounds 14 and 15 (total of 99 sc); continue to work evenly until hat measures 7 inches from center of crown.
Brim: for the first round, increase in every 4th st (total of 124 sc); work evenly until brim measures 2 inches. Working from left to right on the right side, make 1 sc in each st, sl st to 1st sc, fasten off. Weave yarn end under the edge on the right side for about 1 inch.

CHILD'S CAP
For ages 4 to 8.
Materials
4 ozs. wool sport yarn, hook size F
Gauge: 9 sc = 2 inches
Crown: work 13 rounds, following the instructions for hat with brim. Work evenly on 81 sc until hat measures 6½ inches from center of crown, sl st to 1st sc in final round to close.
Cuff: work in rows on the wrong side.
Row 1 (wrong side): 1 sc in sl st of last rnd, 1 sc in each of next 80 sc, ch 1, turn
Row 2: 1 sc in each sc, ch 1, turn
Row 3: 1 sc in each of 1st 2 sc, 1 post dc around front of 3rd sc in Row 1 [yo,

insert hook across front of 3rd sc in Row 1, draw up a loop, yo, draw through 2 loops, yo, draw through remaining 2 loops], *sk 1 sc, 1 sc in each of next 2 sc, 1 post dc around next sc in Row 1*, rep from * across row, ch 1, turn
Rows 4, 5, 6: *1 sc in each st*, ch 1, turn
Row 7: 1 sc in each of 1st 2 sc, 1 post tr in post st 3 rows below, *sk 1 sc, 1 sc in each of next 2 sc, 1 post tr in post st 3 rows below*, ch 1, turn
Rep Rows 4-7 once more, fasten off.
Right side facing you, work 1 row of sl st along edge, then whipstitch back seams together from wrong side. Fasten off; weave end into seam. Turn cuff back.

Crochet stitches

Selecting a pattern stitch
Textures
Shells
Clusters
Motifs
Motifs/patchwork
Meshes
Shaping mesh ground
Filet crochet
Overlaid meshes
Irish crochet
Tunisian crochet
Loop stitches
Multicolor crochet
Charting a pattern stitch

Using a pattern stitch

A **pattern stitch** is a sequence of crochet techniques, repeated continuously to form a fabric. There are two ways of working a pattern—in *rows* or in *rounds*.

To work a pattern in rows, start with a number of chains that can be divided by the multiple (the stitches needed to complete one horizontal motif), plus any additional chains indicated. These extra chains include the ones that will be skipped at the beginning of Row 1, and sometimes a few for balancing pattern motifs. (The chain on the hook is never counted.) After completing all rows in the pattern, you begin again, usually at Row 2; the first row is usually a setting-up row. If a pattern is complex, use a row counter and/or markers to keep tally.

To work a pattern in rounds, you begin with a ring of chain stitches or yarn and work the first round into the ring (see p. 370 for the method). All subsequent rounds are worked with the right side facing you; the item is complete when you have obtained the desired size. It is not necessary to work all rounds.

Whether worked in rounds or rows, there is usually little difference between the two sides of a crochet pattern. Exceptions are some Tunisian stitches, also two-color patterns in which yarn is carried up one side. Unless directions specify otherwise, Row 1 begins the right side.

Most pattern stitches can be classified according to structure. Familiarity with these basic structures will permit you to "read" almost any pattern from a picture or sample, as you gain experience. Patterns in this section are grouped according to type, though in some cases, a stitch fits more than one category. The first group, *textures,* is a selection of compact patterns that are variations of basic crochet stitches. They are firmer and stiffer than the comparable knit stitches.

In selecting a pattern, consider its suitability for both yarn and purpose. A test swatch should show whether the stitch meets your requirements.

Textures

Alternate stitch: Two single crochets worked in every other stitch yield a firm fabric with leaf-like motif.
Multiple of 2 ch plus 2
Row 1: sk 3 ch, 2 sc in next ch, *sk 1 ch, 2 sc in next ch*, ch 2, turn
Row 2: *sk 1 st, 2 sc in next st*, ch 2, turn
Rep from Row 2

Double stitch: Each stitch spans two.
Multiple of 2 ch plus 2
Row 1: sk 2 ch, 1 double st [insert hook in next ch, yo, draw through a loop, insert hook in next ch, yo, draw through a loop, yo, draw through 3 loops], *1 double st, inserting hook first in st where 2nd yo was made for previous double st*, ch 2, turn
Row 2: *1 double st in each pair of sts*, 1 double st inserting hook in last st and top of ch at beg, ch 2, turn
Rep from Row 2

Up and down stitch: A varied texture produced by alternating single and double crochet stitches.
Multiple of 2 ch plus 2
Row 1: sk 2 ch, 1 sc in next ch, *1 dc, 1 sc*, 1 dc, ch 2, turn
Row 2: sk 1st dc, *1 dc in sc of previous row, 1 sc in dc of previous row*, 1 dc in ch 2 of previous row, ch 2, turn
Rep from Row 2

Checkerboard: Alternating bands of single and double crochet stitches.
Multiple of 10 ch plus 6
Row 1: sk 2 ch, 4 sc, *5 dc, 5 sc*, ch 3, turn
Row 2: sk 1st st, 4 dc, *5 sc, 5 dc*, work last dc in top of ch at beginning of previous row, ch 2, turn
Row 3: sk 1st st, 4 sc, *5 dc, 5 sc*, work last sc in top of turning ch, ch 3, turn
Rep from Row 2

Woven stitch: Single crochet stitches worked in single chain spaces.
Multiple of 3 ch plus 3
Row 1: sk 2 ch, 1 sc, *ch 1, sk 1 ch, 1 sc*, ch 2, turn
Row 2: *1 sc in ch sp of previous row, ch 1*, 1 sc in the turning ch sp, ch 2, turn
Rep from Row 2

Crossed stitches: Double crochet stitches worked in reverse order.
Multiple of 3 ch plus 2
Row 1: sk 6 ch, 1 dc in next ch, ch 1, 1 dc in 4th ch from beginning (crossing over the 1st dc), *sk 2 ch, 1 dc, ch 1, 1 dc in 1st of the skipped ch*, 1 dc in last ch, ch 4, turn
Row 2: sk 2 dc, 1 dc in next dc, ch 1, 1 dc in last skipped dc, *sk 1 dc, 1 dc in next dc, ch 1, 1 dc in skipped dc*, 1 dc in 3rd ch of turning ch, ch 4, turn
Rep from Row 2

Diagonal stitch: Long stitch pulled diagonally across each group of three.
Multiple of 4 ch plus 1
Row 1: sk 1 ch, *1 sc in each ch*, ch 2, turn
Row 2: *sk 1 st, 1 dc in each of next 3 sts, insert hook in last skipped st, yo, draw through an elongated loop, yo, draw through 2 loops*, 1 dc in last st, ch 1, turn
Row 3: sk 1 st, *1 sc in each st*, 1 sc in turning ch, ch 2, turn
Rep from Row 2

Open ridge stitch: A firm and heavy, yet airy pattern; especially suitable for a place mat or handbag.
Multiple of 2 ch plus 1
Row 1: sk 1 ch, *1 sc in each ch*, ch 1, turn
Row 2: 1 hdc, *sk 1 st, 1 hdc in next st, 1 hdc between 2 preceding hdc*, sk 1 st, 1 hdc in ch at beg of row, ch 1, turn
Row 3: *1 sc, inserting hook through front loop of each st in previous row*, ch 1, turn
Rep from Row 2

Basket weave: An unusual dimension is created by working *around* the stitches, first to the front, then the back. (See p. 364 for this technique.)
Multiple of 6 ch
Row 1: sk 3 ch, *1 dc in next ch*, ch 2, turn
Rows 2 and 3: sk 1 dc, *(1 post dc around the front) 3 times, (1 post dc around the back) 3 times*, (1 post dc around the front) 3 times, 1 dc in top of turning ch, ch 2, turn
Rows 4 and 5: sk 1 dc, *(1 post dc around the back) 3 times, (1 post dc around the front) 3 times*, (1 post dc around the back) 3 times, 1 dc in top of the turning ch, ch 2, turn
Rep from Row 2

Relief stitch: A 3-dimensional pattern with raised stitches worked around post as in basket weave, above.
Multiple of 2 ch
Row 1: sk 3 ch, *1 dc in each ch*, ch 1, turn
Row 2: *1 sc in each dc*, ch 2, turn
Row 3: *1 post hdc around the front of 1 dc of Row 1, 1 dc in next sc*, ch 1, turn
Row 4: *1 sc in top of post hdc, 1 sc between post hdc and the dc*, 1 sc in the turning ch, ch 2, turn
Row 5: *1 post hdc around the front of 1 post hdc of 2 rows below, 1 dc in next sc*, ch 1, turn
Rep from Row 4

Steps: Pattern progresses on a diagonal.
Multiple of 8 ch plus 3
Row 1: sk 2 ch, *1 dc in each ch*, ch 2, turn
Rows 2 and 3: sk 1 dc, *4 post dc around the front, 4 post dc around the back*, 1 dc in top ch at beg of Row 1, ch 2, turn
Row 4: sk 1 dc, 1 post dc around the back, *4 post dc around the front, 4 post dc around the back*, 3 post dc around the back, 1 dc in turning ch, ch 2, turn
Row 5: sk 1 dc, 3 post dc around the front, *4 post dc around the back, 4 post dc around the front*, 4 post dc around the back, 1 post dc around the front, 1 dc in turning ch, ch 2, turn
Rep from Row 4, moving pattern one st to the left on the even rows

Crochet stitches

Shells

A **shell** is a group of stitches, usually three or more, worked into one stitch or chain space. Stitches come together in close formation at the base and spread out at the top so that they resemble certain types of seashells or fans. The width and depth of a shell depends on the number of stitches that comprise it and the size of the space in which these are worked. The shape, too, can be varied. It is symmetrical when all stitches are the same size, asymmetrical when long and short stitches are combined (see far right, opposite page, for the latter).

The shell is a pretty stitch that has a lacy appearance even in a solid pattern.

Made up in medium-weight or heavy yarns, it is suitable and attractive for a blanket or afghan. Worked with fine yarns, it is appropriate for shawls, dressy garments, and baby clothing. In any yarn type, the shell stitch makes a nice edging because of its curved shape. Examples can be seen on page 401.

Because of the shell's comparatively elaborate structure, it is best suited to smooth yarns. It also requires more yarn than simpler stitch types (textures, for example), a factor that must be considered in estimating yarn for your own design. Guidelines for making yarn estimates are on page 393.

Lacy scallops: Small shells worked in narrow chain spaces form a delicate, open pattern; suitable for a baby garment.
Multiple of 6 ch plus 4
Row 1: *sk 5 ch, (2 dc, ch 3, 2 dc) in next ch*, sk 3 ch, 1 dc in last ch, ch 3, turn
Row 2: *(2 dc, ch 3, 2 dc) in 3-ch sp*, 1 dc in top of turning ch, ch 3, turn
Rep from Row 2

Close scallops: A firm stitch that is moderately scalloped.
Multiple of 6 ch plus 1
Row 1: sk 3 ch, 2 dc in next ch, sk 2 ch, 1 sc, *sk 2 ch, 4 dc in next ch, sk 2 ch, 1 sc*, ch 3, turn
Row 2: 2 dc in 1st sc, *1 sc between 2nd and 3rd dc of next 4-dc group, 4 dc in next sc*, 1 sc in 3-ch sp at beginning of row, ch 3, turn
Rep from Row 2

Wide arches: A moderately large pattern in which the shells alternate with open areas.
Multiple of 8 ch plus 3
Row 1: sk 2 ch, *1 dc, ch 3, sk 3 ch, 1 sc, ch 3, sk 3 ch*, 1 dc, ch 3, turn
Row 2: *1 sc in 2nd ch of 3-ch group, ch 3, 1 sc in 2nd ch of next 3-ch group, ch 1, 1 dc in the dc, ch 1*, 1 dc in the turning ch, ch 3, turn
Row 3: *7 dc in 3-ch sp, 1 dc in the dc*, 1 dc in the turning ch, ch 3, turn
Row 4: *ch 3, 1 sc in the center of the shell, ch 3, 1 dc in the dc*, 1 dc in the turning ch, ch 3, turn
Rep from Row 2

Simple shells: A moderately large motif.
Multiple of 6 ch plus 5
Row 1: sk 3 ch, 1 dc in next ch, *(2 dc, ch 1, 2 dc) in next ch, yo, insert hook in next ch, draw up a loop, yo, draw through 2 loops, sk 3 sts, yo, insert hook in next ch, draw up a loop, (yo, draw through 2 loops) 3 times*, 1 dc, ch 3, turn
Row 2: 1 dc in dc before the ch sp, *(2 dc, ch 1, 2 dc) in ch sp, yo, insert hook in next dc, draw up a loop, yo, draw through 2 loops, sk 3 sts, yo, insert hook in next dc, draw up a loop, (yo, draw through 2 loops) 3 times*, work last st in top of turning ch, ch 3, turn
Rep from Row 2

Arcade stitch: Lacy but firm; the pattern repeats on the diagonal.
Multiple of 6 ch plus 8
Row 1: sk 1 ch, 1 sc in each of next 2 ch, *ch 3, sk 3 ch, 1 sc in each of next 3 ch*, ch 3, sk 3 ch, 1 sc in each of last 2 ch, ch 1, turn
Row 2: 1 sc in 2nd sc, *5 dc in 3-ch sp, 1 sc in 2nd sc of 3-sc group*, turn
Row 3: *ch 3, 1 sc in each of 3 central dc*, ch 2, 1 sc in turning ch, ch 3, turn
Row 4: 2 dc in 2-ch sp, *1 sc in 2nd sc, 5 dc in 3-ch sp, 1 sc in 2nd sc, 3 dc in 3-ch sp, ch 1, turn
Row 5: 1 sc in each of first 2 dc, *ch 3, 1 sc in each of 3 central dc*, ch 3, 1 sc in last dc, 1 sc in turning ch, ch 1, turn
Rep from Row 2

Wave stitch: A popular pattern for baby blankets and afghans. The crest of each wave is formed with one shell stitch; the distance between crests can be varied, if you wish, by adjusting the multiple.
Multiple of 13 ch
Row 1: sk 3 ch, 4 dc in next 4 ch, 3 dc in next ch, 5 dc in next 5 ch, *sk 2 ch, 5 dc in next 5 ch, 3 dc in next ch, 5 dc in next 5 ch*, ch 3, turn
Row 2: sk 1 st, 4 dc in next 4 sts, 3 dc in next st, 5 dc in next 5 sts, *sk 2 sts, 5 dc in next 5 sts, 3 dc in next st, 5 dc in next 5 sts*, on the last multiple, end with 4 dc, sk 1 dc, 1 dc in turning ch, ch 3, turn
Rep from Row 2

Bushy stitch: These shells are a combination of single and double crochet stitches, and are asymmetrical in form.
Multiple of 3 ch plus 1
Row 1: sk 3 ch, (1 dc, ch 2, 1 sc) in next ch, *sk 2 ch, (2 dc, ch 2, 1 sc) in next ch*, ch 2, turn
Row 2: *(2 dc, ch 2, 1 sc) in each 2-ch sp*, ch 2, turn
Rep from Row 2

Fan stitch: Elegant large shells.
Multiple of 14 ch plus 2
Row 1: sk 1 ch, 1 sc, *sk 6 ch, 1 elongated dc [yo, insert hook, draw up a loop ½″ long, yo, draw through 2 loops, yo, draw through 2 loops], 12 more elongated dc in the same ch, sk 6 ch, 1 sc*, ch 3, turn
Row 2: 1 elongated dc in 1st sc, *ch 5, 1 sc in 7th of 13 elongated dc, ch 5, 2 elongated dc in sc between the fans*, 2 elongated dc in last sc, ch 1, turn
Row 3: 1 sc between the 1st 2 elongated dc, *13 elongated dc in the sc worked at center of fan in previous row, 1 sc between the 2 long dc of previous row*, ch 3, turn
Rep from Row 2

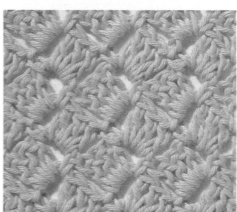

Brick stitch: Squares of asymmetrical shells with openwork between them.
Multiple of 4 ch plus 6
Row 1: sk 3 ch, *2 dc in next 2 ch, (1 dc, ch 3, 1 dc) in next ch, sk 1 ch* 3 dc in last 3 ch, ch 3, turn
Row 2: *(3 dc, ch 3, 1 sc) in each 3-ch sp*, 1 dc between last group of 3 dc and turning ch, ch 3, turn
Rep from Row 2

Starburst: Shells and clusters combined.
Multiple of 8 ch plus 10
Row 1: sk 1 ch, 1 sc, *sk 3 ch, 9 dc in next ch, sk 3 ch, 1 sc*, ch 3, turn
Row 2: sk 1 sc, 4-dc cluster over next 4 sts [(yo, insert hook, draw up a loop, yo, draw through 2 loops) in each st, yo, draw through 5 loops], *ch 4, 1 sc, ch 3, 9-dc cluster over next 9 sts*, ch 4, 1 sc, ch 3, 5-dc cluster, ch 4, turn
Row 3: 4 dc in top of 5-dc cluster, 1 sc in the sc, *9 dc in top of 9-dc cluster, 1 sc in the sc*, 5 dc in top of 4-dc cluster, ch 3, turn
Row 4: sk 1 dc, *9-dc cluster, ch 4, 1 sc, ch 3*, 1 sc in turning ch, ch 1, turn
Row 5: 1 sc, *9 dc in top of 9-dc cluster, 1 sc*, 1 sc in turning ch, ch 3, turn
Rep from Row 2

Ripple stitch: Asymmetrical shell stitches in a compact pattern; also pretty worked in two or more colors.
Multiple of 3 ch plus 1
Row 1: sk 2 ch, 2 dc in next ch, *(1 sc, 2 dc) in next ch, sk 2 ch*, 1 sc, ch 2, turn
Row 2: 2 dc in first sc, *(1 sc, 2 dc) in each sc of previous row*, 1 sc in turning ch, ch 2, turn
Rep from Row 2

Crochet stitches

Clusters

A **cluster** is a group of three or more stitches worked into one stitch or chain space, then drawn together at the top with one loop. Depending on how many stitches are in the group, results may be relatively flat, as in the soft cluster stitch directly below, or extremely chunky, as in the bobble stitch at the lower right. Whatever the type, however, all clusters stand out from a flat surface, thus providing extra texture and dimension in the finished piece.

In an allover pattern (examples below), the cluster makes a warm, somewhat bulky fabric that is suitable for a heavy sweater or a blanket. Used indi-

vidually, or as one row in a plain crochet pattern, it is an attractive accent or trim. It also works well in patchwork motifs (see pp. 378-379), where it contributes symmetry and textural interest.

Generally, clusters look best in heavy or medium-weight yarn. When estimating the yarn quantity, remember that each cluster is composed of several yarn loops, so half again or even twice as much yarn will be needed as for a simpler stitch, such as a mesh or texture.

In working a cluster, the yarn tension should be kept fairly loose to make the clusters soft, and to facilitate drawing the final loop through the top.

Lace clusters: A bubbly texture of thick puffs combined with openwork.
Multiple of 6 ch plus 4
Row 1: sk 3 ch, *(1 dc, ch 2, 1 dc) in next ch, sk 2 ch, 1 puff [(yo, insert hook, draw up a loop) 4 times in same ch, yo, draw through 9 loops], ch 1, sk 2 ch*, (1 dc, ch 2, 1 dc) in last ch, ch 3, turn
Row 2: *1 puff in 2-ch sp between 2 dc of previous row, ch 1, (1 dc, ch 2, 1 dc) under loop that closes the puff in previous row*, 1 puff, 1 dc in 3-ch sp at beg of previous row, ch 3, turn
Row 3: (1 dc, ch 2, 1 dc) in top of puff, *1 puff in 2-ch sp, ch 1, (1 dc, ch 2, 1 dc) in top of puff*, 1 dc in 3-ch sp at beg of previous row, ch 3, turn
Rep from Row 2

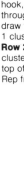

Soft clusters: Relatively flat stitch grouping; looks the same on both sides.
Multiple of 2 ch plus 4
Row 1: sk 3 ch, *1 cluster [(yo, insert hook, draw up a loop, yo, draw through 2 loops) 3 times in same ch, yo, draw through 4 loops], ch 1, sk 1 ch*, 1 cluster, ch 3, turn
Row 2: *1 cluster in ch between clusters of previous row*, 1 cluster in top of turning ch, ch 3, turn
Rep from Row 2

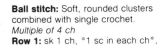

Ball stitch: Soft, rounded clusters combined with single crochet.
Multiple of 4 ch
Row 1: sk 1 ch, *1 sc in each ch*, ch 1, turn
Row 2: 3 sc, *1 ball [(yo, insert hook, draw up a loop) 3 times in same st, yo and draw through 7 loops], 3 sc*, ch 1, turn
Row 3: *1 sc in each st*, ch 1, turn
Row 4: 1 sc, *1 ball, 3 sc*, 1 ball, 1 sc, ch 1, turn
Row 5: *1 sc in each st*, ch 1, turn
Rep from Row 2

Pineapple stitch: A thicker stitch than soft clusters above, but still somewhat flat. In lightweight yarn, a popular stitch for stoles.
Multiple of 2 ch plus 4
Row 1: sk 3 ch, *1 pineapple [(yo, insert hook, draw up a loop) 4 times in same ch, yo, draw through 8 loops, yo, draw through the last 2 loops], ch 1, sk 1 ch*, 1 pineapple, ch 3, turn
Row 2: *1 pineapple in each ch sp of previous row*, 1 pineapple in the turning ch sp, ch 3, turn
Rep from Row 2

Bobble stitch: Solid, 3-dimensional pattern; be sure to allow ample yarn.
Multiple of 3 ch plus 1
Row 1: sk 1 ch, *1 sc in each ch*, ch 1, turn
Row 2: *1 bobble [(yo, insert hook, draw up a loop, yo, draw through 2 loops) 5 times in same st, yo, draw through 6 loops], 2 sc*, 1 bobble, ch 1, turn
Rows 3 and 5: *1 sc in each st*, ch 1, turn
Row 4: *2 sc, 1 bobble*, 1 sc, ch 1, turn
Row 6: 1 sc, *1 bobble, 2 sc*, ch 1, turn
Rep from Row 2

Motifs

A **motif** is composed of stitches worked around a center ring. The formation may be symmetrical or it may not, but each unit is complete and can be used singly or joined with others in a patchwork.

The center ring of a motif is usually a chain joined with a slipstitch. The first row, called a *round*, is worked into this circle, with stitches taken over the chain, and adjusted to fit evenly around. Each subsequent round is worked from the right side and closed with a slipstitch at the starting point (unless the form is a spiral). The last round is fastened off.

Motifs can be used individually as appliqués, for example, or as coasters, place mats, or potholders. Because there is no limit to their size, you can even fashion a rug. The most popular use for motifs, however, is patchwork. Square patterns, familiarly known as "granny squares," are frequently used for this, but any symmetrical design will do. Larger items are easy to manage because motifs can be done one at a time, and joined at your convenience. Motifs are also ideal for using up yarn leftovers, as each round can be worked in a different color (see p. 390 for how to change yarn colors). You can join motifs with an overcast stitch, or crochet them together with slip stitch or single crochet.

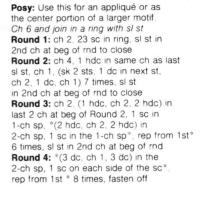

Posy: Use this for an appliqué or as the center portion of a larger motif.
Ch 6 and join in a ring with sl st
Round 1: ch 2, 23 sc in ring, sl st in 2nd ch at beg of rnd to close
Round 2: ch 4, 1 hdc in same ch as last sl st, ch 1, (sk 2 sts, 1 dc in next st, ch 2, 1 dc, ch 1) 7 times, sl st in 2nd ch at beg of rnd to close
Round 3: ch 2, (1 hdc, ch 2, 2 hdc) in last 2 ch at beg of Round 2, 1 sc in 1-ch sp, *(2 hdc, ch 2, 2 hdc) in 2-ch sp, 1 sc in the 1-ch sp*, rep from 1st* 6 times, sl st in 2nd ch at beg of rnd
Round 4: *(3 dc, ch 1, 3 dc) in the 2-ch sp, 1 sc on each side of the sc*, rep from 1st * 8 times, fasten off

Clover: The lucky kind with four leaves. For the traditional variety, turn to page 384.
Ch 5 and join in a ring with sl st
Round 1: 14 sc in ring
Round 2: 2 sc, 1 leaf [ch 4, (yo twice, insert hook in next st, draw up a loop, yo, draw through 2 loops, yo, draw through 2 loops) 3 times in same st, yo, draw through 4 loops, ch 3], 1 sc in each of next 2 sts, 3 more leaves as above, make stem [ch 6, work back along these 6 ch with 1 sc in each ch (or with 1 sl st in each ch if yarn is thick)], 1 sl st in 1st sc to close, fasten off

Daisy: Chain stitches form the petals of this 3-dimensional motif.
Ch 6 and join in a ring with sl st
Round 1: 14 sc in ring, sl st to 1st sc at beg of rnd to close
Round 2: (into front strand of each sc work 1 sc, ch 6, 1 sc) 14 times, sl st to 1st sc to close
Round 3: (into back strand of each sc in Round 1 work 1 sc, ch 8, 1 sc) 14 times, sl st to 1st sc, fasten off

Star: The conventional 5-pointed shape to use as an emblem or decoration.
Ch 2
Round 1: 5 sc in 2nd ch from hook
Round 2: 3 sc in each sc
Round 3: (1 sc in next st, ch 6, sl st in 2nd ch from hook, 1 sc in next ch, 1 hdc in next ch, 1 dc in next ch, 1 tr in next ch, 1 tr in base of starting sc, sk 2 sc) 4 times, sl st in first sc to join, fasten off

Chrysanthemum: Broad petals that curl slightly toward the center.
Ch 4 and join in a ring with sl st
Round 1: 13 sc in ring, sl st to 1st sc at beg of rnd to close, fasten off
Round 2: using 2nd color, make 1 petal into the front strand of each sc of Round 1 [1 sc, ch 5, 1 sc in 2nd ch from hook, 1 hdc in each of next 2 ch, 1 sc in next ch, 1 sc in sc at beg], total of 13 petals
Round 3: make 1 petal into the back strand of each sc of Round 1 [1 sl st, ch 6, 1 sc in 5 of these 6 ch], total of 13 petals, fasten off

Crochet stitches

Motifs/Patchwork

Eyelet square: A simple center motif surrounded by rows of single crochet; more interesting when worked in two or more colors. Round 1 is crocheted over a double yarn strand instead of the usual ring of chains.
Wind yarn twice around tip of index finger to form a ring
Round 1: 16 sc in ring
Round 2: (1 sc, ch 10, sk 3 sc) 4 times, sl st in 1st sc, fasten off
Round 3: using new color, (11 sc in the 10-ch sp, 1 sc in next sc) 4 times, sl st in 1st sc, fasten off
Round 4: using new color, *1 sc in each of 6 sts, 2 sc in next st to form corner, 1 sc in each of 5 sts*, rep from * 3 times, sl st in 1st sc, fasten off
Round 5: 1 sc in each st and 2 sc at each corner, sl st in 1st sc
Rep Round 5 as many times as desired for size, changing colors as it suits you, fasten off

Hawaiian square: Pineapple stitches surround a small flower; a very simple motif.
Ch 8 and join in ring with sl st
Round 1: 1 pineapple st in ring [(yo, insert hook, draw up a loop) 4 times, yo, draw through 9 loops], (ch 2, 1 pineapple st) 7 times, ch 2, sl st in 1st st
Round 2: 1 pineapple st in ch sp before sl st, *ch 2, 1 pineapple st in next sp, ch 2, (1 dc, ch 2, 1 dc) in next pineapple st to form the corner, ch 2, 1 pineapple st in next sp*, after dc group at end of rnd ch 2, sl st in 1st pineapple st
Round 3: 1 pineapple st in sp before sl st, *(ch 2, 1 pineapple st) in each sp up to the corner, ch 2, (1 dc, ch 2, 1 dc) between dc groups at corner, ch 2*, 1 sl st in 1st st
Rep from Round 3, working 1 more pineapple st on each side for each rnd, until there are 6 pineapple sts on each side, or until the square is the desired size; fasten off

Flower in a square: Long chains are the flower petals.
Ch 5 and join in a ring with sl st
Round 1: 12 sc in ring, sl st in 1st sc to close
Round 2: (ch 11, sl st in next sc) 12 times
Round 3: sl st in each of 1st 6 ch of 1st ch loop, *ch 4, 1 sc in central st of next ch loop, ch 4, 1 cluster in next ch loop [(yo, insert hook, draw up a loop, yo, draw through 2 loops) 3 times in same ch loop, yo, draw through all 4 loops], ch 4, 1 cluster in same ch loop to form corner, ch 4, 1 sc in next loop *, rep from * 3 times
Round 4: 2 sl sts in 1st 4-ch sp, ch 3, (yo, insert hook in the same sp, draw up a loop, yo, draw through 2 loops) twice, yo, draw through all 3 loops, *ch 4, 1 sc in next 4-ch sp, ch 4, (1 cluster, ch 4, 1 cluster) in corner sp, ch 4, 1 sc in next 4-ch sp, ch 4, 1 cluster in next 4-ch sp*, rep from * 3 times, ch 4, sl st in top of 1st cluster to close, fasten off

Old America square: This is a traditional type of granny square. It is frequently worked in two or more colors.
Ch 6 and join in a ring with sl st
Round 1: ch 3, 2 dc in ring, ch 2, (3 dc in ring, ch 2) 3 times, sl st in top of beg ch, fasten off
Round 2: join new color with sl st in 1st ch sp, ch 3, (2 dc, ch 2, 3 dc) in same sp to form a corner, (ch 1, 3 dc, ch 2, 3 dc in next 2-ch sp) 3 times for 3 more corners, sl st in top of beg ch, fasten off
Round 3: join new color with sl st in 1st ch sp, ch 3, (2 dc, ch 2, 3 dc) in same sp, *(ch 1, 3 dc) in each 1-ch sp (along the side), (ch 1, 3 dc, ch 2, 3 dc) in each 2-ch sp (a corner)*, sl st in top of beg ch, fasten off
Rep Round 3 as many times as desired for size

Hexagon: A simple, solid pattern.
Ch 6 and join in a ring with sl st
Round 1: ch 2, 2 dc in ring, ch 3, (3 dc in ring, ch 3) 5 times, sl st in top of beg ch to close, fasten off
Round 2: using new color, ch 4, *(3 tr, ch 2, 3 tr) in each 3-ch sp*, sl st in top of beg ch to close, fasten off
Round 3: using new color, ch 3, *1 dc in each tr, (2 dc, ch 2, 2 dc) in each 2-ch sp*, sl st in top of beg ch to close, fasten off
Round 4: using new color, ch 3, *sk 1 st, 1 dc in next st, 1 dc in the skipped st*, sl st in top of beg ch to close, fasten off

Paddle wheel: The rounds are left open in this spiraled hexagon.
Ch 5 and join in a ring with sl st
Round 1: (ch 6, 1 sc in ring) 6 times, do not close the round
Round 2: (ch 4, 1 sc in next sp) 6 times
Round 3: (ch 4, 1 sc in next sp, 1 sc in next sc) 6 times
Round 4: (ch 4, 1 sc in next sp, 1 sc in each of the 2 sc) 6 times
Round 5: (ch 4, 1 sc in next sp, 1 sc in each of the 3 sc) 6 times
Rep for as many rnds as desired, working 1 extra sc in each group on each rnd; beginning with the 10th rnd, make 5 ch in each sp instead of 4

Dogwood: Four lovely petals.
Ch 2
Round 1: sk 1st ch, 8 sc in 2nd ch, sl st in 1st sc to close
Round 2: ch 5, sk 1 st, 1 sc in next st, (ch 4, sk 1 st, 1 sc in next st) twice, ch 4, sl st in 1st of 5 ch at beg of rnd
Round 3: 1 sl st in next ch sp, ch 4, 6 dc in same sp as sl st, (ch 2, 7 dc) in each of next 3 ch sp, ch 2, sl st in top of 4 ch at beg of rnd
Round 4: ch 2, 1 sc in joining sp, (1 sc in each of next 2 sts, 2 sc in next st) twice, ch 3, *(2 sc in next st, 1 sc in each of next 2 sts) twice, 2 sc in next st, ch 3*, rep from * twice, sl st in top of beg ch
Round 5: ch 4, 1 dc in joining st, 1 dc in next st, 2 dc in next st, 1 dc in next st, 2 dc in next st, (1 dc in next st, 2 dc in next st) twice, (1 dc in next st, 2 dc in next st) twice, ch 2, turn
Round 6: (1 sc, 4 dc, 1 sc, ch 2, sk 2 sts) twice, sk 1 st, 1 sl st, fasten off; rep Rounds 5 and 6 for 3 other petals, each time starting with right side facing you

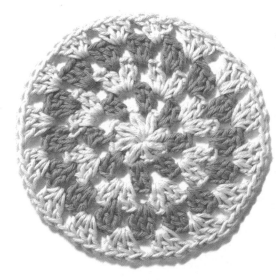

Wagon wheel: A versatile pattern; besides patchwork, it would be suitable for household items such as coasters, mats, or pillow covers.
Ch 4 and join in a ring with sl st
Round 1: ch 3, 1 petal in ring [(yo, insert hook, draw up a loop) twice, yo, draw through 5 loops, ch 1], 7 more petals in ring, sl st in top of beg ch, fasten off
Round 2: join new color in 1st ch sp, ch 2, 1 dc in 1st ch sp, ch 2, (2 dc, ch 2) in each of next 7 ch sp, sl st in 2nd ch at beg, fasten off
Round 3: join new color in 1st ch sp, ch 2, (1 dc, ch 1, 2 dc, ch 1) in 1st ch sp, (2 dc, ch 1, 2 dc, ch 1) in each of next 7 ch sp, sl st in 2nd ch at beg, fasten off
Round 4: join new color in 1st ch sp, ch 2, 2 dc in 1st ch sp, ch 1, (3 dc, ch 1) in each of next 15 ch sp, sl st in 2nd ch at beg, fasten off
Rep Round 4 as many times as desired for size, but after Round 5, ch 2 between dc groups

379

Crochet stitches

Meshes

A **mesh** consists of chain stitches and double crochets combined in such a way that they form open spaces. By itself, or in conjunction with other techniques, it has a wide variety of uses.

Either of the square meshes below can serve as the basic element in **filet crochet** (see p. 382). To produce filet, selected meshes are filled with double crochet to form a pattern. (Or sometimes the reverse: the background is filled and open meshes form the pattern.) Once used extensively for doilies and antimacassars, filet is today used more for trims and accessories. Square meshes also form the background for **overlaid patterns** (see p. 383); in this technique, the spaces are filled with chain stitches, woven yarns, or other material such as ribbon.

Diamond, honeycomb, and diamond picot stitches, at the right, are used in the working of **Irish crochet** (see p. 384); for this purpose, they form the lace background to flower and leaf motifs.

Used alone, any mesh pattern is ideal for a shawl, providing the lightweight warmth desirable in a wrap. Mesh is also suitable for summer garments, evening wear, and baby clothing. To make the most of its laciness, lightweight yarns are best. Good choices are crochet cotton and fingering and sport yarns.

Diamond mesh: A flexible stitch that is especially suitable for a flat round item such as a doily or tablecloth. It is also used in fringe-making and sometimes to join solid sections that have been knitted or crocheted.
Multiple of 4 ch plus 2
Row 1: sk 1 ch, 1 sc in next ch, *ch 5, sk 3 ch, 1 sc in next ch*, 1 sc, ch 5, turn
Row 2: *1 sc in next ch sp, ch 5*, turn
Rep from Row 2

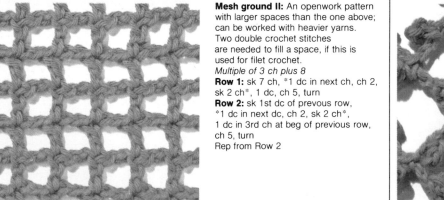

Mesh ground I: A small openwork pattern, suitable for the background in filet crochet and overlaid patterns, or it can be used alone.
Fine yarns are most appropriate.
Multiple of 2 ch plus 6
Row 1: sk 5 ch, *1 dc in next ch, ch 1, sk 1 ch*, 1 dc, ch 4, turn
Row 2: sk 1st dc of previous row, *1 dc in next dc, ch 1*, 1 dc in 3rd ch at beginning of previous row, ch 4, turn
Rep from Row 2

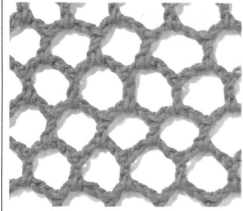

Honeycomb mesh: A popular pattern for background in Irish crochet (p. 384).
Multiple of 4 ch plus 10
Row 1: sk 9 ch, *1 dc in next ch, ch 4, sk 3 ch*, 1 dc, ch 8, turn
Row 2: *1 dc in the 4-ch sp, ch 4*, 1 dc, ch 8, turn
Rep from Row 2

Mesh ground II: An openwork pattern with larger spaces than the one above; can be worked with heavier yarns. Two double crochet stitches are needed to fill a space, if this is used for filet crochet.
Multiple of 3 ch plus 8
Row 1: sk 7 ch, *1 dc in next ch, ch 2, sk 2 ch*, 1 dc, ch 5, turn
Row 2: sk 1st dc of prevous row, *1 dc in next dc, ch 2, sk 2 ch*, 1 dc in 3rd ch at beg of previous row, ch 5, turn
Rep from Row 2

Diamond picot mesh: Another favorite pattern for Irish crochet; this one has been used as the background for pillow cover shown on page 385.
Multiple of 7 ch plus 2
Row 1: sk 1 ch, 1 sc in next ch, *ch 2, 1 picot [ch 5, sl st in 1st of these 5 ch], ch 3, 1 picot, ch 2, sk 6 ch, 1 sc*, ch 2, turn
Row 2: 1 picot, ch 3, 1 picot, ch 2, 1 sc in ch sp between picots of previous row, *ch 2, 1 picot, ch 3, 1 picot, ch 2, 1 sc in ch sp*, ch 2, turn
Rep from Row 2

Solomon's knot: Lengthened chains form an open mesh that is similar in appearance to netting. The lengthened loop can be adjusted as desired. See page 365 for the way to make the knots.
Multiple of 4 ch plus 2
Row 1: sk 1 ch, 1 sc, 1 single knot [lengthen loop on hook to ½″, draw up a loop, take hook across front of lengthened loop and insert it under yarn of ch just completed, work 1 sc], make another single knot to complete the double knot, *sk 3 ch, 1 sc in next ch, 1 double knot*, 1 single knot, turn (total of 3 single knots for turning)
Row 2: *1 sc in center of double knot in previous row, 1 double knot*, 1 single knot, turn
Rep from Row 2

Trestle stitch: A lacy pattern with alternating large and small spaces. Especially suitable for a shawl.
Multiple of 4 ch plus 6
Row 1: sk 5 ch, *1 dc in next ch, ch 3, sk 3 ch*, 1 dc, ch 4, turn
Row 2: *1 sc in 2nd ch of 3-ch group, ch 2, 1 dc in next dc, ch 2*, 1 sc in turning ch of previous row, ch 5, turn
Row 3: *1 dc in the dc, ch 3*, 1 dc in turning ch of previous row, ch 4, turn
Rep from Row 2

Open checks: A large mesh ground with the alternate spaces filled in.
Multiple of 6 ch plus 3
Row 1: sk 3 ch, 1 dc in each of next 2 ch, *ch 3, sk 3 ch, 1 dc in each of next 3 ch*, ch 3, sk 3 ch, 1 dc in last ch, ch 3, turn
Row 2: 2 dc in 1st 3-ch sp, *ch 3, 3 dc in next 3-ch sp*, ch 3, 1 dc in top of turning ch, ch 3, turn
Rep from Row 2

Shaping mesh ground

To decrease a space at the end of a row, do not work the last space (the one formed by the turning chain); instead, chain 4 (for mesh ground I) or chain 5 (for mesh ground II) and turn; work 1 double crochet in the next double crochet. The resulting space will be triangular rather than square.

To decrease a space at the beginning of a row, do not make the usual turning chain; instead, chain 1 and turn; make 1 slip stitch in each chain stitch up to the next double crochet, then 1 slip stitch in the double crochet; chain 4 (for mesh ground I) or chain 5 (for mesh ground II) and continue with the mesh pattern starting with 1 double crochet in the next stitch. Use this method only when decreases must be paired on either side of the work.

To increase a space at the beginning of a row, do not make the usual turning chain; instead, chain 5 (for mesh ground I) or chain 7 (for mesh ground II) and turn; work 1 double crochet in first stitch of the previous row.

Crochet stitches

Filet crochet

Filet crochet is a square mesh pattern with certain spaces filled to form a motif. Appropriate stitches for the openwork are mesh grounds I and II on page 380.

The filling is double crochet, one stitch for a small space, two for a large one. Directions are usually charted, with background meshes represented by blank squares and motif stitches by filled ones. To follow a chart, read from right to left on the odd (right side) rows, from left to right on the even rows. Do the reverse, if you are left-handed. Suitable filet motifs are monograms, geometrics, and flowers. Cotton is the traditional yarn choice, as it shows off the delicacy of filet.

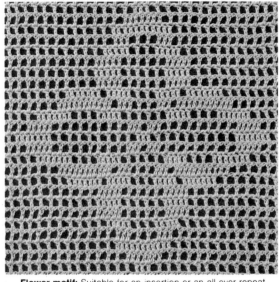

Flower motif: Suitable for an insertion or an all-over repeat.

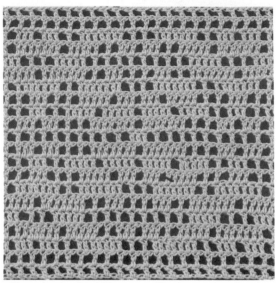

Flower border: A kaleidoscope motif makes an attractive trim.

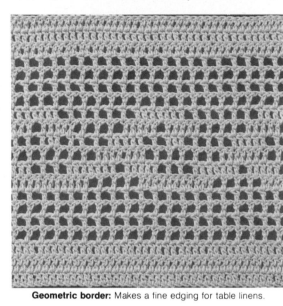

Geometric border: Makes a fine edging for table linens.

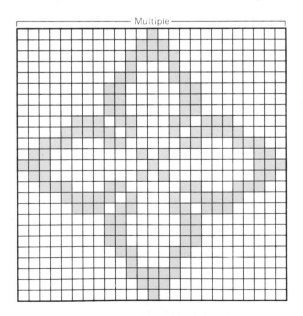

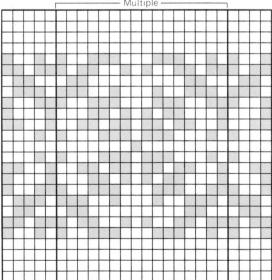

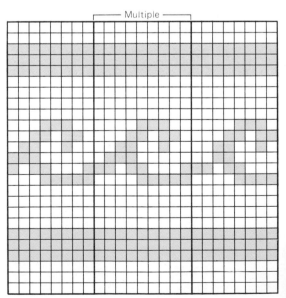

Overlaid meshes

Chained overlay: A mesh background with chain stitches worked in the spaces. An easy and effective way to create a crocheted stripe or plaid. Depending on the weight and type of yarn you choose, this technique can be used for a garment, a place mat, a pillow cover, or a rug. The color sequences should be planned before you begin.

To prepare the background, use pattern for mesh ground I (p. 380).
To work the overlay chains, use 2 strands of yarn; make a slip knot. With right side of mesh facing you, and yarn held behind the work, draw a loop through the first space in the lower right corner, insert hook in space directly above it, draw a loop through the space and the loop on the hook. Continue working this way to the top of the mesh, then begin again at bottom. In forming the chains, take care to maintain an even tension, or the background may be pulled askew.

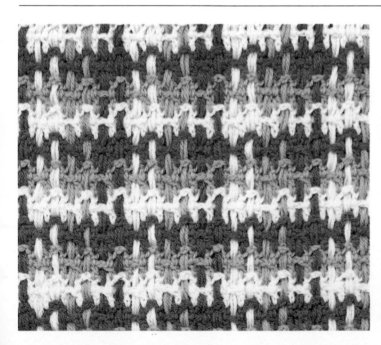

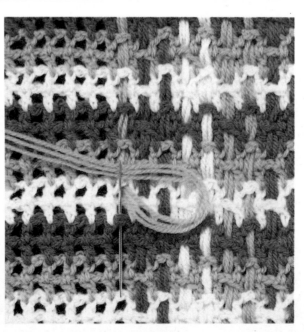

Woven overlay: Yarns intertwined with a mesh background. The fabric produced is thick and firm, usable for outerwear, a place mat, or rug. Though any stitch might be used, a mesh (shown here) is the usual choice. The woven strands can be yarn, fabric strips, or ribbon, and can be worked into the background vertically, horizontally, or diagonally.

To prepare the background, use pattern for mesh ground I (p. 380).
To weave the overlay, use 3 strands of yarn threaded in a tapestry (blunt-pointed) needle. Lace the yarns vertically under and over the chain bars, filling alternate spaces on each row. Yarn should be pulled firmly so that no loops remain, yet not too tightly, or the mesh may pucker.

Crochet stitches

Irish crochet

Irish crochet was developed in the mid-nineteenth century, its style inspired by a popular Venetian lace. The lovely designs are most elegant worked in fine cotton or linen yarns. A typical pattern consists of floral motifs set in a mesh background. The mesh is usually worked around motifs, but in some modern adaptations it is crocheted separately and the motifs applied to it. A three-dimensional look can be given the motifs by working certain portions over an additional yarn strand called a foundation cord. This cord, which is used also to control shaping, should be about twice the thickness of the working yarn.

Shamrock: Wind foundation cord twice around index finger and slip it off
Round 1: 2 sc in ring, 1 picot [ch 4] (10 sc in ring, ch 4) twice, 8 sc in ring, sl st to 1st sc, pull cord so sts lie flat
Round 2: 15 sc over cord only, sk 1 picot and 1 sc, over cord and sts make 1 sc in each of next 7 sc, pull cord so sts lie flat, 18 sc over cord only, sk 1 picot and 1 sc, 1 sc in each of next 7 sc, 15 sc on cord only, sk 1 picot and 1 sc, 1 sc in each of next 7 sc
Round 3: drop cord, around 1st leaf (ch 1, 1 sc) in each of next 2 sts, (ch 1, 1 dc) in each of next 3 sts, (ch 1, 1 tr) in each of next 5 sts, (ch 1, 1 dc) in each of next 3 sts, (ch 1, 1 sc) in each of next 2 sts, sl st in sc between leaves, work other 2 leaves as the 1st, but make 7 tr in 2nd leaf, sl st between leaves
Round 4: pick up foundation cord, sk 1st ch, *3 sc in each of next 2 ch, ch 4*, rep from * around leaf, omitting last ch 4, pull up cord, continue same way around other 2 leaves, sl st to close
Short stem: 30 sc over cord, ch 1, turn, leave loop of cord at end, work back up stem with 1 sc in each sc, sl st to base
Long stem: same as short one but 160 sc

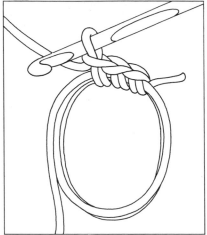

Loop for adjusting stem

To form motif center, wind foundation cord over index finger 1, 2, or 3 times (if number is not in directions, determine it by cord thickness). Slip ring off and work center stitches over it. When ring is complete, pull cord gently to bring stitches close together. Work subsequent rounds over the cord where indicated in directions (sometimes stitches are made over cord alone, at other times over both cord and stitches). As work progresses, pull cord gently to keep stitches close together.
When motif is complete, cut the cord and working yarn, leaving ends at least 6" long. Using a yarn or tapestry needle, weave each yarn end into the motif back for about ½". Cut the remainders.

Leaf: Worked over foundation cord and stitches, pulling up the cord periodically to make stitches lie flat. Ch 15, lay foundation cord over ch
Row 1: sk 1 ch, *1 sc in each ch*, 5 sc in last ch (to form the tip), 1 sc in each loop along opposite side of ch, 3 sc over foundation cord only (to go around base), 1 sc in back loop of each sc on 1st side of ch, ending 4 sc from the center sc in leaf tip, ch 1, turn
Row 2: picking up front loop only, 1 sc in each sc down side, 3 sc in center sc at base, 1 sc in each sc up other side, ending 3 sc from tip, ch 1, turn
Row 3: picking up back loop, 1 sc in each sc down side, 3 sc in center sc at base, 1 sc in each sc up other side, end 3 sc from tip of previous row, ch 1, turn
Rows 4 and 6: as Row 3, working front loop only
Row 5: as Row 3, working back loop only
Fasten off at end of Row 6

Rose: ch 8 and join in ring with sl st
Round 1: ch 6, (1 dc, ch 3) 7 times, sl st in 3rd ch at beg of rnd
Round 2: (1 sc, 1 hdc, 3 dc, 1 hdc, 1 sc) over each 3-ch loop
Round 3: working behind Round 2, make 1 sl st in 1st sl st of Round 1, ch 5, (1 sl st in next dc of Round 1, ch 5) 7 times, 1 sl st in 1st sl st to close
Round 4: (1 sc, 1 hdc, 5 dc, 1 hdc, 1 sc) over each 5-ch loop
Round 5: working behind Round 4, make 1 sl st in 1st sl st of Round 3, ch 7, (1 sl st in next sl st of Round 3, ch 7) 7 times, 1 sl st in 1st sl st to close
Round 6: (1 sc, 1 hdc, 7 dc, 1 hdc, 1 sc) over each 7-ch loop
Round 7: working behind Round 6, make 1 sl st in 1st sl st of Round 5, ch 9, (1 sl st in next sl st of Round 5, ch 9) 7 times, 1 sl st in 1st sl st to close
Round 8: (1 sc, 1 hdc, 9 dc, 1 hdc, 1 sc) over each 9-ch loop, fasten off

Irish crochet pillow top

This lovely pillow top is a fine way to display your talent for crochet. Finished size is 12 inches square, but you could enlarge it by making a bigger grid, adding 8 chains for each inch of mesh.

Materials

2 balls (250 yds. each) of Knit-cro-sheen cotton; 1 ball of Speed-cro-sheen cotton (for the foundation cord); steel crochet hook #5 or size to obtain mesh gauge; tapestry needle; 14″ square of light-colored, smooth fabric such as muslin; pencil; ruler; scissors; basting thread and needle; 1 knife-edge or box-edge pillow 12″ or 13″ square and covered with a plain, smooth fabric

Gauge

For mesh, 8 chains = 1 inch

For motifs, no gauge can be specified, but finished sizes are: *leaf*, 2¼″ from tip to base; *shamrock*, 2¼″ from top to stem; *rose*, 2½″ in diameter

Preparing the grid: Draw a 12″ square on light-colored fabric. Mark off 1″ segments along each side, then use the marks to draw lines diagonally between edges (see photo below). This will serve as a pattern for making the mesh.

Making motifs: Following the instructions on the opposite page, make 1 rose, 8 leaves, 2 shamrocks with short stems facing in opposite directions, 2 shamrocks with long stems facing in opposite directions (to reverse a stem, flip it over just before slip stitching it to the base). Finish off all of the foundation cords except the ones extending from the long shamrock stems. Assemble the motifs and attach them to the grid as directed below.

Making the mesh: Work Rows 1 and 2, then baste the mesh to the grid, right side up, and proceed as directed below under the photograph.

Ch 98 and check your gauge

Row 1 (wrong side): sk 1 ch, 1 sc, *ch 2, 1 picot [ch 5, sl st in 1st of these 5 ch], ch 3, 1 picot, ch 2, sk 7 ch, 1 sc in next ch*, turn

Row 2: ch 10, 1 picot, ch 2, 1 sc in the 3-ch sp between picots of previous row, *ch 2, 1 picot, ch 3, 1 picot, ch 2, 1 sc in the 3-ch sp*, turn

Row 3: ch 2, 1 picot, ch 3, 1 picot, ch 3, 1 picot, ch 2, 1 sc in 3-ch sp, *ch 2, 1 picot, ch 3, 1 picot, ch 2, 1 sc in the 3-ch sp*, work last sc in the 10-ch sp of the previous row, turn

Repeat Rows 2 and 3 for pattern.

After mesh is attached to grid, each right-side row is worked with the grid facing you right-side up; for a wrong-side row, grid must be turned upside down and the mesh pulled away from it slightly. Wherever mesh comes in contact with a motif, slip stitch it to one edge of the motif, then chain enough stitches to move up a row or to continue horizon-

tally on the wrong side of the motif. When mesh is complete, connect diamonds along top and left edges with *ch 8, 1 sc in each 3-ch sp*

Forming a border: Cut a length of foundation cord 60″ long. Starting at one corner, work (5 sc, ch 5) 3 times over cord and each 8-ch group. Pull up the cord periodically to make stitches lie flat. Do not fasten off foundation cord until after cover has been mounted, as some adjustment may be necessary.

Finishing: Detach crocheted piece carefully from grid; remove basting threads. Pin it to one side of pillow, adjusting fit either by stretching gently or pulling on the foundation cord. Sew the border with double thread, taking small stitches through back of border and under pillow fabric; weave foundation cord into back of border for 1 inch; cut remainder. Tack rose to prevent shifting. Steam lightly.

To assemble motifs, lay them out in the arrangement shown. Join 7 leaves first, making small stitches at contact points. Next, attach rose and bottom leaf. Join shamrocks where picots touch, then draw up cords on stems, shaping them as shown. Sew each stem in position, cut its cord, weave end into the back. Center motifs on grid; baste their centers to fabric, leaving edges free.

To crochet mesh around motifs, work first 2 rows, then baste foundation chain to bottom line of grid with the 10-ch group at right edge, mesh lines aligning with grid lines. Work 3rd row of mesh, taking it behind shamrocks as necessary. Continue up right side to top of motifs; fasten off; work left side, then top, basting mesh to grid as work proceeds. Complete border as directed above.

Sew the completed piece by hand to one side of pillow, centering it between finished edges, as shown, or attaching it along the seams (if it fits precisely). Smooth fabric, in a dark or medium color, sets off this lace to best advantage. For laundering, it would be wise to remove lace to avoid the risk of color bleeding. Wash it gently by hand, wet-block it on the grid; re-sew it to pillow when dry.

Crochet stitches

Tunisian crochet

Tunisian crochet (also called afghan stitch) is a cross between knitting and crochet methods. The fabric is similar to a knitted one, but firmer, especially suited to blankets, coats, or suits.

To work these stitches, you need a special tool called an *afghan hook*. This is longer than other types, uniform in diameter, and has a knob at one end to keep stitches from sliding off. The procedure is to work from right to left on one row, leaving all loops on the hook, then from left to right on the next row, never turning the work.

The foundation of most afghan stitches is two basic rows (see below); the finish can be one row of either slip stitch or single crochet. Blocking is essential and must be done carefully, as this fabric tends to pull on the bias.

BASIC TECHNIQUE

Chain the desired number of stitches plus one.
Row 1: sk 1 ch, *insert hook in the next ch, draw up a loop and leave it on the hook*, do not turn work at the end of the row.

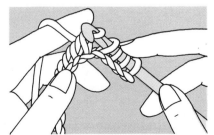

Row 2: yo, draw yarn through first loop on hook, *yo, draw through 2 loops*, do not turn work; the 1 remaining loop counts as 1st st on next row.

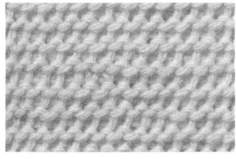

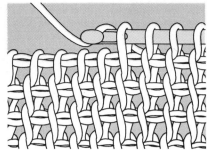

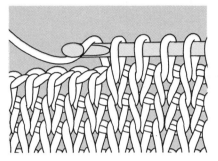

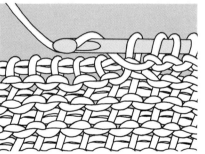

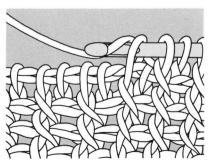

Basic Tunisian (knit stitch): The first two rows of this pattern are used for the foundation of most Tunisian stitches. Its texture, which resembles that of a woven, is especially suitable for cross stitch embroidery.
Multiple is any number of ch plus 1
Row 1: sk 1 ch, *insert hook in next ch, draw up a loop*
Row 2: yo, draw through 1 loop, *yo, draw through 2 loops*
Row 3: ch 1, *insert hook right to left under next vertical st, draw up a loop*
Rep from Row 2

Tunisian stockinette: This pattern looks like the knitted version, except that it is thicker.
Multiple is any number of ch plus 1
Rows 1 and 2: basic Tunisian
Row 3: ch 1, *insert hook front to back in the center of next vertical st loop (the center can be seen more easily if you separate the 2 yarns using thumb and 3rd finger of left hand), draw up a loop*
Row 4: yo, draw through 1 loop, *yo, draw through 2 loops*
Rep from Row 3

Tunisian purl: Yarn is held in front of work as for purl stitch in knitting.
Multiple is any number of ch plus 1
Rows 1 and 2: basic Tunisian
Row 3: ch 1, *holding yarn to the front, insert hook right to left under next vertical st, draw up a loop*
Row 4: yo, draw through 1 loop, *yo, draw through 2 loops*
Rep from Row 3

Tunisian crossed stitch: Pairs of stitches are worked in reverse order.
Multiple is 2 ch plus 1
Rows 1 and 2: basic Tunisian
Row 3: ch 1, *sk 1 vertical st, insert hook right to left under next vertical st, draw up a loop, insert hook right to left under skipped vertical st, draw up a loop*
Row 4: yo, draw through 1 loop, *yo, draw through 2 loops*
Rep from Row 3

Tunisian double stitch: Rows of diagonal stitches alternate with rows of the basic vertical pattern.
Multiple is any number of ch plus 1
Rows 1 and 2: basic Tunisian
Row 3: ch 1, *insert hook right to left under next vertical st, draw up a loop, yo, draw through 1 loop*
Row 4: yo, draw through 1 loop, *yo, draw through 2 loops*
Rep from Row 3

Tunisian popcorn: The nubs are worked on a ground of basic Tunisian. If desired, popcorn size can be increased by lengthening the chain; also, spacing can be varied by adjusting the number of stitches between popcorns.
Multiple of 4 ch plus 5
Rows 1 and 2: basic Tunisian
Row 3: ch 1, draw a loop through each of next 4 vertical sts, *ch 3, draw a loop through each of next 4 vertical sts*
Rows 4, 5, 6: basic Tunisian
Row 7: ch 1, draw a loop through each of next 2 vertical sts, *ch 3, draw a loop through each of next 4 vertical sts*, ch 3, draw a loop through each of next 2 vertical sts
Rows 8, 9, 10: basic Tunisian
Rep from Row 3

Tunisian rib: A combination of the basic and purled Tunisian stitches.
Multiple of 6 ch plus 4
Rows 1 and 2: basic Tunisian
Row 3: ch 1, *3 sts basic Tunisian, 3 sts Tunisian purl*, 3 sts basic Tunisian
Row 4: yo, draw through 1 loop, *yo, draw through 2 loops*
Rep from Row 3

Tunisian honeycomb: Knit and purl stitches are alternated in the same way as for a knitted seed stitch.
Multiple of 2 ch plus 1
Rows 1 and 2: basic Tunisian
Row 3: ch 1, *1 Tunisian purl under next vertical bar, 1 basic Tunisian under next vertical bar*
Rows 4 and 6: yo, draw through 1 loop, *yo, draw through 2 loops*
Row 5: ch 1, *1 basic Tunisian under next vertical bar, 1 Tunisian purl under next vertical bar*
Rep from Row 3

Tunisian bias stitch: Worked in the same manner as Tunisian crossed stitch (opposite page), but pattern is moved one stitch to left on alternate rows.
Multiple of 2 ch
Rows 1 and 2: Tunisian crossed stitch
Row 3: ch 1, draw a loop under next vertical st, *cross next pair of sts*, draw a loop under last vertical st
Row 4: yo, draw through 1 loop, *yo, draw through 2 loops*
Rep from Row 1

Tunisian lace: An exceptionally pretty pattern that is very easy to work.
Multiple of 4 ch plus 1
Row 1: basic Tunisian
Row 2: *ch 3, yo, draw through 5 loops, yo, draw through 1 loop*
Row 3: ch 1, *draw up a loop through the top of each cluster, draw up a loop in each ch of the 3-ch group*
Rep from Row 2

Crochet stitches

Loops

Lattice loop: An airy pattern of elongated loops, especially suitable for a shawl, or one row might be used for a lacy insertion. See below for the way to work a lattice.
Multiple is any number of ch
Row 1: sk 1 ch, *1 sc in each ch*, ch 1, turn
Row 2: lengthen turning ch to height of strip, place strip between the loop and the yarn, draw a loop through the lengthened chain, *insert hook in next st, draw up a loop to top of strip, yo, draw through the long loop, yo, draw through 2 loops*, ch 1, turn
Row 3: *1 sc in each st*
Rep from Row 2

Bouclé loop: Shaggy loops on one side of fabric, single crochet on reverse side. Loops can be worked in two different ways (see below). This stitch is suitable for a pillow cover, rug, or novelty garment; bouclé loop can also be knitted.
Multiple is any number of ch
Row 1: sk 1 ch, *1 sc in each ch*, ch 1, turn
Row 2: *1 loop st in each sc*, ch 1, turn
Row 3: *1 sc in each st*, ch 1, turn
Rep from Row 2

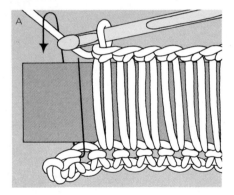

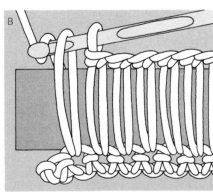

WORKING THE LATTICE LOOP

A lattice can be worked neatly over a large tongue depressor or a ruler. If you do not have one of these in a suitable size, cut a strip of sturdy cardboard about 6″ long and the desired depth of the stitch.
To begin lattice pattern, work a row of single crochet, chain 1 and turn. Lengthen the turning chain to the height of the strip, place strip between loop and yarn, draw a loop through the lengthened chain, *slide hook forward and down and insert it in the next stitch, lower yarn behind the strip until it reaches the hook, draw up a long loop (hooking action is indicated by arrow, illustration A), yarn over (B), draw a loop through the long loop, yarn over, draw through remaining 2 loops*. Repeat from asterisk across the row, removing strip and moving it forward as it becomes filled with stitches, chain 1, turn.
To continue pattern, work a single crochet in each stitch, and on the last stitch, insert hook under the last long loop as well as the two top loops, chain 1 and turn. Repeat the lattice row next or, if preferred, work additional rows of single crochet, then a lattice.

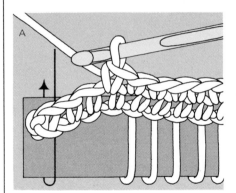

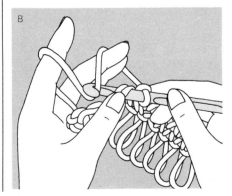

WORKING THE BOUCLÉ LOOP

A bouclé loop can be formed with the aid of an object, such as a pencil, ruler, or cardboard strip, or it can be worked over one or two fingers of the left hand. The first method is a bit more precise; the second is faster once a rhythm is developed. Before you begin, make a swatch to determine how long you want the loops to be. Somewhere between ½″ and 1½″ is the normal range. Once established, the loop length should be consistent throughout the pattern.
To form loops over a strip, first make a foundation row of single crochet, chain 1 and turn. *Bracing strip behind the work with left hand, insert hook in next stitch, transfer strip to right hand and take yarn around strip front to back (see arrow, illustration A) draw up a loop, yarn over, draw through 2 loops*. Repeat from asterisk to end of row, sliding loops off and moving strip forward as it becomes filled.
To form loops over the fingers, first make a foundation row of single crochet, chain 1 and turn. *Insert hook in next stitch, swing 3rd and 4th fingers of left hand forward *under* yarn, then back against the yarn so that a loop is formed over these fingers (B), draw a loop through the stitch, pulling it over top of 3rd finger, yarn over, draw through 2 loops, slip fingers out of the loop*. Repeat from asterisk across the row.

Chain loop stitch: Curly loops are worked on a background of single crochet. Different effects can be obtained by making longer chains, or by working the ground in double crochet. This pattern has the same uses as bouclé loop (left).
Multiple is any number of ch plus 2
Rows 1 and 2: single crochet
Row 3: working into front loop of each st *1 sc, ch 8*, 1 sc, ch 1, turn
Row 4: *1 sc, working into other loop of each st worked in previous row*, ch 1, turn
Rep from Row 1

Broomstick lace: A soft and spongy texture; popular stitch for shawls and baby blankets. The pattern is a combination of large loops, worked over a "stick" (dowel or large knitting needle), and single crochet, worked over a group of 5 loops.
Multiple of 5 ch
Row 1: transfer ch on hook to the stick, *insert hook in next ch, draw up a loop and place it on the stick*, do not turn
Row 2: *insert hook through 5 loops and slide them from stick, draw a loop through the 5 loops, yo, draw through 1 loop, 4 sc over same 5 loops*, do not turn
Row 3: transfer ch on hook to the stick, *draw up loop through next sc, place loop on stick*, do not turn
Rep from Row 2

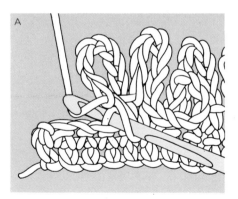

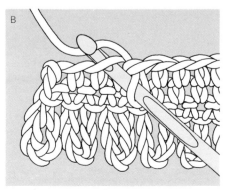

WORKING THE CHAIN LOOP

A chain loop is produced by making a long chain between 2 stitches. The crowding of these loops forces them to curl and form a thick, spongy texture on the fabric face.
To begin a chain loop pattern, work 2 rows of single crochet, chain 1 and turn. *Inserting hook into front loop of each stitch (A), work 1 single crochet, ch 8*. Repeat from asterisk, ending the row with 1 single crochet, chain 1, turn.
To continue pattern, *insert hook into the other loop of each stitch in the previous row (B), work 1 single crochet*, chain 1 and turn.

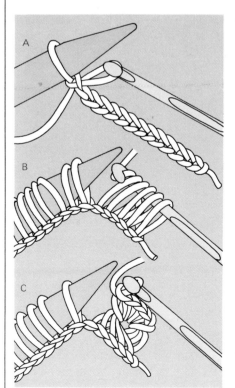

WORKING BROOMSTICK LACE

Broomstick loops are formed over a dowel or thick knitting needle, of a diameter somewhere between ½" and 1", and a length sufficient to hold all stitches. To make a blanket, for example, a dowel 1" thick and 36" long might be required. If using a dowel, several layers of tape or a few rubber bands should be wrapped around one end to keep stitches from sliding off.
To begin broomstick pattern, work a chain of stitches divisible by 5, not counting chain on hook. Transfer chain on hook to the stick and brace the stick under your left arm. *Insert hook in next chain, draw up a loop (A) and place it on the stick*. Repeat from asterisk across the row; do not turn.
To continue pattern, *insert hook right to left through 5 loops, draw a loop through the 5 loops (B), yarn over, draw a loop through the 1 loop, 4 single crochet over the same 5 loops (C)*. Repeat from asterisk across the row; do not turn. All loop rows are worked from left to right, single crochet rows from right to left (the reverse if you are left-handed).

Crochet stitches/Multicolor

Introduction

Attractive effects are possible with the use of two or more colors in crochet. Because stitches are tall, however, results can never be as subtle or finely detailed as in multicolored knitting. As a rule, simple designs, such as geometrics and stripes, work the best, and single crochet permits the greatest flexibility, especially when color changes are frequent.

There are three ways of working colored patterns (also called jacquards), shown on the facing page. Each is suited to a particular situation. Whichever technique you use, a color change is always made the same way—by picking up the new color as the final yarn over in the last stitch of the previous color (second illustration in row at right).

WORKING WITH A COLOR CHART

A chart is often used to give directions for color patterns in crochet. This is a graph in which each square equals a stitch and each line equals a row. Usually, blank squares represent the main color, symbols or colored squares depict the contrasts, and where needed, an accompanying key interprets these usages. To follow a chart, start at the bottom and read from right to left for right-side rows, from left to right for wrong-side rows. It is possible to work crochet from other needlework charts, such as a cross stitch pattern, but a test swatch must be made to determine if the proportions translate attractively, and the color changes are workable.

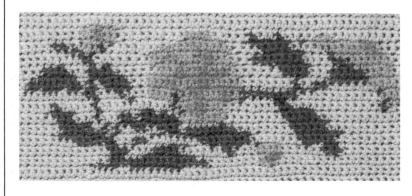

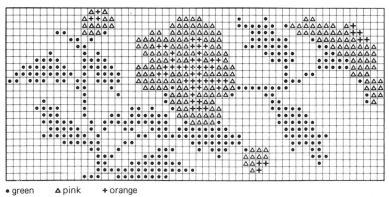

• green   △ pink   + orange

Jacquard techniques

To join in a new color mid-row, lay the yarn end over the row below, introducing it a few stitches before you need it (A). Continue to work with the 1st color, covering the end of the new yarn. Work the 1st color to the final 2 loops of the last stitch, then draw the new color through these last 2 loops (B).

The same technique can be used when changing colors at the beginning of a row by introducing the new color on the last few stitches of the row below. Joining yarn by this method eliminates the need to weave in the yarn ends with a tapestry needle when the project is complete.

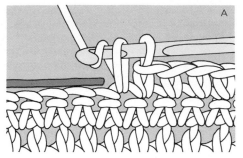

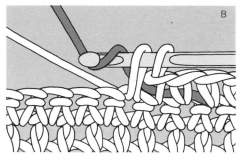

If unused yarn must be carried over more than 3 stitches, it is best to catch it into the work every other stitch. The yarn strands will be less likely to pull or be snagged, and tension will be more even. When using this technique, take care not to apply tension to the yarn being carried, as this will cause the work to pucker.

On a right-side row, insert hook into the stitch, then under the carried yarn at back of the work, catch working yarn with the hook (A), draw up a loop and complete the stitch.

On a wrong-side row, insert hook under the carried yarn, then into the stitch, catch working yarn with the hook (B), draw up a loop and complete the stitch.

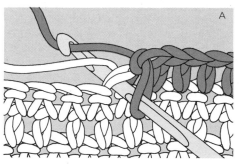

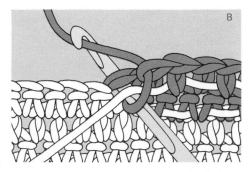

Carrying unused colors across the wrong side is suitable for any crocheted fabric that reveals just one finished surface—a pullover or a pillow cover, for example. If carried over more than 3 stitches, unused yarn should be caught into the work every other stitch (see lower right, opposite page).

To change colors on a right-side row, work the 1st color to the final 2 loops of the last stitch, drop 1st color back and to the left of 2nd color, yo and draw through 2 loops with 2nd color.

To change colors on a wrong-side row, work 1st color to the final 2 loops of the last stitch, drop 1st color forward and to the right of 2nd color, yo and draw through 2 loops with 2nd color.

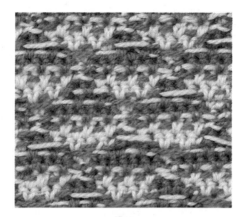

Working over colors not in use is one way to crochet a reversible fabric. This method is faster than cutting and weaving (below), but it consumes more yarn and produces a fabric that is quite heavy. The carried yarn, though covered by the stitches, *is* visible between stitches, and the fabric is attractive or not depending on the design and colors you are working with. Use a hook one size larger than usual to allow for the bulk of the unused yarn.

To carry the unused color, lay it on top of the previous row as you work stitches in the contrasting color.

To change colors, draw a loop of the 2nd color through the final 2 loops of the last stitch in the 1st color.

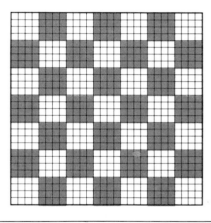

Cutting and weaving the yarn ends is another way to manage color changes on a reversible fabric. An alternative to working over yarn (above), this is a practical approach when unused yarn must be carried a great distance, when colors are changed at the end of a row, or when the pattern is an inset motif, as in the example at the right.

To discontinue a color, work it to the final 2 loops of the last stitch, then draw up a loop with the new color. Cut off the 1st color, leaving a 6″ end. When the work is complete, weave the yarn end through 4 to 6 stitches of the color that matches it; cut off the remainder.

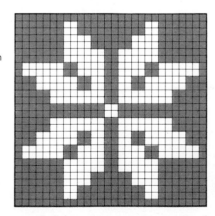

Crochet stitches/Charted

Shorthand symbols

Crochet techniques can be represented by symbols and the symbols used to chart a pattern stitch, or an entire project, visually. Because a chart resembles the actual look of a pattern, it aids in visualizing an unfamiliar stitch. It is especially suited to working in the round.

Listed at the right are symbols, their meanings, and the numbers of pages on which illustrations of the techniques can be found. As a rule, no more than a few symbols are used in one pattern, so it is necessary to remember only the ones for which you have immediate use.

Though crochet symbols are used in many countries, they are not standardized. The ones given here are typical, but not universal, examples. If different pictures would have more meaning for you, or if you should need a symbol that is not included here, you can invent your own.

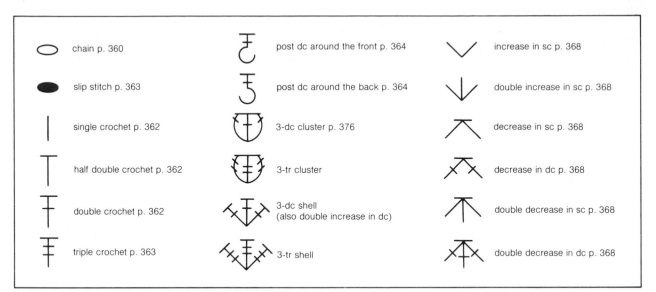

chain p. 360	post dc around the front p. 364	increase in sc p. 368
slip stitch p. 363	post dc around the back p. 364	double increase in sc p. 368
single crochet p. 362	3-dc cluster p. 376	decrease in sc p. 368
half double crochet p. 362	3-tr cluster	decrease in dc p. 368
double crochet p. 362	3-dc shell (also double increase in dc)	double decrease in sc p. 368
triple crochet p. 363	3-tr shell	double decrease in dc p. 368

Charted stitch

Clusters in a square: Directions below, charted form at the right.
ch 6 and join in ring with sl st
Round 1: ch 3, (yo, insert hook in ring, draw up a loop, yo, draw through 2 loops) twice, yo, draw through 3 loops, ch 2, *3-dc cluster in ring [(yo, insert hook, draw up a loop, yo, draw through 2 loops) 3 times, yo, draw through 4 loops], ch 2*, rep from * 6 more times, sl st in top of beg ch
Round 2: ch 3, 2 dc in the 2-ch sp at end of Round 1 (in front of ch 3), ch 2 (3 dc in next 2-ch sp, ch 2) 7 times, sl st in top of beg ch
Round 3: ch 1, *1 sc in 2nd dc, ch 2, 3-tr cluster in next 2-ch sp [(yo twice, insert hook, draw up a loop, yo, draw through 2 loops, yo, draw through 2 loops) 3 times, yo, draw through 4 loops], ch 2*, rep from * 7 more times, sl st in beg ch
Round 4: ch 1, *3 sc in st at top of cluster, (3 dc, ch 2, 3 dc) in next sc, 3 sc in top of next cluster, ch 1, 1 sc in next sc, ch 1*, rep from * 3 more times, sl st in beg ch
Round 5: ch 1, 1 sc in each st or ch, 3 sc in each 2-ch sp at corners, sl st in beg ch, fasten off

Crocheting a garment

Introduction
Designing a crocheted garment
Charting a woman's sweater
How to make a garment chart
Shaping necklines
Shaping armholes and sleeves
Ribbing
Buttons
Buttonholes

Introduction

Time-honored formulas are used to crochet garments. The purpose of this section is to acquaint you with the basic procedures so you can better understand pattern directions, and if you would like to, even design your own garments.

Before crocheting any garment, you need to do the following: (1) Read through the instructions to be sure you understand them; try out any new techniques to see if you can do them correctly. (2) Compare the garment's measurements with those of the person for whom it is intended. (Procedures for taking and using measurements can be found in Knitting, p. 324.) If measurements are not given, you can determine them by dividing a stitch or row total by the gauge. For example, if the shoulder has 18 stitches, and the gauge is 4 stitches to the inch, the shoulder should measure 4½ inches. (3) Check your gauge. Planned garment dimensions can be obtained only by duplicating the gauge in the pattern.

Designing a crocheted garment

There are two ways to design a crocheted garment. One is to alter an existing pattern, making changes to suit your needs; the other is to originate your own. With either approach, you must make a plan, for which you need the following:
1. An accurate set of body or garment measurements (see Knitting, p. 324).
2. A test swatch to determine gauge and, if necessary, to calculate yarn needs.
3. Knowledge of the way to structure certain garment areas (see pp. 396-399).
4. Paper to outline or chart a pattern.

The first thing to do is write down width and length dimensions for each section of the garment you are planning. If your plan is based on body measurements, you must add ease, using for guides other patterns and/or the general criteria listed on page 324. You should also add ¼ inch for seams and plan the overall length, for example, from the underarm to the bottom edge of a sweater.

Next, choose a yarn and stitch pattern, crochet a swatch, or several if necessary, until you are satisfied with the appearance of the stitch, then measure gauge.

To translate garment width dimensions into stitches, multiply the stitch gauge by inches. For example, if you are planning a sweater that measures 18 inches at the bottom edge of the back, and the stitch gauge is 4 stitches to the inch, you would need 72 stitches plus 2 stitches for seams for the back section.

To translate garment length dimensions into rows, multiply row gauge by inches. If a sweater measures 15 inches from bottom edge to underarm, and row gauge is 3 rows to the inch, there would be 45 rows from bottom to underarm.

To determine the number and distribution of decreases for shaping armholes, sleeves, and the neckline, follow the guidelines on pages 396-397. Prepare a chart or outline (see pp. 393-394 for the method), then calculate the quantity of yarn that will be needed.

To estimate how much yarn you will need for your own design, there are several approaches; these are described below. One general rule to keep in mind is that pattern stitches with clusters, shells, or bobbles usually require about half again as much yarn as the basic stitches (single crochet, etc.) and textures (see p. 372 for these types).

One way to estimate your yarn needs is to use the amount specified for a similar pattern that is structured of the same yarn and stitch. (For this purpose, it is useful to keep a notebook of patterns you like.) This quantity may not be precisely what you need, so it is advisable to buy extra yarn to be sure of having enough from the same dye lot. Many stores will accept the return of unused yarn within a reasonable time; check store policy at the time of purchase.

Another approach is to consult with a salesperson in a yarn shop. Salespeople will usually have the experience and/or pattern files from which to make an estimate of your project's yarn needs.

If you cannot find either an appropriate pattern or an able consultant, here is a way to make your own estimate: Buy a skein or ball and measure off a length of yarn that equals about ⅛ of the yardage given on the label. (If yardage is not given, see p. 325 for the way to calculate yarn needs by weight.) Record the length. It might be, say, 18 yards. Make a gauge swatch and record its area; if the swatch is 4 inches by 3 inches, the area would be 12 square inches.

Next, calculate the approximate area for each garment section by multiplying widest dimension by overall length. Add these figures together, then divide the sum by the swatch area and multiply this number by the length of yarn used for the swatch. Here is an example:

Sweater back

across the chest	18 in.
length, neck to bottom	20 in.
total area (roughly)	360 sq. in.

Sweater front

area, same as the back	360 sq. in.

Sweater sleeve

width at upper arm	12 in.
overall length	23 in.
total area, both sleeves	552 sq. in.

Total area for sweater	1272 sq. in.
Sweater area divided by swatch area (12)	106

The number 106 represents the approximate number of 4 × 3-inch swatches needed to crochet this sweater. Multiply 18 yards (the length of yarn in the swatch) times 106 to determine the approximate amount of yarn needed—1908 yards. Deduct 10% of 1908 to allow for shaping decreases; 1717 yards is the estimate.

Crocheting a garment

Charting a woman's cardigan

This tailored cardigan is presented here in both written and charted form so you can compare the two methods. The directions given here are for Misses' size 12 (34 bust).

Materials

14 ounces of wool sport yarn, sizes E and F hooks, 6 buttons, ½" in diameter

Gauge

4 hdc and 3 rows = 1 inch with F hook

BACK: Using F hook, ch 73

Row 1: sk 1 ch, *1 sc in each ch*, ch 1, turn (you should have 72 sc)

Row 2: *1 hdc in each sc*, ch 1, turn

Row 3: *1 hdc in each hdc*

Rep Row 3 until piece measures 14".

Armholes: 1 sl st in each of 1st 4 sts, 1 hdc in each st to last 4 sts, ch 1, turn; dec 1 st at each end of next 4 rows.

Work even on 56 sts until the armholes measure 8 inches.

Shoulders: 8 sl st in 1st 8 sts, 9 hdc in next 9 sts, ch 1, turn; dec 1 st at beg of next row, 1 hdc in each of next 6 sts, 1 sc in next st; fasten off.

Skip center 22 sts; attach yarn and work other shoulder to correspond.

LEFT FRONT: With F hook, ch 37

Row 1: sk 1 ch, *1 sc in each ch*, ch 1, turn (you should have 36 sts)

Row 2: *1 hdc in each sc*, ch 2, turn

Row 3: 1 hdc in each of 1st 14 hdc, 4 post dc around the front of next 4 sc in Row 1, 1 hdc in each of next 18 hdc, ch 2, turn

Row 4: *1 hdc in each hdc*, ch 2, turn

Row 5: 1 hdc in each of 1st 14 hdc, 4 post dc around the front of 4 post dc 2 rows below, 18 hdc in next 18 hdc, ch 2, turn

Repeat Rows 4 and 5 until piece measures 14 inches, ending with a wrong-side row.

Armhole: 1 sl st in each of 1st 4 sts, work to end of row; dec 1 st at armhole edge 4 times. Work even on rem 28 sts until the armhole measures 4 inches, ending at front edge.

Shaping neck: 1 sl st in each of 1st 8 sts, work to end; dec 1 st at neck edge 4 times. Work even on rem 16 sts until armhole measures 8 inches, ending at armhole.

Shoulder: 1 sl st in each of 1st 8 sts; work to end of row; fasten off.

RIGHT FRONT: Work as for left front, reversing the pattern and shapings.

SLEEVES: With F hook, ch 33

Work **Row 1** in sc and **Row 2** in hdc as for left front, but on 32 sts.

Row 3: 1 hdc in each of 1st 14 sts, 4 post dc around the front of next 4 sts, 1 hdc in each of next 14 sts.

Continue in pattern, increasing 1 st at each end, every 4th row, 8 times. Work even on 48 sts until piece measures 16".

Shaping cap: sl st in each of 1st 4 sts, work to last 4 sts, turn; work 1 row; dec 1 st at each end of next and every other row 6 times; dec 1 st at each end of every row 5 times; 18 sts remain; fasten off.

FINISHING: Sew side, shoulder, and sleeve seams. With right side facing you, using E hook, begin at right side seam and work 2 rows of sc along bottom, front, and neck edges of sweater; work 3 sc in each corner st. With yarn scraps, mark 6 buttonhole positions on right front, placing first one ¼" from neck edge, last one ½" from bottom edge, spacing others evenly between them. **Next round,** work in sc, making a horizontal ch-1 buttonhole at each marking and 3 sc at each corner. Work 2 more rounds of sc, decreasing around curve of neck; fasten off. With right side facing you, using E hook, work 5 rounds of sc along bottom of each sleeve. Sew in sleeves. Attach buttons.

A woman's tailored cardigan is worked in hdc with a panel of 4 post-dc on each front and sleeve.

How to make a garment chart

A garment chart is a visual representation of written instructions. There are two different forms—**outline** and **graph.** Either can be used when designing a garment or adjusting an existing pattern.

An outline is a drawing of the exact dimensions of each main garment section, with shaping information written on it. This form gives you a realistic view of garment shape, and can be used later, if desired, for blocking. To make an outline, use sturdy wrapping paper and start by drawing a straight line on it equal to the widest dimension (usually the underarm) of the garment back, then draw a second line perpendicular to and through the center of the first. Using these as reference points, measure the other areas. Draw the sleeve and any other garment sections in the same way.

A graph is worked out on paper marked off in squares. Each square represents a stitch, each line of squares a row. To chart this way, the gauge must already have been determined. You can graph an entire garment section, or just those areas that are shaped (as shown opposite); only half need really be graphed. A graph is a less realistic view of garment shape than an outline, but it is somewhat easier to follow, especially if you use a ruler to keep track of progress.

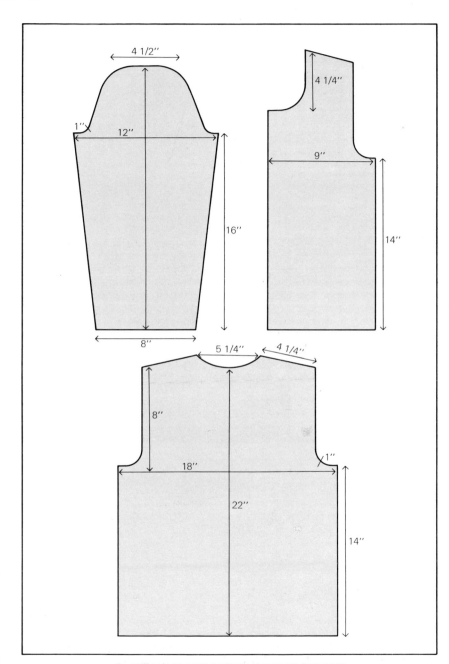

An outline is an exact duplicate of garment dimensions.

1/2 sleeve

24 stitches

48 rows

16 stitches

1/2 back

11 stitches

24 rows

36 stitches

Front

8 stitches

24 rows

36 stitches

In a graph, each square represents a stitch, each line of squares a row.

Crocheting a garment

Shaping necklines

Special care should be taken in crocheting a neckline; this part of a garment is particularly noticeable. In general, the fit should be smooth, with no gaping or wrinkling. In the case of a high neck on a pullover, a slit opening must be provided so that the head can pass through. (There is not enough stretch in crochet for the neckline to expand.)

The neck width calculation is based on shoulder width and equals about one-third of it, or the number of stitches that remain after subtracting the two shoulder lengths. Front neck depth is figured in relation to armhole depth, and varies according to style (see the directions at the right). Usually, a back neck is straight, formed by leaving the stitches unworked just below the last row of shoulder shaping. If a front is a deep scoop or square, the back may be shaped the same way, but would be less deep as a general rule.

In shaping a neckline, work is usually divided, each half crocheted separately, and all decreases made on the right side. Distribution of decreases depends to some extent on stitch height. You can skip one or two rows between decreases for a short stitch (sc or hdc), but should decrease every row for a tall one (dc and taller), or the edge will be jagged.

A crocheted neck edge may be naturally neat—a square neck is an example—but it will hold its shape better and have a more finished appearance if you work an edging. One or more rows of single crochet makes a firm edge. Ribbing is also suitable. It can be crocheted (see p. 398) or knitted by picking up stitches along the edge. Shoulder seams should be joined before the finish is added.

Guidelines for making three basic neck shapings are shown at the right. These represent typical but not all possibilities. If you wish to use them for altering an existing pattern, or designing your own, be sure to chart your design before crocheting it.

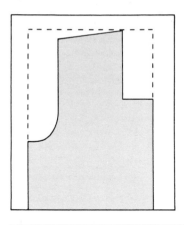

Square neckline shaping is begun 3″ to 6″ below the start of shoulder shaping by leaving unworked all stitches allotted for the neckline opening. (Reminder: The number of stitches for the neck is what remains after subtracting stitches for each shoulder.) There is no decreasing for this style; you work straight up to the shoulder, completing one-half of the neckline at a time.
To make the edging shown here, work 2 rounds of single crochet along the neck edge, starting and ending at one shoulder seam, decreasing 1 stitch at each corner.

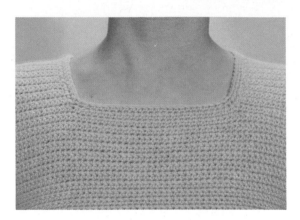

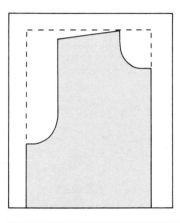

High round neckline shaping is begun about 2″ below shoulder for an adult garment, 1½″ for a child's. One-third of stitches to be decreased are left unworked at the center; another third are allotted to each half of the neck, decreasing at the neck edge 1 stitch every row, then working even to the top of the shoulder.
A slit opening must be provided for this style; usually it is worked at the back by dividing the work at the center, 3″ to 4″ below the shoulder.
To make the edging shown here, work 3 rows of single crochet, starting and ending at the slit, decreasing where necessary (usually in the curved areas) to keep the edging flat.

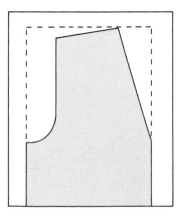

A V-neckline is usually started 6″ to 9″ below the shoulder, or just after the start of armhole shaping. Work is divided at the center and each half is worked separately, decreasing gradually at the neck edge, always on the right side. For a wide V, decrease 1 stitch every row; for a narrower one, every second or third row. If you have an odd number of stitches across the front, decrease center stitch before dividing work.
To make the edging shown here, work 1 round of single crochet on the neck edge, then a second round of reverse single crochet, starting and ending at a shoulder seam, decreasing 2 stitches at the V on each round.

Shaping armholes and sleeves

Armhole and sleeve shapings are important to crocheting a well-fitted garment. Three basic styles are described below—**classic, raglan,** and **semi-raglan.**

To chart an armhole with the formulas given here, you need measurements for *shoulder width,* the *chest* (or underarm) across half the garment, plus the standard *shoulder length* and *armhole depth* for your garment size and *neck circumference* (for raglan only). To shape a sleeve, you should have the *wrist,* the *underarm* *length,* and the *upper-arm* measurements.

The usual way of crocheting a sleeve is from the bottom edge up, increasing the underarm seam gradually and symmetrically between the wrist and the underarm. The armhole and sleeve cap are shaped with decreases. To avoid having a jagged decrease at the underarm, follow the instructions on page 369 for decreasing several stitches at the beginning and end of a row. These methods are appropriate also for shaping the shoulder seam.

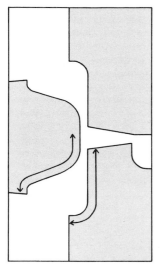

A classic armhole shape is formulated by subtracting the stitches needed for shoulder width from the number at the underarm. Half this figure is the number of stitches to decrease for each armhole. At start of shaping, decrease at least 1″ of stitches, then decrease remainder over next few rows. Work even until correct depth is reached.
For set-in sleeve cap, decrease the same number of stitches as at beginning of armhole. Continue decreasing symmetrically until cap length is the same as armhole length; work 1 more row and fasten off.

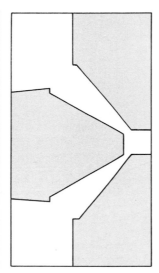

A raglan armhole ends at the neckline and must be planned in relation to it. It is shown here combined with a square neckline, a simple combination often used in crocheted garments. To determine the number of decreases, subtract the stitches for neck width from the number of stitches at the underarm; Start raglan with ½″ of decreases on each side; distribute remaining decreases symmetrically and evenly over the number of rows needed to reach the neckline.
Shape top of sleeves the same way, having 3″ to 6″ at neck edge depending on neckline depth.

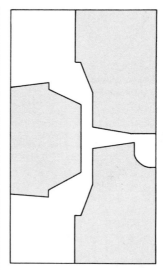

A semi-raglan armhole is shaped like a raglan on the lower half, like a classic armhole on the upper half and shoulder. Calculate the number of decreases as for a classic armhole, but instead of distributing them over the first 4 to 5 rows, space them in a sloped line over half the armhole depth; work evenly for the remaining depth.
For the sleeve cap, decrease symmetrically over the same number of rows as for the armhole; work 1 more row straight across and fasten off.

A set-in sleeve has a symmetrically curved cap.

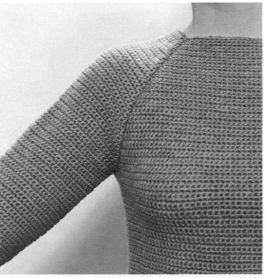

A raglan sleeve is shaped in a continuous slope to neckline.

A semi-raglan sleeve has raglan slope combined with a wide cap.

Crocheting a garment

Knitted ribbings 280
Picking up stitches 297

Working a post stitch 364
How to form a ring 370

Ribbing

Crocheted ribbing is used on the edges of a garment to provide a firm and somewhat elastic finish. Four variations are described below. The easiest of the four to produce is the ridge stitch, in which the ribs are worked horizontally, then turned and the garment pattern worked along one side edge to obtain the vertical effect. All the other rib patterns are worked vertically.

Crocheted ribbing is not as elastic as knitted ribbing and never fits as snugly. You can, if you prefer, knit the ribbed edging for a crocheted garment. The usual method is to work the garment, join the seams, then pick up stitches along the edge. As a general rule, one knit stitch is picked up for each crocheted one. A test swatch should be made to determine the correct needle size to use.

Ridge stitch ribbing: Ridges are formed horizontally, then turned sideways for ribbing. *Multiple is any number of ch that will form desired depth of ribbing.*
Row 1: sk 1 ch, *1 sc in each ch*, ch 1, turn
Row 2: *1 sc in back loop of each st*, ch 1, turn
Repeat Row 2 for the pattern. When ribbing is long enough for the garment edge on which it is to be used, fasten off yarn; sew the ends together, then work the pattern stitch along one side of the ridge pattern.

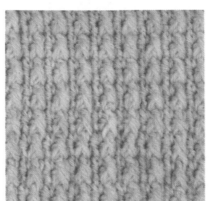

Post stitch ribbing I: Vertical ridges are formed on two sides.
Multiple of 2 ch plus 1
Row 1: sk 1 ch, *1 sc in each ch*, ch 1, turn
Row 2: *1 post sc around the front, 1 post sc around the back*, 1 sc in last space, ch 1, turn
Row 3: *1 post sc around the front, 1 sc under the 2 crossed strands of next post st*, 1 sc in last space, ch 1, turn
Repeat Row 3 for pattern.

Post stitch ribbing II: Vertical ridges are on one side only.
Multiple of 2 ch
Row 1: sk 1 ch, *1 sc in each ch*, ch 1, turn
Row 2: 1 sc, *1 post dc around the front of next stitch, 1 sc in next st*, ch 1, turn
Row 3: *1 sc in each st*, ch 1, turn
Row 4: 1 sc, *1 post dc around front of post st 2 rows below, 1 sc in next st*, ch 1, turn
Repeat Rows 3 and 4 for pattern.

Tunisian crochet ribbing: Ridges are less pronounced than in other crocheted ribbings, but this is a neat pattern, particularly well-suited to a garment of Tunisian crochet.
Multiple of 2 ch
Rows 1 and 2: basic Tunisian
Row 3: ch 1, 1 Tunisian purl under 2nd bar, *1 Tunisian stockinette, 1 Tunisian purl*
Row 4: yo, draw through 1 loop*, yo, draw through 2 loops*
Repeat Rows 3 and 4 for pattern.

Buttons

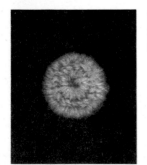
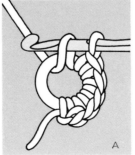

Ring button: Yarn is worked over a plastic ring 1/8″ smaller than desired button size. To start, make a slip knot. Inserting hook through ring to form each st, work around it in sc (A) until ring is completely covered; sl st in first st to close; fasten off. Cut yarn, leaving 12″; thread the end in a tapestry needle. Make an overcast st in each outside loop (B), then pull stitches toward center. Tie beginning and end strands together, then sew an X across the button back for attaching it to the garment.

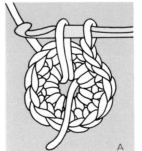
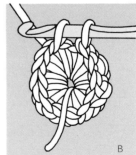

Ball button: Yarn is worked into a 3-dimensional motif; size and thickness depend on yarn weight. *Ch 3 and join in ring with sl st.* **Round 1:** ch 1, 8 sc in ring, sl st to beg ch. **Round 2:** ch 1, (1 sc in next st, 2 sc in next st) 4 times, sl st to beg ch; pull the short yarn end up through center hole. **Round 3:** ch 1, (insert hook through center hole, draw up a long loop (A), yo, draw through 2 loops) 16 times, sl st to beg ch. **Round 4:** 1 sc in every other st (B); fasten off; overcast and finish back as for ring button.

Buttonholes

Horizontal buttonhole, single crochet:
At the beginning of buttonhole placement, make a number of chain stitches that will accommodate the diameter of the button (usually from 1 to 5). Skip the number of stitches for which you have chains, then continue in pattern (A).
Next row: Work *over* the buttonhole chain in single crochet, making the same number of stitches as there are chains (B).

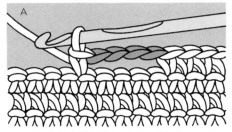

A 4-chain buttonhole completed

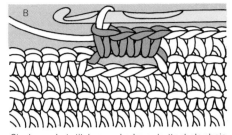

Single crochet stitches worked over buttonhole chain

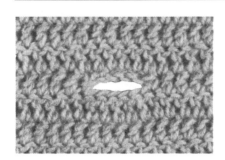

Horizontal buttonhole, double crochet:
At beginning of buttonhole placement, insert hook under the diagonal strand halfway down the stitch just completed (A), *draw up a loop, yarn over, draw through 2 loops, insert hook under left strand at front of stitch just completed*, repeat from * to * for desired length. To complete buttonhole, draw up a loop, skip the same number of stitches as were made for the buttonhole, insert hook in next stitch, draw up a loop, complete a double crochet (B).

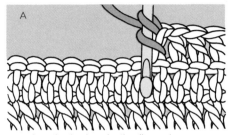

Inserting hook under the diagonal yarn

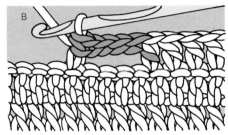

A double-chain buttonhole completed

Vertical buttonhole, any stitch:
On right side of garment, work across the row to buttonhole placement; turn and continue to work this half until depth of buttonhole has been obtained. If the number of buttonhole rows is uneven, fasten off yarn (A), weave into back of work later; if even, leave yarn at side of work. Starting at buttonhole edge, attach yarn, work second half to match the first. Next row, start at side edge and continue in pattern across both sections (B).

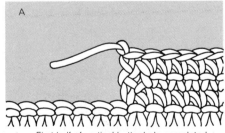

First half of vertical buttonhole completed

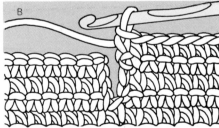

Second half of vertical buttonhole completed

Buttonhole loop of single crochet:
On a right-side row, work to end of buttonhole placement. Make a chain the same length as buttonhole, join it to beginning of buttonhole thus: Slip hook out of chain, insert it front to back through top of stitch, hook chain and pull it through; insert hook in next stitch to the right, yarn over (A), draw a loop through both stitch and chain. Work single crochet over chain, slip stitch in stitch where chain was started (B); continue in pattern.

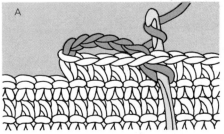

Joining chain to beginning of buttonhole

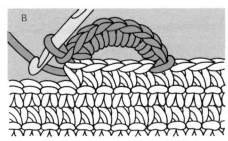

Working single crochet over the buttonhole loop

Assembling and finishing

General information
Joining sections right sides together
Joining sections edge to edge
Crocheted edgings and insertions
Afghan in Tunisian crochet

General information

There are several ways to finish crochet; select methods that suit your needs and work patiently for professional results.

Blocking is generally the first step. This procedure shapes crocheted pieces to specific measurements and, at the same time, usually smooths slight stitch irregularities. There are two basic blocking methods—steam and wet. These and pressing techniques are fully described in Knitting, pages 342-343. Before beginning, check the yarn label; some yarns should not be blocked.

Joining is the step after blocking for any project worked in sections. There are several methods (see below). Selection should be made according to, first, the needs of the situation, then personal preference. Joining with a seam allowance (right sides together) is necessary when edges are uneven; it is often preferred for its firm and neat appearance. Joining edge to edge is possible only when edges are even and have the same number of stitches. This method is especially suitable for ribbings and motifs.

Edging may be applied as a final step to provide extra firmness and a uniform appearance for a crocheted edge. Suggestions for finishes are given opposite.

JOINING SECTIONS RIGHT SIDES TOGETHER

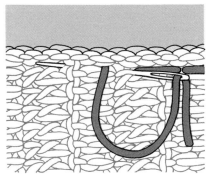

Backstitch: Worked any distance from edge; use for uneven edges or to alter garment.
Bring needle up through 2 corresponding stitches; *insert through 2 stitches behind thread (where thread emerges for last stitch); bring up through 2 stitches in front of the thread.*

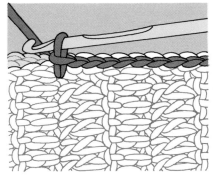

Slip stitch: A firm joining that is suitable for seams in which minimal stretch is required.
Draw up a loop through a corresponding stitch on each section; *insert hook through the next 2 stitches; draw a loop through both stitches and the loop on the hook.*

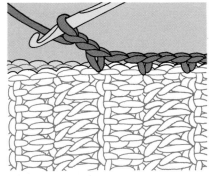

Slip stitch plus chain: A more flexible joining than plain slip stitch; use for bulky yarns or when a greater degree of stretch is desired.
Work slip stitch through 2 corresponding stitches at start of row; *make a chain equal to height of row; work slip stitch at beginning of next row.*

JOINING SECTIONS EDGE TO EDGE

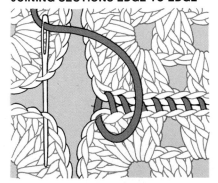

Overcast: Used mainly to join patchwork motifs.
***Insert needle** at a right angle under back loop of a corresponding stitch on each edge; draw yarn through.* When you reach the corners of 2 motifs, continue with the next 2 as shown.

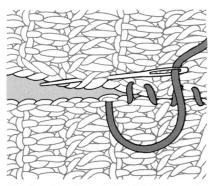

Weaving side edges: An invisible joining, especially suited to taller stitches and filet.
Lay sections right side up. *Take needle under lower half of edge stitch on one piece, then under upper half of edge stitch on adjacent piece.*

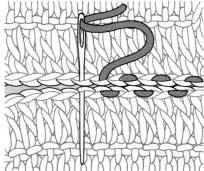

Weaving top or bottom edges: Invisible joining for straight edges with equal numbers of stitches.
Right sides up, *bring needle up through 1 loop, down through next loop on one edge; weave down and up through 2 loops on other edge.*

Crocheted edgings and insertions

Crochet lends itself so naturally to use as a trim that pattern possibilities are nearly endless. Worked along the edge of crochet or knitting (see directly below), it serves to make an edge firm, give it a trim look, and reinforce its shape with a distinctive outline. When applied to a garment, seams should be joined first and the edge stitch begun at one seam. Worked separately, a trimming can be crocheted horizontally (examples in center row) or vertically (bottom row), and sewed to crocheted, knitted, or woven fabrics. Any yarn is suitable as long as it is compatible with the fabric to which it is applied.

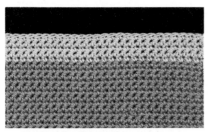

Single crochet edging: Use one to four rows for sleeveless armholes or a neckline, at least 1'' for front or bottom edges of a garment.

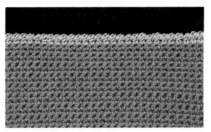

Corded edging: A very firm and neat trimming.
Row 1: single crochet, working right to left
Row 2: single crochet, working left to right

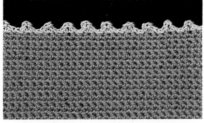

Little picot edging: For a child's dress.
Every row: *1 sl st in each of next 2 sts, 1 sc in next st, ch 3, 1 sc in same st as last sc*

Scalloped edging: Suitable for any lacy item.
Every row: 1 sl st, *sk 2 sts, 5 dc in next st, sk 2 sts, 1 sl st in next st*

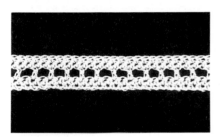

Eyelet insertion: Multiple of 2 ch plus 2
Row 1: sk 1 ch, *1 sc in each ch*, ch 1, turn
Row 2: *1 sc in each sc*, ch 4, turn
Row 3: sk 2 ch, *1 dc in next sc, ch 1, sk 1 sc*, 1 dc in last sc, ch 1, turn
Row 4: *1 sc in each dc, 1 sc in each ch*, ch 1, turn
Row 5: *1 sc in each sc*; fasten off

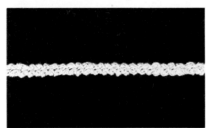

Twisted braid: Multiple is any number of ch
Row 1: sk 1 ch, *insert hook in next ch, draw up a loop, twist hook horizontally and clockwise 1 full turn, yo, draw through 2 loops*; at end of row, ch 1 and continue around opposite side of ch; repeat instructions between asterisks in each loop on that side; fasten off.

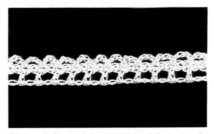

Filet and picot edging: Multiple of 2 ch plus 5
Row 1: sk 5 ch, 1 dc in next ch, *ch 1, sk 1 ch, 1 dc in next ch*, ch 1, turn
Row 2: 1 sc in each st and ch sp, ch 4, turn
Row 3: sk 1 sc, *sl st in next sc, ch 4, sk 1 sc*, sl st in 4th ch at beg of Row 1, fasten off

Fancy scalloped edging: Multiple of 5 ch plus 3
Row 1: sk 1 ch, *1 sc in each ch*, turn
Row 2: sl st in 1st 2 sc, *ch 3, sk 3 sc, sl st in next 2 sc*, turn
Row 3: sl st in 1st 2 sc, *(1 dc, ch 1 in next 3-ch sp) 4 times, 1 dc in same sp, 2 sl sts*, turn
Row 4: *(1 sc, ch 3 in next 1-ch sp) 4 times, sl st in next 2 sl sts*, fasten off

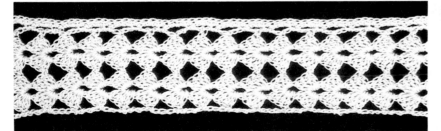

Double shell edging: *Ch 19*. **Row 1:** sk 9 ch, 1 shell [4 dc, ch 3, 4 dc] in next ch, sk 5 ch, 1 shell in next ch, sk 2 ch, 1 dtr in last ch, ch 5, turn. **Row 2:** 1 shell in each 3-ch sp of shell below, 1 dtr in last dc of 2nd shell, ch 5, turn. Repeat Row 2 for pattern, ending last row with ch 2, 1 dc in last dc; do not turn. **Along one edge,** ch 1, 1 sc in loop just formed, *ch 3, 1 sc in next loop* for entire length, ch 1, turn. **Next row:** 1 sc in 1st sc, *3 sc in next 3-ch sp, 1 sc in next sc*, fasten off.

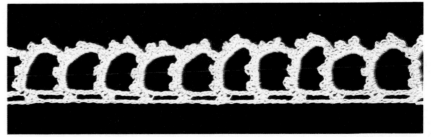

Looped edging: *Ch 13*. **Row 1:** sk 6 ch, 1 tr in next ch, ch 9, sk 5 ch, sl st in last ch, ch 1, turn. **Row 2:** in 9-ch sp (3 sc, ch 3) 5 times, 2 sc in same sp, 1 sc in the tr, 2 sc in 6-ch sp, ch 5, turn. **Row 3:** sk 2 sc, 1 tr in next sc, ch 9, sk 2 3-ch loops, sl st in next 3-ch loop, ch 1, turn. **Row 4:** in 9-ch sp (3 sc, ch 3) 5 times, 2 sc in same sp, 1 sc in the tr, 1 sc in 4th ch of turning ch, ch 5, turn. Repeat Rows 3 and 4 for desired length; fasten off.

Afghan in Tunisian crochet

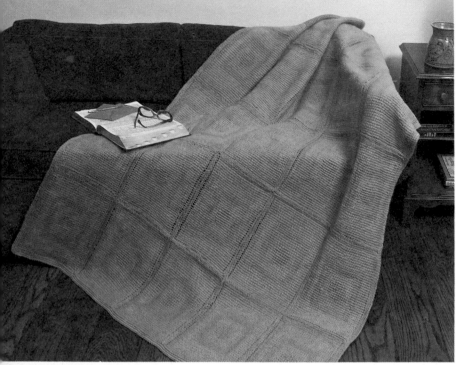

Wool afghan, approximately 48″ by 63″, is worked in Tunisian crochet with single crochet borders.

Geometric blocks (25) form the basis of this afghan. Each block is worked in the basic Tunisian stitch, bordered with single crochet, then embroidered with cross stitch to create the center motif.

Materials

Knitting worsted, seven 4-ounce skeins of blue, eight 4-ounce skeins of beige; size J afghan hook; tapestry needle; large knitting bobbins (optional)

Gauge

4 sts and 3½ rows = 1 inch

Preparation

Wind bobbins—several of each color, or make butterflies (see p. 446 for method), allowing 5 to 6 yards for each one.

MAKING A BLOCK: With blue, ch 34

Rows 1-6: Work in basic Tunisian, omitting ch 1 at beginning of Row 3, and at the end of each row inserting hook under both the last bar and the yarn directly behind it. This approach makes a firm edge on which to work the border.

Row 7: Pick up 3 loops in blue and then *change colors* as follows: Make a slip knot 4 inches from the end of the beige yarn; pull up this loop through the next stitch, leaving short yarn end at back to be woven in later. Pick up 27 more beige loops;

fasten in a new blue yarn with a slip knot; pick up 3 blue loops.

Row 8: Work off 2 loops in blue, then pick up beige yarn from under the blue, thus *twisting* the yarns; draw it through the last blue loop and 1 beige loop. Continue with beige until 1 beige loop remains; pick up blue yarn from under the beige; work off last 4 loops in blue. Continue in pattern, adding new colors where needed (you will have 7 bobbins or butterflies on Row 27), and twisting yarns when changing colors on the return rows. When the square is finished, do not fasten off, but continue with blue.

Border: Across the top work 2 sc under the 2nd bar, *1 sc under the next bar*, 2 sc in the last bar. Continue down the left side with 1 sc under the double loop of each bar; continue along bottom with 2 sc in the first ch, *1 sc in the next ch*, 2 sc in the last ch; work up the right side with 1 sc under both loops of each end st; join with a sl st to the 1st sc; fasten off. Weave all yarn ends into the back.

CROSS STITCHING: Work an oval design in center of each block, following diagram and directions below left.

BLOCKING AND ASSEMBLING: Carefully block each piece so that all are the same size (approximately 9¼ × 12¼ inches). Lay out 10 blocks in 2 rows of 5 each, one row above the other, having all tops facing away from you. Using 1 long strand of blue and working from right to left, overcast adjacent top and bottom edges, taking yarn through each back loop only (see example of this technique, p. 400). Add on 3 more rows of 5 squares each until all squares are joined horizontally. Turn afghan sideways and join all the rows vertically in the same way.

WORKING THE AFGHAN BORDER: With blue, work 2 rows of sc around the outside edge of the afghan, making 1 stitch in each stitch, 2 stitches in each corner, skipping the overcast joining. Fasten off. Gently steam-block all around.

Each afghan block is worked in basic Tunisian, using this chart as a guide. A square in the chart equals 1 stitch and a row represents 2 rows of the afghan pattern; there are 34 stitches and 84 rows. Though the cross stitch pattern in the center appears to be off-balance, the motif, when finished, is actually centered because cross stitches are worked over the upright bars of the extra beige stitch.

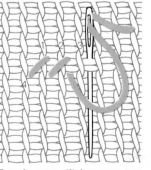

To make cross stitches, use a tapestry needle and one strand of blue yarn. Bring the needle up just below crossbars of stitch **1**; pull yarn through, leaving 4″ at the back; take needle top to bottom behind both crossbars of stitch **2**, then behind crossbars of stitch **3**.

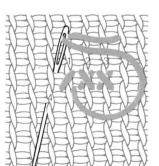

Work back across the same row, inserting the needle behind crossbars as before. To start the next row, weave needle down behind crossbars of stitch **4**; continue making rows of stitches until oval is complete; cut yarn; weave in ends. Stitches should not show on back.

Lacework

404 Needle lace
　　Supplies
405 Making a sampler
406 Needle lace stitches
　　Meshes
408 Bars and picots
409 Insertions/woven
410 Insertions/Russian
　　Edgings
411 Needle lace butterfly
413 Tatting
　　Terms and abbreviations
　　Supplies
414 Tatting techniques
　　Forming the double stitch
415 Practice with one shuttle
416 Points to remember
417 Working with two threads
418 Shawl with tatted border
420 Filet netting
　　Supplies and equipment
421 Making the basic knot
422 Basic mesh techniques
423 Plain square mesh/
　　netting sampler
424 Embroidering the sampler
425 Chinese folk design pillow top
426 Bobbin lace
　　Tools and supplies
427 Preparing the pricking/
　　bobbin lace sampler
428 Winding the bobbins
　　Working the two basic stitches
429 Weaving a design
　　Pinning within stitches
430 Ground patterns
431 Other lace techniques
432 Lace-trimmed apron

435 Lace weaves
　　Supplies
436 Setting up the loom
　　Preparing the weft
437 The weaves
439 Woven lace place mat
440 Hairpin lace
　　Making strips
441 Joining strips
　　Finishing edges
　　Variations
442 Hairpin lace shawl

Lacework projects
411 Needle lace butterfly
418 Shawl with tatted border
425 Filet netting pillow top
432 Bobbin lace-trimmed apron
439 Woven lace place mat
442 Hairpin lace shawl

Duchesse lace (a bobbin lace) with inserts in *point de gaze* motif (a needle lace)/
Belgium, late 19th century/From the collection of Susanna E. Lewis, Brooklyn, New York

Needle lace

Introduction to needle lace
Supplies
Making a sampler
General information on stitches
Meshes
Bars and picots
Insertions/woven
Insertions/Russian
Edgings
Needle lace yoke to stitch

Introduction

Needle lace is what its name suggests—lace made with a needle and thread. The techniques probably evolved from those used for openwork embroidery, but the structure is built entirely of thread, with fabric used only as an anchoring device. While there are several styles of needle lace, just one, called **Battenberg** or **Renaissance lace,** is dealt with in this chapter; it can be executed with minimal needlework experience. To produce this lace, variations of the buttonhole stitch are worked between sections of a narrow tape that has been basted, in the outline of the design, to a backing. When work is completed, the backing is removed, leaving just the lace structure.

Battenberg lace, also called Renaissance lace, was popular in the Victorian era.

Supplies

First consideration is usually given to selecting a tape because thread is then chosen to match or blend with it. For best performance, the tape should be between 3/16 and 1/2 inch wide, flexible enough to mold to curves in a design, constructed loose enough so that it offers little resistance to a thick needle, and demarcated in some way that will guide the spacing of stitches. Braids, eyelets, tape with picot edging, and two rickracks twisted together are suitable possibilities. See examples at the right.

For the thread, medium-weight crochet cotton is recommended because it has the firm twist needed for these techniques and enough body to give character to the stitches. The needle should have an eye large enough to accommodate the yarn; a tapestry needle is preferable because it will not catch in the backing. You will also need a regular needle and sewing thread for basting, sturdy paper for backing, and fabric that contrasts with yarn color to provide visibility. In addition, a transfer pencil is useful because it permits you to hot-iron a design onto a backing fabric. A thimble and small scissors are indispensable.

Making a sampler

A sampler is an easy and practical way to learn needle lace techniques. While developing skills, you produce a reference for future projects and a piece handsome enough in itself to be framed.

Materials

4 yards of tape (see opposite page for suitable choices), 1 ball #5 crochet cotton, tapestry needle, basting thread and needle, medium-weight drawing paper 11″ × 14″, plain, smooth fabric, 11″ × 14″, in color to contrast with yarn.

Preparation

Cut 4 strips of tape 8″ long, 3 strips 12″ long, and one 40″ piece for the border. Lay fabric on the paper and strips on the fabric, arranging them so that the large

center spaces measure 2½″ × 1¾″. Baste strips to fabric and paper through centers; whipstitch tapes to each other at intersections. Baste border over ends of strips, rounding the corners.

Working the stitches

Following key (above right) for stitch placement, work patterns in numbered order (they are arranged by increasing complexity). Directions for all of the stitches are given on pages 406-410.

			37				
27	21	19	20A-B	15	16	17A 17B	27
32	22	1 2 3		4			23	32
33	30	6 8 8 7		9 10 11			5	33
34	31	12 13 14		18			29	34
	28A	24	26 26		25		28B
		35	36	35			

KEY TO SAMPLER DIAGRAM

1. Single net stitch
2. Double net stitch
3. Buttonholed net stitch
4. Brussels net stitch
5. Pea stitch
6. Cloth stitch
7. Eyelets in cloth stitch
8. Embroidered cloth stitch
9. Side stitch
10. Double side stitch
11. Shell stitch
12. Spanish point
13. Twisted Spanish point
14. Twisted Spanish point patterns
15. Twisted bar
16. Double twisted bar
17A, B. Buttonholed bars
18. Branched bar filling
19. Bar with buttonholed picot
20A, B. Bar with pinned picots
21. Bar with bullion picot
22. Woven leaves
23. Open leaves with wheels
24. Beaded insertion
25. Wheel filling
26. Rings
27. Rosettes
28A, B. Spider webs
29. Buttonholed Russian stitch
30. Double Russian stitch
31. Half bars
32. Knotted edging
33. Side stitch edging
34. Pinned picot edging
35. Bullion picot edging
36. Buttonholed picot edging
37. Shell edging

Needle lace stitches

General information

All of the stitches for Battenberg lace are variations of just one, the buttonhole stitch, illustrated below in both right and left formations because most of the patterns are worked back and forth in rows. To produce such variety, the buttonhole

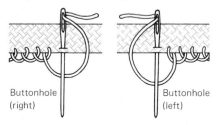

Buttonhole (right) Buttonhole (left)

is worked three different ways: (1) loosely, referred to in directions as a loop; (2) tightly and closely spaced, called stitch or buttonholing; (3) to one side over another loop, known as sideways stitch. For more variety, buttonhole stitch may be combined with embroidery techniques, such as bullion knot or weaving. Page references for these are given where they are needed.

General rules for working:

1. The stitches should be pulled firmly enough to prevent their sagging, but not so taut as to draw in the tape edges.
2. The tape edge is used as a guide in spacing the stitches and rows.

Overcast

3. Overcast stitch (illustration above) is used along tape edges between rows.
4. For a mesh stitch or other type of filling, the number of loops remains constant for a regular space, is increased or decreased as needed for an irregular space, but stitch depth remains the same.
5. For a pattern with a one-row repeat, each row is started with a whole loop, and ended with a half-loop.

Meshes

Meshes are especially suitable for filling large and/or irregular spaces in a lace pattern. They are grouped here and opposite according to the basic way of working each stitch. *Net stitches* (this page) are openwork patterns, each a variation of the single net stitch (right). *Cloth stitches* (top row opposite) are closely spaced in a solid cloth effect; they can be embellished with eyelets or embroidery. *Side stitches* (center row) are characterized by a second stitch that is made sideways over the first and locks it in place. *Spanish points* (bottom row) are similar to single net, but have an extra twist in the loop.

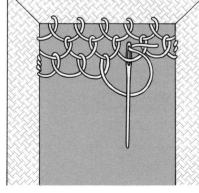

Single net stitch

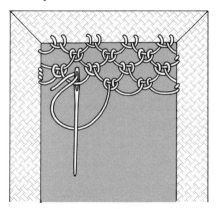

Double net stitch

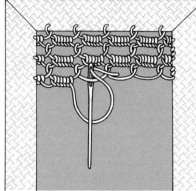

Buttonholed net stitch

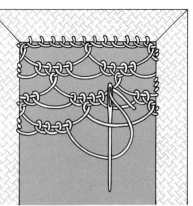

Brussels net stitch

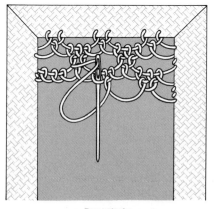

Pea stitch

Single net stitch (4 rows, #1): An open pattern, simplest and most basic of the meshes.
Row 1: work evenly spaced loops, making each loop about as deep as it is wide.
Row 2: repeat Row 1, working each stitch into the center of the large loop above. Repeat this row for the pattern.

Double net stitch (5 rows, #2): This stitch looks better if you make the large loop a bit shallower than for the single net stitch (above).
Row 1: work 1 large loop followed by 2 small loops close together.
Row 2: repeat Row 1, working the 2 small loops in each of the large loops above. Repeat this row for the pattern.

Buttonholed net stitch (8 rows, #3): This stitch is purposely started at the right edge because the second row, closely spaced buttonhole stitches, is easier to execute from left to right. Also, it is evenly spaced, because it has a two-row repeat.
Row 1: working right to left, make widely spaced loops, beginning and ending with a half-loop.
Row 2: working left to right, fill each loop with closely spaced buttonhole stitches (about 6 for each full loop, 3 for each half-loop).
Row 3: working right to left, work large loops in the small spaces between buttonholed bars of the row above.
Repeat Rows 2 and 3 for pattern. For last row in sample, catch tape between buttonholed bars.

Brussels net stitch (#4):
Row 1: make closely spaced loops in multiples of 6 (18 were made on the sampler).
Row 2: make 1 large loop in every sixth stitch above.
Row 3: make 4 medium-size loops on each large loop above.
Row 4: make 1 large loop in the center of the 4-stitch group above.
Repeat Rows 3 and 4 for the pattern.

Pea stitch (#5): Like the two stitches above, this pattern has a two-row repeat and is evenly spaced.
Row 1: make 1 large loop followed by 2 closely spaced loops, ending with 1 large loop.
Row 2: work 3 loops on each large loop above and 1 loop between the 2 small loops, ending with 3 loops.
Row 3: make 2 loops in each 3-loop group above (that is, 1 loop between the first and second, and 1 loop between the second and third stitches).
Repeat Rows 2 and 3 for the pattern.

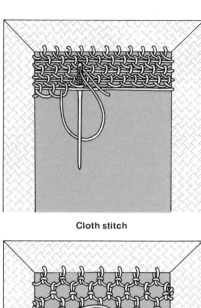

Cloth stitch

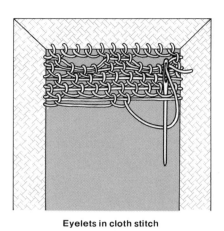

Eyelets in cloth stitch

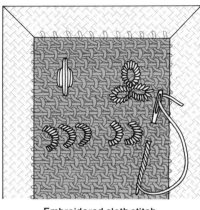

Embroidered cloth stitch

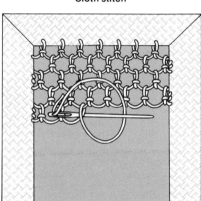

Side stitch

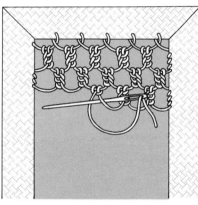

Double side stitch

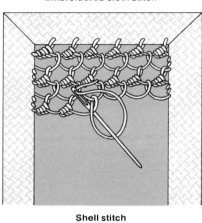

Shell stitch

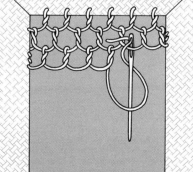

Spanish point

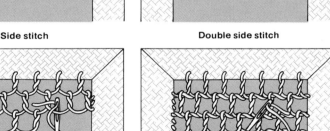

Twisted Spanish point

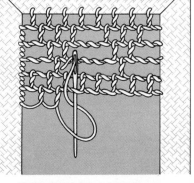

Twisted Spanish point patterns

Cloth stitch (12 rows, #6):
Row 1: working left to right, make closely spaced loops, then pull thread back across the space.
Row 2: again left to right, make a loop into each loop above, going over the loose thread as well. Pull thread back to left side and repeat this row.

Eyelets in cloth stitch (7 eyelets, #7):
Row 1: for each eyelet, skip 3 stitches, carrying thread straight across the empty space. At end of row, pull thread back to the left side.
Row 2: for each eyelet, work 3 buttonhole stitches over the 3 strands.

Embroidered cloth stitch (#8): Center of the raised spot is 2 satin stitches worked over 1 cloth stitch and 4 rows; sides are 2 satin stitches over 1 cloth stitch and 2 rows. Leaves consist of 3 bullions; to hold it flat, each clover leaf is anchored with 1 stitch at the center of its outside curve.

Side stitch (4 rows, #9):
Row 1: left to right, make 1 loose buttonhole stitch; make a second stitch sideways around both threads of first one; pull tightly in place.
Row 2: working right to left, repeat Row 1.

Double side stitch (5 rows, #10):
Row 1: make single loops spaced widely apart.
Row 2: make 1 loose buttonhole stitch into loop above; make a second stitch in same loop; pull it tight. Make 2 sideways stitches below second buttonhole stitch. Repeat this row for pattern.

Shell stitch (6 rows, #11):
Row 1: working left to right, make 1 side stitch, pulling thread firmly so that the sideways stitch lies against the tape and the loop slants left. Make 3 more sideways stitches above the first, each one slightly looser than the preceding one. One shell is now completed; start the next shell abutting it.
Row 2: right to left, work 1 loop between each shell, drawing it up closely under a shell.

Spanish point (4 rows, #12):
Row 1: left to right, make a thread loop that faces right; holding loop with left thumb, take needle through the tape (or stitch above), then through the loop; adjust stitch to desired depth.
Row 2: repeat Row 1, facing each loop to left.

Twisted Spanish point (2 rows, #13):
Row 1: work as for Row 1 in Spanish point.
Row 2: work back along row above; pass needle once behind each bottom loop. Pull thread firmly, but not so tight as to pull bars askew.

Twisted Spanish point patterns (5 rows, #14):
Arrange twisted Spanish point stitches as shown.

407

Bars and picots

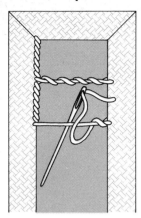

Twisted bar (# 15):
Fasten thread to tape at the left side, stretch it across the space, and take a stitch in tape on opposite side. (Take care, when laying the foundation of a bar, to stretch the thread firmly across the opening, but not so taut that you draw the tape inward.) Work back to the left side, winding the thread 4 times around the bar (for a wider space, you would wind more times to make bar firm).

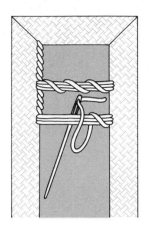

Double twisted bar (# 16):
Lay a foundation across the space as for twisted bar at left, but stretch 3 strands across instead of 1. Work back to the left side, going over the bar 3 times. (Fewer twists are needed for this stitch to make it firm.)

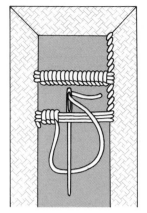

Buttonholed bar (# 17A):
Starting at the right edge, stretch 3 foundation strands across the space, then work closely spaced buttonhole stitches over them. Before starting the stitches, overcast 1 space down on the tape to secure the end of the bar and prevent it from curling. For a thicker bar (# 17B), make buttonhole stitches over 5 strands.

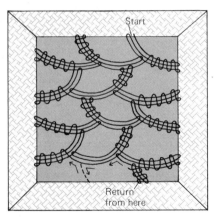

Start

Return from here

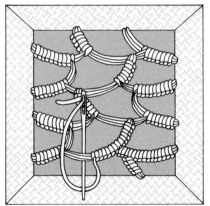

Branched bar filling (# 18):
Each bar should emerge from last one without having to cut and join the thread. Starting in the upper right corner (see diagram), make a foundation of 3 strands; work buttonhole stitches for half its length. Make a new foundation for the next bar, anchoring it through bottom of the last stitch; work buttonhole stitches for half its length. Begin the third and subsequent bars the same way. When all bars have been laid out and partially buttonholed, complete them by working back along each one in reverse order.

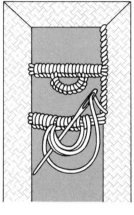

Bar with buttonholed picot (# 19): Make a buttonholed bar, working stitches ¾ of the way across, or 6 stitches beyond where the picot is to start. Take thread back to the left and pass needle between the sixth and seventh stitches, then back to the right and around the bar, then back to the left and between the same 2 stitches (there should be 3 loops hanging below the bar). Work closely spaced buttonhole stitches over the loops, then complete the bar.

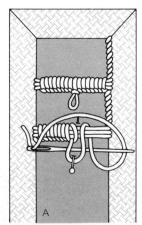

A

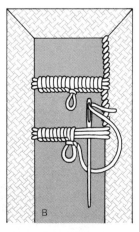

B

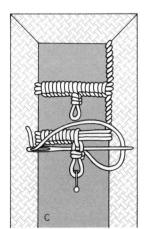

C

Bar with pinned picot (# 20):
Make a buttonholed bar, working stitches to the point where you want the picot; insert a pin to the desired depth of the picot. Pass thread around the pin, then behind the foundation threads to the outside of the loop. Make a side stitch around the loop and the working thread (as shown in illustration A). Complete the buttonholed bar (B). For a longer picot, make 2 or more side stitches, placing the first one down low enough for the additional stitches to fit between it and the bar (C).

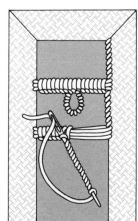

Bar with bullion picot (# 21):
Make a buttonholed bar, working stitches to the point where you want the picot; insert needle partway through the last stitch that was made and wind thread around the needle point 15 times (not too tightly). Pull needle through and draw the bullion into a circle. Complete the buttonholed bar.

Insertions/Woven

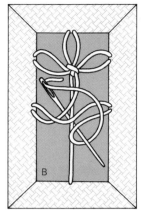

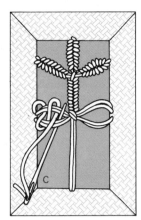

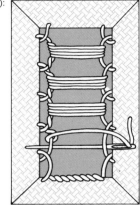

Open leaves with wheels (#23):
Stretch thread bottom to top
and form 3 leaflets tied with
a sideways stitch. Weave
around the center, going over
side leaflets, under stem and
top leaf 4 times. Wind thread
twice around stem before
making next pair of leaflets (A).

Woven leaves (#22): Form
stem and 2 groups of leaflets
1'' apart (B), then retrace foundation, bottom to top, anchoring
through each sideways
stitch. Starting at top, weave
first leaf tip to base, going
over thread groups alternately
on each side; weave stem and
side leaflets the same way (C).

Beaded insertion (#24):
Make 1 row of large, evenly
spaced loops along each long
side of the space (7 loops
were made in the sampler).
Starting at the top left side,
connect opposite loops by
taking the thread 4 times
through each pair; be sure the
thread does not become
crossed or twisted. Before
moving from one group to
the next, overcast
once around the left loop.

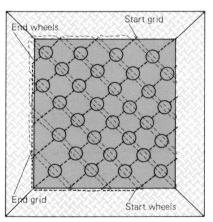

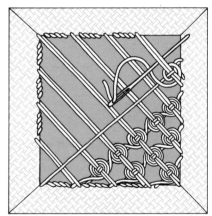

Wheel filling (#25):
First fill the space with
double strands laid diagonally
in parallel rows (see diagram).
Overcast along the tape
between rows. Fasten off the
thread and re-attach it where
indicated. Stretch thread
across the grid, take a
stitch in tape at the opposite
side, and return across
the row. At each intersection,
weave a wheel, going 3 times
under the diagonals and
over the single thread.
Overcast once around single
thread before starting next
wheel. Every other wheel is
wound in the opposite direction.

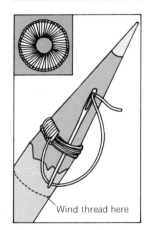

Rings (#26): These are made
separately, then sewed onto the
work wherever desired. Wind
thread around a pencil 15
times, then buttonhole over
all of the strands. (The
buttonholing is easier if you
push the threads up toward the
pencil point.) When ring is
complete, remove from pencil,
flatten, and sew in place.

Wind thread here

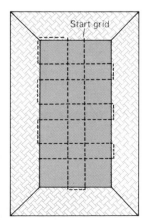

Rosette (#27): This appears
in the sampler as one filler
for a small space. It can also
be worked in multiples to
fill a larger area. First
prepare a grid as in the
diagram, laying 2 pairs of
parallel strands for each
rosette. Notice that the
intersecting areas for each
rosette are spaced 1 stitch
apart and interlaced.
For each rosette, weave a
wheel, going around the circle
4 times, then buttonhole
closely over all threads,
placing 2 stitches between the
parallel strands and
3 stitches at the corners.

Spider webs (#28A, #28B):
This stitch is good for filling
small spaces. First make
4 twisted bars, 2 across the
center in both directions, and
2 diagonally between corners.
Twist the fourth bar only to
the center, work spider web,
then complete the bar.

Woven web (#28A): Working
from the center out, weave
a wheel, skipping 1 bar at the
end of each round so threads
will alternate on each row.

Ridged web (#28B): Starting
at the center, take thread
under 2 bars, then weave in a
circle, going back over 1 bar,
forward under 2 bars.

Needle lace stitches

Insertions/Russian

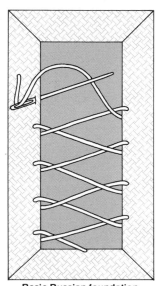

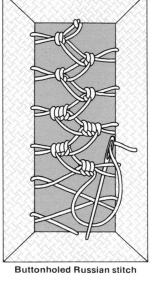

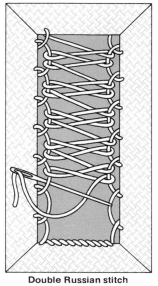

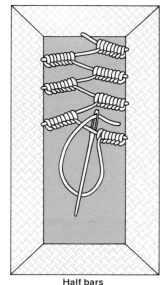

Basic Russian foundation   **Buttonholed Russian stitch**   **Double Russian stitch**   **Half bars**

Buttonholed Russian stitch (# 29): Starting at bottom center of the space, make a basic Russian foundation, looping thread from side to side as in first illustration, left (for sampler, there are 9 loops on each side). Take a small stitch at top center to secure thread, then work down the center of the foundation, making closely spaced buttonhole stitches over each pair of threads. Make 2 stitches over each of the first 4 pairs, 4 stitches over the next 5 pairs, 6 stitches over the next 4, and 8 stitches over the last 4 pairs.

Double Russian stitch (# 30): Make 1 row of evenly spaced loops along the tape on each side of the space (for the sampler, 14 loops). Connect opposite pairs of loops with 2 Russian stitches through each one. Density can be increased by taking 3 or 4 stitches in each loop.

Half bars (# 31): Starting at the top center, make 1 Russian stitch on the right side and pull it up to a loose diagonal; take 1 stitch in the tape to secure the bar, then make 8 buttonhole stitches over the diagonal thread. Repeat this procedure on alternate sides.

Edgings

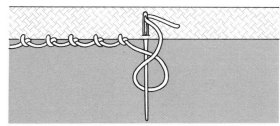

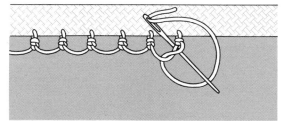

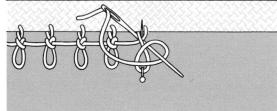

Knotted edging (#32): Make a loop as illustrated; take the needle through the tape edge, then through the loop, going behind the upper and over the lower thread. Work this and all the edgings on the sampler from left to right.

Side stitch edging (#33): Make a buttonhole loop on the tape; over this loop make 1 sideways stitch and pull it up close to the tape. Take the thread through the loop and then make another sideways stitch next to the first one.

Pinned picot edging (#34): Make a buttonhole loop on the tape. Insert a pin to desired depth of picot; take thread around it right to left. Make a second loop in front of the pin; pass the needle through buttonhole and second loop; pull thread tight.

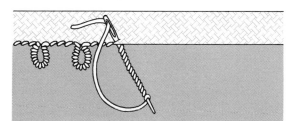

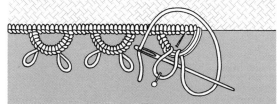

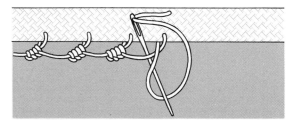

Bullion picot edging (#35): Overcast along the tape to desired place for picot. Insert needle partway through tape; wind thread around needle point 15 times, draw bullion into a tight circle.

Buttonholed picot edging (#36): Work 7 buttonhole stitches along the tape edge. Make a buttonholed picot (see directions, p. 408), adding 1 pinned picot (p. 408) every 5 stitches, if desired.

Shell edging (#37): Make 1 loose buttonhole loop on the tape; make a second stitch sideways around both threads of the first one and pull it tight. Make 3 more sideways stitches above the first.

Needle lace butterfly

Make this spectacular butterfly to adorn the front of a long dress, or mount it in any way that will set off its dramatic look—on the back of a simple evening jacket, for example. As shown here, the butterfly is sewed to a yoke, made from two layers of sheer fabric, on a dress constructed from a commercial pattern. You could apply it also to a ready-made garment; the style should be simple, and the color one that complements all the yarn colors used. If the backing color matches any one yarn, the section worked in that color will blend into the background. For example, if this butterfly had been backed with black fabric, you would not see the black stitches.

Materials for the lace

¼″ tape for outlining the design, 1 yd. black, 1½ yds. beige, 1½ yds. white (in the project shown here, black and beige tapes are rayon president's braid, white tape is a flat polyester braid); pearl cotton, 1 ball each brown, black, and white; medium-weight crochet cotton, 1 ball ecru; tracing paper; transfer pencil; medium-weight drawing paper; 11″ × 14″ piece of plain, smooth fabric, in a color to contrast with the yarns; thread for basting (any color); black thread for sewing lace to garment; tapestry and sewing needles.

Preparation

Using transfer pencil and tracing paper, trace the half-butterfly pattern from page 412. It is essential to trace the tape outlines and branched bar filling stitches (the black stitches at the bottom and just below the antennae); copying of the other stitches is optional. Turn the paper over and trace again, this time just the wing, placing it a few inches from the first tracing. Pin the paper to your fabric and lay these on an ironing board with a piece of aluminum foil beneath them. Using a dry iron at "wool" setting, press firmly against the pattern area where pencil marks are against the fabric, avoiding contact with the area where they are face up; do not slide iron back and forth.

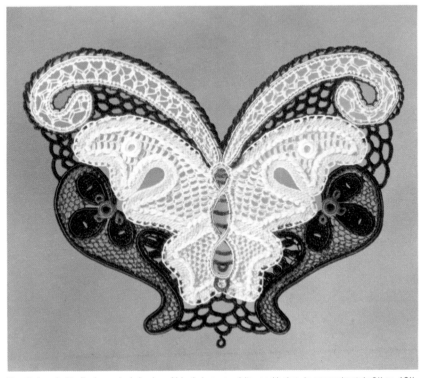

Needle lace butterfly, in neutral shades of black, brown, white, and beige, is approximately 9″ × 12″.

The butterfly is sheer drama on a long dress.

Turn paper over and abut second tracing with the design on the fabric, pinning pattern and fabric to the ironing board to prevent shifting; press this part, then remove pattern. Baste tapes in place using the pattern (p. 412) or the photo (above) as color guide. When you cut tapes, leave ½ inch ends, and tuck each one under an adjacent tape layer. These ends are finished later (see below right). With tiny stitches, join tape edges that touch. Baste fabric to the drawing paper.

Working the stitches

Each stitch used in the butterfly is one that appears in the sampler. The stitch names, also page numbers where directions for them can be found, are next to the pattern. As with the sampler, stitches are numbered in the order in which they should be worked. In this case, each section is worked with filling stitches first, embellishments next, and edgings last. To obtain consistency in the appearance of your stitches, and to minimize the possibility of tangles, always thread the needle with the yarn end that is coming off the ball, then cut the yarn.

Finishing

Clip the bastings, then remove the backing; handle the butterfly gently to avoid stretching it out of shape. On the wrong side, trim each tape end and sew it with whipstitches (tiny overhand stitches) to the tape that it overlaps (see illustration at right). Attach lace to the yoke or garment, taking small stitches through the back of the tape; try to avoid sewing into any of the lace stitches.

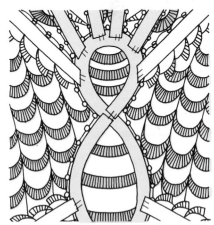

To whipstitch tape ends, insert needle at right angle, picking up a few threads of the end and tape under it. Take care not to pierce right side.

Needle lace butterfly to stitch

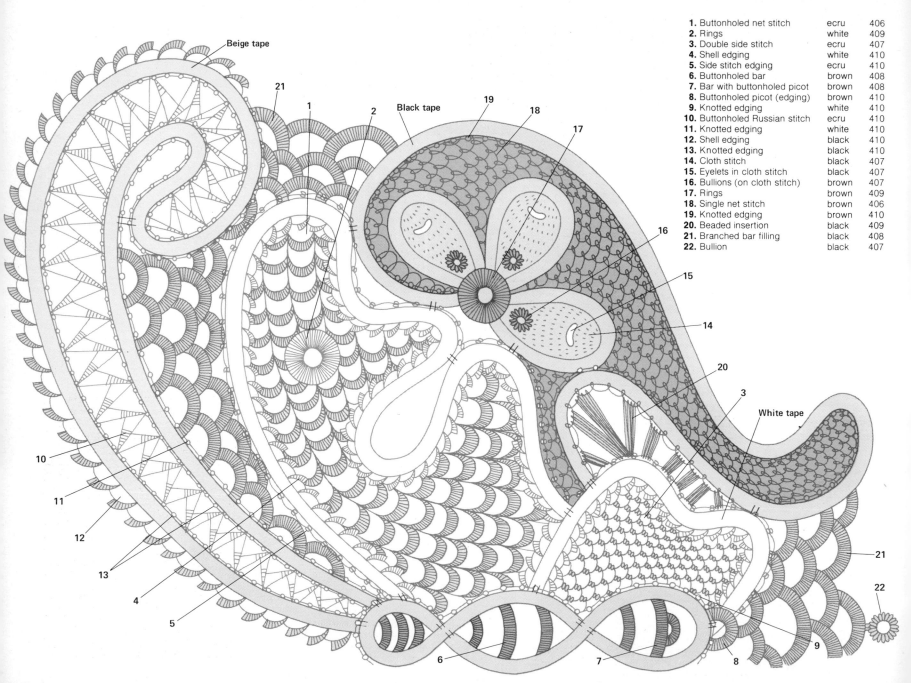

Beige tape

Black tape

White tape

1.	Buttonholed net stitch	ecru	406
2.	Rings	white	409
3.	Double side stitch	ecru	407
4.	Shell edging	white	410
5.	Side stitch edging	ecru	410
6.	Buttonholed bar	brown	408
7.	Bar with buttonholed picot	brown	408
8.	Buttonholed picot (edging)	brown	410
9.	Knotted edging	white	410
10.	Buttonholed Russian stitch	ecru	410
11.	Knotted edging	white	410
12.	Shell edging	black	410
13.	Knotted edging	black	410
14.	Cloth stitch	black	407
15.	Eyelets in cloth stitch	black	407
16.	Bullions (on cloth stitch)	brown	407
17.	Rings	brown	409
18.	Single net stitch	brown	406
19.	Knotted edging	brown	410
20.	Beaded insertion	black	409
21.	Branched bar filling	black	408
22.	Bullion	black	407

Tatting

Introduction
Terms and abbreviations
Supplies
Forming the double stitch
Practice with one shuttle
Points to remember
Working with two threads
Tatted edging for a shawl

Introduction

Tatting is a form of lacework that consists of one knot, called double stitch, worked in groups over a single thread. This thread is pulled to draw stitches into curved formations called rings and chains, and these in turn are joined in larger groupings or motifs. Traditionally, the technique has been used to make edgings and insertions, but a tatting en-thusiast can produce a large item such as a tablecloth. This lace is usually worked with fine cotton thread, so it is delicate looking but very strong.

In the tatting procedure, a continuous thread is used and it is wound on a small shuttle (see below). A loop of thread is held in the left hand while the shuttle, held by the right, is maneuvered around it; double stitches (the same knots are known as lark's head in macramé) form over the shuttle thread. To use the instructions in this section effectively, you should practice a double stitch (p. 414) until your movements coordinate smoothly. Then try each technique in the order presented: they are arranged in order of increasing complexity.

For tatting directions, there are special terms and abbreviations. Those used in this book are listed at the immediate right. These are in common use elsewhere except for slip join and lock join. Most patterns make no distinction between the two, but simply say "join."

Terms and abbreviations

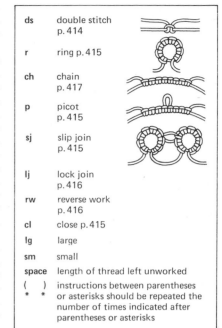

ds	double stitch p. 414	
r	ring p. 415	
ch	chain p. 417	
p	picot p. 415	
sj	slip join p. 415	
lj	lock join p. 416	
rw	reverse work p. 416	
cl	close p. 415	
lg	large	
sm	small	
space	length of thread left unworked	
( ) * *	instructions between parentheses or asterisks should be repeated the number of times indicated after parentheses or asterisks	

Supplies

There are two types of tatting shuttles commonly available. One is metal with a removable bobbin to hold thread, and a hook at the front end for joining rings. This is best suited to fine threads in the 70 to 10 size range. The other shuttle is plastic and has a center post around which the thread is wound, and a tapered point to use in joining. It is more suitable for #5 or #3 (a yarn thicker than #3 is impractical because you cannot wind enough on the bobbin). In addition, you might want a steel crochet hook to use instead of the shuttle point for joining, and you will need needles for finishing yarn ends (see p. 416).

The best yarn for tatting is smooth cotton with a firm twist. Samples made with different yarn types are shown at the far right. For practice when you are learning, #5 crochet cotton is best.

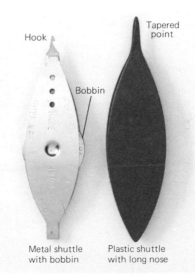

Hook

Tapered point

Bobbin

Metal shuttle with bobbin   Plastic shuttle with long nose

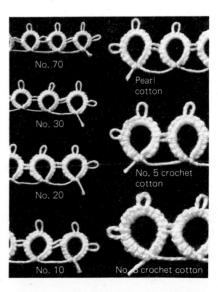

No. 70

Pearl cotton

No. 30

No. 20

No. 5 crochet cotton

No. 10

No. 3 crochet cotton

413

Tatting techniques

Forming the double stitch

The double stitch (ds) is the fundamental technique used in tatting. It is formed in two stages, with the right hand used to maneuver the shuttle around a loop of thread controlled by the left hand. It is this left hand loop that forms the stitches over the shuttle thread. Once you grasp this principle, and master the forward and backward movement of the shuttle, coordination of the tatting movements is fairly easy and a steady rhythm can be established.

Preparing a bobbin: Wind thread firmly to the edges, not beyond; insert bobbin in the shuttle.

Holding the thread: Unwind 16 inches; hold the end firmly between thumb and index finger of left hand. Spread your fingers, wrap thread around them, and grasp thread again after it comes full circle. Hold shuttle horizontally in right hand, with thread unwinding from the back, passing over the top of the hand and supported by raising the little finger (A).

First half of double stitch: Pass shuttle *under* the right hand (shuttle) thread and *under* the top thread of loop held in left hand (B). Still holding shuttle horizontally, slide it backward *over* the same thread (C). Allow thread to slide off the right hand and pull shuttle thread taut. At the same time, relax fingers of the left hand slightly, so that the *loop forms around the shuttle thread* (D).

Second half of double stitch: Hold the shuttle horizontally as before, but instead of passing thread over the right hand, push down on it with the back fingers. Pass the shuttle *over* the top thread of the left hand loop (E), then slide it backward *under* this thread (F). Pull shuttle thread taut, allowing *loop to transfer to the shuttle thread* (G). If the stitch has been formed correctly, you should be able to slide the shuttle thread through it.

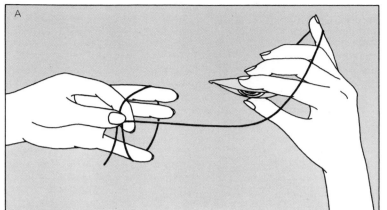

A

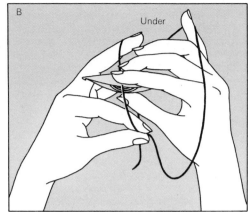

B   Under

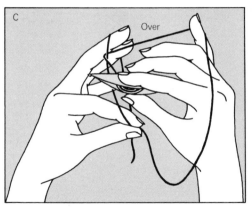

C   Over

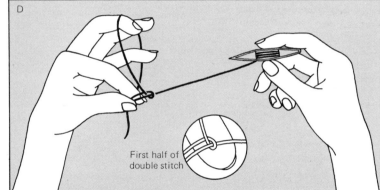

D   First half of double stitch

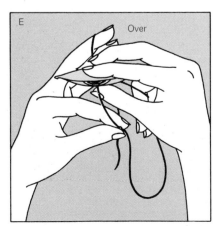

E   Over

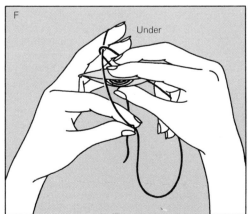

F   Under

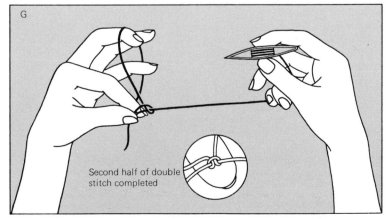

G   Second half of double stitch completed

Practice with one shuttle

Two of the basic elements in tatting are **rings** and **picots.** These should be mastered along with the **slip join** technique (bottom of page) before you proceed to the more complex methods that follow.

A ring is a curved formation of stitches set close together by pulling on the shuttle thread. Its size varies and its shape is a semicircle, a circle, or an oval, depending on how many stitches comprise it and how thick a thread is used.

A picot is a thread loop set between two stitches. It is used for decoration and to join rings. Picot size, too, can be varied, but should be consistent in one pattern, unless picots of different sizes are called for in the directions. As a rule, small picots (⅛- to ¼-inch long) are used for joining rings; large picots (¼-inch or longer) are used to enhance a design.

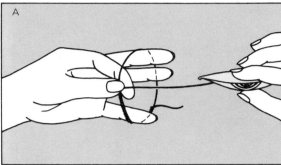

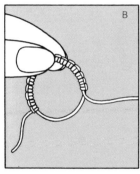

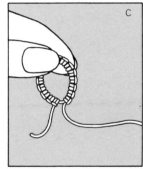

A ring (r) is formed by releasing left hand loop with which double stitches are made, and pulling on the shuttle thread until stitches are drawn into a tight circle or semicircle. In instructions this is called *closing (cl).*
To practice making a ring, wrap thread around left hand and work 20 ds (A), slide thread off left hand, and, holding the stitches between left thumb and index finger, pull shuttle thread gently so stitches are drawn together. Keep pulling until stitches are as closely set as possible (C).

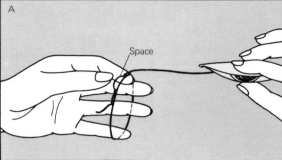

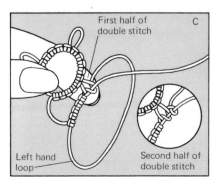

A picot (p) is formed by leaving a length of thread between two double stitches, then sliding the stitches together so that the thread length becomes a loop.
To practice making picots, start with 5 ds, work first half of the sixth stitch, leaving ¼" of space between it and the fifth ds (A), complete the sixth stitch, then slide it next to the fifth, thus pushing up the loop (B). Work (5 ds, p) 2 more times, 5 ds, cl. Remember, the stitch that closes a picot is counted as the first one in the next group of stitches.

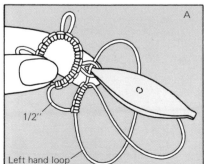

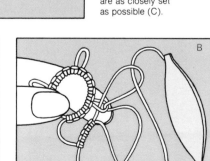

A slip join (sj), made by working a double stitch through an adjacent picot, is the conventional method of joining two rings. **For practice,** make r of 20 ds and 3 p, as explained above right.

Leave ½" space (length of thread) and start second r with 5 ds (A). Lay the third p of the first r over the left hand loop. Using tip of shuttle or a crochet hook, draw up a loop through the p and

pass shuttle through this loop (B). Keeping shuttle thread taut, pull loop close to last ds, taking care not to pull shuttle thread back through the picot (C). The join counts as first half of a ds; complete

the second half (see inset) and count this as the first ds in the next group. Finish r with (5 ds, p) 2 times, 5 ds, cl. Repeat second r as many times as desired to produce a handsome edging.

Tatting techniques

Practice with one shuttle

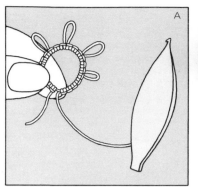

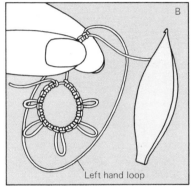

Reversing work (rw) is the turning of a completed element upside-down, so that the next portion is worked with knots facing in the opposite direction. This technique permits a greater variety in design, and also allows you to make wider patterns.

To practice reversing, make this tatted braid:
Make r of 5 ds, sm p, (3 ds, lg p) 3 times, 3 ds, sm p, 5 ds, cl (A); rw, ¼" space, make second r like the first (B), rw, ¼" space, make third r of 5 ds, sj to fifth p of first ring, 3 ds, lg p, (3 ds, lg p) twice, 3 ds, sm p, 5 ds, cl. Repeat instructions for the third ring until braid is the desired length, joining each ring to the fifth picot of the ring adjacent to it.

Left hand loop

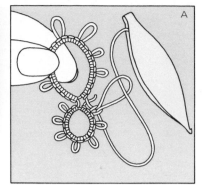

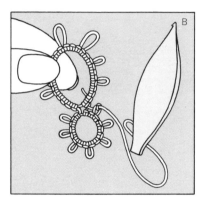

Locking join (lj) is the connecting of two elements with half a slip join. Once made, shuttle thread can no longer be pulled through stitches, so method is limited to completed rings or chains.

To practice locking join, make this medallion:
Make center r of (2 ds, sm p) 7 times, 2 ds, cl; starting next to last ds of center r, make petal of 5 ds, sm p, 3 ds, sm p, (3 ds, lg p) 3 times, (3 ds, sm p) twice, 5 ds, cl; lj to center r by drawing up a loop through first p, passing shuttle through this loop (A), then pulling the loop tight (B). Do not count lj as a stitch. Make 7 more petals as follows: 5 ds, sj to last p of previous petal, 3 ds, sj to next p, (3 ds, lg p) 3 times, (3 ds, sm p) twice, 5 ds, cl; lj to next p in center r.

Points to remember

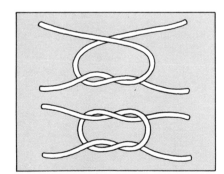

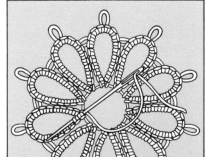

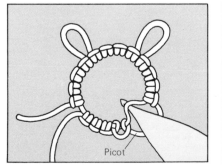

Picot

A new thread is joined only at the end of a ring or chain, before starting the next part of the design. A square knot, illustrated, is an effective way to tie threads together. Leave enough length so that the thread ends can be woven into the back of the completed work.

A thread end is finished most neatly by weaving it under a few stitches, then cutting the remainder. The needle used must have an eye large enough for the thread but thin enough to pass under stitches. An alternative is to whipstitch over the thread ends with matching sewing thread.

A mistake is corrected most easily while a ring is in progress. If it is necessary to open a ring, you have a better chance of success if you pry loose a thread between two stitches of a picot, as illustrated. Otherwise, thread must be cut, then re-joined after eliminating the error.

To avoid confusion, remember:

1. The thread in the left hand is the one to show itself in the stitches; if it is looped, the result will be a ring; if it is draped, the result will be a chain.
2. Work progresses from left to right.
3. The purled loops of the double stitches are facing to the left while a ring or chain is being formed.
4. The term *picot* refers only to a thread loop, not to the double stitch that encloses it. The closing stitch is counted as the first in the next group of stitches.
5. Never set work down in the middle of a ring or chain; it is difficult to resume the correct position and tension.

Working with two threads

Working with two threads considerably enlarges the scope of tatting. It permits introduction of a second color, and allows you to work stitches over the connecting threads between rings—a formation called **chain (ch).** To make a chain, one thread is wrapped over the left fingers and around the little finger to provide tension; the second is used to make double stitches. As with a ring, thread in the left hand forms the stitches.

For working two threads of one color, the preferred method is to use a shuttle plus ball of yarn and work over the ball thread to form chains. Tatting with two colors usually requires two shuttles.

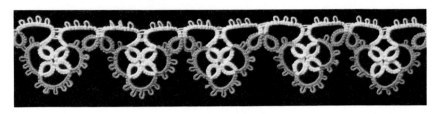

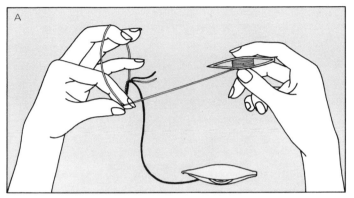

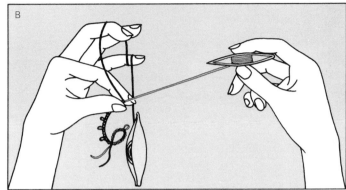

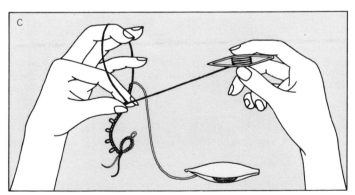

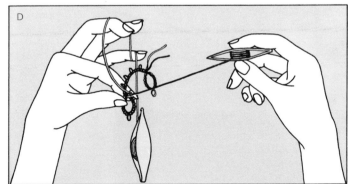

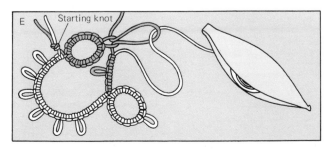

E Starting knot

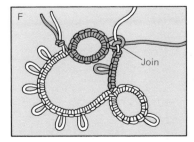

F Join

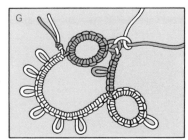

G

Two-color edging: Composed of rings and chains in two colors, this is a good practice piece for mastering the use of two shuttles. Keep in mind that the shuttle not in use rests in the lap or on a table, and whatever color is in the left hand will form the stitches. Wind one shuttle with blue, the other with white; knot the two ends loosely together. Starting close to knot, **with blue,** make r of 8 ds, p, 8 ds (A), cl, rw; **with white** tensioned over left hand and blue in right hand, make ch of (3 ds, p) 6 times, 6 ds (B), do not rw; **with white,** make r of 8 ds, p, 8 ds (C), rw; **with blue** tensioned over left hand and white in right hand, start ch with 3 ds, p, 3 ds (D), sj to p of 1st blue r as follows: pull up a loop of blue, insert white shuttle through it (E), pull loop close to the last ds (F), and complete sj (G), finish ch with (3 ds, p) 3 times, 3 ds, rw; **with white,** make r of 8 ds, sj to p of 1st white r, 8 ds, cl, rw; **with blue,** make ch of (3 ds, p) 5 times, 3 ds, rw; make 2 more sm white rings, connecting them to p of first white r and with a blue ch between them, do not rw; **with white,** make ch of 6 ds, sj to 1st p of opposite white ch, 3 ds, sj to next p, (3 ds, p) 4 times, 3 ds, rw; **with blue,** make r of 8 ds, sj to 2nd p of last blue ch, 8 ds, cl. First repeat is now complete. To begin the next one, do not rw, but make 1st blue r right next to last one, rw; begin 1st white ch with 3 ds, sj to 1st p on opposite ch, finish with (3 ds, p) 5 times, 6 ds. Continue as for first repeat.

417

Shawl with tatted border

The tatted border for the shawl consists of three elements, separately made, then sewed in place. **Tatting** is done with six-cord cotton, one ball each of the colors specified in instructions. **For beading,** you need 180 small glass beads in red-orange (for flowers) and 552 in green (for leaves); 252 4-mm. silver-colored beads for fringe. **Equipment:** Two tatting shuttles; beading needle to transfer the beads to cord (see top illustration, below right); 1½ × 3-inch cardboard gauge for fringe; thread to match tatting.

For shawl: 1½ yds. challis, at least 54 inches wide; ¾ yd. lightweight lining; thread to match challis; 1¼ yds. of wrapping paper to make shawl pattern.

To make the shawl: Trim off selvages; straighten each cut end by drawing out a crosswise thread and cutting along drawn line. Fold fabric on the true bias into a triangle; press fold gently. Baste layers together from center of base to point opposite. Make paper pattern for curve (facing page); use to mark both halves of fabric; cut along marked line.

To attach tatting: Mark center of edge to be trimmed. Starting there, position center border and cluster, then trims at ends. Cut bias lining pieces (for backing) slightly larger than separate groupings; holding backing pieces behind them, pin decorations. Tack pieces in place with matching thread; trim backing.

To hem the shawl, fold it in half with right sides facing; stitch, leaving a 5- to 6-inch opening. Turn right side out; press edge well. Slipstitch opening.

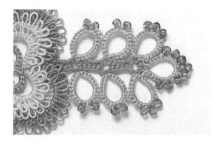

Flowers and leaves (above and below) are separately made and then joined, 2 leaves to each flower. Small glass beads are used in both: red-orange in flowers; green in leaves.

FLOWERS (make 12)

Materials (per flower): Six-cord cotton, 4½ yds. dk. pink, 3½ yds. lt. pink (plus a little extra for beginning and end of shuttle); 15 red-orange beads. Wind dk. pink on one shuttle, lt. pink on the other. Put 15 beads on lt. pink. Note: Wind enough thread on shuttles to make several flowers; add beads just before making each flower.

With lt. pink. Bring 5 beads into loop around hand; let hang at bottom of loop until needed. 4 ds, lg p (bring the 5 beads to top of loop and stretch the picot, not too tightly, across them), 4 ds, close. Place 2 more beads against base of ring (when beginning next ring, make sure these 2 beads remain loose on the thread). *Ring: 4 ds, sj into center p between 1st and 2nd beads, 4 ds, close. Place 2 beads against base of ring* 4 times, putting one bead between each join in center picot, lj to base of 1st ring, rw. Attach second shuttle (dk. pink) to beginning thread of lt. pink with a temporary knot.

With dk. pink. Chain: *10 ds, lj with lt. pink to base of next ring below* 5 times. Do **not** rw.

With lt. pink. Chain: *3 ds, 8 p separated by 2 ds, 3 ds, lj with dk. pink to next space between chains below* 5 times.

With lt. pink. Chain: *3 ds, 10 p separated by 2 ds, 3 ds, lj with dk. pink to next space between chains below* 5 times.

With dk. pink. Chain: *3 ds, 12 p separated by 2 ds, 3 ds, lj with lt. pink to next space between chains below* 5 times.

With dk. pink. Chain: *3 ds, 14 p separated by 2 ds, 3 ds, lj with lt. pink to next space between chains below* 5 times. Cut threads. Tie ends in tight square knot on back; clip close.

LEAF MOTIF (make 24)

Materials: Six-cord cotton, 2 yds. lt. blue for **rings,** ½ yd. green for **chains;** 23 green beads per leaf. One shuttle. Wind shuttle with blue; put on 23 beads; leave green on ball. All joins are sj.

1. Chain: 5 ds, sm p, 1 ds, rw (do not push stitches too close; they should lie in a straight line). **Ring:** (2 beads in loop) 10 ds, bead, 2 ds, bead, 2 ds, p, 10 ds, close, rw.

2. Chain: 5 ds, sm p, 1 ds, rw. **Ring:** (2 beads in loop) 5 ds, j to p of 1st R, 5 ds, bead, 2 ds, bead, 2 ds, p, 10 ds, close, rw.

3. Chain: 5 ds, sm p, 1 ds, rw. **Ring:** (3 beads in loop) 5 ds, j to p of 2nd R, 5 ds, bead, 2 ds, bead, 2 ds, bead, 8 ds, p, 2 ds, close, rw.

4. Chain: 2 ds, rw. **Ring:** (9 beads in loop) 1 ds, j to p of 3rd R, 5 ds, bead, 2 ds, bead, 2 ds, bead, 2 ds, 3 beads together, 2 ds, bead, 2 ds, bead, 2 ds, bead, 5 ds, p, 1 ds, close, rw.

5. Chain: 2 ds, rw (to work ch more easily from here, fold 1st half of leaf toward you, making ds from behind, joins from front). **Ring:** (3 beads in loop) 2 ds, j to p of 4th R, 8 ds, bead, 2 ds, bead, 2 ds, bead, 5 ds, p, 5 ds, close, rw.

6. Chain: 1 ds, j to p of opposite ch by pulling up loop of green and inserting shuttle, 5 ds, rw. **Ring:** (2 beads in loop) 10 ds, j to p of 5th R, 2 ds, bead, 2 ds, bead, 5 ds, p, 5 ds, close, rw.

7. Chain: 1 ds, j to p of opposite ch, 5 ds, rw. **Ring:** (2 beads in loop) 10 ds, j to p of 6th R, 2 ds, bead, 2 ds, bead, 10 ds, close, rw.

8. Chain: 1 ds, j to p of opposite ch, 5 ds. Cut threads; leave ends for tying. To tie 2 leaves to flower, pull one set of threads through space between ch on last row of flower; tie in a tight square knot on back. Leave 2 petals; join 2nd leaf.

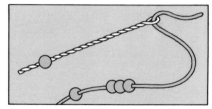

Beads are transferred to cord with needle of fine wire that works like a needle threader. Bead goes onto needle, cord into "eye" at end. Bead passes easily over flexible needle and eye onto cord.

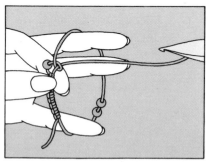

Beads for flowers and leaves are brought into loop around hand before ring is begun; moved into position as needed. Keep beads not in use wound three turns back in shuttle. *Silver beads for the fringe* are put on ball, enough for a section; moved up as fringe is wound, one to a picot.

Fringed swag is made in three sections. Do gray rings first, then yellow edging.

RINGS IN GRAY

Materials: Six-cord cotton, 34 yds. med. gray per section; one shuttle. Edging is designed in repeats of 8 large and 7 small rings—11 repeats to a section.

Large ring: 6 ds, p, 6 ds, p, 6 ds, p, 6 ds, close, rw. Leave a ¼'' space (thread length) between rings.

Small ring: 3 ds, p, 3 ds, p, 3 ds, p, 3 ds, close, rw. Leave space as before.

2nd lg R: 6 ds, sj to 3rd p of 1st lg R, 6 ds, p, 6 ds, p, 6 ds, close, rw. Leave space as before.

2nd sm R: 3 ds, sj to 3rd p of 1st sm R, 3 ds, p, 3 ds, p, 3 ds, close, rw. Leave thread as before.

Continue with 2nd lg and sm R until you have 8 large and 7 small R (one repeat). Begin second repeat with a large R; it will be joined to last small R of first repeat. Similarly, first small R

of this repeat will be joined to last large R of the first repeat. Continue until 11 repeats are completed. Tie off threads close to stitches; clip close.

YELLOW EDGING AND FRINGE

Materials: Six-cord cotton, 23 yds. lt. yellow for chains, 4 yds. dk. pink for rings; 84 silver beads per section. One shuttle; 1½'' × 3'' cardboard gauge for fringe. Wind dk. pink on shuttle; leave yellow on ball; thread 84 beads on yellow. Upper edge will be worked first. Turn gray edging so the first group of small rings at each end faces upward. Attach both threads to the 1st p of the 1st small ring at the *left* end.

Chain: 6 ds, p, 6 ds, lj with dk. pink to top of *next* sm R.

*Chain: 6 ds, p, 6 ds, rw.

Small ring: 3 ds, p, 3 ds, skip one sm R below and sj to top of *next* sm R, 3 ds, p, 3 ds, close, rw.

Chain: 6 ds, p, 6 ds, skip one sm R below

and lj to top of next sm R. 6 ds, p, 6 ds, skip last sm R and lj to top of 1st lg R. (6 ds, p, 6 ds, lj to top of next lg R) 7 times. 6 ds, p, 6 ds, skip 1st sm R and lj to top of next sm R. Repeat from * across top. When next to last sm R has been joined, go around end as follows: 6 ds, p, 6 ds, lj to last p of last sm R, 6 ds, p, 6 ds, lj to 1st p of 1st lg R below, 6 ds, p, 6 ds, lj to top of same lg R. Begin fringe.

Fringes are just very large picots, each with one bead, made on a cardboard gauge for uniformity. Fringe picots (fr p) are made on chains joining lg R. Chains and ring joining sm R are same as above.

Chain: (4 ds, fr p, 4 ds, fr p, 4 ds, lj to top of next lg R) 7 times, then proceed across sm R as above.

To make fringe picot, see below right.

After bottom edge is completed, go around the end same as before; tie ends in a tight square knot and clip close.

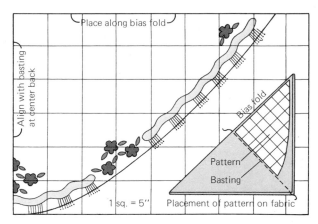

To curve edge of fabric, draw grid of 5'' squares on paper; on it duplicate curve above, square for square. Align pattern with basting on shawl; trace curve on fabric. Flip pattern; trace on other half of shawl.

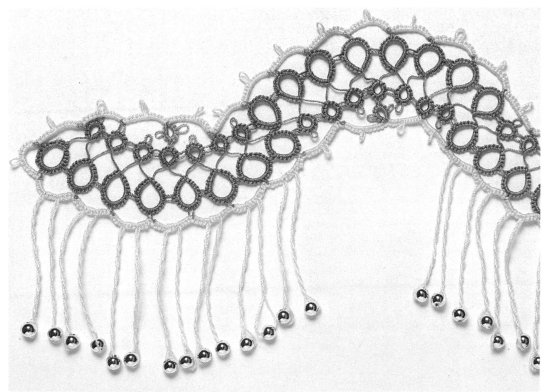

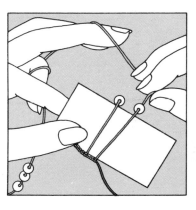

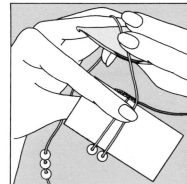

To make fringe picot, after 1st 4 ds in chain, hold cardboard in horizontal position above work. Wrap ball thread, with one bead, once around cardboard, *from* side facing you, *over* top, *to* side away from you; twist thread as you wrap by rolling it between fingers (be sure to twist in the same direction as thread twists naturally). *Make 1st half of next ds* from behind the gauge, nestling it up underneath the gauge next to previous ds stitches (but not too tightly). Complete this ds and 3 more, then make another fr p, 4 ds, and lj to the top of next lg R. Proceed in this way across all the large rings (14 fr p in each group), then remove gauge and arrange the twists and beads to hang properly. Proceed across the small rings as for the top, then again place gauge for next group of fr p.

Filet netting

What is filet netting?
Supplies and equipment
Making the basic knot
Basic mesh techniques
Plain square mesh / netting sampler
Embroidering the sampler
Chinese folk design pillow top

What is filet netting?

Filet netting is a netting of many forms, from tennis nets and hammocks to lace of the delicate kind shown at the right. No matter what form the netting takes, the basic technique remains the same and involves only one knot (see facing page).

In lacemaking terms, filet netting is a mesh worked in diamond or square shape, with a design embroidered on it. (Actually, all mesh is diamond-shaped; it is squared as explained on page 423. Most filet netting is square mesh.)

Netting reached its peak of popularity in 17th-century Europe, when it featured intricate embroidery in many colors and textures. It returned to favor during the Victorian era, but in a less ornate form characterized by geometric patterns in natural-colored cotton and linen thread. Our example typifies this more moderate style, the one associated most closely with the tradition. Today, tradition can be followed with fine, soft crochet cottons. Bear in mind, however, that the knots should look crisp and be nearly invisible; this calls for smooth, tightly twisted cord (but not so hard a twist that knots will be obvious). Embroidery thread can be chosen far more freely; it faces no such restrictions.

Example of filet netting in which both beginning mesh and embroidery are worked in natural colors.

Diamond mesh

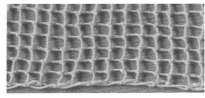

Square mesh

Supplies and equipment

Besides knotting cord, you need heavier cord (about 12 inches) for a **foundation loop,** into which the starting meshes are made; a **shuttle** to hold knotting cord; **mesh stick** to establish mesh size. The number of starting meshes depends on the shape: several for diamond mesh, which starts at an edge (see facing page and p. 422); two for square mesh, which begins at a corner (p. 423). The ideal shuttle for lace is the netting needle below; an alternative, also shown, is two 6-inch upholsterer's needles placed in opposite directions and taped together below the eyes. A good mesh "stick" for lace is a double-pointed knitting needle, with its smooth surface, slim and uniform width, and manageable length.

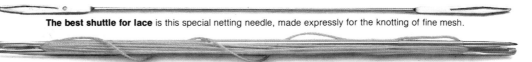

The best shuttle for lace is this special netting needle, made expressly for the knotting of fine mesh.

An alternative shuttle can be made of two 6″ upholsterer's needles, facing in opposite directions and taped together below the eyes.

Good mesh "stick" for filet netting is a double-pointed knitting needle: slim enough to establish small openings, short enough to be manageable.

Making the basic knot

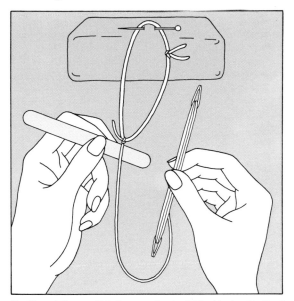

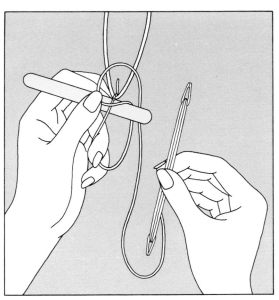

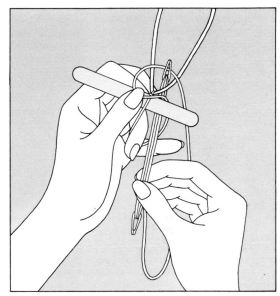

Knot foundation cord into loop; anchor to stable object so it will not pull loose under tension. Thread shuttle; be sure, when wound, it is not larger than mesh stick. Knot end of shuttle thread into foundation

cord. Holding mesh stick between thumb and first finger of left hand and shuttle in right, as shown, pass shuttle thread over stick, around the fourth finger, and back up behind stick. Holding thread against

stick with thumb, loop thread up and around figure-eight style. Pass shuttle through loop on finger, behind stick, through foundation loop, and over top of figure-eight loop.

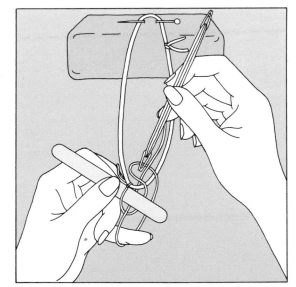

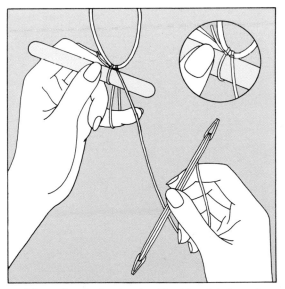

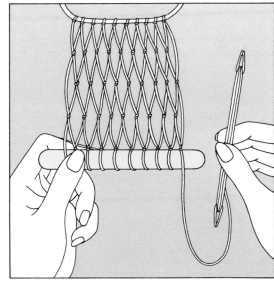

Draw shuttle through and away, *hooking trailing thread on small finger*. Release thumb, then loop on fourth finger; continue pulling until all slack tightens around stick but *do not release thread on*

small finger. Place knot on top of and touching stick, then release small finger, drawing thread toward you and keeping foundation cord taut. This forms first knot. Make starting loops on stick and over

foundation (about 10 for diamond mesh above; for square mesh, see p. 423). Remove stick; turn work (knotting always goes left to right). Continue knotting, except now into loop above.

Filet netting

Basic mesh techniques

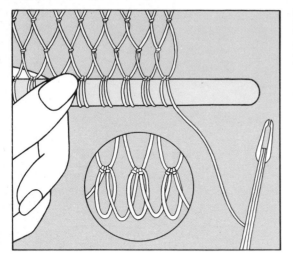

Shaping is accomplished by increasing (left) to widen the mesh, and decreasing (right) to narrow it. These drawings show the basic techniques; for their special use in making square mesh, refer to the facing page.
To increase, form two or more knots in one loop, widening that row, and also those that follow, since you will be knotting into an additional mesh wherever an increase was made.

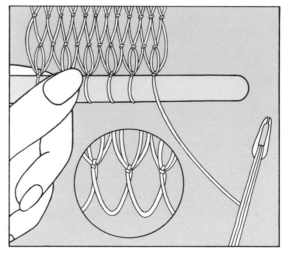

To decrease, work one knot in two or more loops, tying them together, and reducing the number of meshes to be worked in subsequent rows. Though shaping is the primary use for both these techniques, especially by a beginner, fancy filets can be made by alternating decreases and increases from row to row, or at fixed intervals.

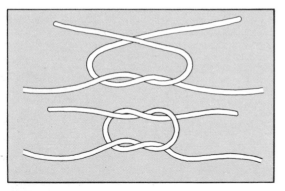

A new thread is best joined at the end of a row. Tie the end of the new thread very close to the last knot that was made, then join the two ends in a weaver's knot as shown. Clip the ends close to the joining knot.

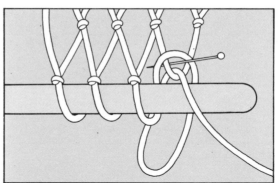

Try to correct mistakes before the knot is tightened. Use a pin to loosen it. If a knot cannot be untied, cut the thread close, untie it, and join a new thread. If you make very tight knots, whole sections of netting can be cut without knots coming undone.

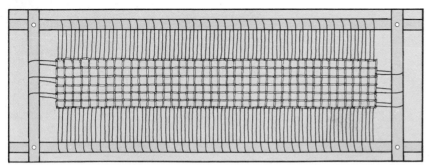

For embroidery, mesh must be stretched in a frame. Be sure to leave at least a 1″ allowance between mesh and inner edge of frame. Wind cord through each mesh and around the frame at top and bottom and through every other mesh at sides. Adjust tension so stretching is even and netting is taut. A mesh too long for a frame can be rolled up and the rolled part finished after the first is completed.

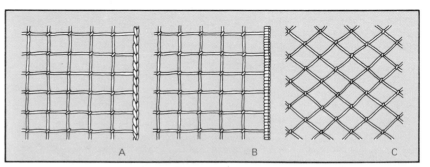

Edge finishes: For any technique, use the same thread as was used for the mesh. In square mesh, the shaping causes side meshes to come out double, to conceal this, and produce a straight, firm edge, good finishing choices are single crochet (A) or close buttonhole stitch (B). The edges of diamond mesh are often cut close to the knots (C). There is no danger of the knots coming undone.

Plain square mesh/Netting sampler

The square mesh being made at bottom is the beginning of the sampler-insertion below (the embroidery directions are on the next page). The directions produce a rectangular mesh approximately 2 by 16 inches, enough for the embroidery charted: 2 repeats, each 32 meshes (about 6 inches) long, *plus* an additional final triangle for balance, *plus* 6 extra meshes at each end—83 meshes in all. To make a longer strip, add meshes in 32-mesh increments for each repeat.

Though the quantities are specifically for the sampler, the technique applies to any square mesh. The progression will be easier to grasp if you remember that the work is turned for each new row.

All work is done with size 20 crochet cotton: the mesh in ecru; embroidery in ecru or white as directed. You also need a mesh stick ⅛ inch wide (or a size 1 knitting needle); a steel netting needle (or a pair of 6-inch tapestry needles faced in opposite directions and taped together below the eyes—see p. 420); a tapestry frame or the equivalent to stretch mesh for embroidery (see opposite page); tapestry needle for working embroidery.

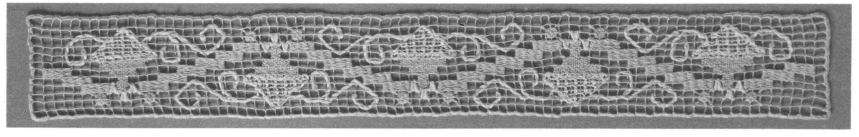

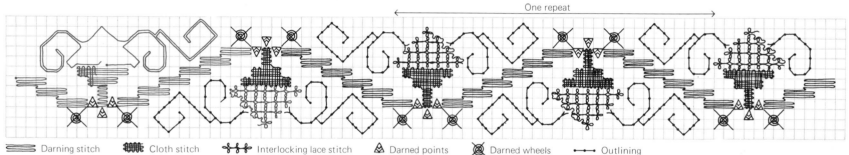

One repeat

〰 Darning stitch   ▦ Cloth stitch   ✚ Interlocking lace stitch   △ Darned points   ⊗ Darned wheels   •—• Outlining

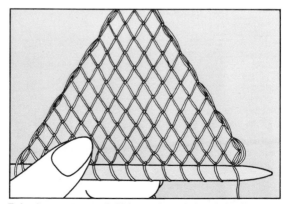

To begin a square mesh: Make two knots in foundation loop; turn work. Starting with second row, *increase one knot in each row* (put two knots in last loop) until you have enough knots for the width—in this case 13, which makes 12 meshes, the width of the sampler.

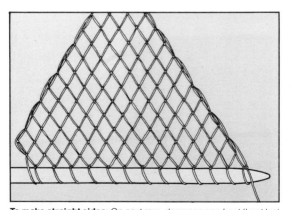

To make straight sides: On next row, *decrease one knot* (knot last two loops together); on following row, *increase one knot* (put two knots in last loop). *Alternate these rows* until long side of mesh is the desired length. In the sampler, this is 83 meshes.

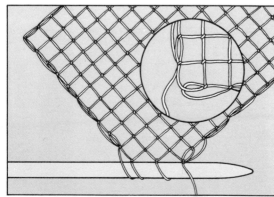

To square the last corner: Beginning with the next row after the length has been established, *decrease one knot at the end of each row* until two loops are left. Knot these two together and cut the threads close. Remove the foundation loop.

423

Filet netting

Embroidering the sampler

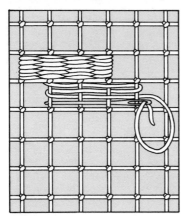

1. Darning stitch (ecru, single thread): In 1st group at left end, tie thread to top left corner of 1st mesh. Weave over and under mesh, from top to bottom, until space is filled—10-12 threads will usually suffice. With next section, attach thread to lower left corner of 1st mesh, and progress upward.

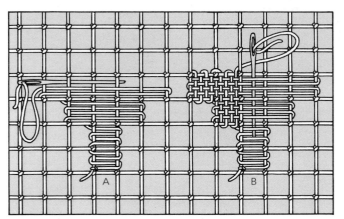

2. Cloth stitch (ecru, single thread): Done in two steps—first warp, then weft threads, in each pattern area. (A) Attach thread at bottom left. Weave single meshes first, over and under, bottom to top, 4 threads per mesh. Weave somewhat loosely; slack is taken up in second step. At next mesh, be sure to weave 1st thread as you did last thread on previous mesh; thread between will be included in next step. (B) Without breaking thread, begin at upper left and weave weft threads back and forth across warp threads. Include all intervening mesh threads in weaving; put in 4 threads per mesh. After each completed row, pull slightly on warp threads so weaving is flat and even.

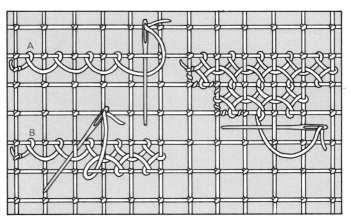

3. Interlocking lace stitch (white, single thread): Done in loop or buttonhole stitch; can be worked diagonally as well as back and forth. Each row takes two steps. (A) Begin with longer row on chart. Attach thread to center of mesh on left side. Make one loop stitch in each mesh, large enough to cover half the mesh. At end of row, make a loop stitch in side of mesh. (B) Going right to left in same row, make loops as before, going over each loop in preceding row and under each vertical mesh. To move to second row, make overcast stitches around last mesh; begin again as in A, except pass needle through bottom loops of previous row to interlock.

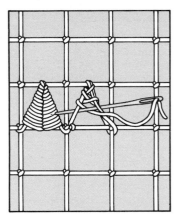

4. Darned points (white, single thread): Darn from top to base. Begin with left point. Attach thread at lower left corner of mesh. Loop around top, down to opposite corner, back up to top. This forms a scaffold for darning. Beginning at top, darn alternately from each side into center—from right a buttonhole stitch, from left a plain stitch; catch in loose end from knot as part of scaffold. When working last stitch on each side, go around bottom of mesh to anchor base of point. Run thread behind mesh to center top of next point and form scaffold as before.

5. Darned wheels (ecru, single thread): Attach thread at center of 4 meshes. Make a bar from there to each corner of 4-mesh square by passing thread around corner, then passing needle twice around it to twist bar. When bars are made, weave thread spirally around center, over bars and under mesh threads, until wheel is desired size (about 4 times). Fasten off on back by passing thread through twists of a bar or tying a square knot with beginning thread.

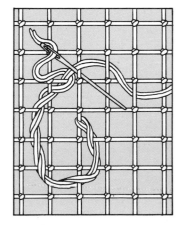

6. Outlining (white, double thread): Begin at bottom center of interlocking lace stitch; weave over and under mesh threads around triangle as indicated by dots on chart. Following chart and photograph, weave first spiral. When center is reached, begin weaving back alongside first thread, except pass thread *under* each mesh thread previously passed *over* and twisting once around previously laid thread. Continue around second spiral, then finish off top of first on way back to triangle. Continue around triangle, making other side the same. Fasten off thread with square knot to beginning thread.

Chinese folk design pillow top

Materials

Small netting shuttle; knitting needle, size 1, for mesh stick; tapestry needle; embroidery scissors; frame and cord to mount mesh (at least 12-inch square inside space); size 20 crochet cotton, 1 ball, ecru; size 8 pearl cotton, 1 ball each, 5 shades of blue; square pillow for the finished piece. It is 56 meshes (about 10 inches) square; for a larger size, use size 10 crochet cotton, size 2 or 3 knitting needle, size 5 pearl cotton.

Making the net (square mesh)

To begin, make two knots into foundation loop; turn. Starting with second row, *increase* one knot at end of each row until you have 57 knots on mesh stick. On next row, net plain (no increase). Next row, begin *decreasing* one knot at end of each row until two knots are left. Knot these

together, cut thread, remove foundation loop. Stretch mesh in frame, winding the cord through every other mesh. Measure edges to be sure they are all the same.

Embroidery

In 5 shades of blue, charted as A, B, C, D, E (lightest to darkest). Stitches are those in sampler, but worked as listed on this page. To secure thread ends during work, run thread back and forth a few times from back (do not make knots). Always thread needle with thread coming from ball nearest needle; this enhances sheen of stitches and keeps thread from untwisting. Turn frame with stretched mesh so the raised mesh threads (you can feel them with your fingers) run vertically and face you; those on back run horizontally. Direction of raised threads make a difference in the darning stitches.

Cloth stitch (fish's body): Numbers on diagram mark starting points for first threads. Follow lines to point where thread turns and second threads are woven in. Weave second threads in as far as possible, then begin at next number before completing first area. Lay in 4 threads per mesh; remember that first thread in each mesh is woven same as last thread of previous mesh. Traveling threads, sometimes needed to get from one row to next, are incorporated into mesh threads during second stage of weaving. Work numbers 1-4 in color A. Complete work in this color before going further. Numbers 5-10 are worked in color B, number 11 in color C.

Darning stitch (fish's fins, tail bars, and eye; all darkest areas in border): Lay in about 12 threads per mesh. Work bars in tail vertically in color B. Raised vertical threads of mesh help "outline" them. Go from bar to bar by passing thread through edge of cloth stitch from back. All other darning is worked horizontally. Fins on left side are worked in colors B and A in that order. Small bars are made after last row is completed by passing thread 3 times around threads, then wrapping twice around threads and going to next small bar. Fins above head are worked, bottom to top, in color D. When top mesh is completed, pull end of thread down so it is doubled, and proceed with outline at top of each fin. Work darning in eye, all border darning, in color E.

Darned wheels (fish's eye; border): Worked somewhat differently from sampler. Thread is brought out from darned area adjacent at corner between first two wheels. Diagonal bars are laid

from center to each corner, but first corner will have only one thread. Its second thread is laid after wheel itself is darned, enabling you to begin second wheel from adjacent corner. After second wheel is completed, thread is concealed in darning and brought around between next two wheels to be worked. In these wheels, corner threads are laid under mesh; darning is done by passing needle over mesh threads and under corner about 3 times. Work fish's eye in color A, border wheels in D.

Interlocking lace stitch (fish's body; border): Work fish's body in color A. Begin in upper left corner and work down. Conceal traveling threads in edge stitches at left side. Work outside border area in color E; begin and end at point indicated. Work inside border area in color C; begin above fish's head and work first row all the way around, putting in diagonal stitches as indicated. Diagram shows how to lay in return row on diagonal (pass needle under mesh knot in same way that you pass it under mesh thread when doing a straight row).

Darned points (fish's teeth): Work in color D, left to right. Scaffold for each point will have one thread on left, two on right.

Outlining (fish's eye, around head; inside border): Use double thread. Outline fish's eye in color A, eye socket in D; top of head, from last tooth to first fin, in color B; bottom of head, from tooth to halfway around back of head, in color A; inside border in color D.

Edging: With double thread in color C, work 4 buttonhole stitches into each mesh all around (one extra at each corner).

Time-honored traditions combine to create a striking pillow top with a remarkably contemporary look. The fish is the carp, a favorite in Chinese folklore, worked in five shades of blue on an ecru mesh. The pillow top is 56 meshes (about 10 inches) square, but can easily be made larger by changing thread and mesh stick (knitting needle) sizes.

A □ B □ C □ D □ E □

Bobbin lace

Introduction
Tools and supplies
Preparing the pricking/bobbin lace sampler
Winding bobbin pairs
Working the basic (half and whole) stitches
Weaving a design
Pinning within a design
Ground patterns
Other lace techniques
Bobbin lace-trimmed apron

Introduction

Bobbin lace is a lace woven of pairs of threads wound on bobbins. Only two basic stitches are involved, half stitch and whole stitch (see pp. 428-430), but from these a variety of designs can be woven. The weaving is done over an actual-size paper pattern mounted on a pillow or padded board (see below). Pins are inserted through the pattern into the pillow to hold threads in place; the pattern is called a *pricking* because it is perforated at specific points in the design to make pins easier to insert. The pillow accounts for another name, pillow lace, by which this lace is also known.

Bobbin lace is an old technique, dating back to the 15th century. As its popularity spread, local styles developed, with patterns and stitches, and their names, reflecting their places of origin. As a result, old pieces of bobbin lace exhibit a wide range of styles, from geometric patterns made with a few pairs of bobbins, to complex floral and pictorial designs requiring hundreds.

Russian braid

Cluny

Honiton

Examples of torchon

Scandinavian (free-form)

Tools and supplies

Though their forms may be different, the elements required for bobbin lace have stayed the same for centuries: appropriate thread, bobbins, a pattern to follow, a pillow on which to mount the pattern. Traditional threads were silk, metallic, or linen, spun very smooth and incredibly fine; for most modern bobbin lace, the choice is a smooth cotton. Bobbins were wood, bone, or ivory, often weighted with glass beads to help hold thread taut. True bobbins can still be found and are easiest to handle, but there are many satisfactory alternatives: slotted clothespins; doweling or pencils cut to 4- to 6-inch lengths and grooved at one end; swizzle sticks; large nails; tapestry or fly shuttle bobbins used in weaving. Traditional prickings were of parchment so they could be re-used; for present purposes, we recommend graph paper. The pillow need only support the work firmly and take pins easily—our simple solution is to use squares of corrugated cardboard well padded with fabric.

Modern pillow "dressed" (traditional term) with bobbins has revolving cylinder suitable for making edgings and insertions. Lace being worked: traditional torchon edging with half-stitch scallops.

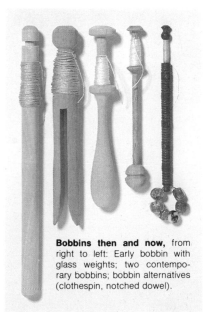

Bobbins then and now, from right to left: Early bobbin with glass weights; two contemporary bobbins; bobbin alternatives (clothespin, notched dowel).

Preparing the pricking/Bobbin lace sampler

The sampler is designed to introduce you to the half stitch and whole stitch, and several of the patterns that can be made from them; and to the pattern, or pricking, that you follow to produce bobbin lace designs. On your graph paper (see equipment list at right), using waterproof ink, copy the diagram below square for square, putting in all dots, lines, and numbers precisely as shown. One ink color is sufficient; three are used here to make the diagram more comprehensible. The right side of the braid-tape that edges the sampler is exactly the reverse of the pattern for the left side.

Pin your pricking at the corners, in the center and as near the top of the pillow-board as possible. Using a pricker (an awl-like tool with a needle point), or a large needle fitted with a dowel or pen-holder handle, punch holes through all dots into the board.

The diagram is labeled with the names of the stitches in the order in which they are worked in the sampler, and the numbers of the pages on which instructions for them appear. You may find it helpful to indicate these stitch names on your diagram, perhaps also the page numbers. Listed below are abbreviations used in the instructions, and some working pointers about the weaving process.

Abbreviations used in instructions

h st	half stitch	**c**	cross
w st	whole stitch	**pr,**	pair,
t	twist	**prs**	pairs

Points to remember:

1. Pairs of bobbins are numbered left to right; numbers refer to their position on the board, not to actual bobbins.

2. In twisting, the right partner crosses over the left partner.

3. In crossing, the right bobbin of the left pair crosses over the left bobbin of the right pair.

4. Pins are placed perpendicular to the board except at the edges, where they are slanted outward.

5. Place pins in their holes *between* the last two pairs of bobbins worked.

6. Always keep bobbins hanging evenly.

7. Do not roll bobbins back and forth on the board; this makes thread unwind. Instead, push them back and forth in pairs.

8. Join a new thread by working both new and old ends into the weaving together; clip when lace is completed.

Equipment specifically for sampler:

Board or "pillow" approximately 26″ square (usable also for project, p. 432). You can make your own with two or more pieces of corrugated cardboard taped together and padded with layers of wool felt or cotton or wool flannel. Acoustical tile or similar soft board will also work well, provided surface is smooth. Insert a few pins in "pillow" to be sure they go in easily and hold firmly. If they protrude at the bottom when pushed in all the way, place thick toweling or some similar padding underneath, or change to a shorter type of pin.

Dressmaker's straight pins (or shorter pins if they are more suitable) to use in weaving. Long T-pins or corsage pins are helpful for pinning bobbins not in use out of the way.

Bobbins, 24, either the traditional style (available in some shops and by mail) or one of the alternatives described under Tools and supplies on the opposite page.

Thread or yarn of almost any kind can be used in contemporary work. For learning, a smooth 3- or 6-cord cotton is best. Sampler calls for one ball of size 10 in white or ecru.

Pricker, or a needle-like equivalent that will make satisfactory pinholes, for perforating the pricking at all of the dots in the design. These are the points at which pins will be inserted, and pricking makes insertion far easier.

Pricking requires two 8½″ × 11″ sheets of graph paper, 6 squares to the inch.

Crochet hook, size 8, 9, or 10, which is used in making sewing joins (see p. 431).

Cloth cover, a 15″ to 20″ square of smooth fabric to protect lace that has been woven as you work on another section, or to cover your project when you put it aside or away.

Dowel, ⅛″ in diameter and about 7″ long, for mounting bobbins so that the sampler is ready for hanging when it is completed.

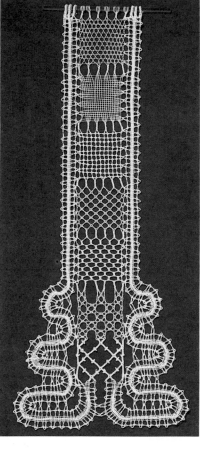

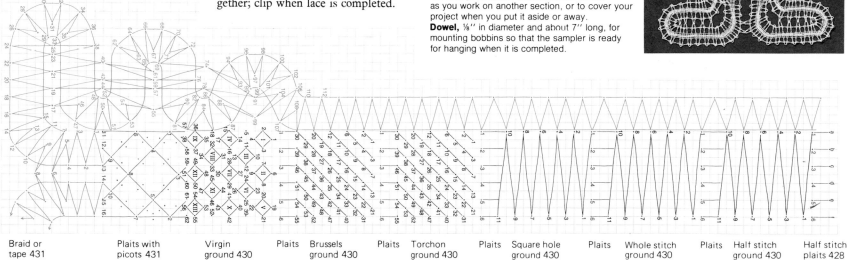

| Braid or tape 431 | Plaits with picots 431 | Virgin ground 430 | Plaits | Brussels ground 430 | Plaits | Torchon ground 430 | Plaits | Square hole ground 430 | Plaits | Whole stitch ground 430 | Plaits | Half stitch ground 430 | Half stitch plaits 428 |

Bobbin lace techniques

Winding bobbin pairs

Measure off enough thread to fill the bobbins but not overload them. For the sampler, this is about 6 yards—3 per bobbin. Wind bobbins from each end toward center, leaving about 18 inches unwound

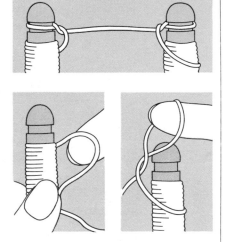

for mounting. Secure thread with noose, made by looping thread as shown, twist-

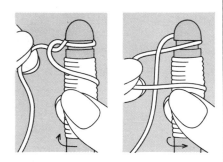

ing bobbin away from you, then slipping noose over head of bobbin. Pull thread to tighten. Noose lets you unwind thread as needed (above left) or wind up excess thread (right) without undoing the knot. Mount two pairs of bobbins together with a lark's head knot (p. 447). Place a pin between each two pairs, just under dowel—points a to f on pricking.

Working the basic (half and whole) stitches

The illustrations below show two bobbin pairs mounted as described at the left. Work is done on the side shown; the reverse side becomes the right side when lace is finished. Two adjacent pairs are woven together, the left pair held in the left hand and the right pair in the right. In directions, pairs are numbered left to right. Numbers indicate board position, not actual bobbins. The first row of drawings shows the steps to a half stitch plait. These occur in the sampler in series of six, made by plaiting all of the pairs as you did prs 1-2 (prs 3-4, pin at #2, prs 5-6, pin at #3, etc.).

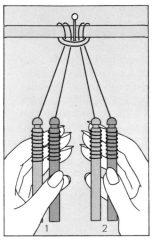

Start weaving, as illustrated above, with pair 1 held in the left hand and pair 2 in the right; pin the other bobbins out of the way.

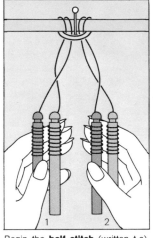

Begin the **half stitch** (written t,c) with a *twist,* worked as follows: Push right member of each pair over left with thumb of each hand.

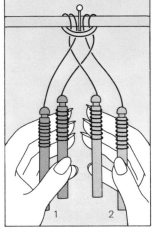

In the *cross,* inside members exchange places, the one on the left crossing over the one on the right. This completes one half stitch.

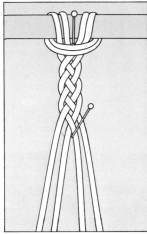

To produce a plait, make half stitches as described down the pricking to the first hole. Place a pin at #1 between the two pairs.

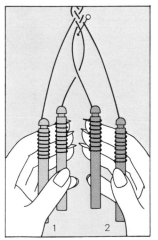

In whole stitch (written c,t,c), pairs are first crossed, then twisted, then crossed again. The illustration above shows the first *cross.*

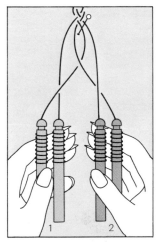

All crosses and twists are worked exactly the same for whole stitch as for half stitch. The *twist* is being worked in the drawing above.

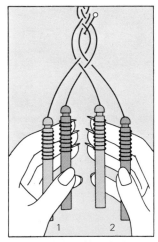

The step illustrated here is the second *cross,* which completes the whole stitch. A plait cannot be made with a whole stitch. When it is re-

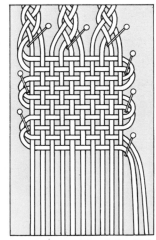

peated, the result is **whole stitch ground,** which is the fourth stitch area in the sampler. For whole stitch ground instructions, see page 430.

Weaving a design

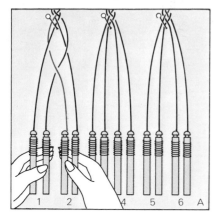

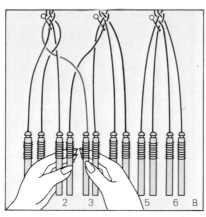

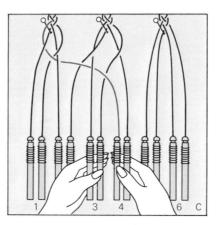

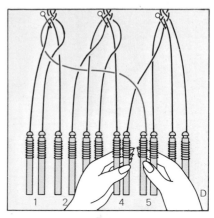

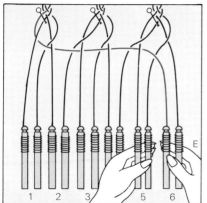

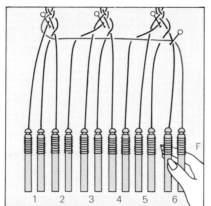

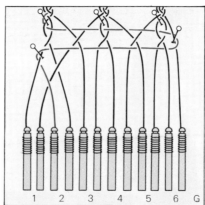

This sequence, of basic steps to half stitch ground, is designed to give a general sense of the interaction of pairs of bobbins. The drawings also clarify what is meant by numbers signifying positions of bobbins on board, not actual bobbins. Space limitations permit showing only 6 pairs of bobbins instead of the 12 used in the sampler, but the principles are the same. In A, the half stitch (t,c) has been completed with prs 1-2; B, C, D, and E show half stitches made with prs 2-3, 3-4, 4-5, and 5-6 respectively; in illustration F, the left-to-right sequence has been pinned. (Unless otherwise indicated, pins are always placed between the two pairs of bobbins involved in the just-completed stitch.) In illustration G, half stitches have been worked in reverse (prs 6-5, 5-4, 4-3, 3-2, 2-1). Stitch is worked the same way regardless of direction. This sequence, repeated, produces the ground.

Pinning within a design

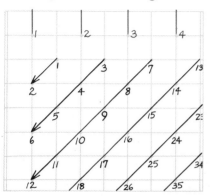

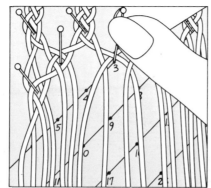

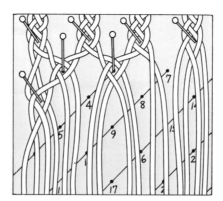

Another pinning principle is demonstrated by torchon ground, a mesh form of the whole stitch ground. It is worked diagonally, making it necessary to place a pin in the center of each whole stitch to hold it in place. The mesh is created by twisting both pairs of bobbins before each whole stitch; the twists force the stitches apart, producing diamond-shaped holes. Edge bobbins are also given an extra twist for added firmness. The drawings show only the start of the procedure; for full instructions, see next page. To begin the stitch, t,c prs 3-2, pin at #1, t,c. This makes a whole stitch with a pin at its center, both pairs having been twisted first. Then t,c prs 2-1, pin at #2, t,c, extra twist to pr 1 (the edge pair). t,c prs 5-4, pin at #3, t,c, and so on down the second diagonal row.

Bobbin lace techniques

Ground patterns

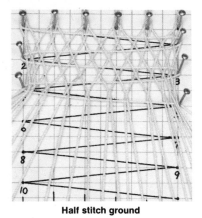

Half stitch ground

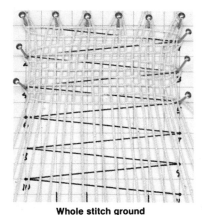

Whole stitch ground

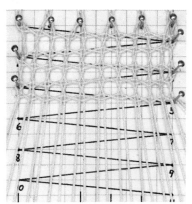

Square hole ground

Plaits are worked at start and between sections. See page 427 for locations, page 428 for technique.
Half stitch ground (also net or lattice ground):
1. t,c prs 1-2 (lay down pr 1, shift pr 2 to left hand and take up pr 3 in right); t,c prs 2-3 (shift prs again); t,c prs 3-4, 4-5, etc., through prs 11-12; pin at #1 between 11-12. Twist pr 12 once more (extra twist makes edge firmer); pull slightly on all bobbins to make threads lie even. *Remember numbers signify board position, not actual bobbins.*
2. Work back across row the same way: t,c prs 12-11, 11-10, 10-9, 9-8, etc., through prs 2-1. Pin at #2 between prs 2 and 1, extra twist to pr 1.
3. Repeat these two rows until space is filled, ending with pin #11.

Whole stitch ground (also cloth stitch and linen stitch), worked over an area, looks like a woven fabric. In this stitch (written c,t,c), pairs are crossed, then twisted, then crossed again:
1. c,t,c prs 1-2, 2-3, 3-4, etc., through prs 11-12. Pin at #1 between prs 11-12, twist pr 12 once more.
2. Work back across row the same way: c,t,c prs 12-11, 11-10, 10-9, etc., through prs 2-1. Pin at #2, extra twist to pr 1.
3. Repeat rows 1 and 2 to pin #11. Occasionally pull down on threads to keep tension even.
In this stitch, an "active" pair passes back and forth through the other "passive" pairs. Variations can be achieved by twisting active, or passives, or both, between stitches or groups of stitches.

Square hole ground, a variation of the whole stitch ground, is worked exactly as above, except both pairs of bobbins are twisted once before each whole stitch is made. The twists force the whole stitches apart, making "square holes."
1. t,c,t,c prs 1-2, 2-3, 3-4, etc., through prs 11-12. Put a pin between prs 11-12 at #1. Edge bobbins do not get extra twists in this pattern.
2. Work back across row the same way: t,c,t,c prs 12-11, 11-10, 10-9, etc., through prs 2-1. Put a pin between prs 2-1 at #2.
3. Repeat rows 1 and 2 to pin #11. Pull threads into position carefully after every row. Do this by pulling down on the bobbins, not by pulling the threads themselves.

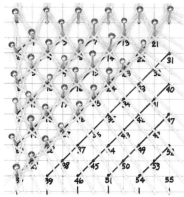

Torchon ground

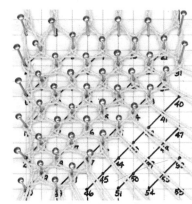

Brussels ground

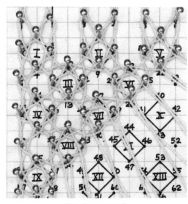

Virgin ground

Torchon ground is like square hole ground, except worked diagonally, making it necessary to put a pin in the center of each w st to hold it in place.
1. t,c prs 3-2, pin at #1, t,c (makes a w st with a pin in its center, both prs having been twisted first); t,c prs 2-1, pin at #2, t,c. Extra twist to pr 1.
2. t,c prs 5-4, pin at #3, t,c; t,c prs 4-3, pin at #4, t,c; t,c prs 3-2, pin at #5, t,c; t,c prs 2-1, pin at #6, t,c. Extra twist to pr 1.
3. t,c prs 7-6, pin at #7, t,c; t,c prs 6-5, pin at #8, t,c; t,c prs 5-4, pin at #9, t,c; t,c prs 4-3, pin at #10, t,c; t,c prs 3-2, pin at #11, t,c; t,c prs 2-1, pin at #12, t,c. Extra twist to pr 1.
4. Continue, always picking up the two prs of bobbins on either side of 1st hole for each new diagonal row. Remember to give pr 12 an extra twist before making stitch at #31, etc., so each edge has 2 twists.

Brussels ground sequence is the same as for torchon ground, except Brussels ground has two whole stitches at each pin, with pin placed between them.
1. t,c,t,c prs 3-2, pin at #1, t,c,t,c (extra twist made after the pin because you cannot cross the same prs twice without twisting them first); t,c,t,c prs 2-1, pin at #2, t,c,t,c. No extra twist needed to prs 1 and 12 in this pattern.
2. t,c,t,c prs 5-4, pin at #3, t,c,t,c; t,c,t,c prs 4-3, pin at #4, t,c,t,c; t,c,t,c prs 3-2, pin at #5, t,c,t,c; t,c,t,c prs 2-1, pin at #6, t,c,t,c.
3. Continue in this way, always starting each new diagonal row by picking up the prs of bobbins on either side of 1st hole.

Virgin ground (also maiden ground) is worked in a series of large diamonds, each in a "box." Whole stitches with a twist between are worked in each corner of diamond and pinned in center. Corners of boxes are completed with one half stitch (no pins).
1. t,c prs 2-3, pin at #1, t,c; extra twist pr 1, t,c prs 1-2, pin at #2, t,c; t,c prs 3-4, pin at #3, t,c,; t,c prs 2-3, pin at #4, t,c; Diamond I complete. Extra twist pr 1, t,c prs 1-2, pin at #5, t,c; t,c prs 3-4. Lower corners of box around Diamond I are now complete. Begin Diamond II.
2. t,c prs 6-7, pin at #6, t,c; t,c prs 5-6, pin at #7, t,c; t,c prs 7-8, pin at #8, t,c; t,c prs 6-7, pin at #9, t,c; t,c prs 7-8 and prs 5-6 to complete lower corners of box around Diamond II.
3. t,c prs 4-5, pin at #10, t,c; t,c prs 3-4, pin at #11, t,c; t,c prs 5-6, pin at #12, t,c; t,c prs 4-5, pin at #13, t,c; t,c prs 3-4 and prs 5-6.
4. t,c prs 2-3, pin at #14, t,c; extra twist pr 1, t,c prs 1-2, pin at #15, t,c; t,c prs 3-4, pin at #16, t,c; t,c prs 2-3, pin at #17, t,c; extra twist pr 1, t,c prs 1-2, pin at #18, t,c; t,c prs 3-4.
5. Continue same way with Diamond V, giving pr 12 an extra twist for a firmer edge. Each diamond begins with prs on either side of its 1st (top) hole—prs 10 and 11 for Diamond V. As Diamond IX, XII, XIII are completed, put pins under half stitches at holes #57-62 to hold them in place for next section.

Other lace techniques

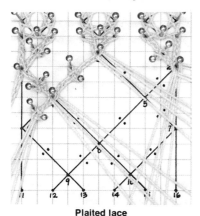

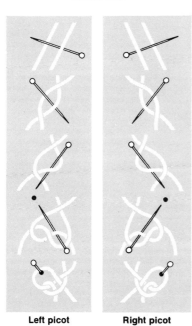

Plaited lace is simply half stitch plaits enhanced with tiny picots and joined. Begin by making a plait with prs 1-2 long enough to reach pin #1. Do not put in a pin yet, but lay the plait aside, and make a plait with prs 3-4 halfway to pin #1. The two holes at this point mark the positions for the picots.

Left and right picots are made with the left and right pairs of bobbins—see diagram. Use a pin to help pull up the loop as shown; then insert pin in the loop and pull down carefully on the two bobbins to lock the picot in place. Continue making the plait to pin #1 and then join this plait to the first by means of a "windmill join" (below).

The windmill join is just a whole stitch, with a pin in its center, made with each pair of bobbins functioning as a single bobbin: Cross pr 2 over pr 3; cross pr 4 over pr 3 and pr 2 over pr 1 (this is the twist). Put pin in #1. Cross pr 2 over pr 3. Join is now completed. Repeat this procedure with prs 9 to 12, putting another join at #2. With prs 5 to 8, make plaits and join at #3. Continue making plaits, picots, and joins as indicated on the pricking. At pins #11 to #16, place pins between the pairs of bobbins in each plait to hold them in position for the next section.

Plaited lace

Left picot   **Right picot**

Windmill join

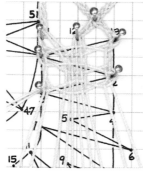

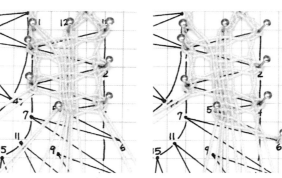

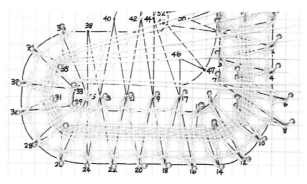

Braid or tape lace, a style popular in Russia and Eastern Europe, is characterized by curving lines and free forms. Although apparently complex, designs require only a few pairs of bobbins, just enough for the width of the tape, which turns, curves, and joins to itself by means of sewings (below). The tape is made like whole stitch ground, varied by twisting the pairs to make openings. Before starting, remove all center pins from the ground patterns, and push in all the way the pins along both edges. Cover the completed lace, but leave the pricking exposed where you will be working the tape. You will be making two sections, one at each side, with six pairs of bobbins for each; 6th pair is active for left side, first pair for right. Pin the right-side bobbins out of the way—left side is made first. At some point, active pair will run out of thread; when it does, re-wind each bobbin with another 3 yards of thread. Weave ends in cloth (center) portion of tape. Ends can be clipped later.

Making the tape:
1. t,c,t,c prs 6-5, t pr 5; c,t,c prs 5-4, 4-3, 3-2; t,c,t,c prs 2-1; pin at #1.
2. t,c,t,c prs 1-2, t pr 2; c,t,c prs 2-3, 3-4, 4-5; t,c,t,c prs 5-6; pin at #2.

Blind pin (pins #5, 9, 13, 27, 31, 35, etc.): To make a smooth curve in the tape, there must be more threads at the outer edge and fewer at the inner edge. To achieve this, the active pair is woven from the outer edge halfway to the inner edge, then woven back out again. For example, after pin #4 has been placed: t,c,t,c prs 6-5; t pr 5; c,t,c prs 5-4; c,t,c prs 4-3; c,t,c prs 3-2; pin at #5; c,t,c prs 2-3; c,t,c prs 3-4; c,t,c prs 4-5; t,c,t,c prs 5-6, etc.

Sewings: As the tape curves, it must be joined to itself at intervals with "sewings," made by joining the active pair of bobbins to previously made portion of tape at a pin. Sewings are made here at pins #6, 8, 17, 19, 21, 23, 25, etc. These pins are placed farther than usual from the edge of the tape, and best given 1 or 2 extra twists for added firmness. Pins #6 and #8 are joined on the other side, so the first sewing comes after pin #36. When it has been placed, weave through tape as usual toward pin #25; extra twist to active pr. Remove pin at #25; with crochet hook, reach down through loop at #25 and pull up thread of nearest bobbin. Insert other bobbin through pulled-up thread, then gently pull both threads back in position. Replace pin at #25, and continue weaving as usual. Sewings are sometimes made without an extra twist on the pair: e.g., at #49, where a sewing is made to #1; at #51, where one is made into the plait; along edges of ground patterns, where tape is joined to sampler edges. After completing tape, finish off dowel by making a plait with each group of 4 bobbins long enough to go around it. End with sewing made through base of plait with each pair acting as a single bobbin. Tie prs in tight square knot; clip close.

431

Bobbin lace-trimmed apron

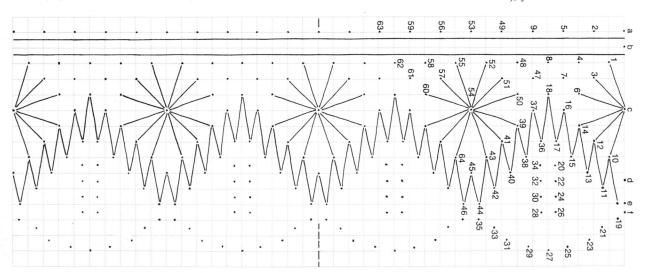

The lace trims consist of an edging in torchon patterns and a medallion in a combination of styles. Ordinarily worked in white, these patterns are worked in three thread colors, to give variety and to make the lace construction easier to understand. For information about prickings, and other details about the individual patterns, be sure to read the introduction to each set of instructions.

Materials needed to make the lace

Board or "pillow," at least 26″ long (the sampler board is suitable)

Dressmaker's pins

Paper for prickings: graph paper for the edging pattern, 4 squares to the inch, enough to make a pricking 24″ long; medium-weight drawing paper for the medallion pattern, shown actual size

Bobbins: 14 pairs for edging; 8 pairs for medallion

Heavy crochet cotton (approximate equivalent of pearl cotton #5), one ball each of white, ecru, and light blue

Crochet hook, size 9, for sewings (in medallion only)

Pricker, scissors, drawing ink (one color is sufficient), yardstick

The edging motifs are all torchon patterns; see pages 429 and 430 for general principles. The medallion is made much like the braid in the sampler (p. 431): a few pairs of bobbins to make a tape in several variations, here both whole and half stitch tapes with occasional picots, joined at various points by sewings. After tapes are completed, fillings are added: Brussels ground in flower petals, half stitch plaits in the background.

To make the apron, you need 1 yard of 36″- or 45″-wide dressweight linen or cotton, and sewing thread to match.

From fabric, cut an *apron front* 25″ wide by 23½″ long; a *pocket lining* the shape of the medallion, plus ⅝″ seam allowance all around; *waistband* 4¼″ wide by 17¼″ long; two 2½ by 27″ *ties.*

To finish side edges of apron, stitch ¼″ from edge, turn, topstitch in place. Turn ¼″ again and topstitch. Finish both long edges and one end of ties the same way. To hem apron, turn cut edge under and topstitch; turn up a 3¼″ hem and topstitch in place. Place the scalloped edge of the edging on hemline; stitch lace in place along top and sides. Stay-stitch along seamline of pocket lining. Turn back seam allowance; clip and notch as needed. Stitch in place with two rows of straight stitch or one of zigzag; trim excess. Center pocket lining, seam allowance up, on right half of apron, bottom edge 5½″ up from top of lace. Topstitch in place; hand-sew lace to pocket.

Divide top edge of apron into three 8″ sections; place gathering stitches along seamline of first and last parts. Turn under seam allowance at each end of the waistband; place a pin 4″ in from fold. With right sides together, pin waistband to apron front, gathering fullness to fit 4″ spaces at ends of the waistband. Stitch; trim seam allowances. Turn waistband to right side, turn under second seam allowance, slipstitch band in place. Slip unfinished end of a tie into each end of waistband; topstitch in place.

Lace edging and medallion, worked in pretty pastels, make plain linen apron feminine and fashionable.

Make a complete pricking for the edging with 10 complete repeats of the fan, putting in all dots, lines, and numbers exactly as shown.

EDGING (3½″ by 24″)

This pattern introduces three traditional torchon motifs: spider (white), made with 6 pairs of bobbins; zigzag (ecru), often worked in half stitch but here in whole stitch; fan (blue), also in whole stitch, with twists between stitches. The straight edge is the **footing;** the opposite side, which hangs freely, is the **heading;** ground pattern is torchon.

Prepare pricking, using graph paper as specified, with 10 complete repeats of fan. Spider begins and ends at its center pin. Broken line indicates last row. Pin prepared pricking as near as possible to top of board and a place or two on the sides. Prick through all dots.

Prepare 14 pairs of bobbins as follows: 2 prs white, 1½ yds. each bobbin; hang both pairs at b. 10 prs white, 2 yds. each bobbin; hang 2 prs at a, 6 prs at c, 1 pr each at d and f. 1 pr ecru, 4½ yds. each bobbin; hang at e. 1 pr blue, 5½ yds. each bobbin; hang at e. To secure bobbins around pins, w st prs 1-2. At e, place ecru pr left, blue pr right. Make w st and place pin between two prs at first hole below e (has no #), t both prs and make another w st. Ecru should be left, blue right. With prs 5 to 10 at c, work as follows: w st prs 8-7, 7-6, 6-5. w st prs 9-8, 8-7, 7-6. w st prs 10-9, 9-8, 8-7. Draw up around pin carefully, making sts lie as flat and tight as possible. Then twist prs 5, 6, 7 twice, prs 8, 9, 10 three times.

Torchon ground and footing:

t pr 2 twice, w st prs 2-3, w st prs 3-4. t,c prs 5-4, pin # 1, t,c.

Footing: t pr 4, w st prs 4-3, w st prs 3-2, t pr 9, w st prs 9-10, 10-11, pin # 13. t pr 2 twice, w st prs 2-3, w st prs 3-4. (Hint: Pull down on both passive prs and up on the active pr before placing pin.)

t,c prs 6-5, pin # 3, t,c. t,c prs 5-4, pin # 4, t,c. Rep footing, pin # 5, t,c prs 7-6, pin # 6, t,c. t,c prs 6-5, pin # 7, t,c. t,c prs 5-4, pin # 8, t,c. Rep footing, pin # 9.

Zigzag, 1st half: w st prs 12-11, w st prs 11-10, pin # 10.

*Pattern repeat begins here
t pr 10, w st prs 10-11, w st prs 11-12, pin

11. t pr 12, w st prs 12-11, 11-10, 10-9, pin # 12. t pr 9, w st prs 9-10, 10-11, pin # 13. t pr 11, w st prs 11-10, 10-9, 9-8, pin # 14. t pr 8, w st prs 8-9, 9-10, pin # 15. t pr 10, w st prs 10-9, 9-8, t pr 7, w st prs 8-7, pin # 16. t pr 7, w st prs 7-8, 8-9, pin # 17. t pr 9, w st prs 9-8, 8-7, t pr 6, w st prs 7-6, pin # 18.

Fan, bobbin prs 9 to 14 (draw up sts carefully after each row): t,c,t,c prs 13-14, pin # 19. t,c,t,c prs 14-13, 13-12, 12-11, 11-10, 10-9, pin # 20. t,c,t,c prs 9-10, 10-11, 11-12, 12-13, 13-14, pin # 21. t,c,t,c prs 14-13, 13-12, 12-11, 11-10, pin # 22. t,c,t,c prs 10-11, 11-12, 12-13, 13-14, pin # 23. t,c,t,c prs 14-13, 13-12, 12-11, pin # 24. t,c,t,c prs 11-12, 12-13, 13-14, pin # 25. t,c,t,c prs 14-13, 13-12, pin # 26. t,c,t,c prs 12-13, 13-14, pin # 27. t,c,t,c prs 14-13, 13-12, pin # 28. t,c,t,c prs 12-13, 13-14, pin # 29. t,c,t,c prs 14 to 11, pin # 30. t,c,t,c prs 11 to 14, pin # 31. t,c,t,c prs 14 to 10, pin # 32. t,c,t,c prs 10 to 14, pin # 33. t,c,t,c prs 14 to 9, pin # 34. t,c,t,c prs 9 to 14, pin # 35. t,c,t,c prs 13-14.

Zigzag, 2nd half, prs 6 to 13:

t pr 6, w st prs 6-7, 7-8, t pr 9, w st prs 8-9, pin # 36. t pr 9, w st prs 9-8, 8-7, pin # 37. t pr 7, w st prs 7-8, 8-9, t pr 10, w st prs 9-10, pin # 38. t pr 10, w st prs 10-9, 9-8, pin # 39. t pr 8, w st prs 8-9, 9-10, t pr 11, w st prs 10-11, pin # 40. t pr 11, w st prs 11-10, 10-9, pin # 41. t pr 9, w st prs 9-10, 10-11, t pr 12, w st prs 11-12, pin # 42. t pr 12, w st prs 12-11, 11-10, pin # 43. t pr 10, w st prs 10-11, 11-12, t pr 13, w st prs 12-13, pin # 44. t pr 13, w st prs 13-12, 12-11, pin # 45. t pr 11, w st prs 11-12, 12-11, pin # 46.

Torchon ground and footing, 2nd part, prs 1 to 7: t,c prs 6-5, pin # 47, t,c. t,c prs 5-4, pin # 48, t,c. Rep footing, pin # 49. t,c prs 7-6, pin # 50, t,c. t,c prs 6-5, pin # 51, t,c. t,c prs 5-4, pin # 52. t,c. Rep footing, pin # 53.

Spider, prs 5 to 10: t prs 5 to 10 three times each pr. *w st prs 8-7, 7-6, 6-5. w st prs 9-8, 8-7, 7-6. w st prs 10-9, 9-8, 8-7*, pin # 54 (between 8 and 7). Draw up carefully around pin. Rep * to *. Draw up carefully again. Twist prs 5, 6, 7 twice, prs 8, 9, 10 three times.

Torchon ground and footing, 1st part, prs 1 to 7: t,c prs 5-4, pin # 55, t,c. Rep footing, pin # 56. t,c prs 6-5, pin # 57, t,c. t,c prs 5-4, pin # 58, t,c. Rep footing, pin # 59. t,c prs 7-6, pin # 60, t,c. t,c prs 6-5, pin # 61, t,c. t,c prs 5-4, pin # 62, t,c. Rep footing, pin # 63.

Zigzag, 1st half, prs 6-13: t pr 13, w st prs 13-12, 12-11, 11-10, pin # 64.

*Repeat from *

To finish off, tie bobbin prs together in tight square knot around last pin. Clip close to knot or weave ends back with tapestry needle. Steam lace if desired (footing especially may need it if it has pulled in slightly).

MEDALLION (about 7½″ wide, 8″ deep at widest and deepest points)

Pricking (p. 434) is half the total pattern (a bit more for orientation) shown actual size. Flower (worked first) is in red; vine, stems, and leaves are blue; fillings are black. Dots are pinholes; second rows of dots mark picots. Circled dots are sewings; two circles signify two sewings at the same place. Tie off bobbin pairs with sewings to start of tape; touch knots with glue if necessary.

Trace half given, reverse paper, trace again, matching carefully in center. Second half mirrors first, except for working direction of flower fillings—left to right on both sides. Trim paper about ¼″ around design; pin to center of board.

FLOWER

Center: 6 prs bobbins. 4 prs blue and 1 pr white, ½ yd. each bobbin; 1 pr white, 1¼ yds. each bobbin (active pr). Hang 2 prs blue each at a and b; 2 prs white at c with the active pr outside. *t,c,t,c prs 6-5, t pr 5, w st prs 5-4, 4-3, 3-2, 2-1, pin # 1. t pr 1, w st prs 1-2, 2-3, 3-4, 4-5, t,c,t,c prs 5-6, pin # 2, repeat from *. After pin # 3, place a pin at # 4. Twist active 3 times, go around pin, t twice, and continue as usual. Do this each time where indicated; the last time, t 3 times, make a sewing through all loops at # 4, t twice. Tie off threads at beginning.

Petals: Large portion of petal done in h st with one white pr at each side in w st to form an outline. Small area at inner curve between crosshatchings is done in w st with a blind pin hole. 6 prs bobbins. 2 prs white, 1½ yds. each; 4 prs blue, 2½ yds. each. Hang 1 pr white and 1 pr blue at a with white at outside, 2 prs blue at b, 1 pr blue and 1 pr white at c with blue at outside. *Begin w st area:* t pr 6, w st through pr 2, t pr 1, w st prs 2-1, pin # 1. t pr 1, w st through pr 6, pin # 2. t pr 6, w st through pr 2, t pr 1, w st prs 2-1, sewing at # 3. *Blind pin hole:* t pr 1, w st through pr 4, pin # 4. w st back through pr 1, pin # 5. Remove pin # 4 and pull on actives gently, do not replace pin # 4. Repeat this procedure for pin # 6 and sewing at # 7. Continue with w st through all prs until pin # 11 is reached. *Change to h st ground:* *t,c,t,c prs 1-2. h st prs 2-3, 3-4, 4-5, t,c,t,c prs 5-6, pin # 12. t,c,t,c prs 6-5, h st through pr 2, t,c,t,c prs 2-1, pin # 13. Repeat these two rows until crosshatched bar indicates change to w st. First picot occurs after pin # 20. These are made exactly as in the sampler

(directions, p. 431). After placing the pin for the picot, work the knot so that it lies snugly against pin # 20, then continue as before. Work all around the 5 petals, fastening off thread to the beginning of the tape.

VINE, STEM, LEAF

These are worked all in one braid, beginning with the scroll on the right and ending with the scroll on the left. The tape works down the right side, across the bottom center to the left side of the loop. The left stem and leaf are worked next, then the top of the bottom loop, then the right stem and leaf. The bottom loop is then completed with the tape passing over the completed tape at bottom center and continuing up the left side.

Before starting, remove the pins of petal picots, which will be covered by subsequent work. 6 prs bobbins. 3 prs ecru, 2½ yds. each bobbin; 1 pr white, 1¼ yds. each bobbin; 2 prs white, 4 yds. each bobbin. Hang the two large prs of white bobbins, one at a and one at c. Hang 2 prs ecru at b. The last 2 prs of bobbins will be added after completion of the scroll. The scroll is worked with these 4 prs in w st ground (refer to sampler if necessary). Blind pins are made through two prs of passives. Two sewings are made along the way, with a third at a, then the work is stopped at A. At this point, the last two prs of bobbins are added: the ecru pr to the two ecru prs at b, and the white prs to the white pr at c, all with sewings.

Vine: Now begin the vine down the right side, which is worked exactly like the Russian braid in the sampler (refer if necessary), with sewings where indicated; be careful not to undo the knot on the picot when tightening the sewing. Continue across the bottom center and up the left side of the bottom loop to point B. Pin the active and the first passive pr (both white) out of the way. The stem and leaf are made with the remaining 4 prs with the remaining white pr as active.

Stem, lower half: Made with 4 prs in w st ground exactly as for the scroll with the white pr as active. The bottom half of the stem is made first, with the upper half being made after the leaf is completed and attached with sewings all the way down the center. Begin by taking up pr 4 (white pr) at C, t, and w st across, pin # 1, then continue up the bottom half of the stem. The blind pin near the top is taken through two prs. Stem ends at point D.

Leaf: The upper half is made first, in w st, then the lower half in h st, with sewings down the center, and picots at the edge. To begin: Continue w st ground for pins # 1 and 2. After pin # 2 and through pin # 14, t the active pr once between each st to separate the sts. Then continue around the tip in plain w st ground, going through 2 prs for the blind pins,

Bobbin lace-trimmed apron

and pulling down sts very carefully to make the tip firm and even. Stop work when pin is placed at E. Begin h st: Take up pr 1, which is hanging from pin #14, and h st prs 1-2, 2-3, t,c,t,c prs 3-4, pin F, make picot. t,c,t,c prs 4-3, h st through pr 1, make sewing. Continue to point D.

Stem, upper half: At G, remove pin and replace between prs 4 and 3. Begin w st ground with pr 4, making a sewing at center of stem. Continue down stem, with a sewing at the leaf tip, ending at point H.

Continue vine: Take up the first two prs at B and continue with the Russian braid pattern, starting with prs 1 and 2. Remove the pin at H and re-use it as the first pinhole for the continuation of the vine.

Second stem and leaf: These are worked like the first except that the upper half of the stem and lower half of the leaf are worked first.

Continue vine to point B. At H, begin stem as before, with the white pr as active. Work stem to point G. Place pin between prs 1 and 2 at D and begin h st with prs 1 and 2 with w st through the white pr as before, using hole at G as first pinhole (replace pin). Then continue to pin # 2, remembering the extra twist around the center pins. Work to pin #14, then: t pr 1, h st prs 1-2, 2-3. Place pin at E between prs 3 and 4. t pr 4, w st prs 4-3, 3-2, blind pin. Continue around tip with w st as before, making a sewing at the tip and another at pin #14. Continue with w st ground as before, twisting actives once between each st, to pin #2. Continue in plain w st ground, making a sewing at D, and work down stem to C. Pick up bobbins at B and continue vine, using pinhole at C twice.

Rest of vine and scroll: Remove pins that will be covered, and continue working the vine right over the first part at bottom center, making

sewings in the four corners. At A, pin prs 1 and 2 aside and work around scroll as before. Make sewing with active pr at a and tie off. Make sewings with remaining bobbins, one or two prs together, and tie off.

Fillings: 8 prs bobbins, each wound with 2 yds. white. All fillings are made with these pairs, without re-winding, which means that the ends of each pair are knotted together at the beginning of each section, then attached to the work with a sewing so that the knot is placed against the sewing the same as when finishing off.

Brussels ground (filling for petals of flower): Attach one pr each at a,c,d,f and 2 prs knotted together at b and e. Make Brussels ground (see sampler) with sewings at sides where indicated (t pr once before making sewing).
prs 2-1 #1, sewing pr 1 at g. prs 4-3 #2, prs 3-2 #3, prs 2-1 #4, sewing pr 1 at h. prs 6-5 #5, prs 5-4 #6, prs 4-3 #7, prs 3-2 #8, sewing pr 2 at i. prs 8-7 #9, sewing pr 8 at j. prs 7-6 #10, prs 6-5 #11, prs 5-4 #12, prs 4-3 #13,

sewing pr 3 at k. prs 8-7 #14, sewing pr 8 at l. prs 7-6 #15, sewing pr 7 at m. prs 6-5 #16, sewing pr 6 at n. prs 5-4 #17, prs 4-3 #18, sewing pr 3 at o. prs 6-5 #19, sewing pr 6 at p. sewing prs 5-4 together at q. Tie off all prs and move to next petal.

Plaits (continue with same bobbins, 4 pairs): Attach with sewings two prs together at A and B. Make two plaits with windmill joins at crossings (see p. 431) and sewings where indicated (sewings may be made with one pr or both prs together, as you prefer). At C, knot and cut off bobbins and re-attach at F. With other plait, make sewing at D, continue plait to E, making sewing, and start next section with bobbins hanging at F. Plaits are continued across the stems to bottom section (will not show from front)—from blue H to blue C and from leaf tip to G. Tie off at H and I and re-attach at J for center section. Tie off at K and complete plaits on other side. Making sure that all knots are secure, remove all pins, turn lace over, and sew to pocket of apron.

Pricking for medallion is actual size, but only gives half the design, plus a bit more for orientation. The broken line near the bottom shows exact halfway point.

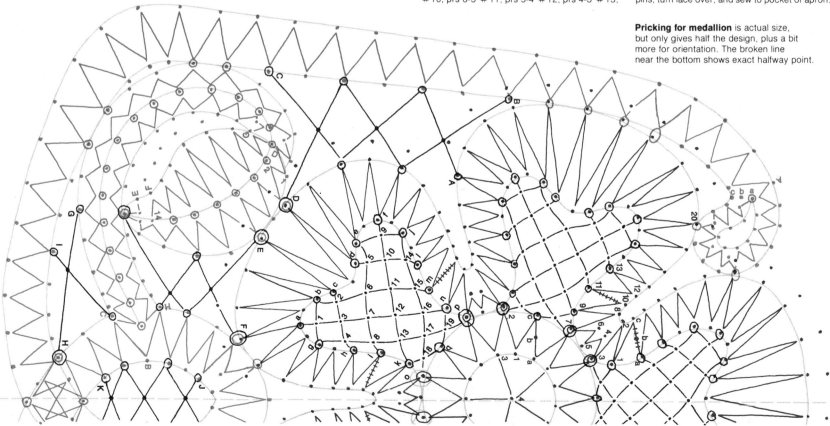

434

Lace weaves

Introduction
Supplies
Setting up the loom
Preparing the weft
The weaves
Woven lace place mat

Introduction

Lace can be created by the technique of weaving, which is the interlacing of two sets of threads, the warp and the weft, to produce a textile. In most forms of weaving, all warp threads are parallel to each other and all weft threads are parallel to each other, with the warp and the weft perpendicular to one another. In lace weaving, warp and weft are diverted somewhat from their parallel course to form spaces in the weave. The resulting textile is open and airy, characteristically what we consider lace.

Lace weaving can be worked on a simple frame loom or a complex mechanical one. Whichever loom is used, lace weaving is maneuvered by the weaver. The technique, in fact, is called weaver- or finger-controlled because, to manipulate warp or weft threads, the weaver uses her fingers or a stick-like instrument rather than the mechanism of the loom.

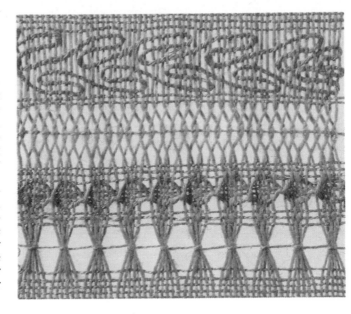

The woven lace sampler, left, incorporates a variety of the lace weaves shown on pages 437 and 438. They are, from top to bottom: Spanish lace, Mexican lace, Danish medallion, and Brook's bouquet.

Supplies

Lace weaves can be worked on any loom. The purpose of the loom is to keep the warp threads evenly spaced and under tension while the weft is passed over and under them. We chose to work on a frame loom because it is simple to use and inexpensive. The weaves shown on pages 437 and 438, however, can be woven on almost any loom you may have.

To make a frame loom, you will need canvas stretcher bars, available at art supply stores in 1-inch increments. You will need one set of two bars for the width of the frame, and one set of two bars for the length of the frame. To determine what size frame you need for the size weaving you want to make, see page 436. To assemble the stretcher bars into a frame loom, see page 436.

For the weaving process, you will also need a shuttle, a tool used for carrying the weft; a shed sword or shed stick, a tool used to help in manipulating the warp threads; and appropriate thread.

Canvas stretchers, sold at art supply stores, can be used to make a frame loom. Their size is designated by the outside measurement.

A shuttle is a flat wood stick with a deep indentation at each end; the weft thread is wrapped on the shuttle (see p. 436).

Yarns for lace weaving include fine, strong linen thread in sizes 10/1, 10/2, or 10/5. For an explanation of the sizes, see page 459.

A shed sword or pick-up stick is a flat stick pointed at one end. It is slightly longer than width of weaving.

Lace weaves

Setting up the loom

On a frame loom, the maximum size of the textile you can weave is slightly less than the dimensions of *the frame opening*. Maximum width is 1 to 2 inches less; maximum length is about 6 inches less because warp threads become too tight to work with as a consequence of what is called *take up*. Take up is the small amount of warp that is used up as the warp threads curve over and under the weft. Since stretcher bars, which are 1½ inches wide, are sold by their outside length measurement, you must use a frame that is larger than the size weaving you want. If, for example, you want to weave a 10-by-16-inch textile, you will need a 16-by-26-inch stretcher frame.

To estimate the amount of warp thread you will need, multiply number of warp threads per inch (see Step 2, below) by width of weaving by *length of loom*. To estimate the amount of weft, multiply number of weft threads per inch by width of weaving by *length of weaving*.

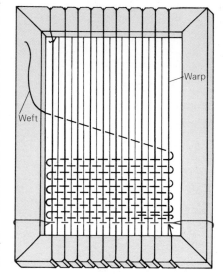

Weaving is the interlacing of weft threads and warp threads. On a frame loom, warp threads are first wrapped around the loom so they are held taut. Weft is woven over and under the warp.

Preparing the weft

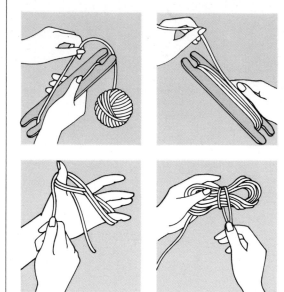

To wind thread onto a shuttle, hold thread end against shuttle with your thumb (left). Wind thread around shuttle so thread end is secured (right). Continue winding thread, making sure you do not pull it as you wind. Do not wind too much thread on shuttle or it will not pass easily through the warp.

To make a butterfly, wind thread in a figure-eight around your thumb and little finger (left). Slip the bundle off your fingers and secure it in the center with a rubber band (right).

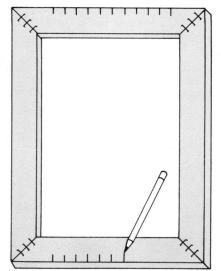

1. Assemble the stretcher bars by fitting the corners together. Be sure corners make a true square; staple them to secure the joining. With a pencil, mark off inches along top and bottom of the frame on the outer edge.

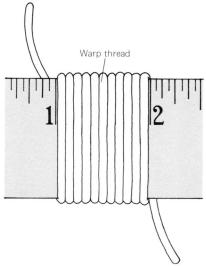

2. To determine number of warp threads per inch, wind thread around ruler. Count wraps; divide in half; multiply by width to be woven. For example, if there are 10 threads per inch and a 12-inch-wide project, you need 120 warp threads.

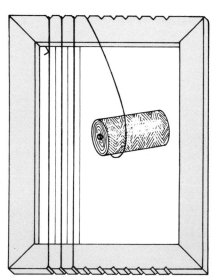

3. Mark threads per inch along frame top. With small saw, make a notch at each mark; sand frame. Tie warp to frame at top left. Bring warp down the front, around bottom edge, and up the back, keeping thread in the notches.

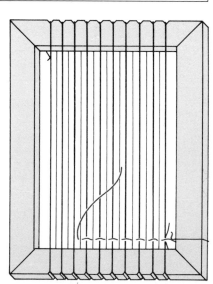

4. As you warp the loom, keep the tension slack but not loose. Threads are now in two layers—in front and back of loom. To make them one layer, weave a piece of string, called a heading, over top and under bottom threads. Tie at sides.

The weaves

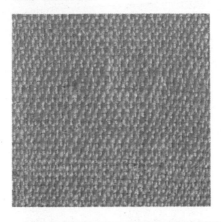

Plain weave is the simplest weave; the weft goes over one warp thread and under the next across the row. On a frame loom, one shed or space between warp threads is already created by the loom. The first weft shot (term for passage of weft) goes in this shed; pass the shuttle through this space (A), leaving a 3'' tail. Pack the weft in with a fork. For next row, weft goes in the *countershed,* created by weaving shed stick *over* threads on top of loom and *under* threads behind it. Turn stick on its side and pass the shuttle through the space made by it (B). Put tail in this shed. Repeat these rows.

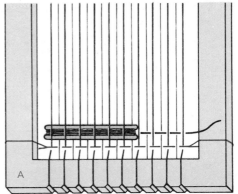 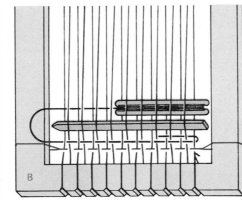

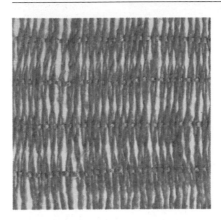

Gauze or leno weave is created by manipulating warp threads so they change places with one another. If *one* warp thread changes places with one other, the lace is 1/1 gauze; if *pairs* of threads change places, the lace is called 2/2. Starting at the right side, pick up the far right thread and bring it to the left over the second thread. Pick up the second thread with the shed stick, letting the first thread fall beneath it. Work across the row this way (A). Turn stick on its side and insert the weft. Then work a row of plain weave left to right (B). Continue alternating these two rows.

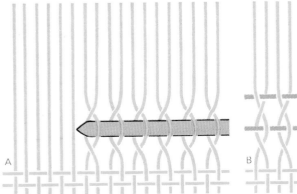 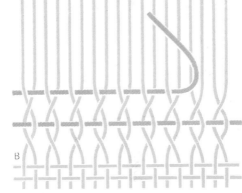

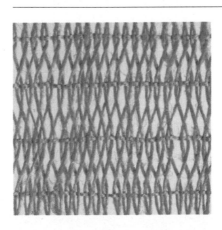

Mexican lace is a variation of the gauze weave. Starting at the right, twist first thread over third, pick up third. To begin pattern, twist second thread over fifth, pick up fifth. Twist fourth thread over seventh, pick up seventh. Continue across the row this way, twisting the next untwisted even-numbered thread with the next odd-numbered one three threads away (A). Turn the shed stick on its side and insert the weft. Then work a row of plain weave to maintain the twists (B). Repeat these two rows.

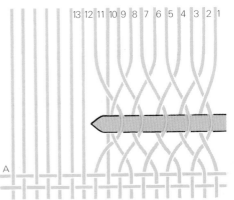 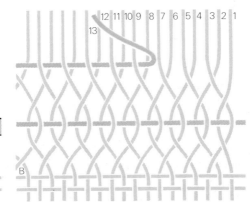

Lace weaves

The weaves

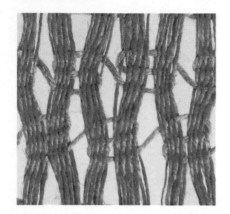

Spanish lace is worked with a butterfly rather than a shuttle. Starting on the right, weave a small group of warp threads in plain weave, going back and forth as many times as you like. Here, it is three times (A). Carry the weft to the next group of warp threads and weave this group the same number of times as the first. Continue across the row this way. Many variations in this pattern can be made with the second row of weaving (B) by changing the groups of threads, varying the number of warp threads in each group, and alternating and splitting groups.

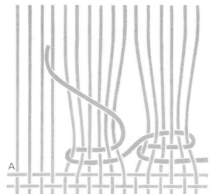 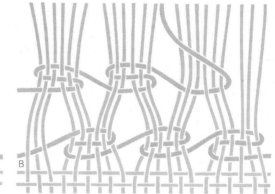

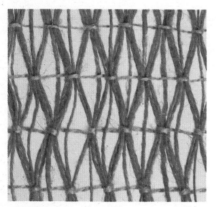

Brook's bouquet is a lace pattern that uses the same technique as the backstitch in embroidery. The weft is carried over warp threads and then back under them. Begin this weave after several rows of plain weave. Bring the weft under a group of warp threads, up over the threads, and back under them. Pull the weft to gather the warp threads (A). Continue gathering groups, leaving one warp thread between them as shown here, or no threads between groups. For second row, alternate the placement of groups, centering them between two groups in the previous row (B).

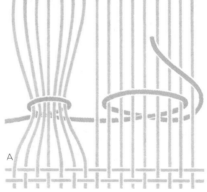 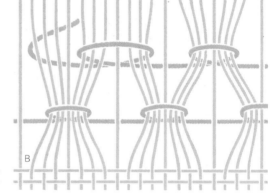

Danish medallion consists mostly of plain weave using two different weft threads. Primary weft thread is usually the same as the warp; secondary weft contrasts in color, weight, or texture. To begin, weave a row of secondary weft from left to right. Change to primary weft and weave several rows of plain weave. Determine where you want the medallions to be; use a crochet hook to pull up a loop of secondary weft half as high as the plain weave (A). Weave secondary weft from right to first loop; pull weft through loop with crochet hook (B). Weave to next loop and pull weft through it. Repeat.

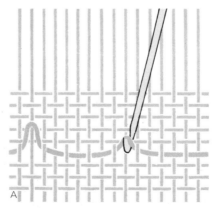 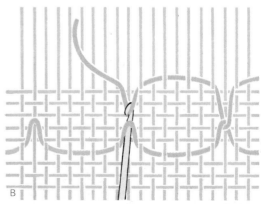

Woven lace place mat

Lace bands on place mat are 2/2 gauze or leno, a variation of 1/1 gauze shown on page 437.

The 12-by-18-inch linen place mat has a dusty rose warp and a pale blue weft. A 2-inch-wide area of lace, called 2/2 leno or gauze (see below), is woven on either side of the center area.

Materials needed

100 yards of 10/2 linen thread (for an explanation of thread size, see p. 459) for the warp for one place mat
60 yards of 10/2 linen thread for the weft for one place mat
18″ × 30″ wood stretcher frame
Pencil
Ruler
Small saw
Sandpaper
½ yard string
Shuttle
Shed stick

The mat

The place mat is worked from side edge to side edge. The width of the weaving in this case is the height of the place mat; the height of the weaving is the width of the place mat. The place mat is mainly plain weave (see p. 437), with a lace insert on either side of 2/2 leno or gauze weave, a variation of the 1/1 gauze weave shown on page 437. In 2/2 gauze, pairs of warp threads are twisted around each other so they change places and create a space in the weave.

Setting up a frame loom

To make the loom and to attach the warp threads, see page 436. There are 10 warp threads per inch (see p. 436). Make 10 marks along each inch marked on the frame loom. Saw a small notch at each mark; sand the edge to eliminate any splinters. Wind the warp onto the loom, keeping the tension of the threads even as you wind. Weave a heading (a piece of string) over the top threads and under the bottom ones (see p. 436).

Weaving

With the weft thread, weave 2 inches of plain weave (see p. 437). End the plain weave with the weft going from left to right; then start the lace weave. At the

right, use your fingers to pull the two threads at the far right toward the left and over the next two threads to the left to create a twist. Pick up the second two threads with the shed stick, letting the first two threads fall under the stick (see A, below). With these two threads still on the stick, pull threads 5 and 6 to the left over threads 7 and 8. Pick up threads 7 and 8. Continue this way across the row, each time picking up the two threads on the right after the twist is made. When you finish the row, turn the stick on its side to create a shed or space for the weft and put the weft through the shed from right to left. For the next row, work a row of plain weave but go over and under *pairs* of threads rather than single ones; this will retain the twist (see B, below). Continue alternating these two rows until the lace measures 2 inches. Then work the plain weave for 10 inches and the lace weave for 2 inches; finish with 2 inches of plain weave. To end the weft, cut off the excess, leaving a 2-inch tail. Wrap the tail around the end warp thread and put it back in the shed.

Fringing

At top and bottom of loom, cut pairs of warp threads; tie in overhand knot (see below). Knot as you cut; do not cut all threads at once. Trim the ends.

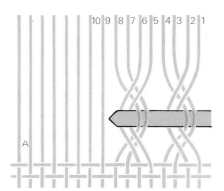

For 2/2 gauze weave, bring two end warps to the left over the next two threads. Pick up second pair on shed stick. Continue to end of row.

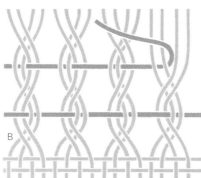

For second row, work row of plain weave, going over and under *pairs of threads* to keep twist created in first row. Alternate these two rows.

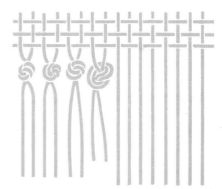

To keep the ends of the place mat from unraveling, knot each pair of warp threads with an overhand knot as shown. Trim the ends even.

439

Hairpin lace

Making strips
Joining strips
Finishing edges
Variations
Hairpin lace shawl

Making strips

Hairpin lace is a type of crochet worked with a two-pronged fork, or hairpin, and a crochet hook. Yarn is wound around the prongs of the hairpin to form a series of large loops held together by a row of crochet stitches worked in the center, called the spine. The strips produced by this process are then joined together. The width of the strips is determined by the distance between the prongs. In the past, a hairpin loom was U-shaped; to make strips of different widths, a variety of hairpins was necessary. A modern hairpin loom consists of two metal rods connected at the top and bottom with removable plastic bars. These rods can be adjusted to different widths. A number of yarn weights can be used; each will give a different look to the lace. Directions for the basic crochet stitches appear on pages 361-363.

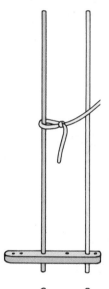

1. To begin, remove the top bar of the loom. Make a slip knot in the yarn and slide the loop that it forms onto the left prong; replace the top bar. Adjust the knot so that it is in the center between the prongs.

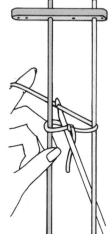

2. Wind the yarn around the right prong, front to back, and hold it taut with your left hand. Insert the crochet hook under the front strand of the loop. Pick up the yarn at the back and bring it through the loop to form a loop on the hook.

3. With the crochet hook, pick up the yarn at the back again. This is called yarn over hook, or simply yarn over.

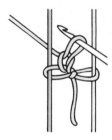

4. Draw the yarn through the loop on the hook; you will have one loop on the hook. This completes the joining of the first loop on the right to the center.

5. Remove the hook from the loop. From the back, insert the hook in the dropped loop. Turn the loom from right to left in front of you.

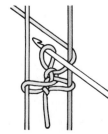

6. Turning the loom causes the yarn to wrap around what is now the right prong to form another loop. The crochet hook is now in the front of the loom.

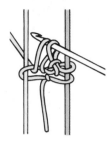

7. This new loop is secured in the center with a single crochet stitch. To do this, insert hook under front strand of left loop, yarn over and draw through the left loop so you have two loops on the hook.

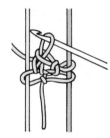

8. Yarn over hook and draw through both loops on the hook. Continue making the strip by repeating Steps 5, 6, 7, and 8. Each new loop is formed by turning the loom at the completion of the single crochet stitch in the center.

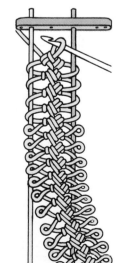

9. When the loom is full, remove the bottom bar and slide all but the top four loops on both sides off the prongs. Replace the bar and continue working.

Joining strips

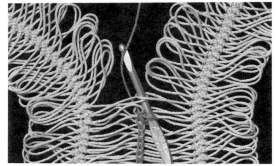

Slip stitch: With a crochet hook and extra yarn held underneath the work, join the strips by inserting hook into one loop from left and one loop from right strip. Slip stitch them together by catching yarn on hook and drawing it through the three loops.

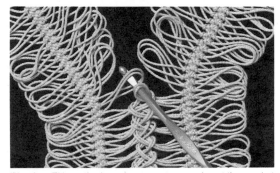

Weaving: This method requires no extra yarn. Insert the crochet hook into one, two, or three loops of one strip, then into the same number of loops of the other strip. Draw the second group through the first. Continue along the length of the strips.

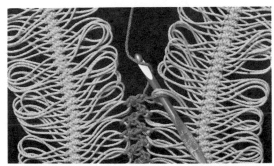

Chain stitch: With a crochet hook and extra yarn, pick up two loops from one strip and work a single crochet stitch (p. 362) in the space. Chain 2 (p. 361), pick up two loops from the other strip and work a single crochet in the space, chain 2. Repeat.

Finishing edges

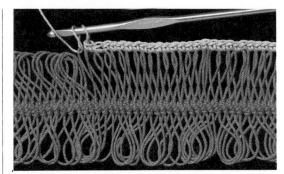

A single crochet stitch along the edge is the simplest way to finish the outside loops of a strip. To do this, make a loop on the hook with a separate length of yarn. Work a single crochet stitch into each loop along the length of the strip.

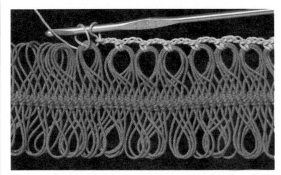

To group the loops, pick up several loops, keeping the twist in them. Work a single crochet stitch in the center space of the group of loops. Make a chain between groups of loops that has one stitch less than the number of loops you picked up.

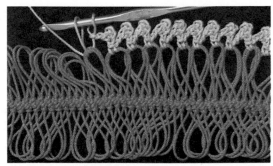

To make a picot edging, work a single crochet stitch into first two loops held together. Chain 4, work a single crochet stitch into third chain from hook, chain 2, work a single crochet stitch into next two loops held together. Repeat from the chain-4.

Variations

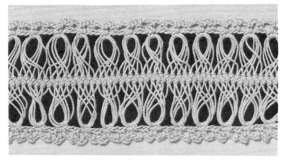

An insertion: Make a strip of the appropriate length. To edge each side, work 1 sc (for abbreviations, see p. 366) in first 4 loops, keeping the twist in them, ch 3. Repeat for the length of the strip. For second row, work 1 sc in sc of previous row, ch 3, sc in center stitch of ch-3 loop, ch 3. Repeat across row.

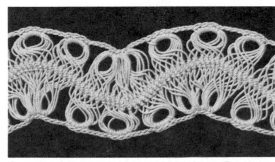

A wavy band: Make a strip of the appropriate length. To edge one side, work (4 sc in 6 loops held together, ch 4) 3 times, then work (1 sc in 6 loops held together) 3 times, ch 4. On the other side, start with second group of stitches—single crochet without chain stitches—so groups are opposite each other.

Fringe: Make two strips of the appropriate length. Join the two strips by weaving them together. Fold the resulting band in half so the weaving is on top. To finish this edge, work 1 sc in the first space, ch 2, work 1 sc in the next space, ch 2. Repeat along the strip. For fringe, cut the loops.

441

Hairpin lace shawl

The shawl is made of one long strip of hairpin lace laid out in a spiral shape and crocheted together with chain stitches. The fringe is a second long strip.

Materials needed

Rayon chenille yarn (approximately 30 yards per ounce)

   27 ounces of a light color

   16 ounces of a dark color

Adjustable hairpin lace loom

Crochet hook, size I

Safety pins to use as markers

Making the strip

Directions for making the basic hairpin lace strip are on page 440. The abbreviations of crochet stitches used here are explained on page 366. To begin the shawl, with light color yarn on a 3-inch loom, *make a strip with 15 sc (8 loops on one side, 7 on the other). Then make a bobble: dc in front thread of last loop, ch 1, (yo, insert hook under dc, draw up loop, yo, draw through 2 loops only) 4 times. Yo, draw through all 5 loops on hook, ch 1.* Repeat between* until you

have 151 bobbles; end strip with 16 sc. During work, as loops are dropped from the loom, group 8 loops together with a safety pin on the right side, then next 8 loops on the left side; leave 8 loops between pins free.

Edging the loops

With dark color, attach yarn to first sc at the beginning of strip, ch 2, *insert hook through 8 loops pinned together, remove the pin, work 4 sc through 8 loops at once. This will automatically put a twist in the group of loops. Ch 1 (1 sc, ch 1 in next loop, twisting it) 8 times, ch 1.* Repeat between * along the length of the strip. To work around end of strip: ch 2, sc in last sc of strip, ch 2. Continue pattern between * down the opposite side of the strip. End with ch 2; fasten off yarn in first sc of strip.

Joining the strip

On a clean, flat surface, lay out strip in a spiral (see diagram, below left). Begin joining at outside edge and work inward. Pattern for joining straight edges is shown in red; pattern for joining curves is shown in blue. All joining is done with light-colored yarn.

Straight joining: *Ch 1, 1 sc in 4th (center) space between single loops in strip below; ch 4, sk 2 loops and sc in next space above; ch 4, sk 2 loops and sc in next space below; ch 8, sk last 2 loops and sc in space between last loop and the 4-sc in strip above; ch 8, sk last 2 loops and sc in space between last loop and 4-sc below; 1 sc in center of 4-sc below, ch 1, make a bobble, ch 1; 1 sc in space between 4-sc and 1st single loop of next group below; ch 8, 1 sc in space between 4-sc and 1st single loop of next group above; ch 8, sk 2 loops and sc in next space below; ch 4, sk 2 loops and sc in next space above; ch 4, sk 2 loops and sc in next space (center) below; ch 1, sk 2 loops and sc in next space (center) above.* Repeat between *. Center space below will have 2 sc in it.

Curved joining: *Ch 1, sc into 4th (cen-

ter) space between single loops below; ch 4, sk 2 loops and sc in next space above; ch 8, sk 4 loops and sc in space between last loop and 4-sc below; sc in center of 4-sc below, ch 1, make a bobble, ch 1; sc in space between 4-sc and 1st single loop of next group below; ch 8, sc in same space as previous sc above; ch 4, sk 4 loops and sc in center space between loops below; ch 1, sc in center of 4-sc above; ch 1, sc in same space below as previous sc; ch 4, sk 2 loops and sc in next space above; ch 8, sk 4 loops and sc in space between last loop and 4-sc below; sc in center of 4-sc below, ch 1, make a bobble, ch 1; sc in space between 4-sc and first single loop of next group below; ch 8, 1 sc in same space as previous sc above; ch 4, sk 4 loops and sc in center space between loops below; ch 1, sk 2 loops and sc in center space above.* Repeat between *. Note three exceptions to the above: *To taper strip end,* at the beginning fasten yarn to center space of single loops above and put 1st sc at beginning of single loops below. When working next sc below, sk 4 loops instead of 2. *The very end of the joining* ends with 2 extra sc with ch-1 between and a bobble. *On the last curved repeat,* the 2 center sc with ch-1 between are omitted.

Fringe

With dark-colored yarn and 5-inch loom, make a strip with 480 loops on each side or 960 sc. Put markers at convenient intervals on one side to aid in counting. To weave the fringe to the shawl, insert hook into space between single loops and the 4-sc, draw up 1st 2 loops of fringe, twisting them once together. Retain on hook. Insert hook into next space (to the left of the 4-sc), draw up next 2 loops of fringe, twisting them together, and bring them through the 1st 2 loops on hook. Repeat. In every 4th (center) space between single loops, draw up 4 fringe loops instead of 2. Continue around the edge this way; fasten last loops to first loops with a separate piece of yarn.

Shawl is a hairpin lace strip in an oval shape.

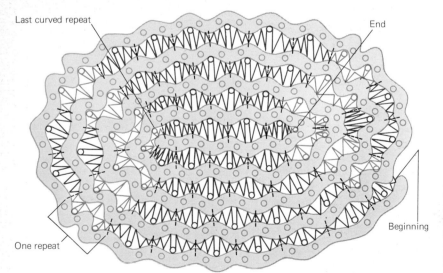

Last curved repeat

End

One repeat

Beginning

To join strip, lay it in oval shape. Begin joining at outside edge and work in toward center. Straight joining is shown in red, curved joining in blue. Pattern repeats are marked with dotted lines; joining begins with seven repeats of straight pattern, then one repeat of curved.

442

Macramé

444 Introduction to macramé
Cords and supplies
446 Setting up
Terms and abbreviations
Making a butterfly
447 Basic macramé knots
Lark's head knot and sennits
448 Double half hitch
449 Shaping with double half hitches
450 The square knot and sennits
451 Alternating square knots
The bobble
Gathering square knot
452 Additional techniques
The overhand knot
Picots
453 Cavandoli work
Josephine knot
Berry knot
454 Adding beads
Replacing short cords
Adding cords
455 Subtracting cords
Finishing edges
Designing macramé
456 Fringing
Determining fringe measurements
457 Fringing fabric
Attaching cords to fabric
Adding to macramé fringe
458 Turning a corner
Finishing fringe ends
Making a tassel

Macramé projects
459 Woman's macramé belt
460 Window screen

Introduction to macramé

History
Cords
Supplies
Setting up
Terms and abbreviations
Making a butterfly

History

Macramé, the art of ornamental knotting, originated as a decorative way of securing the ends of a piece of woven fabric, creating a lacy edge. Later macramé was worked separately and attached to both household items and garments as a trimming. By the Victorian era, entire items, such as tablecloths, bedspreads, and curtains, were made of macramé.

The word macramé is derived from the Arabic word *migramah,* which translates as towel or shawl or the fringe on either one. It now means the process itself, regardless of the finished item.

There is some evidence that macramé fringes were used in Arabia as early as the thirteenth century. From there, the art of macramé spread very quickly. The Spanish learned it from the Moors; from Spain the technique spread to Italy and to France. The use of macramé for clothing decoration in these countries is documented in paintings. In England, Queen Mary, wife of William of Orange, taught her ladies-in-waiting to macramé.

British and American sailors are credited with perpetuating the craft. It was known as McNamara's Lace or Square Knotting to sailors because of the predominance of square knots in their work. The sailors knotted to while away the long hours at sea, and then used the belts, hammocks, and bottle covers they had made for barter when they went ashore.

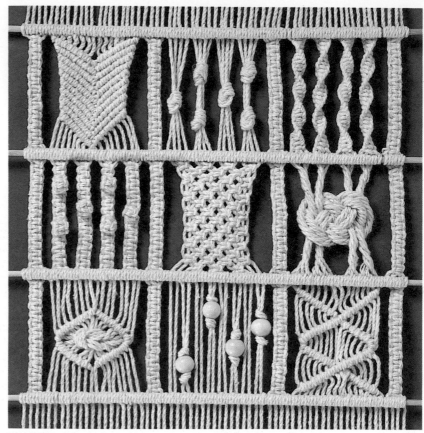

Sampler of macramé knots includes the basic knots as well as variations of them. The vertical dividers are sennits of square knots; the horizontal dividers are rows of double half hitches.

Cords

Cords for macramé need not be expensive or specially purchased. A search through most households will reveal a number of materials appropriate for knotting. The cords should be strong enough to withstand the abrasion of repeated knotting and should not have excessive give or elasticity. Household string, butcher's twine, or venetian blind cord are types that work well; knitting yarns are not suitable because they are too elastic.

Natural-fiber cords are used most often in macramé. *Cotton, linen,* and *jute* are some of the most popular natural materials because they are readily available, knot easily, have the requisite strength, come in a variety of weights and colors, and can be dyed. Jute is not colorfast, so it should not be made into a project that will be used outdoors. Certain *wool* yarns can be used if they are fairly regular in texture and are not too elastic; weaving wools are better than knitting wools. *Silk* cord produces a beautiful knot but it is expensive and not always easy to obtain.

Synthetic-fiber cords include acrylic and polyester, which knot easily and are weather-resistant. They are usually available in bright colors, and can also be dyed. Nylon and rayon are silky, shiny fibers that tend to slip during knotting and so are best used by experienced knotters. Synthetics are often combined with natural fibers to give added strength and durability to a cord.

Construction of the cord is another way to group macramé cords. Most cords are constructed of several lengths of fibers tightly twisted together. Each length is called a *ply*. A three-ply cord is composed of three separate lengths twisted together. The number of plies is not the same as the size measurement. A five-ply cord made of thin fibers can be smaller than a three-ply cord of thicker fibers. The size of a cord is given by its diameter measurement. Some cords are composed of lengths of fibers that are braided rather than twisted together. Venetian blind cord is an example of a braided cord.

Cords with regular texture are best suited for macramé. They can be thick or thin, smooth or rough, but their thickness should not vary and they should not be nubby. However, cords not suitable for whole projects, such as nubby or elastic yarns, can often be introduced into a piece in small quantities.

Suppliers for cords are almost as diverse as the cords themselves. Besides local yarn or hobby shops, you can try such industrial and consumer outlets as variety and hardware stores, cordage companies, marine stores and army-navy surplus outlets, weaving supply stores, and stores dealing in drapery and upholstery supplies. Cords for macramé are sold either by length in prepackaged balls or skeins, or by weight, with the cord unwound from a large ball or tube and weighed on a scale. When buying by weight, don't assume that a bulkier cord will cost less than a thinner one in the long run. Thick cords are used up more rapidly and of course weigh more per comparable length.

Before you purchase a large amount of cord for an entire project, you may want to buy a small amount and test it. Knot a 3- or 4-inch-square sample to see how the cord handles and what the knot pattern looks like worked in that particular cord. If the knotted item is going to be laundered or used outdoors, wash a piece of cord to test it for shrinkage and color-fastness. If you are making a garment in which size is important, you can use the sample to make an estimate of the number and length of cords that you will need.

Cotton cable cord

Waxed linen

Rayon

Linen

Leather

Crochet cotton

Rug yarn

Cotton seine

Synthetic jute (acrylic and nylon)

Lightweight jute

Heavyweight jute

Supplies

Macramé is one craft that requires very few tools other than the knotting cords. There are a few items, however, most of which can be found around the house, that will make the process of knotting easier and the end result more uniform.

Macramé is usually worked, especially by a beginner, on a flat surface called a *knotting board*. The board has to be thick enough to support the work but porous enough to have pins inserted in it. Some suitable boards are insulating material, fiberboard, a clipboard, or a thick slab of foam rubber. To keep the cords and the knots even, the board may be covered with paper marked off in 1-inch squares. A *C-clamp* attached to a table makes a good anchor for working lengths of macramé, as for a belt.

Cords to be knotted are mounted on a support so they can be tied under tension. A support can be another length of cord, a dowel, a ring, or a belt buckle. A stretcher frame can also be used as a support. The finished macramé can be removed or, if you wish, left on, with the stretchers forming a frame.

Pins that can be used to hold cords to the board include straight pins with colored heads, push pins, T-pins, U-pins, and upholstery pins. You will also need a sturdy pair of scissors for cutting the cords, a tape measure or yardstick for measuring off lengths of cord, rubber bands to hold bundles of cord called *butterflies* (see next page), and clips to hold the cords that are not being used out of the way of the working area.

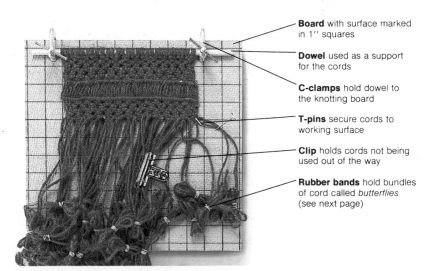

Board with surface marked in 1″ squares

Dowel used as a support for the cords

C-clamps hold dowel to the knotting board

T-pins secure cords to working surface

Clip holds cords not being used out of the way

Rubber bands hold bundles of cord called *butterflies* (see next page)

445

Introduction to macramé

Setting up

Estimating cord length: There is no exact formula for estimating the length of cords necessary for a particular macramé project, but a good way to start is with individual cords that are seven to eight times the length of the finished piece. This means that when the strands are folded over and mounted, each working cord will be three and one-half to four times longer than the finished piece. As a beginner, add a little extra to your estimate because there are many factors that determine how much cord is needed. If a design is predominantly vertical, as a belt or plant hanger would be, less cord will be required than for a design with many horizontal areas. If a design has lots of knots, it will take more cord than a design with areas of floating cords (cords without knots). Tightly tied knots require more cord than loosely tied knots. Thick cords are used up more rapidly than thin cords. As you gain experience, you will become better at estimating how much cord is needed for a particular project. It is ideal to start with cords that are long enough to finish the project, but if you should happen to run short in the middle of a project, there are several ways to add to cords (see p. 454).

Estimating the number of cords: To determine how many cords you will need, you must first decide how wide the piece is to be. A belt may be 2 inches wide; a wall hanging may be 15 inches wide. Take the cord you have chosen and lay strands side by side until they equal one inch. Multiply the number in one inch by the number of inches in your piece to get the total number of cords needed. For example, if you are making a 15-inch-wide wall hanging, and there are four cords to the inch, you will need sixty cords; since each length of cord is folded over when mounted, you will actually need thirty lengths of cord.

Measuring and cutting cords: Measuring and cutting long cords can be cumbersome but there are several ways to accomplish it efficiently. The simplest method is to measure one length with a ruler or yardstick, cut it, and use that length to measure all subsequent cords. If you have many cords to cut, you can attach two C-clamps to the edge of a table, setting them a distance apart equal to half the length of your cord. Tie the end of the cord to one C-clamp, wrap the cord around the other, and bring it back to the first. This span is equal to the length of one cord. Continue wrapping until you have the appropriate number of cords, then cut the cords at the first C-clamp. The cords are already halved and ready for mounting.

You can also measure cords using the backs of two chairs that are set a certain distance apart. Or you can wind the cord around two doorknobs or between the handles of kitchen cabinets. A weaver's warping board, a flat board that has pegs projecting at certain distances, is handy to use if one is available.

Anchoring cords: Macramé knots must be tied with the cords held under tension. The way this is accomplished varies with the particular project, the working materials, and the amount of working space available. If you have never worked macramé knots before, it is advisable to do the work on a board (described on the previous page) so that you can pin cords to the board and follow the path of the cords. As you become more adept at tying the knots, you may want to dispense with the knotting board. There are several alternatives for anchoring the cords. If the cords are attached to a dowel, you can slip the dowel between the handles of two kitchen cabinets. Or you can put the dowel behind a ladder-back or slatted chair. If the chair is not sturdy enough to supply the necessary tension, it can be weighted down with a stack of books. Articles that are long and narrow, such as belts and plant hangers, can be kept under tension by tying one end to a doorknob or the handle of a dresser drawer.

Terms and abbreviations

Terms used in macramé have evolved so that cords can be identified by their function as a piece is being worked. *A mounting cord* is the support on which the other cords are tied. This does not always have to be a cord; a dowel, a ring, or a belt buckle can function as a mounting cord. *Knotting cords* are the cords that are actually tied in any given knot. *Anchor cords* are those cords within a knot that are not tied, as in the center of a square knot (see p. 450). *A holding cord* or *knot-bearing cord* is a cord on which other cords are tied, as in the double half hitch knot (see p. 448). *Floating cords* are any cords within a design that are not knotted; areas of floating cords contrast nicely with knotted areas. *A sennit* is a chain made up of a series of one kind of knot.

Abbreviations are used in macramé directions so that the names of the individual knots (which are discussed on the pages that follow) do not have to be repeated. Where abbreviations are used, a key is provided; this is especially helpful because some knots are known by more than one name. These are the abbreviations of the knots used here:

ask	alternating square knot	**jk**	Josephine knot
ddhh	diagonal double half hitch	**lh**	lark's head knot
dhh	double half hitch	**ok**	overhand knot
hdhh	horizontal double half hitch	**rlh**	reverse lark's head knot
hk	half knot	**sk**	square knot
hc	holding cord	**vdhh**	vertical double half hitch

Making a butterfly

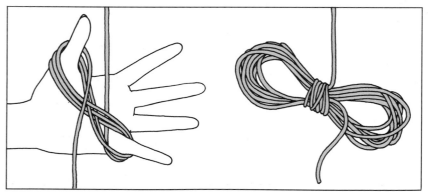

Handling long cords during knotting can be unwieldy. One way to avoid this awkwardness is to make a butterfly. Leave a foot or two of cord below the mounting knot. Wind the remainder of the cord in a figure-eight shape around your thumb and little finger (above left). Slip the bundle off your hand and secure it in the center with a rubber band (above right). Do not start winding at the bottom end of the cord or the excess cord will not pull out from the bundle as it should. If you are working with two cords together, wind both cords into the same butterfly. Otherwise, wind each cord separately so you can release as much of each cord as you need. Another method of handling long cords is to wind them around knitting bobbins, or use a small piece of cardboard.

Basic macramé knots

- Lark's head knot
- Lark's head sennit
- Double half hitch
- Shaping with double half hitches
- Square knot
- Square knot sennits
- Alternating square knot
- The bobble
- Gathering square knot

Lark's head knot

The lark's head knot is a mounting knot. Because macramé knots must be tied under tension, the cords are mounted on a support, such as a length of cord, a dowel, or a ring. The lark's head knot is used to mount the knotting cords on that support. A series of lark's head knots form a definite horizontal ridge along the bottom of the dowel or other support. If you do not want this ridge, use *the reverse lark's head knot.* When the cords have been mounted, each half is considered a separate cord.

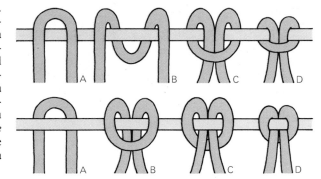

To tie a lark's head knot, fold a cord in half; place loop *in front of dowel* (A). Bring loop back and under dowel (B). Put two ends through loop (C); pull it tight (D).

For reverse lark's head knot, place loop *behind dowel* (A). Bring loop down in front of dowel (B). Pull ends through loop (C) and tighten the knot (D).

Lark's head sennit

A chain of lark's head knots worked vertically is called a *lark's head sennit.* The anchor cord (the cord around which knots are tied) can be made up of more than one strand. A sennit can be worked with the left cord tied around the right cord as shown (right), or the right cord can be tied around the left cord. An attractive way to vary sennits of three or more cords is to alternate a knot with the left cord and a knot with the right cord around a center cord.

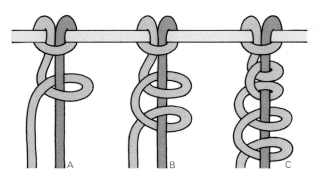

To tie a lark's head knot vertically, bring knotting cord *over* anchor cord, around *behind* it, and through space between the two (A). Then bring knotting cord *under* the anchor cord, around *in front* of it, and down through space between knotting and anchor cords (B). Tighten knot and repeat (C).

Variations

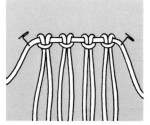

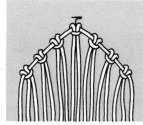

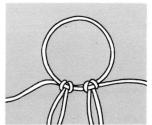

A holding cord can be used as a support in place of a dowel. Mount the cords with lark's head knots; the holding cord becomes two additional knotting cords, one at each side.

To begin a belt, mount an odd number of cords on a holding cord. Pin the center knot to hold it, then angle the sides down. The holding cord becomes knotting cords at the sides.

To attach cords to a ring, use lark's head knots for each cord. To completely cover the ring, work lark's head knots around the ring with one long cord (see vertical knotting above).

For a loop, make a circle with mounting cord, overlapping ends. Place first knots at joining to secure. Add other cords. Mounting cord can become knotting cords, or ends can be trimmed.

Basic macramé knots

Double half hitch

The double half hitch, also called the clove hitch, and the square knot (see p. 450) are the two basic knots used in macramé. The double half hitch is two half hitches knotted in succession. The half hitch is rarely used by itself, although it can be added to the double half hitch to make a triple half hitch.

The double half hitch requires two cords: one is the knotting cord; the other is the holding cord, which is held taut during the knotting process. The double half hitch is tied in multiples. A series of knots is used most often to make straight lines; the position of the holding cord, horizontal or diagonal, determines the position of the lines. Rows of double half hitches can be combined to form a great number of designs, such as diamonds or crosses, that involve diagonal lines (see sampler, p. 444).

The vertical double half hitch is a variation of this knot; it can be tied in horizontal rows or it can be worked vertically to form a chain or sennit.

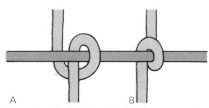

To make a half hitch, start the knotting cord in back of the holding cord. Bring it under the holding cord, then up and over it. Put the end through the loop (A). Tighten the knot (B).

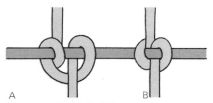

To form a double half hitch, follow the steps given above for the half hitch. Then bring the knotting cord up and over the holding cord, putting the end through the loop formed by the knotting cord (A). Pull the knot tight (B).

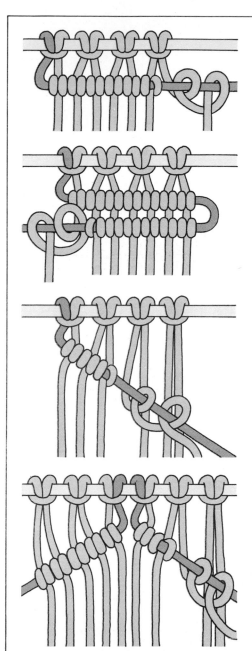

Horizontal double half hitches: Place the left cord in a horizontal position across the other cords in the row. Tie a double half hitch with the second cord on the left. Then tie a similar knot with each of the cords across the row.

When the last cord is knotted, turn the holding cord in the opposite direction and tie a double half hitch with each cord, working from right to left.

To make a diagonal line of double half hitches going from upper left to lower right (shown), place first cord on left diagonally across the knotting cords. Make a double half hitch with each cord. To make a diagonal line from upper right to lower left, place the last cord on the right diagonally across the cords and knot from right to left.

Diagonal lines do not have to start at the edges; any cord can be used as a holding cord. Shown at left are diagonal lines worked from the two center cords out to the sides.

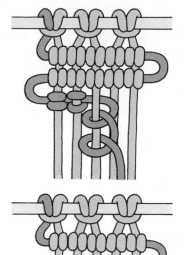

Vertical double half hitch knot is a variation of the double half hitch; the way it is made differs from the basic knot technique in that the holding cord becomes the knotting cord and each of the knotting cords becomes a holding cord. To work vertical double half hitches in a row from left to right, use the holding cord to tie a double half hitch vertically around the first knotting cord. Then tie a knot on each knotting cord in row.

To work a row from right to left, tie a double half hitch with the holding cord around the first cord on the right. Continue tying a knot on each cord from right to left across the row.

A sennit of double half hitches makes a chain that twists around itself (see drawing A).

One variation of a double half hitch sennit using four cords (see drawing B) is to tie left and right cords in a double half hitch alternately around two center cords. This sennit lies flat.

Shaping with double half hitches

To make angled edges, the double half hitch is worked in solid blocks consisting of horizontal and vertical rows. The angled edges that result are a departure from the straight parallel edges usually associated with macramé. The angle can protrude from either side of the piece. To make the angle extend to the right, you use the first cord on the left as the holding cord and work double half hitches from left to right. You then use each cord in turn as the holding cord. To make the angle extend to the left, you start with the right cord and work the knots from right to left.

Narrow zigzag shapes, which can be made in the center of a piece, are achieved with four cords angled the same way as the cords described at left. Two shapes, knotted separately, can be overlapped.

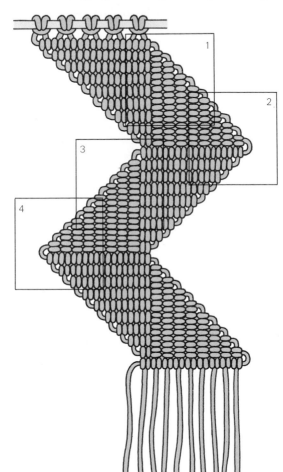

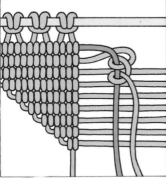

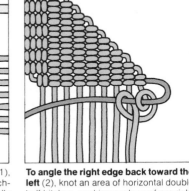

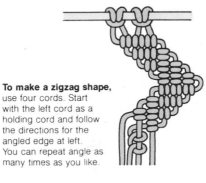

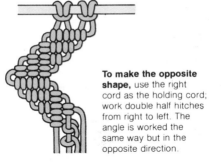

To make a zigzag shape, use four cords. Start with the left cord as a holding cord and follow the directions for the angled edge at left. You can repeat angle as many times as you like.

To make the opposite shape, use the right cord as the holding cord; work double half hitches from right to left. The angle is worked the same way but in the opposite direction.

Sharply angled edges are created by alternating areas of horizontal with areas of vertical double half hitches. To begin, the left edge is angled toward the right with an area of horizontal double half hitches. Each cord, starting with the first cord on the left, is used as a holding cord for a row of knots. The cords are left hanging on the right side. The details above show the directional changes (horizontal to vertical double half hitches and vice versa) on either edge.

To angle the right edge to the right (1), work an area of vertical double half hitches. To begin, lay the top cord vertically across the other cords and tie a vertical double half hitch with each cord in turn. Then use the second cord, which is now on top, as the holding cord and tie a knot with each cord in turn. Using each of the cords as a holding cord, work a row of knots with the other cords.

To angle the right edge back toward the left (2), knot an area of horizontal double half hitches, working each row from right to left. To begin this area, place the first cord on the right horizontally across the other cords and make a knot with each cord, working from right to left. Using each of the cords as a holding cord, work a row of horizontal double half hitches with each cord.

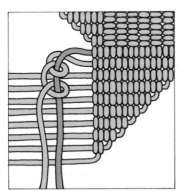

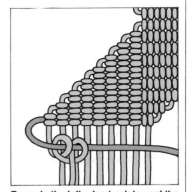

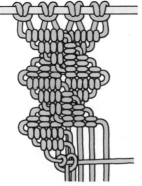

To angle the left edge to the left (3), work an area of vertical double half hitches. To begin this area, lay the top cord vertically across the other cords and tie a vertical double half hitch with each cord in turn. Using each of the cords as a holding cord, tie a row of vertical double half hitches with the other cords.

To angle the left edge back toward the right (4), work an area of horizontal double half hitches. To begin, place the first cord on the left horizontally across the others and tie a knot with each one in turn. Then use each cord as a holding cord. Design can be repeated from here; area is the same as the beginning.

Intertwine the zigzag shapes by overlapping the angles as shown.

Basic macramé knots

The square knot

The square knot is one of the two fundamental macramé knots; the other is the double half hitch (p. 448). The basic square knot is tied with four cords; the two inside cords are anchor cords, the two outside cords are knotting cords. A square knot lies flat. When only half a square knot (a half knot) is tied in a sennit or chain, it will twist around itself. The square knot and the half knot can be tied with the left cord going over the center cords and the right cord under them for a left-hand knot. Or the left cord can go under center cords and the right cord over them for a right-hand knot. Either is correct; you can make whichever is more comfortable for you. We show the left-hand knot in the detail (right) and use it for all the variations (below and on the facing page).

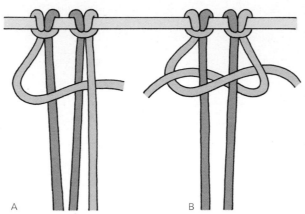

A B

Working with four cords, put the left cord over the two center cords and under the right cord (A). Then bring the right cord under the center cords and up through the loop formed at the left (B). This completes the **half knot** and is the first half of the square knot. Make the opposite knot by placing left cord under center cords, right cord over them.

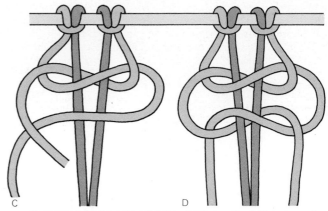

C D

To continue the square knot, bring what is now the right cord over the two center cords and under the left cord (C). Then bring the left cord under the two center cords and up through the loop formed by the right cord (D). Tie the opposite knot by putting the right cord under and the left cord over the center cords after initial half knot has been tied.

Square knot sennits

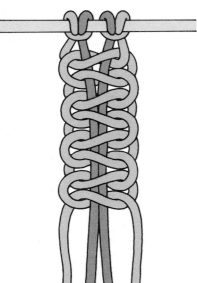

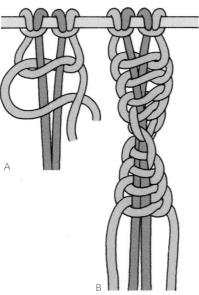

A

B

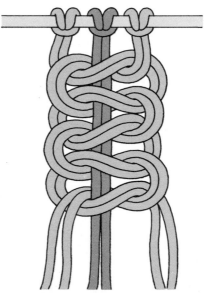

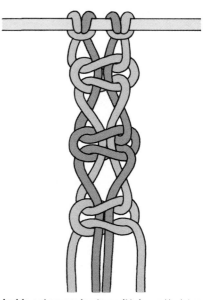

A square knot sennit or chain uses four cords and is formed by tying a series of square knots in a row. The result is a flat, braid-like chain that, by itself, can be used as a belt, a bracelet, a handle, or a dog leash. The sennit can also be incorporated into larger designs.

A half knot sennit is formed by repeating the half knot (A). After about four knots are tied, the chain will twist around itself (B). As it turns, be sure to continue using the cord that is on the left. If knots are tied with the right cord, the chain will twist in the opposite direction.

A multiple-strand sennit is a series of square knots that uses two or more knotting cords on each side and two or more anchoring cords in the center. Hold each set of knotting cords together and tie a basic square knot around the center cords. Do not twist the cords as you tie the knot.

Inside-out square knot sennit is formed by interchanging knotting and anchor cords. To begin, tie a square knot. Bring knotting cords into center to be anchor cords and tie another knot with former anchor cords as knotting cords. For the next knot, return cords to their original positions.

Alternating square knots

The alternating square knot pattern is formed by exchanging the knotting cords and anchor cords in succeeding rows of square knots. The first row is made up of square knots tied with groups of four cords; the second row makes use of cords from two adjacent knots in the first row. The pattern alternates the two rows. Alternating square knots can have a lace-like appearance if the knots are widely spaced, a solid texture if the knots are tied close together.

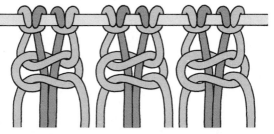

For the first row, make a basic square knot with each group of four cords. The total number of cords in the row will vary with the design.

For the second row, put aside the first two cords. Tie a square knot with two cords from the first knot and two cords from the second knot. For the next square knot, use two cords from the second knot and two cords from the third knot. Continue this way across the row. Leave last two cords untied.

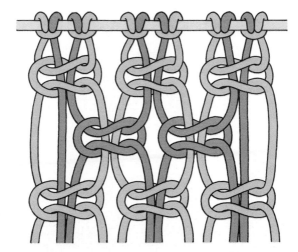

The third row repeats the first row; square knots are tied with the original groups of four cords. The pattern is formed by repeating the two rows.

The bobble

The bobble is a three-dimensional knot formed by pulling a square knot chain up and through itself. The knot can be used for additional surface texture on a flat macramé piece, or as a button closure on a vest or belt.

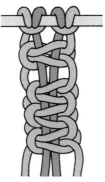

To make a bobble, leave a space in the knotting where you want the bobble to be. Then tie three square knots close together. The bobble is made with at least three square knots; use more knots if you want the bobble to be larger.

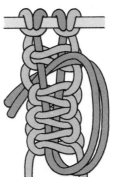

Bring the anchor cords up over the knots and between anchor cords in the space at the top. Pull the cords through so knots roll into a ball.

Tie a square knot directly below the bobble to hold it securely. You can tie just one bobble or make several of them in a row.

Gathering square knot

A gathering square knot is one that uses multiple cords; it is worked at a point in a design where it is desirable to have many cords come together. This knot is tied the same way as the square knot described on the opposite page.

Multiple anchor cords tied into a square knot with one knotting cord on either side form a type of gathering square knot that brings many cords together in one thick knot.

Four knotting cords, two on either side, make the square knot more visible against the many anchor cords. This type of gathering square knot can be used with any number of anchor cords.

Another variation of the gathering square knot is possible only if total number of cords is divisible by four. Divide cords into four equal groups; make a square knot using each group as one cord.

451

Additional techniques

The overhand knot
Picots
Cavandoli work
Josephine knot
Berry knot
Adding beads
Replacing short cords
Adding cords
Subtracting cords
Finishing edges
Designing macramé

The overhand knot

The overhand knot is the simplest of the additional knots used in macramé; it is the same knot that is tied at the end of a length of sewing thread. The knot itself requires only one cord, which is unusual in macramé. However, there are several variations of the overhand knot, some of which require more than one cord. The variations are an overhand knot tied with a filler cord, intertwining overhand knots, and the barrel knot, which is an overhand knot that is made with the working end of the cord wrapped around the loop several times.

Both overhand knots with filler cords (left) and intertwining overhand knots (right) can be worked into a mesh-like pattern by alternating the position of the knots in alternate rows.

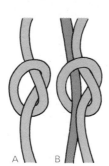

To tie an overhand knot (A), make a loop and bring the end of the cord through the loop. Pull to tighten the knot.

To tie an overhand knot with a filler cord (B), make a loop around the filler cord and tie the knot. Pull the end to tighten the knot.

To tie intertwining overhand knots, tie an overhand knot with one cord. Before you pull it tight, slip the second cord through the loop and tie an overhand knot with it. Pull both knots tight.

To tie a barrel knot, make a loop with the cord and wrap the end around the loop several times; pull it tight. The more wraps you make, the longer the knot will be.

Picots

Picots are decorative elements added to macramé either along the top edge or at the sides. If they are added to the top edge, picots are worked before the cords are mounted or as they are being mounted. This is accomplished by pinning the midpoint of the cord above the dowel and working a decorative knot above the dowel. Cord ends are then mounted to the dowel with double half hitches (p. 448). If picots are added to the sides, they are made during the knotting process.

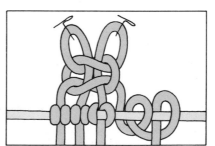

To make a simple loop picot, pin the midpoint of the cord above the mounting cord or dowel; the higher it is above the cord, the larger the loop will be. Attach each of the cord ends to the mounting cord or dowel with a double half hitch.

To make a square knot picot, pin the midpoints of each of two cords next to each other above the dowel. Using center cords as filler cords and outside cords as knotting cords, tie a square knot (see p. 450). Mount cord ends with a double half hitch.

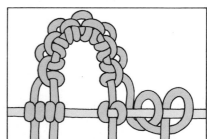

To make a lark's head picot, mount one end of each of two cords onto a dowel. With the left cord, tie lark's head knots (see p. 447) over right cord. The more knots you make, the larger the loop will be. Mount cord ends with double half hitches.

Cavandoli work

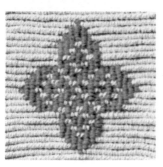

Cavandoli work is a technique that consists of closely worked horizontal and vertical double half hitches in two colors; horizontal knots are used for the background and vertical knots form the design. The technique originated in Italy where it was taught to young school children.

A design to be knotted in Cavandoli work can be graphed. Each square represents one double half hitch knot. The white squares are the background worked in horizontal knots; the colored squares represent the design and are worked in vertical knots.

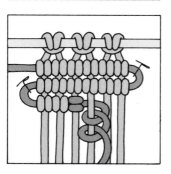

To work Cavandoli, mount cords in the background color onto a dowel; there should be as many cords as there are squares in the graph. Use a separate cord in a second color as a holding cord. Using the graph as a guide, tie a horizontal double half hitch for each white square on the graph. For a colored square, tie a vertical double half hitch, using the holding cord as a tying cord.

Tie a horizontal double half hitch where there is a white square on the graph. The tying cord in the background color will cover the holding cord. Tie knots across each row, following the graph for placement.

Josephine knot

The Josephine knot is also known as the Carrick bend. It can be made small or large depending on the number of cords used. It is often tied with two cords held together as shown, but four or six can be used. The knot can be left loose or pulled tight.

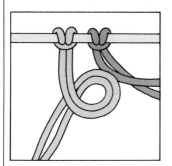

Mount two cords at their midpoints so you have four working cords. Make a loop with the left cords, placing the working end under the beginning end, as shown.

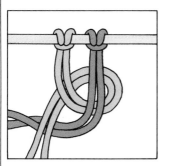

Place the right cords on top of the loop that was formed with the left cords. Bring the ends of the right cords under the ends of the left cords.

The right cords are woven over and under the other cords, going from upper left to lower right. To do this, bring the right cords around and over the first pair of cords, under the second pair, over the third pair, and under the last pair. Pull cord ends to make loops even and tighten knot as much as you wish.

Berry knot

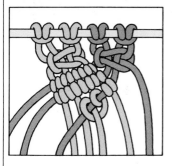

The berry knot, also known as the hobnail, is another knot that adds surface texture to a macramé piece. The berry knot is a variation of the double half hitch. To make the knot, a series of double half hitches are puffed up and kept in place with square knots. This knot requires eight cords.

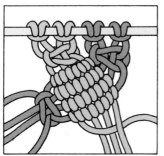

Tie a square knot with each group of four cords. Place the fifth cord diagonally across the first four cords and tie a double half hitch with each of the first cords. Use the sixth, seventh, and eighth cords as holding cords and tie double half hitches with the first four cords.

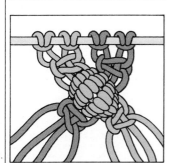

When the second four cords have all been used as anchor cords, tie a square knot with these four cords (they are now on the left). As you make the knot, put one finger behind the berry and push it up until it is rounded.

To hold the rounded, puffy shape of the berry knot, make another square knot with the first four cords (they are now on the right). Tie this knot tightly to keep the shape of the berry.

453

Adding beads

Adding beads to a macramé piece creates textural variety. Beads are available from many sources. They can be pieces of old jewelry, purchased at craft shops, or handmade. A bead can be attached to one or more cords depending on the size of the bead, the size of the hole in the bead, and the particular knotting pattern. When choosing beads, make sure the hole in the bead is large enough to accommodate the thickness of the cord you are using. Small beads can be added to almost any design. Large beads look best if the knotting pattern is designed to accommodate their size.

With an overhand knot: Tie an overhand knot above point where you want bead. Slip the bead onto the cord; tie another knot below to secure it.

With a square knot: Tie a square knot above point where you want bead. Slip bead onto filler cords. Tie a square knot below bead to secure it.

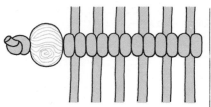

With horizontal double half hitches: If separate holding cord is used, ends can be secured with a bead. To do this, tie overhand knot in end of cord, slip bead on, and use cord as holding cord.

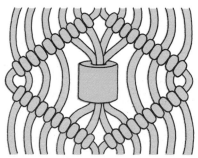

With double half hitches in diamond shape: Bead can be emphasized by being placed inside a configuration of knots. Here, upper knots are worked, bead slipped on, then lower ones worked.

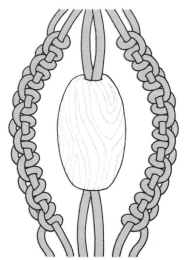

With lark's head sennits: Using six cords, bead is slipped on center two. Outside cords are knotted into sennits that echo curve of the bead.

Replacing short cords

Regardless of how carefully you plan and how accurately you measure the cords, it will occasionally be necessary to replace a cord that is too short. There are several ways to do this. The least visible, though most time-consuming, is to unravel the end of the old cord and the beginning of the new one, then splice and glue them together. Some faster ways of adding to cords are shown below.

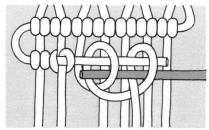

To add to a holding cord in horizontal double half hitches, place the new cord next to the old one and tie several knots over both cords.

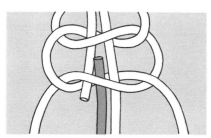

To add to a filler cord in a square knot, place the new cord so that it overlaps the old one and continue tying square knots over both cords.

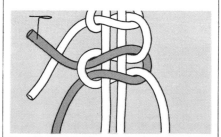

To add new knotting cord, pin new cord to board. Drop old cord and use new one. When piece is completed, tie ends together and trim.

Adding new cords

Additional cords can be required in macramé for different reasons. The dimensions of some projects will have to be changed as the piece is being worked; an example is a piece that starts out narrow and grows wider. In other projects, color may be added as work progresses. There are several ways to add cords to available spaces so the addition looks natural and is not immediately visible.

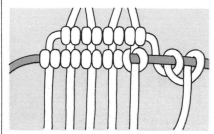

A new holding cord can be introduced in a row of horizontal double half hitches. The cord ends can become knotting cords in subsequent rows.

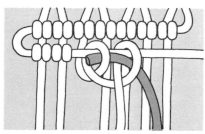

A new cord can be added as a knotting cord in a row of horizontal double half hitches. Make several knots over the end of the cord to secure it.

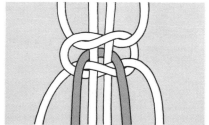

Two new cords can be added by slipping one long cord through the filler cords of a square knot so the midpoint of the new cord is behind the knot.

Subtracting cords

Cords will sometimes need to be eliminated, either gradually or suddenly. The simplest way to drop a cord is to knot over it, leaving it hanging at the back of the piece where later it can be cut off. Of the other methods of eliminating cords shown below, which can be used depends on whether the cord in question is in the center of the work or at the edge, and on the knotting pattern used.

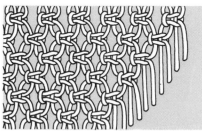

Cords at the edges can be eliminated simply by not knotting them. The cord ends can be woven into the back when the piece is finished.

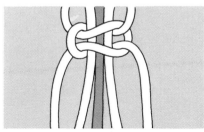

You can knot over unwanted cords by using them as filler cords in a square knot. The ends can be trimmed off after several knots have been tied.

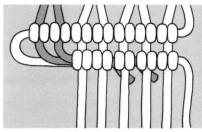

Unwanted cords can be eliminated by knotting over several of them with horizontal double half hitches; trim off ends on back of piece.

Finishing edges

The method used to finish the edge of a macramé piece contributes to the overall look of the work. The most common way is to let the cord ends hang loose to form fringe (see pp. 456-458). If fringe is not suitable to your particular piece, you can weave the ends into the back of the work, finish the edge with bias tape, or wrap groups of cords together. All these techniques are shown below.

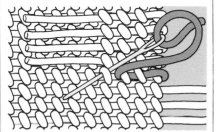

To weave cord ends into the work, thread each cord end into a large yarn needle and bring the needle under several knots on back of work.

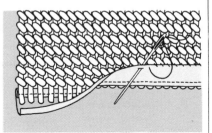

To face edge with bias tape, trim cord ends to ½". Machine-stitch tape to right side of macramé. Fold tape to back; stitch to macramé by hand.

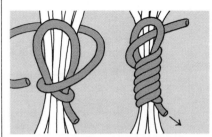

To wrap ends, place loop over bundle; wrap from bottom up. Put working end in loop; pull starting end so loop and working end go under wrapping.

Designing macramé

The overall design of a macramé piece is composed of several elements: the size of the piece, the type of cord or yarn, the color or colors, and the knotting pattern. If you will be designing for the first time, keep the size of the piece and the complexity of the design in line with your ability and the time that you want to spend working on it.

You will want to decide if the piece is going to be **functional** or **decorative**. A functional piece will have to conform to its intended purpose in terms of size, texture, and finishing techniques; a purely decorative piece permits great freedom in all of these areas.

The size of a piece is determined by its outer dimensions and the size of the cord that is used. A thick cord will work up quickly and will give the impression of being a larger piece.

Texture is a product of both the cord and the knotting pattern. A smooth cord shows off the configuration of the knots better than a nubby one. Usually the fiber content of a cord determines the texture of the cord. For example, jute makes a rough, scratchy cord while linen makes a smooth one; both of these cords hold knots securely. Nylon makes a smooth and shiny cord that is difficult to work with because it is slippery. An interesting texture can be introduced into a macramé piece by using a variety of materials in the same color family—cords smooth and rough, thick and thin, dull and shiny. How knots are tied also contributes to the texture of a piece. Knots tied tightly and close together create a compact, dense texture while knots tied loosely or spaced far apart create a lacy look.

The knotting pattern is the result of both the particular knots used and the way in which the knots are combined with each other. The most frequent design elements in macramé are horizontal, vertical, and diagonal lines and areas featuring small patterns. Circles, curves, and flowing lines are possible, but they do require some knotting experience.

Color can be used in macramé in a variety of ways. The usual way is to work in one color only, with the color merely enhancing the pattern. Or a knotted piece can be mostly one color, with just a few cords in a contrasting color to highlight a certain area of the piece. Using several shades of a single color can add depth to a work. A bold color contrast looks best when it is used with a simple knotting pattern.

Whether to add such ornaments as beads, feathers, or shells is a matter of personal taste. Bear in mind that each of these additions can greatly enhance a macramé piece if its size, color, and general feeling is in harmony with the piece to which it is being added.

A bold color contrast of black, brown, and beige cords is used with a simple knotting pattern consisting of double half hitches and square knots.

Fringing

Introduction
Determining fringe measurements
Fringing fabric
Attaching cords to fabric
Adding to macramé fringe
Turning a corner
Finishing fringe ends
Making a tassel

Introduction

Any kind of fringe, whether used to complete a macramé project or added to a fabric garment, utilizes macramé knots. The purpose of fringe is to gather individual thread ends or cords into a decorative pattern. With a coarse fabric, such as heavy linen, canvas, some wools, fringe can be made from the fabric's own threads. This is done by drawing out the crosswise threads, then knotting the remaining lengthwise threads. For fabrics that lack the requisite coarseness, you can add yarn or cord to the edge of the fabric after it has been hemmed. Fringe on a macramé piece does not have to be limited to the number of cords used in the piece itself; others can be added in several different ways, the choice depending on the knotting pattern that is used at the end of the piece.

To form fringe, cords can be attached to the hemmed edge of fabric and tied in a variety of knots. Here, linen cord was attached to printed fabric with lark's head knots. The cords were then tied to form two rows of diamonds; the first row of diamonds is formed by rows of diagonal double half hitches and the second row is square knot sennits woven over and under each other. Cord ends are gathered into groups and wrapped.

Determining fringe measurements

Adding fringe to an item requires some planning. You must first decide how many cords you want to use and how far apart they will be; cords can be added individually or in groups. On fabric, cords can be mounted ⅜ to ¾ inch apart, depending on the thickness of the cords. Fringes made from fabric threads will be a fixed distance apart. The number and spacing of macramé fringes can be adjusted by adding cords. Decide on the thickness of cord you will use according to the look you want. On a macramé piece, you will add more of the same cord that was used to knot the piece. When adding fringe to fabric, you can use many thin cords in each group or a few thick ones, depending on the knotting pattern you plan to use. Cords are mounted at their midpoint so cut length must be twice the mounted length. However, to allow for knotting, cut each cord four times as long as you want the finished fringe to be; this will assure that mounted length is twice as long. Trim off any excess cord when knotting is complete.

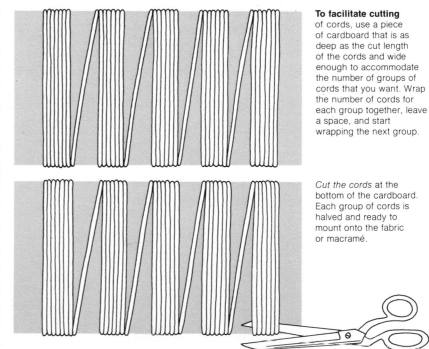

To facilitate cutting of cords, use a piece of cardboard that is as deep as the cut length of the cords and wide enough to accommodate the number of groups of cords that you want. Wrap the number of cords for each group together, leave a space, and start wrapping the next group.

Cut the cords at the bottom of the cardboard. Each group of cords is halved and ready to mount onto the fabric or macramé.

Fringing fabric

If the fabric you are working with is coarse enough, which means the individual fabric threads are thick enough to manipulate, fringe can be created with the fabric threads. Fringe that is made from fabric threads will be much finer than fringe made of added cords, and will look like an integral part of the fabric rather than a separate entity. To fringe fabric, gently draw out the crosswise threads and knot the remaining lengthwise threads. Fabric fringe looks best when the fabric is a solid color.

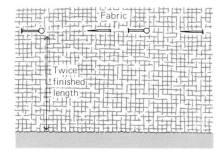

To make fabric fringe, pin-baste a line on fabric that is twice the length finished fringe is to be.

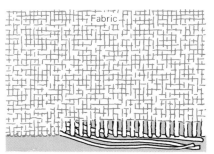

With a pin, push each crosswise thread down. Work each one separately or the threads will knot.

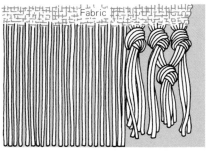

Knot groups of lengthwise threads to form fringe. Trim ends even after knotting is complete.

Attaching cords to fabric

To attach extra cords to fabric, allow at least ½ inch beyond the edge of the fabric for a hem. (Make the hem deeper if this is necessary for the item you are making.) Fold hem allowance under ¼ inch twice, and stitch the fold to the fabric. Besides finishing the raw edge of the fabric, the hem creates a firm base on which to mount the extra cords. Take care that the cord chosen for the fringe is not too thick for the fabric. If you are using groups of cords, make sure the groups are not so thick that they tear the fabric as they are being mounted.

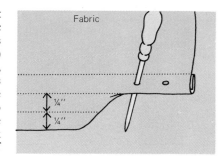

Use a dressmaker's awl or a sharp knitting needle to make holes in the fabric at predetermined distances. Keep the holes within the hem.

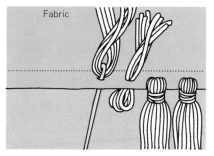

To attach cords, insert a crochet hook through the hole from the back. Catch the center of a cord or group of cords and pull through the hole.

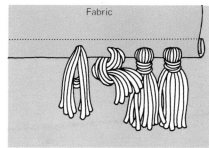

Put ends of cord or bundle through the loop and pull it tight. Repeat with each cord or group of cords. This forms a lark's head knot (see p. 447).

Adding to macramé fringe

If the cord ends on a piece of macramé are left hanging, they will act as a natural fringe at the end of the work. If you want to make an elaborate fringe that requires more cords than are in the piece, you can add cords at the bottom of the work; the appropriate way depends on the particular knotting pattern used and the configuration of knots that occurs at the end of the work. Shown at the right are several ways to add cords to a macramé piece that ends with either a row of horizontal double half hitches or a row of alternating square knots.

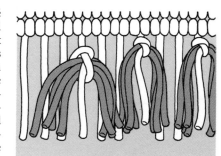

To add groups of cords, tie each group onto the macramé, using one cord from the existing fringe. Leave a space of several cords between groups.

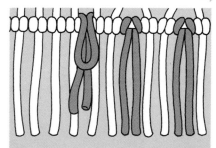

If the macramé ends with a row of horizontal double half hitches, add new cords to the holding cord with a reverse lark's head knot (see p. 447).

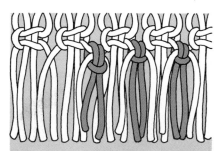

If the macramé ends with square knots, add new cords with a lark's head knot (p. 447) tied over the knotting cords from two adjacent square knots.

457

Fringing

Turning a corner

If fringe is to be put on two adjacent sides of a piece of fabric, on two edges of a shawl, for example, cords must be added to the corner area as it is being worked so that the design of the knots can continue around the corner. Begin by inserting extra cords into the corner hole in the fabric. Then, as the work progresses, you can add more cords (see p. 454) so that the macramé will turn the corner without drawing up.

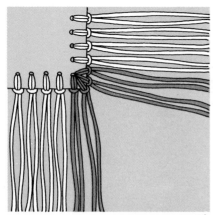

In the corner hole, insert three extra cords. With groups of cords, insert one group that contains four times as many cords as the other groups.

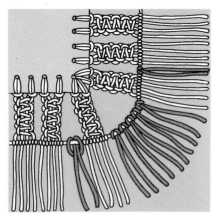

As the work progresses, add more cords both to the corner area and to the space on either side of the corner—enough to fill any gaps.

Finishing fringe ends

Although fringing is the customary technique for finishing the cord ends on a macramé piece, fringe can begin to look worn and frayed very easily. There are a number of ways to prevent or compensate for this; several are shown below. Which one you select will depend on the look you want your fringe to have.

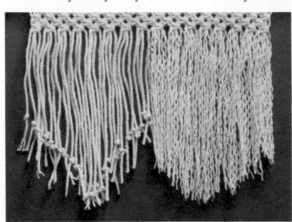

If each individual cord end is going to hang separately, tie an overhand knot where you want the fringe to end, then trim the fringe off right below the knot (far left).

Another way to finish fringe is to unravel the individual plies that comprise each cord (near left). Before you unravel the fringe, unravel a small piece of leftover cord to see if you like the separated effect with the cord you are using.

A further possibility with individual cord ends is to divide them into groups of two or four cords and tie them into sennits. The sennits illustrated are, from left to right, overhand knots tied with two cords (see p. 452), alternating half hitches tied with two cords (see p. 448), and alternating lark's head knots tied with two cords around two filler cords (see p. 447).

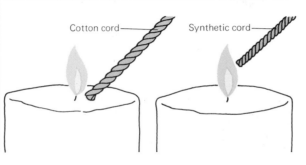

Cotton cord — Synthetic cord —

If you prefer to let the individual cord ends hang free, there is a simple way to protect ends and keep them from unraveling. If the cord is cotton or linen, dip the end into melted candle wax (far left). With nylon cord, melt the plies together by placing the cord end in a candle flame (near left).

Making a tassel

A separate tassel can be made from extra lengths of the same cord that is used to make the fringe. Tassels add bulk and weight to a fringe; this may be desirable if the fringe is on the end of a wall hanging where the added weight will make the piece hang nicely. To determine how much extra cord you will need, decide how long you want the tassels to be. Cut a piece of cardboard that is as high as the tassel is long. Wrap cord around the cardboard until you have the thickness of tassel that you want. Unwind the cord and measure it; multiply this amount by the number of tassels you want to make.

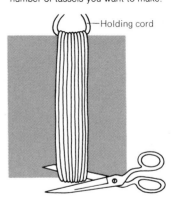

— Holding cord

To make a tassel, wrap cord around cardboard. Tie a holding cord around the cords at the top; cut the cords at bottom.

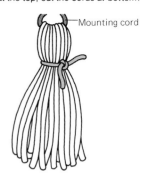

— Mounting cord

Tie separate cord one-quarter of distance from top. To mount, put mounting cord in space at top; remove holding cord.

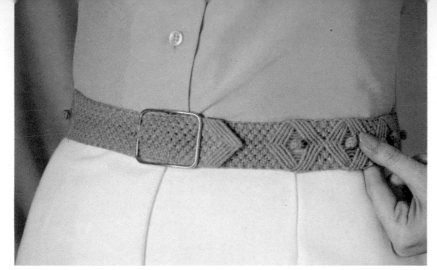

Linen belt uses only two basic knots—square knot and double half hitch—and their variations.

Woman's macramé belt

Macramé belt, tied with sturdy but soft linen cord, has a repeat design of diamonds composed of diagonal double half hitches with a bobble in the center.

Materials needed
Ten 10-yard lengths of 10/5 linen cord
Belt buckle with 1½″ center bar
Knotting board marked off in 1″ squares
T-pins
Rubber bands

Introduction
Finished belt fits a 26-inch waist. It has 12 motifs and measures 29½ inches; the length can be changed in 1¾-inch increments (the length of one motif). To do this, you lengthen or shorten the cut length of each strand by 24 inches for each motif you want to add or subtract. Size of linen cord is indicated by two numbers, such as 10/5. The first stands for the thickness of each ply; the higher the number, the thinner the ply. The second is the number of plies in the cord; the higher the number, the more plies, so the thicker the cord. Linen cord comes in 15-yard skeins or 8-ounce tubes.

Knotting
To begin belt, fold each 10-yard strand in half; mount on center bar of buckle with a lark's head knot (p. 447). Wind cord ends into butterflies and secure with rubber bands (p. 446). Tie alternating square knots (p. 451) for 2½ inches. To shape square knots to conform to point of first motif, continue knotting each side separately, decreasing one knot each row until there is only one knot on each side (see Step 1).

The motif
To work motif, tie cord 10 in a double half hitch (see p. 448) over cord 11 in center of belt. Bring cord 11 diagonally across first nine cords and cord 10 diagonally across the last nine cords. Using these cords as mounting cords, tie diagonal double half hitches (referred to as ddhh) with each of the other cords. Tie three more rows of ddhh (see Step 2) to form top half of diamond. Mounting cords from previous rows are not used as knotting cords so the number of knots in each row decreases. Leave the mounting cords hanging at the sides; they will also be mounting cords for the bottom half of the diamond. Make a bobble (see p. 451) with center four cords, placing it ⁵⁄₁₆ inch below inner point of upper half of diamond. Use five square knots and secure with a sixth knot.

To make bottom half of diamond, bring cord 11 diagonally across first nine cords so it is ⁵⁄₁₆ inch below bobble. Tie ddhh with next nine cords, working from left to right. Place cord 10 diagonally across cords on the right; tie ddhh from right to left, using the mounting cord from the left side (cord 11) as the last knotting cord. Tie three more rows of ddhh in the same way to complete bottom half of diamond.

Between motifs
To fill triangular shapes between motifs, work alternating square knots as shown in Step 3. Do not use center four cords. Repeat motif, using the last mounting cord on the right as first mounting cord placed diagonally from center to left.

Finishing
After twelfth motif (or last motif for your size), work 6 inches of alternating square knots from lower point of last motif to point of shaped end (see Step 4). Using last cord at left edge, tie ddhh from left to center, following shape of point. Repeat with last cord on right side, using mounting cord from left side as last knotting cord. Work three more rows of ddhh in same way as bottom half of diamond. With a needle, work cord ends into macramé on the back (see p. 455). Trim off excess cord. You can glue the ends in back if you prefer.

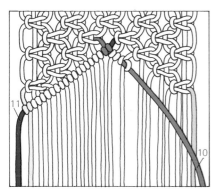

1. For first motif, work square knots as shown. Tie cord 10 in a double half hitch over cord 11; use cord 11 as holding cord for row of knots on left side, cord 10 as holding cord on right side.

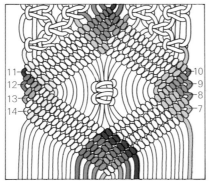

2. Motif that is repeated along length of belt consists of a diamond shape formed by four rows of diagonal double half hitches. Bobble is worked in center when top half of diamond is complete.

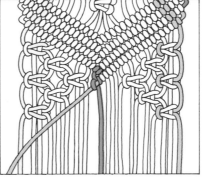

3. To fill triangular shapes between motifs, work alternating square knots as shown. Do not use center four cords. Last holding cord on right from previous motif becomes first holding cord on left.

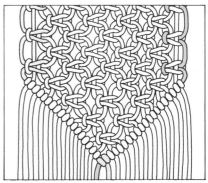

4. After last motif, work 6″ of alternating square knots. To shape point at end of belt, continue tying knots, decreasing one knot on each side in successive rows until there is one knot in center.

Window screen

Window screen, worked in natural-color jute, uses variations of two basic knots.

Materials needed

One 10-pound cone of heavyweight, 3-ply, natural-color jute
⅝-inch dowel, 36 inches long
3 × 3½-foot knotting board
T-pins
Rubber bands
C-clamps
Paper and pencil
Wide felt-tipped marker

Setting up

To enlarge design, make a grid with 1-inch squares and copy design square for square (see p. 14). Go over design lines with felt-tipped marker so you will be able to see them under the jute. Secure enlarged design to knotting board with tape or T-pins. Attach dowel to knotting board with C-clamps. Cut 22 cords that are 9 yards long; 42 cords 12 yards long. Mount the cords at their midpoint with lark's head knot (p. 447) in this order: 11 short cords, 42 long, 11 short. You will have 128 working lengths. Wrap each cord end into a butterfly (p. 446).

Knotting

Work alternating square knots in Section A. Line 1, a row of double half hitches, is worked from top of three points down; arrows indicate knotting direction. For holding cords, use cords indicated on diagram below. Always tie left cord over right cord first. For example, tie cord 36 in double half hitch over cord 37, then use these two cords as holding cords. Work Line 2 the same as Line 1; hold floating cords (cords without knots) taut. Work Line 3, then the top diamond.

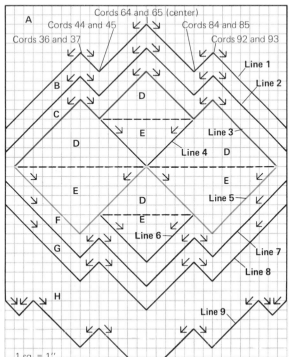

To enlarge design, make a grid with 1″ squares and copy design square for square (see p. 14).

Key

A: Alternating square knots (p. 451)
B and C: Floating cords (p. 446)
D: Half knot sennits (p. 450)
E: Alternating square-knot bobbles (p. 451)
F and G: Floating cords
H: Alternating square knots
Lines 1 and 2: One row of double half hitch (p. 448)
Lines 3, 4, 5, 6: Two rows of double half hitch
Lines 7, 8, 9: One row of double half hitch

Window screen, 30″ by 39″ without tassels, is made with heavy 3-ply jute; cord is ⅛″ in diameter.

Make half knot sennits to just below middle of diamond; work alternating square knot bobbles in bottom half. Bobbles are made with four square knots, secured with a fifth. To make bobbles, you will have to unwind butterflies so cord ends fit through space in square knots. Work Line 4, knot centers of the two large diamonds, then work Line 5. There are 6 floating cords between the side of each large diamond and side edge of piece. Work center of bottom diamond, then knot Line 6. Knot Lines 7 and 8, keeping floating cords taut, then make alternating square knots in Section H. Knot Line 9.

To finish, weave cord ends into back of work (p. 455); glue them if you wish, and trim ends. Make five 11½-inch-long tassels with 38 cords in each (p. 458). To secure tassel, wrap a separate length (p. 455) around cords for 1 inch. Tie tassels to the five points at bottom edge. Trim ends after piece is hung at window.

Rug-making

462 Hooking and knotting
Hooked and knotted rug types
463 Equipment for hooked rugs
464 Equipment for knotted rugs
465 Frames
Design transfer equipment
Finishing equipment
466 Designing principles
467 How to draw circles, semicircles, and ovals
468 Preparing the rug base
Methods of design transfer
470 Preparing for and working a hooked rug
Estimating and preparing fabric for hand hook method
Estimating and preparing yarn for punch needle method
471 Setting a rug base into a frame
472 Hand hook method
Basic techniques
473 Working a design; shading
474 Punch needle method
Basic techniques
475 Working a design
Special techniques
476 Preparing for and working a knotted rug
Estimating and preparing yarn for latch hook method
Estimating and preparing yarn for Rya stitch method
477 Latch hook method
Additional techniques
478 Rya stitch method
Additional techniques
479 Working a charted design
Trimming and sculpturing pile

480 Finishing techniques
Finishing hooked rugs
482 Finishing knotted rugs/canvas
484 Finishing knotted rugs/Swedish backing
485 Care of handmade rugs
Repairing hooked rugs
486 Braiding
Materials
487 Equipment
Making fabric strips
488 Making a three-strand braid
Round rug
489 Oval rug
Rectangular rug
490 Lacing
Joining fabric strips
491 Tapering off
Butting
492 Multiple braiding

Projects using rug methods
494 Chair cushion
495 Wall hanging
496 Braided rug

Hooked rug with set-in braided rug circles, probably late 19th century/
From Shelburne Museum, Shelburne, Vermont

Hooking and knotting

Types of hooked and knotted rugs
Equipment for hooked rugs
Equipment for knotted rugs
Frames
Design transfer equipment
Finishing equipment
Designing principles
How to draw circles,
semicircles, and ovals
Preparing the rug base
Methods of design transfer

Types of hooked and knotted rugs

A hooked or a knotted rug consists of a pile surface attached to a rug base. The primary difference between the two types of rugs is the way that the pile is attached to the base. With a hooked rug, the pile is "threaded" through the rug base; with a knotted rug, the pile is "tied" onto the rug base. There are two ways of forming a hooked rug—with a hand hook or with a punch needle. There are also two ways of forming a knotted rug—with a latch hook or with a tapestry needle and

Rya stitches (also known as Ghiordes knots). Examples of all four types of rugs are shown below. Notice that the quality of the pile differs from sample to sample. These differences are a result of both the method and the materials most commonly used for each rug type. In general, the pile of a hooked rug is short and, in most cases, its loops are uncut (as shown below). The pile of a knotted rug is long and shaggy. If a knotted rug is made with a latch hook, it will have a cut pile; if it is

made with Rya stitches, the pile can be cut or uncut (uncut pile is shown in the example). As with any other needlework technique, variations can be introduced once you become familiar with the necessities of the craft. Materials for the four rug methods and tips about designing them are given on the next five pages. For detailed instructions on the two hooked rug methods, see pages 470-475; for the two knotted rug techniques, see pages 476-479.

HOOKED RUGS

Hand hook method

Punch needle method

KNOTTED RUGS

Latch hook method

Rya stitch method

Equipment for hooked rugs

Different equipment is needed for each of the hooked rug methods. For a hand-hooked rug, you need a base fabric (usually burlap), fabric strips, and a hand hook to pull small loops of the strip up through the base fabric, thus forming the pile surface. The texture of the pile depends on the width of the strip and the fabric used to make it. Medium-weight, finely woven wools, such as flannel, work best. Wool resists soil and wears better than other fibers; a flannel can be cut into narrow ($^3/_{32}$ inch), medium ($^1/_8$ inch), or wide ($^1/_4$ inch) strips. Hooks

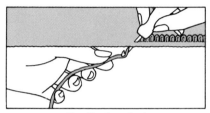

Hand hook method

come in different sizes to suit the various strip widths. Strips can be cut by hand or machine (p. 470).

To make a rug by the punch needle method, you need a base fabric, yarn, and a punch needle. The pile is automatically formed by bringing the threaded needle in and out of the base fabric. Monk's cloth makes a suitable base; burlap can also be used. Although yarn need not be a particular weight or texture, rug and tapestry yarns work best. Punch needles come in several sizes to suit different weights of yarn. Be sure the yarn can pass easily through the eye of the needle.

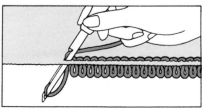

Punch needle method

HAND HOOK METHOD

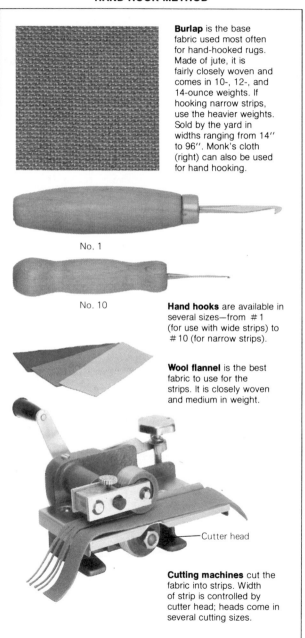

Burlap is the base fabric used most often for hand-hooked rugs. Made of jute, it is fairly closely woven and comes in 10-, 12-, and 14-ounce weights. If hooking narrow strips, use the heavier weights. Sold by the yard in widths ranging from 14″ to 96″. Monk's cloth (right) can also be used for hand hooking.

No. 1

No. 10

Hand hooks are available in several sizes—from #1 (for use with wide strips) to #10 (for narrow strips).

Wool flannel is the best fabric to use for the strips. It is closely woven and medium in weight.

Cutter head

Cutting machines cut the fabric into strips. Width of strip is controlled by cutter head; heads come in several cutting sizes.

PUNCH NEEDLE METHOD

Monk's cloth is a soft, closely woven fabric used as a base for rugs made with a punch needle. Made of cotton, it is sold by the yard in widths up to 15 feet. Some monk's cloths have a guideline woven in every 2″ (shown here). Burlap is also an appropriate base fabric for a rug made with a punch needle.

Size 6

Pile gauge

Size 6

Size 5

Punch needles, sizes 5 and 6, are used for rugs. Some brands have removable needle tips. Pile gauge is used to automatically shorten pile height.

Tapestry yarn

Rug and tapestry yarns are smooth and work well with the punch needle. Of the two, rug yarn (far left) is heavier. Both come in different fibers, with wool being preferred.

Rug yarn

Hooking and knotting

Equipment for knotted rugs

A knotted rug made with a latch hook is one in which cut yarns are "tied" onto the crosswise threads of a rug canvas with the aid of a latch hook. The character of the pile is determined by the type of yarn used and its length before knotting. Rug and Rya yarns are the most popular types for the purpose. Rug yarn is heavy and smooth; Rya is lighter and has a rope-like twist. Both types are available in packages of cut pieces. Rug yarns in packs are 2½ inches long (to produce a 1-inch pile) and Rya yarns are 4½ inches long (for a 2-inch pile). If other

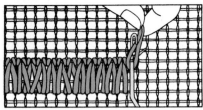

Latch hook method

yarns are used, they must be cut into pieces that are twice the desired pile length plus ½ inch for the knot.

The pile of a true Rya rug is formed by making Rya stitches (also known as Ghiordes knots) on the exposed lengthwise threads of a Swedish backing fabric. Rya stitches are made with a large tapestry needle (size 13) and Rya yarns. The loops that connect the stitches can be left uncut or can be cut. A Rya-like rug can be formed on rug canvas with a latch hook and precut Rya yarns; Rya stitches can also be worked on a rug canvas. See pages 477-478 for both variations.

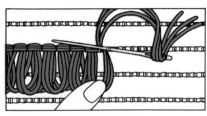

Rya stitch method

LATCH HOOK METHOD

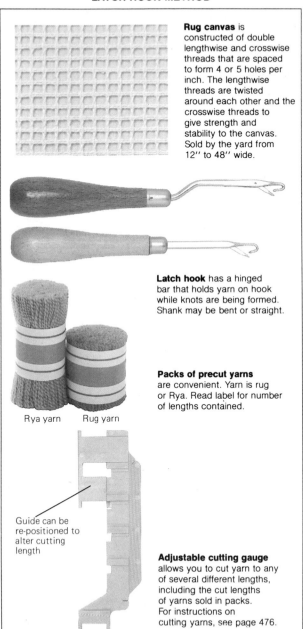

Rug canvas is constructed of double lengthwise and crosswise threads that are spaced to form 4 or 5 holes per inch. The lengthwise threads are twisted around each other and the crosswise threads to give strength and stability to the canvas. Sold by the yard from 12″ to 48″ wide.

Latch hook has a hinged bar that holds yarn on hook while knots are being formed. Shank may be bent or straight.

Packs of precut yarns are convenient. Yarn is rug or Rya. Read label for number of lengths contained.

Rya yarn   Rug yarn

Guide can be re-positioned to alter cutting length

Adjustable cutting gauge allows you to cut yarn to any of several different lengths, including the cut lengths of yarns sold in packs. For instructions on cutting yarns, see page 476.

RYA STITCH METHOD

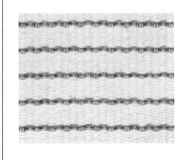

Swedish backing is a heavy, woven fabric whose lengthwise threads are left exposed at ½″ intervals across the full width of the fabric. Comes by the yard in widths from 17″ to 47″. Also available in a few standard-size pieces; in these cases, all four edges are finished.

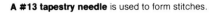

A #13 tapestry needle is used to form stitches.

Needle threader (yarn-sized) facilitates threading yarn through eye of needle.

Heavyweight Rya

Lightweight Rya

Rya yarn is a two-ply yarn having a rope-like twist. Available in skein form in heavy or light weights. Is also sold in packs of cut lengths to use with latch hook rug method. Rya yarn in skein form is wool; precut Rya may be wool or other fibers.

Frames

Hooked rugs should be worked on a frame. Two frames recommended for rug use are shown below. Both are strong and capable of holding many different sizes of rugs, from very small to quite large. A needlepoint frame or a quilting hoop could also be used for a small rug.

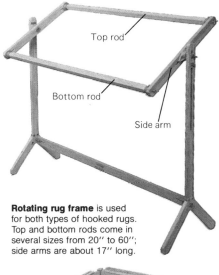

Rotating rug frame is used for both types of hooked rugs. Top and bottom rods come in several sizes from 20″ to 60″; side arms are about 17″ long.

Frame with carding strips can handle many sizes of hand-hooked rugs (not used with punch needle method). Wires in strips hold rug in place. Can be used as a lap frame or on a stand (shown).

Design transfer equipment

If you are designing your own rug, you will have to transfer the design to the rug base. There are four ways of transferring a design; the method used will depend mainly on whether the rug base is fabric or canvas. If it is a *fabric base*—burlap, monk's cloth, or Swedish backing—there is a choice of three transfer methods. One is to re-draw the lines of the design with a **special transfer pencil** and apply heat to the re-drawn lines so they will transfer to the fabric. Second is the pricking transfer method, in which **pounce** (a powder) is used with a **dressmaker's pencil.** The lines of the design are perforated and pounce is patted through the holes onto the fabric; the pencil is used to connect the dots. The third fabric method is to trace the design with dressmaker's **carbon paper** and a **tracing wheel.** If rug base is *canvas,* transfer the design by slipping the drawing under the canvas and using a wide-tipped **felt marker** to draw the design onto the canvas. For instructions on all four of these methods, see pages 468-469.

Finishing equipment

Some pieces of equipment needed to finish rugs (pp. 480-484) are unique to rug-making; others, like heavy needles and threads or a thimble, are common to many other types of needlework. The equipment shown at the right is exclusively for rug-making. **Rug binding,** a strong woven tape, is used to finish the edges of some rugs. It is 1½ inches wide and is available by the yard in neutral colors, such as tan. **Latex** is useful in two ways. Applied to the back of a hooked rug, it "glues" the pile to the rug base. Its other purpose is to form a skid-proof surface on the back of any rug, hooked or knotted. The **rug scissors** are unique in the way that they are bent. The bend permits the blades to be held parallel to the pile while you are trimming yarn ends to an even, uniform length.

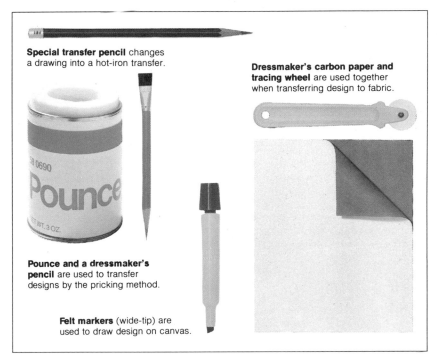

Special transfer pencil changes a drawing into a hot-iron transfer.

Dressmaker's carbon paper and tracing wheel are used together when transferring design to fabric.

Pounce and a dressmaker's pencil are used to transfer designs by the pricking method.

Felt markers (wide-tip) are used to draw design on canvas.

Rug binding is a strong cloth tape that is used to finish the edges of some rugs.

Latex is applied to the back of a rug to secure the pile or skid-proof the rug.

Rug scissors are bent so that blades can be parallel to the pile during trimming.

Hooking and knotting

Designing principles

While working on the design of a hooking or knotting project, you should consider several things. First, decide what the finished project will be—a rug, a pillow top, a purse, a belt. Once its purpose is established, you can think about its finished size and shape, and what type of design will look best in that shape. Should the design be extremely detailed and realistic or undetailed and abstract? Will it be best if the design fills the entire shape, or should it be a center motif surrounded by a plain background?

Very often it is the design that determines what rug method should be selected for a project. In general, both of the hooked methods (hand hook and punch needle) are better suited to executing a detailed or realistic design than are the two knotted methods (latch hook and Rya stitch). The knotted techniques are better for carrying out undetailed designs. These differences stem from the base on which each method is worked and the pile that each method forms.

Two rug bases, burlap and monk's cloth, are used interchangeably for the hooked rug methods. Each of these is a fairly closely woven fabric. The fineness of the weave allows the loops of the pile to be set close to each other and thus to follow any drawn line fairly accurately. The worked pile stands up from the drawn line and tends to reinforce it. The first sample below was done on burlap with the hand hook method and fabric strips. It shows a row of loops forming a line with opposite curves. The drawn line above the row of loops is identical to the marked guideline on which the loops were formed. Notice that the row of loops is almost an exact duplicate of the drawn line. If the sample had been worked with a punch needle and rug yarn, the resulting row would have looked almost the same. There would have been fewer loops per inch, however. This is because the rug yarn used with a punch needle tends to be thicker than the fabric strips used for hand hooking.

Bases used for the knotted rug methods are rug canvas and Swedish backing. The canvas can be used for either latch hook or Rya knotting; Swedish backing is for Rya only. Both bases are constructed so as to predetermine possible placement of the knots. With rug canvas, 4 or 5 knots per inch can be formed across and up and down. With Swedish backing, about 4 knots per inch can be formed across, but only 2 to 3 rows of knots up and down. Because knots can be formed only in certain places, many drawn lines, especially those that are curved or diagonal, have to be adapted to follow the preset placement. The second sample below was done on rug canvas with the latch hook method. The drawn line above the row of knots, an adaptation of the curved line used for the first sample, is the same as the guideline used for placing the knots. Notice how the curves had to be "stepped" to conform to the places where knots are possible on rug canvas. If the sample had been done on Swedish backing, there would have been fewer knots up and down. With either of these two methods, the line on which the row is based becomes feathered and almost lost. This is because a knotted pile, being shaggy and long, has a tendency to fall to one side of the line. This falling tendency decreases, however, after several rows of knots have been worked, the rows having a stabilizing effect on one another.

It should not be concluded from these precautionary comments that a detailed design cannot be done with a knotted rug method, or an undetailed design with a hooked method. Detail can be achieved with a knotted rug method if the areas are large enough to permit the number of knots needed to execute the design. Also the pile should not be too long; a short (about 1-inch) pile will stand up and reinforce the lines of the details better than a longer pile would. If you should want to work an undetailed design with a hooked method, the areas for the elements would not have to be changed. There would be a noticeably different effect—a greater crispness in the overall design would be produced because of the crisper pile.

At the top of the opposite page there are four samples, each worked with a different rug method and illustrating the primary textural effects achievable with that method. What these samples do not show is how to produce a pile variegated in color, a technique that can be useful in producing a rich and interesting design. With the hand hook method, variegation in color is achieved by cutting the fabric strips for the pile from a multicolored fabric, such as a plaid. A similar effect can be produced with the punch needle by threading the needle with multiple strands of a finer-than-usual yarn, each one a different color (p. 475). With the latch hook method, color variegations can be accomplished in two ways. One way is to alternate colors from knot to knot; the other is to use several strands and colors of a finer yarn for each knot (p. 477). The multicolor effect is produced with the Rya stitch method by using yarns of several colors to form stitches (p. 478).

As you formulate your design, keep the drawing of it to a manageable size within the intended finished shape. For help in drawing circular, semicircular, and oval shapes, see the bottom of the facing page. Color your drawing, but bear in mind that the actual shades will depend on the color range of the yarn or fabric that will be used to work the design. Before transferring the design to the rug base (p. 468), enlarge the design to finished size (p. 14), then mark its center. The dimensions of your rug base must be at least the finished size, plus any necessary margins for finishing edges (pp. 480-484). For guidance in estimating the amount of fabric or yarn for a hooked rug, see page 470; for a knotted rug, see page 476.

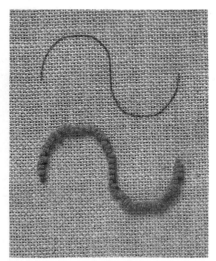

The bases for hooked rugs are fairly closely woven fabrics. Because of their weave, the loops can be formed at almost any point on the base and can therefore be made to follow almost any kind of drawn line in a design.

The bases for knotted rugs preset the possible points where knots can be placed. Because of this, many lines, especially curved and diagonal lines, have to be adapted. The stepped line used above is an adaptation of curved line at left.

Hand hook method

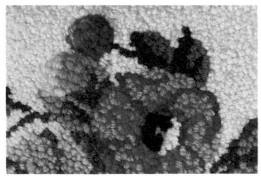
Punch needle method

Hooked rug methods were used to make the two samples at left. The top sample was worked with the **hand hook method,** the lower sample with the **punch needle method.** Although the two samples look slightly different from each other, each was based on the same design in the same amount of space. The differences were caused by the technique and the materials used to form the pile in each sample. The sample done with the hand hook method has finer line and color detail than the one done with the punch needle method. This is because it is possible to form more loops per inch with narrow fabric strips than with the rug yarn used in the punch needle method. With the hand hook method, it is even possible to work several values of a color to mimic the shading that occurs when light hits a three-dimensional object—its high points become lighter in color value than its lower points. With the punch needle method, dimensional detail can be achieved by altering the height of the pile. A fuzzy texture can be produced by cutting some of the loops. For more information on the hand hook and punch needle methods, see pages 470-475.

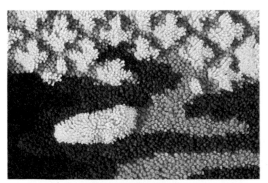
Latch hook method

Rya stitch method

Knotted rug methods were used to make the two samples at left. The **latch hook method** was used to form the top sample, the **Rya stitch method** was used for the lower sample. Both were based on the same design within the same amount of space. Any differences in line were caused by the preset knot placement of rug canvas (in top sample) and Swedish backing (in lower sample). The textural differences between the samples are caused by differences in the character of the pile. With the latch hook method, the pile is always cut because precut lengths of yarn are used to form the knots. With the Rya stitch method, the loops that connect the stitches and form the pile can be cut or uncut. Both methods allow for variations in pile length. The pile formed with each method can even be sculptured to produce a definite dimensional contour. A cut pile is sculptured by trimming it to the shape of the contour; an uncut pile is sculptured by forming the loops between stitches to the lengths required to form the contour. For more information on the two knotted rug methods, see pages 476-479.

How to draw circles, semicircles, and ovals

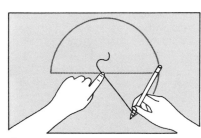

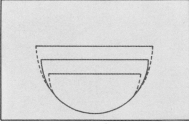

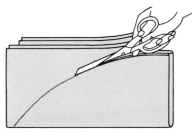

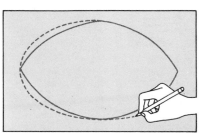

Circle: Draw a line equal to desired width of circle; mark center of line. Tie a string to the end of a pencil. Place pencil point at end of drawn line; hold in place. Stretch string taut and hold at center of line, then swing pencil around to draw the circle.

Semicircle: Draw the bottom half of a circle. To make the semicircle *shallower,* draw a new line below straight edge of semicircle; adjust curved ends to meet new line. For a *deeper* semicircle, draw a new line above the straight edge and adjust curved ends.

Oval: Cut out a rectangle the same height and width as the intended oval. Fold the rectangle in half, then into quarters. On the top quarter, draw a gently curved line to connect the top and the outer cut edges. Cut through all layers along the curved line.

Unfold the paper; place it on a larger piece of paper, trace around its outer edge. Remove the cut shape. It may be necessary to refine the curves of the traced outline to round the ends or make the oval more symmetrical.

Hooking and knotting

Preparing the rug base

The rug base should measure the same as the finished rug, plus margins at each edge if necessary. For a hooked rug, add a minimum 3-inch margin at each edge so the base can be set into a frame. Margins will be used later when the rug is being finished. For a knotted rug, add margins equal to the amount needed to finish each edge (pp. 482-484). No margins are needed for a piece of Swedish backing woven to the required finished-rug size. Before working any rug, finish all raw edges so they will not unravel as you work. To transfer the design, you must first mark the exact center of the base and the center of each edge.

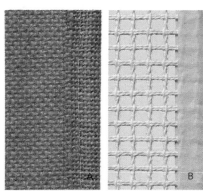

If necessary, join lengths to produce the required width. *If using a fabric base* (burlap, monk's cloth, Swedish backing): Cut lengths to be joined to the rug base length required (see above). Place side by side and trim selvages. Lap edges 1'' (be sure rows in Swedish backing align); stitch through both layers. When working, form pile through both layers.

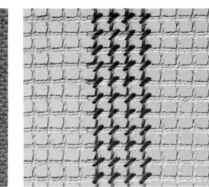

If using a canvas base, cut the lengths to be joined and trim their selvages as explained for fabric rug bases (see left). Lap the cut edges 4 lengthwise threads; match all the lengthwise and cross-wise threads. Then, working down each row of matched lengthwise threads, form a whipstitch over each matched mesh. When working the rug, form the pile through both layers.

Finish the raw edges of the rug base so they will not unravel while the rug is being worked. If the rug base is *fabric*, turn under each raw edge ½'' and machine-stitch in place (A). If the rug base is *canvas*, finish the raw edges by wrapping them with 1''-wide masking tape (B).

Mark the exact center of the rug base as well as the center of each of its edges. Use a dressmaker's pencil to mark a *fabric* base; use a wide felt-tipped pen to mark a *canvas* base. These markings will be used as guides when the design is being transferred to the rug base.

Methods of design transfer

To transfer a design to a fabric rug base (burlap, monk's cloth, Swedish backing), use either the **pounce method,** a **hot-iron transfer pencil,** or **dressmaker's carbon paper and tracing wheel.** If the rug base is canvas, use the **canvas method.** With any of these methods, only the lines of the design are transferred. If you should wish to do so, the areas of the design can be colored in on a

POUNCE METHOD

If hand hook or Rya stitch method will be used, proceed this way: **1:** Using a heavy needle, form holes along the design lines. A quicker way to do this is to "sew" along the lines with an unthreaded sewing machine set for a long straight stitch.

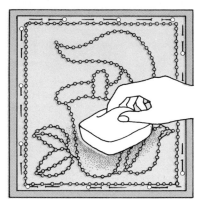

2. With its *wrong side down,* center the perforated drawing on the rug base; pin it in place. Sprinkle some pounce over the holes; then, using a felt pad or a thick wad of fabric, rub the pounce through the holes of the drawing and onto the rug base.

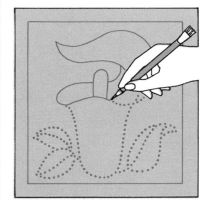

3. Remove the drawing from rug base, being careful not to smudge the dots of pounce. Using a dressmaker's pencil, connect the dots to produce the lines of the design. When all the lines have been drawn, shake the base to remove the excess pounce.

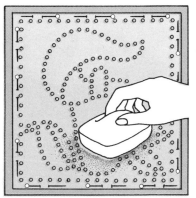

If punch needle method will be used: Perforate the drawing as in Step 1. With its *right side* facing the base, center the drawing on the rug base and pin it in place. Sprinkle pounce and rub through holes as in Step 2. Remove drawing and connect dots (Step 3).

canvas base; this is usually not done on a rug base made of fabric.

It is when the design is transferred that the face and back sides of a rug are determined. (The face side is the pile side of the finished rug.) If the rug will be made with the *hand hook, Rya stitch, or latch hook method,* the side to which the design is transferred becomes the face side because it is the side where the pile will be.

If the *punch needle method* will be used, the side to which the design is transferred becomes the back side of the rug; the pile will be on the opposite, or face side. To ensure that the design takes the proper direction on the face side of the rug, the design is transferred to the back side of the rug base in the direction opposite to what it will be on the face side. See below for specific instructions.

HOT-IRON TRANSFER PENCIL METHOD

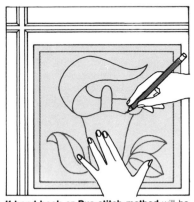

If hand hook or Rya stitch method will be used: **1.** Turn the drawing of the design to its *wrong side* and hold it up to a sunny window. Using the hot-iron transfer pencil, re-draw the lines of the design on the wrong side of the drawing.

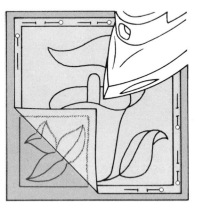

2. With *wrong side* of drawing down, center it on base; pin it in place along the edges. Working an area at a time, press hot iron down on the drawing and lift up after a few seconds. Repeat if lines have not transferred. Be careful not to scorch rug base.

If the punch needle method will be used, transfer the design in the following manner: **1.** Using a special hot-iron transfer pencil and working on the *right side* of the drawing of the design, carefully re-draw all the lines of the design.

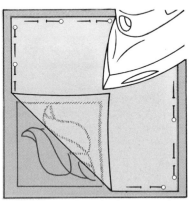

2. With *right side* of drawing down, center it on rug base and pin in place along outer edges. Working an area at a time, press the hot iron down on the drawing and lift up after a few seconds. Repeat if lines have not transferred. Be careful not to scorch rug base.

DRESSMAKER'S CARBON PAPER AND TRACING WHEEL METHOD

If using hand hook or Rya stitch methods: *Wrong side* down, center drawing on base. *Carbon side down,* slip carbon paper under drawing. Trace lines with wheel. Re-position carbon to work various areas of design.

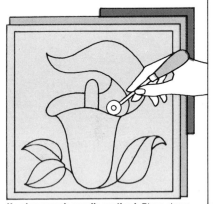

If using punch needle method: Place drawing, *wrong side* down, on base. Slip carbon paper, *carbon side up,* under the rug base. Trace lines with wheel; re-position carbon to work various areas of design.

CANVAS METHOD

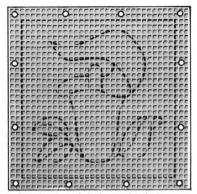

1. Slip drawing of design under the canvas and center it. Tack layers together.

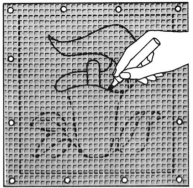

2. Using a wide felt-tipped marker, draw the lines of the design onto the canvas.

Preparing for and working a hooked rug

Estimating and preparing fabric for hand hook method
Estimating and preparing yarn for punch needle method
Setting a rug base into a frame
Hand hook method
Punch needle method

Estimating and preparing fabric for hand hook method

Fabric, cut into strips, is used to form the pile of a rug that is made with the hand hook method. The amount of fabric necessary for strips is roughly equal to the combined measurements of four layers of fabric, each layer the same size as the finished rug. This total should be apportioned among the colors in the design and, as a precaution, 15 percent added to each color's total. If you are using finer strips or a higher pile than usual, increase the amount proportionally; if strips are wider or pile is lower, decrease the amounts. The soundness of your estimate can be tested if you are careful as you work the first few areas of the rug.

Before the fabric is cut, it should be washed and preshrunk. Shrinking tightens the weave so the cut strips will be less likely to ravel. Always cut the fabric and strips on the straight (lengthwise or crosswise) grain, never on the bias. To make the strips easier to cut, first cut the fabric into small (about 4-by-12-inch) pieces. If you are cutting strips by hand, use a fabric thread as a width guide. If you are cutting by machine, be sure to use a cutter head of the correct size and follow the specific cutting instructions that accompany the machine.

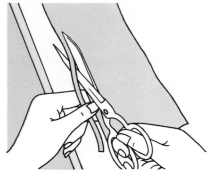

To hand-cut the strips, use a fabric thread as a guide to a uniform strip width.

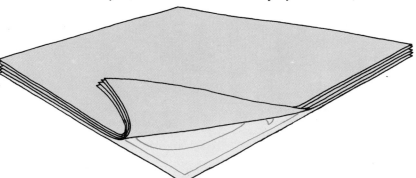

The amount of fabric needed for the pile strips is roughly equal to the combined measurement of four layers of fabric, each layer the same size as the finished rug.

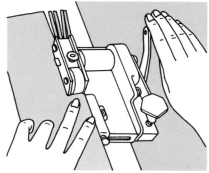

To cut strips by machine, use correct size cutter head; guide fabric carefully through machine.

Estimating and preparing yarn for punch needle method

Yarn, usually in rug-weight, is used to form the pile of a rug that is made with the punch needle method. The basic formula for estimating the required amount of rug yarn is: Allow 110 yards of yarn for every square foot of design area; calculate the total yardage by multiplying the number of square feet in the design by 110. Then apportion the total among the colors used in the design. As a precaution, add 15 percent to the amount of each color. This formula is based on the rug's being worked with a ½-inch pile, the height that is achieved by using a #6 punch needle without the pile gauge. If you intend to use a higher pile, or a thinner yarn, increase the amounts proportionately. For example, you will need about twice as much tapestry yarn as rug yarn because about twice as many rows of loops will be formed with tapestry yarn as with rug yarn. Test the accuracy of any estimate by recording how much yarn was actually used in the first few areas worked.

Before working the rug, wind the yarn into balls (p. 271) so that it will feed easily through the punch needle. Winding will be easier if you open the skein of yarn and place it over the back of a chair.

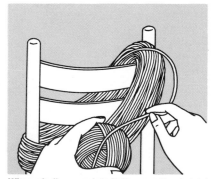

When winding yarn into balls, open the skein of yarn and place it over the back of a chair.

Setting a rug base into a frame

A hooked rug should be worked while it is stretched taut in a frame. The loops will be easier to form and they are less likely to slip out of the rug base. Frames made especially for rug-making are the best ones to use. Instructions are given below for setting a rug base into the two rug frames most frequently used. The rotating rug frame is suitable for either of the hooked rug methods; the frame with carding strips should not be used to make a rug with the punch needle method. If the rug is small, a needlepoint frame or a quilting hoop can be used. For instructions on setting a base into a needlepoint frame, see page 184; to set a base into a quilting hoop, see page 249. When you set any type of rug base into any type of frame, be sure that its design side is facing up.

ROTATING RUG FRAME

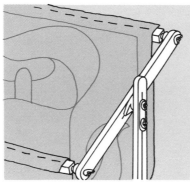

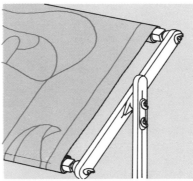

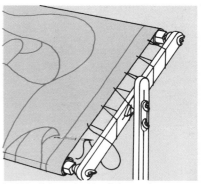

1. Assemble stand and attach side arms. Insert the ends of the top and bottom rods into the top and bottom ends of each side arm. If necessary, refer to the instructions that accompany the frame and stand.

2. Lap the top edge of the rug base over the top rod of the frame. Center the rug base on the rod and tack or staple it in place. Attach the bottom edge of the rug base to the bottom rod of the frame in the same way.

3. Loosen the screws that hold the top and bottom rods in the side arms. Turn rods to take up the excess rug base. As you take up the excess, center the area to be worked. When it is properly centered, tighten the screws.

4. Whipstitch each side of the rug base to an arm, using a heavy needle and thread. Begin stitching with a knot; end it with a few backstitches in the rug base. To re-position base, remove stitches and repeat Steps 3 and 4.

FRAME WITH CARDING STRIPS

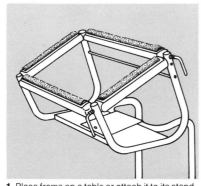

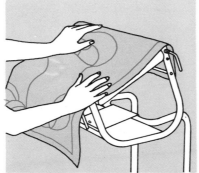

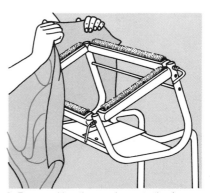

1. Place frame on a table or attach it to its stand. Check that the adjusting handles on the top and side carding strips are aligned with the tubing of the frame. If necessary, turn the handles clockwise to make them align.

2. Decide on the area to be worked and center it in the frame. Press the base down onto the four carding strips so that the needles in the strips catch the base. Smooth out any excess rug base between the strips.

3. Gently turn the handle on the top carding strip until the rug base is taut. Then gently turn the handle on the side carding strip until the base is taut. Always turn the handles in a clockwise direction.

4. To re-position the rug base on the frame, proceed as follows: Lift the rug base off the frame and return the handles to their starting position (Step 1). Determine the area to be worked next and repeat Steps 2 and 3.

Preparing for and working a hooked rug

Hand hook method

Strips of fabric are used to produce the pile of a rug that is made with the hand hook method. The strips can be cut to a number of different widths; which width to use depends on the amount of detail in the design and the amount of space allowed for the detail. In general, the greater the quantity of detail and the smaller the space given to it, the narrower the strips should be. A medium strip width is ⅛ inch; a strip this wide can achieve an average amount of detail within an average space. (The project on page 494 was carried out with ⅛-inch-wide strips.) For instructions on cutting strips, see page 470. Hand hooks are available in several sizes; the size used should be suitable to the strip width. A #10 hook is used with strips $^3/_{32}$-inch wide, a #4 hook with ⅛-inch strips, and a #1 hook with ¼-inch strips. The loops, as a rule, should be about as high as the strip is wide. For example, if the strips are ⅛-inch wide, make the loops ⅛-inch high. The basic techniques for the hand hook method are explained below; for more specialized working techniques, refer to the facing page.

Basic techniques

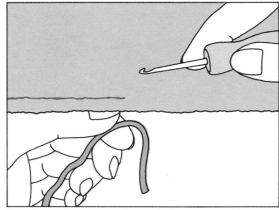

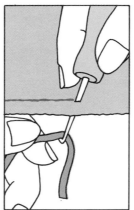

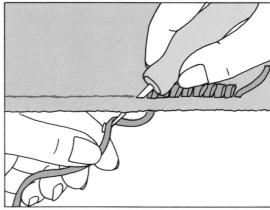

Position hands so that your left hand is below the rug base holding the fabric strip and your right hand above the base holding the hook. Work rows from right to left. (If you are left-handed, reverse the position of hands and the working direction of rows.)

To start a fabric strip, push hook down through the rug base and place one end of the fabric strip over the hook. Then pull the hook and the end of the strip up through the rug base. Ends of strips will be cut even with pile when the rug is finished.

To form loops, push hook down through base, catch fabric strip, and bring it up in the form of a loop. If you have trouble pulling the loop up, push back on hook to enlarge the hole. The space between loops will depend on the strip width (see facing page).

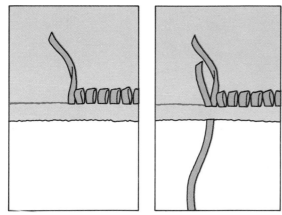

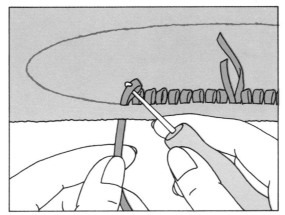

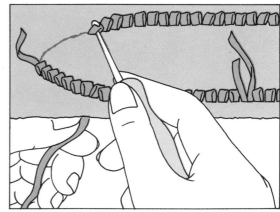

To end a fabric strip, bring its cut end up through the rug base. If the strip is still quite long, pull up a large loop, cut it, and pull the excess out through the back. Begin next strip in the hole where the last strip ended. Ends will be evened off later.

Loop height is controlled by the pull on the hook. As you pull up loops, keep each one even with the others. If you should pull up too large a loop, keep the hook in the loop and pull down on the strip until the loop is the correct height.

Work rows, especially long rows, from right to left as much as possible. If row starts to swing in opposite direction, end it, and work rest of row from right to left to meet it (as above). Work short rows continuously, in any direction necessary.

Working a design

To make a rug with the hand hook method, work the details of the design first and then the background area. Unless the detail will be shaded (see below), first form rows of loops to outline the shape of the detail, then work additional rows to fill in the area (see right). As was explained with Basic techniques (facing page), work the rows from right to left, stopping and starting the rows whenever necessary to maintain the proper row-working direction. The amount of space between loops and rows of loops will depend on the strip width. In general, if the strips being used are $^3/_{32}$ - to $^1/_8$-inch wide, leave two of the base fabric's threads between loops and rows of loops; if the strips are $^1/_4$-inch wide, leave two to three threads. If the rug starts to buckle, increase the amount of space between loops and rows; if the rug base can be seen between loops from the pile side of the rug, decrease the intervening space. As you work, do not carry the strip from one section to another; this causes a bulge that will wear out quickly when the rug is in use. If the design calls for pile of variegated colors, cut the strips for the pile from a multicolored fabric, such as a plaid or a herringbone.

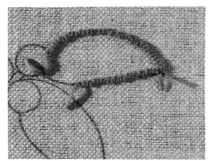

Outline a detail first. Work the rows from right to left. Start and stop rows as necessary to maintain the proper row-working direction.

Fill in the outlined area with additional rows. The rows can be made to follow the contours of the outlined shape (A), or they can be worked across

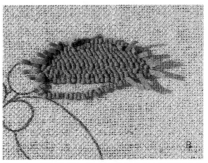

the area (B). Again, stop and start rows whenever necessary to maintain the proper row-working direction (see Basic techniques opposite).

The amount of space between loops and rows of loops depends on the strip width. The wider the strip, the more space between loops and rows.

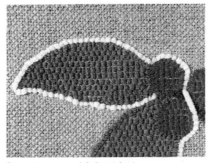

Do not carry a fabric strip from one area to another. Instead, end the strip in the one area and start it again in the other.

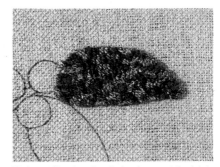

To form pile of variegated colors, cut the fabric strips from a multicolored fabric that contains the colors you want or need for the pile.

Shading

Shading is the hooking of a detail with several color values to imitate the way a real, three-dimensional object changes in value with the angle at which light hits its contoured surface. An example of a shaded detail is shown at the right. When planning how to shade a detail, imagine how its color will vary when it is exposed to a hypothetical light source. The number of values worked will depend on the real-life shape of the object, the amount of space allowed for the detail on the rug base, and the width of the strips being used. The larger the space for the detail and the narrower the strips, the greater the possible number of values. Assign the lightest value to the area that receives the most light, the darkest value to the area that receives the least. Then, depending on the amount of space you have left, assign intermediate values to the remaining areas according to the relative amount of light each receives. When working the detail, work its inner areas and outer edges simultaneously. This differs from the approach to a simple detail (top of page). If there is enough space to allow it, work the rows in a slight zigzag; the colors will blend together better.

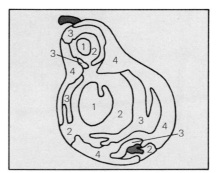

Indicate the color values on drawing of detail. Give the lightest value to highest area (1), the darkest value to the lowest (4).

Work rows of loops within each color value area. If the space allows, work rows in a slight zigzag; the color values will blend better.

473

Preparing for and working a hooked rug

Punch needle method

The punch needle method is named for a hollow needle used to "thread" yarn in and out of a fabric base. This type of needle comes in several sizes, two of them suitable for rug-making. The #6 needle is used with rug-weight yarn; the #5 is appropriate for those that are lighter in weight, such as tapestry yarn. All punch needles are equipped with a removable pile gauge, a device that, when attached to the needle, produces a shorter pile. Without the pile gauge, for example, a #6 needle forms ½-inch pile; with the gauge, it forms ¼-inch pile.

The punch needle rug method is easy to do and the pile works up fast. The basic techniques of the method are shown below, more specific techniques on the facing page. In forming the pile, it is very important not to lift the needle too far above the surface of the rug base.

When the needle is lifted too high, excess yarn is pulled through it and sometimes loops already formed are pulled out. If either of these situations should occur, place the point of the needle where the next loop is to be, pull the excess yarn back through the needle, and continue.

Basic techniques

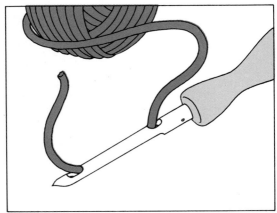

To thread a punch needle: Insert cut end of yarn down through the eye near the handle, then up through the eye at the point of the needle. Tug on the cut yarn end until the yarn seats itself into the hollow shank of the punch needle.

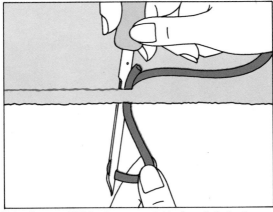

To begin a yarn: With back or grooved side of needle facing the way the row will be worked, plunge needle into fabric as far as it will go. Pull cut yarn end all the way down through the rug base. Withdraw needle until point touches surface of base.

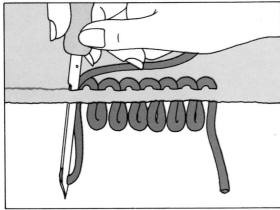

To form loops: Slide the point of the needle along fabric for a few threads. Then plunge needle into fabric as far as it will go and bring it out to form the next loop. Spacing between the loops will depend on the weight of the yarn (see facing page).

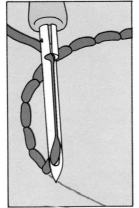 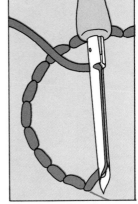

To change row-working direction: Turn the needle so its grooved side is facing in the new direction. If the grooved side of the needle is not facing in the same direction as the row to be worked, the yarn will not feed through the needle properly.

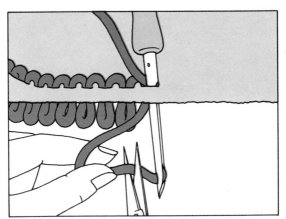

To end a yarn: Plunge the needle into the fabric. Tug on yarn supply, then cut the yarn behind the eye at the point of the needle. Bring the needle out. The starting and ending yarn ends should be trimmed even with the pile when the rug is finished.

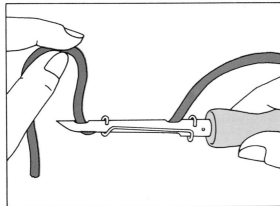

To attach pile gauge: Unthread needle and slip the pile gauge in place. Re-thread needle, then tug on yarn to make sure gauge is not interfering with yarn supply. Pile gauges and the way they are attached will vary from one needle brand to another.

Working a design

When working a rug, work the details of the design first, then its background. Begin each detail by forming a row of loops to outline its shape, then work rows to fill the shape. Fill-in rows can be worked in two ways (see right); each way has a different effect on the clustering of the pile. These same two row-working directions can be applied to the filling-in of the background area. The amount of space that is skipped between loops and rows will vary according to the weight of the yarn being used. For rug-weight yarn, leave about three base-fabric threads between loops and rows; for a tapestry-weight yarn, leave about a two-thread space. Since thread counts will vary slightly among rug bases, alter the spacing if necessary. Generally, if the rug starts to buckle, the loops and rows are too close together; if you can see base fabric between loops on the pile side of the rug, they are too far apart. As you work the areas, do not "travel" the yarn over one area to get to another (see right). From time to time, check the pile side of the rug. If you discover that some loops are uneven, lift them with a knitting needle until they are even with the rest of the pile.

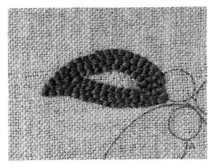
Outline the shape of each detail with a row of loops that follow the line on the rug base. Alter direction of row as many times as necessary.

Fill in the outlined area with additional rows. The fill-in rows can be worked in two different directions—to follow the contour of the outlined shape

(A) or in straight rows across the outlined shape (B). Each way has a slightly different effect on the way the pile looks.

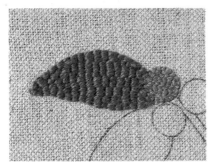
Spacing between loops and rows varies with the yarn weight. For a rug-weight yarn, leave about 3 threads; for tapestry-weight, 2 threads.

Do not travel yarn from one area to another. Instead, cut and end the yarn in the first area, then start it again in the next.

If some loops are uneven, slip a knitting needle through several and pull up on them to make them even with the rest of the pile.

Special techniques

Pile made with the punch needle method can be varied in several ways. A multicolored pile can be produced by threading the needle with several strands of a lightweight yarn, each a different color. Dimensional detail can be added to a design by forming the pile to different heights and by cutting only the higher loops (those about ½ inch high). Differences in pile height are achieved by forming loops both with and without a pile gauge; those formed without the gauge are about twice as high as those made with it. The actual high and low of any pile depends on the needle size.

For a multicolored pile, thread the needle with several strands and colors of a lightweight yarn. Work the loops in the usual way.

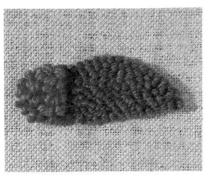
To vary pile heights, work some loops without the pile gauge, others with the gauge attached. Use different needle sizes for more variation.

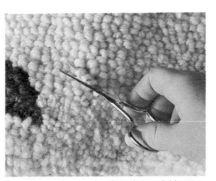
To cut loops, remove rug from frame; fold area to be cut over hand. Working several loops at a time, slip scissors blade through loops and cut.

475

Preparing for and working a knotted rug

Estimating and preparing yarn for latch hook method
Estimating and preparing yarn for Rya stitch method
Latch hook method
Rya stitch method
Working a charted design
Trimming and sculpturing pile

Estimating and preparing yarn for latch hook method

The amount of yarn needed to make a rug with the latch hook method will depend on the number of knots needed to form the design and the number and length of the strands used in the knots (see the facing page). The cut length of a yarn strand used in any knot should be twice the desired pile length plus ½ inch. The length is double because the strand becomes halved when knotted; the ½ inch is taken up in the knot. Yarn for the knots can be purchased in packs of cut strands or in skein form (p. 464).

To calculate yarn amounts, first estimate the number of knots in the design (the number of knots in a square inch of canvas times the number of square inches in the design). Then determine the number of yarn strands required for the knots (knot count times the number of strands needed for each knot). Apportion the resulting strand count among the colors and yarn types in the design and add 15 percent to each total. If you are buying packs of precut yarns, divide the total strand count of the rug by the count of one pack; the result is the number of packs needed. If the yarn will be purchased in skeins, you must translate the total strand count into yards (multiply the strand count by the cut length of the strands, then divide by 36). Yarn to be cut is wrapped around a cutting gauge, then cut at top and bottom. An adjustable gauge (see right) can be set to the correct cutting length. You can make your own gauge of cardboard, cut to the length of the strand and wide enough to accommodate several wraps of yarn.

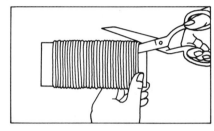

Yarns being cut on a cardboard gauge

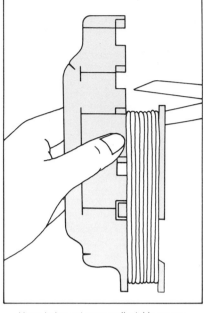

Yarns being cut on an adjustable gauge

Estimating and preparing yarn for Rya stitch method

The Rya stitch rug method is the formation of Rya stitches (Ghiordes knots) on the exposed lengthwise threads of a Swedish backing fabric (see p. 478). Each knot spans two lengthwise threads and is made with three or more strands of yarn (usually Rya). The pile formed by the knots is usually 2 inches long but can be as short as ¾ inch or as long as desired. To calculate the amount of yarn needed for a Rya stitch rug, first determine how much yarn is needed for each knot, then multiply this amount by the total number of knots in the design. The quantity of yarn needed for one knot made with a single strand of yarn is twice the desired pile length plus ½ inch. This much is required because the yarn is halved when knotted; the ½ inch is absorbed in the knot. If the knot will be made with several strands, the amount of yarn needed is the length needed for a single-strand knot multiplied by the number of strands that will be used to form the knot. To determine the total amount of yarn needed for the rug, multiply the length needed for one knot by the number of knots in the rug. (If the pile length varies, make a calculation for each pile length.) Apportion these totals among the colors and yarn types used in the design, add 15 percent to each total, then divide by 36 to arrive at yardage amounts. To prepare the yarn for work, cut it to equal lengths of about 55 inches. Skeins of Rya yarn can usually be opened up and cut at one end to produce many equal lengths, each about 55 inches long. The skein structure of other yarns, however, may necessitate pulling the yarn out as a single strand and cutting the working lengths individually (see below).

An open skein of yarn being cut into equal working lengths

Individual lengths being cut from a pullout skein

Latch hook method

With the latch hook method, cut yarns are knotted onto the crosswise threads of a rug canvas with the aid of a latch hook. The knots are worked row by row across the canvas and from the bottom edge of the design up. This direction for working ensures that the latch hook can slip easily through the canvas while the knots are being formed. As a rule, single strands of rug yarn, 2½ inches in length, are used to form the individual knots (see right); the pile length produced is 1 inch. When using this type of yarn, form a row of knots across every set of crosswise threads of the canvas. Quite often, however, three or four strands of Rya yarn (or tapestry), 4½ inches long, are used to make the knots (see below); the pile length produced with these is 2 inches. When forming a knot with several strands of yarn, treat the multiple strands as a single unit. To produce a thick pile with *multiple-strand knots,* form a row of knots across every set of crosswise threads; for a less dense pile, and one that will fall, form a row across every other set of crosswise threads. If the design of the rug calls for it, a *multicolored pile* can be formed with either single- or multiple-strand knots; the procedure differs with each type of knot (see below).

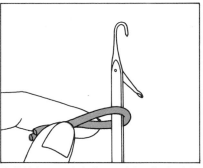

1. Fold the yarn in half around the shank of the latch hook; hold both of the cut yarn ends between your thumb and index finger.

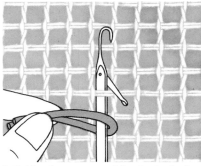

2. Holding the yarn around the shank, slip tip of hook under a set of crosswise threads and push it through until the bar of the hook falls open.

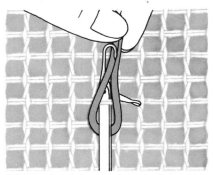

3. Still holding the yarn ends, and with the latch hook remaining open, bring the yarn up and around into the open latch hook as shown.

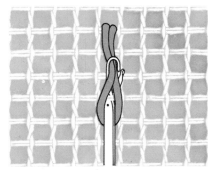

4. Carefully pull the hook down under the cross-wise threads. When the bar of the hook closes, release both of the cut yarn ends.

5. Continue to pull the hook down and under the crosswise threads. The yarn ends will be pulled with the hook to form the knot.

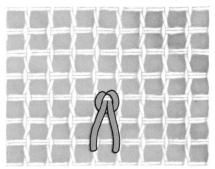

6. Tug on the cut yarn ends to tighten the knot around the crosswise threads and to bring both cut yarn ends even with each other.

Additional techniques

To form a multiple-strand knot, treat strands as a single unit. Fold all yarns around hook and form knot as described at top of page.

Rows of multiple-strand knots can be worked on every set of crosswise threads, or on every other set of threads as shown above.

To form a multicolored pile with *single-strand knots,* alternate the colors of knots across each row; stagger placement of colors from row to row.

If using multiple-strand knots, use strands of different colors to form the knots. Form rows on each set or every other set of crosswise threads.

Preparing for and working a knotted rug

Threading a needle 19

Equipment for knotted rugs 464
Methods of design transfer 468-469

Rya stitch method

A Rya stitch rug is produced by working Rya stitches (Ghiordes knots) row by row across a Swedish backing fabric, from the bottom of the design up. A # 13 tapestry needle is used to work the stitches (knots); the loops that connect the stitches form the pile of the rug. The quality of the pile depends on the type and amount of yarn used for the stitches, the length of the loops, and whether or not the loops are cut. Rya stitches are generally made with three or four strands of Rya yarn, the loops are 1 to 2 inches long, and they are cut after all the stitching is done. Loop length is controlled by you as you work the stitches. The rows of exposed lengthwise threads on a Swedish backing fabric are spaced ½ inch apart and can be used as loop-length guides. The loops can be as long as desired; they must be at least long enough to cover the tops of knots worked in the row immediately below. The loop length and yarn color or type can be changed as they occur in the design across a row. If the design calls for a multicolored pile, use yarn strands of different colors to make the knots. Rya stitches can also be done on a rug canvas; the main difference with canvas is that the rows of stitches can be placed closer to each other because of the closer spacing of the rows of lengthwise threads. If you are left-handed, work the stitches and the rows from the right to the left and with the needle pointing to the right.

1. Begin at lower left. Slip the needle under one lengthwise thread (1 to 2) and pull it through until yarn end is the length of the desired loop.

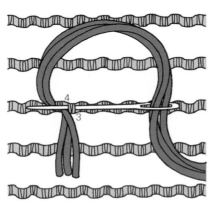

2. With excess yarn up and out of the way, slip needle under next lengthwise thread (3 to 4); pull needle and yarn through to complete the stitch.

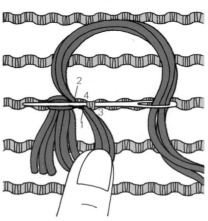

3. Work across row to the right, forming a loop of the desired length and holding it in place as you form the next and each successive stitch.

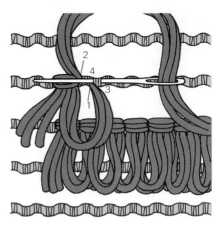

4. Work each new row from left to right, above row just done. When stitching is finished, trim yarn ends even with pile; cut loops (below) if desired.

Additional techniques

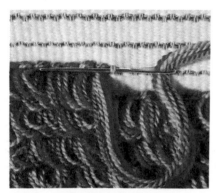

To form a multicolored pile, thread the needle with strands of yarns in the colors needed for the pile. Form stitches in the usual way.

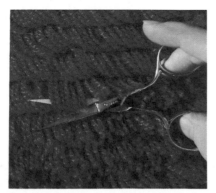

To cut loops, slip blade of scissors through a few loops, tug on them slightly and cut. Proceed to next group of loops and cut them the same way.

To form a Rya stitch on rug canvas, separate a double lengthwise thread; slip needle under one thread (1 to 2), then the other (3 to 4). You can

work stitches across every row of lengthwise threads, or skip one or more between stitch rows. Loops must cover tops of knots in row below.

478

Working a charted design

Sometimes a design intended for use with one of the knotted rug methods will be presented in chart form. In chart form, each stitch (knot) in the design is represented by one square on graph paper. In addition to the location of the stitches (knots), a chart will usually specify the color and type of yarn and the length and number of strands to use in each stitch (knot). If these elements are not described, they are up to you to determine. Colors are represented by filled squares on the chart, filled either with the colors intended for the knots or with symbols to represent them. The yarn type, length, and number of strands can also be denoted by symbols but are usually explained in a written statement. If

symbols are used, their meanings are defined in a listing known as a key. A row of blank squares on a chart usually signifies an unworked row on the rug base.

The amount of rug base needed to work a charted design is equal to the number of threads required to form the stitches called for by the chart across and up and down. To this amount should be added any margins necessary along each edge of the rug base (p. 468). When you calculate the amount of rug base, also determine the amount of yarn needed to work the design (p. 476). Read and follow the chart to work the design onto the rug base. Work and read from left to right and from the bottom edge of the design up.

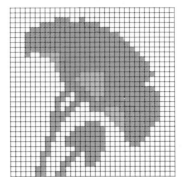

When a design is charted, each square on the chart means a stitch or knot on the rug base. Shown above is a charted design; at right, the same design worked on rug canvas with latch hook method. Sample is shown from reverse side.

Trimming and sculpturing pile

The last step in working a latch hook or Rya stitch rug is to trim any stray yarn ends even with the rest of the pile. Do this with a pair of specially bent rug scissors; these can be held parallel to the pile as you cut the yarn ends (see p. 482).

With knotted rugs in which certain areas of the design have been worked with longer cut pile than others, trimming can mean something more explicit. It can mean cutting the pile in an area to a shorter, more suitable length (as in the

first sample below) or the sculpturing of the pile to produce a specifically shaped, three-dimensional contour (second and third samples). All three samples are parts of the rug on page 495. Trimming to shorten pile length or to form a con-

toured shape is not applicable to a Rya stitch rug worked with uncut loops. Here the loops must be formed, as the rug is being worked, to the length or lengths that will produce the desired pile or contoured shape.

To cut pile to a shorter length, hold several of the strands straight up and cut them straight across to the desired length. Proceed to the next group and cut them the same way.

To sculpture an area, cut the pile to the lengths needed to form the desired shape. The area above is being cut so that the strands at one edge are shorter than those at the opposite edge.

This area is being sculptured to form a mound. The strands at the edges are being cut shorter than those in the center. If a mistake is made, re-work the knots and cut them again.

Finishing techniques

Finishing hooked rugs
Finishing knotted rugs/canvas
Finishing knotted rugs/Swedish backing

Finishing hooked rugs

Before you begin a finishing process for a rug made with either the hand hook method or the punch needle method, check the front of the rug to make sure that all the fabric and yarn ends have been cut to the same length as the pile. Check the back of a rug made with either of these methods to see if there are any long crossover stitches. If there are, cut them in the center and pull the ends to the front; trim the ends even with the pile. The finishing techniques shown below and opposite include applying latex; hemming and binding; making a lining for a rug; and making a pillow.

APPLYING LATEX

Latex, a viscous rubber available in either liquid or aerosol form, is used to cement the pile firmly to the base fabric. It is essential to use latex on a rug made with the punch needle method or the pile will pull out when the rug is used. Traditionally, latex is not used on a rug made with the hand hook method; however, you may use it if you wish. Latex makes a rug more durable and also makes it skid-proof. Spray latex is faster to use than liquid but it does not cover the base fabric as well. When using latex, let the rug dry thoroughly, following package directions. When the rug is dry, you can proceed with a finishing technique. Whether you plan to hem or bind the edges of the rug, you will have to use a sharp needle and a thimble to help push the needle through the coated fabric.

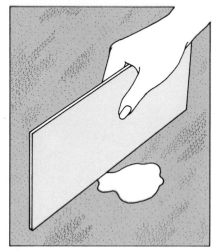

To apply liquid latex, pour a small amount in the center of the base fabric. Use a piece of stiff cardboard or an old spatula to spread it.

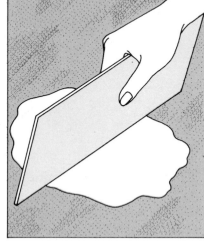

Spread the latex into as thin a layer as possible. Continue applying a small amount at a time until the entire back of the rug is coated.

HEMMING

It is possible to hem the edges of a rug made with the hand hook or the punch needle method if the base fabric is monk's cloth and if the rug is not too large. The fibers in monk's cloth are pliable so the excess fabric can be turned under and hemmed; the fibers in burlap, being stiff, crease when folded and are likely to crack in time. If you have used burlap as a rug base, you should bind the edges (see opposite page). In general, use binding on any rug that is large and will get a lot of use—bound edges are far more durable. Binding also makes a neater edge for a round or oval rug. For hemming, you will need button-and-carpet thread or any heavy-duty cotton thread, a sharp needle, and a thimble.

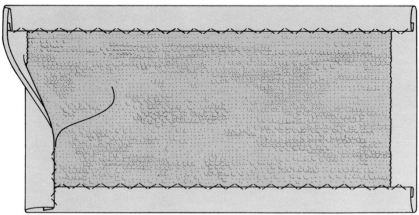

To hem a rug, trim the excess base fabric to 2″ on all four sides. Fold under (toward the back) ¼″ on all edges; then fold the excess fabric to the back, making this fold as close as possible to the last row of pile. Stitch the hem first on two opposite sides, then turn up the remaining sides. On the last two sides, stitch the fold to the hemmed edge and then to the rug back as shown.

BINDING

Binding is the best finishing technique if you want to create a strong edge for a rug. It is essential to use binding if the edges of the base fabric have become frayed from being stretched in a frame. It is also necessary to use binding if you have used burlap as the base fabric, because exposed burlap threads tend to crack and wear out in time.

Rug binding is a 1½-inch-wide woven cotton tape; it comes in tan and other neutral colors. Since the binding does not show, it is not necessary for the binding to match the colors in the rug, but you can dye rug tape if you wish. When buying rug binding, be generous. You will need enough to go around the outside measurement of your rug, plus a 2-inch overlap. You will also need a heavy linen or cotton thread, such as button-and-carpet thread, and a needle. If latex has been applied to the back of the rug, you will also need a thimble to push the needle through the fabric.

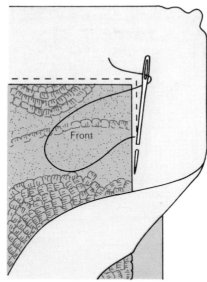

To bind a square or rectangle, trim base fabric to ¾" from edge of last row of loops. Lay rug tape on right side of rug with edge of tape even with last row of loops. With heavy thread, stitch tape to rug about ⅛" from edge of tape.

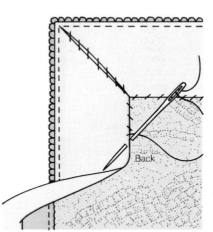

Fold tape to back of rug and pin in place. At corners, form miter by folding excess tape under as shown. Sew tape to rug with an overcast stitch; sew miter line closed at corners. Stitch loosely so edges do not gather up and pucker.

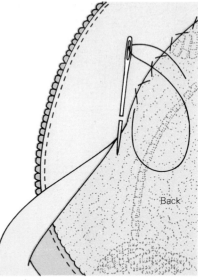

To bind a round or oval rug, you will have to make bias tape (see p. 258) because it is not available in widths for rugs. Apply tape by stretching outer edge of tape slightly as you stitch it to rug; ease inner edge to fit rug shape.

LINING

If a rug you have made is to be used in an area where it will get a lot of traffic, it would be wise to add a lining. It will protect the rug against wear and thus make it more durable. There are two ways to make a lining. The first method requires turning the rug inside out; it is limited to small rugs and pillows. If a rug is too large to turn, you can make a lining by folding under the edges of lining fabric and base fabric and stitching the two together, as shown far right.

For a lining fabric, choose a sturdy, firmly woven cotton, such as twill or duck. If you are making a pillow top, you can select a less durable and more decorative fabric for the backing. To make the pillow, follow the directions at the near right, and insert a pillow form or loose polyester batting through the opening before you stitch it.

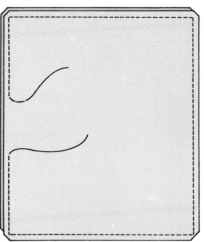

To make a lining, cut lining fabric 1" larger than rug. Trim excess base fabric to ½". With right sides facing, stitch lining to rug ½" from edge. Leave opening for turning. Trim corners; turn right side out; stitch opening closed.

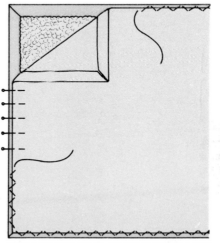

If rug is too large to turn, cut lining fabric 2" larger than rug; press under 1" on all sides. Trim excess base fabric to 1", then fold to back of rug. Pin lining to rug back so that the folds meet, then stitch them together.

PRESSING

A hooked rug should be steam-blocked. If you are going to apply latex, block the rug first. If not, block after hemming or other finishing technique is completed. To block, press the rug with a steam iron and a pressing cloth; this sets the loops and gives a finished look to the rug. To do this, place the rug face down on an ironing board. If the rug is too big for this, place it face down on any clean, flat, firm surface. For a pressing cloth, wet a towel or a piece of heavy cotton fabric and wring it out; cloth should be damp but not wet. Spread the cloth on the rug and iron over it. As the pressing cloth dries, dampen it again. Continue until the entire back of the rug has been pressed. You can turn the rug face up and repeat the entire procedure on the right side of the rug. Let the rug dry thoroughly before you use it.

Finishing techniques

Finishing knotted rugs/Canvas

Before you begin a finishing process for a rug knotted on a canvas base, examine the back of the canvas to see whether you have missed any areas; missed areas are more easily seen from the back. Knot any such areas. The cut ends of a knotted pile can be somewhat uneven. To trim the ends evenly, use a pair of specially bent rug scissors (see p. 465) as shown below. To sculpture pile by cutting ends to different lengths, see page 479.

BINDING

To apply binding to a rug that has been knotted on a canvas backing, you will require 1½-inch-wide rug binding, a heavy-duty needle, and strong cotton or linen thread. When the knotting is completed, trim excess canvas to 1 inch on edges; trim corners diagonally. On a square or rectangular rug, it is not necessary to fold this excess canvas to the back of the rug and stitch it down; however, you can stitch it down first if you find it easier to work with this way. On a round or oval rug, do stitch excess canvas to the back of the rug first; this makes it easier to apply binding as shown below.

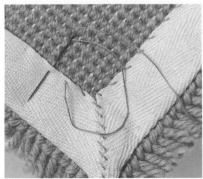

With rug right side up, place tape face down along edge. Overlap ends 2″. Stitch from wrong side, keeping tape close to first row of knots.

Fold tape to back of rug, covering excess canvas, and stitch. At corners, fold tape to form miter. Stitch diagonal miter line to close it.

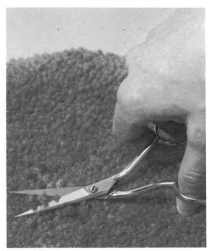

To trim yarn ends on cut knotted pile, use bent-handled rug scissors. They allow space for fingers yet keep blade flat against pile.

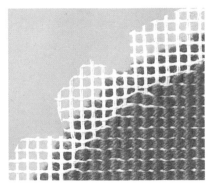

On oval or circle, trim canvas to 1″. Cut out notches so canvas will not fold on itself when turned back. Do not cut up to last row of knots.

Fold excess canvas to back of rug, making sure sections of canvas lie next to each other but do not overlap. Stitch canvas to back of rug.

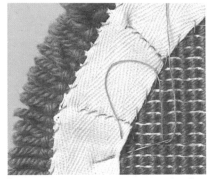

Stitch tape to back of rug along outer edge. Sew inner edge of tape to rug back, folding excess tape into darts as needed; stitch darts closed.

LINING

To add a lining to a rug or make a pillow, follow the directions for hooked rugs on page 481, taking note of two exceptions: If you are making a pillow or lining a small rug, make sure that the longer yarn ends are pushed toward the center of the work; stitch carefully so the yarn ends do not get caught in the seam. If you are lining a large rug, fold back the excess canvas and stitch it to the back of the rug. It will prove to be much easier to attach the lining to the rug if the excess canvas has been secured first.

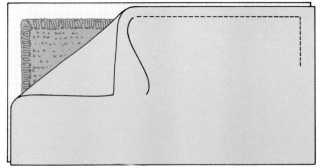

When backing a small rug or making a pillow, push yarn ends to the center so they do not get caught in the stitching.

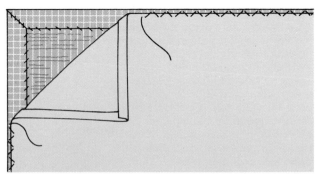

When lining a large rug, fold excess canvas to back of rug and stitch in place. Press under 1″ on lining fabric; stitch fold to edge of canvas.

STITCHED BORDERS

Another way to finish the edges of a canvas rug base is to stitch a border with yarn that matches or coordinates with colors used in the rug. If you want to add a stitched border, this must be decided before you start the rug because the canvas must be turned under around all edges and secured by working knots at the outer edges through two layers of canvas. If you have used precut yarn, purchase a skein of the same type of yarn for the border. If you have used Rya or tapestry yarn, use at least two strands for the border stitches so the border will be thick enough to cover the canvas.

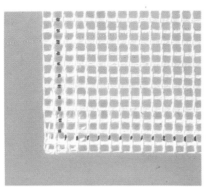

Before you begin, fold back excess canvas, leaving one row of holes free past design. Secure canvas with knots at edges through both layers.

For buttonhole stitch, see page 26. Leave 2'' tail of yarn. Make at least 3 stitches in each hole to cover canvas. Work over tail at end.

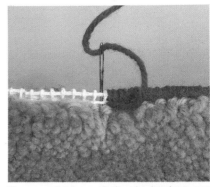

To overcast, take needle from back to front, over canvas, then back to front again. Work enough stitches in each hole to cover canvas.

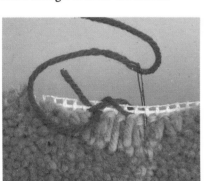

To work braided or plaited stitch, bring needle from back through 1st hole; go over edge and put needle through 5th hole. Go over edge and bring

needle through 2nd hole; go over edge and bring needle through 6th hole. Continue this way, going from next hole on left to fourth hole from it.

To combine plaited border with binding, a technique used on round and oval rugs, sew excess canvas to rug back (see facing page), leaving one

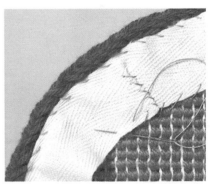

row of holes around edge. Work plaiting in this row. Place binding so edge abuts plaited stitch; sew binding in place (see facing page).

FRINGE

If you decide to add fringe to a rug that has been worked on canvas, you can use long strands of the same yarn that was used for the knotting. Or, if you want to simulate the look of fringe on an Oriental carpet, you can use strong string or cotton crochet yarn in beige or ecru. Oriental carpets have fringe on two ends only; other rugs can have fringe on all edges. Cut the yarn into strands that are slightly more than twice as long as the finished fringe length. You can add binding after you have knotted the fringe if you wish.

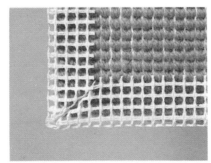

To fringe four sides of a rug, fold back excess canvas so that one hole is exposed on all edges. Stitch canvas to back of rug (see facing page).

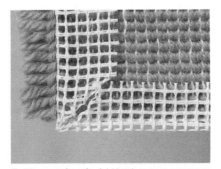

To fringe ends only, fold back excess canvas so no canvas shows on two long sides; one row of holes is exposed on ends. Stitch canvas to back.

To attach fringe, fold yarn in half and pull through canvas hole from the back with a crochet hook. Put ends through loop; pull to tighten.

Finishing techniques

Finishing knotted rugs / Swedish backing

The Swedish backing fabric used for Rya rugs is specially woven so that it provides evenly spaced areas of exposed lengthwise threads. It is available in a variety of widths; you can purchase the width you want with selvage edges on both sides. The knotting is worked right up to the selvage edges; they do not have to be turned under and hemmed. You will need to finish only the top and bottom edges. Swedish backing is also available in squares and rectangles of various sizes; these have selvage edges on all four sides

and do not require any finishing technique. When the knotting is complete, the rug is complete.

If you are making a small pillow, you may have raw edges on all four of the sides. These edges will be enclosed when the pillow backing is sewed to the knotted base fabric, as shown at right.

The finishing techniques shown below include applying binding to the top and bottom edges and adding fringe. Fringe is added, traditionally, only to the top and bottom edges of a Rya rug.

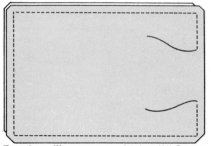

To make a pillow, cut excess fabric to ½''. Sew to backing ½'' from edge, leaving an opening.

Trim corners; turn right side out. Insert pillow form or loose polyester fiber. Sew opening.

BINDING

Because Swedish backing fabric has selvage edges on the sides, you only have to apply binding to the top and bottom. Binding is sewed along the row of spaces (exposed lengthwise threads) above the first row of knots and below the last row. When the binding is folded to the back of the rug, there will be a small area (less than ⅜ inch) of backing fabric showing. The loops will cover this when the rug is placed on the floor. In addition to the binding, you will need a heavy-duty needle and a strong thread, such as button-and-carpet thread.

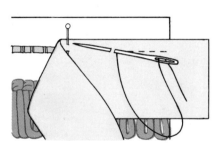

Cut rug binding to rug size plus 2''. Place binding on rug, leaving 1'' extended on either side. Stitch binding to rug along row of spaces.

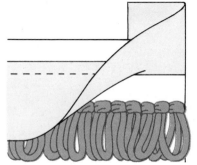

Before you fold the binding to the back of the rug, fold the 1'' extensions on both sides to the back to create a clean side edge.

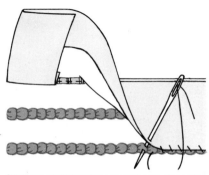

Stitch the binding to the rug as shown. Then slip-stitch the fold of the binding to the rug base fabric along the side edge.

FRINGE

Traditionally, fringe is added only to the top and bottom edges of a Rya rug stitched on Swedish backing fabric. Make the fringe with the same Rya yarn used for the rug. To add fringe, you stitch a row of the same knots used in the rug, placing them in the row of spaces (exposed lengthwise threads) immediately below the last row of knots and immediately above the first row of knots. Make the loops of fringe at least twice as long as the loops in the rug; you can make them longer if you like. You can cut the fringe or leave the long loops. Apply binding to the fabric edges after the fringe is attached.

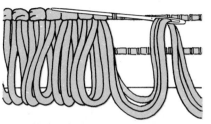

To add fringe, make a row of the same knots as in the rug, placing them in the row of spaces above the first row and below the last row of knots.

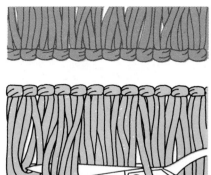

Make the loops of fringe at least twice as long as the loops in the rug. You can cut the fringe or leave it in long loops, as you prefer.

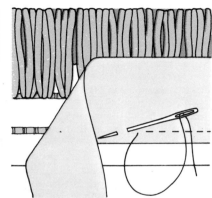

Apply rug binding (above) after fringe has been worked. Sew binding along row of spaces just above top row of fringe and below bottom row.

Care of handmade rugs

Skidproofing, padding, vacuuming, removing spots, dry cleaning, washing, repair, and storage

A handmade rug will look better and last longer if certain precautions are taken with its care and handling.

Skidproofing: To prevent accidents, a small rug should be anchored by placing a nonskid pad underneath it. This can be a thin mat that is all rubber or rubberized on one side only. If a small rug is in an area that does not get a lot of foot traffic, you can simply sew small pieces of rubber mat at each corner of the rug. If you have used latex on the back of the rug to secure the pile, the latex will help prevent skidding also.

Padding: Small handmade rugs are often used on top of carpeting, which acts as a cushion for the rug. If a rug is used on a bare floor, it will wear better with a waffle cushion underneath it. Without a cushion, the pile surface will become flattened and will wear out sooner.

Vacuuming: Handmade rugs can and should be vacuumed regularly. Wool has great resistance to soil; a vacuum will pick up loose dirt on the surface. Small rugs can be turned over and vacuumed on the back as well. Rya and latch hook rugs, if they are small enough, can be picked up and shaken to dislodge loose dirt. Since the pile is higher on these rugs, it is easier for dirt to get caught in the yarn. Shaking before vacuuming will loosen the dirt so the vacuum can pick it up; it will also make cleaning easier because you will not have to run the vacuum over the rug repeatedly.

Removing spots: A spot that occurs on a rug is much easier to remove if steps are taken immediately. Use a reliable spot remover, following package directions. A spot that is not removed immediately tends to get ground into the rug and is difficult to remove later.

Dry cleaning: All handmade rugs can be dry-cleaned; if the rug gets a lot of use, it should be dry-cleaned as often as once or twice a year. Take it to a reputable dry cleaner and specify that it is a handmade rug so the dry cleaner will take care in handling it.

Washing: Rugs should never be washed in such a way that they become saturated. There are several commercial rug cleaners available in both dry and liquid forms. A dry rug cleaner is sprinkled on the rug, allowed to remain for a while, then vacuumed off. Liquid rug cleaners are applied with a damp towel. Before you use either type of rug cleaner, vacuum the rug thoroughly to remove loose dirt. Some rug cleaners are toxic; read directions carefully and make sure the room is properly ventilated.

Repairing: If you save a few pieces of yarn or fabric strips in the colors used in your rug, you can use these to repair a small area that has been damaged by a burn, a tear, or a stain that will not come out. To repair a damaged spot, outline the area with a row of pins (see below). Turn the rug over and carefully cut the damaged yarn or fabric from the back. Hook or knot the area with your leftover material. Trim any ends. If a stitched border becomes damaged, pull out the yarn in that area, and work ends under adjacent stitches. With matching yarn, re-work the border stitches.

Storing a rug: To store or transport a rug, roll it with the loops on the outside. This keeps the loops from getting wrinkled and does not put unnecessary strain on the backing fabric. Never fold a handmade rug. If you are going to store the rug for a period of time, wrap it in an old sheet to keep it clean. Do not use plastic because it does not breathe. Most wool yarns intended for rug use are mothproofed; you may want to use mothballs as an extra precaution.

Repairing hooked rugs

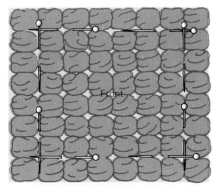

To repair a damaged area, outline it on the front of the rug with straight pins. Push the pile aside, if necessary, to insert the pins.

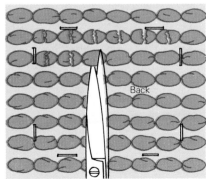

Turn the rug over. Cut the yarn or fabric strips within the pinned area. Carefully remove yarn or fabric strips, bringing ends to the front.

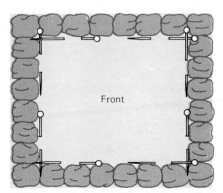

Using yarn or fabric strips of the same color, hook the area. Bring ends to front and trim them even with the pile. Remove the pins.

485

Braiding

Materials
Equipment
Making fabric strips
Making a three-strand braid
Round rug
Oval rug
Rectangular rug
Lacing
Joining fabric strips
Tapering off
Butting
Multiple braiding

Materials

Braided rugs probably originated as mats braided of straw or grass and used to cover dirt floors. Braided rugs as we know them started out as a way to utilize fabric scraps. Many braided rugs are still made from leftover fabric or worn clothing that is cut into strips. Whether you braid with new or used fabric, there are certain guidelines to follow.

The fabric: Heavy or medium-weight wool is the best fabric for a braided rug because it wears so well. The wool should be heavy and closely woven, soft but firm. Loosely woven fabrics wear out more quickly than those that are tightly woven; stiff wools, such as gabardine, are difficult to work with. Avoid using cotton, linen, or silk; fabrics of these fibers do not wear well. Synthetics attract static and will not stand up to the wear that a rug is given. Do not use fabrics of different fiber content in the same rug.

Assembling the fabric: If you use new fabric, buy manufacturer's remnants by the pound to keep the cost down; rugs require a great deal of fabric. Check in your area for woolen mills; most of them sell wholesale only but will probably be glad to get rid of mill ends.

The most economical way to make a rug is with fabric from old coats, suits, skirts, and blankets. If you do this, make sure all of the wool is approximately the same weight. Be sure, with old clothing, to remove any zippers, linings, collars, and pockets. Open darts and cut along seamlines. Cut out any worn areas, such as elbows, knees, and seats. Also remove any areas damaged by moths. Wash the fabric in a machine or by hand, using a mild detergent and cool water. Hang it up to dry; do not put wool in a dryer. You may also want to wash new wool remnants before using them.

Amounts: If you are purchasing fabric by the yard, allow about 1 yard of 54-inch-wide fabric for 1 square foot of braiding. A 2-by-3-foot rug would require approximately 6 yards of fabric. If

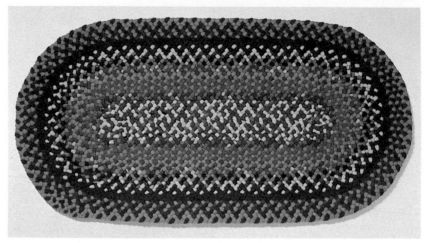

Oval braided rug, worked in shades of brown and gold, is started with a straight center braid.

you are purchasing or assembling wool by the pound, allow about ¾ to 1 pound for 1 square foot of braiding. The amount will vary, depending on how wide you cut your strips, and how tightly you braid. Weigh garments after the lining, zipper, and collar have been removed. When buying wool by the pound, allow from 10 to 20 percent for waste. If you are buying strips of fabric, allow extra length for braiding; it takes up approximately one-third of the strip. Each braid tends to be about 8 inches longer than the braid in the previous row. If you have planned a color scheme, buy or collect the maximum amount of fabric suggested before you start so that you will not run out of a particular color.

Using color: There are several ways to employ color in a braided rug. The easiest, especially for a beginner or for anyone who is using old fabrics, is called the hit-or-miss pattern. This is simply a combination of any colors you have. The most common design in a braided rug is stripes or bands of color. In planning a color scheme, there are several design guidelines to bear in mind. Lighter shades look better in the center than dark

ones; a dark center tends to look like a bull's eye. Dark colors on the edge of a rug, however, have the effect of a frame. Keep the size of the center of the rug in a pleasing proportion to the size of the overall rug. To determine what the center size should be, make a sketch of the rug and color the rows. With this to guide you, you can decide how many rows to use in the center. Braids need not be a solid color. Since they consist of three strips, there can be three colors in them. Solid fabrics can be braided with checks, tweeds, or small plaids for an interesting texture. Bright colors look best combined with beige, tan, or other neutrals. Remember that the appearance of a color can change according to the color surrounding it.

Work gradually to change colors in a rug. Add a new color to the rug by having one strip of the new color in the first braid, two strips in the second, three strips in the third and subsequent braids for a solid band of the new color. Always change colors of braids on a curve near the end of a round, in approximately the same place each time, to make the change less obvious.

Equipment

A braided rug is made of braided strips of fabric either sewed or laced together. In addition to the fabric strips, you will need a *sewing needle and carpet-and-button thread* to stitch the first bend of the braid to itself. The remainder of the rug is laced together with a *blunt-edged lacing needle and heavy thread,* such as upholsterer's twine or carpet thread. You will need a clip *clothespin* to keep the end of the braid from unraveling when you stop braiding.

There are several other braiding accessories that are not necessary but will help speed the work. *Braiding cones* are tubes that automatically fold a fabric strip. These are sold in sets of three; each strip of fabric requires one. The cones eliminate the whole process of folding and basting the fabric strips. Some braiding cones come with a *reel attachment* that keeps a long strip of fabric from tangling during braiding. *A braid holder* is a metal clamp that attaches to a table; it holds the braid under tension. *A cloth cutter* is a machine that cuts uniform strips of fabric; it adjusts to cut various widths.

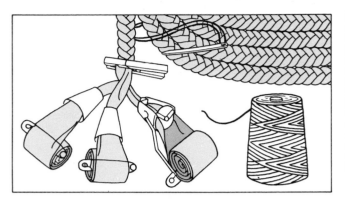

Braid is shown at left being made with braiding cones that automatically fold the fabric strips; one cone has a reel attachment to prevent the strip from tangling. A clothespin holds the end of the braid. A blunt-edged lacer and heavy thread are used to lace the braids together.

Making fabric strips

Fabric strips for braiding can be folded and sewed together by hand, or fed into braiding accessories that fold them automatically. With either method, you must first cut the fabric into strips 1¼ to 2½ inches wide, the width depending on the weight of your wool and the width you want the braid to be. Always cut the strips with the grain of the fabric; cut either lengthwise or crosswise, whichever will give you the longest strips. To determine the most desirable braid width, cut sets of three strips to various widths; fold and braid them, then use strips in the width that produces the braid width you find you prefer.

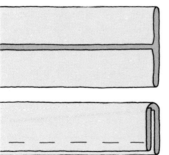

Fold fabric strip by bringing each raw edge to the center (top). Then bring folded sides together (bottom). To keep the folded edges together, you can sew a long basting stitch along the open edge.

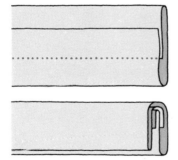

You can add bulk to fabric strips of lightweight fabric by folding the raw edges beyond the center (top). Then bring folded edges together (bottom) as usual and baste open edges together if you wish.

Handling of folded strips will be easier if you wind each one into a coil. The coil will unroll easily when you are ready to braid with it. Also folded fabric strips can be stored more conveniently in flat coil form.

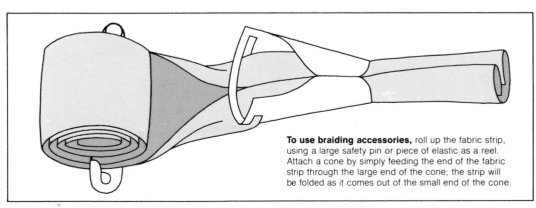

To use braiding accessories, roll up the fabric strip, using a large safety pin or piece of elastic as a reel. Attach a cone by simply feeding the end of the fabric strip through the large end of the cone; the strip will be folded as it comes out of the small end of the cone.

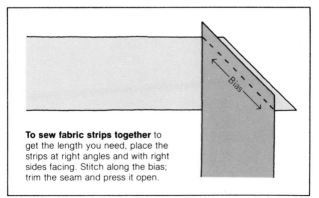

To sew fabric strips together to get the length you need, place the strips at right angles and with right sides facing. Stitch along the bias; trim the seam and press it open.

Braiding

Making a three-strand braid

The simplest type of braid is composed of three strips of fabric. It is possible to braid with four or more strips (see pp. 492-493) but larger multiples do not conform as well to the shaping of a rug. When braiding, anchor the strip ends by tacking them to a board or using a table clamp so that the ends are under tension. Always keep the open edges of strips to the right. To make a tight braid, pull each strip to the side, not down, as you braid. When you stop braiding for any reason, clip a clothespin to the braid end to hold it. The length of the braid you make to start will depend on the shape you want the rug to be.

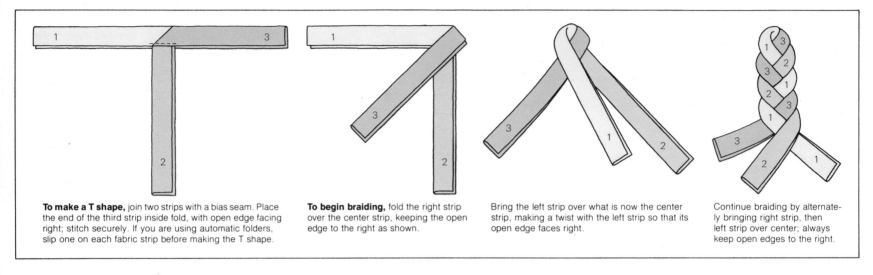

To make a T shape, join two strips with a bias seam. Place the end of the third strip inside fold, with open edge facing right; stitch securely. If you are using automatic folders, slip one on each fabric strip before making the T shape.

To begin braiding, fold the right strip over the center strip, keeping the open edge to the right as shown.

Bring the left strip over what is now the center strip, making a twist with the left strip so that its open edge faces right.

Continue braiding by alternately bringing right strip, then left strip over center; always keep open edges to the right.

Round rug

For a round rug to lie flat, it must be started correctly in the center. To do this, you make a variation in the braiding that is called either a *round turn* or a *modified square corner;* this variation makes it easier to coil the braid around itself. The turn is repeated from six to twelve times to form the center circle, then regular braiding is continued. How many times you repeat the turn depends on the weight of the fabric you are using, the width of the strips, and how tightly you braid. When the center of the rug is formed so the braid coils around itself and lies flat, the rest is worked in regular braiding.

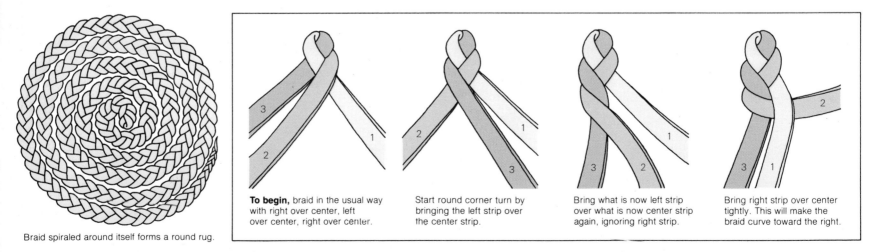

Braid spiraled around itself forms a round rug.

To begin, braid in the usual way with right over center, left over center, right over center.

Start round corner turn by bringing the left strip over the center strip.

Bring what is now left strip over what is now center strip again, ignoring right strip.

Bring right strip over center tightly. This will make the braid curve toward the right.

488

Oval rug

An oval rug is made by coiling a braid around a length of straight braid. The length of the center braid is determined by the overall size of the rug: length of rug minus width equals length of center braid. For example, a 3-by-5-foot oval rug has a 2-foot-long center braid. To start the rug, make a braid of the appropriate length; then make three round turns as described for a round rug (see facing page) so the braid turns the opposite way. Continue regular braiding until you reach the starting end of the braid; make three round turns around the starting end. Continue regular braiding for the remainder of the rug.

In oval rug, braid coils around straight center.

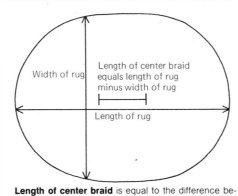

Length of center braid is equal to the difference between the length and the width of the finished rug.

3 round turns

3 round turns

For oval center, make braid of appropriate length; work three round turns. Straight braid to the next turn; make three round turns so braid wraps around starting end.

Rectangular rug

A braid can be made into a rectangular rug, although this shape is not as traditional as a round or an oval. To shape the braid into a rectangle, you make a variation in the braiding that is called a *square turn*. This produces a right angle in the braid so that it can turn a corner. The length of the center braid of a rectangular rug is determined in the same way as with an oval rug: the length of the center braid is equal to the length minus the width of the rug. The rectangular rug is made with regular braiding along the sides and a square turn at each of the four corners of the rug in each row of the braiding.

Rectangular rug has square turn at each corner.

To begin a square turn, bring left strip over center, then left strip over center again.

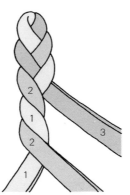

Bring left strip over center again for total of three times. (Right strip is not yet braided.)

Bring right strip over center and pull it tight. The braid will turn toward the right.

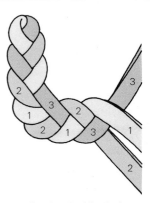

Continue braiding in the regular way with left strip, then right strip over center.

489

Braiding

Lacing

The center of a braided rug, where the braid first turns on itself, is sewed together; the rest of the rug is laced. Lacing is faster than sewing and makes a sturdier rug. For sewing, use any carpet-and-button thread and a sharp needle. For lacing, use a blunt-edged needle, called a lacer, and a heavy waxed thread, such as upholsterer's twine or carpet thread. Always use a double length of thread. Lace with one continuous strand; when a length of thread is used up, tie another length to it with a square knot. Work on a table or other flat surface so the rug lies flat; do not let it hang over the side or it will be distorted. Pull the lacing thread tight as you work so it is hidden in the loops of braid; if it does not show on either the top or the bottom of the rug, the rug will be reversible.

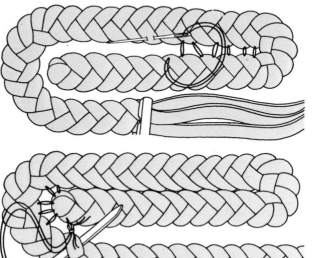

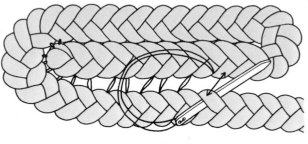

1. To sew first loops of braid together, start at first bend of braid (start of oval rug is shown). Knot thread; hide knot inside braid. Stitch through the folds of the inside loops of braids, working from one braid to the other. Keep thread concealed as you stitch.

2. Continue stitching loops together until you are just beyond the second bend. Thread lacer with waxed thread; attach this to the end of the sewing thread with a square knot.

3. To lace, position braids so they are not side by side but at an angle. Lacing cord goes between loops; it does not penetrate fabric. Bring lacer diagonally under inside loop of each braid; pull thread tight so it does not show. Lace all straight edges this way.

4. To lace curves of round or oval rug, loops must be skipped (on braid, never on rug) so rug will lie flat and not buckle. Decide when to skip a loop after thread is through loop on rug. If next loop on braid is even with or in back of the thread, you should skip it.

Joining fabric strips

As you braid, you will need to add to the fabric strips because it is too cumbersome to start with strips that are long enough to make an entire rug. This is done by splicing a new strip onto the working strip. To avoid a bump in the braid, begin with fabric strips of uneven lengths so the splicing of each one will fall in a different place. If you want to change colors, you can splice a strip of the new color onto the old strip. Plan your color changes so they will occur at the same place on each round (see p. 486); planned color changes give a more uniform look to a rug.

Always splice a strip when it is in the center after it has been in an *over* position so the seam you make will be hidden by another strip going over it.

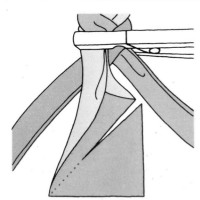

Before you begin splicing, secure the braid against unraveling with a clothespin. Unfold short strip and cut it on the bias.

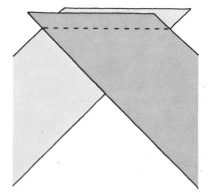

Place the old and new strips together, with right sides facing, and stitch along the bias. Trim the seam allowance to ⅛″.

Re-fold the spliced strip and continue braiding; make sure the seam is hidden when the next strip is placed on top of it.

Tapering off

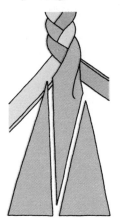

When the rug has reached the desired size, taper each strip into a long, thin point that extends for about 5″ to 7″. Cut each strip to a slightly different length so they do not end in the same place.

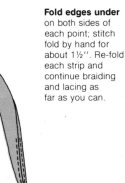

Fold edges under on both sides of each point; stitch fold by hand for about 1½″. Re-fold each strip and continue braiding and lacing as far as you can.

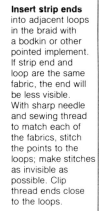

Insert strip ends into adjacent loops in the braid with a bodkin or other pointed implement. If strip end and loop are the same fabric, the end will be less visible. With sharp needle and sewing thread to match each of the fabrics, stitch the points to the loops; make stitches as invisible as possible. Clip thread ends close to the loops.

Butting

Butting—joining the beginning and end of a braid to form a complete circle—is an advanced technique that permits distinct color changes. Although an entire rug can be made by this method, it is most often used on the final rows of a rug for a finished look. To prepare a braid for the final row of a rug, attach a safety pin 1 inch from the ends of three folded strips. Make a braid long enough to go around the rug, and place it so its ends will not be butted at the same point where the previous row was tapered. Leaving four loops of braid free at the beginning, lace the braid to the rug; leave about four loops of braid free at the end. Remove safety pin. To butt the ends, follow directions below.

1. Put starting end of braid in front of you, finishing end above it. If your three strips are not identifiable by different colors, put a piece of colored thread on corresponding strip ends to identify them. Start butting with strips in the position shown.

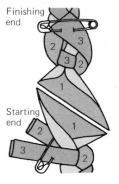

2. Pin Strips 2 and 3 out of the way. Unfold both ends of Strip 1 and cut the ends along the bias.

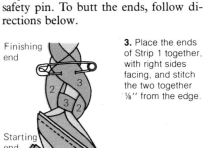

3. Place the ends of Strip 1 together, with right sides facing, and stitch the two together ⅛″ from the edge.

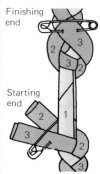

4. Fold Strip 1 back into a tube; the seam allowance will be on the inside.

5. At finishing end, braid Strip 3 over Strip 1, concealing the seam. Braid Strip 2 over Strip 3 and bring Strip 2 under Strip 1. At starting end, bring Strip 2 out from under Strip 1. Both ends of Strip 2 should be on the right side of the braid.

6. Pull both ends of Strip 2 out of the braid slightly so you can butt the ends together. If you don't pull the ends out slightly, the butted strip will be too long to fit in the braid and will bulge. The braid will be somewhat distorted now but will be put back in shape later.

7. Butt the ends of Strip 2 and fold the strip back into a tube, following the directions given for Strip 1. Pull both ends of the braid so it is smooth again.

8. At starting end, bring Strip 3 under Strip 2. At finishing end, pull Strip 3 out from under Strip 2.

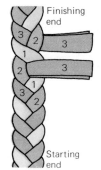

9. Butt the ends of Strip 3 together, using directions given above for Strip 1.

Braiding

Multiple braiding

The pages to this point have dealt only with three-strand braiding not because more strands cannot be used, but because the result would not be flexible enough to be formed into the oval, round, and rectangular rugs being described. Braids of more than three strands can be formed into an oblong rug, but only by running them lengthwise, then lacing the braids together along the length of the rug and hemming the raw edges under at the strip ends. Other uses for multiple braids include handbag handles and luggage straps, belts, and headbands.

To start a multiple braid, secure the ends of the folded fabric strips with a large safety pin, or sew across them so they lie flat. Multiple braiding can be somewhat confusing at the beginning. It will help to use fabric of a different color for each strip so you can follow their individual paths to understand the configuration of the braid. Any multiple braid, like a three-strand braid, should be worked under tension.

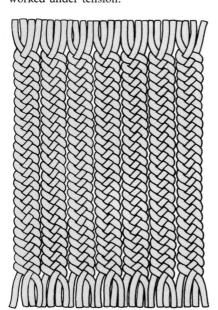

Multiple braids can be made into an oblong rug.

4-STRAND BRAID

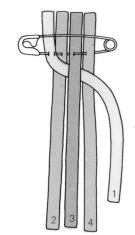
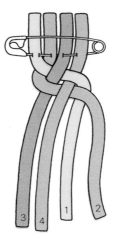

To begin four-strand braid, bring first strip on left over the second, under the third, and over the fourth.

Bring what is now first strip on the left (it was second strip) over the next strip, under the next, over the last.

Continue braiding by repeating the motion of over, under, over, always using strip on the left.

4-STRAND VARIATION

For a variation on a four-strand braid, braid the four strips as if they were three (see p. 488) by holding the first two strips together as you braid.

5-STRAND BRAID

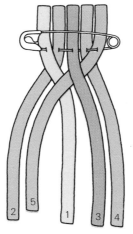
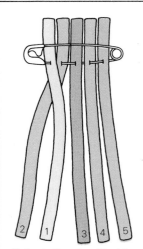

To begin five-strand braid, bring the left strip over the strip to its right.

Bring the right strip over the strip to its left, under the next strip, and over the one after that.

Continue braiding by repeating these two steps, always using the outer left and right strips.

5-STRAND VARIATION

For a variation, braid five strips as if they were three (see p. 488); hold the first two strips together and the last two strips together as you braid.

6-STRAND BRAID

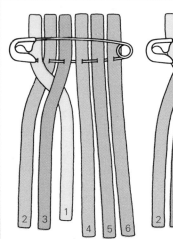

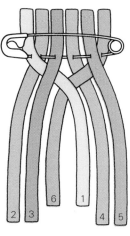

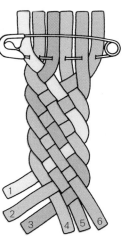

To begin six-strand braid, bring the outer left strip over the second strip and under the third.

Bring the outer right strip under the strip to its left, over the next strip, under what was the first strip.

Continue braiding by repeating these two steps, always using outer left and outer right strips.

6-STRAND VARIATION

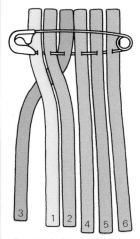

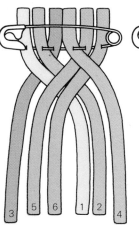

For a variation on six-strand braid, hold first two strips together as one and bring them over the third strip.

Hold last two strips on right together as one; bring them under fourth strip and over what were first two strips.

Continue braiding this way, keeping first two and last two strips together and using them as one.

7-STRAND BRAID

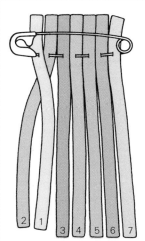

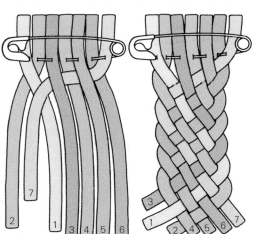

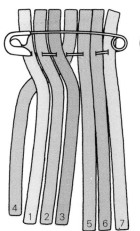

To begin seven-strand braid, bring outer left strip over the strip to its right.

Bring outer right strip over sixth, under fifth, over fourth, under third, and over what was the first strip.

Repeat these two steps. The braiding sequence is the same for any odd number of strips.

7-STRAND VARIATION

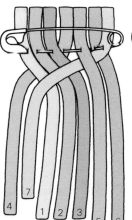

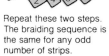

For seven-strand variation, hold the first three strips together and bring them over the fourth strip.

Bring last strip on right over sixth, under fifth, and over the first three strips, which were held together.

Repeat these two steps, always holding the first three strips together and using them as one.

493

Chair cushion

Intricacy of floral design chair cushion is made possible by technique used—hand hook method.

½-inch squares; copy the design square for square (see p. 14). Finish the edges of the burlap and mark the centers (see p. 468). Transfer the design to the base fabric (pp. 468-469). Put the burlap in a rug frame (see p. 471). Cut the flannel into ⅛-inch-wide strips (see p. 470). To hook rug, refer to pages 472 and 473.

Shading
Guidelines for shading with different colors of fabric strips can be found on page 473. This piece was shaded as follows: Each flower is worked in four different shades of one color. To simplify references, we designated the lightest shade as the first shade and the darkest as the fourth. The spokes are worked in the third shade, the shadows behind the spokes are in the second shade, the petals are filled in with the first shade. The fourth, or darkest shade is used for accents along the outline of the flower itself and the outline of the individual petals. The flower buds are worked in three shades of one color. The yellow buds

start with the darkest shade near the enveloping leaf and work out to the lightest shade at the upper tip. In the red buds, the three shades are used to make the bud appear round: the lightest where the light would strike; the darkest where the bud would be in shadow. The leaves are worked in three shades of green, some in an olive-green combination, the others in hunter greens. Stems and leaf veins are worked in darkest shade; two lighter shades are used to fill in the shapes.

Finishing
When you have finished hooking the seat cushion, trim the excess burlap and attach the rug binding (see p. 481). Before you stitch binding to rug, you can insert the chair ties. To do this, cut the grosgrain ribbon in half. Place the cushion on the chair and mark the place on the circle nearest the chair spokes or slats you want to use to anchor the cushion. Fold each piece of ribbon in half; slip the fold between cushion and binding. As you sew the binding, you will catch the ribbon.

Floral design cushion is worked in hand hook method because of the intricacy and detail possible with this technique.

Materials needed
20-inch-square piece of burlap
Size 4 hand hook
1 yard rug binding
1 yard ¼-inch-wide grosgrain ribbon
Heavy-duty needle and thread
Wool flannel in square-inch amounts:
  20 each of 4 shades of gray
  24 each of 4 shades of blue
  45 of light red
  26 each of 3 darker shades of red
  12 each of 3 shades of yellow
  26 each of light and dark olive green
  8 of medium olive green
  30 each of 3 shades of hunter green
  7 of black
  (or ⅛ yard of each of the above)
  455 of white (or ¼ yard)
Rug frame

Preparation
To enlarge the design, make a grid with

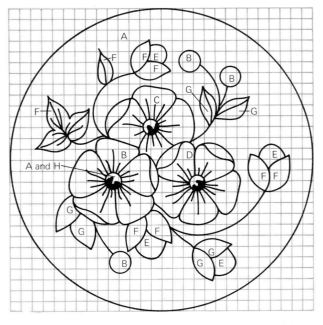

To enlarge design, make a grid with ½″ squares and copy the design square for square (see p.14).

Key

A	White
B	Red
C	Blue
D	Gray
E	Yellow
F	Olive green
G	Hunter green
H	Black

494

Wall hanging

Wall hanging, 20″ × 32″, is mainly one pile height, with areas of white Rya yarn in a higher pile.

G (see detailed chart below)

To enlarge design, make a grid with 1″ squares and copy design square for square (see p.14). To transfer the design to canvas, see page 469.

A Light blue, 2½″ lengths
B Tweed (see p. 477) of light and medium blue, 2½″ lengths
C Pink, 2½″ lengths
D Brown, 2½″ lengths
E Olive green, 2½″ lengths

F Blue-green, 2½″ lengths
G Charted design at left (see p. 479): light blue background, 2½″ lengths; white crosses, 4″ lengths
H White, 4″ lengths
I White, 6″ lengths

The 20 × 32-inch wall hanging is made with a combination of precut rug yarn and Rya yarn cut to various lengths.

Materials needed
Paper and pencil
Waterproof felt-tipped marker
26″ × 38″ piece of rug canvas with four holes per inch
Masking tape
4 yards rug binding
Latch hook
Three 3.6-ounce skeins (160 yards in each) of lightweight white Rya yarn
Precut rug yarn, the following number of 2½-inch-long pieces:
3700 light blue
1300 medium blue
200 pale pink
1300 brown
1400 olive green
1250 blue-green
Five ½″ plastic rings
½″ dowel, 30″ long

Knotting
To enlarge the design, make a grid with 1-inch squares; copy the design square for square (see p. 14). Bind the edges of the canvas with masking tape and mark the center (see p. 468). Transfer the design to the canvas (see p. 469). You can fill in the areas with colored felt-tipped markers or you can simply tie a piece of yarn in that area so you know which color yarn to hook.

With the precut yarns, use one length for each knot. The Rya yarn must be cut; prepare 2000 4-inch lengths and 1100 6-inch lengths. Make certain that the two lengths are in separate piles. Use four lengths of Rya yarn for each knot. Knot the rug, following the chart above and the directions on pages 477 and 479.

Finishing
When the knotting is complete, sculpture the long white areas. Trim the crosses at the top to ¼ inch above the top of the blue pile. Cut them straight across by holding the scissors parallel to the rug.

Trim the two white areas in the lower left corner so that each one is shorter on the right side and longer on the left side. The four white areas above these are rounded so they are shorter on the inner and outer edges, longer on top.

To finish the wall hanging, trim excess canvas to 1 inch. Attach rug binding to the edges, following the directions on page 482. To equip the rug for hanging, sew the five rings to the rug binding at the top of the rug, spacing them evenly across the top. To hang the rug, slip the dowel through the rings and balance the dowel on nails or hooks that have been put in the wall.

Another view of this oval braided rug, worked in shades of brown and gold, is shown on page 486.

Braided rug

Fabrics in the rug pictured are mainly solid shades of brown, gold, and white. One plaid fabric was used in some braids to create an interesting tweed.

Materials needed

Fabric—the following amounts of 54-inch-wide heavy-weight wool:

1½ yards each of gold and brown
1 yard tarnished gold
⅔ yard brown-and-white plaid
½ yard off-white
⅓ yard each dull gold and light brown
¼ yard dark brown

Button-and-carpet thread
Sewing needle
Lacing thread
Lacer

Preparation

Prepare the fabric by cutting it into 2-inch-wide strips, cutting along the crosswise grain. If you are going to fold the strips by hand, see page 487. If you are using braiding accessories, slip a braiding cone onto the ends of three strips in the following colors: off-white, tarnished gold, and plaid. With either method of preparing strips, the next step is to make a T-shape (see p. 488). Anchor the strip ends by tacking them to a board or using a table clamp; make a 24-inch-long braid (the length of the rug minus the width) for center of rug.

Beginning an oval rug

When the center braid is 24 inches long, work three round turns (see p. 488) so that the braid will turn and go in the opposite direction. Continue braiding until you reach the starting end of the braid. Make three round turns so that the braid will turn around the starting end (see p. 489). Continue forming a straight braid for the remainder of the rug. To lace the rug together, see page 490.

Color changes

To duplicate the color changes in the rug pictured, follow the schematic drawing and chart below. The chart shows, for each row, the length of braid necessary for that row and the three colors of fabric used to make the braid. The schematic drawing shows where the color changes are made—on the curve in the same place in each round. To join fabric strips of a new color, see page 490.

Finishing

When the rug reaches the size you want, taper the ends of the three fabric strips as illustrated on page 491. Stitch the ends to loops of braid, using sewing thread to match each fabric color.

Center braid length is equal to length minus width of rug; 2′ by 4′ oval rug has 2′ center braid.

	Row	Braid length	Colors of strips
	1-3	14 feet	Off-white; tarnished gold; plaid
	4	6 feet	Dull gold; tarnished gold; plaid
	5-6	12 feet	Dull gold; tarnished gold; gold
	7	7 feet	Gold; tarnished gold; gold
	8	7½ feet	Gold; tarnished gold; plaid
	9	8½ feet	Gold; dark brown; plaid
	10	9 feet	Off-white; brown; plaid
	11	9½ feet	Off-white; brown; brown
	12	10 feet	Brown; brown; brown
	13-14	22 feet	Brown; light brown; gold
	15	12 feet	Brown; gold; gold

Index

Complete Guide to Needlework, as you will see, is indexed in an unusual way: Instead of the customary overall index covering the entire book, there is a separate index for each section. They are arranged in alphabetical order as follows:

Appliqué	Macramé
Crochet	Needlepoint
Embroidery	Patchwork
Knitting	Quilting
Lacework	Rug-making

Such an arrangement, the editors feel, makes it easier to find a particular craft, and specific aspects of that craft, than it would be with a standard index.

That will only be true, however, if readers know precisely what appears in each section. Usually that will be obvious. In some instances it will be less so, because of unfamiliarity with the book or uncertainty about the classification into which certain crafts fall. The list below will help you to locate most such subjects.

Subject or craft name	Section that includes it
Bargello	Needlepoint
Blackwork	Embroidery
Braiding	Rug-making
Broomstick lace	Crochet
Crewel work	Embroidery
Florentine embroidery	Needlepoint
Fringing	Macramé
Hairpin lace	Lacework
Hooking	Rug-making
Huckwork, huck darning	Embroidery
Tatting	Lacework
Trapunto	Quilting
Weaving	Lacework

Appliqué

pages 191–206

Bias strips, making and using 199

Corners, how to handle
for hand method 194, 195
for machine method 197
Curves, how to handle
for hand method 194, 195
for machine method 197
Cut-through (reverse) appliqué
description 201
hand method 205
machine method 206
Cutting out appliqués
for fusing method 197
for hand method 194
for machine method 196

Decorating appliqués 200
Designs in appliqué
basic types 192-193
methods of obtaining
free cutting 192
free drawing 192
paper cutouts 193
tracing 192
using fabric prints 193
transferring 193

Embroidery used to decorate appliqué 200

Fabrics for appliqué 192, 194
for reverse appliqué 201
prints used as design 193
Fusible webs, use of 197
Fusing appliqué 197

Hand appliqué
cutting 194
securing 195

Interfacing appliqué 199

Layering appliqués of two or more pieces 198

Machine appliqué
reverse (cut-through) appliqué 206
straight-stitch method 196
zigzag method 196-197
Molas (San Blas appliqué) 201

Needles for appliqué 192

Overhand stitch, use of 195

Quilting used to decorate appliqué 200

Raised appliqué 199
Reverse appliqué 201-206
cut-through technique 205-206
San Blas technique 202-204
types, description of 201

San Blas (reverse) appliqué
basic technique 202
description 201
using patches 204
using slits 203
using three fabric layers 203
using two fabric layers 202
Securing appliqués
by fusing 197
by hand 195
by machine 196-197
Slipstitch, use of 195
Staystitching 194
Stitches in hand appliqué
used to decorate 200
used to secure 195
Straight-stitching appliqué (machine method) 196
Stuffing of appliqué 199

Templates, making and using 193, 194, 196, 197
Thread for appliqué 192
Tools and supplies 192
Transferring appliqué designs 193

Zigzag-stitching appliqué (machine method) 196-197
cut-through (reverse) appliqué 206

Crochet

pages 357—402

Abbreviations used in crochet 366
Afghan hook 359, 386
Afghan (Tunisian) stitches 386-387, 402
Armholes and sleeves 397
Around-the-post technique 364
Assembling and finishing 400-401

Ball button 398
Basic crochet, rules for 363
Basic crochet techniques 360-363
Blocking techniques 342-343, 400
Buttonholes for garment 399
Buttons, how to make 398

Carrying yarn on wrong side 391
Chained overlay 383
Chain ring, how to form 370
Chain stitch
 made left-handed 361
 made right-handed 360
Chains, used for turning 363
Charting a pattern stitch 392
Charting a woman's sweater 394-395
Circles, shaping of 370
Color charts, how to read and work
 with 390
Colored patterns (jacquards) 390-391
Concentric shaping 370
Crocheting in rounds 370
Cross stitching on afghan crochet 402

Decreasing 368-369
Designing a crocheted garment 393
Double crochet, forming of 362
Double-hook needle 359
Double shell edging 401
Double triple crochet, forming of 363

Edges, finishing of 400-401
Edgings, crocheted 401
Elementary stitches 362-363
Elementary techniques, variations
 of 364-365
Equipment 359
Estimating yarn quantity 393
Eyelet insertion 401

Fancy scalloped edging 401
Fastening off 367
Filet and picot edging 401
Filet crochet 382
Finishing edges 400-401
Finishing yarns ends 367
Flat row counters 273, 359
Following crochet instructions 366-370

Garment, crocheting a 393-401
 armholes 397
 blocking and assembling 400
 buttonholes 399
 buttons 398
 charting 394-395
 designing 393
 edges, finishing of 400-401
 measuring for 393
 necklines 396
 ribbing 398
 sleeves 397
 yarn estimating 393
Gauges, testing or measuring of 366
Geometric shapes 369-370
 worked in rounds or rings 370
 worked in rows 369

Half-double crochet, forming of 362
Hooks
 how to hold left-handed 361
 how to hold right-handed 360
 types 359

Increasing 368
Instructions, how to follow 366-370
Irish crochet 384-385

Jacquard (multicolor) tech-
 niques 390-391
Jiffy hook 359
Jiffy lace needle 359
Joining a new yarn 367, 390
Joining sections 400
Jumbo hook 359

Knitting aids useful for crochet 273, 359

Left-handed crochet method 361
Little picot edging 401
Looped edging 401
Loop stitches, forming of 388-389

Markers, coiled ring 273, 359, 368
Measuring stitch and row gauge 366
Meshes 380-383
 overlaid 383
 used in filet 382
Mesh ground, shaping of 381
Motifs 377-379
Multicolor (jacquard) crochet 390-391

Necklines, types of 396
Needles, tapestry 359

Octagons, shaping of 370
Openwork meshes 380-381
Ovals, shaping of 370
Overlaid mesh patterns 383

Patchwork motifs 377-379
Pattern stitches 372-389
 clusters 376
 filet 382
 Irish crochet 384-385
 loops 388-389
 meshes 380, 383
 motifs 377-379
 shells 374-375
 textures 372-373
 Tunisian 386-387
Post stitch ribbings I and II 398

Raglan sleeve 397
Regular hook 359
Right-handed crochet method 360
Rings, forming and working around 370
Round neckline 396
Rounds, working in 370
Row counters 273, 359
Row gauge measurement 366
Rows, working geometric shapes in 369
Rules for basic crochet 363

Scalloped edging 401
Securing yarn ends 367
Semi-raglan sleeve 397
Set-in sleeve 397
Shapes, geometric 369-370
 worked in rounds or rings
  circle 370
  octagon 370
  square 370
 worked in rows
  oval 369
  square 369
  triangle 369
Shaping mesh ground 381
Shaping techniques
 decreasing 368-369
 increasing 368
Shorthand symbols used in crochet 392
Single crochet edging 401
Single crochet, forming of 362
Sleeves and armholes 397
Slip stitch, forming of 363
Solomon's knot (mesh) 381
Spaces in mesh, how to increase
 and decrease 381
Spiral shaping 370
Square neckline 396
Squares, shaping of 369, 370
Steel hook 359
Stitches, individual names of
 afghan 386
 alternate 372
 arcade 374
 ball 376
 basic Tunisian 386
 basket weave 373

Stitches, individual continued
 bias (Tunisian) 387
 bobble 376
 bouclé loop 388
 brick 375
 broomstick lace 389
 bushy 375
 chain loop 389
 checkerboard 372
 chrysanthemum 377
 close scallops 374
 clover 377
 clusters in a square 392
 crossed 373
 crossed (Tunisian) 386
 daisy 377
 diagonal 373
 diamond mesh 380
 diamond picot mesh 380
 dogwood 379
 double 372
 double (Tunisian) 387
 eyelet square 378
 fan 375
 flower border 382
 flower in a square 378
 Hawaiian square 378
 hexagon 379
 honeycomb mesh 380
 honeycomb (Tunisian) 387
 knit (Tunisian) 386
 lace clusters 376
 lace (Tunisian) 387
 lacy scallops 374
 lattice loop 388
 mesh grounds I and II 380
 old America 378
 open checks 381
 open ridge 373
 paddle wheel 379
 pineapple 376
 popcorn (Tunisian) 387
 posy 377
 purl (Tunisian) 386
 relief 373
 rib (Tunisian) 387
 ripple 375
 simple shells 374
 soft clusters 376
 Solomon's knot 381
 star 377
 starburst 375
 steps 373
 stockinette (Tunisian) 386
 trestle 381
 up and down 372
 wagon wheel 379
 wave 375
 wide arches 374
 woven 373
 woven overlay 383

Stitches, types of
 clusters 376
 loops 388-389
 meshes 380, 381-383
 motifs 377-379
 shells 374-375
 textures 372-373
 Tunisian 386-387
Stitch formation
 basic stitches 360-363
  chain 360-361
  double 362
  double triple 363
  half-double 362
  single 362
  slip stitch 363
  triple 363
 variations on basic stitches 364-365
  under one loop 364
  around the post 364
  between stitches 364
  double chain 365
  double-faced double 365
  double knot 365
Stitch gauge measurement 366
Stitch pattern selection 372
Symbols used in crochet 366, 392

Tapestry needle 359
Terms used in crochet 366
Test swatch, how to make 366
Triangles, shaping of 369
Triple crochet, forming of 363
Tube, shaping of 370
Tunisian crochet 386-387, 402
Tunisian crochet ribbing 398
Turning chains, instructions on 363
Twisted braid 401

Under-one-loop variation 364

V-neckline 396

Working around the post 364
Woven overlay 383

Yarn ends, joining and securing 367
Yarns
 estimating amounts for garment 393
 types 358

Embroidery

pages 7—110

Algerian eye stitch (in blackwork) 57
Assisi embroidery 69

Backstitches 22-25
Blackwork embroidery 56-65
Blanket stitches 25-27
Blocking finished embroidery
  basic technique 55
  board and pins for 11
Bokhara couching stitch 33
Brick stitch 49
Bullion knot stitch 43
Buttonhole stitches 26-27
  in cutwork 91
  in drawn threadwork 82

Cable stitch (in smocking) 94
Chain stitches 28-32
Charting colors and stitches 21
Chessboard filling stitch (in pulled
  threadwork) 76
Chevron stitch 24
Chinese (Pekinese) stitch 23
Cleaning finished embroidery 54
Cloud filling stitch 53
Coil filling stitch (in pulled thread-
  work) 75
Colors
  charting 21
  choosing for a design 13
Coral stitch 31
Couching stitches 32-34
Cretan stitches 41
Cross stitch embroidery 66-69
  Assisi 69
  on gingham 68
Cross stitches 35-38
Cutwork embroidery (by machine) 102
Cutwork embroidery (see Open-
  work 90-91)

Darning (see Huck embroidery 70-73)
Darning stitches 46-47
Darning stitch (in drawn threadwork) 84-85
Designs and designing 12-15
  charting colors and stitches 21
  color selection 13
  design sources 12
  enlarging a design 14
  interpreting designs in embroidery 12
  reducing a design 15
  stitch selection 21
  transferring designs
    materials for 11
    methods of 16-17
Dove's eye filling stitch
  in drawn threadwork 82-83
  in Hardanger 89
Drawn fabric embroidery (see Open-
  work/Pulled threadwork)
Drawn threadwork (see Openwork/
  Drawn threadwork)

Enlarging a design 14

Fabrics
  basic types 9
  binding edges of 16
  cutting to size 16
Featherstitches 39-41
Filling stitches 42-45
  detached 42-43
  laid 44-45
Filling stitches (in openwork)
  in drawn threadwork 82-83
  in Hardanger 88-89
Finishing embroidered pieces 54-55
  blocking 55
  cleaning 54
  pressing 54
Fishbone stitch 41
Fly stitch 43
Four-sided stitch (in pulled threadwork) 75
Framed cross stitch (in pulled threadwork) 76
Frame types 10
Free-motion work (in machine
  embroidery) 100-101
French knot stitch 42

Hardanger embroidery (see Open-
  work 86-89)
Hemstitching (by machine) 101
Hemstitching (see Openwork/Drawn
  threadwork 78-83)
Herringbone stitches 36-38
Holbein stitch 47
Honeycomb stitch (in smocking) 95
Hoops
  basic types 10
  using a hoop in hand work 18
  using a hoop in machine (free-
    motion) embroidery 100
Huck embroidery 70-73

Japanese darning stitch 47

Kloster blocks (in Hardanger) 87

Laidwork 44-45
Laundering finished embroidery 54
Lazy daisy stitch 28
Long and short stitch 50
Loopstitch
  in drawn threadwork 83
  in Hardanger 88-89

Machine embroidery 98-102
  cutwork 102
  free-motion work 100-101
  hemstitching 101
  mock smocking 102
  with straight stitch 98, 100
  with zigzag stitches 99, 101, 102

Needles
  basic types 10
  correct handling 20
  threading methods 19
Needleweaving
  basic stitches 51-53
  in drawn threadwork 84-85
  in Hardanger 88-89

Openwork 74-91
  cutwork 90-91
  drawn threadwork 78-85
  Hardanger 86-89
  pulled threadwork 74-77
Outline (stem) stitch (in smocking) 94
Overcast stitch
  in drawn threadwork 84-85
  in Hardanger 88-89

Pekinese stitch 23
Preparing a design to be worked
  choosing colors 13
  design transfer
    materials 11
    methods 16-17
  embroidery fabrics
    basic types 9
    preparation 16
  embroidery yarns and threads
    basic types 8
    preparation of 19
  enlarging a design 14
  reducing a design 15
  tools and accessories 10-11
Pressing finished embroidery 54
Pulled thread embroidery (see Open-
  work/Pulled threadwork 74-77)

Raised needleweaving stitch 52
Reducing a design 15
Reverse faggot stitch (in pulled thread-
  work) 77
Ringed backstitch (in pulled thread-
  work) 77
Rosette chain stitch 32
Roumanian couching stitch 34
Running stitches 46-47

Satin stitch (in machine embroidery)
  99, 101
Seeding stitch 42
Sheaf filling stitch 43
Smocking 92-97
  adding to a garment 93
  English method 94-96
Smocking (by machine) 102
Spider web stitch 53
Split stitch 23
Stem stitch 23
Stem stitch (in smocking) 94
Stitches, basic embroidery 21-53
  backstitches 22-25
  blanket stitches 25-27
  buttonhole stitches 26-27
  chain stitches 28-32
  couching stitches 32-34
  cross stitches 35-38
  darning stitches 46-47
  detached filling stitches 42-43
  featherstitches 39-41
  filling stitches 42-45
    detached 42-43
    laid 44-45
  herringbone stitches 36-38
  laid filling stitches 44-45
  running stitches 46-47
  satin stitches 48-51
  weaving stitches 51-53

Stitch selection 21
Straight stitch 51
Straight stitch (in machine embroi-
  dery) 98, 100
Surface honeycomb stitch (in smock-
  ing) 95

Threading a needle 19
Threads and yarns
  basic types 8
  separating strands 19
Tools and supplies 8-11
  design transfer materials 11
  fabrics 9
  hoops and frames 10
  needles 10
  yarns and threads 8
Transferring designs 16-17
Trellis stitch (in smocking) 96
Turkey work 24

Vandyke stitch 38
Vandyke stitch (in smocking) 95

Wave stitch 52
Wave stitch (in smocking) 96
Weaving stitches 51-53
Working embroidery
  basic techniques for 16-20
  binding fabric edges 16
  cutting fabric to size 16
  following design lines 20
  handling a needle 20
  preparing yarns 19
  starting and ending stitching 20
  threading a needle 19
  transferring designs
    materials 11
    methods 16-17
  using an embroidery hoop 18

Yarns and threads
  basic types 8
  separating strands 19
Zigzag stitch (in machine embroidery) 99, 101, 102

Knitting

pages 269—356

Abbreviations used in knitting 286
Adjusting garment fit 347
Alphabet for embroidering 349
Aran knitting 315
Armholes, how to shape 332-333
Assembling a garment 344-345

Bar increase 291
Binding-off techniques 282-283
Blind-hemming stitch 336
Blocking 342-343
Body measurement charts 325
Body measurements, how to take 324
Borders 335
Buttonholes 341

Cable cast-on method 274
Cable stitches 310-311
Cabling techniques 294-295
Casting off 282-283
Casting-on methods 274-275
Charted patterns 322-323
Circular needle 272
  knitting with 298
Collars, how to shape 330-331
Colors, knitting with two or
  more 316-321
Continental (left-handed) knit stitch 277
Continental (left-handed) purl stitch 279
Corners, mitered 292-293, 335, 337
Counters and markers 273
Crocheted bind-off 283
Crocheted joining of knitted
  sections 345
Crossed stitches 308-309
Crossing stitches, techniques
  of 294-295
Cuffs for long sleeves 334

Darts used to shape garment 328-329
Decreasing methods 292-293
Designing a garment 325
Diagonals , shaping of 328-329
Diagonal stitches 303
Double cast-on method 275
Double chain edge 284
Double decreasing 293
Double garter edge 284
Double increasing 291
Double picot edge 284
Double-point needles 272
  knitting with 298-299
Dropped stitches, how to pick up 296
Duplicate stitch, how to make 348

Ease allowances 324
Elastic, adding to garment 347
Elementary stitch patterns 280
  variations 281
Elongated stitches 288
Embroidering on a knit 348
English (right-handed) knit stitch 276
English (right-handed) purl stitch 278
Equipment needs 272-273
Errors, how to correct 296-297
Eyelets, how to make 341

Facings 336-337
Foldlines for hems 336
Fringe, tasseled, how to make 285

Garment, knitting a 324-341
Garter stitch 280
Gauge, checking the 287
Gauge ruler 273
Grafting 344

Hems and facings for garment 336-337

Inside pockets 338-339
Invisible bind-off technique 283

Joining techniques 344-345

Knit stitch, how to form 276-277
Knitting aids, types of 273
Knitting basics 274-284
Knitting hem edge to garment 337
Knitting one below 288
Knotted stitches 314

Lace (openwork) stitches 304-307
Lengthening a garment 347
Lining a knitted skirt 355
Looped cast-on method 275

Measurement charts 325
Measurements, how to take and use 324
Mistakes, how to correct 296-297
Mitered corners, how to shape 292-
  293, 335, 337
Moss increase 291
Multicolor knitting techniques 316-321
  changing colors at end of row 316
  stranding 318-319
  twisting 317
  weaving 320-321
  working from a chart 317
Multiple, definition of 287

Necklines, how to shape 330-331
Needles, types and sizes 272
Novelty stitches 312

Picking up stitches
  along an edge 297
  dropped 296-297
Picot edging
  for hem 336
  for pocket 338
Plaited stitch, how to form 281
Pleats 329
Pockets
  inside 338-339
  patch 340
Pompon, how to make 353
Pressing 342-343
Purl stitch, how to form 278-279

Raised increase 290
Repeat, definition of 287
Reverse stockinette stitch 280
Rib stitches 280-281, 302
Ring markers 273
Row counters 273

Seed stitch 280
Selvages
  bottom 274-275
  side 284
  top 282-283
Shaping a garment 328-333
Shortening a garment 347
Single cast-on method 275
Single chain edge I and II 284
Single garter edge 284
Single-point needle 272
Skirts, techniques for shaping 328
Sleeve finishes 334
Sleeves, shaping of 332-333
Slipping a stitch 288
Slipstitching an edge 345
Slip stitch joining of seams 345
Stitch and row counters 273
Stitch-by-stitch hemming 336, 345
Stitches, elementary 280
Stitch patterns 300-322
  Aran patterns 315
  baby fern 306
  basket stitch 301
  basket weave 308
  basket weave rib 308
  bluebells 305
  bobble 314
  bowknot 312
  braided cable 310
  broken ribbing 302
  butterfly 307
  cellular stitch 304
  chain cable 311
  chain stitch 309
  changing rib 302
  chevron lace 306
  chevron rib 303
  chevron seed 300

Stitch patterns, continued
  coiled cable 315
  coiled rope 310
  crossed cables 311
  crossed ribs 311
  crossed ribs with fagoting 311
  crossed-stitch ribbing 308
  daisy stitch 312
  diagonal couching stitch 303
  diagonal lace stripe 306
  diagonal rib 303
  diamond seed 300
  double drop stitch 307
  double rickrack 309
  drop stitch lace 307
  eyelet stitch 304
  fancy trellis 306
  fern stitch 306
  gathered stitch 301
  hazelnut stitch 314
  herringbone 301
  herringbone twill 303
  honeycomb (cable) 311
  honeycomb (smocks) 313
  horizontal openwork 307
  horseshoes 305
  hyacinths 305
  knotted cross stitch 308
  lace and cable pattern 322
  lace insert 307
  lace rib 305
  lace zigzag 305
  lattice stitch 310
  linen stitch 301
  loop stitch 312
  minaret stitch 310
  moss stitch rib 302
  network 304
  oblique openwork 304
  oblique seed stitch 303
  palm fronds 309
  popcorn 314, 315
  quilted diamonds 301
  ribbed cables 302
  rib stitches 280, 302
  ridge stitch 301
  ripple 303
  sand tracks 310
  7 × 3 flat rib 302
  simple cable rib 310
  simple seed 300
  small diamonds 309
  smocked stitches 313
  steps 303
  stocking heel stitch 302
  striped fagoting 307
  tracks 300
  traveling vine 305
  tree of life 315
  trellis stitch 311
  trinity stitch 314
  tweed stitch rib 302

Stitch patterns, continued
  twigs 309
  twill rib 309
  Turkish stitch 304
  Vandyke stitch 306
  waffle 301
  wasps nest 308
  waved welt 301
  wild oats 310
Stitch patterns/multicolor 316-321
  abstract diamond 319
  argyle plaid 317
  checkerboard 318
  chevron stripes 316
  diamond jacquard 321
  fleur-de-lis 318
  flower border 319
  geometric border 319
  Greek key 321
  horizontal stripes 316
  houndstooth check 318
  ladders 316
  Norwegian tile 321
  sand stitch 316
  star stitch 316
  striped ribbing 318
  woven stitch 316
Symbols used in knitting 286
Symbols used to chart pattern
  stitches 322

Taking in garment width 347
Tape, how to add to garment 346
Tapestry (or yarn) needle 273
Tasseled fringe, how to make 285
Terms used in knitting 286
Texture or fabric stitches 300-301
Turning
  darts, shoulder 329
  sock heel 352
Twisted stitch, how to form 281
Two-needle casting-on methods 274

Washing knitted articles 343
Weaving seams together 344
Whipstitching
  instructions for 345
  of a hem edge 336

Yarn, attaching new 285
Yarn-end weaver 273
Yarn needed for garment 325
Yarn (or tapestry)needle 273
Yarn-over increase 289
Yarns
  buying tips 271
  chart of basic types 270
  selecting appropriate 271
  winding into balls 271
Yarn tension guidelines 281

Zippers, how to insert 346

Lacework

pages 403—442

Bobbin lace 426-434
Abbreviations 427

Blind pin 431
Bobbins, selecting and using 426-429
Braid (tape) lace 431

Cloth cover, description and use of 427
Crochet hook (used in sewings) 431
Cross 427, 428, 429

Ground patterns 430

Half stitch 428
    half stitch ground 429, 430
    plaits 428

Joining a new thread 427

Picots 431
Pillow-board 426-427
Pins and pinning 426-429
Plaited lace 431
Plaits, half stitch 428
Pricking, how to prepare 427

Sampler 427, 428-431
Sewings, joining by means of 431

Tape (braid) lace 431
Thread choices 426, 427
Tools and supplies 426, 427
Torchon ground and variations 429,
    430, 432-434
Twist 427, 428, 429

Whole stitch 428
    whole stitch ground and
    variations 430
Winding bobbins 427
Windmill join 431

Filet netting 420-425
Diamond mesh 420, 421, 422

Embroidery stitches 424
Embroidery, stretching mesh for 422

Foundation loop 420, 421-423

Knot, making the basic 421

Mesh (netting) 420-423
Mesh stick 420, 421-423

Netting needle (see Shuttles)

Sampler 423-424
Shuttles 420, 421-423
Square mesh 420, 421, 423

Thread selection 420
Tools and supplies 420

Hairpin lace 440-442
Finishing edges 441

Hairpin (fork) 440

Joinings 441

Strips, making and joining 440-441

Variations
    fringe 441
    insertion 441
    wavy band 441

Lace weaves 435-439
Brook's bouquet lace 438
Butterfly, making a 436

Canvas stretcher bars 435, 436

Danish medallion lace 438

Finger-controlled weaves 435
Frame loom 435, 436

Gauze or leno weave 437

Lace weaves 437-438
Leno or gauze weave 437

Mexican lace 437

Pick-up stick 435
Plain weave 437

Shed (space between threads) 437
Shed stick 435
Shuttle 435, 436
Spanish lace 438

Warp 435, 436
Warping a frame loom 436
Weaver-controlled weaves 435
Weft 435, 436

Needle lace 404-412
Bars and picots 408
Beaded insertion 409
Brussels net stitch 406
Buttonholed net stitch 406
Buttonholed Russian stitch 410

Cloth stitch and variations 407

Double net stitch 406
Double Russian stitch 410
Double side stitch 407

Edgings 410
Embroidered cloth stitch 407
Eyelets in cloth stitch 407

Half bars (Russian stitch) 410

Insertions 409-410
    Russian 410
    woven 409

Meshes 406-407

Open leaves with wheels 409

Pea stitch 406
Picots, bars and 408

Rings 409
Rosette 409

Sampler 405
Shell stitch 407
Side stitch 407
Single net stitch 406
Spanish point and variations 407
Spider webs 409
Supplies 404

Tape selection 404
Twisted Spanish point 407

Wheel filling 409
Woven leaves 409

Tatting 413-419
Beads, addition of 418-419
Bobbin, shuttle with 413, 414

Chain, making a 417

Double stitch, forming the 414

Fringe, addition of 419

Joins 415, 416

Picots, formation of 415

Reversing work 416
Rings, formation of 415

Shuttles 413
    working with two 417
Supplies 413

Techniques 414-417
Terms and abbreviations 413
Thread selection and use 413, 415-417

Macramé

pages 443—460

Abbreviations, terms and 446
Alternating square knots 451

Barrel knot 452
Beads 454
Berry knot 453
Bobble 451
Butterfly, making a 446

Cavandoli work 453
Cords
    additional 454
    anchoring 446
    attaching to fabric for fringe 457
    length and number, estimating 446
    measuring and cutting 446
    ring, attaching to 447
    short cords, replacing 454
    subtracting 455
    suppliers of 445
    types of 444-445
    wrapping ends 455

Design principles 455
Diagonal double half hitch 448
Double half hitch 448
Double half hitch sennit 448

Edges
    angled 449
    finishing 455

Fringe ends, finishing 458
Fringe measurements, determining 456
Fringing 456-458
Fringing fabric 457

Gathering square knot 451

Half hitch 448
Half knot sennit 450
Horizontal double half hitch 448

Inside-out square knot sennit 450

Josephine knot 453

Knots, basic macramé 447-453
    alternating square knot 451
    barrel 452
    berry 453
    bobble 451
    Cavandoli work 453
    diagonal double half hitch 448
    double half hitch 448
    gathering square knot 451

Knots, basic macramé *continued*
    half hitch 448
    half knot 450
    horizontal double half hitch 448
    Josephine knot 453
    lark's head 447
    overhand 452
    picots 452
    reverse lark's head 447
    square knot 450
    vertical double half hitch 448
Knotting board 445

Lark's head knot 447
Lark's head sennit 447
Length of cords, estimating 446

Making a butterfly 446
Making a tassel 458
Measuring and cutting cords 446
Multiple-strand square knot sennit 450

Number of cords, estimating 446

Overhand knot 452

Picots 452

Reverse lark's head knot 447

Sennits
    alternating half hitch 448
    alternating lark's head 458
    double half hitch 448
    half knot 450
    inside-out square knot 450
    lark's head 447
    multiple-strand square knot 450
    overhand 452
    square knot 450
Shaping with double half hitches 449
Square knot 450
Square knot sennit 450
Suppliers for cords 445
Supplies 445

Tassel, making a 458
Techniques, working
    anchoring cords 446
    attaching new cords 454
    finishing edges 455
    replacing short cords 454
    shaping with double half hitches 449
    subtracting cords 455
Terms and abbreviations 446

Vertical double half hitch 448

Wrapping cord ends 455

Zigzag shapes 449

Needlepoint

pages 111—190

Algerian eye stitches 151
Asymmetrical designs 162, 167, 172

Backstitches 138
  in stem stitch 130
  oblong cross stitch with back-
    stitch 141
  with Algerian eye stitch 151
  with diamond eyelet stitch 153
  with leaf stitch 154
Bargello
  description 113
  Florentine stitch used in 133-134
  how to design and work 173-182
Basketweave stitch 120, 121
Blocking
  equipment for 117
  making paper pattern for 164
  step-by-step techniques 185
Box charts 166
  making your own 172
Brick stitches 132
Brighton stitch 156
Byzantine stitches 123

Canvas (general)
  available types 114
  basic preparation 164
  determining and selecting gauge 114,
    162-163
  how to hold for stitching 119
  joining canvas lengths 164
  making a pattern of 164
  marking canvas centers 164, 167
  repairing ripped canvas 183
Canvas (for specific design types)
  full design charts 167
  partial design charts 168-169,
    170-171, 176-182
  uncharted designs 164-165
Canvas stretchers 116, 184
Cashmere stitches 127-128
Changing stitch direction 163, 169
Charting
  a design 172
  an area 165
  Bargello 174, 176, 178,180-181
Charts, interpreting ready-made 166
Chart types
  full design 166, 167
  partial design 166, 168-171, 173-182
Checker stitch 125, 126
Color schemes 174-175
Compensating stitches 161
Composite stitches 151-156
Condensed cashmere stitch 127, 128

Condensed mosaic stitch 124, 125
Condensed Scotch stitch 125, 126
Continental stitch 120, 121
  in jacquard stitch 123
Crossing stitches 139-150
Cross stitches 139-144
  in Brighton stitch 156

Darning stitch 137
Design elements in needlepoint 162-163
Design transfer materials 117
Design transfer methods
  for charted designs 166-171, 173-182
  for uncharted designs 164-165
Diagonal stitches 120-130
Diamond eyelet stitch 153
Double cross stitch 142, 143
Double herringbone stitch 148
Double leviathan stitch 143, 144
Double stitch 141, 142
Double straight cross stitch 143

Embroidery hoop in needlepoint use 116
Encroaching slanted Gobelin stitch 122
Encroaching straight Gobelin stitch 131
Enlarging and reducing designs 14-15
Expanded ray stitch 152

Fern stitch 147
Fishbone stitch 147
Flame stitch 133, 134, 174
Florentine stitches 133-134
  in Hungarian grounding 135, 136
  old Florentine stitch 136, 137
  use in Bargello 173-182
Four-way designs 173, 180-182
Frames 116, 184
French stitch 145
Full design charts 166, 167, 172

Gobelin filling stitch 132
Gobelin stitches
  Gobelin filling 132
  slanted 122
  straight 131
Graph paper
  description 117
  used in charting 165, 166, 172
Greek stitch 148, 149

Half-charts 168, 170
Half-cross stitch 120
Herringbone stitches 148
Hungarian diamond stitch 135
Hungarian grounding 135, 136
Hungarian stitches 135-136

Jacquard stitch 123

Kalem stitches 130
Knotted stitches 145-146

Large Algerian eye stitch 151
Leaf stitch 154
Left-handed stitching 161
Leviathan stitches 143-144
Line charts 166
  making your own 172

Milanese stitches 128-129
Mosaic stitches 124-125
Motif designs 173, 178-179, 181, 182
Multiple-color stitching 160
Multiple-repeat designs 170-171

Needlepoint rod 116, 184
Novelty stitches
  defined 113
  effect on design 113, 162-163
  instructions for forming 122-159, 161

Oblong cross stitches 141-142
Old Florentine stitch 136, 137
Oriental stitch 128, 129

Parisian stitches 136-137
Partial design charts 166, 168-171
  row charts 173-182
Pattern of prepared canvas
  how to make 164
  use in blocking 185
Perspective stitch 149, 150
Pile stitches 157-159
  cutting pile stitches 158
Plaited stitch 149
Projection mirrors (used to develop
  Bargello designs) 175-181

Quarter-charts 168, 169, 170, 172

Ray stitches 152
Reducing and enlarging designs 14-15
Rice stitch 146
Rococo stitch 145, 146
Row charts (Bargello) 173-182
Row designs 173, 176-177
Rya stitch 157

Scotch stitches 125-126
Slanted Gobelin stitches 122
Stem stitch 130
Stitches, basic needlepoint 118-159
  composite stitches 151-156
    Algerian eye stitch 151
    Brighton stitch 156
    diamond eyelet stitch 153
    expanded ray stitch 152
    large Algerian eye stitch 151
    leaf stitch 154
    ray stitch 152
    triangle stitch 155

crossing stitches 139-150
  cross stitch 139-140
  double cross stitch 142, 143
  double herringbone stitch 148
  double leviathan stitch 143, 144
  double stitch 141, 142
  double straight cross stitch 143
  fern stitch 147
  fishbone stitch 147
  French stitch 145
  Greek stitch 148, 149
  herringbone stitch 148
  knotted stitch 145
  leviathan stitch 143, 144
  oblong cross stitch 141
    with backstitch 141
  perspective stitch 149, 150
  plaited stitch 149
  rice stitch 146
  rococo stitch 145, 146
  upright cross stitch 142
diagonal stitches 120-130
  basketweave stitch 120, 121
  Byzantine stitch 123
  cashmere stitch 127
  checker stitch 125, 126
  condensed cashmere stitch 127, 128
  condensed mosaic stitch 124, 125
  condensed Scotch stitch 125, 126
  continental stitch 120, 121
  encroaching slanted Gobelin
    stitch 122
  half-cross stitch 120
  jacquard stitch 123
  Kalem stitch 130
  Milanese stitch 128
  mosaic stitch 124
  Oriental stitch 128, 129
  Scotch stitch 125-126
  slanted Gobelin stitch 122
  stem stitch 130
  tent stitches 120-121
pile stitches 157-159
  Rya stitch 157
  Surrey stitch 157, 159
  velvet stitch 157, 158
straight stitches 131-138
  backstitch 138
  Bargello 133-134, 173-182
  brick stitch 132
  darning stitch 137
  encroaching straight Gobelin
    stitch 131
  Florentine stitch 133-134, 173-182
  Gobelin filling stitch 132
  Hungarian diamond stitch 135
  Hungarian grounding 135, 136
  Hungarian stitch 135
  old Florentine stitch 136, 137
  Parisian stitch 136
  straight Gobelin stitch 131

Stitching fundamentals
  basic stitch formation 118-119
  changing stitch direction 163, 169
  compensating stitches 161
  holding canvas for stitching 119
  left-handed stitching 161
  multiple-color stitching 160
  securing yarn ends 119
  stitch coverage 118
  stitch durability 112, 163
Straight Gobelin stitches 131
Straight stitches 131-138
Surrey stitch 157, 159
Symmetrical designs 162, 168-169, 172

Tent stitches 120-121
  effect on a design 113, 162-163
  in checker stitch 126
Tools and supplies 114-117
Transferring design to canvas
  charted designs 166-171, 173-182
  uncharted designs 164-165
Triangle stitch 155

Upright cross stitches 142-143
  in Brighton stitch 156

Velvet stitch 157, 158

Working techniques
  basic canvas preparation 164
  basic stitch formation 118-119
  blocking 185
  calculating yarn amounts 183
  changing stitch direction 163, 169
  charting a design 172
  compensating stitches 161
  joining canvas lengths 164
  left-handed stitching 161
  making pattern of prepared
    canvas 164
  multiple-color stitching 160
  removing stitches 183
  repairing ripped canvas 183
  securing yarn ends 119
  setting canvas into a frame 184
  techniques for charted designs 166-
    182
  techniques for uncharted designs
    164-165

Yarn basting (to mark canvas
  centers) 167
Yarns
  calculating amounts 183
  securing ends 119
  separating strands 19, 119
  types and selection 115, 162-163
  weight (related to stitch coverage) 118

Patchwork

pages 207—234

Abutted seams 233-234
Appliquéd block-unit patchwork (see Basic types of patchwork)
Appliquéd dividers and borders 215
Appliqués in patchwork
   designing 212, 214, 216-217
   multiple-layer appliqués 214, 226-229
   pieced appliqués 212, 214, 226-229
   single-layer appliqués 214, 226-228
   techniques for sewing 226-229
   use on dividers and borders 215

Basic types of patchwork
   basic types defined 208
   block-unit/appliquéd
      designing 212, 214, 216-217
      how to construct 209, 218-219, 226-231
   block-unit/pieced
      designing 212-213, 216-217
      how to construct 209, 218-225, 230-231
   one-shape patchwork
      designing 213, 232-234
      how to construct 209, 218-219, 232-234
Blindstitch, instructions for 225
Block-unit patchwork (see Basic types of patchwork)
Borders 215, 217, 230

Charting a patchwork 209, 217
Circles, designing with 212-213
Color in patchwork 210-217, 232-234
Compass, use of in designing 212-213
Cornered edges, turning back 226-227
Cornered seams 222-223
Curved edges, turning back 226-227
Curved seams 223
Cutting fabric 219
Cutting templates 218-219

Designing
   appliqués 212, 214
   crazy patchwork 214
   dividers and borders 215
   one-shape patchworks 213
   pieced blocks 210-211, 213
Designs, traditional patchwork
   Baby Blocks
      designing 213
      how to construct 233
   Basket of Flowers
      designing 214
      how to construct 229
   Crazy patchwork
      designing 214
      how to construct 225
   Dresden Plate
      designing 212
      how to construct 229
   Drunkard's Path
      designing 213
      how to construct 223
   Eight Point Star
      designing 210
      how to construct 222
   Grandmother's Flower Garden
      designing 213
      how to construct 234
   Log Cabin
      designing 211
      how to construct 224
   Rose
      designing 214
      how to construct 228
   Shell
      designing 213
      how to construct 232
   Simple Star
      designing 210
      how to construct 221
   Snowflake
      designing 214
      how to construct 228
Diagonal lines, designing with 210-211
Diamond shapes, designing with 213
Dividers 215, 217, 230-231

Edges, turning back 226-227
Equipment and supplies 209

Fabrics 219
   selecting fabrics 209, 219
Featherstitch, instructions for 225
Finger-pressing of edges 226-227

Geometric shapes 210-214
Grid, forming a 210-213

Hand-sewing of seams 220
Hand stitches, instructions for
   blindstitch, featherstitch, slipstitch 225
   running stitch 220
   whipstitch 233
Hexagons, designing with 213

Joining sequence for
   appliquéd block units 209, 226-231
   dividers and borders 215, 230-231
   one-shape patchworks 209, 232-234
   pieced block units 209, 220-225, 230-231

Layering of appliqués 226, 228-229
Lapped seams 225, 226-229, 232

Machine-sewing of seams 220
Marking seams 219
Marking templates
   making 218
   using as a pressing guide 226-227
   using to make paper backing 233-234
   using to mark seamlines 219
Multiple-layer appliqués 214, 226-229

One-shape patchwork (see Basic types of patchwork)
One-way layouts 219

Pieced appliqués 214, 226-227, 229
Pieced block-unit patchwork (see Basic types of patchwork)
Pieced dividers and borders 215
Plain seams 220-223
Placement of color
   in block-unit patchwork 216-217
   in one-shape patchwork 232-234
Planning
   block-unit patchwork 209, 216-217
   one-shape patchwork 209, 217, 232-234
Pressing seams 220
Pressing turned edges 226-227
Protractor, use of in designing 212

Rectangles, designing with 210-211
Rhomboids 210-211, 219
Running stitch, instructions for 220

Seams
   abutted 233-234
   cornered 222-223
   curved 223
   lapped 225, 226-229, 232
   plain 220-223
   straight 220-221
   through a base fabric 224-229
Single-layer appliqués 214, 226-228
Slipstitch, instructions for 225
Squares, designing with 210-214
Staystitching, use of 226-227
Straight seams 220-221
Strip quilt, definition of a 215
Supplies and equipment 209

Templates
   defined 209
   making and using 218-219, 226-227, 232-234
Triangle, designing with 210-211

Whipstitch, instructions for 233

Yardage, how to calculate 219

Quilting

pages 235—268

Adding to a garment 238, 244
All-over quilting 239
Assembling layers 248

Basting layers together 248
Batting and other fillers 236
Border designs 242-243
Bound edges (separate binding) 258-260

Care of quilts 261
Chalk-marking of designs 244
Constructing a frame 237
Corded (trapunto) quilting 254
Cutting quilt parts 247

Designs and designing 238-245
   design types 239-241
      all-over quilting 239
      borders 242-243
      ornamental motifs 240-241
      outline quilting 239
   producing a design
      design tools and supplies 238
      planning a design 238
      transferring and marking 244-245
Dividing a quilt into sections (see Sectional quilting)
Drying a quilt 261

Echo quilting (see Outline quilting)
Edge finishes 257-260
English quilting (see Padded quilting)
Extended binding (edge finish) 257

Fabric panels, joining 247
Fabrics for quilting
   appropriate types 236
   estimating yardage 246
Fillers for quilting
   basic types 236
   cutting 247
Finishing edges 257-260
Frames and hoops
   basic information 237
   constructing a frame 237
   setting quilt into frame 248-249
   setting quilt into hoop 249

Garments, adding quilting to 238, 244
Guide-bar attachment (for machine quilting) 251

Hand quilting techniques 250

In-frame marking of designs 244

Laundering a quilt 261
Layers, assembling 248
Lining and underlining a quilt 260

Machine quilting techniques 251
Marking of designs 244-245
Measuring bed to determine quilt size 246

Needle-marking of designs 244
Needles for quilting 237
No-frame quilting method 249

Off-frame marking of designs 244-245
Ornamental motifs 240-241
Outline quilting 239

Padded (English) quilting 253
Perforated patterns for marking designs 244, 245
Pillow quilting 256
Pressing a quilt 261
Puff quilting 256

Quilter guide-bar attachment 251
Quilting in units 255-256
   pillow quilting 256
   puff quilting 256
   sectional quilting 255

Repairing damages 261
Running stitch in quilting 250

Sectional quilting 255
Self-finished edges 257-258
Size of quilt, measuring for 246
Slipstitched edges 258
Stencils for marking designs 245
Storing a quilt 261
Straight-line designs, how to mark 244

Templates for marking designs 245
Thread for quilting 237
Tools and supplies
   for designing a quilt 238
   for quilting 236-237
      fabrics and fillers 236
      frames and hoops 237
      needles 237
      thread 237
Transferring designs 244-245
Trapunto (see Corded quilting)
Tufting a quilt 252
Tying a quilt 252

Underlining and lining a quilt 260
Unit quilting 255-256

Washing a quilt 261

Yardage needed, estimating 246

Rug-making

pages 461—496

Braiding rugs 486-493
Butting 491

Cutting fabric strips 487

Design principles 486

Equipment 487

Fabric selection and
    preparation 486-487
Finishing techniques 491
Five-strand braid 492
Four-strand braid 492

Joining (splicing) fabric strips 490

Lacing 490

Methods of braiding
    3-strand braid 487-491
    4-, 5-, 6-, 7-strand braids 487,
        492-493
Multiple braiding 492-493

Oblong braided rug 492
Oval braided rug 489

Padding braiding strips 487

Rectangular braided rug 489
Round braided rug 488

Selecting and preparing fabric 486-487
Seven-strand braid 493
Six-strand braid 493
Splicing (joining) fabric strips 490
Strip width 487

Tapering off braid ends 491
Three-strand braid 487-491

Hooking and knotting rugs 462-485
Binding 481, 482, 484
Blocking 481
Borders, stitched 483
Braided (plaited) stitch, instructions
    for 483
Buttonhole stitch, instructions
    for 26, 483

Caring for hand-made rugs 485
Charted design, working a 479
Circles, drawing 467

Cleaning rugs 485
Cutting
    fabric strips 470
    loops 475, 478
    yarns 476

Design, enlarging or reducing a 14-15
Design principles 466-467
Design transfer
    equipment 465
    methods 468-469
Drawing circles, ovals, semicircles 467

Enlarging or reducing a design 14-15
Equipment 463-465
Estimating and preparing
    fabric for hand-hooked pile 470
    rug bases 468-469, 479
    yarns 470, 476

Fabric for hand-hooked pile
    estimating and preparing 470
    selecting 463
Fabric strips
    cutting 470
    determining width 463, 470, 472
Finishing techniques 480-484
Frames 465, 471
Fringe, applying 483, 484

Ghiordes knots (Rya stitches) 478

Hand hook method 472-473
Hemming 480
Hooked rug methods
    hand hook 472-473
    punch needle 474-475
Hooking rugs 462-475

Knotted rug methods
    latch hook 477, 479
    Rya stitch 478, 479
Knotting rugs 462-469, 476-479

Latch hook method 477, 479
Latex, applying 480
Lining 481, 482
Loops, cutting 475, 478

Multicolored pile
    hand hook method 473
    latch hook method 477
    punch needle method 475
    Rya stitch method 478

Ovals, drawing 467
Overcasting stitch, instructions
    for 483

Padding 485
Pile
    basic types of 462
    cutting loops 475, 478
    multicolored 473, 475, 477, 478
    sculpturing 479
Plaited (braided) stitch, instructions
    for 483
Preparing and estimating
    fabric for hand-hooked pile 470
    rug bases 468-469, 479
    yarns 470, 476
Pressing 481
Punch needle method 474-475

Reducing or enlarging a design 14-15
Removing spots 485
Repairing 485
Rug bases
    estimating and preparing 468-
        469, 479
    selecting 463, 464
Rya stitch method 478, 479

Sculpturing pile 479
Selecting
    fabrics for hooked pile 463
    rug bases 463, 464
    yarns 463, 464
Semicircles, drawing 467
Shading 473
Skidproofing 480
Stitched borders 483
Stitches
    braided (plaited) 483
    buttonhole 26, 483
    overcasting 483
    Rya (Ghiordes knots) 478
Storing 485
Strips (fabric) for hand-hooked pile
    cutting 470
    determining width 463, 470, 472

Transferring designs 468-469

Winding yarn into a ball 271
Working a
    charted design 479
    hooked rug 462-475
    knotted rug 462-469, 476-479

Yarn
    cutting 476
    estimating and preparing 470, 476
    selecting 463, 464
    winding into a ball 271

Projects

Appliqué/Patchwork/Quilting
262 Man's patchwork vest
263 Boy's coveralls/machine appliqué
264 Baby quilt
266 Cut-through appliqué wall hanging
267 Patchwork floor pillow
268 Quilted evening bag

Crochet
367 Tote bag
371 Three hats
385 Irish crochet pillow top
394 Woman's cardigan
402 Afghan

Embroidery
103 Monogramming/machine embroidery
104 Crewel picture
106 Place mat and napkin/pulled thread
107 Table runner/huck embroidery
108 Cutwork embroidery on caftan
109 Cross stitch for a child's dress
110 Corded pillow/blackwork

Knitting
285 Scarf
315 Aran-pattern pullover
326 Man's pullover
350 Children's sweaters and hats
352 Sport socks
353 Mittens and hat
354 Evening skirt, top, and shawl
356 Knitted trims for sheets
    and pillowcases

Lacework
411 Needle lace butterfly
418 Shawl with tatted border
425 Filet netting pillow top
432 Bobbin lace-trimmed apron
439 Woven lace place mat
442 Hairpin lace shawl

Macramé
459 Woman's macramé belt
460 Window screen

Needlepoint
186 Initialed eyeglass case/Bargello
188 Oriental-design footstool cover
189 Man's belt
190 Address book cover

Rug-making
494 Chair cushion
495 Wall hanging
496 Braided rug